ISLAM UNDER THE CRUSADERS

Books by the Same Author

Islam under the Crusaders is number two in a continuing series of related but independent works on crusader Valencia. The following have appeared or are ready for press:

The Crusader Kingdom of Valencia: Reconstruction on a Thirteenth-Century Frontier. Cambridge, Mass.: Harvard University Press, 1967.

Islam under the Crusaders: Colonial Survival in the Thirteenth-Century Kingdom of Valencia. Princeton: Princeton University Press, 1973.

Medieval Colonialism: Postcrusade Exploitation of Islamic Valencia. Princeton: Princeton University Press, forthcoming.

The Crusader-Muslim Predicament: Colonial Confrontation in the Conquered Kingdom of Valencia, in preparation.

ISLAM UNDER THE CRUSADERS

Colonial Survival in the Thirteenth-Century Kingdom of Valencia

Robert Ignatius Burns, S.J.

PRINCETON UNIVERSITY PRESS
PRINCETON, NEW JERSEY

LCC: 72-4039

ISBN: 0-691-05207-7

Library of Congress Cataloging in Publication data will be found on the last printed page of this book.

Publication of this book has been aided by a grant from the Louis A. Robb Fund of Princeton University Press.

This book has been composed in Linotype Granjon

Printed in the United States of America by Princeton University Press, Princeton, New Jersey

We cannot sell the Moors and Mooresses,
Yet beheading them would gain us nothing.
Let them live among us, since we hold the sovereignty;
We'll be guests in their houses, and they will serve us.

Song of the Cid
(canto i)

I have many Saracens in my country. My dynasty kept them formerly in Aragon and Catalonia; I keep them in the kingdoms of Majorca and Valencia. All retain their Law just as well as if they were in the country of the Saracens.

King James I, *Book of Deeds*
(ch. 437)

CONTENTS

CONTENTS

ILLUSTRATIONS

MAPS

PREFACE

SEEN IN THEIR full range, the crusades were far more than the brief and localized outbursts which tend to monopolize the term. They comprised a sustained confrontation between East and West, inherited to a surprising degree from distant Hellenic times, though restated in terms of its legatees, the religious communities of Islam and Christendom. At one time or another they raged around the whole inner perimeter of the Mediterranean world. While less important to the vast Islamic cosmos, they became Europe's history as viewed from one vantage. After the manner of a musical theme, recurring in multiple idioms, they underwent the wildest transpositions of extrinsic form and mood in their millennial evolution. At their heart, below the brave campaigns or the barbaric idiosyncrasies at once foreign and fascinating to the modern mind—the romantic froth which became the stuff of novels and drama—the crusades represented an encounter between two Mediterranean societies, fellow inheritors of the Hellenic past, drawn together at almost every level, yet simultaneously repelled by their respective, engulfing ideologies.

As if they were a battling married couple, basically incompatible yet unable to disengage, the two worlds lived side by side, erupting or subsiding in eccentric schedule. The drama changed its locale, replaced its cast, varied its costuming and scenery, translated its language, and provocatively paraphrased its script, like some frantic experimental theater, yet clung to its identity. No dialogue of cultures, no chapter of "race" prejudice or persecution so combines intense feeling, unremitting action, broad but shifting scale, and expanse of time as does this perennial seesaw of conquest between Cross and Crescent.[1]

[1] With men like Ramón Menéndez Pidal and Johannes Vincke, I find the traditionalist concept of crusade or holy war as excluding Spain to be inadequate both to historical facts and to logic. Like Muḥammad 'Inān (Enan), dean of modern Muslim historians on Spain and the Christian-Islamic conflict, I see more sense in the above position, though it distresses the traditionalists. The evolution of the concepts of crusade and holy war, and their applicability to the early phases of the struggle or to Spain, has inspired its own bibliography. The point at which Islam and Christendom became opposed cultures, as distinguished from areas divided by religious differences or clashing in almost wholly political wars, is not

The inner reality of crusades as confrontation consequently lies as much in their colonial interims as in the brave show of battlefields. Like the overt military story, this colonial development metamorphosed into a hundred shapes from generation to generation and according to the changing complexion of the communities involved. To appreciate it, one must seize upon a circumstanced moment, freezing and dissecting it painstakingly in the historian's laboratory. Strangely, the Holy Land does not seem to offer a proper specimen. Such able specialists as Richard, Munro, and Prawer separately experimented there without bringing away more than bare outlines of the subjected society and its interaction with the conquerors.[2] Perhaps Cahen's observation helps explain the failure—that its Muslims and Christians experienced relatively little interpenetration or mutual understanding, and less social intermingling than in Sicily or Spain.[3]

---

easy to fix. The Valencian crusade, of course, was formally proclaimed by the papacy, involved the usual crusade privileges, attracted many foreign combatants, and received its share of the Holy Land Tithe.

[2] Jean Richard, *Le royaume latin de Jérusalem* (Paris, 1953), ch. 10. Dana C. Munro, *The Kingdom of the Crusaders* (Port Washington, [1935] 1966), ch. 5. Emmanuel Guillaume Rey, in his *Les colonies franques de Syrie au xiime et xiiime siècles* (Paris, 1883), devoted ch. 5 to Muslims and other natives, excluding the Christian natives treated in ch. 4, yet could muster only ten pages, and those drawn largely from Ibn Jubayr. Claude Cahen, in *La Syrie du nord a l'époque des croisades et la principauté franque d'Antioche* (Paris, 1940), found that a chapter sufficed to cover the question of contact and interpenetration (part 2, ch. 5; but see below, n. 3). Joshua Prawer's studies, like "The Settlement of the Latins in Jerusalem" (*Speculum*, XXVII [1952], 490-503), his "Colonization Activities in the Latin Kingdom of Jerusalem" (*Revue belge de philologie et d'histoire*, XXIX [1951], 1063-1118), his "Étude de quelques problèmes agraires et sociaux d'une seigneurie croisée au xiiie siècle" (*Byzantion*, XXII [1952], 5-61, XXIII [1953], 143-170), and the brief chapter in his *Histoire du royaume latin de Jérusalem* (rev. and trans. G. Nahon, 2 vols. [Paris, 1969-1970], I, 502-535) with its sequel *The Crusaders' Kingdom: European Colonialism in the Middle Ages* (New York, 1972), pp. 46-59, have little to offer about Muslim subjects of the crusaders. Some excellent accounts of the crusader kingdom virtually ignore its Muslim population. The most ambitious effort to date, Aharon Ben-Ami's *Social Change in a Hostile Environment: The Crusaders' Kingdom of Jerusalem* (Princeton, 1969), is able to do little more than point up the conclusions of standard authors in the framework and terminology of the sociologist, concentrating on changes introduced within both independent politico-cultural systems because of the confrontation rather than penetrating the problem of colonial imposition on a subject people.

[3] Claude Cahen, "Crusades," *Encyclopaedia of Islam*, 2d edn. rev., 4 vols. to date (Leiden, 1960ff.), II, 66; R. C. Smail agrees, discussing at length the school of

The fallen Valencian kingdom on Spain's eastern coast (roughly the same size as the kingdom of Jerusalem in its prime)[4] during the central thirteenth century does offer such an opportunity. The expanse of territory taken raises the Valencian experience above mere local history, while its compact organization allows exploration in exhaustive nuance. The period catches the urbanized Mediterranean West at a moment of technological advance, intellectual sophistication, administrative competence, aggressive expansionism, and self-consciousness, in patterns which differentiated it ever more sharply from its companion civilization, Islam; crusader Aragon was swirling along on these currents of change. The time span enters as a factor here—one generation or some fifty years of evolution; the story comes to a close when the crusaders are old men, watching their sons taking over their world. The deaths of Peter III of Aragon (1285), Alfonso X of Castile (1284), and Abū Yūsuf of Marinid Morocco (1286) mark the end of an era. Finally, Valencia's maximum Mudejarism affords the genuine colonialist amalgam—a dissident majority intimidated by an alien conqueror's military-administrative overgrid and reduced to near invisibility by the dominant

French historians which defends the contrary point of view, in *Crusading Warfare (1097-1193)* (Cambridge, 1956), ch. 3, esp. parts 1 and 4. H. G. Preston came to the same conclusion in *Rural Conditions in the Kingdom of Jerusalem during the Twelfth and Thirteenth Centuries* (Philadelphia, 1903), pp. 26-30. After his *Syrie du nord*, Cahen explored the scanty materials on landlord-peasant relationship in "Notes sur l'histoire des croisades et de l'orient latin: le régime rural syrien au temps de la domination franque," *Bulletin de la faculté des lettres de Strasbourg*, XXIX (1951), 286-310, and in "La féodalité et les institutions politiques de l'orient latin," *Atti del convegno di scienze morali, storiche, e filologiche* (Rome, 1957), 167-197. The problems of interpretation and of insufficient documentation underlay his "Indigènes et croisés, quelques mots à propos d'un médecin d'Amaury et de Saladin," *Syria*, XV (1934), 351-360.

[4] Palestine from Tyre and Dan in the north to below Gaza and Beersheba is 150 miles, and from above Beirut to Gaza some 180 miles; the width varies from 28 miles (Acre to the sea of Galilee) to 55 miles (Gaza to the Dead Sea), increasing very much, of course, beyond the Jordan. In comparison, Valencia from its northern border down to Murcia city—the area conquered by James I—is 180 miles; the width varies from 40 to 60, both measurements being typical. The Holy Land of the crusaders had withered to a much smaller remnant by the thirteenth century and was about to die. At its best it had never been so purely Islamic in its population as Valencia, since it accommodated large and dynamic non-Muslim minorities, particularly in the cities.

minority's quiet arrogance in intruding, as a superior norm, their own social and religious patterns.

This book approaches Islam's predicament under a crusader regime, and the mystery of its acculturative devolution from a proud, celebrated community into a provincial appendage of Aragon, by analyzing the elements of its survival in a series of steps. First, it sketches Islamic Valencia's political, geographical, economic, and social contours at the moment of the crusaders' impact; these preliminary adumbrations take on detailed substance as the work progresses. Secondly, it places the community in its postcrusade constitutional setting—a framework which surrounded all its social and individual life—proposing the result to be at once traditional and unique in Spanish Mudejarism. Thirdly, it pursues this analysis of social processes and dynamic forms down through the religious, educational, and juridical matrices. Finally it dwells upon the Mudejar in his political dimension as he finds his place in the Christian feudal order at the nobiliary and patrician levels; and culminates with a chapter which probes below the political sphere to reveal the interlocking "establishment" comprising the community's inmost strength.

Though the book covers a great deal of ground, economic realities have reduced its original version by half, stripping away extraneous themes like Muslim-Christian relations and brutally excising a welter of detailed subthemes like Mudejar dress, diet, and language, the role of the Jews as intermediaries between the two societies, and the process by which town *morerías* formed. The essential story of how the subject Islamic majority survived as a society, and on what terms, now stands uncluttered. The achievement has exacted its price. It has necessitated the amputation of all consideration of tax records, which not only reveal the revenue structure and economic life of town and country Moors of all classes, especially the farmer majority at their immemorial rounds, but which also disclose myriad homely glimpses of Mudejar life. Early chapters merely adumbrate these topics, reserving their details to two companion volumes in preparation: *Medieval Colonialism* and *The Crusader-Muslim Predicament*. This book must also refrain from plunging into the correlative phenomena of emigrants and immigrants, the hemorrhage of Muslim population to North Africa versus their deliberate importation into Valencia. A major subject by itself, population movement raises in turn the moot problem of expulsion and requires construction of an interpretative chronology of the several Valencian revolts. The present work may reflect some attitudes implicit from knowledge of the patterns by which Mudejar presence diminished.

Above all, though this book never ceases to deal with an intermeshing of two peoples and their social forms, it has no room to do so explicitly. It focuses on the Islamic society and especially on its more obvious boundary-maintaining mechanisms. It omits the darker story of prejudice and persecution, mutual tensions and alienations, restrictive legislation, acculturative intrusion, osmotic interborrowings, movements of conversion and apostasy within each camp, the kingdom-wide riots at the end of King James's reign, and all the assimilative-antagonistic milieu. Such omissions demand an ascetic response from the reader, a reasonable willingness to forego subsidiary themes of real importance, abstaining so as to build in orderly progression the essential context.[5] Christian-Muslim confrontation will provide yet another sequel in this series.

My previous book, *The Crusader Kingdom of Valencia: Reconstruction on a Thirteenth-Century Frontier*,[6] showed how the conquerors managed to prescind from Muslim omnipresence and to lay down a psychological base for the colonialist regime by means of the handy "church"; this term church covered a congeries of institutions, services, centers, and personnel, representing a multitude of disparate, autonomous energy sources and acting as a nucleus which embodied the settlers' values, customs, aspirations, and springs of action. Here the institutional, symbolic, and human planes converged with formidable dynamism to stamp the conquered land as both Christian and European. *Crusader Kingdom* approached the settlers' total social order—not excluding crop variety, theater, or abortive university—as observable from a particularly well-docu-

[5] For this reason, too, the spirited debate over Hispanic-Islamic cultural exchange and interpenetration enters this book only tangentially; its escalating bibliography is still dominated by older authors like Asín Palacios, Castro, Menéndez Pidal, and Sánchez-Albornoz. The same is true of the western-approaches-to-Islam bibliography, so ably represented by writers like d'Alverny, Daniel, Kritzeck, Malvezzi, Southern, Sweetman, and Monneret de Villard.

[6] 2 vols. (Cambridge, Mass., 1967).

mented vantage point. Though readers of the present study would profit from familiarity with that background, they can also dispense with it. *Islam under the Crusaders* is designed to stand by itself, requiring no previous initiation as long as the reader remains conscious of the complex European society hovering at the Mudejar perimeter, pressing and distorting Islamic activity. Eventually this series will culminate in a volume on the colonial society itself, at which point the full range of interacting factors can be appreciated. Meanwhile it has been a privilege to rescue the people we are about to meet and to give them passports into our own lives. They have much to say to us.

MUDEJAR studies proper are scanty, the later Morisco problem absorbing the attention of historians from Janer (1857) and Boronat (1901) through Halperín Donghi (1956) and Lapeyre (1959) to Fuster (1962) and Reglá (1964). Morisco studies have enjoyed a special renaissance during the past two decades.[7] Nineteenth-century historians did occupy themselves now and again with Mudejarism—Circourt (1846), Pedregal Fantini (1898), and especially the solid Fernández y González (1866)—laboring with sparse materials and unsatisfactory results. In our own day Cagigas attempted an overview of the subject, unfortunately losing himself in the allied politico-military encounter.[8] Though the task seemed formidable,

[7] Florencio Janer, *Condición social de los moriscos de España, causas de su expulsión y consecuencias que este produjo en el orden económico y político* (Madrid, 1857). Pascual Boronat y Barrachina, *Los moriscos españoles y su expulsión, estudio histórico-crítico*, 2 vols. (Valencia, 1901). Tulio Halperín Donghi, "Un conflicto nacional: moriscos y cristianos viejos en Valencia," *Cuadernos de historia de España*, XXIV-XXV (1955), 5-115, and XXV-XXVI (1957), 82-250; "Recouvrements de civilisation: les morisques du royaume de Valence au XVIe siècle," *Annales, économies, sociétés, civilisations*, XI (1956), 154-182. Henri Lapeyre, *Géographie de l'Espagne morisque* (Paris, 1959). Juan Fuster, *Poetes, moriscos, y capellans* (Valencia, 1962). Juan Reglá Campistrol, *Estudios sobre los moriscos* (Valencia, 1964). See also the complementary volume by Juan R. Torres Morera, *Repoblación del reino de Valencia después de la expulsión de los moriscos* (Valencia, 1969). Rachel Arié surveys the flowering of Morisco studies after the appearance of Fernand Braudel's brilliant *La méditerranée et le monde méditerranéen a l'époque de Philippe II* (Paris, 1949), in "Les études sur les morisques en Espagne à la lumière de travaux récents," *Revue des études islamiques*, XXXV (1967), 225-229.

[8] Isidro de las Cagigas, *Los mudejares*, 2 vols. (Madrid, 1948-1949). A. [Anne M.J.A.], comte de Circourt, *Histoire des mores, mudejares et des morisques, ou des arabes d'Espagne sous la domination des chrétiens*, 3 vols. (Paris, 1845-1848). José Pedregal y

interest always remained high, expressing itself largely in journal publication. Macho Ortega examined the early Renaissance Mudejars of upland Aragon proper, confining himself to two articles, later reissued in separate cover (1922). Estenaga published an address on Toledo's subject Moors (1924); and López Martínez confected a light work on those of Seville (1935). The Tortosa region along Valencia's northern border attracted some attention from Font y Rius (1953), and from Liauzu using Lacarra's documents (1968), but especially from Bayerri, whose eight-volume history of Tortosa offered animadversions from time to time on the Mudejar minority (1933-1960). Orti Belmonte, editing the Cordova code of 1241 that was so influential in Andalusia, especially in its Sevillian form, added comments on provisions affecting the minorities, but allowed only some ten pages to the thirteenth-century Mudejar (1954). Researching the Murcian conquest and settlement, Torres Fontes compiled an article on its Mudejars (1961), supplementing his more general excursion into the later Mudejar-Morisco problem (1960). Mobarec Asfura essayed a juridical interpretation of the Mudejar condition (1961). Recently Ledesma Rubio has commented briefly on Mudejarism in western Aragon (1968), while Ladero Quesada has treated more extensively the late fifteenth-century situation in Castile (1969), and Lourie has offered an article on the free Mudejars of the Balearics (1970). Special topics like Mudejar costume have focused the efforts of scholars like Arié, while Sanchis Guarner and Vernet have opened fresh linguistic vistas. Little by little, though rarely with an eye on the thirteenth century, preliminary studies about the Spanish Mudejar are accumulating.[9]

Fantini, *Estado social y cultural de los mozárabes y mudéjares españoles* (Seville, 1898). Francisco Fernández y González, *Estado social y político de los mudejares de Castilla, considerados en sí mismos y respecto de la civilización española* (Madrid, 1866).

[9] Francisco Macho y Ortega, "Condición social de los mudéjares aragoneses (siglo xv)," *Memorias de la facultad de filosofía y letras de la universidad de Zaragoza,* I (1922-1923), 137-231, and his "Documentos relativos a la condición social y jurídica de los mudéjares aragoneses," *Revista de ciencias jurídicas y sociales,* v (1922), 143-160, 444-464. Narciso Estenaga Echevarría, "Condición social de los mudéjares en Toledo durante la edad media," *Real academia de bellas artes y ciencias históricas de Toledo,* VI (1924), 5-27. Celestino López Martínez, *Mudéjares y moriscos sevillanos: Páginas históricas* (Seville, 1935). José M. Font y Rius, "La comarca de Tortosa a raíz de la reconquista cristiana (1148), notas sobre su fiso-

On the most promising sweep of territory, Valencia, a handful of articles holds the field. Gual Camarena, drawing especially from the *cartas pueblas* and ranging from the thirteenth up into the sixteenth centuries, contributed two able essays (1949, 1959), matched in quality by Piles Ros's social study of crown Moors in the fifteenth century (1949) and Roca Traver's review of the first century of Mudejarism (1952). For northern Valencia, García y García compiled a seven-page appendix to his book on Christians from data in Mudejar charters (1943). García Sanz published a brief companion-piece for Castellón (1952) and Grau Monserrat a larger article on the same area, unfortunately derivative in its thirteenth-century parts. I have explored aspects of the story in ten articles, containing much material not included in this book (1960-1971).[10] This meager

nomía político-social," *Cuadernos de historia de España*, XIX (1953), 104-128. Jean-Guy Liauzu, "La condition des musulmans dans l'Aragon chrétien au xie et xiie siècles," *Hespéris-Tamuda*, IX (1968), 185-200. Enrique Bayerri y Bertoméu, *Historia de Tortosa y su comarca*, 8 vols. to date (Tortosa, 1933ff.). Miguel Ángel Orti Belmonte, "El fuero de Córdoba y las clases sociales en la ciudad: mudéjares y judíos en la edad media," *Boletín de la real academia de Córdoba*, XXV (1954), 5-94. Juan Torres Fontes, "Los mudéjares murcianos en el siglo xiii," *Murgetana*, XVII (1961), 57-90, and as repaged offprint. Norma Mobarec Asfura, "Condición jurídica de los moros en la alta edad media española," *Revista chilena de historia del derecho*, II (1961), 36-52. M. L. Ledesma Rubio, "La población mudéjar en la vega baja del Jalón," *Miscelánea ofrecida al ilmo. sr. Dr. J. M. Lacarra y de Miguel* (Zaragoza, 1968), 335-351. M. A. Ladero Quesada, *Los mudéjares de Castilla en tiempo de Isabel I* (Valladolid, 1969). Elena Lourie, "Free Moslems in the Balearics under Christian Rule in the Thirteenth Century," *Speculum*, XLV (1970), 624-649. Work currently in progress includes a doctoral dissertation on the riverine Mudejars of thirteenth-century Tortosa by Roser Argeni de Ribó; some attention to the neo-Mudejars of Málaga in a study of the local *Repartimiento* by the archivist Francisco Bejarano Robles; a volume on Christian attitudes toward the Mudejars of Aragon by Elena Lourie; and an article by Pierre Guichard on the Mudejar barony of Crevillente, a Castilian enclave which entered the kingdom of Valencia at the end of the thirteenth century and lost its Mudejar lord early in the fourteenth.

[10] Miguel Gual Camarena, "Mudéjares valencianos, aportaciones para su estudio," *Saitabi*, VII (1949), 165-190; "Los mudéjares valencianos en la época del Magnánimo," *IV Congrés d'història de la corona d'Aragó* (Palma de Mallorca, 1959), pp. 467-494. Leopoldo Piles Ros, "La situación social de los moros de realengo en la Valencia del siglo xv," *Estudios de historia social de España*, I (1949), 225-274. Francisco A. Roca Traver, "Un siglo de vida mudéjar en la Valencia medieval (1238-1338)," *EEMCA*, V (1952), 115-208. Honorio García y García, *Estado económico-social de los vasallos en la gobernación foral de Castellón* (Vich, 1943), pp. 70-76. Arcadio García Sanz, "Mudéjares y moriscos en Castellón," *BSCC*, XXVIII

direct bibliography for early Valencia can be fleshed out with subsidiary, fragmentary, incidental, or derivative exercises such as my notes and bibliography cite. Thus Rodrigo y Pertegás described the topography of the later *morería,* Arribas Palau a fifteenth-century piratical episode, Danvila and Ardit Lucas the fifteenth-century sack of the capital's *morería,* and Mateu y Llopis some numismatic and nomenclatural sources, while Glick touched tangentially on Mudejar irrigation.[11] The list of offerings is very short, and its quality uneven. Roca Traver rightly comments that, while Valencian Mozarabs and Jews have received ample attention, her Mudejars "have been the most neglected" group. Lapeyre's monograph on Spanish Moriscos complains particularly that Valencia's thirteenth-century Mudejar development, "the decisive" stage, "has not yet been completely elucidated," to the detriment of Morisco studies.[12] Little wonder that modern historians, unable to avoid comment on so large a piece of the Spanish story, have generalized unwisely on attendant problems of Mudejar Valencia like expulsion, tolerance, and the root identity of both peoples.

Meanwhile, researches into precrusade Islamic Valencia, fragmentary at best, have resulted in articles by men like Chabás, Gui-

(1952), 94-114. Manuel Grau Monserrat, "Mudéjares castellonenses," *BRABLB,* XXIX (1961-1962), 251-275. Robert Ignatius Burns, see esp., "Journey from Islam: Incipient Cultural Transition in the Conquered Kingdom of Valencia (1240-1280)," *Speculum,* XXXV (1960), 337-356; "Social Riots on the Christian-Moslem Frontier: Thirteenth-Century Valencia," *American Historical Review,* LXVI (1961), 378-400; "Irrigation Taxes in Early Mudejar Valencia: The Problem of the *Alfarda,*" *Speculum,* XLIV (1969), 560-567; "Baths and Caravanserais in Crusader Valencia," *Speculum,* XLVI (1971), 443-458; and "Christian-Islamic Confrontation in the West: The Thirteenth-Century Dream of Conversion," *American Historical Review,* LXXVI (1971), 1386-1434.

[11] José Rodrigo y Pertegás, "La morería de Valencia, ensayo de descripción topográficohistórica de la misma," *BRAH,* LXXXVI (1925), 229-251. Mariano Arribas Palau, *Musulmanes de Valencia apresados cerca de Ibiza en 1413* (Tetuán, 1955). Manuel Danvila y Collado, "Saco de la morería de Valencia en 1455," *El archivo,* III (1889), 124-129. Manuel Ardit Lucas, "El asalto a la morería de Valencia en el año 1455," *Ligarzas,* II (1970), 127-138. Felipe Mateu y Llopis, "La repoblación musulmana del reino de Valencia en el siglo xiii y las monedas de tipo almohade," *BSCC,* XXVIII (1952), 29-43; and his "Nómina de los musulmanes de las montañas de Coll de Rates del reino de Valencia en 1409," *Al-Andalus,* VI (1942), 299-335. Thomas F. Glick, *Irrigation and Society in Medieval Valencia* (Cambridge, Mass., 1970).

[12] Roca Traver, "Vida mudéjar," p. 116: "el mas descuidado." Lapeyre, *Géographie de l'Espagne morisque,* p. 27.

chard, Ribera Tarragó, Torres Balbás, and Vernet, together with the surveys of Piles Ibars and Sanchis Guarner, but they have tended to stop short of the murky Almohad twelfth and thirteenth centuries.[13] Huici laments this "sad" lack, as well as the paucity of source materials on institutions and society, in his multivolume history of Islamic Valencia (1969-1970). The pattern of available Arabic sources confines his own account almost exclusively to a dynastic-military chronicle at the most elevated ruling levels; in this respect his hundred closing pages devoted to the Almohad period can only continue the annalistic data of his excellent political history of the Almohad empire (1956-1957).[14] This period consequently awaits any illumination the early Mudejar era can cast back on the precrusade generation. Around these several shores washes an ocean of Islamic researches, while from Hispanist ports have gone forth exploratory studies like Dufourcq's recent opus concerning external relations between Hispanic and Islamic countries.[15] The study of all these areas may draw benefit from the Valencia story.

THE TASK OF excavating early Mudejar Valencia falls to the Hispanist rather than to the Arabist. Pertinent Arabic documents are rare to the point of being negligible. Survivals such as the marriage contract or the rebel's surrender agreement cited at appropriate

[13] Multiple articles by Chabás, Ribera y Tarragó, and Torres Balbás will be cited in footnotes; Guichard's theories will receive special attention. The standard older work by Andrés Piles Ibars, *Valencia árabe* (Valencia, 1901), was never completed. Manuel Sanchis i Guarner displaces it with his "Època musulmana," last segment of the symposium *Història del país Valencià*, ed. Miguel Tarradell Mateu, 1 vol. to date (Barcelona, 1965).

[14] Ambrosio Huici Miranda, *Historia musulmana de Valencia y su región, novedades y rectificaciones*, 3 vols. (Valencia, 1969-1970); *Historia política del imperio almohade* (Tetuán, 1956-1957); on the deficiency of primary and secondary materials, see I, 8-10.

[15] Charles Emmanuel Dufourcq, *L'Espagne catalane et le Maghrib aux xiiie et xive siècles, de la bataille de Las Navas de Tolosa (1212) à l'avènement du sultan mérinide Abou-l-Hasan (1313)* (Paris, 1966). The standard authors on North Africa and Islamic Spain appear in my footnotes. The only good general history of Islamic Spain, by Évariste Lévi-Provençal, comes to an end with the fall of the early caliphate; I cite its Spanish version in preference to the French because it has been revised in translation and is more accessible in libraries: *España musulmana hasta la caída del califato de Córdoba (711-1031 de J.C.)*, trans. Emilio García Gómez, 2 vols., in *Historia de España*, ed. Ramón Menéndez Pidal, 12 vols. to date (Madrid, 1957ff.), IV and V.

places in the text do little more than add frills to the substance already in hand. Careful Arabists like Ribera and Huici have gone over the ground minutely, and a generation of archivists has kept a sharp eye out for these precious relicts, to no great avail. This is not surprising. Islam did not organize in the corporative way of the West, where archives consequently proliferated. Her Spanish sector dissolved into tumult and death in the thirteenth century, even the Granada rally not serving to recoup the loss. Beyond the Mudejar pale, Muslims seemed unconcerned with the inner life of their lost brothers; a sufficiency of fragmentation and disaster distracted their own attention. The Valencian silence nonetheless seems more encompassing than one expects after the finds elsewhere in Spain. Literary exercises do exist—rhetorical letters, histories, geographies, and poems. They contribute something to this study, but their content, often conventional and inflated, is soon exhausted and in any case largely applies to background or mood. By way of background, too, extraneous materials can serve. Because the Islamic world differed strikingly from place to place, however, one cannot merely transfer apparently similar terms or institutions; but with due caution comparative material about Muslims and their institutions from the Islamic East, Christian Sicily, and especially cognate North Africa may illumine a practice or supply an analogy.[16]

The researcher, foiled on the Islamic side, finds himself thrown back upon Christian sources, which prove unexpectedly rich. Archival originals by the hundreds, law codes, privileges, Dominican reports, trial records, tax lists, memoirs, and treaties lie at hand. The variegated picture of Mudejar life which emerges tempts one to give a running comparison with the similar status of Christians under Islam, whether to indicate a model for crusader attitudes or to demonstrate a parallel mentality common to Mediterranean politics whose foundations antedated both peoples. Though mutual causality and osmotic imitation were surely at work on this Muslim-Christian frontier, extension of inquiry in that direction would overburden a book already heavily laden. Finally, though the documentation at hand demands of its interpreter expertise concerning

[16] Numbers of poets, historians, geographers, and the like are cited for example in the first five chapters; very few of these voices come from within the Mudejar community, and some are distant in place or time.

the Arago-Catalan medieval scene, the discussion must nevertheless touch on myriad aspects of medieval Islamic life; one or other interpretation will inevitably reveal hidden chasms of nescience. No man can be omnicompetent; Islamologists must content themselves with the Hispanic plenty.

PROCEDURAL minutiae demand a word. I shall not recapitulate the paleographical and chronological problems discussed in the preface to *Crusader Valencia*, except to note that the nativity and incarnational calendars coincided from December 25 to March 25, rendering many dates ambiguous. The complex question of the several moneys current and their relative values is less pertinent here; the most common unit was the Valencian solidus, of which about 370 comprised a knight's annual revenue. Something over three solidi equaled a silver besant. Land measures varied according to extrinsic factors like productivity or water supply; the most common of these variables was the fanecate (831 square meters), six of which made a cafiz, with six cafizes comprising a jovate. My conviction that the Valencian Mozarabs had disappeared as a community in Islamic Valencia, though some do not share it, explains the infrequent reference to them.[17] The bracketing dates of about 1235 or 1245 to about 1285 are guidelines rather than straitjackets; Mudejar materials from much earlier or later periods are marked lest they mislead. Similarly, occasional parallels or analogies come from contemporary conquests, from Valencia's neighbors the Balearics and Murcia; less frequently they are drawn from alien quarters like Castile.

A number of puzzling terms such as sheik, *faqīh*, or notable, when they occur casually either before the appropriate place for discussing them or so long afterward as to strain the memory, can be clarified if necessary by using the index. Some useful and rather obvious words have been adopted or Anglicized—notably huerta for an intensely irrigated plain, aljama for a community, Mudejar[18] for the normally privileged Moorish subject, solidus, Hadith, and Ifriqiya. Some Arabic words are already commonly received and

[17] See Chapter I, n. 17.

[18] On the origin and meaning of *mudéjar* (Catalan *mudèixar*), its accent problem, and its relation to the terms Moor and Saracen, see p. 64 and note.

ensconced in English dictionaries, such as imam, Koran, muezzin, sheik, Sufi, and Sunna. The Hafsid, Marinid, and Nasrid dynasties lose their marks, assimilating more comfortably to their Anglicized predecessors the Almoravids and Almohads. Tunisia appears indifferently for Hafsid Ifriqiya, which in fact was a larger entity. In these arbitrary choices I have tried to keep to a minimum the suffering of opposing classes of readers—specialists, purists, the plain human, and medievalists of varied stripe disadvantageously scattered over a broad spectrum of interest.

Names pose a problem to which any resolution seems unsatisfactory. I continue the practice described in *Crusader Valencia.* Geographical names usually appear in their modern Spanish forms, since most maps give them thus; exceptions include the Guadalaviar River and Murviedro for which I have retained the medieval names rather than the Roman-cum-modern ones, Turia River and Sagunto. Some common English forms replace their Spanish counterparts (Cordova, Seville, but not the less universally accepted Saragossa). Following a practice usual enough among historians today, I prefer to Anglicize the given names (James rather than Catalan Jaume and Jacme or the Castilian Jaime; Peter rather than Pere or Castilian Pedro). One does reach a dubious borderland, so I am willing to accept Blasco and compelled to accept Jazpert. Alfonso (Alfons, Castilian Alfonso) seems firmly established in popular usage for the Castilian kings, to whom it is largely confined in this book; consequently it can serve also for the occasional Catalan king or other bearer; if the *Encyclopaedia Britannica* has recently retreated from Alphonso to Alfonso, who can stand? To retain the surname's accent in the resultant combinations, though bad usage ordinarily, is acceptable in technical works and has its advantages. In the debatable land of surnames, especially when joined by the connective de, I follow a common practice of Anglicizing them (Godfrey of Bouillon, William of Tyre, Raymond of Penyafort), unless a consecrated form already holds the field beyond all cavil (Thomas Aquinas, Hernando de Talavera). This usage, with its illogical but regularized results, was inculcated by an apprenticeship in confecting eighty biographies for five encyclopedias; it offends some but on balance seems a reasonable precedent to follow. Some Catalan surnames call for the less distracting Castilian version under which numerous Catalan families have entered Spain's modern history (Alagón for Alagó, Pérez for Pèreç); the knowledgeable reader can easily render these back into Catalan. In the mixed result, I have retained the surname's accent as probably more helpful than distracting to the reader.

Muslim names raise a different problem, and here I defer to the practice of many Islamologists. In a host of recent studies they have accustomed us to their arsenal of diacritical marks. An older school stands firm against the tide. (Sir Ernest Gowers in the latest Fowler's *Usage* decries it, but he also inveighs against any spelling except Mahomet, having a passionate go at this bugaboo twice.)[19] I shall allow myself to be carried by the tide, even retaining an isolated Muḥammad or 'Alī for the sake of uniformity. A rare name, widely established, may retain another form (Saladin). Good authors unabashedly throw not only names but Arabic words into the English possessive, an awkward appearance I avoid as far as feasible, as also the making of bastard plurals. In transliterating Arabic—in this case Middle Arabic with some departures from the classical—seven national systems contend within an international set of equivalents, further confused by occasional idiosyncratic preferences. Ibn Khaldūn may appear for example as Jaldūn or (international) Ḫaldūn. I follow the international program but spare the reader several of its more cumbersome devices, choosing dh over ḏ, gh over ġ, j over ǧ (Spanish ŷ), kh over ḫ, and sh over š. With a few exceptions—notably th for t͟h, j for dj (international ǧ), and q for ḳ—the equivalences coincide with the widely used scheme of the *Encyclopaedia of Islam*. The elision of al- with words beginning in d, dh, n, r, s, ṣ, sh, t, ṭ, z and ẓ (ash-Shaqundī, aṭ-Ṭanjī) is a speech pattern, which may be reproduced or disregarded in writing; I have kept it, as useful for correlating the Latin and Romance distortions with the Arabic.

The reader should know that a Muslim's personal name could carry as embellishment a selected group of ancestors, especially his father, linked by the repetitious ibn or its abbreviation b., "son of"; sometimes ibn introduces a family name, even of place or quality. On the other hand the personal name might be extended by a pa-

[19] H. W. Fowler, *A Dictionary of Modern English Usage*, ed. Sir Ernest Gowers, 2d edn. (Oxford, 1965), pp. 129, 348-349.

ternal or possessive abū complex, "father of," "possessed of," or "referable to." Sometimes more important than either was the ultimate appendage, one or more epithets denoting his or his family's social, economic, or geographic origins, or supplying a description, nickname, or honor. Thus the anti-Almohad hero Ibn Hūd was in full: Abū 'Abd Allāh (his *kunya*), Muḥammad (his personal or given name) b. Yūsuf b. Hūd (his ancestry), al-Mutawakkīl 'ala Allāh ("he who trusts in God"), with the formal titles Amīr al-Mu'minīn ("commander of the faithful") and Nāṣir ad-Dīn ("defender of the faith"). He could be addressed *inter alia* as Ibn Hūd, or Abū 'Abd Allāh, or al-Mutawakkīl, or occasionally as Muḥammad. The bar in Abu before 'l, retained by some authors, should disappear as the vowel shortens in elision; the first edition of the *Encyclopaedia of Islam* excluded the bar in such combinations as Abu 'l- and Dhu 'n-, though the current edition prefers to retain it. Spanish names displayed quirks of their own. Gothic forms perdured, such as Ibn Garsiya (García), Ibn Mardanīsh (perhaps Martínez), Bashkuwāl (Pascual), and Zidri (Isidro in the genitive). Ibn Yannaq (Iñigo, Latin Ennecus) died at Játiva in 1153, and a wealthy Mudejar subject of King James bore the mixed name Abyhuc aben Rodrich—probably Ibn Hūd b. Rudhrīq. Common Romance names remained popular in translation, as with Sa'īd for Felix. 'Abd ar-Raḥmān Shanjwilo or Sanchuelo was a pretender to the caliphate. The Latin diminutive -ellus could affix itself, as in Muḥammaḍāl for Muḥammad-ellus. The augmentative -on reinforced or added to the similar Semitic augmentative, so that names like 'Abdūn for 'Abd Allāh, Georges Colin tells us, were more common in Spain than anywhere else in Islam. Latin -ensis survived faintly, yielding oddities like al-Gharnāṭishī for "the Granadan" instead of a more orthodox al-Gharnāṭī.[20]

[20] Lévi-Provençal sees the Banū Qaṣī as deriving from the Roman Cassius clan, but this is improbable. It is common to follow Dozy in making Mardanīsh the genitive Martinis, rather than Codera's Byzantine Mardonios or something from the excremental root merda; Huici, while not endorsing Dozy, concludes it must be of Romance origin. Simonet's and Slane's Banū "Chica Lola" is moot (see M. J. Rubiera Mata, "El significado del nombre de los Banū Ashqīlūla," *Al-Andalus*, XXXI [1966], 377-378). An el ending was diminutive or belittling; the ending -un or -on could be an augmentative or honorific. Of particular interest in the search for Romance and other origins is Francisco Codera y Zaidín, "Apodos ó sobrenombres de moros españoles," *Mélanges Hartwig Derenbourg* (Paris, 1909), 323-334.

Most Islamic names in the Valencian story belonged to people now obscure. They entered the Catalan ear of the local scribe, passed out onto his paper in one or several Latin approximations, and then suffered the vagaries of multiple transcription, even when spared the modern reading of an editor. Reconstituting such names etymologically is often impossible. The Hispanist can proceed from the analogy of known names, similarly deformed, to a reasonable reconstruction, though an especially recalcitrant garble can reduce him to guessing. Reconstituted names provide their original within the text, allowing the reader equipped with a sufficiency of contemporary Spanish variants to try his own hand at the puzzle. One important name requires comment; the Arabist Cagigas has misled many by calling Valencia's last Muslim king Abū Sa'īd, instead of Abū Zayd. A Jew might have both a Hebrew and a Romance name; King James's celebrated subject Rabbi Moses b. Nahman (Nahmanides) of Gerona was also Bonastruc de Porta. He could have an Arabic form as well, often cognate to the Hebrew, thus confusing the unwary reader. Those serving the crown of Aragon I assimilated to that realm, Anglicizing the given names and leaving some surnames in unaccented Romance mood (David Almascarán, Moses Alconstantini, Judah b. Manasseh). In keeping with this distinguishing pattern, Ibn Vives becomes, less equivocally for the average reader, Ben Vives.

This book took shape over many years, five of them in the archives of Europe. I began it in 1955, innocent of how extensive its ramifications would soon prove. By 1960 it was obvious that the church-as-frontier theme, by reason both of its thousands of documents and its unique impact, had to be amputated as a separate work. A 1963-1964 Guggenheim fellowship allowed me to return to Spain, partly to put finishing touches to *Crusader Valencia* but mostly to research the final stages of the present work. In 1970 a National Endowment for the Humanities grant, supporting a sequel to *Islam under the Crusaders*, similarly permitted finishing touches in Spain's archives and libraries to this parent volume. Two faculty grants from my own university aided pilot projects which were eventually absorbed into the larger work. A fellowship from the American Council of Learned Societies in 1971, and an appointment to the Institute for Advanced Study at Princeton, both involving a further project, supported the final editorial stages of this book. For this generous assistance I express my gratitude. Many other hands have aided in the construction of the book, including the unfailingly helpful staffs at the various European manuscript collections specified in detail in my *Crusader Valencia,* but especially Felipe Mateu y Llopis, director of the Biblioteca Provincial in Barcelona; José Martínez Ortiz, director of the Archivo Municipal in Valencia; Ramón Robres Lluch, canon and director of the Archivo Catedral at Valencia, and his fellow-canon and historian Vicente Castell Maiques; Rosa Rodríguez Troncoso de Tormo, director of the Archivo General del Reino in Valencia; and most notably Federico Udina Martorell and all his colleagues at the Archivo de la Corona de Aragón at Barcelona. Michel Mazzaoui and Philip Hitti (emeritus), of Princeton University's Near Eastern Studies department, gave technical help during final editing.

A number of Arabists have been kind enough to give the finished manuscript a careful reading: Claude Cahen of the University of Paris, his colleague Rachel Arié, H.A.R. Gibb, now retired from Oxford and Harvard Universities, Ira Lapidus and James Monroe of the University of California at Berkeley, Felix Pareja, S.J., of the University of Madrid and the Instituto Hispano-Árabe de Cultura, and Gerard Salinger of the University of California at San Diego. I have incorporated many of their valuable suggestions. Their names appear here solely to convey my gratitude for this arid service; the themes of the book, its interpretations, conjectural reconstructions, and data must all stand on their own feet.

ROBERT IGNATIUS BURNS, S.J.
UNIVERSITY OF SAN FRANCISCO

Valencia
1972

ABBREVIATIONS

ACCV	*Anales del centro de cultura valenciana*
AEM	*Anuario de estudios medievales*
AHDE	*Anuario de historia del derecho español*
Aldea Charter	Carta puebla de Aldea, February 12, 1258
Alfandech Charter	Carta puebla de Alfandech, April 15, 1277
Arch. Cat.	Archivo de la Catedral de Valencia
Arch. Cat. Tortosa	Archivo de la Catedral de Tortosa
Arch. Crown	Archivo de la Corona de Aragón
Arch. Mun.	Archivo Municipal de Valencia
Arch. Nac. Madrid	Archivo Histórico Nacional
Arch. Reino Val.	Archivo General del Reino de Valencia
Arch. Vat.	Archivio Segreto Vaticano
Aureum opus	*Aureum opus regalium priuilegiorum ciuitatis et regni Valentie*
Bibl. Univ. Barc.	Biblioteca, Universidad de Barcelona (MSS)
Bibl. Univ. Val.	Biblioteca, Universidad de Valencia (MSS)
BRABLB	*Boletín de la real academia de buenas letras de Barcelona*
BRAH	*Boletín de la real academia de la historia*
BSCC	*Boletín de la sociedad castellonense de cultura*
Chelva Charter	Carta puebla de Chelva, August 17, 1370
Chivert Charter	Carta puebla de Chivert, April 28, 1234
Colección diplomática	A. Huici, ed., *Colección diplomática de Jaime I*
Congrés (I, III, IV, or *VII)*	*Congrés d'història de la corona d'Aragó*
EEMCA	*Estudios de edad media de la corona de Aragón*
EI[1], *EI*[2]	*Encyclopaedia of Islam*, old and new editions
Eslida Charter	Carta puebla de Eslida, May 29, 1242
Fori	*Fori antiqui Valentiae* (1967, Latin text)
Furs	*Fori regni Valentiae* (1548, Catalan text)
Itinerari	J. Miret y Sans, *Itinerari de Jaume I*
Játiva Charter	Carta puebla de Játiva, January 23, 1251 or 1252
Llibre dels feyts	James I, *Crònica* (autobiography)
RIEEIM	*Revista del instituto egipcio de estudios islámicos en Madrid*
Second Eslida Charter	Rephrased Carta puebla de Eslida, June 27, 1276
Tales Charter	Carta puebla de Tales, May 27, 1260
Tortosa Charter	Carta puebla de Tortosa, December 1148
Tudela Charter	Carta puebla de Tudela, March 1115
Uxó Charter	Carta puebla de Uxó, August 1250
Valencia Capitulation	Surrender Treaty for Valencia City, September 28, 1238

The Kingdom of Valencia
Showing Major Natural Divisions as Grouped Administratively in the Tomás López Map of 1788

THE PHYSICAL-HISTORICAL MILIEU

CHAPTER I

The King's Other Kingdom

CAPITAL OF A princely realm, Valencia stood like a giant among the cities of Islamic Spain. Muslim poets risked blasphemy to apply to Balansiya the Koranic themes of Paradise. Christians as far away as England spoke of it with awe as "famed Valencia" and "Valencia the great." It rose abruptly from a flat green countryside laced with irrigation canals, framed by the Mediterranean and by a far circle of austere hills. The broad Guadalaviar—the Wādi 'l-abyaḍ or White River—wound along the city's northern flank to the sea. Within its walls a teeming populace thrived on commerce with far-flung ports of the Islamic world. Valencia's name evoked memories of great men of letters, mystics, and voyagers. Ash-Shaqundī (d. 1231) praised its inhabitants as compassionate to strangers, constant in friendship, and valiant in repulsing "the closeness of the enemy" Christians. Ibn 'Idhārī in 1224 admired its peculiarly light-filled air. All agreed that Valencians lived with grace in a land of high prosperity.

Serpents come, and paradises must end. On the eve of Valencia's tragedy, her poet Ibn Ḥarīq (d. 1225) reflected contemporary unease in his wryly humorous verses:

> "Valencia is the dwelling of all beauty."
> This they say both in the East and in the West.
> If someone protests that prices there are high,
> And that the rain of battle falls upon it,
> Say: "It is a paradise surrounded by
> Two misfortunes: famine and war!"[1]

[1] Abu 'l-Ḥasan 'Alī b. Muḥammad al-Makhzūmī, called Ibn Ḥarīq, teacher of Ibn al-Abbār, in *Hispano-Arabic Poetry and its Relations with the Old Provençal Troubadours*, trans. A. R. Nykl (Baltimore, 1946), p. 331. Ismā'īl b. Muḥammad Abu 'l-Walīd ash-Shaqundī, *Elogio del Islam español* (*Risāla fī faḍl al-Andalus*), trans. Emilio García Gómez (Madrid, 1934), p. 115. Ibn 'Idhārī al-Marrākushī, *Al-Bayān al-mugrib fi ijtiṣār ajbār muluk al-Andalus wa al-Magrib: Los almohades*, trans. Ambrosio Huici, 2 vols. (Tetuán, 1953-1954), I, 302-303. On "Magna Valentia" as a term used by contemporaries, see Robert Ignatius Burns, *The Crusader*

The year Ibn Ḥarīq died, Christian crusaders invaded his homeland, harbingers of its downfall a decade later. The capital itself surrendered on a fall day, the seventeenth of the month of Ṣafar in the year 636 from the Hegira, or in the infidels' calendar Tuesday, the vigil of the feast of St. Michael the Archangel, September 28, 1238. By a few strokes of the pen, the peace of defeat descended upon Balansiya, a brooding atmosphere soon carried over into the letters and poems of its population in exile.[2]

The Survivors

The red and gold bars of Aragon flew from the massive northeastern tower called 'Alī Bufāt. The stone battlements, which al-'Udhrī had admired as among the most formidable in Spain, now

---

Kingdom of Valencia: Reconstruction on a Thirteenth-Century Frontier, 2 vols. (Cambridge, Mass., 1967), II, 370, with citations to Matthew Paris and the Cistercian statutes. "Valencia famosa civitas" is the expression in *Crónica latina de los reyes de Castilla* (ed. M. D. Cabanes Pecourt [Valencia, 1964]). Some idea of Valencia's creative past may be gained from Julián Ribera y Tarragó, "Moros célebres valencianos en literatura y viages," *El archivo*, I (1886-1887), 136-140; Pascual Meneu, "Moros célebres de Onda," *El archivo*, II (1887-1888), 175-186; Francisco Pons, "Escuela de Abú Alí en Játiva," *El archivo*, II, 2-5.

[2] The story and bibliography of the crusade is given briefly in my *Crusader Valencia*, I, 1-9, II, 307-308, 370-372. Surveys are in Huici, *Historia musulmana de Valencia*, III, 252-270; Ferran Soldevila, *Història de Catalunya*, 3 vols. (Barcelona, 1934-1935), I, 225ff.; rev. edn. (3 vols., 1962), I, 279ff., 290ff.; J. Lee Shneidman, *The Rise of the Aragonese-Catalan Empire, 1200-1350*, 2 vols. (New York, 1970), I, 128ff.; Ferran Valls-Taberner and F. Soldevila, *Historia de Cataluña*, trans. Nuria Sales, 3 vols. (Barcelona, 1955-1957), in *Obras selectas de Fernando Valls-Taberner*, ed. Ramón d'Abadal and J. E. Martínez-Ferrando, 3 vols. (Barcelona, 1952-1957), III (double volume), I, 159-160; and Martínez-Ferrando in Miguel Tarradell *et alii*, *Història dels Catalans*, 3 vols. to date (Barcelona, 1961ff.), II, part 2. See also R. B. Merriman, *The Rise of the Spanish Empire in the Old World and in the New*, 4 vols. (New York, 1918-1936), I, 293ff.; H. J. Chaytor, *A History of Aragon and Catalonia* (London, 1933), ch. 6; Ferdinand Lot, *L'art militaire et les armées au moyen âge en Europe et dans le proche orient*, 2 vols. (Paris, 1946), II, 302-307; Teodoro Llorente, *Valencia*, 2 vols. (Barcelona, 1887-1889), I, chs. 3 and 4; Vicente Boix y Ricarte, *Historia de la ciudad y reino de Valencia*, 3 vols. (Valencia, 1845-1847), I, 118ff. and 505ff. See also Miguel Gual Camarena, "Reconquista de la zona castellonense," *BSCC*, XXV (1949), 417-441; J. M. Font y Rius *et alii*, *La reconquista española y la repoblación del país* (Zaragoza, 1951), pp. 85-126. The new history of Valencia by Tarradell *et alii* has only reached the crusade. See too the biographies of the king listed below in n. 11, and Muslim writers in n. 4.

stood empty of soldiers. In the maze of streets below, the clangor of armed men had given way to the bustle of civilians preparing for exile. All the efforts of the past months had come to nothing—the flame and catapults, the bloody sallies, the secret embassy to north Africa, followed by the heartbreak of watching a Tunisian relief fleet repulsed, and finally the deathwatch as Christendom's army fastened its grip while famine decimated the populace. In the end Abu 'l-Ḥamlāt, the ruler's nephew, had to ride out to the pavilion of Aragon's king—Jāqmo, "the tyrant born to rule Spain"—to bargain for the lives of Valencia's people. The terms, though minimal, spared the population a mass sack such as these armies had recently loosed upon Majorca's capital. Evacuation of the city had to be accomplished within five days, the exiles bearing away whatever their backs could hold; safe passage without search or harassment prevailed south to Cullera for a period of twenty days. A seven years' truce stabilized the Christian-Muslim battlefront along the line of the Júcar River.[3]

For three days Valencia city churned with hasty preparations. Muslims sacrificed their nonportable treasures for whatever money the crusaders cared to offer, "rich quilts of samit and fine drapings and sumptuous coverlets and much fair cloths of silk and gold and caparisons."[4] On the third day the city emptied itself in a great flux

[3] The Valencia Capitulation is conveniently at hand in Fernández y González, *Mudejares de Castilla*, appendix, doc. 15; Jaime Villanueva, *Viage literario a las iglesias de España*, 17 vols. in 22 (Madrid, 1803-1852), xvii, 331; Charles de Tourtoulon, *Don Jaime I el Conquistador, rey de Aragón, conde de Barcelona, señor de Montpeller, según las crónicas y documentos inéditos*, 2d edn. rev. and trans. Teodoro Llorente y Olivares, 2 vols. (Valencia, 1874), i, 379-380, doc. 15; Janer, *Moriscos de España*, p. 192; *Colección de documentos inéditos para la historia de España*, ed. Martín Fernández Navarette, Miguel Salvá, Pedro Sáinz de Baranda, *et alii*, 112 vols. (Madrid, 1842-1896), xviii, 84-86, doc. 26. Before the surrender, Valencia's poet-ambassador pleaded for help at Tunis on August 17 (Joaquín Vallvé Bermejo, "Un privilegio granadino del siglo xiii," *Al-Andalus*, xxix [1964], 233-242), returning through the siege lines again. James began the siege on or before April 26. See the *Itinerari de Jaume I "el Conqueridor,"* ed. Joaquín Miret y Sans (Barcelona, 1918), p. 131. Contrast the Muslims' dates below in Chapter II, n. 13. On Abu 'l-Ḥamlāt, see Chapter XIII, n. 19. For the "great number" who perished of famine and for the "tyrant," see Ibn Khaldūn, *Histoire des Berbères et des dynasties musulmanes de l'Afrique septentrionale*, trans. Baron de Slane, rev. edn., Paul Casanova and Henri Pérès, 4 vols. (Paris, 1925-1956), p. 311.

[4] Bernat Desclot, *Crònica*, ed. Miguel Coll y Alentorn, 4 vols. (Barcelona, 1949-1950); trans. F. L. Critchlow, *Chronicle of the Reign of King Pedro III of Aragon*,

of humanity—men, women, and children of all ages and every status. King James estimated the throng at fifty thousand, a gross exaggeration which conveys his sense of wonder at so immense a mob. The Conqueror himself, "with knights and armed men about me," punctiliously escorted the fugitives out onto the open fields stretching south between the city and the suburb of Ruzafa.[5] Brutal incidents marred the occasion's military correctness. The prospect of helpless Muslims carrying their wealth roused the greed of escorting soldiers; some set about robbing their charges, even spiriting

2 vols. (Princeton, 1928-1934), ch. 49: the few direct quotations will be from the version by F. L. Critchlow, whose chapter numbers do not always correspond to those of the standard editions as used here. The very early historians of Valencia like Beuter and Escolano provide colorful but inaccurate accounts. On the Islamic side an eyewitness account of the surrender ceremonies is in "Un Traité inédit d'Ibn al-Abbār à tendance chiite," ed. A. Ghedira, *Al-Andalus*, XXII (1957), 31-54, esp. 33n. For Valencia's fall, from a near-contemporary view, written ca. 1312, see Ibn 'Idhārī al-Marrākushī, *Al-Bayān al-mugrib*, I, 306, 321, II, 124-125. Less detailed is Muḥammad b. 'Abd al-Mun'im al-Ḥimyarī, *Kitāb ar-rawḍ al-mi'ṭār fī ḫabar al-aḳṭār*, in *La péninsule ibérique au moyen-âge*, ed. and trans. Évariste Lévi-Provençal (Leiden, 1938), pp. 40-42; also translated by M. P. Maestro González (Valencia, 1963), pp. 72-74, the version hereafter cited. See Ibn Khaldūn, a compilation made a century later, *Histoire des Berbères*, II, 306-312; and the early modern history of Aḥmad b. Muḥammad al-Maqqarī (d. 1631), *The History of the Mohammedan Dynasties in Spain*, 2 vols. (London, [1840-1843] 1964), II, book 8, ch. 4, which represents an abridged adaptation by Pascual de Gayangos rather than a translation. The recent history by Muḥammad 'Abd Allāh 'Inān (Enan), *The Age of the Almoravides and Almohads in Maghreb and Moslem Spain*, English title, Arabic text, 2 vols. (Cairo, 1964-1965), includes the conquest of Valencia and eastern Spain in the latter part of the second volume; 'Inān continues his political survey in *The End of the Moorish Empire in Spain and the History of the Moriscos*, 2d edn. rev. (Cairo, 1958). 'Alī b. 'Abd al-Wahhāb an-Nuwayrī (d. 1332), in reviewing the loss of Valencia and the other five main cities captured by crusaders in the thirteenth century, laments the consequent break in historical narrative materials, so that little remains but their date of conquest; of Valencia he knows the details of siege and terms. An-Nuwayrī devotes several pages to the fall of the Almohads; see his *Historia de los musulmanes de España y África*, trans. Mariano Gaspar Remiro, 2 vols. (Granada, 1917-1919), II, 198-249, esp. pp. 245ff.; Valencia on p. 277. See also Huici, *Historia musulmana de Valencia*, III, 259-260; and Muslims like Ibn al-Khaṭīb cited below in Chapter II, n. 13.

[5] James I, *Llibre dels feyts*, ed. as *Crònica* by Josep M. de Casacuberta, 9 vols. in 2 (Barcelona, 1926-1962), ch. 283; translations, when not my own, are from the version by John Forster, *The Chronicle of James I, King of Aragon, Surnamed the Conqueror* (*Written by Himself*), 2 vols. (London, 1883). A useful variant in Latin (1313) by Pere Marsili is among the Bibl. Univ. Barc. MSS. The original version was put together in two parts, part 1 at Játiva in 1244 and part 2 at Barcelona in 1274.

away women and children for sale as slaves. Angry at this affront to his honor, the Conqueror incontinently executed the culprits. More enterprising crusaders bypassed the convoy, penetrating into the Islamic zone beyond the point of safeguard so as to fall upon the refugees in the mountain passes. The exodus rolled on, many Muslims purchasing passage by sea on Barcelona merchantmen but most making their way overland, a long line creeping like a wounded serpent toward the safety of Cullera.

The grief of Valencia's population found eloquent expression as they abandoned their green country, their homes, bazaars, farms, graveyards, mosques, and places holding memories. Their letters and poems, lamenting the homeland, convey a stunned sense of loss. "Is it a dream?" asks a refugee. "No, never in a dream could such a reality be seen." One outcast mourns "this immense woe," as though a "sea of sadness swells its waters," while "Valencia becomes the residence of an infidel leader." The lost city had been "lovely, a garden." "Tears show in every eye and cries of sorrow rise on all sides," the victims write; friends are scattered and brothers dead, and "a deluge of affliction has burst on us." All that was gracious, all that was sound is lost.

Ibn al-Abbār, vizier to Valencia's exiled ruler, cried out in pain: "Where is Valencia and its homes, its warbling birds and the moan of its doves?" Forever gone is its fresh, green countryside, like time long passed. "Has Valencia committed some crime," he asked, "that such should be its fate?" The Valencian intellectual Abu 'l-Muṭarrif b. 'Amīra bewailed the choice of slavery or death. "What friends have gone away, what companions have left their fatherland," he declaimed. "Everywhere one hears only mourning and weeping"; in every eye one reads suffering. Evil has pierced to the heart of our country; the hawk has seized its prey; the lion has slain our brothers, whose loss makes us weep. "Valencia the beautiful, the elegant, the brilliant!" The infidels have silenced in it the call to prayer and have stifled the breath of Islam's faith. Valencia, "metropolis of the coast, capital of sea and land, admiration of the gifted, which shone with rays of beauty and of light"—Valencia is gone!

The anguish echoed abroad. In the south the poem of al-Qarṭājannī (d. 1285) had the rivers of Moorish Spain running tears, Valencia's Guadalaviar matching the woe of Seville's Guadalquivir, while the Júcar below Valencia turned mad with grief. In ar-Rundī the elegiac note swelled to organ tones:

> A curse smote her Muslims and the bane gnawed her,
> Until vast regions and towns were despoiled of Islam.
> Ask Valencia what became of Murcia,
> And where is Játiva, or where is Jaén?

To some extent these were poetical conceits, an arabesque of conventional images, belonging to a fall-of-cities theme adopted by Hispano-Muslim poets since the conquest of Barbastro in the eleventh century. The tragedy of Valencia's fall supplied occasion for evoking platonic nostalgia, a thirst for the One beyond transitory creation. For the exiles, however, the tragedy was real.[6]

While literary Muslims indited these laments, Christian notaries briskly listed the deserted properties, assigning them to crusaders or immigrants. Approximating as best they could the odd Arabic names, they rudely gave away the pleasure gardens of Avixelo, of Habenadin, and of Dolonseri; the small house of Aladip and the larger one of Alahant; and the complex of buildings owned by Alboegi. Barons and bishops fell heir to the proud establishments of Valencian aristocrats, while shoemakers and soldiers took over homes belonging to displaced persons of humbler station whose lowly names and sorrow are perpetuated down the centuries on

[6] See the letters and poems gathered in Lévi-Provençal, *Péninsule ibérique,* pp. 61-67, and Claudio Sánchez-Albornoz y Menduiña, *La España musulmana según los autores islamitas y cristianos medievales,* 2 vols. (Buenos Aires, 1946), II, 335-338. See also Adolfo Federico von Schack, *Poesía y arte de los árabes en España y Sicilia,* 2d edn., 3 vols. (Madrid, 1872), I, ch. 5, esp. pp. 139-141. Nykl supplies a translation of the long lament by Ṣāliḥ Abu 'l-Baqā' ash-Sharīf ar-Rundī, as well as a Spanish version of the brief verses by Abu 'l-Ḥasan Ḥāzim b. Muḥammad b. Ḥāzim al-Anṣārī al-Qarṭājannī (d. 1285), in his *Hispano-Arabic Poetry,* pp. 334-335, 337-339. As background to my own selection of poet's texts, see the general study of specifically Valencian themes by Elías Terés Sádaba, "Textos poéticos árabes sobre Valencia" (*Al-Andalus,* XXX [1965], 291-307), including the application of Koranic lines on paradise by Ibn az-Zaqqāq, among others, and the unkind revelation by al-Gharnāṭī of a flaw: "something intolerable, the mosquitoes." The great traveler Ibn Jubayr "the Valencian," born at Valencia or Játiva to a high functionary in 1145 (d. 1217), gives keen expression to the homesickness and attachment to place he and his shipmates felt as they approached Valencia's shores (*Voyages,* trans. Maurice Gaudefroy-Demombynes, 4 vols. [Paris, 1949-1965], III, 407).

these lists. In the countryside, especially, many properties continued to function as before, their Muslim tenants accommodating themselves to the Christian heirs. The *Repartimiento* or book of land division represents an inventory of such local treasures as a dovecote, an orchard, a park, a villa, and a garden around "a large palm tree." To run through the catalogue of transferred properties, with one faceless 'Alī or Muḥammad succeeding another, becomes a poignant experience.[7]

The fall of Valencia was merely the most dramatic episode in a long crusade against the Islamic kingdom of Valencia. The clearing of the city and partitioning of its surrounding territory create an impression of victory and Christian presence belied by the facts. The illusion is fortified by the continuing conquests in the south, by the imposition of Christian institutions ecclesiastical and civil throughout the conquered kingdom, and by the circumstance that the mass of documentation from this time forward virtually ignores the resident Muslims. So much was this true that it is possible to write a considerable history of Christian Valencia with no more than an infrequent glance at the Muslim remnant. From the start a handful of Christians assumed possession of the main cities, ports, and defenses, inaugurating a dynamic life in which Mudejars persisted largely as labor force and social problem. Bemused by the process, an earlier generation of scholars entertained the strange idea that the Muslims had been "expelled," or that only the rural or seignorial categories remained, or at best that Muslims stayed on as oppressed serfs, except for isolated communities whose strategic position had won them fairer terms. On the contrary, the majority of the conquered remained in the kingdom, their society and institutions wounded and withdrawn but still omnipresent. What is more, they remained as organized communities and as a respectable

[7] *Repartiment de Valencia*, facsimile edn., ed. Julián Ribera y Tarragó (Valencia, 1939). The standard but badly done edition is by Próspero de Bofarull y Mascaró, *Repartimiento de Valencia*, in the *Colección de documentos inéditos del archivo general de la corona de Aragón*, 41 vols. (Barcelona, 1847-1910), XI, 143-656; see, e.g., the *viridarium* and *palumbarium* on p. 195, and the *orticulum* "in quorum uno est quedam magna palma" on p. 488. Occasionally a famous name appears; in 1242 the Christian lord of Rebollet succeeded to the Denia property of the Banū Maymūn, who had supplied a long line of admirals there (see Huici, *Historia musulmana de Valencia*, III, 116).

military force. This dissident majority formed a sea on whose sullen surface Christian immigrants at first had to cluster like infrequent atolls.

Valencia continued to look much like other Islamic lands; when the muezzin called over the countryside, it even sounded much the same. Islamic courts passed judgment; Moorish officials administered affairs as usual. Arabic names, uneasy on the Catalan tongue, defined the realm from top to bottom and obtruded at many turnings within the cities. External landmarks tended to persist—boundaries of political units, roads, baths, ovens, mills, vineyards, merchants' inns, markets, and even the kinds of houses.[8] Many customs carried over. "Ancient Moors" were cited to court to settle precedents for Christians. "As was the custom in the former days of the Saracens" became a repetitious formula in the royal registers, for Christians as well as Moors. The crown prescribed irrigation procedure "as anciently was the custom in the time of the Saracens." The Burriana irrigation system functioned, according to its 1235 Christian charter, "just as it was in the time of the Saracens." The irrigation networks in the central part of the realm were assigned to the control of Valencia city a year after the conquest, "so that with them you can irrigate according as was anciently the custom."[9]

[8] Examples of such continuities are documented in succeeding chapters. Many vineyards, mills, ovens, baths, and the like can be indexed from the *Repartimiento.* Any number of Arabic place names paradoxically had Romance origins; the Low Latin diminutive Silvella ("little woods") entered Arabic as Xilvella, becoming the crusaders' Chiribella; Penacatella became Benicadell; conversely, Arabic names sometimes turned into pseudo-Romance, like Montaverner or Cebolla; the Romance Boayal acquired the Arabic prefix al, as Albal. Julián Ribera Tarragó gives further examples in his *Disertaciones y opúsculos* (Madrid, 1928), II, 355-357. Even when a locale changed hands, its elements often perdured, as at Segorbe where the Christian market was placed "in illo loco quo antiquitus tempus" the Moors had theirs (*Itinerari,* pp. 378, 380, documents of September and October 1265).

[9] Arch. Crown, James I, Reg. Canc. 15, fol. 90 (April 10, 1268): "ad rigandum illos quattuor campos . . . prout antiq[u]ius tempore sarracenorum fuit consuetum." *El "Repartiment" de Burriana y Villarreal,* ed. Ramón de María (Valencia, 1935), p. 41: "sicut fuerunt in tempore sarracenorum" (Burriana). *Aureum opus regalium priuilegiorum ciuitatis et regni Valentie* (Valencia, 1515), doc. 8, fol. 2r, v (Dec. 29, 1239): "ita quod ex eis possitis rigare secundum quod est antiquitus consuetum." A property dispute between two Játiva townsmen, the physician Baldwin and Cresque or Crescas of Gerona, was settled by consulting the previous Moorish situation (Arch. Nac. Madrid, Ords. Milits., Montesa, privs. reales, no. 130). A long disagreement over boundaries, carried on by Oropesa with its neighbors, was even-

Despite the imposition of a Valencian money and a Christian calendar, the Islamic calendar served the domestic needs of the Muslim majority, and Arabic coins continued to be minted here by the Christian king.

Beneath the surface of the kingdom of Valencia lay a submerged kingdom much more populous—King James's other realm, his Muslim vassals and subjects. What were to be the relations between the two peoples? How would James manage his Islamic kingdom and how would he fit it into his realm? He could not simply treat Valencians like the negligible Muslim minorities back in Aragon and Catalonia; on the other hand, he did not dare regard his conquest as a remote tributary appendage. Valencia was a special kingdom, for which the king had special plans.

The Crusaders

James I of Aragon controlled a mixed set of realms. Aragon proper, whence his royal title derived, comprised a feudal upland region not unlike its neighbor Castile. Catalonia, a progressive mercantile coastland with modified feudal survivals, belonged to the urban world of Languedoc, Provence, and Italy. The two areas were unevenly yoked, differing in psychology, resources, social structure, institutions, and even languages. The Catalans, speaking a language related to Limousin, formed an integral part of the troubadour culture. Many parts of lower Languedoc were bound to the Catalan king by feudal links. But the Roussillon region, and Montpellier with its university, belonged more directly to King James's realms, as much as Catalonia or the Pyrenean counties. All these entities, with their multiple law codes, privileges, and parliaments, found their center of unity only as part of the "Crown" of Aragon. To the distress of those who inherited the more dominant or Catalan culture, historians speak loosely of all as Aragonese and of their realms as Aragon.[10]

---

tually settled by appeal to antecedent Moorish custom. The first Christian laws of Valencia forbade interfering with or changing "vie antique, quibus itur ad hereditates, vineas, alquerias seu ad alia quelibet loca" (*Fori antiqui Valentiae*, ed. Manuel Dualde Serrano [Valencia, 1967], rub. 11, no. 7).

[10] The standard histories are in n. 2. On Catalan literary culture see Martín de Riquer and Antonio Comas, *Història de la literatura catalana*, 4 vols. to date (Barce-

Though the king was the essential symbol and key of unity, he did not reign unchallenged. Like contemporary kings he liked to surround himself with Roman lawyers, affecting the imperial prerogatives and trappings of a true monarch. Neither the feudal barons, who saw him rather as a first-among-equals suzerain, nor the townsmen, who accepted him more as a partner and a guarantor of communal semiautonomy, acquiesced completely in the royal vision. The political regime of the crown of Aragon was a *modus vivendi*, a constant readjustment of relationships between the several self-views held by its component parts. This may explain why King James (1213-1276) was not merely a man of letters and the author of an excellent autobiography but preeminently, in the best sense of the word, a politician. He was also a passionate defender of the Christian religion, a notorious womanizer, and a formidable crusader. Attended by a retinue of lawyers and counselors, he wandered restlessly back and forth over his unwieldy realms, spending a third of the last forty years of his rule within the kingdom of Valencia.[11]

Unlike his father, Peter the Catholic (1196-1213), who had lost his life fighting to retain control of Languedoc against the encroaching Albigensian crusade, James the Conqueror reserved his military strength for expansion into the Mediterranean world, first to the east to absorb the Balearics, then south to annex Valencia. The time

---

lona, 1964). The expression "Crown of Aragon" for the several realms may represent a late (1286) formulation; and "feudalism" in the context of James's kingdom should be understood less in the socioeconomic sense of northern Europe than as a loose suzerain-baronage-vassal set of relations (see below, Chapter XII).

[11] Biographies of James I include C. R. Beazley, *James of Aragon* (Oxford, 1890); Ferran Soldevila, *Els grans reis del segle xiii, Jaume I, Pere el Gran* (Barcelona, 1955), his later *Vida de Jaume I el Conqueridor* (Barcelona, 1958), and his *Els primers temps de Jaume I* (Barcelona, 1968); F. D. Swift, *The Life and Times of James the First, the Conqueror, King of Aragon, Valencia and Majorca, Count of Barcelona and Urgel, Lord of Montpellier* (Oxford, 1894); and Tourtoulon, *Jaime I.* Ambrosio Huici has edited a *Colección diplomática de Jaime I, el Conquistador*, 3 vols. (Valencia, 1916-1922). Joaquín Miret y Sans has constructed a day-by-day documentary in his *Itinerari de Jaume I.* Specialists in the era assembled essays on aspects of James's reign as the symposium *Congrés d'història de la corona d'Aragó, dedicat al rey en Jaume I y a la seua época*, 2 vols. (Barcelona, 1909-1913). F. Elías de Tejada clarifies the political trends in *Las doctrinas políticas en la Cataluña medieval* (Barcelona, 1950); see also Percy Schramm, "Der König von Aragon, seine Stellung im Staatsrecht (1276-1410)," *Historisches Jahrbuch*, LXXIV (1955), 99-123; and Ferran Valls-Taberner, "Les doctrines politiques de la Catalunya medieval," *Estudios histórico-jurídicos*, in his *Obras selectas*, II, 210-216.

spared from feudal or foreign wars and from other business he devoted to these conquests and their troublesome consolidation. In the enterprise of Valencia James associated his son and successor, the troubadour king Peter the Great (1276-1285). James was an Homeric figure, larger than life both in physique and in exploits; Peter gained more substantial fame as heir to the Hohenstaufen, by blunting French expansion during the War of the Sicilian Vespers and by absorbing Sicily. For both men, the same thrust toward Mediterranean empire appears in the creation of an extensive North African sphere of influence.[12]

The peoples who together comprised the crown of Aragon in the thirteenth century stood among the most advanced in Europe, panoplied in commerce, finance, and the varied contrivances of urban prosperity. The forward-looking elements of their commonwealth were enclaved in towns which amounted to semiautonomous city-states, each governing itself and its dependent villages by an elected complex of legislative council, executive jurates, and judicial justiciar. In this century the realms boasted one of the greatest universities of Europe at Montpellier, incomparably the greatest lawyer in Penyafort, a famous scholastic philosopher in Lull, and a mature vernacular literature. The towns of northern Italy sought the leadership of James against Emperor Frederick II; southern Italy found its champion in Peter. Even the Mongol khan, knowing Aragon's strength, courted alliance. The men of this federated realm were a courtly and successful people whose armies and navies moved across the central stage of world affairs in this and the following century.

When they invaded the kingdom of Valencia they brought with

[12] Besides the brief Soldevila biography of Peter in the *Els grans reis* above, see his larger *Vida de Pere el Gran i d'Alfons el Liberal* (Barcelona, 1963), but especially his ample work in progress, *Pere el Gran*, 4 vols. (Barcelona, 1950-1962). Two outstanding contemporary historians wrote lengthy works on the reigns of James and Peter: the Valencian Ramón Muntaner (1265-1336), a diplomat and crown administrator; and Bernat Desclot, probably the royal functionary Bernard Escrivá (d. 1289), prominent in Valencian affairs (see above and below, nn. 4 and 20). For Peter's Italian wars see Steven Runciman, *The Sicilian Vespers: A History of the Mediterranean World in the Later Thirteenth Century* (Cambridge, 1958), passim. Charles Dufourcq surveys Aragonese relations with North Africa, 1212-1331, in *L'Espagne catalane et le Maghrib.* For the episodes of the khan and Frederick II see my *Crusader Valencia*, I, 1-2.

them this atmosphere of dynamism and color, promptly creating an extension of their world of communes and commerce, of hospitals and elementary schools, of Gothic art, guilds, parliaments, scholasticism, and modern financial techniques. No sooner had they installed themselves than they confected for the conquered kingdom the first fully practical Romanized law code of Europe and established a university. They organized their proliferating religious institutions at the center and south into a diocese of Valencia; those at the north became part of the diocese of Tortosa; an intervening fragment struggled briefly to survive under Castilian auspices as the unwelcome diocese of Segorbe. Since Muslims so outnumbered immigrants from Catalonia, Aragon, and southern France, success in altering the appearance and atmosphere of Moorish Valencia provides a lesson in colonial technique.

The crusade itself can be summarized in a few paragraphs. King James's predecessors had ambitioned Valencia's conquest and raided it without notable success. The memory of the Cid's exploit had lured them on. James's grandfather had advanced his frontier down around the arid western flank of the kingdom as far as Teruel; at the north he had pushed, by mid-century, just beyond Tortosa. Here the power of Aragon had bogged, surrounding the upper part of the Islamic principality but shut out from its wealth and beauty. The kings took care now, by treaties with Castile in 1151 and 1179, to reserve Valencia as their own zone of conquest. Through the terrible days after Islam's victory over the allied Christian kingdoms at Alarcos in 1195, and through the glorious days after Las Navas de Tolosa—the Christian victory which countered Alarcos in 1212—the Arago-Catalans never forgot Valencia. Peter the Catholic could effect little, because of his involvements in Languedoc, but James dreamed of this conquest from the time he was a child. As early as 1225 the seventeen-year-old king led his first crusade south against Peñíscola, an offshore Gibraltar in northern Valencia. The result was a failure so painful that James wiped it from his memory and memoirs. From the debacle he salvaged a promise of tribute and a needed lesson in caution. Comparing the king's memoirs with the documentation, an historian recently concluded that James never entertained realistic hopes of taking the Valencian kingdom; he encouraged his barons to raid and occupy frontier zones, continuing the traditional seesaw interaction along the Christian-Islamic frontier, until internal circumstances and the fortunes of war revealed the dazzling opportunity of acquiring a kingdom.[13] Insurmountable obstacles, realistically appraised, do not cancel out dreams however; the jealous greed demonstrated by the treaties with Castile, together with the wild ambition confessed in the memoirs, kept the dream alive and later transmuted opportunity into conquest.

Valencia by its nature resisted annexation. It extended over a considerable portion of the Spanish peninsula's eastern coastline, comprising today the provinces of Castellón, Valencia, and northern Alicante. By its acquisition James's mainland domain was to increase from 87,000 to over 104,000 square kilometers. Valencia's coastal plains, displaying a series of irrigated huertas, river valleys, and prosperous towns, lay secure within bastions of bleak highlands and mountain ranges. By the easiest routes an unimpeded traveler required over a week to cover the length of the kingdom. Much of the northern country formed a rough borderland difficult for troops to operate against; at the southern extreme, where the kingdom was widest, a tumble of imposing sierras called the Alcoy massif also favored the defense. Valencia bristled with some fifty castles and strongholds. Its ports allowed provisioning from the sea or relief by the allied fleets of North Africa. Its south was buttressed by the kingdom of Murcia, itself backed against the bulwark of Granada. The armies of Islamic Valencia, as the crusade proved, equaled those of Arago-Catalonia in bravery, skill, and weapons.[14]

No other area of Islamic Spain, not even Granada, boasted such a combination of wealth, manpower, natural defenses, fortifications, and amplitude of territory. Shortly after its conquest, while acting as neutral arbiter for a royal inheritance dispute, the lawyer-pope Innocent IV summed up the findings of his experts: Valencia "in

[13] Antonio Ubieto Arteta, "La conquista de Valencia en la mente de Jaime I," *Saitabi*, XII (1962), 117-139.

[14] Geographical and allied detail on the area formerly comprising the kingdom of Valencia will be found abundantly in the massive volumes *Geografía general del reino de Valencia*, ed. Francisco Carreras y Candi, 5 vols. (Barcelona, 1920-1927). The estimate of seven days' travel is in *Llibre dels feyts*, ch. 128; al-Marrākushī, a Spanish traveler writing in 1224, reckoned the distance from Peñíscola to Valencia as three days, from there to Játiva two days and to Denia a full day, and from Játiva to Murcia three days.

revenues and income much exceeds the county of Barcelona."[15] He wrote this when the Catalan county of Barcelona, the central portion of the realms of Aragon, was in its glory, playing a significant role in international commerce. In short, the crusaders had set out in 1232 not to annex a province but to swallow whole a powerful realm. It is not too much to say that the acquisition of the Balearics and Valencia was the turning-point in Arago-Catalonia's history, making possible its extraordinary maritime and commercial expansion.[16]

King James had to rely on an army which operated by brief, bold strikes and then melted into oblivion. Feudal levies owed only a short service; town militias and the supply of foreign crusaders were an unpredictable quantity; money for expensive adventures was desperately hard to come by; and rebellious turmoils distracted the royal strength at home. Stubbornly James persisted. First he removed the flanking strength of the Balearics, taking Majorca in 1229 and neutralizing Minorca in 1231. He then settled down grimly to a fifteen-year struggle of intermittent campaigns against Valencia—fighting, intriguing, besieging, negotiating, acquiring supplies by trickery or pressure, mustering support by appeals to every available motive, and in the end inexorably moving forward. From 1229, when he intruded into a Valencian civil war by joining the more legitimate Muslim faction, until 1245, when Biar fell in the south, the new Cid clung to the kingdom like a bulldog. In 1232, while heady from his successful Majorca crusade, James publicly announced his determination to win Valencia. The north—the modern province of Castellón—he gained from 1232 to 1235. The major event among these early campaigns was the siege and fall of Burriana in 1233; the city's Muslims gained by their heroic defense only the concession of mass emigration.

External factors distracted the king and contributed to the lengthening of the crusade—especially his attempt to annex Navarre, his taking of a new wife, and his embroilments in Languedoc. In 1236

[15] Arch. Vat., Reg. Vat. 22, Innocent IV, fol. 88v, curiales, ep. 46 (March 5, 1251): "quod in redditibus et proventibus comitatum barchinonensem multum excedit."

[16] This is the conviction also of Gonzalo de Reparaz, "L'Activité maritime et commerciale d'Aragon au xiiie siècle et son influence sur le développement de l'école cartographique de Majorque," *Bulletin hispanique*, XLIX (1947), 422-451.

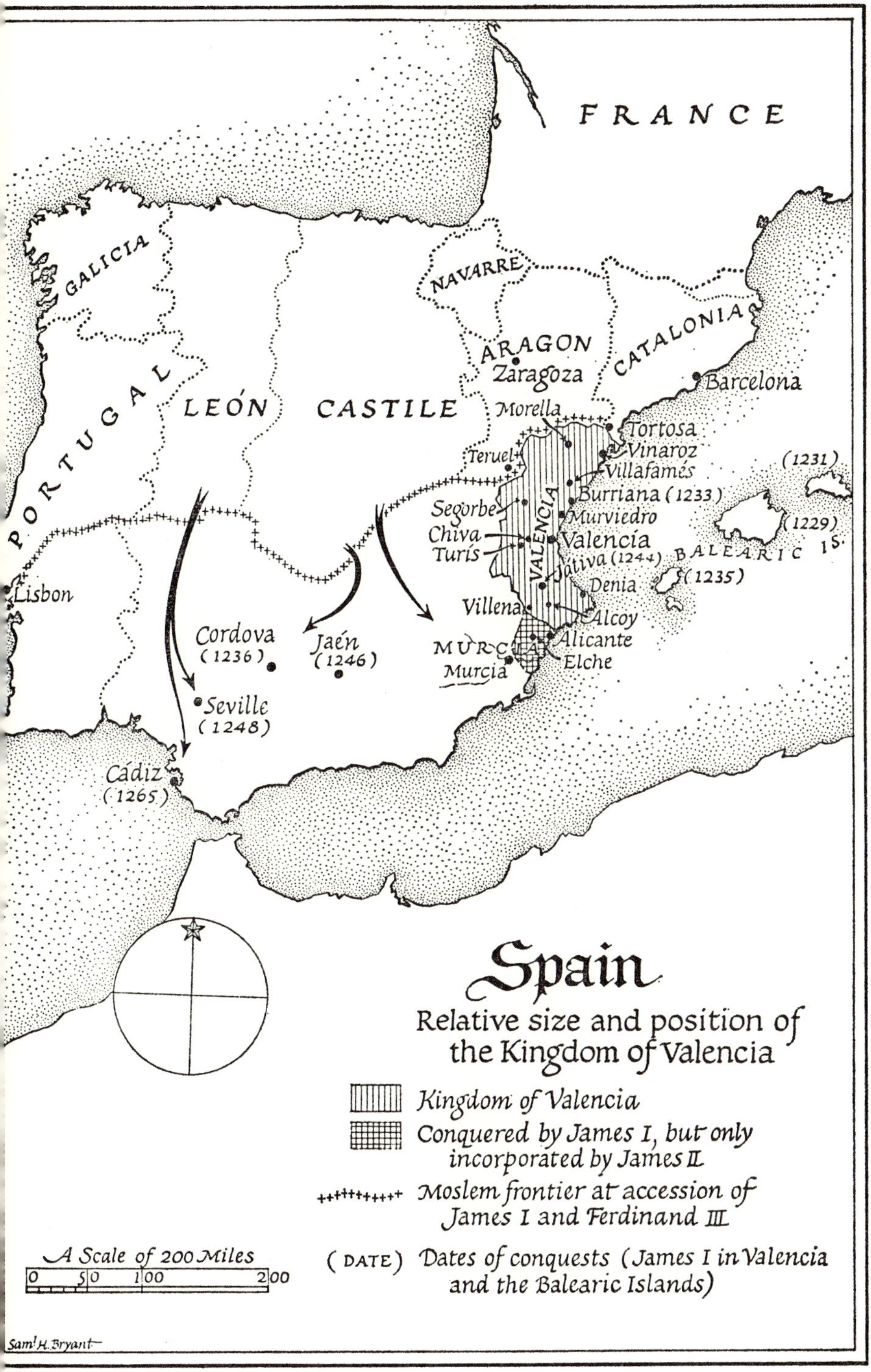

Thirteenth-Century Spain
(Reprinted from *The Crusader Kingdom of Valencia* by Robert I. Burns, S.J., Harvard University Press)

a fresh phase of the crusade opened. James rallied support in a general parliament at Monzón, and as symbol of his new determination adopted the title "King of Valencia." In the same year he ensconced his crusaders at Puig, a strategic hillock rising above the huerta within sight of Valencia city. After enemy assaults had failed to dislodge the Christian garrison, the Conqueror strengthened morale by vowing not to return north until the capital city had fallen. Town by town he cleared the zone just above the Guadalaviar. As crusaders poured south he put the capital city under siege, repelled the Tunisian relief fleet, and with relentless violence tightened his grip by the month. The Muslims watched their cause grow dimmer, their sallies fewer and less vigorous, their doom more sure. Like Burriana they neglected to surrender in time and in 1238 had to settle for the same fate of mass expulsion.

The Moors' battle line retreated now to run along the Júcar River, while their whole camp fell into confusion. King Zayyān retreated to Alcira, then to Denia, to Murcia, and finally to Alicante. At the end he pleaded for tributary governorship over Minorca in exchange for Alicante; James refused on the ground that Alicante lay within the zone already conceded to Castilian conquest. By January 1244 King James had thrown a strangling siege around Játiva, keystone to the south. Next year Biar, the southernmost effective stronghold, collapsed. Demoralized and outflanked, the last Moorish castles still sustaining the war hastened to surrender, from the Júcar down to the borders of Murcia.

The spectacle of a crusade led jointly by a Christian king and a deposed Almohad governor might seem bizarre—a crusade undertaken for a Muslim ruler, with Muslim and Christian contingents fighting side by side. Such a program fitted comfortably enough, however, into the wider history of Spain, which was not merely a story of Cross versus Crescent but a complex interplay of ideological struggle and expediency. King James was at home in this shifting world of international power politics, and played the game constantly and with skill. His negotiations with the Mongol khan, his attempt from about 1260 to capture the Egyptian trade, and his alliances with the Tunisian caliph in the 1260's and 1270's were all part of that interplay.

Consolidation and Reconstruction

James set about reorganizing and garrisoning his new kingdom, bringing settlers, parceling out lands, promulgating a law code, and arranging jurisdictions, taxes, and new money. Merchant ships crowded into the ports. Craftsmen set up their workbenches. Dioceses appeared, busily arranging their parish networks. An array of religious orders descended, to intrude their monasteries and priories. Churches and town halls were devised from abandoned mosques. Schools opened. Gothic edifices arose. Communal officers were sworn and electoral machinery created. Islamic Valencia drifted peacefully into its new orbit.

One element which might have eased this raw transfer of power and styles was missing. In the conquered kingdom no Mozarabic community remained. Had this Christian residue, immemorially assimilated to Islamic culture, interpreted Muslim to Christian and facilitated the take-over, Valencian history might have followed a less bitter and tumultuous course. The Mozarabs had long disappeared, however, melted away in the crucible of Almohad persecution, their remnants having fled into exile in the wake of Christian raiders. Whatever family units remained were statistically negligible. Some historians have argued that an inconsiderable nucleus still huddled around St. Vincent's shrine outside the south walls of Valencia city; the evidence is flimsy and unconvincing. King James never mentions such a group in all his voluminous records or autobiography. The closest research has not yielded a half-dozen individuals, though a scattering must have survived. James's clergy had to consecrate anew the Mozarabic church of St. Vincent's, just as they did the other mosques requisitioned for Christian use. Northern Christians had played a role in the Moorish kingdom's commercial life, and a small quarter stood reserved for their use; the crusade tumult seems to have emptied this.[17]

[17] Sanchis Guarner argues that the Mozarabs were "virtually annihilated" in the twelfth century here, and therefore practically invisible to the historian; he accepts the St. Vincent's group ("Època musulmana" in Miguel Tarradell, *Història del país valencià*, I, 338). He presents interesting linguistic deductions bearing on the problem in his *Introducción de la historia lingüística de Valencia* (Valencia, 1950), pp. 135ff., 147-148. The "carraria illa quam mercatores christiani uti tem-

Troubles disturbed the Christian camp. Just as the Majorcan crusade proved a field of exploitation for the seafaring Catalans, so Valencia represented opportunity for the landlocked people of Aragon proper. The Aragonese did expand across the Valencian border to some extent, but the mass of settlers fanning out over the kingdom were Catalans. Lérida and Urgel sent many families south, while others came from troubled Languedoc. The Catalans even advanced beyond Valencia, populating the Castilian area, so that cities like Murcia and Cartagena became as Catalanized as Orihuela and Alicante. The solid Catalan presence in Valencia, flaunting its own language, laws, sociopolitical forms, and peculiar psychology, constituted an affront to the Aragonese.

The Castilians for their own reasons resented the rapid advance of King James, though Castilian armies had not been idle. Town for town, the Castilian reconquest had surged forward parallel to that of Aragon. Cordova fell in 1236, Jaén in 1246, and Seville in 1248; Murcia yielded in 1243-1244, at least as garrisoned protectorate. Suspecting that Aragon might slyly continue south into Murcia, reserved by treaty to Castilian conquest, the future Alfonso X precipitated its premature surrender himself, consequently becoming entangled in a border dispute within Valencia. Difficulties were resolved by a treaty drawn at Almizra near Orihuela in 1244, sealed later by James's neighborly restoration of rebellious Murcia. At the

---

pore sarracenorum sollebant" appears in a property transaction of 1240, apparently located outside the Boatella gate (Arch. Cat., perg. 1,308, Oct. 21, 1240). The evidence for a Mozarabic community, based on the conventional phrase "place or church" in a grant of 1232 along with (anticipated) tithes there, can be seen in Roque Chabás y Lloréns, *Episcopologio valentino, investigaciones históricas sobre el christianismo en Valencia y su archidiócesis, siglos i a xiii*, 1 vol. only (Valencia, 1909), I, 64-66. See also Francisco Fernández y González, "Ampliación sobre los mozárabes valencianos," *El archivo*, v (1891), 28-30; Chabás, "Los mozárabes valencianos," *El archivo*, v (1891), 6-28, in *BRAH*, XVIII (1891), 19-49, and as an appendix to Josef Teixidor, *Antigüedades de Valencia: Observaciones críticas donde con instrumentos auténticos se destruye lo fabuloso dejando en su debida estabilidad lo bien fundado*, 2 vols. (Valencia, [1767] 1895), I, 391-420; L. Torres Balbás, "Mozarabías y juderías de las ciudades hispano-musulmanas," *Al-Andalus*, XIX (1954), 172-199. Cagigas, *Los mozárabes* (2 vols., Madrid, 1947) does not reach our period but furnishes useful background and a sound general bibliography. For older general works like Simonet, see my Bibliography. For the tangled case of St. Peter Pascual, perhaps a Valencian Mozarab at this time, see my *Crusader Valencia*, p. 309 and bibliographical note.

turn of the century, James II was to acquire the Alicante-Orihuela region, but for the present the work of reconquest in Valencia had to be essentially consolidation and reconstruction.

To place Valencia beyond jealous interference by Aragon proper, and beyond a too obvious link with Catalonia, King James set it up as a distinct kingdom. Its urbanism acted as a lever for royal against baronial power, while its wealth and extent made it a compensating balance for political reverses in Aragon. The Roman law fostered by King James conferred title to all the conquered territory to the crown; feudal precedent and practical considerations dictated his sharing with fellow crusaders and with the copowers of his realms. This sharing fulfilled the crusade promises of reward, gave his subjects a stake in the new project, and rendered local government possible. Important barons received estates, which they managed almost like little kings; dioceses, religious and military orders, and clerics of all kinds secured similar estates, graced also with a measure of exemption and independent power. In contrast to these seignorial domains were the regalian or crown lands, including most of the cities. Property-holding was diversified; the lord who presided over his nearly independent barony might also hold warehouses, residences, and farms on regalian territory. García y García, who has studied in depth the politico-economic organization of the northern part of the Valencia kingdom, reckons that the barons and church (who were at their strongest in that segment) held respectively 900 and 2,800 square kilometers out of a total of 5,000, while the king kept 1,300.[18]

Each of these three classes of landholder could improve an estate by attracting settlers. Piecemeal distribution to individuals, crowned by issuance of a local integrating charter or a set of privileges, sometimes proved less effective than previous issuance of a charter to an entrepreneurial agent or company who then lured settlers to some small locality and divided its available free land. Whether the contract or constitution was individual, communal-antecedent, or communal-prior, the lord might in feudal fashion stress such factors as military service and homage or else in capitalist spirit orient the arrangement rather toward maximum income. The king as largest landholder did not necessarily rule directly, through

[18] García y García, *Estado económico-social de Castellón*, pp. 26-27.

crown officers and the machinery of municipal government, but in a number of places interposed vassal knights or subrenters, arranging some acceptable division of the private rents and public taxes. Depending on the law code prevalent in a lord's homeland, on the compromises required to attract settlers, and on the converging mixture of Islamic practice with customs cherished by the several kinds of settler, conditions of life in the new realm varied. King James preferred to frame the local constitutions or contractual grants of Christian settlers, wherever feasible, in the wider context of Valencia city's new code and growing book of privileges.[19]

Being so huge, the kingdom of Valencia never acquired enough settlers to guarantee its safety; near the end of his life James complained to the people of Barcelona that only 30,000 had established themselves when security required a minimum of 100,000. The small, steady immigration diversified itself by sudden surges from time to time, as expulsion of Muslims threw open desirable tracts. Because of mass expulsions at Burriana and Valencia, as well as postrevolt expulsions at places like Morella, those areas became Christian. Settlers favored the cities, each family acquiring also an extramural farm. If Catalans had less experience in living and coping with Muslims than did the men of Aragon proper, the southern French contingents from Montpellier, Marseilles, Perpignan, Narbonne, and the trans-Pyrenean area generally, were even more innocent. To turn from crusader into neighbor and colleague was difficult for them.

Settlement of rural farmlands corresponded to antecedent Moorish patterns of specialization and intense cultivation in the huertas and valleys, preserving what a recent historian calls multiple minifarms. At Murcia James I and to some extent Alfonso X were to prefer the contrary expedient of presenting large sweeps of huerta to relatively few owners. That the northern part of the conquered kingdom of Valencia had been almost wholly abandoned by its Muslims is a common assumption; in any case Christian settlement proved

[19] Without elaborating a full bibliography on such topics as land tenure, or anticipating the sections below on the peculiarities of Valencian feudalism and the details of taxes, rent, and government, the reader may be referred to García y García's careful analysis of the system at work in what is now Castellón province, especially ch. 4 on the *carta puebla*, ch. 6 on the condition of the settlers, ch. 7 on their rights, and ch. 13 on the administrative offices.

sparse there except for the swift influx at Morella and Burriana. Clutches of Christians did assemble slowly at northern places like Peñíscola and Castellón, but the effect was patchy. The military orders and the powerful secular magnates were prominent up north. In the central area, between the Mijares and Guadalaviar rivers, the crown was the main landlord; barons held scattered towns, especially Chelva and Liria, and for a time Segorbe was alienated from royal control. Resettlement there seems to have been meager, except for Murviedro, with some quickening after the revolt and expulsion of Muslims in 1247.

Below this heavily Moorish area lay the confiscated countryside belonging to Valencia city. Over two-thirds of its Muslims may eventually have left; consequently the area bore the brunt of Christian immigration, long remaining the nucleus of settlement in the realm. From the Júcar south, Muslims remained in force until the 1247 troubles; Christians appeared in numbers at a few places like Denia, and comprised a peppering of strangers in other attractive regions like Alcira and Játiva. Local mass exodus after the 1247 revolt only partially improved the situation, Alcira, Valldigna, and the Játiva country especially receiving settlers, while Gandía and some other points acquired small accretions. Throughout the mountainous lower frontier the scattering of Christian settlement was a little heavier—some 40 at Luchente, 300 in the Albaida valley, 50 at Alcoy, 40 in the Jalón valley, 125 around Guadalest, 40 at Altea, and so on. These estimates by Sobrequés represent a fair statement of immigration patterns insofar as they are visible to the historian.[20]

[20] The basic data is in the *repartimiento* of the Valencia kingdom (editions above in n. 7), with analogous materials in the *Repartimiento de Murcia,* ed. Juan Torres Fontes (Madrid, 1960), the *Repartimiento de Mallorca,* ed. Próspero de Bofarull y Mascaró, *Colección de documentos inéditos del archivo general de la corona de Aragón,* XII, 1-141, and the *Repartimiento de Sevilla,* ed. Julio González (Madrid, 1951). Surveys of the Valencia settlement are in Font y Rius, "Reconquista y repoblación," and in Santiago Sobrequés Vidal, "Patriciado urbano," in Jaime Vicens Vives *et alii, Historia social y económica de España y América,* 4 vols. to date (Barcelona, 1957ff.), II, part 1, ch. 1; J. E. Martínez-Ferrando, "Estado actual de los estudios sobre la repoblación en los territorios de la corona de Aragón (siglos xii al xiv)," *VII Congrés d'història de la corona d'Aragó,* 3 vols. (Barcelona, 1962-1964), I, esp. 172-180. Miguel Gual Camarena has plotted the settlements according to law codes in his "Contribución al estudio de la territorialidad de los fueros de Valencia," *EEMCA,* III (1947-1948), 262-289; and Ramón de María concentrates on one locale in *"Repartiment" de Burriana.* On the Catalans populat-

Further penetration may be possible by using evidence from tithes and by closely examining the parish network in the three dioceses of the Valencian kingdom.[21]

In 1270 the crown regularized its previously piecemeal distribution of lands through a general auditing and adjusting of the records. Though mostly tenanted with Mudejars under Christian landlords and with patchwork clusters of Christian farmers, the realm by this time featured several Christian cities with Mudejar ghettos, a larger number of towns unequally divided between the two peoples, and a multitude of predominantly Moorish villages. The northern part of the realm displayed large estates and a drowsy cattle industry, while the coastal strip continued to boast a thriving urban and commercial economy surrounded by a small-farming hinterland. Throughout the new realm the crown was the largest single landholder. It controlled as well the cities and most of the large towns. Only the north showed extensive baronial estates, and only the northwest resembled the feudal uplands of Aragon. Much of the countryside was parceled to rural knights, whose status did not differ greatly from that of the small farmer or landlord. Important cities in the north included Peñíscola and Burriana on the coast and Morella in the mountains. At the center along the coast stood Murviedro, Valencia, and Cullera, with Liria and Segorbe inland to their north, and Alcira at the south linked by river to the sea. In the southern part of the realm, Játiva loomed above its huerta on a

ing the Murcia kingdom see Ramón Muntaner, *Crònica*, ed. Enrique Bagué, 9 vols. in 2 (Barcelona, 1927-1952), ch. 17; King James's *Llibre dels feyts*, ch. 453; and the *Crónica del rey Don Alfonso X*, ch. 15; Juan Torres Fontes, "Jaime I y Alfonso X, dos criterios de repoblación," *Congrés VII*, III, 331, 333, 339. Miguel Gual Camarena takes up the problem of the post-1266 repopulation of the Murcian huerta in "La corona de Aragón en la repoblación murciana," *Congrés VII*, concluding that 45 percent of the immigrants were from King James's realms (including 3 percent from Aragon and 39 percent from Catalonia, southern France, Majorca, and Valencia itself), 18 percent from Castile, and 17 percent of unknown origin (see esp. p. 309). See also the allied studies of Joaquín Espín Rael, "De la conquista y repartimientos de tierras a los conquistadores y pobladores de Lorca," *ACCV*, XVIII (1957), 93-102, though Torres Fontes has corrected his chronology and interpretation, and J. M. Font y Rius, "El repartimiento de Orihuela (notas para el estudio de la repoblación levantina)," *Homenaje a Jaime Vicens Vives*, ed. J. Maluquer de Motes, 2 vols. (Barcelona, 1965), I, 418-430.

[21] Done in detail in my *Crusader Valencia*; see esp. I, 44-53; 76-87, with parish maps for each diocese; and on the tithe see chs. 8-9.

rocky inland ridge, while Gandía and Denia looked seaward from the coast, and mountain towns like Alcoy survived in the rugged sierra. Below that massif, Castilian Alicante and Orihuela dominated the farther flatlands. All this was now part of Christendom. The map of Europe extended down the western coast of the Mediterranean, with European cities penciled on it from Peñíscola to Murcia and beyond.

Jostled aside and all but ignored, the Muslim majority seemed at first to accept all changes. It declined into a huge ghetto, absorbed in its own parochial daily round, a faceless sea around the colonial atolls. But from time to time the Moors revealed their secret unhappiness, flaring into revolt, riding again in their thousands behind some patriot leader. In each successive decade rebellion made Valencia again a land of decision—in the late 1240's, 1250's, 1260's, and 1270's. Valencia was a land of constant crusade, its dissident majority a permanent problem. As in later colonial countries, the problem lurked just below the rim of visibility, surfacing savagely, if infrequently. The dominant minority contrived to create the illusion of a single presence, an illusion which could assume strength and a certain reality only as the decades passed.

On the Conqueror's tomb his people incised the boastful legend, "Contra Sarracenos semper praevaluit" ("He always triumphed over the Saracens").[22] The inscription, however, came only in the following century. At the time of King James's death the kingdom of Valencia, enmeshed in an Islamic countercrusade, was unsafe for such leisured niceties. His warriors interred him at Valencia city hurriedly. Only in 1278 did a lull in the war allow them to honor his last request by ceremoniously translating the corpse to Poblet monastery.

[22] The full inscription and story is in Ricardo del Arco, *Sepulcros de la casa real de Aragón* (Madrid, 1945), ch. 13, esp. p. 192.

CHAPTER II

Death of an Islamic Empire

THE CONTEXT OF Moorish weakness renders more explicable Valencia's stunning fall. In a moment of insane fratricide Islam left her doors open to the conqueror. Though Valencia was technically not a kingdom, the Christians' use of the term *rex* or king for an Almohad *sayyid* does convey her isolation and furnishes a clue to the malaise of contemporary Spanish Islam.[1] A quarter-century before the Valencian crusade, Islamic Andalusia stood solid as a rock. Sharing an imperial serenity which evokes images of the Roman empire,[2] she presented to the hostile northerners a strong frontier running from just below Lisbon in an upward slanting line almost to the Ebro River, bending in the center of Spain to accommodate a Christian salient at Toledo and Calatrava. Within the salient the Moors had just won their victory at Alarcos in 1195. "Never was such a defeat heard of in Spain," wrote Ibn Khallikān a half-century later. The Moroccan caliph lacked the resources to exploit it, and the victor himself gave way only four years later to a far less able ruler; but in 1200 the Almohad empire still loomed in the sunset of that triumph, with its caliph installed behind the rose walls of Marrakesh on the edge of the Sahara, and with its movement of religious reform and military zeal still apparently charged with primal energy.[3]

[1] Islamic *malik* or king, unlike the Christian *rex*, held no necessary connotation of sovereignty, having long been used as well for governor, nor would the legal significance be the same as the European even for a sovereign; see Chapter XV, section 1.

[2] Emilio García Gómez returns several times to this comparison, e.g., in his *Poemas arábigoandaluces* (4th edn., Madrid, 1959), p. 40.

[3] A sturdy guide through the maze of chronological and interpretative difficulties is Huici, *Imperio almohade*, esp. II, ch. 7; on Las Navas, see II, 425-429; on the technical *sayyid* category, originally of more modest significance, under the Almohads, appendix 2; his introduction surveys the sources as well as Western and Arabic historians of the dynasty. He summarizes the Spanish part of the story briefly in his *Historia musulmana de Valencia*, III, 219-226. See also Robert Brunschvig, *La Berbérie orientale sous les ḥafṣides*, 2 vols. (Paris, 1940-1947), I, chs. 1 (to 1277) and 2 (to 1318); Charles André Julién, *Histoire de l'Afrique du nord,*

The Almohad Crisis

Beneath the imposing facade a vast erosion was at work. The empire lacked cohesion, its local parts heaving in uneasy stability, its past history punctuated with revolts. Its military despotism, functioning without popular roots, remained a stranger to the native

---

Tunisie-Algérie-Maroc, de la conquête arabe à 1830, rev. Roger Le Tourneau, 2 vols. (Paris, 1951-1952), II, ch. 3, esp. pp. 118ff., of which vol. II is available in English as *History of North Africa: Tunisia, Algeria, Morocco, from the Arab Conquest to 1830*, ed. Roger Le Tourneau and C. C. Stewart (New York, 1970); Henri Terrasse, *Histoire du Maroc des origines à l'établissement du protectorat français*, 2 vols. (Casablanca, 1950), II, ch. 1 (to 1269); Roger Le Tourneau, *The Almohad Movement in North Africa in the Twelfth and Thirteenth Centuries* (Princeton, 1969), and his interpretative essay, "L'occident musulman du milieu du viie siècle à la fin du xve siècle," *Annales de l'institut d'études orientales*, II (1936), esp. pp. 166-167. Focusing more on the Spanish story see, besides Huici, Cagigas, *Mudejares*, II, chs. 3, 4, and esp. 6; his *Sevilla almohade y últimos años de su vida musulmana* (Madrid, 1951), pp. 19-28; Sánchez-Albornoz, *España musulmana*, II, parts 5-6; Henri Terrasse, *Islam d'Espagne: Une rencontre de l'orient et de l'occident* (Paris, 1958), ch. 5. Useful older works include the adaptation from al-Maqqarī, *Mohammedan Dynasties in Spain*, II, 327-340. For Valencia see Sanchis Guarner's segment of Tarradell *et alii, Història del país Valencià*, I, part 2, ch. 5, and Piles Ibars, *Valencia árabe*, esp. chs. 14, 15. Though Lévi-Provençal's detailed histories stop short of this period, his article "Balansiya," *EI²*, I, 985-986, sketches his basic information. J. E. Martínez-Ferrando devotes a rather summary chapter to "La dominació aràbiga a la Catalunya nova, València i les illes" in his *Baixa edat mitjana (segles xii, xiii, xiv, xv)*, in Ferran Soldevila, *Història dels Catalans*, 3 vols. to date (Barcelona, 1961ff.), II, ch. 2. Dufourcq supplies background on each of the states emerging in North Africa out of the Almohad breakup, carefully tracing their diplomatic-commercial relations with thirteenth-century Aragon (*L'Espagne catalane et le Maghrib*, passim). Among older works, the *Geografía general del reino de Valencia* has a substantial section on Arabic Valencia, I, 348-362, and useful notes passim. Extreme care is required both as to chronology and interpretation in accepting source or secondary writings. An example of misleading Arabic works is Ibn Abī Zar' al-Fāsī, part 3 of whose popular history of western Islam, written before 1326, deals with the Almohad era; he has Valencia city fall in 1245 and is often misinformed, yet he conveys the spirit and general movement of the times. See his *Rawḍ al-qirṭās*, trans. Ambrosio Huici, 2d edn., 2 vols. (Valencia, 1964), II, 455ff., 476ff., 529 (1st edn., *El cartás* [Valencia, 1918], pp. 279-282). Ibn Khaldūn has penetrating comments on Almohad North Africa and Spain in his *Muqaddimah* as cited below passim, and especially in his *Histoire des Berbères*, II, 212-257, from the Alarcos battle through the first quarter of the thirteenth century, 235ff., 280ff., 319, and passim. The quotation is from Ibn Khallikān, *Biographical Dictionary*, trans. Baron de Slane, 4 vols. (Paris, 1843-1861), IV, 310, and see pp. 335-351. See also the Muslim authors above, Chapter I, n. 4, and below, n. 13.

Spanish Muslim. Ibn Khaldūn, descendant of exiled aristocrats from conquered Seville, recorded that the Spaniards "detested this domination" by "Almohad Berbers"; the Almohad "oppression weighed heavily upon them, and their hearts were filled with hate and indignation" against the aliens.[4] Even the Almohad religious enthusiasms, the dynasty's *raison d'être*, were not fully shared by Spanish Muslims. Monolithic governments tend to take on a peculiar brittleness in moments of crisis anyway; uncertainty and fear counsel each local leader to look to himself, to hoard his reserve of power, and to enter upon a political course of irresponsible feudalism. If the handsome but lazy new caliph (1199) proved a lesser man than the victor of Alarcos, his successor in turn (1213) was a footling youngster. Worse still, Christendom had reacted to the humiliation of Alarcos by abandoning its own factionalism and moving massively to crusade. The Christian victory at Las Navas de Tolosa in 1212 led directly to the fragmentation of Islamic Spain. A combatant at Las Navas recorded how the great bonfires destroying the enemy's stores of lances and bows lit up the summer sky, so that the victors needed no other light by which to celebrate through the night. The leaping flames proved to be the funeral pyre of a mighty culture.[5]

When the Christian states of the peninsula began systematically to exploit the results of Las Navas two decades later, the great regional centers of Spanish Islam from the Atlantic to the Mediterranean succumbed to their armies with dismal regularity. "The Spanish Muslims had to suffer the conquest of their castles, the

[4] Ibn Khaldūn, *The Muqaddimah: An Introduction to History,* trans. Franz Rosenthal, 2d edn., 3 vols. (Princeton, 1967), I, 334-335. Huici reaches the same conclusion, *Imperio almohade,* II, 576. The contemporary warrior-bishop and primate of Spain, Rodrigo Jiménez de Rada, had already reported this feeling: "cismarinos Arabes adeo crudeli dominio opprimebant quod de facili Abenhuti proposito consenserunt"; *De rebus Hispaniae,* lib. IX, c. 13, in his *Opera* (Valencia, [1793] 1968), p. 202, though the authorship is moot. Ibn 'Abdūn illustrates the same popular perception of the Berber as alien when speaking of Seville's Almoravid rulers (*Séville musulmane au début du xiie siècle, le traité d'Ibn 'Abdūn,* trans. Évariste Lévi-Provençal [Paris, 1947], pp. 19-20, 62).

[5] Jiménez de Rada, *De rebus Hispaniae,* lib. VIII, c. 11, p. 188. Le Tourneau, *Almohad Movement,* pp. 83ff., 86, on the significance of Las Navas as symptom and symbol; pp. 93ff. on the "complete" collapse by 1248, the Marrakesh enclave until 1269, and the negligible enclave until 1275; and pp. 100-101 on civil wars.

pillaging of their territory, the loss of their provinces, the occupation of their towns, and the ruin of their properties," Ibn Khaldūn reported in his fourteenth-century history of the Maghrib. "In 1239 [637] the count of Barcelona conquered the city of Valencia," and "in eastern Andalusia the power of the independent chiefs was destroyed." Despite stubborn resistance, convulsive countercrusades, desperate little rebellions, and ready alliances with North Africa, nearly all of Andalusia by mid-century or shortly afterwards lay in Christian hands, with only the small state of Granada remaining under Muslim control, as an autonomous vassal of Castile. The multitude of poets and mystics of Spanish Islam, all the builders, philosophers, and statesmen, found themselves unroofed, strangers immersed beneath the chilling floodwaters of the onrushing Christian world.

The interior story of western Islam during the 1220's, 1230's, and 1240's is painful even in outline. Disintegration was so confusingly kaleidoscopic that the mere retelling imposes some repetitive doubling-back. North Africa suffered increasingly violent convulsions and fragmentation. Autonomous from 1229, Tunisia declared its independence in 1236 under the Hafsid family, who soon usurped the title of caliph; in 1283 it broke into two parts, Bougie and Tunis. Near the end of the Valencian crusade the Zayyanid dynasty created the kingdom of Tlemcen between Tunis and Morocco. Morocco itself thrashed through decades of civil war until the Almohads lost their capital Marrakesh in 1269, a decade after the Mongols overran Bagdad and ended the glories of the Abbasid caliphate; henceforth the new dynasty of Marinids governed Morocco from Fez. Tying the sieges of Valencia, Cordova, and Seville with those of Marrakesh and Bagdad, Ibn Khaldūn mourned that Islam had been left without a caliph in either East or West.[6]

While bloody disorders racked North Africa, Spanish rule devolved into ancient localisms, each area further disintegrating into fractional squabbles. The governor of Murcia, refusing to accept his uncle as the new caliph in 1224, gained Marrakesh under the caliphal title al-'Ādil, but without establishing a firm military foundation. His brother al-Ma'mūn, seizing power first at Cordova and Seville,

[6] Ibn Khaldūn, *Histoire des Berbères*, II, 306, 373; IV, 74. The Marinid sultans did not accept the title caliph until the early fourteenth century.

repeated the adventure in 1227-1229. He had the foresight to negotiate for a truce and 500 Castilian cavalry (not the legendary 12,500) from King St. Ferdinand III, and to amass an army from African garrisons throughout Spain.[7] Below the surface of intra-Almohad governmental disturbances, riot and disorder further splintered Andalusia. The Almohad governor of Valencia and his brother the governor of Cordova and Jaén repudiated al-'Ādil. To forestall Christian and Muslim enemies each brother had made overtures to Castile by 1225, buttressing his shaky independence with its overlordship and auxiliaries. The spectacle of Almohad complicity with the infidel Christians in turn sparked revolts by the older native aristocracy of Islamic Spain; these families had stayed relatively aloof from the urban mainstream, Ibn Khaldūn explains, and clung to a military role in lesser centers. As "the Almohad lords handed over many of their strongholds to the Abominable [Christian ruler] in order to gain his support for their attempts to capture the capital city of Marrakesh," and as Spain had already been stripped of many Almohad garrisons to aid this convulsive effort, anti-Almohad revolutions broke out within the existing rebellions.[8]

A hero arose at Murcia named Abū 'Abd Allāh Muḥammad b. Yūsuf b. Hūd al-Mutawakkil. One Christian chronicle dismisses Ibn Hūd as a rootless plebeian demagogue; another exalts him as a descendant of the rulers of Islamic Zaragoza; Ibn 'Idhārī relates that his ancestors had held high office locally. Building upon a reputation as a rashly valiant soldier and stirring the populace by his religious fanaticism, Ibn Hūd seized Murcia in 1228 and proclaimed himself emir for the distant Abbasid caliph of Bagdad. His triumphant forces wrested or welcomed city after city for the black flag of the Abbasids, beheading Almohad partisans and washing out the mosques tainted by Almohad worship. His anti-Almohad

[7] On the legend see Huici, *Imperio almohade*, II, 471-472; and his *Historia musulmana de Valencia*, III, 241-242. See also Ibn Khaldūn, *Histoire des Berbères*, II, 235, as against the *Rawḍ al-qirṭās*; Cagigas, *Mudejares*, II, 346; J.F.P. Hopkins, *Medieval Muslim Government in Barbary until the Sixth Century of the Hijra* (London, 1958), pp. 76-78; Charles Emmanuel Dufourcq, "Les relations du Maroc et de la Castille pendant la première moitié du xiiie siècle," *Revue d'histoire et de civilisation du Maghreb*, v (1968), p. 43.

[8] Ibn Khaldūn, *Muqaddimah*, I, 335; see also p. 313 and II, 129. On II, 116, he used the Almohad breakup as a classic illustration of how a dynasty fragments.

movement blazed like a fire out of control, briefly winning almost all Islamic Spain to a single unity. Inevitably this unity in turn began to dissolve as rival factions rallied. Important local families with a stake in Almohad posts remained cool to his revolt. The Castilians bloodily repulsed his attempt to mount a holy war. What was worse, the demagoguery which gave Ibn Hūd a power base among the lower classes occasioned an aristocratic counterrevolution from 1232. Ibn al-Aḥmar or "(the son of) the Red," its leader, "rose to power and opposed Ibn Hūd's propaganda," acting on behalf of the rebel Almohad splinter-state at Hafsid Tunis and with the aid of Marinid chieftains "from across the sea" in Morocco.[9] Ibn al-Aḥmar founded the Nasrid principality of Granada, whose red flag was destined by mid-century to fly over the sole remnant of Islam's glories in Spain. Ibn Hūd, though driven to invoke the tributary protection of Castile, exercised power vigorously for some six more years; at his murder in 1238 the fragile unity of his diminished state dissolved in a welter of local uprisings. These excitements of larger scope over more than a decade were punctuated by a dizzying succession of assassinations, beheadings, reprisals, depositions, intrigues, betrayals, restorations, riots, ephemeral lesser rebellions, vindictive massacres, noisy tumults, bloody battles, and disconcerting losses of territory to the armies of Castile and Aragon.

[9] Ibn Khaldūn, *Muqaddimah*, I, 335; *Histoires des Berbères*, II, 224-225. Ibn Abī Zarʿ, *Rawḍ al-qirṭās*, pp. 476ff., 526ff. Muḥammad b. ʿAbd Allāh b. al-Khaṭīb, Lisān ad-Dīn, *Islamische Geschichte Spaniens, Übersetzung der Aʿmāl al-aʿlām und ergänzender Texte*, ed. Wilhelm Hoenerbach (Zurich, 1970), pp. 488-493. The career of Ibn Hūd, elaborated by a number of Muslim authors, like the contemporary Ibn ʿAskar, is also reviewed by historians of Murcia like Mariano Gaspar Remiro, Antonio Ballesteros Beretta, and most recently by Juan Torres Fontes, *La reconquista de Murcia en 1266 por Jaime I de Aragón* (Murcia, 1967), ch. I. See also al-Maqqarī, *Mohammedan Dynasties*, II, 327ff.; Huici, *Historia musulmana de Valencia*, III, 227-249. Antonio Prieto y Vives sees Ibn Hūd as a vulgar demagogue, his assassination a public-relations fiction, and his intention of helping Valencia against James I a face-saving invention by the chroniclers (*Formación del reino de Granada* [Madrid, 1929]), pp. 7-11. On Granada's rise, see also Miguel Ladero Quesada, *Granada, historia de un país islámico (1232-1571)* (Madrid, 1969), pp. 73ff. and ch. 2, with corresponding ch. 3 on Castile; Henri Terrasse, "Gharnāṭa," *EI*², II, 1012-1020. Ibn ʿAskar, first Nasrid *qāḍī* of Malaga from 1238, characterized Ibn Hūd as brave, generous, disliking violence, but a poor administrator (Joaquín Vallvé Bermejo, "Una fuente importante de la historia de al-Andalus, la 'Historia' de Ibn ʿAskar," *Al-Andalus*, XXXI [1966], 237-265).

Valencia at Bay

An exception to these hectic enthusiasms was the Valencia region. Though its history paralleled the disorders, it reflected them in its special pattern. The dynasty governing for the Moroccan Almohads remained loyal to the old traditions. Even when the Almohad pretender al-'Ādil began his move from Murcia toward the Marrakesh throne, the one Almohad governor refusing to support the upstart was the Valencian, who belligerently put his province on a war footing. This was the *sayyid* Abū Zayd, *wālī* or governor over the regional entities of Valencia, Alcira, Denia, Játiva, and in some tutorial fashion over the governorship of Murcia. His title *sayyid* designated him as an Almohad prince of the blood; of his nine brothers, one became caliph at Marrakesh, another was narrowly cheated of the title by assassination, and a third administered conquered Seville for Ferdinand III of Castile.

In documents for Christians Abū Zayd described himself by accommodation as king (*rex*); his kingdom comprised the larger part of Spanish Islam's eastern coast, stretching from the borders of Aragon near Tortosa down into Murcia. Ibn Khaldūn styled him "governor of Valencia and of eastern Spain," and King James was to receive from him a tribute out of the taxes both of Valencia and of Murcia. This personage signed the sonorous name *sayyid* 'Abd ar-Raḥmān b. *sayyid* Abū 'Abd Allāh (Muḥammad) b. *sayyid* Abū Ḥafṣ ('Umar); a final element related his connection as grand-nephew of the awesome 'Abd al-Mu'min, founder of the Almohad caliphate and successor to the founder of the Almohad sect. Abū Zayd incorporated on his official seal this descent from the caliphal Amīr al-Mu'minīn or "Commander of the Believers."

He had come to power at about the same time as King James, though he died a decade sooner than the Conqueror. Abū Zayd was contending with the aggressive al-'Ādil when Valencia sustained its first invasion by the crusaders of Aragon, the abortive siege of Peñíscola in 1225. Fortified by an accommodation with Castile that same year, the embattled *wālī* bought off the trouble-makers from Aragon by signing away as permanent tribute in 1226 a fifth of the public rents throughout both Valencia and Murcia. The humiliation hardly helped the Almohad cause. Three years later Ibn Hūd erupted at Murcia and routed the Valencian armies sent to help. The attention of Abū Zayd soon became diverted by a challenge within his heartland. The revolutionary enthusiasm had precipitated an Abbasid-oriented revolt at Onda north of Valencia city in 1228 under Ibn Mardanīsh or Zayyān. Abū Jamīl Zayyān b. Abi 'l-Ḥamlāt Mudāfi' b. Abi 'l-Ḥajjāj b. Sa'd b. Mardanīsh, to give this aristocratic rebel his full name, was a grandnephew of the celebrated King Lobo or Lūb of Valencia (Muḥammad b. 'Abd Allāh b. Sa'd b. Mardanīsh). Dead only fifty years, this last pre-Almohad ruler of the region, praised by pope and princes, now lent an air of glory to his descendants. Branches of his Banū Mardanīsh controlled such strategic centers as Alcira, Denia, and Játiva. The rebel chief of Onda displayed his royal relative's name like a flag in his public dealings; even the Christian crusaders acknowledged his status later when accepting Valencia's surrender, addressing him in Latinized style as "King Zayen, nephew of King Lupus and son of Modef."[10]

Abū Zayd, insecure before the encircling Banū Mardanīsh centers to his south and southwest, withdrew from his capital north into the Segorbe-Jérica-Alpuente region, backed against Aragon proper. Triumphantly Zayyān entered Valencia city in January 1229, installing himself in its abandoned alcazar. He coined his own

[10] The only study of Abū Zayd is Roque Chabás y Lloréns, "Çeid Abu Çeid," *El archivo*, IV (1890), 215-221, V (1891), 143-166, 288-304, 362-376. See also Huici, *Imperio almohade*, II, 617ff., the closing chapters of his *Historia musulmana de Valencia*, and Piles Ibars, *Valencia árabe*, ch. 15, esp. pp. 591-595. James's tribute is in *Llibre dels feyts*, ch. 25; the quotation from Ibn Khaldūn is from his *Histoire des Berbères*, II, 223. The papal legate's story, "sicut idem nobis [Juan, bishop of Osma?] retulit viva voce," is in "Chronique latine des rois de Castille jusqu'en 1236," ed. Georges Cirot, *Bulletin hispanique*, XV (1913), 272-274; see also the later chronicler on p. 273n. On the incorrect form Abū Sa'īd, see my Preface. Ibn al-Abbār, counselor both to Abū Zayd and to Zayyān, gives the latter's name as Abū Jamīl Zayyān b. Mudāfi' b. Yūsuf b. Sa'd al-Judhāmī ("Un traité inédite," p. 32); Huici substitutes Abū Jumayl (*Historia musulmana*, III, 252). Ibn Khaldūn has Zayyān b. Abi 'l-Ḥamlat Mudāfi' b. Yūsuf b. Sa'd ("Histoire des Benou 'l-Ahmar, rois de Grenade," trans. Maurice Gaudefroy-Demombynes, *Journal asiatique*, XII [1898], 311, 327n.); he makes Zayyān a confidante of Abū Zayd, who imitated Ibn Hūd as a rival and lost Alcira to a pro-Hūd rebel (pp. 312-313). See also Ibn al-Khaṭīb, *A'māl* (Hoenerbach), p. 481. Ladero Quesada sees him as a lower-class *caudillo* (*Granada*, p. 73). The Valencia Capitulation has: "Zayen regi, neto regis Lupi et filio de Modef." On "rey lop," ruler of Valencia-Murcia from 1147 to 1172, see Huici, *Historia musulmana*, pp. 129-170, and Cagigas, *Mudejares*, II, 263-266.

money called "zayyans," welcomed the influential Ibn al-Abbār as vizier after that poet-politician dramatically abandoned the neo-Christian Abū Zayd, and settled into a decade of uneasy sovereignty. He was never able to secure decisive victory or even the full acquiescence of his familial allies. Alcira, Denia, and Játiva soon swung over to the side of Ibn Hūd, so that Zayyān found himself besieged in his new capital by that more formidable rebel until a Castilian threat drew Ibn Hūd south again. Meanwhile the white flag of the last Spanish Almohad continued to fly stubbornly from castles in the truncated northern parts, while the principality of Valencia plunged deeper into civil war. "The tumult of battle," writes Ibn Khaldūn, "resounded everywhere in that unhappy region."

The turmoil invited renewed Christian invasion; this time the invitation came from Abū Zayd. He had already maneuvered against renewed Christian attack by sending "secret agents" to Pope Gregory IX and to King James, indicating that he and his realm were ripe for conversion. Gregory dispatched the cardinal legate John of Abbeville, who held unsuccessful conversations with Abū Zayd in 1228. Though the reforming legate confided to a chronicler that these talks formed the principal purpose of his trip to Spain, they proved abortive. Hard-pressed by Zayyān now, and grimly clinging to his northern remnant, Abū Zayd signed a second treaty early in 1229 with Aragon, not a truce as at Peñíscola but an alliance, ceding in free alod whatever places King James could reconquer from the rival Moorish king, plus a fourth of revenues everywhere. He also promised to turn over six strategic castles and to have Christians temporarily administer any areas reconquered by his Muslim troops. The treaty, making the Almohad a puppet for Aragon, was a measure of the exile's desperation. Abū Zayd had more than mounted a counterattack; he had joined King James's crusade. As concomitant to these policy shifts, James tried to come to an understanding likewise with Játiva, sending envoys to negotiate with its incumbent.[11]

Since King James was on his way to conquer the Balearics, only a few Aragonese contingents helped hold the north for Abū Zayd

[11] This episode, long ignored by historians, appears in a conversation of 1231; Peter López of Pomar and others had served as envoys ("por missatgeria nostra") to the Játiva *qā'id*. Their lively enthusiasm suggests that these travels were recent (*Llibre dels feyts*, ch. 129). Játiva followed the lead of Ibn Hūd for a time, inimical to both leaders of the Valencian civil war.

during the next two years. Unable to deliver the pledged castles, the Muslim puppet had to agree to a third pact in 1232, surrendering all his rents from the city of Valencia and its huerta. These cold northern winds chilled the pure fervor of Ibn Hūd; overextended and currently embarrassed by an aristocratic revolt, he abandoned his central principle and in 1232 appeased the Castilians by surrendering thirty frontier forts and accepting a vague overlordship by Ferdinand III. At this time King James launched his systematic campaign, overrunning all the north from 1232 to 1235. Zayyān fell back on Valencia city; he had managed to refuse Christian help until 1235, but now, like Ibn Hūd, he felt it prudent to offer informal homage to Ferdinand. In 1236, the year of the crusade parliament at Monzón and the fortifying of Puig above Valencia city, Abū Zayd put his signature to a fourth and final agreement confirming the previous treaties and proclaiming his dynasty the vassals of Aragon. He still styled himself king and would continue to do so for a while, but before the year was out King James was usurping even that title.[12] The pitiful survivor, clinging the while to his imperial Islamic nomenclature, had by now transformed himself into the Christian baron Vincent.

The anti-Almohad armies of Valencia, Alcira, and Játiva suffered a major defeat from Aragon on an August Thursday of 1237, at the pitched battle of Puig or Anīsha. The next year visited a plenitude of woes on Islam's cause. Ibn Hūd seems to have planned now to come to the aid of Zayyān; instead his sudden death triggered a series of revolts. Then the Tunisian fleet made a brave show but failed to relieve Valencia city and had to fall back ignominiously upon Denia. Zayyān found himself forced to surrender Valencia

[12] In transferring many towns to the Segorbe church by his *ius patronatus* in 1247 Abū Zayd declared: "nos eripuimus de manibus paganorum" (conveniently reproduced in Chabás, "Çeid Abu Çeid," p. 166). Transfer of his strongholds to Christendom by his status as converted vassal may account for the expression, but such an interpretation is strained; on the other hand, it may refer to recovery of this territory during the rebellion beginning in 1246, though this would also be as a crusader for James. García y García suggests that Abū Zayd was left with only Villamalefa, Ludiente, Eslida, Bounegre, and Zucaina, and that his conversion triggered a revolt, thus allowing King James to acquire Eslida (*Estado económico-social de Castellón*, p. 13). Grau Monserrat incorporates the thesis, which is more provocative than convincing, and dates it 1236 ("Mudéjares castellonenses," p. 253).

city to the Aragonese and to retire to Alcira; involving himself in Murcia's internecine intrigue, he led a victorious faction to power there, setting himself up in 1239 as emir of eastern Spain for the Tunisian Hafsids. Meanwhile the Christian crusade swallowed up the Alcira region and overran Cullera. The demoralized Murcians revolted again in 1241, installing in power an uncle of Ibn Hūd. While Zayyān fled further south to bide his time at Alicante, the new ruler of Murcia came to terms with the deteriorating situation; hard-pressed by Granada, he arranged in 1243 for Murcia-Orihuela to become a more strictly tributary state under Castile. Játiva surrendered the following year, as did Alicante in 1246. Zayyān abandoned Spain for Tunis, where he saved the sultan's life in an armed action against plotters in 1250, then drifted into obscurity until his death twenty years later. His relative ruling at Denia also found his way to the Hafsid court.[13]

Of the major Muslim leaders in eastern Spain Abū Zayd had come off best, though hardly as a hero of Islam. The stages by which he had found himself transformed into puppet and then into crusader did not result from cynical betrayal by King James. The barons of Aragon at first had seized upon a chance to raid and grab; they were not sympathetic to a sustained war of conquest, much less to a philanthropic war. Emboldened by their surprising success in the Balearics, and confident that Abū Zayd could rally enough support to take central Valencia himself, they acquiesced in the more demanding second treaty of 1232. Sometime during the subsequent campaign it became obvious that the Moor could provide at best

[13] Ibn Khaldūn, *Histoire des Berbères*, II, 280-312. Al-Maqqarī, *Mohammedan Dynasties*, II, 333-336. Ibn al-Khaṭīb, *A'māl*, pp. 482-484. Al-Ḥimyarī, *Kitāb ar-rawḍ al-mi'ṭār*, and Ibn 'Idhārī, *Al-Bayān al-mugrib*, as cited above in Chapter I, nn. 1, 4. Muḥammad b. Ibrāhīm az-Zarkashī, *Chronique des almohades et des hafçides*, trans. Edmond Fagnan (Constantine, 1895), pp. 27-29, 36-37; and men like Ibn al-Abbār already cited. Muḥammad b. Shanab (Bencheneb) has collated Reconquest dates from Arabic sources, giving Onda's fall as between July 1, 1242, and June 20, 1243; Alcira's as June 30, 1242; Játiva's as between Dec. 30, 1247, and January 1248; and Valencia as sieged from Thursday, April 22, 1238, and surrendered on September 29 ("Notes chronologiques principalement sur la conquête de l'Espagne par les chrétiens," *Mélanges René Basset, études nord-africaines et orientales*, 2 vols. [Paris, 1923-1925], I, 70-76). On Alcira and on the complicated fall of Játiva, see below, pp. 342n., 363n. See also the Tunisian background and reaction in Brunschvig, *Berbérie orientale*, I, 32ff. Huici reviews the career of Zayyān in his *Historia musulmana de Valencia*, III, 252-264.

auxiliary efforts. Master of the north by 1236, Aragon just might be able to conquer central Valencia but only by a convulsive mustering of all her realms on a large-scale crusade. The Monzón crusade-parliament, the public appearance of Abū Zayd as the convert Vincent, James's abrupt assumption of the Valencian royal title, and the final treaty with his puppet demonstrate that Christian and Muslim allies had been driven to reassess their situation. Hopes for restoration fading, Abū Zayd as a vassal crusader announced his "seizure from the hands of the pagans" of large portions of the kingdom and his patronal disposition of their future churches; under the title of crusader he also received his share of the general conquest, especially family lands of his mother and father.

Everywhere on the eastern coast the infidel invaders stood triumphant. The old spirit of Spanish Islam was deeply wounded, though not yet dead. Local heroes would arise to lead the hosts of Islam. The dynasty of the dead Ibn Hūd, clinging to a shadow of power under Castilian overlordship, provided one such man, whose war of independence occasioned the definitive conquest of Murcia in 1266 by James of Aragon for Castile. Granada still stood firm, despite its superficial status as tributary to Castile; under Ibn al-Aḥmar as Muḥammad I, builder of the Alhambra, it began aggressive raids against Castile from 1261 which broadened into larger hostilities in 1264-1265 and into the sustained war of the 1270's.

Revolt: The Constant Crusade

Heroes of Islam were abroad other than Zayyān and Ibn Hūd. Each will take the stage at his proper cue. For the moment our focus is not on personalities or resources but upon the general movements of revolt which shook the kingdom of Valencia in the late 1240's, 1250's, 1260's, and worst of all 1270's.[14] These wars, never closely examined by historians, are of extraordinary importance for the history of the conquered kingdom. Their significance for the psychology of the Valencian Muslim can hardly be exaggerated; they kept alive the flame of resistance. Because of their protracted nature, they amounted to a continual time of troubles, and must be viewed not as isolated episodes but as persistent atmosphere. The

[14] On al-Azraq see Chapter XIV, section 1; on Albocor see section 2.

first two revolts especially formed part of a single pattern, representing crucial stages in prolonged guerrilla disturbances during the decade after formal closure of the crusade. The fiercely fought initial phase in 1247-1250, though premature and badly coordinated, made inevitable the eventual formal campaign of 1258. Later historians isolated its more impressive stages as separate wars, but King James rightly saw the decade of troubles as a single war.[15]

"The sad fate of Cordova and of her sisters Seville and Valencia had been promulgated to all parts of the [Islamic] world," Ibn Khaldūn writes, including the story of how "the lord of Barcelona and Catalonia had conquered eastern Spain." Holy war obsessed North Africa, but only Tunis found itself sufficiently free from interior troubles to offer help. The Marinids, not yet masters of Fez, much less of Marrakesh, started an expedition in 1245, which the Almohads cut off at the straits. The Marinids did manage the passage of a troublesome nephew, 'Āmir b. Idrīs, and his tribe in 1262: "more than three thousand Marinid volunteers left with them," to form a permanent nucleus for foreign adventurers, giving the armies of Granada new efficiency and morale.[16] Granadan envoys plotted at the Marinid and Hafsid courts, while a web of intrigue united Mudejar with Islamic Spain. The Murcians, quiescent under Castilian tributary occupation since 1243, grew increasingly restive, and aired their grievances to the Castilian monarch and even to Rome.[17]

With explosive simultaneity the Mudejars rose from Jerez to Murcia in the spring of 1264, while Granada threw its armies on the offensive and a Marinid contingent hurried over from Morocco.[18] At Murcia the rebels stormed the alcazar, slaughtered Castilian mer-

[15] See also below, pp. 327ff., 344ff.

[16] Ibn Khaldūn, *Histoire des Berbères*, IV, 48, 75, 460; the Islamic year was 661 (1262-1263).

[17] Fernández y González, *Mudejares de Castilla*, p. 104. Torres Fontes, *Reconquista de Murcia*, pp. 73-74. On the Roman episode, see below, p. 287.

[18] Torres Fontes, *Reconquista de Murcia*, a meticulous reconstruction of chronology and events, corrects the common misdating of 1261, based on an error of Alfonso's chronicle (see chs. 4, 5), suggesting some time between May 10 and June 5. The Murcian war became a papal crusade, preached in Aragon as well as Castile, with crusade calls sent in May 1265 to the metropolitan at Tarragona and to the bishop of Valencia against "the Saracens of Spain and Africa" ("Itinerario de Alfonso X, rey de Castilla," ed. Antonio Ballesteros Beretta, *BRAH*, CIX [1936], docs. on p. 405).

chants, and welcomed a Granadan army in support of al-Wathīq, the son of Ibn Hūd. Though Castile clung to Lorca, Orihuela, and some lesser places, and contrived to recapture Alicante, she had to call on Aragon to regain full control of the Murcian kingdom. The course of the larger war, with its renewal of Spanish Islam's suicidal factionalism, makes a confused story. In its Murcian phase Prince Peter of Aragon twice led armies of invasion, in the spring and summer of 1265; King James conducted the third and final campaign, forcing the capital's surrender in early 1266, restoring the realm to Alfonso X, and initiating the subsequent inpouring of Christian settlement.[19]

The chronicler Desclot asserts that the war had its sympathetic echo in Valencia.[20] No details on such disturbances survive. Soldevila believes a rising might have occurred either in 1261 or in 1262-1263.[21] King James, in asking his barons for help, makes it clear that Valencia had not been able to join the rebellion at its outset, but that Islam had an excellent chance of recovering "all it had lost" in Spain, including Valencia. This supplied a major motive for his intervention.[22] Fortunately, the recent local risings had allowed James to break the power of strategic Mudejar chiefs; the use of Valencia as staging area for his three expeditions further inhibited the spirit of revolt; and immediately upon terminating the Murcian war James established a frontier host for the border area, with a smaller force patrolling the Biar-Alicante roads.

In May 1267 he sent Peter back to Murcia, apparently as observer and as a timely forewarning to the Granadans during their current war with Castile. In 1272, when a small countercrusade came over

[19] Torres Fontes, *Reconquista de Murcia*, chs. 7-10. Soldevila, *Pere el Gran*, part I, I, 123-124. Torres Fontes sums the Muslim and Christian chroniclers for the war, relating them ingeniously to the documentation. Some of the latter might bear other interpretation, depending upon the chronology assigned; see esp. *Itinerari*, p. 347 (Feb. 4, 1264); fleet "against the Saracens," p. 348 (Feb. 6); the king's son Peter Ferdinand as admiral of this fleet, p. 349 (March 19); James to head an army personally from Alcañiz in Easter week, pp. 353-354 (July 10); provisioning for "the greatest quantity of knights against the king of Granada and other enemies of the Christian faith," pp. 353-354 (July 13-14); galleys for the war, p. 356 (Aug. 3); a galley, p. 362 (Nov. 12); Prince James gets Montpellier's revenues for a year to support the invasion; and so on.

[20] Desclot, *Crònica*, ch. 65.

[21] Soldevila, *Pere el Gran*, part I, I, 119n.

[22] *Llibre dels feyts*, esp. chs. 378, 382.

from Morocco, King James went down to Alicante for talks with King Alfonso.[23] In 1273, worried over the alliance of Granada with Castilian rebels, James sent another army promenading through Murcia, shrewdly following this in 1274 with an extended personal visit to assess, from behind a facade of gala diversion, the stability and defenses of this buffer realm. Valencia was obviously at the center of this sustained concern; it was better, James explained to his barons during the Murcian war, to fight one's battles on a neighbor's soil than on one's own.[24] The greatest of the rebellions was yet to come; Valencia's potential for resistance still lay largely untapped.

The war of 1275-1277 culminated the other episodes. It amounted to a determined effort at reconquest by Islam;[25] here the Valencian story becomes submerged in the general countercrusade. King Peter summarized this war just after its close when sending a legal challenge to the count of Pallars. In effect Peter was rebuking irresponsible nobles who had raised domestic tumults during the frontier crisis. He reminded them how "the lord king was personally in the kingdom of Valencia and stayed there a lengthy time, because the Saracens resident in the said realm rose up against the aforesaid lord king and his land and rebelled with many castles and strongholds." Not only did the rebels win great areas by means of domestic strength, but they "also imported into the land of Valencia Saracen knights from the regions of Granada and the regions of Barbary, to the deep dishonor and expense of his realm and of all Christendom." As a result, "the said lord king was compelled to assemble

[23] Ibn Khaldūn has the 1272 "brilliant" episode (*Histoire des Berbères*, IV, 58-59); it may or may not relate to the Alicante talks.

[24] *Llibre dels feyts*, ch. 388. Torres Fontes covers the several visits and the aftermath generally, *Reconquista de Murcia*, ch. 11.

[25] Ibn Khaldūn, *Histoire des Berbères*, IV, 74-81, 361, 469 and passim. This wider story has its own ample documentation; for the Castilian wars see Antonio Ballesteros y Beretta, *Alfonso X el Sabio* (Madrid, 1963), chs. 15, 17, and documentary appendix; in its Valencian aspect the best synthesis is Soldevila, *Pere el Gran*, part I, III, ch. 16, which unfortunately breaks off at mid-1276; his less ambitious *Vida de Pere el Gran*, chs. 6 and 11, esp. pp. 53, 57, 108, 117-121, and Dufourcq, *L'Espagne catalane et le Maghrib*, part 2, ch. 1, esp. pp. 193-205, supply useful information; see also al-Maqqarī, *Mohammedan Dynasties*, II, 345-346. A number of small points in each author can be challenged: e.g., Soldevila allows Hafsid contingents in the 1275 invasion, while Dufourcq dates his "truce of Játiva" as August rather than September 1276, and believes it lasted a year instead of three months.

large armies against these Saracens and with great slaughter, labor, and expense to conquer these Saracens and by the help of God's grace reduce them to his rule." Peter goes on to say that "hardly was the affair of the Agarenes [the Muslims] so concluded, with the king distant and residing in the aforesaid realm of Valencia, for the reorganizing of that land so cruelly and frequently devastated by the aforesaid faithless Saracens," when the baronial discord erupted.[26]

North Africa, previously absorbed in internecine strife, had finally rallied to the cause in a formidable coalition. Concomitantly the Marinid dynasty, master of all Morocco, inaugurated a religious revival and holy war euphoria. The founder of Nasrid Granada, Ibn al-Aḥmar, grown fearful of his ally Castile before his death in 1273, had counseled his son Muḥammad II to rely upon Marinid power. Though Hafsid Tunis lay neutralized by treaty, the technically neutral regions of central Barbary were ready to contribute forces. In Spain even quarrelsome Málaga and Guadix reconciled themselves to Granada and girded for victory. Too long, Ibn Khaldūn writes, "had the Spanish Muslims suffered the seizure of their strongholds, the violation of their territory, the loss of their provinces, the occupation of their towns and ruin of their properties," while cities like Valencia fell and "in eastern Spain the power of the independent chiefs was destroyed." Now Abū Yūsuf Ya'qūb of Morocco, "always preoccupied with making an expedition into Spain" but always frustrated in his plans, stood ready "to take up the defense of the Spanish Muslims." Previously, "every time the sultan Abū Yūsuf Ya'qūb suspected the loyalty of a prince of his family, he sent him into Andalusia" to join the heroic volunteers

[26] Arch. Crown, Peter III, perg. 266 (Aug. 23, 1281): "quod cum ipse dominus rex esset in regno Valencie et fuerit etiam longo tempore pro eo quia sarraceni in dicto regno existentes erexerant se contra predictum dominum regem et terram suam et rebellarunt cum multis castris et fortaliciis contra eundem dominum regem adducendo etiam milites sarracenos ad terram Valencie de partibus Granate et de partibus Barberie in maximum desonorem et dispendium terre sue et tocius christianitatis, in tantum quod idem dominus rex coactus fuit magna contra ipsos sarracenos exercitus congregare, et cum magnis cedibus, laboribus et expensis ipsos sarracenos devincere divina gracia iuvante sue dicioni reduxit vix itaque agarenorum negocio sic peracto eodem domino rege in ipso regno permanente . . . predicto domino rege absente et in predicto regno Valencie existente pro reformacione ipsius terre crudeliter quam plurimum prout dictum est a predictis sarracenis perfidis devastate [bands of nobles raised tumults]." The Agarenes were supposedly descendants of the Scriptural Hagar.

from all over North Africa. This time, leaving Fez for Tangier, he put himself at the head of "all the forces of his empire"—a grand roll call enumerated by Ibn Khaldūn—and embarked for Spain in mid-1275. From the central Maghrib various "sons of kings" set out, "with all the men of their respective tribes they could gather," so that "Spain filled with princes and great chiefs." Though the coalition had Castile as its primary target, it meant to harass and ultimately recover adjacent territory; in the event, Valencia became a second theater of war.

The hosts of Islam rolled back the Castilian defenders. When Nuño González of Lara rallied the main frontier forces for a stand near Écija, his army went down in shameful defeat. The highest prelate of Spain, Toledo's primate-archbishop Sancho, who was the son of James of Aragon, soon met the same fate, captured in battle and executed. The Muslims, hailing their victory as the redress for Las Navas, posted Nuño's head to Granada, which forwarded it to the court of Castile. Alfonso the Learned, rudely awakened from his fantasies of becoming Holy Roman emperor, organized a desperate resistance and begged James of Aragon to help Christendom as he had helped a decade ago in Murcia. By November James was able to commission Prince Peter to march to the aid of Castile, though this project may later have aborted.

The kingdom of Valencia meanwhile had fallen into disorder—partly social tumults, partly anti-Moor pogroms, and partly incipient rebellion—forcing King James to go there in person at the end of 1275. He also sent an army to Jijona under Raymond Moncada, and a second under the royal bastard Peter Ferdinand against a brigand force led by Michael Pérez. There were rebel Mudejars abroad even then, as a letter of James's dated December 13 reveals, but they seemed a minor problem alongside the civil tumult. The king soon had occasion to revise his estimate of the situation. On March 13, 1276, he called for an army to rendezvous from all his realms at Easter, because the Muslim rebels had conquered three castles and were awaiting outside help. A week later, better informed, he disclosed that "many" castles had fallen and that outside aid was on its way.

By mid-June, when forty castles were in Muslim hands, the king had assembled a "multitude" of knights and soldiers at Valencia city and had established his base at Játiva. The enemy by now had received Granadan-Moroccan allies. Rebels had ambushed and destroyed one relief force, and though repulsed at Liria had retained Tous; the Christians had recaptured Beniopa but lost Luchente; and the exiled rebel al-Azraq had returned with a Granadan troop to rally his Valencian followers. At this moment both sides suffered grievous loss. Al-Azraq fell in late April, while leading his army to capture Alcoy; and an Islamic force of 500 horse and 3,000 foot around June 20 shattered the Christian host on the field of Luchente between Játiva and Gandía.[27]

Prince Peter arrived at Játiva by June 27, just before King James was laid low by the mortal illness which carried him off one month later. Peter was destined to spend his first fourteen months as king grimly struggling to retain Valencia. "Assuredly it can well be said," wrote the contemporary Muntaner, "that the lord prince Sir Peter conquered part of the kingdom of Valencia a second time."[28] The Montesa siege alone consumed over two months; other important sieges included Alfandech and Eslida. Peter employed every resource —organizing a fleet, mounting diplomatic missions to North Africa, and neutralizing strongholds by timely concessions. Combat was so stubborn and intense that he had to postpone both his own coronation and the transfer of his father's corpse from a provisional grave. A three-month truce in September 1276 with the most troublesome of his remaining foes allowed him to accept crown and title at Zaragoza, to dispatch an embassy to Morocco and Tlemcen, and to arrange an exodus of rebel leaders. By this time areas like Segorbe-Jérica and Tárbena-Guadalest appear in the records as loyal or at

[27] The documents of December 13, 1275, and of the first half of 1276 are indicated in the *Itinerari*, with long excerpts. On the moot question of al-Azraq's role, see below, p. 331. James sent Peter with 1,000 knights and 500 foot into Murcia, setting up defenses, strengthening garrisons, and raiding into Granada; after the Moroccan forces withdrew from Spain, Peter returned to Murcia for a personal inspection of the situation (Torres Fontes, *Reconquista de Murcia*, pp. 199-200). Some of the activity of King James's bastard, Peter Ferdinand, is reflected in a document of June 9, 1276, about his raid toward Fuente Encarroz, though directly concerning the slaves "Abraphim, qui fuit de cavalcata quam Petrus Ferrandiz filius domini regis fecit apud Fontem de Rebolleto, et una[m] çubayam de Penaguille nomine Uxam" (Miret y Sans, "La esclavitud en Cataluña en los ultimos tiempos de la edad media," *Revue hispanique*, XLI [1917], 15).

[28] Muntaner, *Crònica*, ch. 10: "segurament hom pot be dir, que dit senyor infant En Pere conques altra vegada partida del regne de Valencia."

least pacified; others like Gandía remained war zones. Though Castile also secured a truce in 1276, fighting erupted in July 1277 as Abū Yūsuf disembarked a second invading army from Africa and began scouring the countryside around Jerez and Seville. Alfonso X cautiously refused battle and soon contrived a renewal of the truce. During Aragon's truce that fall, King Peter repaired the walls of Burriana, facilitated the return of refugees to Benaguacil and other towns, garrisoned castles, and replaced castellans.

As the Valencian truce drew to an end in December, he was amassing supplies; by the end of that month Eslida had fallen to him, followed shortly by Torres Torres, Chelva, and in February Serra. Bechí suffered such damage that it was written off as "destroyed by the Saracens."[29] This line of strongholds, running west to northeast across the face of the kingdom just north of Valencia city, underlines the previous success of the rebels. To the south, centers like Finestrat above Alicante were collapsing. Like flares illuminating a night battle, the 1277 documents in the crown registers reveal glimpses of progress—a local truce in February; brisk action against Muslims in May around Orcheta; townsmen dragooned from Murviedro all the way to Gandía in order to cut down the April harvest of the rebels; another general summons of knights and militia throughout the realms; the emergence of Montesa—to the west of Játiva and with a lifeline into Granada—as rebel headquarters; heavy fighting in June and July; and another general mobilization in August to confront renewed invasion by Moroccan forces.

The decisive campaign came in the fall. Crusade armies closed in on Montesa, which held out until the end of September 1277. A month of mopping up brought hostilities to an end. Echoes of the war resounded for a year or two, the crown facilitating emigration of defeated leaders, disposing of Montesa captives in a prolonged slave auction, introducing Christian and Muslim settlement into abandoned areas, building new bridges over the critically important Mijares and Júcar rivers, arbitrating boundary disputes, punishing civil discord the length of the realm, granting amnesties and rewards, promoting the restructured movement by Dominicans for

[29] *Rationes decimarum Hispaniae (1279-1280)*, ed. José Rius Serra, 2 vols. (Barcelona, 1946-1947), I, 176 (1280): "item capellanus de Belxi, nichil solvit nec computavit tres anni sunt, quia locus a sarracenis fuit destructus."

converting Valencian Muslims, and reassuring the chastened Mudejar population by confirming past privileges and allowing tax reductions until prosperity returned.[30]

Foiled in Aragon and Castile, with factions springing up again like weeds, the grand coalition for Islam fell to pieces. Granada mistrusted the Marinid ambition to create an Almohad-type empire. After a localized Castilian war against Muslims in 1278-1279, the crusade picture altered dramatically. In Castile's civil war which ensued, the rebel heir Sancho allied with Granada, so that Alfonso X had to call in its rival Morocco to restore the balance. The spectacle of the erstwhile invader, the devout Marinid ruler of Morocco, leading his armies in 1282 freely to the very center of the peninsula in a holy war[31] to aid his crusader enemy provides an ironic ending to an epic story. The gods made a similar jest for Aragon. Under pretense of crusading against North Africa that same year, King Peter assembled together a powerful amphibious force, then swooped down upon Angevin Sicily; the resultant alliance of France and Castile to make him disgorge the island drove Peter instead to join forces with Morocco.

There would be Spanish crusades again and holy war invasions by Islam, but when Alfonso X died in 1284, Peter III in 1285, and Abū Yūsuf of Morocco in 1286 clearly an era had come to its end. Islamic Valencia had fought valiantly both alone and in conjunction with the larger holy wars; rebels and patriots had abounded; courage was a commonplace. Nothing availed; nothing in the pathetic rebellions of the future would avail. The old glories were departed. Sharq al-Andalus,[32] fabled golden east of Islamic Spain, was dead beyond resurrection.

[30] The details are assembled from Peter's registers. Ibn Khaldūn describes four separate countercrusades by Abū Yūsuf into Spain (*Histoire des Berbères*, pp. 85-103 for the second, 106-110 for the third, 110ff. for the fourth).

[31] Ibn Khaldūn designates it a holy war, and adds that the sultan took Alfonso's crown as pawn (*Histoire des Berbères*, IV, 105, 306, 310). French but not peninsular sources note that Abū Yūsuf camped near Játiva in Autumn of 1282, a friendly visit to lost Valencia, during which he sent a message to the king of France (Leopoldo Torres Balbás, "Játiva y los restos del palacio de Pinohermoso," *Al-Andalus*, XXII [1958], 149).

[32] By the thirteenth century this general designation for the eastern or Mediterranean seaboard, from the Ebro delta down through Murcia, had constricted in meaning to the area we call Valencia kingdom.

CHAPTER III

The Physical Setting

KING JAMES WAS personally active in the kingdom he had conquered, returning year after year until a considerable portion of his total reign was spent there. For twenty-two of the thirty-seven years of rule after the capital's fall, he passed at least a fourth of every year within the new kingdom's boundaries. No other part of his realms so absorbed his attention. If Lérida was the effective capital of his Arago-Catalan confederation, as Miret y Sans has demonstrated, with Zaragoza and Barcelona the respective subordinate regional capitals,[1] Valencia preoccupied James and devoured his time far more than any other single area. During the intervening absences he left behind a politico-military lieutenant to handle crises, an expedient demanded by the continuing numerical dominance of Muslims. The Conqueror's heir, Prince Alfonso, assumed this post of procurator general; Prince Peter supplanted him from 1251, but more definitively from 1260 after Alfonso's death.

COLONIAL RULE

Christian and Mudejar Valencia received its higher government in 1240, some years before the crusade ended. It included a substitute alter ego, more permanently present than the princely procurator general but with less generous powers. Of these secondary procurators or lieutenants, five succeeded each other through King James's reign, the second being the baron Simon Pérez, whose son married the daughter of ex-king Abū Zayd. The lieutenants in turn employed subordinate lieutenants, usually dividing the delegated administration by the Júcar River. These officials the crown commended to the loyal obedience of Christian and Muslim alike: "as the Christians, so the Jews and the Saracens are to have and recognize you as procurator."[2]

[1] *Itinerari*, p. 542; a schematic analysis of James's places of residence is constructed by Miret y Sans on pp. 545-567, and by Chabás on p. 568.

[2] Any lieutenant might have his jurisdiction limited, as when Gerald of Cabrera

A corresponding office centering on revenues and property was that of bailiff general, also normally divided by the Júcar into two offices; it ramified through a multitude of local bailiffs who were often tax farmers. Valencia, unlike King James's other realms, did not receive its bailiff general until 1282. Local bailiffs were frequently Jews, who played an important role in Valencian administration and finance; in 1278, for example, the crown entrusted all its rents from Valencia to Moses Alconstantini.[3] Castles were garrisoned under Christian castellans, a number of them vicars for the absentee bailiff-castellans enjoying the revenues. Some places possessed both a bailiff and an alcalde or a castellan; others united these offices in a single man. Whether the king's representative was a bailiff or an alcalde, the two titles often seem for practical purpose identical.[4]

---

in 1286 became lieutenant for all Valencia above the Júcar except Alcira. On the governmental framework see Jesús Lalinde Abadía, *La gobernación general en la corona de Aragón* (Zaragoza, 1963), part 1, ch. 4, and part 2, ch. 6. The order, "mandantes . . . tam christianis quam iudeis quam sarracenis quod vos habeant et teneant pro procuratore," is in doc. 5 (1286), p. 504. On the early procurators see Josefina Mateu Ibars, *Los virreyes de Valencia: Fuentes para su estudio* (Valencia, 1963), pp. 49-57. See also J. M. Font y Rius, *Instituciones medievales españolas: La organización política, económica y social de los reinos cristianos de la reconquista* (Madrid, 1949), chs. 1-3. On the procurator and his lieutenants see F. A. Roca Traver, "La gobernación foral del reino de Valencia: una cuestión de competencia," *EEMCA*, IV (1951), 177-214.

[3] On Jews in administration see pp. 253-254 and note. The financial aspects are treated in my forthcoming *Medieval Colonialism: Postcrusade Exploitation of Islamic Valencia* (Princeton).

[4] Historically the bailiff in Catalonia had been an administrator over temporalities as agent for king, lord, or cleric, an office which could include judicial or civil functions and which came to cover also guardianship of a minor or the feudal lord's defense of monastic interests; see Eulalia Rodón Binué, *El lenguaje técnico del feudalismo en el siglo xi en Cataluña (contribución al estudio del latín medieval)* (Barcelona, 1957), pp. 33-38, and Antonio M. Aragó Cabañas, "La institución 'baiulus regis' en Cataluña en la época de Alfonso el Casto," *Congrés VII*, III, 139-142. The *alcaydus* was castellan, the alcalde more a civil figure; but the two are often difficult to distinguish, as with their counterparts the *qā'id* and the *qāḍī* (see below, p. 370). A crown letter to the Valencian kingdom, preparing for a war in 1275, addressed these officials: the bailiff and alcalde of Játiva with Sumacárcel, the bailiff and alcalde of Gandía with Palma, the bailiff and alcalde of Denia-Calpe-Segarra-Pego, the bailiff of Alcira, the alcaldes of ten other places, and separately the bailiff and alcalde of Biar (*El archivo*, IV [1890], p. 311, doc. 41). Two years earlier Simon Guasch held both offices for Denia with Calpe, and was responsible for the revenues "de baiulia et alcaidia castrorum et villarum Denie et Calpi." In 1262 a crown feudatory was allowed to name both a bailiff and an *alcaydus* for Pego, over Christians and Moors (document in *Congrés I*, p. 66).

Seignorial and ecclesiastical proprietors had their own agents. The superstructure should not convey an impression of regional organization; unlike the large areas of France, overseen by crown agents, Valencian administration in its actual workings betrayed a markedly local character, a system facilitated by already existing Islamic divisions.

Procurator and bailiff with their subordinate officers enjoyed judicial as well as administrative functions; these could overlap. The confusion became compounded when a town's justiciar or its governing jurates found their local jurisdiction entangled with the royal or seignorial interests in a given case. The crown often addressed the bailiff or the justiciar in matters regarding the protection of Muslims. In Mudejar affairs the procurator emerged from his long bickering with the bailiff as the stronger of the two offices.[5] Beneath the higher Christian officialdom, whether crown or seignorial or municipal, the component elements of the old Islamic polity perdured. This infrastructure was affected by many colonialist factors, such as the map of Christian public and private law, the disposition of Catalan as against Aragonese rural estates, the balance of crown holdings versus baronial or alodial lands, the rhythm and pattern of immigration, and the religious psychology of the settlers.

The Eslida charter of the Moors mentions "alcadi [sic] castrorum" and the "baiuli." The two *baillis* King James set over several districts he conquered in Majorca were rather governors or representatives, both being important men of the royal household (*Llibre dels feyts*, ch. 71). Roca Traver's distinction of bailiff as representative for a crown aljama, and *alcayde* for the feudal lord, does not seem satisfactory ("Vida mudéjar," pp. 130-131); his documents 22 and 24 show that the Muslims "montanearum nostrarum" beyond the Júcar have both "baiuli dictarum montanearum" and "alcadii." Antonio M. Badía Margarit discusses the equivalence of alcalde and the judicial-administrative bailiff, as well as the mechanics by which ḍ became ld in the passage of *al-qāḍī* to alcalde ("'Alcalde,' difusión de un arabismo en Catalán," *Homenaje a Millás-Vallicrosa*, 2 vols. [Barcelona, 1954-1956], I, 67-82, esp. pp. 67, 74); some derive *alcalde* from Latin *caput ville*, i.e., *captellus* or Romance *caudillo*.

[5] Thus Peter in 1279 ordered the Valencia city justiciar to investigate the case of an illegally sold Muslim (Arch. Crown, Reg. Canc. 41, fol. 113), and the justiciar and bailiff of Játiva to prevent extortionate taxation of Muslims that same year (*ibid.*, fol. 101v). Referring back to previous practice, King Alfonso in 1290 ordered the bailiff not to interfere with the procurator's jurisdiction over Muslims, a control prevailing ever since the incumbency of Roderick Simon of Luna in 1277-1282 (Reg. Canc. 81, fol. 59).

The structures sustaining the Valencian Christian—administrative, ecclesiastical, judicial, or economic, and especially his semi-independent city commune—require no elaboration. The thirteenth-century contemporary of Dante, Assisi, and Aquinas, though remote, is not too mysterious a figure. The same does not hold true for the thirteenth-century Muslim. An impression remains, like an ocular afterimage vagrant and diminishing, of unstructured uniformity, of the oppressed Mudejar serf tilling the countryside while his urban brothers huddled in reduced numbers within *morerías* or ghettos. They had fallen into the mass condition of "subject Moors," humiliatingly suffered by Christian authorities like strangers or gypsies along the fringes of real society. Understanding must begin with the larger outlines, and the Mudejar must be set within the frame of historical geography which continued to affect his administration and which helped to shape his character.

The Topographical-Administrative Landscape

Despite much writing around the subject, Islamic Valencia's administrative divisions and evolution remain obscure. The Roman focus on major cities had tended to persist in Spain, and to surface again through the superimposed grid of provinces by which the Cordova caliph governed. The Arab geographer Yāqūt Ḥamawī, writing in the 1220's, noted that the word for a district like Syria or China (*iqlīm*) meant for a Spanish Muslim his city—any large and populous town. This was unusual in Islam; in the East the urban center normally depended upon its province (*ḳūra*), and related to its larger agricultural region more as a component element. Lévi-Provençal, and after him most scholars writing on this point, emphasized a Spain administered over the centuries through more-or-less equal provinces. Within the province however, local traditions and military necessity evolved multiple city-based entities, sometimes overseen by a military *qā'id* rather than by a civil administrator. The city in this case included satellite towns englobed within its own small countryside. The sturdy outlines of this system appear clearly during the Valencian crusade.[6]

[6] Yāqūt b. 'Abd Allāh al-Ḥamawī (1179-1229), *The Introductory Chapters of Yāqūt's Mu'jam al-Buldān*, trans. Wadie Jwaideh (Leiden, 1959), p. 40. See the dis-

In times of chaos central government gave place to both city and semiautonomous or feudal units, combining and recombining fluidly in kaleidoscopic patterns. A hinterland like Alpuente could pose briefly as a princely power. Denia, on the coast south of Valencia city, rose for a time to a dominating position in the maritime history of the western Mediterranean.[7] When a bloc of such cities, or a wide extent of more rural area, did combine as a "kingdom" or a province, forces more ancient than Roman were at work. The pre-Roman tribal grounds comprised a hidden map that underlay all the later administrative history of eastern Spain. They worked in a kind of dialogue with the Roman and Visigothic cities—themselves not unrelated in origin to the tribal groupings—and with more transitory units of power like religious sects or ethnic factions, as well as with all the chance expedients and opportunities of a given moment.

A current theory, relating to a belief in early Berberization, argues for deurbanization of the Valencian zone during the earlier caliphal era, leaving it a marcher region involving undistinguished townlets and a courtesy capital, a dissident and neglected periphery of Spanish Islam. Shrunken cities probably persisted in embryo throughout Valencia even under ruralization, however, especially since the colleague provinces retained their full-blown city orientation. Whether reborn on the multiple analogue of their neighbors or expanded from diminished survivals, Valencia's cities flourished mightily from at least the eleventh century. Deurbanization can be overdrawn. The tenth-century history designating "the *ḳūra* of Valencia and Játiva," for example, does not so much demote Valencia city as recognize the yoking of two disparate city regions.[8] Primitive Játiva, of the

---

cussion below on pp. 387ff., especially the theory of Ḥusayn Mu'nis as opposed by Sánchez-Albornoz. See also Jacinto Bosch Vilá, "Algunas consideraciones sobre 'al-Ṯaġr en al-Andalus' y la división político-administrativa de la España musulmana," in Emilio García Gómez *et alii, Études d'orientalisme dediées à la mémoire de Lévi-Provençal* (2 vols., Paris, 1962), I, 22-23; he notes that Muslim authors applied the terms *iqlīm, 'amal,* and *ḳūra* so indifferently as to defy an absolutely uniform meaning, while the involvement of a *ḳūra* in the logistics of a relatively remote war might make it a *thaghr*, as happened with Valencia in the thirteenth century (p. 31).

[7] On Alpuente, Denia, and other entities, see works cited in n. 19.

[8] Pierre Guichard, "Le peuplement de la région de Valence aux deux premiers siècles de la domination musulmane," *Mélanges de la casa de Velázquez*, v (1969), 103-158, esp. pp. 118-120. On Játiva as autonomous, see below, Chapter XIV, section 3.

not properly Iberian tribe of Contestanes, had stood apart from Valencia; and, under Diocletian's reorganized Roman empire, Játiva-Denia fell to the Cartagena province, while Valencia went to that of Tarragona. This double-gaited history repeated itself in precrusade Valencia, and the crusaders formalized the division for administration and taxes. The deurbanization thesis does help explain the adventitious unity binding together the unwieldy and even unrelated "kingdom of Valencia" under both Abū Zayd and King James: the kingdom comprised all that country which had stood neglected during the early centuries between the brighter entities of Tortosa to the north and Murcia to the south.

The twenty-one provinces of the Cordova caliphate, each under its temporary *wālī* or governor, included three in the Valencia region: Valencia, Játiva, and Murcia (called Tudmīr after the Visigothic ruler Theodmir). Running north to the mouth of the Ebro, the Valencian province or *ḳūra* embraced at least two areas of diverse pre-Roman origins. Much of its northern half still centered more naturally upon Tortosa, to whose region it belonged at one point, while in the south Denia retained its own vitality. At the dissolution of the caliphate, the Valencian area from the northern border of Murcia up the Ebro divided itself for a while among four principalities: Alpuente, Denia, Valencia, and Zaragoza. The kingdom of Valencia, in its several appearances in history, altered variously both in shape and size. The celebrated geographer al-Idrīsī (d. 1154) recorded some nonadministrative groupings for its coastal region: Enguera, including Denia, Játiva, and Alcira or the Júcar River area; the Alpuente-Albarracín country; Tortosa with the north; and Murcia.

By Almohad times Moorish Spain comprised five provinces: Seville, Cordova, Granada, Murcia, and Valencia. The English writer Walter of Coventry, describing his king's cruise of the Catalan coast in 1190, reduced the "principal kings" to the last four provinces, omitting Seville since that city was the Almohad administrative center for Spain.[9] The subregions persisted. Thus the cosmographer

[9] *Memoriale Fratris Walteri de Coventria,* ed. William Stubbs, 2 vols. (London, 1872-1873), I, 407; on p. 404 Denia is described as a notable "civitas magna." The kingdom is "terra regis de Valencia qui est frater predicti Almiramimoli: in cuius dominatione sunt Oedeeb castellum et Stuve castellum et Valencia civitas et Bur-

ad-Dimashqī (b. 1256) listed the dependencies of Valencia city as Alcira, Játiva, Villanueva de Castellón, Almenara, Bairén, Murviedro, Peñíscola, Jérica, Morella, and three negligible forts, including Puig; Denia and its country formed an enclave somewhat apart.[10] Here the Spanish pattern stands out for eastern Islamic Spain, by which a province divided not into large cultivated districts, each with its several urban and village entities, but rather by tighter, individual city and town units.

Some of the more unexpected units in the series owe their appearance to the prominence accorded strategic towns and castles in time of crisis. Peñíscola and Morella for instance were the first targets of King James's crusade, in 1225 and 1232; in the end he had to acquire both by negotiation. The importance of the Bairén fortifications near Gandía is underlined at length in James's memoirs. A glance at a physical map of the country shows the wisdom of holding Murviedro, at the mouth of a major valley, and Jérica, upstream in the general Segorbe region. Lesser forts like Almenara and Puig had their importance in this context. Other forces may have been at work, such as tribes or local military figures, to make one stronghold rather than another the current administrative center. Morella dominated the mountainous northwest corner of the kingdom, a region relatively isolated after the fall of Tortosa and exposed to raids from Aragon proper. It seems also to have enjoyed a special place in the plans of Abū Zayd as he retreated north from his victorious rival in Valencia's civil war. A contemporary monk described it as a "principal castle" whose loss did "grievous damage" to Is-

riana civitas et Penisc[o]le et alia castella multa." Stuve may stand for Shuqr (Júcar), a common name for Alcira; Oedeeb may be a corruption of Shāṭiba, Játiva, by way of an erratic Latin Iatib.

10 Shams ad-Dīn Muḥammad b. Abī Ṭālib al-Anṣārī ad-Dimashqī, *Manuel de la cosmographie du moyen âge*, trans. A. F. Mehren (Copenhagen, 1874), p. 351. On the caliphal province system see Lévi-Provençal, *España musulmana*, v, 27-28. The description of the world written by al-Idrīsī in 1154 at the court of Roger II of Sicily divides eastern Spain below Tortosa and above Murcia into an Alcira bloc—including Alcira, Denia, and Játiva—and a Murviedro bloc—including Burriana, Murviedro, and Valencia; see Muḥammad b. Idrīs al-Idrīsī, *Description de l'Afrique et de l'Espagne*, ed. and trans. R. Dozy and M. De Goeje (Leiden, [1864-1866] 1968), section 1, p. 15.

lamic Valencia.[11] King James, repudiating the claim of Morella's conqueror, the powerful lord Blasco of Alagón, explained that it was too princely a region for a baron: "with its dependencies, this is a castle equivalent to a county."[12] The Christian documentation, by revealing Morella's significance, illumines the status of other regional capitals listed by ad-Dimashqī.

Al-Ḥimyarī, assessing the towns of Spain notable for their power or history, singled out a number of Valencia's centers, mixing into the list a few surprises. He gave Alcira, Alpuente, Bairén, Burriana, Denia, Játiva, Murviedro, Onda, Ondara ("a great city of eastern Spain, ruined by the Berbers"), Peñíscola, and Valencia city; neighboring Murcia had its own list.[13] Alcira's importance in the crusade era, deriving from its superb natural defenses as an island, appears from James's autobiography, from its choice as residence by Zayyān immediately after his surrender to the crusaders, and from its mili-

[11] *Chronica Alberici monachi Trium-Fontium*: "quoddam nobilissimum castrum . . . hoc anno recuperavit unde maximum incurrerunt detrimentum"; Miret y Sans, citing Alberic's description, can only conjecture Torre de Foyos and expresses his puzzlement (*Itinerari*, p. 119); but Morella, won in 1232, had its ownership settled by formal agreement between King James and Blasco of Alagón on May 11, 1235, a documentary trace which explains Alberic's including it in the king's affairs for that year. For the conveyance of Morella to James by Abū Zayd in 1229, see *Itinerari*, p. 77; see also pp. 104, 117.

[12] *Llibre dels feyts*, ch. 136: "Don Blasco, ben sabets que aquest goany no tany a vos per aquesta rao: car aquest es i castell que val tant con un comptat ab ses pertinencies." Al-Ḥimyarī does not bother to include Morella in his elaborate descriptive listings of Spanish cities and castles.

[13] Al-Ḥimyarī gives less than a dozen notices of Valencian towns, only half of them in any detail, plus some Murcian places; see, e.g., Alpuente (*Kitāb ar-rawḍ al-mi'ṭār*, p. 120), Alcira (p. 213), Bairén (p. 128), Burriana (p. 95), Denia (p. 158), Murviedro, whose dependent towns make a frontier with those of Burriana (p. 361), Peñíscola (p. 120), Onda (p. 71), Ondara (p. 71), and Valencia (pp. 100-118). Al-Idrīsī includes in his similar but smaller list Alcira, Bocairente, Burriana, Cullera, Denia, Játiva, Murviedro, Peñíscola, and Valencia city. He describes Bocairente as a stronghold ranking "in importance with the cities," a market and excellent cloth-manufacturing center; Cullera castle at the Júcar mouth "is well fortified"; Peñíscola supported a farming hinterland. Denia held "a great number of fortified places"; Burriana was an attractive town with many resources (al-Idrīsī, *Description de l'Afrique et de l'Espagne*, pp. 36-38). Of the older writers, the most famous was ar-Rāzī; he describes the cities, commerce, and aspect of the Valencian region (Aḥmad b. Muḥammad b. Mūsā ar-Rāzī, "Description de l'Espagne," trans. Évariste Lévi-Provençal, *Al-Andalus*, XVIII [1953], pp. 70-72).

tary centrality during the crusade; when Zayyān gathered his forces for his one pitched battle against King James, the main fight remembered by Islamic historians, "he assembled the populations of the Játiva and Alcira districts."[14]

Al-Waṭwāṭ, near-contemporary to the crusade generation (d. 1319), included the Valencian region in his description of Spain, and put under the capital city more than a dozen regional centers—Alcira, Almenara, Bairén, Bechí (?), Burriana, Castellón (?), Cervera, Cullera, Játiva, Morella, Murviedro, Peñíscola, Requena, and several places of obscure spelling.[15] Ibn Khaldūn, arranging a bookish compendium of geography a century after the crusade, counted the old centers of eastern Spain above Murcia as Valencia, Alcira [Júcar], Játiva, and Denia.[16] He ranked Denia as an island in the class of Cyprus and Sicily, probably because the same word would apply to Denia if viewed as a peninsula. The divisions based in natural, economic, and primitive organization show through also in Valencia's pre-Islamic ecclesiastical structure. The boundaries and towns of the Visigothic dioceses of Alpuente, Denia, Játiva, Segorbe, Tortosa, and Valencia turn up in descriptions like that of King Wamba, which show Valencia extending to Alpuente, Chelva, Murviedro, and the sea. Later, when the Cid claimed tribute from this region, he took an annual 52,000 dinars from the ruler at Valencia city; 50,000 from the Játiva-Denia axis with allied Tortosa; 10,000 from the Muslim lord of Alpuente; 8,000 from the lord of Murviedro; 6,000 from Segorbe's lord; 3,000 from Jérica; 3,000 from Almenara; and 2,000 from Liria. The *Historia Roderici*, mixing strategic forts and cities into its general narrative, emphasizes Almenara,

[14] Ibn Khaldūn, *Histoire des Berbères*, II, 306; he reports a siege of Alcira later; on Alcira in the crusade, see below, pp. 363-365. King James reports Zayyān gathering his great army "from Játiva to Onda" (*Llibre dels feyts*, ch. 217). Both Ibn Khaldūn and al-Ḥimyarī speak rather of the Júcar region than Alcira town, but the context clarifies their meaning. Al-Idrīsī makes Alcira the central town of the Alcira-Denia-Játiva triangle or region, praising its pleasant aspect, great number of fruit trees, and teeming population (*Description de l'Afrique et de l'Espagne*, p. 37).

[15] Muḥammad b. Ibrāhīm b. Yaḥyā al-Kutubī al-Waṭwāṭ, *Extraits inédits relatifs au Maghreb (géographie et histoire)*, ed. Edmond Fagnan (Algiers, 1924), p. 64.

[16] *Muqaddimah*, I, 98 and 141, with Rosenthal's notes. Ibn Khaldūn contrasts North Africa, having "few cities and towns," with Spain, which was organized by cities and districts. Piles Ibars, *Valencia árabe*, pp. 1-4.

Alpuente, Bairén, Benicadell, Burriana, Játiva, Liria, Morella, Montornés, Murviedro, Ondara, Onteniente, Olocau, Oropesa, Puig, Valencia city with its several suburbs, and Villena; the adventures of the Cid involved other important places, like Alcalá, Alcira, Culla, Cullera, Denia, Jérica, Oropesa, and Polop.[17]

The Local Scene

Below or beyond the princely and regional units, a multiplicity of castles or towns dominated their local *termini*. Sometimes the castle presided, rather than its inconsiderable town or collection of townlets; sometimes the town swallowed up its attendant castle; sometimes the walled town comprised its own governing castle. The countryside or *terminus* of any such entity included some castles or fortifications standing isolated and farming complexes equally without subjurisdiction, as well as lesser towns and castles each boasting its own jurisdiction like a mirrored image of the englobing larger entity.[18] The smaller regions embraced by the large blocs each displayed its individual characteristics; they comprise the innumerable *termini* within *termini* which recur in postcrusade documents. Corbera with its more local *terminus*, for example, formed a part of the Alcira *terminus*. The word itself merely meant boundaries; the smallest, innermost of such bounded units, with or without jurisdiction, were described by King James in a legal decision of 1268. The king noted that every alqueria in the kingdom of Valencia preserved "no other fixed boundaries except only those boundaries which the Saracens of the same alqueria were accustomed to farm," and from whose limits they were able to return "from their work the same day to that alqueria." These natural or convenient units large and small the crusaders recognized and largely preserved

[17] Their relative importance emerges from the several episodes involving each; see Ramón Menéndez Pidal, *La España del Cid*, 4th edn. rev., 2 vols. (Madrid, 1947), I, 390; the *Historia Roderici* appended in its second volume; and the Valencian towns severally in its index.

[18] García y García explains the units comprising northern Valencia, in his *Estado económico-social de Castellón*, pp. 5-8, 23; he sees it as a reflection of the Roman *municipium praefecturum* working through its *loci, vici, pagi*, and fortifications. See also the documentation and works cited below in Chapter XVI, which examines the system of city governance under the Muslims.

for administrative purposes. It is difficult to define their functions except to say that in Christian times the whole *terminus*, larger or internal, shared some common life under the head town, coming under its customs, privileges, obligations, administrators, or in general under its organization. This organic unity may have been quite loose, visible mostly at the intermediate political, juridical, and tax levels, and even there sporadically, but operating nonetheless to lend cohesiveness and common tone to the unit. Such jurisdictional spheres or areas of countryside, whatever their remote origins, constituted for the crusading generation a relic of the immediate Islamic past. They afford a precious glimpse into precrusade local government.[19]

Examples abound. The king confirmed Onteniente in 1250 as retaining "in perpetuity all those jurisdictional boundaries which the Saracens of Onteniente had and held in Saracen times." The jurisdictional boundaries of Culla and Cuevas de Vinromá in 1235 stayed "just as ever the Saracens had and held and possessed those castles

[19] Arch. Crown, James I, Reg. Canc. 15, fol. 135r, v (Jan. 29, 1268): "aliqua alqueria regni Valentie non habet terminos certos nisi illos terminos tantum quos sarraceni eiusdem alquerie laborare consueverint redeundo inde eadem die de sua laboracione ad ipsam alqueriam." Regional and local histories can shed some light on these *termini*. Enrique Bayerri's *Historia de Tortosa* devotes vols. 7 and 8 to Islamic and postconquest Tortosa. The ecclesiastical and early colonial period of the Valencian portion of Tortosa is treated in my *Crusader Valencia*, ch. 3 and passim; plate 3 shows Cavanilles' eighteenth-century map of the Benifasá *terminus* in detail. Sarthou Carreres compiled the volume *Provincia de Castellón* on this northern area of Valencia, in the *Geografía general del reino de Valencia* (above, Chapter I, n. 14). Regional or local histories include Felipe Mateu y Llopis, *Alpuente, reino musulmán* (Valencia, 1944); Carlos Sarthou Carreres, *Datos para la historia de Játiva*, 4 vols. (Játiva, 1933-1935); Roque Chabás y Lloréns, *Historia de la ciudad de Denia*, ed. F. Figueras Pacheco, rev. edn. (Alicante, 1958-1960); José Segura y Barreda, *Morella y sus aldeas*, 3 vols. (Morella, 1868); and the histories of towns like Alcira, Cullera, and Burriana. Martín Almagro Basch is directing an ample *Historia de Albarracín y su sierra*, a flanking and overlapping territory on Valencia's west, 4 vols. (Teruel, 1959); Jacinto Bosch Vilá contributed volume II, *Albarracín musulmán*. The EI^2 provides a number of able if brief local histories, such as those by Ambrosio Huici Miranda, "Al-Bunt" (Alpuente), I, 1309-1310, "Dāniya" (Denia), II, 111-112, and "D̲jazīrat S̲huḳr" (Alcira), II, 526. The Uxó Charter (see Chapter VI, n. 7) makes reference to taxation within "the Tinença of Valencia," apparently referring to all the kingdom or at the least to its central part. From the Latin *tenentia*, it bears meanings such as jurisdiction, holding, and fief. The area later called the Tinença de Benifasá was land held by the Benifasá monastery, but such lands tended to be assigned according to preexistent pattern.

and those towns." Gorga remained as "ever it was at its best in the time of the Saracens." The grant of Montornés near Burriana to Peter Sánchez in 1242 kept "the jurisdictional boundaries pertaining to the aforesaid castle in the time of the Saracens." The king granted Cervera to the Hospitallers in 1235 to continue as it had in Islamic times. He solved a land dispute by conceding Almazora to the bishop of Tortosa in 1245 "with the jurisdictional boundaries, in length and in width, which it had in Saracen times." Blasco of Alagón as lord of Morella set the region's limits by enlisting the memories of four Muslims. The formulas employed and the uniform manner of reconstructing boundaries betray a mentality, an approach to handling the division of the new kingdom. They suggest, too, that one can reconstruct the physiognomy of precrusade Valencia by following the continuing and better documented divisions of Christian Valencia.[20]

The theme recurred in several disputes. When Cocentaina quarreled with Alcoy, Penáguila, Travadell, Planes, Perpunchent, Bocairente, and Agres concerning respective spheres, the king instructed his commission to resolve the dispute by judicial inquiry among local Christians and Muslims as to historical boundaries. In the important case of distinguishing the areas proper to the towns of Puzol and Puig, Muslim witnesses entered depositions. For the Navarrés-Bolbaite limits, the king ordered the testimony of Moors to be taken at Montesa, Enguera, Chella, and elsewhere. In 1268 a suit went forward between "Giles Garcés of Azagra on one part and Giles Simon

[20] *Colección diplomática,* doc. 374 (April 29, 1250): "teneatis in perpetuum omnes illos terminos quos sarraceni de Ontinyent habebant et tenebant tempore sarracenorum . . . prout sarraceni eiusdem loci sarracenorum tempore eos melius habuerunt et tenuerunt." Doc. 139 (May 11, 1235): "sicut sarraceni unquam illa castra et illas villas habuerunt et tenuerunt et possederunt." Doc. 989 (Feb. 26, 1274): "sicut unquam melius, tempore sarracenorum." Montornés in the "Colección de cartas pueblas," no. 14, *BSCC,* IX (1928), 86-87: "cum terminis tempore sarracenorum predicto castro pertinentibus," and in *Itinerari,* p. 157 (1242). Bibl. Univ. Val., MSS, no. 154, doc. 10, Cervera grant (Dec. 23, 1235). Arch. Cat. Tortosa, cart. VIII, fol. 59 (June 10, 1245): "sicut maiores terminos habuit tempore sarracenorum et longiores." Burriana charter (Jan. 1, 1235), in *"Repartiment" de Burriana,* p. 41; "sicut fuerunt in tempore sarracenorum." *Itinerari,* p. 115: "habeat suos terminos sicut habere solebat tempore sarracenorum." For Morella see Joan Puig, "Senyors de Morella durant el segle xiii," *BSCC,* XXXI (1955), 89-90, where Blasco uses Mahomet Aman, Maça Abenmaçot, Aben Baço, and the local "Cavaçala" (on this office see below, p. 190).

of Segura on the other, over the townships of Gayanes and of Foncesielles," the former asserting the villages to lie within the district of Perpunchent; the court rejected the claim, on "the testimonies of the oldest and most ancient Moors" that the places "are villages by themselves." When argument arose as to the extent of the town of Chíu, James decreed that it comprised only those lands cultivated by local Moors before the conquest.[21] Thus the exiguous and episodic notices left by Muslim authors like al-Ḥimyarī concerning the lesser localities fall into an ample context, taking on patterned meaning.

The chronicler Muntaner makes a litany of some ninety more important towns and castles taken by the crusaders, indicating some sort of local jurisdictions. Similar lists can be devised, depending upon one's interpretation of the relationship between the lesser and greater *termini*. Sanchis Sivera in his geographic catalogue for Valencia analyzed numerous such entities. He gathered the names of forty-four Islamic alquerias surrounding the castle and town of Albaida, and an incomplete list of forty-six alquerias belonging to Alcira. Arabic authors convey some jurisdictional information, though a given item may represent political rather than permanent natural entities; thus Abu 'l-Fidā' in his contemporary geography located Játiva as a dependency of Valencia city but with its own territory, three of whose charming spots he described; he put the strongholds of Bocairente and Bairén as dependencies of Denia.[22]

King James organized his land distribution around twenty-five major *termini*, assigning one book to each town "with its alquerias." Surely these had previously been the most important centers of Islamic Valencia—allowing for a few additional centers not in royal hands and for the three centers already organized, Morella, Burriana, and Valencia city. Above the Júcar River these centers were

[21] Arch. Crown, James I, perg. no. 1,971 (March 16, 1268). Arch. Cat., perg. 2,372 (an. 1250) for Puzol-Puig. Arch. Crown, Peter III, Reg. Canc. 42, fol. 243 (April 3, 1280), on Navarrés-Bolbaite. Arch. Crown, James I, Reg. Canc. 15, fol. 82 (Feb. 27, 1267-1268): "don Gil Garçes Daçagra de la una part e don Gil Exemeniz de Segura de la otra, sobre las alquerias de Gayanas e de Foncezels"; "las testimonias de los mas veyllos e mas ancianos moros"; "son alquerias por simismas." For Chíu see Arch. Crown, James I, Reg. Canc. 15, fol. 135 (Jan. 29, 1268).

[22] José Sanchis y Sivera, *Nomenclátor geográfico-eclesiástico de los pueblos de la diócesis de Valencia* (Valencia, 1922), pp. 25, 35-39. Abu 'l-Fidā' (1273-1331), *Géographie d'Aboulféda*, ed. and trans. M. [J.T.] Reinaud, 3 vols. (Paris, 1848), I, 240, 257-258. Muntaner, *Crònica*, ch. 9.

Almenara, Liria, Murviedro, Onda, Peñíscola, and Segorbe; from the Júcar down were Albaida, Alcira, Alcoy, Almizra, Bocairente, Calpe, Castalla, Cocentaina, Corbera, Cullera, Denia, Guadalest, Játiva, Jijona, Luchente, Onteniente, and Rugat. The quantity of business entering the registers of King James from the Valencian kingdom confirms this thesis; Valencia city, Alcira, and Játiva in that order account for the three highest numbers of items in the registers; Burriana, Murviedro, Morella, and Gandía each contribute roughly half the number of a first-class city; Peñíscola, Segorbe, Cullera, and Denia are in turn half as important as the second class; unlisted Alfandech ranks between the second and third. The eighteen other places in the king's book list surpass all remaining locales for the realm of Valencia, by this test, except for seven which equal them in business and presumably in rank: Altea, Beniopa, Gallinera, Pego, Penáguila, Tárbena, and Villarreal.[23]

After exposing the permanent pattern—that of smaller *termini* comprising larger *termini*, with each centering upon a city or town—and after allowing for the castle center or the precipitate rise of a local strong man at some unexpected point, one can soften the stark outline by noting the organizational factors which cut across these tidy lines or which further defined them in their local context. An extensive pastoral zone for wandering flocks could depend upon its nearby city; Arab and Berber tribes favored these for settlement, so that tribal affiliations and peculiarities marked such expanses. A river often tied its valley to a city, even by name, as with the Ríu de Chelva. In Valencia the valley as often took the name of its fort or center, combining with other units into a larger *terminus*.

A unity imposing itself everywhere was the water system, which came to be regarded almost as distinctive of Valencia—the thirty-five rivers of the kingdom, supplemented by springs, wells, cisterns, tunnels, huge canals drawing water aside, smaller canals radiating from

[23] Arch. Crown, James I, Reg. Canc. 16, fol. 192 (June 7, 1270), transcribed by J. E. Martínez-Ferrando in the introduction to his *Catálogo de los documentos del antiguo reino de Valencia*, 2 vols. (Madrid, 1934), I, xiv; the register statistics are approximate, compiled from the catalogue's indexes. Morella formed a strong geographical and political unity, with some twenty-five dependent towns. Carmelo Giner Bolufer has studied the eight valleys comprising the Pego unity, with maps and history, in "Topografía histórica de los valles de Pego," *ACCV*, xv (1947), 46-74.

these to divert the water in multiple directions, and tiny ditches in fields and terraces to distribute it widely. A German tourist, observing the system in a more elaborated stage at the opening of the nineteenth century, was struck by how much the domestic economy of Valencia focused on water. "Every field, with its principal canal and its numberless ramifications, exhibits in some measure a miniature representation of the whole province."[24] It seems appropriate that when the kingdom of Valencia first organized in 1010 at the breakup of the Cordova caliphate, it was an irrigation official who assumed the governance at Valencia city, and another at Játiva. This overarching unity of repetitive water communities recurs in the Valencia story, the members bound together in assiduous, disciplined activity.

The smallest communal unit was that survival from the Roman villa, the alqueria or farm-hamlet of an important landlord. Akin to a manor, it amounted to an agricultural complex, a center of population grouped in relation to itself. In Islamic Valencia this farm center with its mills and ovens had evolved into a sort of neighborhood or territory with a nascent personality of its own. At times it evolved into a considerable village or even a walled town surrounded by its tiny district. The precrusade promises of King James obliged him to divide the ownership of the component elements of many alquerias, though they allowed him to keep the complex itself intact. Away from the irrigated huertas, in the *secà* or drier lands and uplands, the alqueria's counterpart was the aldea complex (Arabic *ḍay'a*), a hamlet centered around the landholder's fort.[25] Missing from Valencia was the great latifundium estate such as survived into and beyond Islamic times in Aragon and Andalusia. A local establishment not unlike the alqueria was the mill, its wheels moved by the waters of river or canal, its encompassing

[24] Christian A. Fischer, *A Picture of Valencia, Taken on the Spot; Comprehending a Description of that Province . . .* , 2d edn., trans. F. Shoberl (London, 1811), pp. 40-44, 100-103, 113-115. Lévi-Provençal, *España musulmana*, v, 160ff., with bibliographical notes.

[25] On the historical or technical evolution underlying this later *aldea*, see Claude Cahen, "Ḍay'a," *EI*², I, 187-188. S. D. Goitein found that *ḍay'a* in his eastern documentation applied to either a farm-estate or a village, arguing a similar evolution; see *A Mediterranean Society: The Jewish Communities of the Arab World as Portrayed in the Documents of the Cairo Geniza*, 2 vols. to date (Berkeley, 1967ff.), I, 117.

manor house with stables and gardens and outbuildings all planted comfortably in the landscape.

Single residences varied. King James described a typical Valencian landscape when recalling the view around Islamic Játiva; scattered in the green huerta below the city and castle stood "more than two hundred farmhouses and in addition alquerias many and dense." The whitewashed *barraca* of cane and mud, with steeply canted roof protecting an attic storey for fodder, survives today in parts of Valencia. An object of affection and scholarly attention with antecedents extending beyond Islam into prehistory, it was much less common in medieval than in modern times; its locale was mostly humid areas of intense cultivation. It could stand independently or as part of an alqueria. The *raal* or *rafal* (Arabic *raḥl*) ranged from farmhouse or hamlet to a country estate; 'Alī al-Khaṭṭāb (Ali Alhatap) was able to sell one such domain, granted him by King James, to the Christian community of Cocentaina in 1268 at 600 solidi "for constructing houses and other buildings." The Chivert charter allowed its Muslim population free acquisition of "wood from pines and all other trees in the wastelands, for roofing buildings and making window-frames, doors, trim, and coverings, and for all work necessary for them." Other references to wood-gathering were more ambiguous and possibly were concerned less with construction than with the task of garnering firewood. To learn of enemy plans, for example, the crusaders at Puig sent raiding parties toward Valencia city, who brought back twelve men and fifty women "who had gone out from the city, some for wood, and others for food," an enumeration which incidentally suggests that wood-gathering was women's work in Islamic Valencia or that it fell to them in wartime.[26]

[26] Arch. Crown, James I, Reg. Canc. 15, fol. 91 (April 17, 1268): "reallum Concentanie quam dederamus Ali Alhatap." Another extensive *raal* is below in Chapter XIV, n. 52. Chivert Charter: "habeant posse frangendi vel talliandi fusta de pinis et aliis arboribus omnibus in heremo ad cohoperiendum domos et faciendum postes, portas, limina, et tegellos et ad omnia opera que sunt eis necessaria." Cutting of wood for building houses was one of the first privileges granted to the Christian settlers of Valencia city (1239); the *Aureum opus* copy erroneously puts "stone," but the grant is more carefully transcribed in the *Fori antiqui Valenciae* (rub. II, no. 5, with note). *Llibre dels feyts,* chs. 318 (Játiva) and 225; the preponderance of women captives may also have resulted from their being less agile, but the king's scouts were probably equal to the agility or ferocity of male civilians.

A farmer or craftsman therefore might reside in some alqueria or aldea, or maintain his cottage in the fields, or dwell in a city, suburb, or lesser town. Whatever his status, he normally had or rented a home of his own. The landlord who collected rents from his tenants might live at one of his rustic hamlets or else choose a more pleasant absentee existence in a suburban or urban mansion. Local organization after the conquest was by aljama or community, inevitably a designation covering diverse situations. Some communal units, though independently aljamas under one aspect, might comprise elements in a larger complex or aljama which paid the taxes, signed the surrender treaties, and the like. The ascent from alqueria to aljama to smaller countryside (*terminus*) to larger countryside to region may not have been so neat in practice. Hints of the existence of some such order crop up, however, for Mudejar taxation, justice, or similar limited purposes. Possibly the cities of Tortosa, Valencia, and Játiva each continued to have a special relation to a great segment of the Mudejar population, with the Júcar River and perhaps the Mijares River as dividing boundaries.[27] Preexisting dynastic units like Alcira and Cullera surely enjoyed some continuing role. Since the king's announced policy was to remove or mitigate Islamic appearances, geographic survivals pose a paradox.

These categories, while facilitating an understanding of the complicated kingdom, can mislead by their neatness. The eighteenth-century German traveler, already quoted in connection with irri-

---

On houses see J. M. Casas Torres, *La vivienda y los nucleos de población rurales de la huerta de Valencia* (Madrid, 1944), pp. 85ff., 124-135; on the alqueria, see pp. 141-161, on the mill, pp. 168-169. See also Leopoldo Torres Balbás, "Algunos aspectos de la vivienda hispanomusulmana," *Mélanges d'histoire et d'archéologie de l'occident musulman*, 2 vols. (Algiers, 1957), II, 169-175; Manuel Sanchis Guarner, *Les barraques valencianes* (Barcelona, 1957), esp. ch. 10 on history and name, with bibliography; Julio Caro Baroja, *Los pueblos de España, ensayo de etnología* (Barcelona, 1946), pp. 419-422; Reinhart P. A. Dozy and William H. Engelmann, *Glossaire des mots espagnols y portugais dérivés de l'arabe*, 2d edn. rev. (Amsterdam, [1869] 1965), pp. 97 (*aldea*), 236-237 (*barraca*) and 328 (*rafal, rahal*). For comparison with the houses familiar to Christian immigrants and influential for the evolution of domestic architecture in postcrusade Valencia, see José Puig y Cadafalch, "La casa catalana," *Congrés I*, II, 1041-1060.

[27] The Júcar, administrative division for the new Christian kingdom, had also provided an interior division for the Romans (Eugène Albertini, *Les divisions administratives de l'Espagne romaine* [Paris, 1923], p. 97).

gation, caught the essential note of contrast which characterizes Valencia. "Few countries exhibit, in so small a compass, such a variety and such striking contrasts as the kingdom of Valencia; in the northern and western part we find nothing but wild, inclement, and mountainous regions, while the middle and southern portion is occupied by the most fertile and delicious plains, which extend to the coast."[28] Within this larger disposition lay a remarkably varied and broken environment, each differing region forming a closed bloc where the country's general features combined into their own peculiar balance of forces. The single elements of any such pattern in the Middle Ages "nuanced infinitely."[29] Farm areas of similar general nature betrayed this heterogeneity. Huerta differed from huerta by size, location, and water source; the arid areas ranged from huerta hillside or unirrigated farm to forest, upland, mountain zone, or uninviting badland. Arid and watered areas commonly intermixed, a dry zone focusing on its oases-like green lands, or a series of huertas interlacing with dry lands, so that a farmer owned bits of each. That symbiotic relation was not univocal, but diversified from place to place according to the quality of each element and the multifarious factors framing it: city, villages, or sweep of land; seacoast, river network, plains, mountain range, hill valley, or pastoral stretch; and access to markets, ethnically rooted differences, communications, or political influences. Islamic Valencia, like its Christian successor, was a conglomerate terrain. It shaped its local communities accordingly.

[28] Fischer, *Picture of Valencia*, pp. 235-236.

[29] Halperín Donghi, "Recouvrements de civilisation," p. 155, and his general discussion of this peculiarity. J. M. Houston concludes his detailed analysis, "Land Use and Society in the Plain of Valencia" (*Geographical Essays in Memory of Alan G. Ogilvie*, ed. R. Miller and J. W. Watson [London, 1959]), by confessing the area to be so complex as to intimidate the geographical researcher (pp. 192-193).

CHAPTER IV

The Human Geography

CONTEMPORARIES called Muslims "Moors," a word by now scarcely bearing any echoes of North Africa. *Moros*, with its Latin counterpart *mauri*, occurred often in legal as well as informal usage to designate Valencian Mudejars. Formal usage, and the several Romance memoirs detailing Valencian and North African adventures, inclined rather to "Saracens," the common European and Byzantine name; ecclesiastical documentation preferred the term, reposing as it did for clerics upon a pseudoetymology involving Abraham's wife Sara. The proper distinction, setting Saracens as Muslims of the East against Moors of the Maghrib or West, does not occur in Valencian documents. Muslims and Mudejars alike became *sarraceni* in Latin, or in Catalan *sarrains, sarrahis, sarrahins*, and similar variants. Valencian Christians apostatizing to Islam became "Saracens"; in a single passage of his autobiography, King James speaks of the Valencian Muslims both as "Moors" and "Saracens." "Arab" generally confined itself to the language or customs of these Saracen-Moors. The term universally employed by modern historians for such subject Moors as the Valencians, "Mudejar," was absent from the vocabulary of the crusader generation. Raymond Martí's contemporary Arabic-Latin word list did include its Arabic form as meaning "tributary," and the Mozarabs, like the Muslims, were familiar with its meaning. Apparently it gained currency among Christians only from the late fifteenth century. The Catalan form *mudèixar* derived from the Castilian *mudéjar*, which was based in turn upon the Arabic *mudajjan*—"allowed to remain" as a permanent, tributary, protected community of subjects.[1]

[1] The plural of *mudéjares* received a moot accent, sometimes dispensed with, in fairly recent times; on this problem and Christian terms for Muslims, see also Cagigas, *Mudejares*, I, 58-64, and Dozy, *Glossaire*, pp. 321-322, with supplement on p. 425. Ibn Baṭṭūṭa gives an example of popular usage in Byzantium; at the approach of his party, Constantinople's palace guard cried out the warning "Sarākinū, Sarākinū, which means Muslims" (*Travels* [1325-1354], trans. H.A.R. Gibb, 3 vols. to date [Cambridge, 1958-1971], II, 504). For James's usage, see *Llibre dels feyts*, chs. 100, 331. For Martí, see Chapter V, n. 38.

ETHNIC STRAINS

As the westerly Muslims formed a separate region of Islam, Spanish Muslims comprised a distinct entity within this western bloc. To state it so flatly, however, distorts the complex reality. In discerning the Spanish difference, one cannot read history backwards from modern times; Spain was no phenomenon starkly separate from Africa, a land mass neatly isolated by the natural boundary of the sea. Against the truth of former Visigothic or Roman provincial unity lay the deeper, opposing truth of a common seacoast economy; the Mediterranean peoples lining the territory on both banks were joined by facile water routes and in some ways by similar conditions of life. Their experience in shared living had roots going back past Islam, Christianity, and pagan Rome. It was only natural that post-Almohad Islam dreamed of regaining its lost Spanish peninsula, and that the Christian crusaders entertained no thought of stopping on their side of the sea. Both Aragon and Castile dispatched African crusades, like Castile's ill-fated amphibious assault in 1260 against Salé on the Atlantic coast of Morocco and her ambitious push in the early fourteenth century.[2] Eventually and much later, history would record the accident that Spain ceased to expand at Gibraltar, and that Islam was unable to return beyond North Africa. The channel bridging two regions had turned into a moat. In the thirteenth and fourteenth centuries the prospect of this permanent stalemate would have disheartened both Muslim and crusader.

The wider question of medieval Spain's self-vision as a European unity, and its relative dependence from ancient times upon the East or even Europe as against North Africa, are not at issue here. Skirting the several embattled positions in this debate, whose protagonists shelter behind bulwarks of special bibliographies, it is enough to see that the regions of Spain related directly to the regions of North Africa, even though each division was marked by nuances and a character apart. Wherever the crusading wave washed over Spanish territory, the cultural frontier surged along. Had it moved into Africa, the littoral brotherhood could have been united under Christianity as it had been under Islam; instead it stopped short, disturb-

[2] C. E. Dufourcq, "Un projet castillan du xiii siècle: la 'croisade d'Afrique,'" *Revue d'histoire et de civilisation du Maghreb,* 1 (1966), 26-51; Henry III of England and other prospective allies failed to participate.

ing the western Mediterranean's physical unity, while a wary but inevitable substitute union grew between the Christian states of Spain and their Muslim colleagues in Granada and North Africa—an interchange or assimilation in diplomacy, commerce, war, fashion, and at some levels in manner of life. The Spanish paradox of unity and diversity is slippery to grasp; a number of factors worked for union, but the two cultures ensured division. All discussion of the Spanish enigma must deal with this paradox; any theory of shared *Hispanidad* among Christian and Muslim Spaniards, unless skillfully steered, can shipwreck on it.[3]

The ethnic origins of Valencian Moors have been the subject of erudite study and conjecture. They were basically descended from the original pre-Islamic inhabitants of each locality. These Iberians the Romans had grouped into three main tribes: the Ilercaones in the north down to the Mijares River with a capital at Tortosa, the Edetanes of central Valencia down to the Júcar with a capital at Liria, and the Contestanes from the Júcar to Segura with a capital at Cocentaina. Segorbe had its branch of the Celtiberians; other enclaves like Sagunto held their own tribes. The groups represented a long evolution with further evolution to come, modified by drastic cultural change and by intermarriage with whatever peoples conquered or immigrated at a given point. The volume of Islamic newcomers—whether Arab, Syrian, Berber, cosmopolitan immigrant or merchant, mercenary soldier, or the so-called slave class introduced from the four quarters of the Mediterranean world—served to dilute but not displace the underlying groups. Though the blanket term Hispano-Muslim covers all varieties, allowance must be made not only for a more Arabized and later Berberized aristocracy, but also for pronounced regional and even very local heterogeneity.

[3] A plethora of historico-philosophical writings exists on the Hispanic character in its relations to Islam, North Africa, and the crusades, with champions like Claudio Sánchez-Albornoz and Américo Castro prominent in the battle. Miguel Tarradell recently surveyed the modern bibliography on one phase, the modern demotion of North Africa's role in pre-Roman Spain, seeing rather a cultural movement south from Spain into Africa ("Una hipótesis que se desvanece: el papel de África en las raíces de los pueblos hispánicos," *Homenaje a Jaime Vicens Vives,* I, 173-181). On the creation of the legend of the "Goths" or Europeans, spread especially in the *Historia gothica* written by the Toledo primate Rodrigo Jiménez de Rada at about the time of the Valencian crusade, see Cagigas, *Mudejares,* II, 358. See also José Maravall's *El concepto de España en la edad media* (Madrid, 1954), ch. 5 and passim.

The traditional history of early Islamic Valencia, resting on scraps of information, assimilates the region to the more Arabized sections of caliphal Spain, including the Ebro Valley to the north and Murcia to the south. By this account the original Arab aristocracy, small but powerful in the land, took over the plains and huertas in two successive and antipathetic blocs inclusively termed Yemenite and Syrian. With peculiarly Arabic pride of family their descendants never lost sight of these remote divisions. Within each bloc the many tribal groups perpetuated friendships and feuds which were sometimes pre-Islamic in origin. Ribera Tarragó, who identified a number of Arabic tribes in the kingdom of Valencia, believed that interrelations and rancors influenced their choice of places to settle, thus creating a map of factions permanently incised into the landscape.[4] Not only could locale thus be set against locale, but factional alliances and connections ramified to many cities in and beyond the kingdom. Yemenites predominated—like the Anṣār at Liria, Uxó, and Murviedro, the Ma'āfir at Játiva and Valencia, and the Banū 'Ubāda of the Anṣār at Jérica (giving it the nickname "Castle of the Nobles"). This picture is not appreciably altered by the probability that the Yemenite-Syrian factions originated during the Umayyad reign at Damascus, each subsequently pressing its largely fabricated genealogies back to ancient times. A prominent stratum atop the Arabs was the class of "slaves"—often really freemen of European antecedents, who previously manned upper levels in the military and bureaucratic machinery or served as clients to the Arab ruling classes. They were strong in the Valencian region, particularly from Murviedro down. Their new aristocracy, continually

[4] Julián Ribera y Tarragó, "Las tribus árabes en el reino de Valencia," *El archivo,* I (1886), 83-85; "La nobleza árabe valenciana," *ibid.*, pp. 349-350, 355-357, and II (1887), 49-53, 200-205, IV (1890), 86-91; both reprinted in his *Disertaciones,* II, 210-243, as part of fourteen studies comprising his "Historia árabe valenciana" (pp. 177-336). See also Huici, *Historia musulmana de Valencia,* III, 71-77; Isidro de las Cagigas, *Andalucía musulmana: Aportaciones a la delimitación de la frontera del Andalus* (*ensayo de etnografía andaluza medieval*) (Madrid, 1950), pp. 17-42; the general study by Henri Pérès, "Les éléments ethniques de l'Espagne musulmane et de la langue arabe au ve-xie siècle," in Emilio García Gómez *et alii, Études d'orientalisme,* II, 717-733, with Valencian Arab families on p. 721; Elías Terés Sádaba, "Linajes árabes en al-Andalus según la 'Ŷamhara' de Ibn Ḥazm," *Al-Andalus,* XXII (1957), 55-112, 337-376; Caro Baroja, *Los pueblos de España,* ch. 18; Manuel Sanchis Guarner, *Els parlars romànics de València i Mallorca anteriors a la reconquista,* 2d edn. rev. (Valencia, 1961), pp. 19ff. with map.

replenished, married into resident wealthy classes, as had the Arabs. Such was not the practice of the Afro-Berbers; these tribes, especially from the Sahara and southern Maghrib, came with their families in a mass immigration in the eleventh and twelfth centuries. The backbone of Almohad power, they tended to be standoffish and at times hostile to the Arabs.

Guichard is currently challenging one element of this picture, thus altering the earlier history dramatically. Few Arabs made their way at first to the remote Valencian region, by this account not enough to establish an important aristocracy. They found themselves in a deurbanized, town-and-country marcher region, at the neglected periphery of the caliphal state both politically and culturally. The new order imposed itself less by Yemenite-Syriac groupings, with Berber immigrants relegated to hills and hinterland, than by a small but generalized Berber influx; Arabized but disdained by the purer Arab tradition, they related to the more widespread Berberized hinterlands throughout Spain. An Egyptian wavelet with perhaps a few Syrians soon followed; later a steady influx began, consisting of rebels and fugitives from troubles in the more traditionally Arabic provinces, overseas arrivals, local highland people drawn down by the reviving city life of this ethnically sympathetic area, and, from the eleventh century onward, a considerable number of immigrants displaced by the Christian advance from all over Spain. The early Berber blocs assumed an Arabized style of life, swiftly adopted the language, affected Arabic names or clientage, settled in among the Arab families, and viewed their North African colleagues—especially the twelfth-century Almoravid flood—as uncultivated aliens. Like Yemenites and Syrians, they too imported preexistent antagonisms, aligning as mutually hostile (al-Butr or al-Barānis) tribal complexes. Al-Yaʿqūbī could describe the late ninth-century Valencian regions as distinguished by Berber tribal groupings which dominated rich areas like the Júcar Valley and refused allegiance to Umayyad rule. Valencia's peculiar evolution thus left the so-called slave population in a position of surprising power in comparison with the fairly negligible stratum of traditional Hispano-Arab aristocracy.[5]

[5] Guichard, "Peuplement de la région de Valence," pp. 108-109, 111, 113 (Egyptians), 116-117, 119 (al-Yaʿqūbī), 122-136, 150, and passim. Julián Ribera Tarragó,

Guichard's thesis affects only the background of the crusade era; from the eleventh century the converging elements assembled into a society typical of the Arabic provinces, as the Valencian cities assumed a brilliant role in the cultural and economic history of Islamic Spain. The thesis does imply for the crusade era a more open and exciting social mix, with elements more variegated and less rooted, their combinations less predictable, their relations with seacoast neighbors at Majorca and North Africa and even with their own hinterland more intimate, and their sympathy for or dependence on the Cordova-Marrakesh axis basically looser. If the ethnic tradition perceived as Arabic, as against both Arabized Berber or stricter Berber, rose to prominence centuries later than hitherto admitted, how does this jibe with Ribera's stress on Yemenite prevalence? More significantly, how does it jibe with Glick's recent findings that the Syrian irrigation's proportional measurement prevailed on such huertas as Castellón, Gandía, and Valencia, while the Yemenite time-unit model characterized far-southern places like Elche, Novelda, Lorca, and the southern small-oasis huertas? Attracted by Braudel's theory of Mediterranean colonization as deliberate reduplication of the settlers' home environment, Glick discerned in Valencia city's landscape a re-creation of the Damascus environment and institutions. Accepting this, one can surmise that the earliest mix of populations differed from the later, or that the irrigation system blossomed later in the caliphal period under an influx representing the Syrian faction (Glick rejects Roman authorship). The shattered pattern of all the Valencian groups, though collocating into a stable social structure, did not fuse but continued lastingly to mark

"Influencias berberiscas en el reino de Valencia," *El archivo,* I (1886-1887), 169. On the local movement from hinterland to coast just before the crusade, see his "Musulmanes de Valencia originarios de Albarracín," *Opúsculos dispersos* (Tetuán, 1952), pp. 31-33. César E. Dubler reviewed Berber settlement in Spain by epochs, finding heavy settlement in southern Valencia in the early period; see his "Über Berbersiedlungen auf der iberischen Halbinsel," *Sache, Ort und Wort, Jakob Jud zum sechzigsten Geburtstag* (Geneva, 1943), pp. 182-196 with map, esp. pp. 190-194. Jacinto Bosch Vilá, as part of a forthcoming book on Berber settlement, examines the pre-1050 evidence at leisure in "Establecimiento de grupos humanos norteafricanos en la península ibérica, a raíz de la invasión musulmana," *Atti del I Congresso internazionale di studi nord-africani* (Cagliari, 1965), pp. 147-161, esp. pp. 155ff. on the eastern regions.

the evolving Valencian scene. Just as the postconquest Granadan society observed by Caro Baroja maintained its factions and jealously preserved its genealogies, so crusader Valencia's families surely reflected the old balances while each "followed fully the Islamic patriarchal organization."[6]

Searching out Valencia's ethnic and family or kin profile in its more developed, concluding stage during the crusade generation, the philologist, toponymist, and anthroponymist struggle today to shape their ambiguous data to some instructive purpose. Their episodic researches must ripen further before they can clarify the situation just described; already they have added substantially to the invaluable information left from the chapter on Spanish tribes by the Cordovan Ibn Ḥazm and to the fragments recoverable from biographical encyclopedias and stray texts. Piling tribal names into a jumbled map serves no purpose at this stage. One may profitably search the crusade era for representatives of Onda's Banū Aws, Jérica's Banū Khazraj, Masalavas' Banū Hawāzin, Liria's Banū Makhzūm, or the region's numerous Banū Kināna and Banū Maʿāfir. Our current list of Valencian family names also helps to identify signatories to crusade treaties, functionaries in the early Mudejar aljamas, the tribes and people generously listed in the crusaders' book of land grants,

[6] Glick, *Irrigation in Medieval Valencia*, pp. 169, 186, 214-215; and on the Roman influences, chs. 8-9. Quotation from Julio Caro Baroja, *Los moriscos del reino de Granada, ensayo de historia social* (Madrid, 1957), p. 1023. The geographer Houston suggests that the place names of the 144 alquerias listed for the Valencian vega by the 1244 land division mark them as Berber and perhaps Almohad settlements ("Land Use in the Plain of Valencia," p. 191). The early stages of Guichard's development would have meshed with a wider crisis in Spain, which in turn reflected a movement previously in eastern Islam. Two minorities contended for hegemony in controlling society: the hitherto dominant establishment who identified themselves as "Arabs," and the larger, rival stratum of neo-Muslims or non-"Arabs" who sought social and political equality. Though the adversaries cannot be neatly divided, the Spanish contest lay to some extent between the landed agrarian aristocracy and the urban-mercantile, middle-class patriciate; between the alien absentee landlord and the families of native and mixed immigrant origins; and between centralist government allied with rigid orthodoxy and local loyalties with more open religious orientations. As a neo-Muslim stronghold, eastern Spain attracted heavy immigration by non-"Arabs" in the eleventh century. The varied elements adjusted into a new balance, newly Arabized, but Ibn Khaldūn was able to discern a double patriciate thereafter, of somewhat opposing life styles. See James T. Monroe, *The Shuʿūbiyya in al-Andalus: The Risāla of Ibn García and Five Refutations* (Berkeley, 1970), pp. 1-21.

and in general the leading spirits of the time. Information on the disposition of Mudejar aljamas during the decades immediately after the crusade, as well as on the rate of Muslim emigration or displacement, will affect the applicability of familial data. Christian documents reflect the Islamic family groupings in terms of their European counterparts. They adverted to a Muslim's "lineage" as coordinate kin of relatively equal status, presumably sharing affluence, political influence, a common life-style, and inherited glory. The data recorded in such documents is too sparse to encourage application of sociological or anthropological categories, or to probe below the imposed European pattern to local realities of the Islamic grouping. A *qā'id* who sold Bullent village to a Christian did so with "his kin" (*consanguinei*); a number of Mudejars were identified in documents as nephews or relatives of important men; "friends," perhaps clients, who might avenge wrong appeared in a legal context; and charters provided formally for traveling "to go visit relatives wherever they wish." Family groupings, taken in a special context, will come up for discussion again in the final chapter, where they help supply a clue to the inner nature of Islamic society in Valencia.[7]

[7] Arch. Crown, James I, Reg. Canc. 11, fol. 192 (Jan. 18, 1260): "de alcaydo et consanguineis suis." Eslida Charter: "possint ire visum parentes ubicumque voluerint." The Spanish section of Ibn Ḥazm is in Terés, "Linajes según la Ŷamhara," esp. pp. 74, 87-89, 90-91, 95-97, 101-102, 104, 338-340, 344, 349-350, 355. Of Vernet, see esp. "Antropónimos de etimología árabe en el Levante español: ensayo metodológico," *RIEEIM*, XI-XII (1963-1964), 141-147; "Antropónimos árabes conservados en apellidos del Levante español," *Oriens*, XVI (1963), 145-151; and "Antropónimos musulmanes en los actuales partidos judiciales de Falset y Gandesa," *Homenaje a Jaime Vicens Vives*, I, 123-127. Examining telephone and name lists, Vernet finds more Arabic derivatives in Valencian rural areas and in the south, deciphering, for example, the family Massot as Mas'ūd, Ambros as 'Amrūs, and Bijaldon as Ibn Khaldūn. Working in the topographical tradition of Asín Palacios (*Contribución a la toponimia árabe de España* [Madrid, 1944]), Sanchis Guarner considered areas like Benifasá, Culla, Cullera, and Mislata in "De toponímia aràbigo-valentina," *Revista valenciana de filología*, I (1951), 259-271; he relates some twenty families to places in the Pego Valley alone in the introduction to his study of local jingles, "Dictados tópicos de la comarca de Denia, Pego y La Marina," *Revista valenciana de filología*, V (1955-1958), esp. pp. 12-13. See also Mateu y Llopis, "Nómina de los musulmanes," passim; Hermann Lautensach, *Maurische Züge im geographischen Bild der iberischen Halbinsel* (Bonn, 1960), esp. pp. 24-26 with maps 1-2; and older researches such as Ribera y Tarragó's articles, along with local traditions as gathered into the alphabetic entries of the Sanchis Sivera *Nomenclátor* for Valencia.

Arab, "slave," and Berber aristocrats, with their more plebeian countrymen in larger numbers, formed merely the framework or main outline in the social physiognomy of Valencia's patrician class. Apostate Iberian, Roman, and Gothic families flourished, displaying Arabized names and pseudo-Arabic genealogies. Castle commanders, ambitious intellectuals, holy men, and social-climbing merchant families rose swiftly to local prominence whenever the central or provincial governments collapsed into chaos. A region so rent with cliques and factions always rested in unstable equilibrium. It might fragment in a dozen different patterns, according as the winds of new doctrine or of political opportunity blew. Muslim commentators of the crusade era voiced astonishment over the extremes to which this Valencian tendency carried. No common bonds, no deep political allegiance, bound this diversity into more than an accidental unity. Religion could not always be counted on to rally these forces; it was as effectively employed in fragmenting them, as when Abū Zayd's necessary compromises with the Aragonese led his political enemies to drive him wholly into the Christian camp and to split Islamic Valencia.

Population Figures

It is impossible to say how many Muslims inhabited Valencia at any period in the thirteenth century, or how populous were their villages. Just as the problem of Muslim distribution depends on the prior problem of tracing Christian immigration patterns, so the question of numbers can be settled only after deciding which groups the Christians expelled. As each aljama of the kingdom comes into sight in this book, and as each Muslim official is noticed, a tentative map might be devised to mark at least population distribution and important centers.[8] The besant or household tax might provide basis

[8] Piles Ros listed at random a series of two dozen "important" aljamas of the fifteenth century: Alfara, Algar, Algemesí, Almonacid Valley, Argelita, Benaguacil, Bétera, Castellmontán, Cirat, Eslida, Fanzara, Gayer (Gayanes ?), Játiva, Matet, Montán, Murviedro, Náquera, Navajas, Paterna, Soneja, Sueras, Toga, Torres-Torres, Uxó, and Veo ("Moros de realengo en Valencia," p. 236; I have altered the spellings). Winfried Küchler supplies eight tax lists from 1415 to 1461, naming fifteen Valencian aljamas, with Játiva, Valldigna, and Uxó as very important ("Besteuerung des Juden and Mauren in den Ländern der Krone Aragons während des 15. Jahrhunderts," *Gesammelte Aufsätze zur Kulturgeschichte Spaniens*, XXIV [1968], 227-256).

for conjecture if more totals were available; it does indicate that Valencia city and Játiva, at a time when relatively few Muslims remained within these respective jurisdictions, each boasted an aljama of some 300 households. Comparative measurement of the Moorish quarter of Valencia city, which covered about an eleventh of the city's superficies, tends to confirm this figure of some 1,300 people.

Later tax lists may shed light, though a methodology for their interpretation is lacking. Thus in 1304, for Christmas preparations to support the royal household at Valencia city, authorities made a levy of chickens on Valencian Mudejar centers—20 pairs from Castellón de Burriana, 30 from Játiva, and 80 from Uxó. Two years later, for a similar Easter celebration, the Valencia city aljama had to dispatch 20 pairs, and Játiva 50 pairs, plus 10 goats; a collector gathered the Valencia city offerings, the Játivans sending theirs on the aljama's own animals. Another clue to numbers is the Christian tithe for areas heavily Muslim, though this tax fell mostly upon Christians. The seignorial third of the Eslida-Ahín-Ennueyo tithe was rented to Teresa Giles Vidaure in 1272 for 130 solidi. This implies a minimum personal tithe of some 500 solidi or a seignorial income of 5,000; if the tithed rental from Muslims amounted to a fifth of profits, the income retained by Muslims in this area was at least 20,000 solidi, minus the income of the infrequent Christian tenants there. This would indicate over 800 Mudejar farmers at the minimum, and perhaps double that number. A similar amount is indicated for Muslims under the lord of Buñol and Ribarroja.[9]

Valencia city as capital and pacesetter particularly attracts the eye. Torres Balbás, measuring the walled city of Valencia at 45 hectares and postulating 333 persons per hectare as an average for contemporary Hispano-Islamic cities, arrived at a population of some 15,000 for the capital, not counting its adjoining suburbs, slaves, or unhoused destitute. In a subsequent study he adjusted the density ratio to 58 houses or 348 persons per hectare. Julio González, in his edition of the book of land division for conquered Seville, reckoned that contemporary Valencia held 1,615 houses containing over 8,000

[9] J. E. Martínez-Ferrando, *Jaime II de Aragón, su vida familiar*, 2 vols. (Barcelona, 1948), II, docs. 26 (1304), 34 (1306). Teresa's tithe is in *Itinerari*, p. 462; on the tithe see my *Crusader Valencia*, chs. 8 and 9, and my "Mediaeval Income Tax: The Tithe in the Thirteenth-Century Kingdom of Valencia," *Speculum*, XLI (1966), 438-452, with works cited.

souls; he felt 24,000 a not unreasonable population for Seville. Chantal de la Véronne, working from documents of land distribution, concluded that there were in Islamic Valencia 3,481 owners of buildings, including 103 Jews, and that 3,191 Christians replaced most of these owners by 1244, only 34 remaining; but she had no way of allowing for multiple owners like the man who had 21 buildings, nor for relating owners to residents, nor for being certain that all buildings were included. Her figures, taken as they stand, and supposing 4.5 residents per building, yield an intracity population of just under 15,000. Sobrequés counted 2,600 buildings involved in the distribution of city properties to the Valencia crusaders; his listing is necessarily incomplete and the descriptive term building imprecise.[10] An item in the crusaders' property distributions speaks loosely of 503 houses as comprising a fifth of the inner-city housing available for grants, indicating something over 2,500 buildings with a minimum intramural population of 11,300.[11]

The half-dozen larger cities during King James's reign, Barcelona and Zaragoza aside, each contained probably less than 10,000 people; most of his cities counted less than 1,000. Dufourcq estimates the population of Barcelona as 25,000, rising in the first half of the fourteenth century to perhaps 35,000 when Catalonia proper held some

[10] Leopoldo Torres Balbás, "La población musulmana de Valencia en 1238," *Al-Andalus*, XVI (1951), 167-168; "Extensión y demografía de las ciudades hispanomusulmanas," *Studia islamica*, III (1955), 35-39. Chantal de la Véronne, "Recherches sur le chiffre de la population musulmane de Valence en 1238 d'après le 'Repartimiento,'" *Bulletin hispanique*, LI (1949), 423-426. Sobrequés, "Patriciado urbano," p. 35. *Repartimiento de Sevilla*, I, 316. See also my parish figures for the city in *Crusader Valencia*, I, 98-99 and II, 418. Bayerri, from his voluminous research into medieval Tortosa, estimates its city and countryside together as much below 20,000 for the larger part of the thirteenth century (*Historia de Tortosa*, VII, 332, 618-622). See also the posthumous book by Torres Balbás, derived from his articles, *Ciudades hispanomusulmanas*, ed. Henri Terrasse, 2 vols. (Madrid, 1971), pp. 93-110, esp. p. 106; the *Repartimiento* of Valencia designated its houses as *domus optimae* or *maximae* or *bonae* or *mediocres* or *parvae*, or *parvissimae* (p. 99); probably each house held but a single family, perhaps with as many as six people (p. 101). Huici believes the Islamic city's houses were smaller than in the subsequent Christian city, so that Valencia had been overcrowded; the new settlers would have had to join houses or enlarge them (*Historia musulmana de Valencia*, I, 32).

[11] *Repartimiento de Valencia*, p. 177 (with p. 531): "damus universitati de Barchinona qui voluerint populare et habitare in Valentia quintam partem domorum civitatis."

half-million people; Valencia city grew to contain 20,000, but the total population of Valencia kingdom at the time hardly reached 200,000.[12] In 1400 Játiva and Morella, the largest cities of Valencia outside the capital, each had 10,000 people; no other Valencian city at the time mustered 500 except Villarreal at 598, through Liria, Cullera, and Onteniente were fairly big. Such late figures are of limited use for the earlier period, because serious changes like the Black Death had intervened. For the crusade era, it is no surprise to find Mudejar Játiva assembling a hundred notables for a ceremonial occasion. Granting that some must have represented surrounding villages, that the term notable suffered inflation proportionately as a town was smaller, and even that a single family may have contributed more than one notable, the figures still suggest a population of four to five hundred well-off Muslims, not counting the less affluent, transients, slaves, or indeed any from nonnotable families.

Can estimates directly from thirteenth-century observers help? Numbers reported in King James's memoirs seem at first unreliable. Assuming that the text reflects the king's own witness in some realistic fashion, one might ascribe the results of his calculation to the medieval mentality, which sat lightly to the task of assessing numbers. In the next century the politician-historian Ibn Khaldūn addressed himself to this problem; his judgment can apply to Christian as much as to Muslim observers. "Whenever contemporaries speak about the dynastic armies of their own recent times, and whenever they engage in discussions about Muslim or Christian soldiers, or when they get to figuring the tax revenues and the money spent by the government, the outlays of extravagant spenders, and the goods that rich and prosperous men have in stock," the Muslim historian concludes, "they are quite generally found to exaggerate,

[12] Dufourcq, *L'Espagne catalane et le Maghrib*, p. 67. At the surrender of Islamic Zaragoza in 1118, José Lacarra estimates that space was available within the walls for 20-25,000 people, though much of this must have gone to free space and some even to agriculture; in 1495 the town held nearly 20,000 people; a Muslim contemporary has 50,000 flee the conquered city, an absurd number ("La repoblación de Zaragoza por Alfonso el Batallador," *Estudios de historia social de España*, I [1949], p. 208). Luis García de Valdeavellano y Arcimís puts the Islamic population in the tenth century at 15,000 for Valencia city, 17,000 for Zaragoza, 26,000 for Granada, 37,000 for Toledo, and 100,000 for Cordova (*Curso de historia de las instituciones españolas de los orígenes al final de la edad media* [Madrid, 1968], p. 656).

to go beyond the bounds of the ordinary, and to succumb to the temptation of sensationalism." Real figures, he believed, were "a tenth" of those usually published; he deplored number exaggeration as a common fault of historians, traceable to a natural lack of discipline. In King James's case other factors came into play. After watching a mass of exiled Moors milling out of Valencia city under the weight of bulky possessions, the king guessed them to total 50,000. He was preoccupied with making a point: that his troops safely convoyed a huge mob with inconsiderable loss. He was not really interested in statistics here and may not even have attended to that aspect.[13]

A newly discovered methodology helps make sense of King James's reckoning. Recent study reveals that practiced assessors of crowds, whether judging for purposes of police control or for public information, unwittingly overestimate them by twice or three times the actual size. The Wisconsin journalist Herbert A. Jacobs has devised a corrective method; working from enlarged aerial photographs he has computed a minimum of four square feet per individual, varying according to such factors as density and mobility. His formula for a rapid rough estimate involves adding the crowd's length to its breadth, multiplying the result by ten for a dense grouping and by seven for a loose one. On the assumption that King James meant to assess real numbers in this episode, rather than to exploit them in some symbolic or derivative fashion, the modern principles of crowd-counting can be applied.[14] Allowing for the special difficulties presented by an unwieldy, overloaded swarm of refugee Muslim families in constant movement, the king's total thus revises itself to a figure near 15,000. This accords with the best independent estimates of the population within Islamic Valencia's walls. One might further adjust the number to allow for a remnant left behind, who comprised the initial Moorish quarter, their places

[13] *Llibre dels feyts,* ch. 283. Ibn Khaldūn, *Muqaddimah,* I, 16, 18-19.

[14] Jacobs, then lecturer in journalism at the University of California, presented his "How Big Was the Crowd? And a Formula for Estimates" at the California Journalism Conference in Sacramento, February 24-25, 1967; *Time* kindly supplied my xeroxed reference typescript. Jacobs added that distortion enters when crowds are less than 500 or more than 5,000, when the area is not roughly square, or when the crowd is volatile, or has more front than depth; he allows a 20 to 25 percent margin of error.

in the crowd being filled by refugees from the suburbs and to some extent from the surrounding countryside. Since Zayyān simultaneously surrendered all his castles above the Júcar River, a certain number may have traveled out of neighboring strongholds, especially from the wealthy classes, to swell the convoy leaving Valencia by several thousands.

In the equivalent surrender at Burriana, "so that people may know how many men were in Burriana, counting men and women and children, there were 7,032." It is reasonable to revise this number, on analogous grounds, to about 2,500. Since the crowd was smaller, the element of deception may have been correspondingly less and the king's figure more exact. After 125 years of immigration and growth however, Burriana in a census of 1362 counted 597 hearths or something over 2,500 people. Interpreting other numbers in the king's autobiography requires caution. Army and battle figures particularly demand their own methodology, as when the Valencia Muslim rebels concentrated their fighting force of 60,000 at Montesa, not counting "women and children"; or when 20,000 Moors died in the crusaders' sack of Palma de Mallorca, while in the confusion 30,000 more escaped to the hills; or when the crusading army at Valencia city consisted of 1,000 knights and 60,000 foot, with the besieged defenders numbering 10,000 horse and foot. Though some sense can be made of such figures, it is not appropriate to attempt the task here.[15]

A final total must be confronted. In discussing the mass expulsion from the kingdom of Valencia, which King James suggests involved nearly all Muslims remaining at the time of the first rebellions, he relays a description of the trek as given to him by the convoying knights; they told him that the human stream stretched for twenty miles, the refugees being as thick as Christian warriors at the battle of Las Navas de Tolosa. Contemporary assessments of combatants engaged in that monumental battle are untrustworthy; after careful examination of the numbers, González can conclude only that both armies "were very large," while Huici sets the maximum possible figure at 70,000 Christians and 100,000 Muslims. Conceding 60,000 therefore and reducing it by the crowd-counting technique to 30,000 or 20,000, a more reasonable total emerges. It might

[15] *Llibre dels feyts*, chs. 178, 258, 265, 368-369.

be further reduced by allowing for the circumstance that men remembered Las Navas by this time only in general terms as an assemblage of unprecedented magnitude.

James clarifies the comparison by offering an exact number for the Valencian exiles; he says that when the fugitives, both men and women, paid the besant to the Castilians at the border customs station, 100,000 besants were collected. This reckoning, he confesses, was "according to what they told me." In the king's account, therefore, besides the problem of counting a crowd, there is the added uncertainty of hearsay, the question of how much money actually came in, and especially the anxiety of James to reprove his detractors by emphasizing his zeal in expelling Muslims. Even so, the total is only double that given for Valencia city; the circumstance may furnish some clue, leaving room for the guess that these later expellees totaled a maximum of 30,000 and possibly half that number.[16]

Abundant statistics on Valencian population available from the sixteenth and seventeenth centuries are remote from the thirteenth-century situation; but these figures can serve as a framework, suggesting something of the past and its dispositions. Several observers tallied the Valencian Moriscos—the late remnants of the conquered Muslims, who had been superficially converted by force during the early Renaissance. Because they lived intractably in their inherited alien style, the crown systematically deported them. The Valencian group had not completely lost its fighting spirit, and managed to raise revolts both in 1526 and 1609. A Valencian mathematician in the sixteenth century totaled the local Moriscos at 19,000 families as against 45,000 "Christian" families. He assessed them under four headings: 8,238 households to 20,271 "Christian" households in the Valencia area proper; 9,043 to 13,730 in the Játiva area; 1,154 to 9,450 in the Castellón area; and 1,535 to 6,969 in the Orihuela area. Applying to his figures the reasonable coefficient of 4.5 persons per hearth, a population appears of 90,000 Moriscos as against 200,500 Christians. Demographers have brooded over the proper coefficient

[16] *Ibid.*, ch. 113. Julio González, *El reino de Castilla en la época de Alfonso VIII* (Madrid, 1960), I, 1047-1051. Huici, *Imperio almohade*, pp. 425-429, esp. p. 427. Christian losses were high, a circumstance suggesting that cool observation by combatants was difficult. Both Archbishop Jiménez de Rada and Alfonso VIII of Castile put the Moorish cavalry as 80,000; the former says the victors filled only half the conquered Muslim camp.

to apply. Where authorities listed Morisco persons as well as hearths, the contemporary coefficient can be seen to vary from 4.5 to 4.7. King James, speaking of the unconquered portion of Majorca island in the thirteenth century, assumed a coefficient of six—3,000 warriors with 15,000 dependent women and children.[17]

The most elaborate recent analysis, deriving from all Morisco statistics, estimates 30,000 hearths in the kingdom of Valencia or 135,000 individual Moriscos, as against 3,000 individuals in Granada, 5,000 in Catalonia, 61,000 in Aragon, 16,000 in Murcia, 30,000 in Andalusia, 45,000 in the Castiles, and a total of 300,000 within the Spanish population of eight to nine million. Reglá, the latest scholar to publish a volume on Valencian Moriscos, assesses them at 170,000 for the kingdom or 34 per 100 population; this is 10,000 more than Sobrequés allows, and 35,000 more than Lapeyre. The percentage, roughly a third of the total population, agrees with the reckoning of Halperín Donghi for 1609. At that, the balance in favor of Christians tipped to the Reglá proportion largely as a result of the immigration floods from about 1525. In 1635, after subtraction of many Moriscos by expulsion, the Dutch geographer Blaeu credited the kingdom of Valencia with 100,000 families of every kind; presumably this came to 450,000 people, a figure close to the total of 300,000 recently proposed by Sanchis Guarner for the late fifteenth century. Blaeu located them in 4 cities, 60 walled towns, and 1,000 villages. As for Moriscos, it seems clear that the majority lived on seignorial lands by that time, the main exceptions being city ghettos and some two dozen Morisco towns of the crown. In the countryside they dominated the less valuable *secà* or dry farming and upland areas, leaving the huertas or *regà* mostly in Christian hands except at Játiva and Gandía. From the Mijares River south, the mountains and

[17] Roque Chabás, "Los moriscos de Valencia y su expulsión," *El archivo,* IV (1890), 230-234, with documents on pp. 373-388. The huerta around Valencia city and its mountains, according to a census of 1563, held 1,144 Morisco houses; a later list gave 1,158, plus Christian houses totaling 1,017, a grand total of 2,175 or perhaps a population in this countryside of almost 9,800. Lapeyre, *Géographie de l'Espagne morisque,* pp. 204, 212. *Llibre dels feyts,* ch. 113. Benzion Netanyahu in his study of sixteenth-century Marranos favors the coefficient of six; see *The Marranos of Spain from the Late XIVth to the Early XVIth Century according to Contemporary Hebrew Sources* (New York, 1966), p. 237, influenced by Javier Ruiz Almansa, "La población de España en el siglo xvi," *Revista internacional de sociología,* III (1943), pp. 117-119, 136.

much of the hill country were Morisco. Below the Júcar, the Christians held the cities in countrysides nearly wholly Muslim; but above the river Muslims were rare in huertas, while in the dry lands they clustered in satellite villages around Christian towns. A tax list of 1602 numbered the Valencian Morisco households according to regions, village by village. From several such lists, it is clear that at least 450 towns or villages in Valencia were predominantly Morisco as against 301 which were predominantly Christian.[18]

Closer to the crusade period, Vicens Vives puts Moors at two-thirds of Valencia's population in 1400; he contrasts this with 35 percent for Aragon and 3 percent for Catalonia. In 1337, just less than a century after the fall of Valencia city to the crusaders, Archbishop Arnold of Tarragona, as metropolitan over the Valencia region, reported to the pope that the Valencian Moors could still muster from forty to fifty thousand warriors; despite emigration and some expulsion therefore, the kingdom held at least 100,000 Mus-

[18] Lapeyre, *Géographie de l'Espagne morisque*, pp. 24-25, 204, 212, ch. 1 passim, and appended documents 1-4, 8, 16. See also the lengthy double article by Tulio Halperín Donghi, "Un conflicto nacional: moriscos y cristianos viejos en Valencia," with excellent maps. For the statistics by Willem Janszoon Blaeu (1571-1638) see my *Crusader Valencia*, I, 5-6, II, 372. Although by the end of the fifteenth century the Valencia kingdom was reputed to hold 370,000 people, the demographer Josiah Russell reports that his own researches into the fragmentary evidences of the fourteenth century yielded only 125,400 ("The Medieval Monedatge of Aragon and Valencia," *Proceedings of the American Philosophical Society*, CVI [1962], p. 497). Gaspar Escolano put the 1610 population at under 100,000 houses, which might add up to 450,000 people (*Décadas de la historia de la insigne y coronada ciudad y reino de Valencia*, ed. Juan B. Perales, 3 vols. [Valencia, (1610-1611) 1878-1880], I, ch. 24). Antonio Cavanilles gave a total population of 255,080 for 1718, the Moriscos having long departed; sudden growth sent the 1761 census up to 604,612, the 1768 census to 716,886, and the 1787 census to 783,084; for 1794 he counted 207,145 houses and estimated therefore 932,150 inhabitants; see his *Observaciones sobre la historia natural, geografía, agricultura, población y frutas del reyno de Valencia*, 2 vols. (Madrid, [1795-1797] 1958), I, 13, II, 404). See also the interpretations of James Casey, "Moriscos and the Depopulation of Valencia," *Past and Present*, L (1971), 19-40. There had been previous population leaps in the fourteenth century. Louis García de Valdeavellano thinks the Mudejars in the areas conquered by Aragon in the thirteenth century totaled 150,000, and that Castile-León's population of four to five million after the conquests of the same century included 300,000 Mudejars (p. 306); before the Black Death struck in 1348, he estimates the total population of Valencia was 200,000, of the Balearics 50,000, of Catalonia 450,000, and of Aragon 200,000; in the last third of the fourteenth century Valencia held 300,000, including Mudejars, in a total population of over a million for the crown of Aragon (*Instituciones españolas*, p. 656).

lims—allowing two arms-bearing males per household—and possibly half that number again. King James thought 30,000 Christians a dangerously small immigration by 1272, urging fresh immigration to raise the number at least to 100,000. If these figures represent households as Soldevila thinks, then the Muslim population at the time of King James's death had to be much larger than the Morisco in the seventeenth century. If they are individuals, as Dufourcq and others assume, it is still apparent that the colonists found themselves outnumbered by three to one and perhaps by much more. In any case, the proportions are instructive and all such figures help convey some appreciation of the continuing presence of Islam's sons.[19]

The City Complex

Quite different from its Christian counterpart, an Islamic city like Valencia comprised a tangle of almost independent, unrelated quarters.[20] Around the nuclear public complex—with its citadel (itself at times a mini-city), bazaar, main mosque, and residences—grew any number of miniature sectors, each locked in upon itself, some sealed away more tightly by ethnic, occupational, or sect identities, every area an anarchy of blind passageways and twisting alleys proliferating around lesser mosques, the noisy commercial areas contrasting with the silence of the more residential districts. The jumble of houses and passages comprising each neighborhood related to the center by means of a traffic street less mindless than its meandering feeder lanes. No communal life, corporative identity, or republican participation joined these units. In union with the sub-

[19] *Colección diplomática*, doc. 1341 (Nov. 1270), a trustworthy figure because it served as a foundation for a rebuke, inviting retort. My *Crusader Valencia* argues from the interpretation that 30,000 represented households (I, 80-81). See Dufourcq, *L'Espagne catalane*, p. 184. Vicens Vives, for all the realms of Aragon around 1300, puts the non-Christian population at 40 percent.

[20] The physical details of Islamic Spanish cities were exhaustively studied by Leopoldo Torres Balbás in his *Ciudades hispanomusulmanas* and in his many related articles (see his bibliography). See too his smaller summations in *Resumen histórico del urbanismo en España* (Madrid, 1954), esp. pp. 9-33; and his "Les villes musulmanes d'Espagne et leur urbanisation," *Annales de l'institut d'études orientales*, VI (1942-1947), 5-30, or in Spanish as "Las ciudades hispanomusulmanas y su urbanización," *Revista de estudios de la vida local*, I (1942), 59-80. See also Huici, *Historia musulmana de Valencia*, I, ch. I.

urban elements just beyond the walls, and like the strangely urban villages farther out, the city residents clung to a single unity less by visible organization than by a kind of spiritual gravity. A city like Valencia reveals itself as Islamic theology in buildings—reflecting the fierce individualism and overarching brotherhood of that theology, its cosmopolitan makeup and its factionalism, its unconcern for the merely political and its identification of all concerns with religion.[21]

The streets and neighborhood sections of Valencia city at its moment of transition materialize in the crusaders' schedule of property grants. King James designated fifteen quarters, assigning them respectively to contingents from Barcelona, Calatayud, Daroca, Jaca, Lérida, Montblanc, Montpellier, Rápida, Tarazona, Tarragona, Teruel, Tortosa, Tremp, Villafranca, and Zaragoza. A sixteenth,

[21] On the city as an expression of Islam, see Xavier de Planhol's brief "essay of religious geography," *The World of Islam* (Ithaca, N.Y., 1959); William Marçais, "L'islamisme et la vie urbaine," in his *Articles et Conférences* (Paris, 1961), esp. pp. 59, 61, 67. See also Évariste Lévi-Provençal, *Las ciudades y las instituciones urbanas del occidente musulmán en la edad media* (Tetuán, 1950), also published as "Les villes et les institutions urbaines en occident musulman au moyen âge," *Conférences sur l'Espagne musulmane* (Cairo, 1951), 75-119; his *España musulmana*, v, ch. 6; Edmond Pauty, "Villes spontanées et villes créées en Islam," *Annales de l'institut d'études orientales*, IX (1951), 52-75; and Ira Marvin Lapidus, *Muslim Cities in the Later Middle Ages* (Cambridge, Mass., 1967), pp. 85ff. Some voices have been raised against the "mystique of cities" in Islamic studies as an overworked, even distorted theme; against too stark an opposition of rural versus urban, and against elevation of the dominant city rather than the regional grouping of cities in close relation to their countrysides. In "Muslim Cities and Islamic Societies" (*Middle Eastern Cities: A Symposium on Ancient, Islamic, and Contemporary Middle Eastern Urbanism* [Berkeley, 1969]), symposium editor Lapidus sees the large "city of cities" as a focus of cultural life and center of such unifying *functions* as one's law group, reserving the real community(s) often for the rural-cum-city region; not denying "distinctions between urban and rural habitats, nor the important differences between city and country people, nor the great variety of geographical and ecological relationships," he would substitute for absolute "urban-rural dichotomy" the regional community scattered into "non-contiguous, spatially isolated settlements" (pp. 47-49, esp. 67-68; pp. 74ff.). Grunebaum and others offer demurrers or cautions (pp. 74ff.). See also Grunebaum's entries in my bibliography, especially his "Nature of the Islamic City" in *Islam, Essays*; and the useful survey of *Urban Life in Syria under the Early Mamlūks* by N. A. Ziadeh (Beirut, 1953), ch. 3. In *The Islamic City: A Colloquium* (Philadelphia and Oxford, 1969), the editors A. H. Hourani and S. M. Stern survey in the first two chapters the current soul-searching by Islamologists over the city question, nuancing traditional positions which now seem too generalized and aprioristic.

rather large area went to the Jews.[22] Suburbs provided for the Navarrese, Roussillonese, Mudejars, and the men from Almenara and Huesca. Most of the intramural groups represented whole regions, as with Tortosa and Tarragona; between them the communal beneficiaries represented all the realms of Aragon. A few towns stand in the list independently of the great regional centers, perhaps by reason of distinguished service or subsidies. Barcelona, apparently including older Catalonia with cities like Gerona and Vich, acquired a full fifth of the city; Almenara, Lérida, Montblanc, and Tremp got precincts so small that they may have formed subsections of larger units. Nobles, prelates, knights, and favored folk, as well as volunteers from beyond Aragon's borders, apparently took their rewards in and around these blocs or received lands elsewhere than at the capital. Small wards went to orders or trades, like the fifty buildings of the Templars at the northeast corner, or the three streets of the shoemakers called Paradise Valley located near the city walls and near the sectors of Zaragoza, Tarazona, and the drapers.[23]

[22] Ninety-five Jews, presumably households, received grants there by the *Repartimiento* listings. Unless the previous aljama had been destroyed or much reduced by Almohad persecution, like the Mozarab community, and assuming they did not leave with the mass of exiles at surrender, the number may have to be increased to include them. At the turn of the thirteenth century, Valencia city had 250 Jewish taxpayers, all named in a tax list; the Jewry was enlarged in the second half of the fourteenth century to accommodate growth. Despite crown effort to attract Jewish settlers, Castellón, Játiva, and Murviedro had only 50 families each, representing the largest aljamas after Valencia city. On the other hand, Barcelona probably had only 200 families and Lérida 100, with smaller communities at places like Tarragona, Gerona, and Tortosa. Spain boasted the largest Jewish aljamas in Europe, but 200 to 400 families represented maximum numbers. See Yitzhak [Fritz] Baer, *A History of the Jews in Christian Spain*, trans. Louis Schoffman, 2 vols. (Philadelphia, 1966), I, 194-195, 405. A town of 15,000 divided into fifteen equal quarters would accommodate something over 200 families in each; unequal quarters, as at Valencia, puts the Jewish aljama among the larger segments.

[23] *Repartimiento de Valencia*, pp. 233-234, 253 (Almenara); pp. 177, 181, 314, 325, 383, 527, 531, 615 (Barcelona); 566, 630, 651 (Calatayud); 301, 592, 593, 600, 643, 645 (Daroca); 236 (Huesca); 156, 238, 611 (Jaca); 241, 262, 315, 582, 592, 639 (Lérida); 193, 261, 306, 307, 579 (Montblanc); 180, 225, 252, 539, 622 (Montpellier); 237 (Navarre); 224, 537, 621 (Rápida); 319, 509, 559, 629 (Tarazona); 252, 301, 619, 620 (Tarragona); 171, 227, 600, 602, 615 (Teruel); 211, 224, 253, 275, 276 (Tortosa); 282, 542 (Tremp); 225, 273, 538, 539 (Villafranca, a communal sector?); 319, 509, 544, 551, 623 (Zaragoza); 224, 240, 290, 304, 307, 620 (Jews); 253, 319, 568, 632 (Moors); 319, 508 (three *carrariae* to shoemakers). On the orders' shares, see my *Crusader Valencia*, I, chs. 10-13, 15.

Do these districts virtually exhaust the city's divisions, so that other beneficiaries arranged themselves according to this prior map? And were they true wards, forming neighborhood closes? The listings convey that impression, and statistics tend to confirm it. Sobrequés reached a total of 2,600 buildings by his methodology, and Torres Balbás 2,610 by his; the contemporary description of Barcelona's quarter described its 503 houses as comprising "a fifth part of the city's houses," yielding a total of over 2,500 distributed.[24] The houses in the quarters just described add up to nearly four-fifths of the totals reached by these several methods; with the nuclear cathedral precinct and the 500 sailors installed along the western wall, they fairly exhaust the area available for districts. Were these districts true wards?[25] The unequal numbers comprising them, from 25 to 500, probably reflect an artificial division based upon proportionate representation in the crusading army. If that were the only factor, why furnish separate small divisions to places like Montblanc and Tarazona? Why concentrate most Catalans in one huge lump, while dividing an equivalent number of the rival Aragonese cities into five separate parts? If these were to balance the five cismontane Catalan towns on the list, why strain to do so by providing large and tiny segments on both Catalan and Aragonese sides of the ledger? The reasonable assumption is that these compartments were already on hand and served to house and honor the contributing cities according to the contribution of each, half the districts going to Catalans and half to Aragonese, with important cities like Huesca or Vich unaccommodated because a tiny ward was less honorific than assimilation to a more important colleague city or than a large outside grant. The Montpellier partition, one of the biggest, symbolically recognized

[24] The Torres Balbás total derives from his figures of 45 hectares and 58 houses per hectare.

[25] *Repartimiento de Valencia*, pp. 209 (sailors) and 578 (*partida* of St. Mary's); cf. p. 556, *vicus* of the marketplace. C. H. Moore sees the real community unit of the Islamic city as "not the heterogeneous quarter but rather the [innermost] neighborhood defined by alley ways and impasses," with the quarter supplying basic needs and with its officials or notables (with status from nongeographical groups) becoming politically significant only in crises (in the symposium *Middle Eastern Cities*, p. 77). Are some inner neighborhoods reckoned into the Valencian accounting? Goitein stresses the lack of guilds as a unifier at this time, but also less interneighborhood factionalism such as developed under later tyranny and insecurity (pp. 93-94).

the southern French contingents. Each distinct grouping had room for people from another grouping and for aliens from places like Béarn, Hungary, Navarre, and Toledo.

In short, the wards corresponded to the available Islamic enclosures, a conclusion buttressed by observing that the nine most important of the three dozen mosques, strategically disposed about the city, immediately became parish centers (plus a parish altar at the

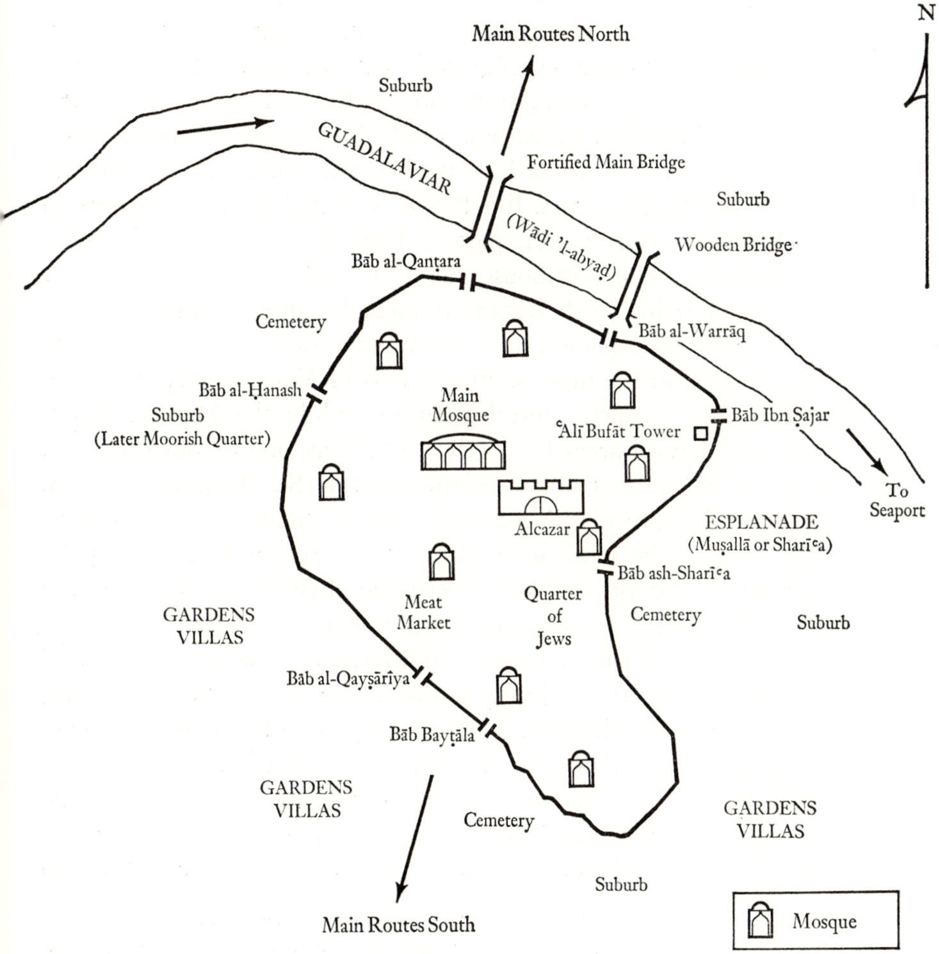

Islamic Valencia City in the Thirteenth Century

cathedral-mosque). Added to the Jewry, the parishes suggest eleven important divisions, including the alcazar nucleus, with smaller enclaves interspersed within or between. Close examination of the property allotments does reveal the central area ringed by nine great intramural segments (Barcelona, then the lesser but considerable wards of Calatayud, Daroca, Montpellier, Tarragona, Teruel, Tortosa, Zaragoza, and the Jews), with four small compounds, which in effect added up to about one more such large district. The disposition of Valencia city's dozen baths and public ovens adds confirmation and precrusade names for some quarters. The pattern corresponds with that of Majorca's capital, where the crusaders divided the city into eight partitions. It has echoes in other fallen capitals; if the parish measure is valid, Seville enclosed twenty-four very unequal sections, Cordova twelve, and Jaén eleven. Valencia recalls other Islamic cities. Ibn Baṭṭūṭa counted thirteen quarters in the old or decayed western part of Bagdad, "each a city in itself, with two or three bathhouses, and in eight of them are main mosques." Fez in North Africa comprised eighteen units.[26]

The Jaca, Montpellier, and Tarragona departments ran from center to west in the more southerly part of Valencia city; the Léridan occupied a north-central position; while the Daroca, Montblanc, and Jewish areas lay to the east. Barcelona or old Catalonia occupied the southernmost salient, around St. Andrew's church. Just beyond the walls, Almenara's "street" made a typical suburb to the west of the south gate and its marketplace. Establishing the existence of the presumably precrusade divisions is more to the point, however, than locating them under Christian names. The property lists call such a quarter indifferently *vicus* or *partida,* and occasionally *barrio*; the Jewry is *calle, barrio,* and *partida.* Going beyond the group districts, street and neighborhood names widen this range of synonyms. In the nomenclature of the listings as a whole, Chabás distinguished as equivalent terms *vicus* (used 45 times), *carraria* (35 times), *barrio* (25 times), *çucac* (Catalan *atzucac* or *assucach,* a dead-end street, 22 times), *calle* (18 times), *via* (16

[26] *Repartimiento de Mallorca,* p. 116. *Repartimiento de Sevilla,* I, 354ff. Ibn Baṭṭūṭa, *Travels,* II, 331. For the parishes and their area distribution see my *Crusader Valencia,* I, chs. 4, 5.

times), *partida* (14 times), and *rabat*[27] (10 times); dismissing repetitions, the 185 descriptions become a possible 165 streets and enclaves defining the capital's interior, each doubtless nourishing a web of nameless, insignificant alleys.[28] This equivalence of terminology underlines the semidetached nature of Islamic neighborhoods.

Even after crusaders had flooded in and the religious houses had come to engulf large areas, thrusting a new skyline above the city walls, much of Valencia's external appearance persisted. Municipal authorities in the following century recorded how the city remained "as it had been built by the Moors according to their custom, straitened and tortuous, with many narrow twisting streets and other deformities"; they complained of "the deformities which are in this city of Moorish streets and other such inconveniences." Despite demolitions and improvements carried through when the 1356 circle of walls went up, Eiximenis, the Catalan theorist of urban beauty, complained as late as 1383 of the city's being "quasi-Moorish."[29] In the following century Valencia still abounded in quirks which carried the stamp of Spanish Islam. Intergrown like something living, the insubstantial buildings contrived—by means of overhangs, arcades, covered bridges, patio enclosures, blind walls, and similar devices appearing frequently in thirteenth-century Valencian property records—to maximize inner space and privacy.

As in other Hispano-Islamic towns, some streets would have been

[27] This *rabat* is derived, not from the *ribāṭ* and *rābiṭa* discussed below on p. 197, but from *ar-rabaḍ*. Denoting a quarter or suburb, it yields the Catalan *raval* or *arraval* and the Castilian *arrabal*. Whatever ambiguity they incorporate, nine distinct "rabats" turn up at Valencia city in the *Repartimiento*, perhaps all enclaves or subsections of wards: in the Abendin or Avindin sector (p. 262), in the Alborg area at the Boatella gate (p. 237), at Açolta just outside the suburb of Ruzafa (p. 249), in the Almafaqui area of the Boatella suburb (p. 236), in the Almugeyt area in the same suburb (*ibid.*), in the Macalcama area there (p. 237), near the baths of Aliasar or Alicar (p. 294, cf. 226), in the Hatoix sector (p. 544), and the Alcadus or Rabatalcadus below in Chapter IX, n. 49. These appear in other forms like *rahalalcadi, ravalalcadi*, and *rahabatatoix*; the *rebathelli* on p. 196 may be additional.

[28] Roque Chabás, "El libro del repartimiento de la ciudad y reino de Valencia," *El archivo*, III (1889), 217-218. For example, the *çucac* on p. 307 becomes *vicus* on p. 542, that on p. 298 becomes *vicus* on 262, and appears elsewhere as *barrio*.

[29] *Ibid.*; Francesc Eiximenis (1340-1409), "quasi morisca," from his *Regiment de la cosa pública*.

so narrow that windows faced each other only an arm's breadth apart, many quarters being too confined to admit a horseman carrying a lance. The effect in back alleyways would have varied, depending on the extreme of coagulation reached, from serenity to a sense of dank melancholia, replaced in active streets by a hive-like hurlyburly. The markets, sealed off by heavy gates, consisted of tiny stalls multiplied in a maze of streets, where merchants and craftsmen clustered in rows according to their specialties. Booths of scribes and officials insinuated themselves into this mélange, while grander establishments reared up here and there, such as the fonduks or public caravanserais. The baths of the city served as important social centers, bright and sensuous, with their paraphernalia of boilers, pipes, steam rooms, and pools.[30] Valencia's commercial medina was well known in the Islamic world, but its residential areas were more widely admired. These were not the teeming quarters of the common folk, but the more affluent suburbs with their hidden patios and luxuriant gardens, the pleasure groves of the countryside, and the country houses of the wealthy.

All this remains a skeleton; the people, who fleshed it with life and made its stony reaches ring with sound, have dropped from sight. Obscured behind the dust of crusading armies and then vanished away, they have left behind only vagrant traces in the archives of their enemy. Can that generation be resurrected, its aljamas revisited, its sheiks and literati once more convoked around their leaders? Can the historian hope to piece together at least the external structure of their life under the crusader kings, and to retrieve something of this people's spirit and stubborn pride and their functional continuity in the new order? Rummaging among the Christian records, the historian can salvage sufficient glimpses into that past to revive it in detail. As a first step, he must arrange some data so as to expose to view the general classes and occupational strata which defined individuals in that society. This broader view can then yield to close-up scenes from varied angles, and ultimately to portraiture.

[30] See my "Baths and Caravanserais in Crusader Valencia," pp. 443-458.

CHAPTER V

City and Country: Basic Classes

THOUGH SPIRITUALLY democratic, Islam was not a leveling religion. Every class comes to light in postconquest records, from military aristocrats to slaves. The professional stratum, especially administrative and legal, was much in evidence. Great landowners remained. The townsmen, like the rustics to whom they felt superior, stayed on while political and social change swirled above them. As with boundaries and customs, traditional social groups persisted in the new Valencia. Muslim theorists variously divided their people; in his penetrating analysis of medieval Near Eastern cities, Lapidus discerns four levels in these discussions and in the reality they reflect: the governing elite with bureaucratic functionaries, the intermediating notables or religious and community leaders (at least within some category, district, or trade), the respectable workers and peasants undistinguished by learning, wealth, office, or political influence, and the despised masses, including the rootless, the menials, the mendicants, the underworld, and the disreputable occupations.[1]

The standard or textbook groups in caliphal Spain had been the upper class, the masses, slaves, and a clientage stratum contributing especially to civil service and army. In later Morisco Granada, Caro Baroja discerns also a warrior type, old Mudejar immigrants from the north, a commercial and Europeanized kind of immigrant able to pass when expedient as Christian, a considerable group distinct as descendants of Christians-turned-Muslims, the lords of small estates, mountain bandits, holy men, and seventy-four trade groups, including schoolmasters. Multiple geographical origins became immediately evident from the speaker's Arabic accent.[2] Such exercises in

[1] *Muslim Cities*, pp. 80-82. See his more general discussion on "Classes of the Population" in cities, pp. 79-95; Reuben Levy, "Grades of Society in Islam," in his *Social Structure of Islam* (Cambridge, 1957), ch. 1; and Goitein on class consciousness and upward mobility in Islamic society (*Mediterranean Society*, I, 75-77).

[2] *Moriscos de Granada*, pp. 68-69, 73, 116, 160. Huici mentions social classes only for early Valencia, dividing them into aristocracy, middle or bourgeois elements, and the mass of artisans and laborers together with rural proletariat, Jews, and Mozarabs (*Historia musulmana de Valencia*, I, 74-77).

classifying social strata demand a word of warning. Peculiarities of the Islamic social structure make strict categorization by class inappropriate; interpenetration of categories opened each to the others. Reflection on this phenomenon, however, requires as a first step a preliminary conspectus of class and economic patterns, despite the risk of making these sound too European or too modern.

Artisan Strata

Though higher classes may be left to the chapters analyzing the nobiliary and the coordinating socio-intellectual elites, the varied middle and lower groups demand some notice. Crafts remained, together with the class managing or serving them. Muslim artists, millers, barbers, bakers, and shopkeepers formed a lively part of the Valencian scene. Workshops, because they yielded a regalian tax, turn up frequently. At Valencia city a general privilege allowed Muslims "to keep your workshops or stores open and to practice your crafts publicly" on all except four of the Christian holy days. King James further regulated Moorish craftsmen with a law prohibiting their working in public view on the feast days, "but within their buildings" only. The conquerors encouraged trades of all kinds, as when the king in 1267 issued an invitation for any Muslim coming to Valencia city to remain there under protection and "to practice his craft [*officium*]."[3] Individuals also appear. "Muḥammad the painter

[3] *Fori regni Valentiae* (Monzón, 1548), lib. I, rub. VIII, c. 2; hereafter cited as *Furs* to distinguish it from the Latin variant of similar title cited above in Chapter I, n. 9; though the *Furs* was substantially in Catalan, it too contains Latin documents intermixed. See the interpretation by Roca Traver, "Vida mudéjar," pp. 164, 170. Arch. Crown, James I, Reg. Canc. 15, fol. 81v (Feb. 26, 1267): "possitis operatoria vestra sive tendas tenere aperta et officia vestra publice in vestris tendis . . . exercere." The standard survey of Islamic Spain's industry and economic life is César E. Dubler, *Über das Wirtschaftsleben auf der iberischen Halbinsel vom xi zum xiii Jahrhundert, Beitrag zu den islamisch-christlichen Beziehungen* (Erlenbach-Zurich, 1943); his map of Spanish craft industries from the eleventh to the thirteenth centuries leaves the northern part of Valencia kingdom bare but locates the active centers to the south (facing p. 98). More recent but less useful is S. M. Imamuddin, *Some Aspects of the Socio-Economic and Cultural History of Muslim Spain, 711-1492 A.D.* (Leiden, 1965), chs. 6, 7. Goitein, though his sources stress the centuries immediately preceding the thirteenth, provides a mine of information on industrial and commercial classes of Mediterranean Islam. See, e.g., his dissection of the artisan and proletariat groups in "The Working People of the

and 'Abd Allāh the carpenter, Saracen brothers, residents of Segorbe" won total tax exemption for life from King James in 1259 in return for free services whenever required. Woodwork was a prized Mudejar skill in Spain, so 'Abd Allāh may have been an artist rather than a mere builder. 'Alī of Gallinera, barber, received a similar exemption plus crown protection but without obligation.[4]

The term craft covered every kind of handiwork involving special skills in a shop—work such as that done by shoemakers, bookbinders, tailors, and carpenters, as well as more creative efforts like the manufacture of rugs, metalware, and pottery. The average shop or stall opening onto the street seems to have used its inner recess as a workshop. A law of 1274 distinguished shopkeepers (*tenderii*), who served "stalls," from craftsmen (*ministrales*), "who worked their crafts" in their "workshops"; probably the two were often identical.[5] Small villages supported necessary crafts; the two Muslim "artisans" appointed as community leaders in 1259 to the Montes and Carrícola aljamas appear to have been prosperous members of this class.[6] Shops and shopkeepers enter the Valencian story in strength. A wide range of economic differences must have distinguished them, from the shabby peddler to the sleek merchandiser and from the sturdy craft laborer to the skilled creator of luxury items like brocade.

Mediterranean Area during the High Middle Ages," *Studies in Islamic History and Institutions* (Leiden, 1966), ch. 13, and his elaboration of Geniza data on these same classes in *Mediterranean Society*, I, part 2.

[4] Arch. Crown, James I, Reg. Canc. 11, fol. 154 (Oct. 10, 1259): "Mahometum pictorem et Abdela fusterium"; fol. 157v (Dec. 21, 1259): "Ali de Gallinera barbitonsor."

[5] On Islamic Spanish crafts, see Dubler, *Wirtschaftsleben*, ch. 8, "Die Zünfte." Ibn 'Abdūn has much to say of Seville's craft groups and their organization; see his *Séville musulmane, le traité*, e.g., pp. 70-71, the group of water-carriers; p. 95, artisans grouped by quarter; p. 105, members of trade groupings; p. 111, dyeing establishments ought to be put outside town; p. 119, the *amīn* or overseer of each trade; p. 133, parchment makers. Goitein has sensible cautionary remarks; he tells of the difficulties of government officials trying to centralize branches of industry into separate markets—51 such locations in twelfth-century Damascus and 24 in Cairo, representing hundreds of minutely specialized processes (*Studies*, pp. 267-270; see also his *Mediterranean Society*, I, 83). Lapidus denies real guilds, either on the European or Byzantine understanding of the term, and finds the concept repugnant to the authorities of religion and government; this did not inhibit a natural cohesion and even the formation of "solidarities" among artisans of the same type (*Muslim Cities*, pp. 98-107).

[6] See document in Chapter X, n. 84.

Linen manufacture had distinguished Játiva since Roman times; during the Aragonese campaign against the town, an agent from Castile plausibly covered his espionage activities by commissioning a luxurious tent.[7] Valencia city was known for its textiles and especially for brocade.[8] When the Játiva pact guaranteed the movable goods of the average Muslim, the only item it expressly specified was *suppellectilia*—carpets and coverlets.[9] At the surrender of Valencia city, as the exiled residents sold their most precious movables, the description explicitly mentioned only drapes and sumptuous cloths.[10] Luxury items like the vestments in the Templar chapel in Peñíscola castle, requisitioned for the king's chapel at the order's suppression, were surely local products; they included a linen alb embroidered in gold with "Saracen work" and with "Arab letters of brilliant color."[11] Muslims continued to produce such hangings and vestments after the crusade. Cloth processing, a staple industry in the western Mediterranean, finds its documentation at conquered Valencia particularly in dyeing operations. These valued, specialized processes comprised a public monopoly under both Islamic and Christian rule. The crown gave Játiva Muslims a special tax exemption to attract dye masters from other lands. Special tax relief for one "master of dyes" mentions shop, equipment, and kinds of cloth treated.[12] Silk processing at Játiva was similarly privileged.[13] The famed sheep-runs of the kingdom insured as well a ready supply of wool. Moorish

[7] *Llibre dels feyts*, ch. 339. Ibn Khaldūn has a section on kinds and demand (*Muqaddimah*, II, 67-69). See also Dubler, *Wirtschaftsleben*, pp. 61-63; and, for Christian textile manufacturing in James's realms, García de Valdeavellano, *Instituciones españolas*, pp. 281-282. Miguel Gual Camarena lists the textile centers of thirteenth-century Valencia, with glossary, map, and documents in his "Para un mapa de la industria textil hispana en la edad media," *Anuario de estudios medievales*, IV (1967), esp. pp. 113, 122-123, 127-128, 134-157 passim.

[8] Ash-Shaqundī praised brocade as an export specialty (see his *Elogio del Islam español*, p. 116).

[9] Játiva Charter (see Chapter VI, n. 9).

[10] Desclot, *Crònica*, ch. 49.

[11] Martínez-Ferrando, *Jaime II*, I, 76-77: "cum opere sarracenico"; "cum literis arabis lividi coloris."

[12] *Itinerari*, p. 493 (Feb. 11, 1274), including "almagels et alquinals" made and sold by this "officium purpurarum."

[13] *Ibid.* ("pannos siricos"). A document of 1303 in Martínez-Ferrando's *Jaime II* (II, doc. 8) has two non-Valencian Muslim masters of the silk craft being rushed to the king at Barcelona.

and Arago-Catalan influences were to meet forcefully in the general textile trade of Valencia, whose major centers became Alcira, Alcora, Alfandech, Burriana, Játiva, Valencia city, Valldigna, and Villarreal.

Ceramics formed a specialty which postcrusade generations continued and dramatically improved. The Valencia city museum of ceramics today exhibits over six hundred pieces of the twelfth and thirteenth centuries from Paterna alone, not all of them necessarily Moorish. Others have come to light from Murviedro and Valencia city. The Játiva surrender pact protected the "masters" who made pitchers, tiles, and pots; open plazas where they worked went free of tax. An ample plaza "in which jugs were sold in the time of the Saracens" became the butcheries of Christian Játiva in 1248.[14] The *Furs* of Valencia gave tax relief to makers of pots, pitchers, tiles "and any other product made of earth or glass"—perhaps an encouragement for Christians to enter the local craft.[15] There were also shipyards at Denia, timber on the upper Júcar, and all the skills involved in fisheries, marine activity, and international seaports. A traditional specialty, the making of books, may not have died altogether with the exiling of Valencia city's population. The book of land division

[14] Játiva Charter: "magistri qui faciant cantaros, ollas, tegulas, et raiolas." *Repartimiento de Valencia*, p. 439: "placiam sibe carrariam . . . ubi modo est macellum et corallum in quo vendebantur cantari tempore sarracenorum"; a *cànter* or *càntir* is a special kind of jug, narrow at the bottom in inverse pear-shape. José Martínez Ortiz and Jaime De Scals Aracil list the Paterna and similar items in their lavishly illuminated study *Colección cerámica del museo histórico municipal de Valencia, ciclo Paterna-Manises* (Valencia, 1962), pp. 75-109. The monumental study of Manuel González Martí, *Cerámica del levante español, siglos medievales* (3 vols., Madrid, 1944-1952), covers our region in exhaustive technical detail; see, e.g., I, 95ff. on themes, pattern, and coloration; pp. 170-181 on animals pictured; p. 651 for a chronological index, extended in II, 682, and III, 725. Felipe Mateu y Llopis examines one of many modern finds in his "Hallazgos cerámicos en Valencia," *Al-Andalus*, XVI (1951), 165-167. Among evidences of Murcian activity is the entry in its *Repartimiento* (p. 225): "a los moros olleros, para sacar terra de que fiziessen su mester, ii alffabas menos quarta en Almunia." See also Dubler, *Wirtschaftsleben*, p. 34. For a broad introduction to non-Hispanic work, with bibliographical orientation and industrial techniques, see Jean Sauvaget, "Introduction a l'étude de la céramique musulmane," *Revue des études islamiques*, XXXIII (1965), 1-68.

[15] *Fori antiqui Valentiae*, rub. CLXIV, no. 5, lists the "olle, cantari, et quodlibet opus de terra," and covers manufacture of "ollas, canters, teulas rayolas, et quodlibet aliud opus de terra, et vitrum: rotumbas, cupas et quodlibet aliud opus de vitro." Ceramics of Valencia were to become most famous only in the following two centuries, largely still a Mudejar industry.

listed a "maker of parchment" resident in the "Saracen quarter."[16]

The most celebrated Valencian industry was the manufacture of paper at Játiva. Though Almoravid and Almohad persecution had diminished the town's monopoly a little by driving Jews north to found small rival centers at Manresa and Gerona, Játiva's mills flourished heartily. Their capture proved a boon for the royal archives and a source of pride for the Christians. King James encouraged Muslims in the paper industry, as he did those engaged in dyes.[17] Not long afterwards, Muntaner found it natural to say that in writing about the political "crimes" of the Genoese and Pisans he "would not have enough space with all the paper made in the town of Játiva."[18] Unlike the single-shop workers in most medieval crafts, paper-makers probably occupied large plants. Al-Idrīsī in the mid-twelfth century had praised Játiva's product, "the like of which is not found in all the world; it is sent to the east and the west"; the

[16] On the Denia shipyards, dependent on pine coming down the Júcar, see Leopoldo Torres Balbás, "Atarazanas hispanomusulmanas," *Al-Andalus*, xi (1946), esp. p. 183; and al-Ḥimyarī, *Kitāb ar-rawḍ al-miʿṭār*, pp. 158-159. For Valencian products large and small, including the very local trade, see my *Crusader Valencia*, i, 149-153; on fishing, see i, 145, 152, 157, 221-222, and esp. pp. 169-170 on the separate sea-fishery tithe. Ibn Khaldūn speaks of commercial hunting and fishing (*Muqaddimah*, ii, 315). The Chivert Charter (see Chapter VI, n. 3) dismisses taxes for Muslims "in omnibus piscacionibus aque salse et dulcis." The "R. pargaminero" living "in vico sarracenorum" in the *Repartimiento de Valencia* (p. 568) may possibly be a Christian, but more likely belongs with the Moors also listed here; he may have been a convert, as was perhaps the "Thomasius pargemenarius" at Alcira (p. 422). Other trades crop up in stray notices. Ibn Khaldūn discusses the well-rooted crafts and entertainment tradition of Islamic Spain, exceeding that of many other countries, and continuing at that time in Granada (*Muqaddimah*, ii, 349-350); Ibn ʿAbdūn rebukes the entertainer class a number of times.

[17] Arch. Crown, James I, Reg. Canc. 19, fol. 99v (Feb. 8, 1273), reduction of tax by threepence per ream. See also Dubler, *Wirtschaftsleben*, pp. 81-84, and Sarthou Carreres, *Datos para la historia de Játiva*, ii, 47ff. Oriol Valls i Subirá supplies background in his "Characterístiques del paper de procedència o escola àrab en els documents del reial arxiu de la corona d'Aragó: pacte de Cazola, repartiment del regne de València i cartes diplomàtiques àrabs," *Congrés VII*, iii, 319-329; see also his more elaborate *Paper and Watermarks in Catalonia*, 2 vols. (Amsterdam, 1970), i, passim. The *Fori antiqui Valentiae*, in its customs list of some 250 local products, includes "caxia paperii," at four solidi, a *caxa* being defined in a 1284 document as 16 *raymes* or reams (rub. cxliv, no. 4). Ibn ʿAbdūn provided regulations for the industry at Seville (*Séville musulmane, le traité*, p. 107).

[18] Muntaner, *Crònica*, ch. 282.

crusading kingdom continued to export reams of it as a principal commodity.[19] At the beginning of the next century the principal Valencian industries continued to reflect the Islamic past—ceramics, paper, processing of raisins, and the typically Moorish work in leather and metal.[20]

The specialization of lower and middle classes—when they did not fall under industrial, commercial, administrative-functionary, intellectual-professional, or agricultural categories—varied widely. The Valencia kingdom held Muslim robber bands, *almogàver* irregular troops, rowdy retainers, falconers, huntsmen, entertainers, and the despised class of bath attendants. Presumably the usual proletariat, the tinder for precrusade demagogues, continued in the larger towns; provision for almsgiving in the surrender treaties recalls the presence of the destitute. Even a stratum of prostitutes and their protectors manifests itself. A crown privilege of 1258 allowed the Biar aljama to disperse theirs: "We grant to you that you may expel if you wish from the town of Biar all the Saracen whores or prostitutes without any person impeding."[21] A more universal document in 1281, imposing a special tax on every Mudejar household in Valen-

[19] Al-Idrīsī, *Description*, p. 37.

[20] J. E. Martínez-Ferrando, *La València de Jaume II, breu aplec de notícies* (Valencia, 1963), p. 25. On Valencian tanneries see Dubler, *Wirtschaftsleben*, pp. 80-81. The *Repartimiento* lists an "adobaria" or tannery for 1241 (p. 282).

[21] *Itinerari*, pp. 275-276 (June 16, 1258): "concedimus autem vobis quod possitis expellere si volueritis de villa de Biar omnes putas seu meretrices sarracenas sine impedimento alicuius persone." Prostitution flourished in the Maghrib, despite legal concubinage and polygamy (Brunschvig, *Berbérie orientale*, II, 173-174). Ibn 'Abdūn provides for control of this class in twelfth-century Seville (*Séville musulmane, le traité*, p. 113, 157n.). On male and female prostitution in Spanish Islam see Lévi-Provençal, *España musulmana*, v, 289-290. On Valencian prostitution from 1311 to 1483, including the role of Moors, see Manuel Dualde Serrano, "Misión moralizadora del lugarteniente general Juan de Lanuza en el reino de Valencia," *EEMCA*, v (1952), esp. pp. 488-489; and Manuel Carboneres, *Picaronas y alcahuetes ó la mancebía de Valencia, apuntes para la historia de la prostitución desde principios del siglo xiv hasta poco antes de la abolición de los fueros, con profusión de notas y copias de varios documentos oficiales* (Valencia, 1876). On fifteenth-century Mudejar prostitution in Valencia city, with its list of licensed women coming from places like Buñol, Carcer, Paterna, and the Alfandech Valley, see Piles Ros, "Moros de realengo en Valencia," p. 270. In his novel *Blanquerna* Lull introduces Saracen women from a brothel, soliciting at a city gate (ed. Lorenzo Ribera 2d edn. [Madrid, 1959], ch. 71). The prostitutes' quarter in Valencia was just north of the Mudejar quarter beyond the northwest gate.

cia kingdom, singled out only one class for individual notice, "Saracen women prostitutes"; on a scale adjusted for prosperity by landholding, each prostitute paid the highest rate, "twenty solidi apiece."[22]

Merchants

The Valencian littoral was a hive of domestic and foreign commerce. Custom, surrender charters, and the profit motive consecrated the continued participation by Muslims; indeed the kingdom's trade must have been dominated by Muslims for some years after the crusade. Commerce can be distinguished from the craft, industrial, or shopkeeping activities. Regulating the groups engaged in commerce throughout the kingdom—including wholesale and retail shopkeepers and the financier-bankers—King James listed the properly merchant class as *mercaders*. They exported, imported, and distributed, in a variety of patterns ranging from the direct buyer-transporter-seller to the contract group conducting an extensive business. King James explicitly included Muslims in this class, specifying only that the merchant be a freeman and at least twenty years of age.[23] In 1261 the king's concession or confirmation of Valencia city's market protected Muslims as well as Jewish and Christian merchants traveling to it.[24] Tax reliefs or privileges applied equally to Muslim and Christian merchants, and protection of the crown covered both indiffer-

[22] Arch. Crown, Peter III, Reg. Canc. 50, fol. 231 (Jan. 17, 1281): "et de mulieribus sarracenibus meretricibus viginti solidos pro qualibet." This may be for each prostitute, or possibly for each brothel; Spanish Islam's prostitutes, taxed by their government also in precrusade days, more commonly worked out of the fonduks, but brothels did exist (Lévi-Provençal, *España musulmana*, v, 289).

[23] Fermín Cortes Muñoz, "Aportación al estudio de las instituciones mercantiles de la Valencia foral, la condición jurídica de los mercaderes," *BSCC*, XXIV (1948), 218-221. Goitein delineates the ideological justification and even superiority gained by the merchant in medieval Islam (*Studies*, ch. 11); the contrast with Mediterranean Europeans, either in practice or among theoreticians like Thomas Aquinas, was not so much as he assumes. See also his more complex *Mediterranean Society*, I, part 3. In 1154 al-Idrīsī described Valencia city as "one of the largest cities of Spain [and] its population consists of merchants" (*Description*, p. 36).

[24] The privilege of market is in Arch. Crown, James I, Reg. Canc. 11, fol. 214 (Aug. 20, 1261) but does not include the safeguard; this was added by James, however, to the version of the privilege published in the *Aureum opus* (doc. 61, same date).

ently. A typical law, part of the Valencian *Furs*, was King Peter's decree of 1283 confirming the right of the kingdom's Muslims, crown and seignorial, to buy or sell anywhere, conducting business with Christian, Jew, or fellow Muslim; or his 1278 postrebellion confirmation of the right of Valencian Muslims to trade with any country of Islam.[25] Overseas trade and travel to Islamic lands, as well as hospitality to foreign Muslims, were always integral to Valencian Mudejar trade. None of this seemed strange to the crusaders. A generation before, the rabbi tourist Benjamin of Tudela had encountered at so northerly a port as Montpellier Muslim merchants from many parts, including Egypt.[26]

Apart from the traumatic change represented by transfer of supreme power from Muslim to colonialist Christian, probably no other factor was so effective as commerce in the acculturative process within the Mudejar communities of Valencia. An omnipresent obsession, with dramatic rewards for the lucky, it crossed all boundaries of religion, language, culture, and holy war hostilities. Dufourcq rightly sums the contemporary Catalan peoples, including the Valencians, as preeminently merchants. "In short, princes, nobles, bourgeois, lower classes, Christians, Jews, Muslims, the Catalans of the mainland and of the islands, sell, buy, resell, traffic, charter boats, are merchants, carriers, and coastal shippers."[27] War and peace, profoundly affecting commerce, were themselves influenced by business exigencies; crusade and commerce lived in a fitful love-hate relationship. The thirteenth-century circle trade between the Catalan-Valencian-Majorcan shores and the North African shore has been minutely explored by Dufourcq, who views it under the aspect of Aragon

[25] Arch. Crown, Peter III, Reg. Canc. 40, fol. 63 (Feb. 14, 1278). The confirmatory decree, in reg. 46, fol. 126 (Nov. 30, 1283) is also in Fernández y González, *Mudejares de Castilla*, doc. 53.

[26] Benjamin ben Jonah of Tudela, *The Travels of Rabbi Benjamin of Tudela, 1160-1173*, ed. Manuel Komroff, in *Contemporaries of Marco Polo* (New York, 1928), part 4, p. 254. Among the concourse of dignitaries who greeted Pope Alexander III at Montpellier in 1162 was a North African prince, emissary of the king of the Muslims; see the *Liber pontificalis*, ed. Louis Duchesne, 2 vols. (Paris, 1886-1892), II, 404; see also Marshall W. Baldwin, *Alexander III and the Twelfth Century* (New York, 1968), pp. 60, 171.

[27] *L'Espagne catalane et le Maghrib*, p. 67. Dufourcq distinguishes between this "international" capitalism and the "urban patriotic" variety of individualists like the contemporary Genoese (p. 62).

expanding its commercial life in range and intensity. One may see it instead as a readjustment of existing trade patterns, and as crown advocacy and regulation of the older, Muslim-to-Muslim Valencian trade; intrusion of Christian merchants and politics required accommodations by both sides. Under Christian tutelage the ports of entry achieving official, monopolistic status by the early fourteenth century remained the traditional precrusade ports (newly founded Castellón excepted); from north to south these were Peñíscola, Castellón, Burriana, Murviedro, Valencia, Cullera, Gandía, and Denia.[28]

In a war-torn country like Mudejar Valencia, trade could suffer hindrance. During the revolt of the 1270's, for example, the crown restricted "each and every Saracen" of the Valencia kingdom in trading with the rebels; such commerce had to pass through a specially licensed contractor. In 1280 Cerveri Ça Nera of Barcelona, a functionary of the royal household, received this monopoly; notice went out to Valencian Muslims to trade south only through him.[29] After pacification of the Valencian kingdom in the wake of the 1277 revolts, when King Peter forcibly imposed order upon baronial, urban, and Muslim elements, the main beneficiary proved to be trade, particularly internal commerce. It was primarily in mercantile terms that the junior contemporary Muntaner assessed Peter's military operations: peace of such a nature had ensued "that merchants could move about with bags of florins and gold doubloons," and everyone else could travel in safety.[30]

Besides the wide-ranging trade there were fairs, markets for single products, and general markets at the local level. The Játiva aljama took care to write into their charter a general market every Friday. At Valencia city, as at Burriana, the expulsion with consequent influx of Christians may have pushed the Muslim merchant into the background, but it did not eliminate him; the Moorish quarter at Valencia city was soon flourishing. The Uxó aljama's charter specified freedom of movement overseas, the common condition for

[28] *Ibid.*, p. 33.

[29] Arch. Crown, Peter III, Reg. Canc. 48, fol. 128 (August 16, 1280), also in Roca Traver, "Vida mudéjar," doc. 11. Roca Traver reads the name as Cenuario, Martínez-Ferrando as Cerviano; is this a garbled form of Cervià Sarriera, a wealthy merchant from Barcelona (*Itinerari*, pp. 512-513 [Feb. 4, 1275])?

[30] *Crònica*, ch. 29: "que ab lo sach dels florins e dels doblons podien anar mercaders, e tot altre hom per tota sa terra salvament e segura."

Valencian Muslims though involving a port tax. Eslida's charter especially protected *negotia* from interference by Christians at the regional level. The Chivert charter offered tax exemption "on all their merchandise, sales, and purchases by sea or fresh water and on or off the road."[31] As the generations passed, interior commerce took on more prominence for Mudejars, so that by 1380 they were minimally involved in maritime affairs but very active inland and with other countries overland.[32] This was a later development, however, explicable by factors like the shifting balance of population and wealth, the increasing restrictions on Muslims, and gradual loss of town population and dynamism by the aljamas. The crusade generation and their sons had fared much better.

Merchants continued to form a creative minority helping to supply tone and definition to the essentially urban aljamas of Valencia which dominated the overwhelmingly agricultural ambience. The progressive capture of merchant leadership and of town life generally by the colonial conquerors required time, in some places a great deal of time. During this twilight period of Mudejar Valencia, the old merchant culture persisted.

Farmers and Stockmen

It was not the warrior, merchant, craftsman, and landlord who made up the bulk of the population. As in most medieval societies, or in modern societies until recent times, farmers supplied the backdrop against which the more dynamic urban minority moved. This was especially true of Islamic Spain; Ibn Khaldūn records that Spaniards, "of all civilized people, are the ones most devoted to agriculture; it rarely happens among them that a man in authority or an ordinary person has no tract of land or field or does not do some

[31] Játiva, Uxó, and Eslida Charters; Chivert Charter: "sint franchi in omnibus suis mercedibus et vendicionibus et empcionibus in aquis salsis et dulcibus et in camino et extra caminum"; for these charters, see Chapter VI, nn. 3, 4, 7, and 9. On markets and fairs see Dubler, *Wirtschaftsleben*, ch. 7; García de Valdeavellano says that fairs in the crown of Aragon, because of her abundant commerce, were always local (*Instituciones españolas*, p. 276; see also p. 281 on the relation of commerce in conquered Valencia to that of Barcelona and Majorca in the general boom).

[32] Desamparados Pérez Pérez and Elena Pascuale-Leone Pascual, "Algunos aspectos del comercio valenciano a fines del siglo xiv," *Congrés VII*, II, 537; metals were a major item.

farming; the only exceptions are a few craftsmen and professional people, or fighters in the Holy War who are newcomers to the country." Ibn Khaldūn had particular reference to fourteenth-century Granada, but viewed it in the general perspective of Islamic Spain's history.[33]

This involves no contradiction to his description elsewhere of Spain as an unusually urbanized area. The townsman was obviously also a small farmer, as in many Christian towns, or at least the partner of his tenant sharecropper. Crusaders settling at Valencia and receiving a personal residence or, for a group, a full street or section also got the corresponding garden farm for each house. King James gave the Barcelona crusaders a fifth of Valencia city, for example, together with its corresponding extramural farmland—"a sixth of the farms in the Valencian countryside." The *agricultores* of Valencia city and countryside soon organized a brotherhood guild. Town militias, who abandoned the Valencia crusade regularly for the mid-June harvesting, also testify to this double orientation of the townsman. There was a difference, however, as tithe records show at mid-century, between this amateur Muslim or Christian grower and the professional who seriously marketed his crops in bulk.[34] The division between rural and urban, though not exclusive, was real. Farmers themselves differed as owners, renters, sharecroppers, or laborers; as wealthy, poor, or in-between; as returning by night to city and village or residing in cottage and cottage cluster; as working predominantly "dry" lands and uplands for grain, olives, figs, nuts, and especially vines, or as enjoying the fruit and vegetable crops of lush riverine, spring, or elaborately canaled farms, not to mention marsh-

[33] *Muqaddimah*, II, 279. Ibn 'Abdūn lauded agriculture, especially cereals, as "the base for civilization" and the foundation below increasing wealth (*Séville musulmane, le traité*, p. 9).

[34] *Llibre dels feyts*, chs. 166, 403; Muntaner contrasts areas like Murcia, where "in April they begin already to reap the wheat," with the later harvests of the north (*Crònica*, ch. 14). On townsmen in Valencia having extramural farms and their amateur status, see my *Crusader Valencia*, I, ch. 9, esp. p. 151; see passim for other examples. At the contemporary non-Valencian town of Cortes an aljama functionary had the duty of unlocking the gates "de nocte quando los mauros habent opus ire ad rigandum" ("Documentos para el estudio de la reconquista y repoblación del valle del Ebro," ed. José M. Lacarra, 3d series, *EEMCA*, v [1952], doc. 399). On rural-urban relations, see also above, Chapter IV, n. 21.

lands. In a territory so varied, with a crazy quilt of juxtaposed zones, the farmer fell into no single classification.

A tax instruction embracing all Mudejars of the Valencia kingdom, except those paying rents directly to the king's bailiff without intermediate landlord, divided them into landholding and nonlandholding households. The tax in question affected each household, whether headed by a man or a woman; perhaps the crown considered shopkeepers and craftsmen adequately covered by their own proper taxes, and therefore took care to scale this levy heavily against land. Every household in a royal city, town, or castle—and their countrysides—paid twenty solidi if it held a farm under a landlord other than the crown; the Mudejar with no farm, living under a noncrown landlord in the same areas, paid only six solidi. The same division applied in castles and countrysides which were noncrown—the household with farm paid twelve solidi, however, and the nonfarm six. The instruction reveals a community split not so much into rural and urban as into independently landed and nonlanded classes, each of them sizable.[35]

A decade earlier the Valencian law code had touched upon the nonlanded Mudejar stratum. The notice, inserted at the end of a rubric on slaves, involved the correlative class of domestics or household members. It provided that if a nonowner, working Christian land as a formal resident of the region and presumably as a permanent tenant, abandoned his farm and moved elsewhere, the Christian owner could recover the farm and any properties the Mudejar had had in that *terminus* or place, though the owner was not allowed to

[35] David Romano Ventura, "Los hermanos Abenmenassé al servicio de Pedro el Grande de Aragón," *Homenaje a Millás-Vallicrosa*, II, doc. 4 (Jan. 17, 1282): "sive masculi aut mulieres pro quolibet casato sarracenorum comorancium infra terminos civitatum, villarum, et castrorum nostrorum regni Valencie qui teneant laboraciones ab aliquibus aliis preter a nobis, viginti solidos regalium; et pro quolibet casato aliorum sarracenorum infra dictos terminos comorancium in hereditatibus aliorum licet non teneant aliquas laboraciones, sex solidos regalium; item de quolibet casato sarracenorum comorancium in castris vel terminis castrorum que per se terminos habeant et non sunt in terminis civitatum, villarum, et castrorum nostrorum, qui teneant laboraciones, duodecim solidos regalium; et pro casato aliorum qui non tenent laboraciones, sex solidos." Whatever the status of the "alii" having Mudejars on lands within crown jurisdiction, at least the division here of the Mudejars themselves by *laboraciones* is clear.

interfere with the tenant's leaving, with his person, or with what he could carry beyond that district. The decree cautioned that such power of local confiscation did not extend beyond the class of *habitator* working an alien farm, and that a Saracen nonowner who had "promised to live and work the Christian's farm for a period of time" not only did not fall under this law "but on the contrary, as soon as his time is up, can go away with all he owns."[36] Besides landowners of various levels, consequently, there were at least two kinds of nonowning tenants. The year before this law appeared, King James adverted to a special group of nonowners, exempting "each and all Saracen laborers resident in Campanar in the district of Alcira, who do not own farms or any possessions there" from all taxes except the tributary besant.[37]

The small farmer appearing in Valencian land contracts was called by Christians an *exaricus*, from *ash-sharīḳ* or sharer. The exaricate was not an oppressive status devised by the Christians to control subject Muslims. Its conditions did not differ notably from those experienced under Muslim rulers. The term had previously concealed a variety of rental contracts; time and the busy pens of jurists had assimilated these to the general status of Christian farmers, while simultaneously simplifying and elevating the exaricate. The *exaricus* had become not a concessionaire or serf farming an integral part of an estate as Hinojosa concluded but rather a free farmer capable of selling his property even though it was permanently englobed in the larger economic unit of his landlord and burdened with rents or taxes.[38] He may therefore be described as a contract-tenant or ten-

[36] *Fori antiqui Valentiae*, rub. LXXXIII, no. 19.

[37] Arch. Crown, James I, Reg. Canc. 16, fol. 217 (Oct. 2, 1270): "universis et singulis sarracenis laboratoribus habitantibus in Campanar termini Aliazire qui non habetis hereditates seu possessiones aliquas ibidem"; the language and the need for legislation suggests a sizable stratum.

[38] The term *exaricus* was translated *particeps* in the word list attributed to the Dominican missionary in Valencia at this time, Ramón Martí, *Vocabulista in arabico pubblicato per la prima volta sopra un codice della biblioteca riccardiana di Firenze*, ed. Celestino Schiaparelli (Florence, 1871), p. 511, and in E. K. Neuvonen, *Los arabismos del español en el siglo xiii* (Helsinki, 1941), pp. 128-129. On *exarici* see Eduardo de Hinojosa, "Mezquinos y exáricos, datos para la historia de la servidumbre en Navarra y Aragón," *Homenaje á D. Francisco Codera en su jubilación del profesorado, estudios de erudición oriental*, ed. Eduardo Saavedra *et alii* (Zaragoza, 1904), pp. 523-531; Lévi-Provençal, *España musulmana*, v, 151; and J. M. Lacarra in Font y Rius *et alii, Reconquista española*, pp. 71-72. Bayerri has some

ant-owner, something between a serf and a free-renter. Occasionally even a slave would set up as an *exaricus*, under contract to work for the price of his freedom. The exaricate was already the common status in the Ebro Valley before the conquest of Valencia. A distinguishing mark of an *exaricus* was his tributary fifth to lord or king. Liauzu's interpretation of him as a lowly serf, vaguely unfree, and capable of being sold with his land, does not fit the Valencian scene, nor do the Ebro Valley documents on which the interpretation rests justify the description. Affluent and relatively exalted landowners answered to the designation without shame. When King James confirmed the estates of three sons of the ex-king Abū Zayd at Ricla near Zaragoza in 1268, each still possessed the proud Almohad title *sayyid*; yet he called them with affection his *exarici*: "Muḥammad 'Abd ar-Raḥmān our *exaricus*" together with his brothers "Mūsā and Ismā'īl" (Muça, Azmal), who were "our very own and special *exarici*." A quarter-century later, a revenue document records these same "sons and heirs of Don Abū Zayd" who were "the *exarici* of the lord king."[39]

The status can be stretched to include the proprietor-farmer who paid his rental share only by way of tax to lord or king. Such a proprietor, if he had tenant *exarici* of his own, must have assimilated rather to the landlord or lord stratum. A transient tenant with no rights to sell his land, at the other extreme, must have assimilated somewhat to that of the hired laborer. Taking *exaricus* as an analogous term embodying a proportional relationship rather than a univocal meaning, the prime analogue was a contract-tenant with real

---

comments on the Tortosa exaricate, *Historia de Tortosa*, VII, 333-336. For the contrasting material conditions of the Holy Land peasant, under his Islamic or Frankish absentee landlords little better than the northern European serf, see Cahen's "Régime rurale," esp. pp. 287, 299ff., and his reinterpretation of Ibn Jubayr in "Indigènes et croisés," pp. 351-360.

[39] Liauzu, drawing on Lacarra's "Documentos" from earlier centuries in the Ebro Valley-Tortosa region, admits that the serf *exarici* concept is not clear; his categories, while interesting, waver in the course of discussion; and his sale documents concern proprietarial rights in tenanted land rather than serf-cum-holding ("Musulmans dans l'Aragon chrétien," pp. 187-188, 192, 197-198). The Ricla grant is in Chabás, "Çeit Abu Çeit," pp. 302-303: "xariqui nostri . . . nostros proprios et speciales xaricos." The revenue document of 1294 is in *Rentas de la antigua corona de Aragón*, ed. Manuel de Bofarull, in *Colección de documentos inéditos del archivo general de la corona de Aragón*, XXXIX (Barcelona, 1871), p. 247.

but limited ownership rights; independent owners, bound to pay tribute of a share of produce as tax to king or magnate, in their own manner also fitted the term. Lesser tenants, with hardly any rights beyond sharing, perhaps might assimilate at least in general appearances and social status to neighboring *exarici*. Despite difficulties and semantic obstacles, therefore, it seems reasonable to see as an *exaricus* any Muslim left behind by the tide of conquest who engaged with some degree of independence in full-time small-farming. The exaricate system or policy contrasted with the very different system in Castile; even in the realms of Aragon, Catalonia knew it in a more progressive and rationalized form than did Aragon proper. Under what conditions did the *exaricus* hold his land? In the case of the true *exaricus* or prime analogue, the usual contract, which derived from Byzantine jurisprudence, was an hereditary and perpetual lease at fixed rent, formally renewable; a tenant defaulting on his rent became liable to loss of his land, yet he could also treat the property as his own, selling or alienating it with its concomitant obligations. Mudejars undoubtedly enjoyed other forms of contract in the Valencian kingdom; in the development of new areas, for example, the Catalan *complant* may have served, where a pioneer got half his tract outright but paid rent on the other half.

Though Mudejar farmers differed grossly in a variety of accidental ways, a keenly felt difference with repercussions in law separated city-dwelling farmers from the mere "bumpkins" (*rustici*) of the countryside alquerias.[40] An appreciation of the meaning *rusticus* had for Christian readers of this Muslim privilege, and by implication therefore something of its meaning for Valencia's Mudejars, can be drawn from Valencia's *Furs* or code, which distinguished the right to duel at three levels of the Christian population, specifying that each level was to fight within its own category and each to post its own pledge—300 Alfonsine morabatins for "knights," 200 for "citizens," and 100 for either "tenants" or "rustics."[41] Besides clarifying

[40] Játiva Charter: "aliquis rusticus sarracenus habitans in alqueriis, qui non sit habitator ravalli praedicti."

[41] *Fori antiqui Valentiae*, rub. CXXXIII, nos. 4-6, 12. Two sections ambiguously join "villani et rustici" and "rustici sive villani"; another separates the battlers as "burgenses cum burgensibus, villani cum villanibus, rustici cum rusticis." The *Usatges* of Catalonia seem to distinguish *rustici* from *pagenses* (countrymen or tenants), but its Catalan versions translated one for the other; that code did divide

rustics somewhat, the *Furs* took direct notice of certain distinctions among Muslim tenants, such as hired labor, permanent settlers, and those "already resident." The tax-collecting procedures categorized Muslim farmers as "all the Moors of the bishop and of the orders and of the alquerias of the knights and of the townsmen," or more simply "all the Moors of the church and of knights and of orders and of other persons."[42] Whatever the distinctions formalized by law, the underlying pattern in Valencia from Roman to modern times has been small-farming by owners or subowners paying rental taxes to a local overlord or landlord. Beneath the differences in Mudejar Valencia, this design persisted. It is important to stress that the crusade did not destroy the farming classes by driving them from fertile regions onto the dry areas and backlands; such a view of Mudejar-Christian division of lands derives from a later period.[43]

A preliminary conspectus of Valencian crops is available in the 1268 tithe settlement negotiated by King James for the new kingdom. Muslims normally paid no tithe; but it is most unlikely that the kinds of local produce falling under the tithe, and their relative importance, had altered drastically within twenty-three years after

---

low class *rustici* in law from a wealthier category called *baccallarii,* who apparently owned several farms like a landlord over an estate (see the discussions of the three, with citations, in Rodón Binué, *El lenguaje técnico*, pp. ix, xvi-xvii, 32, 186, 257). The Valencian Francesc Eiximenis in the next century outlined the Christian population of the realms of Aragon in three estates: the upper class (barons, prelates, counts, knights, and urban patriciate), the middle class or *mitjans* (bureaucrats, professional men such as jurists, physicians, and financiers, and the merchants), and the lower class or *poble menut* (craftsmen, respectable workers, sales people, proletariate, and suburban rural folk); see his *La societat catalana al segle xiv,* texts arranged by Jill Webster (Barcelona, 1967), chs. 4, 6, 7; and García de Valdeavellano, *Instituciones españolas*, pp. 315-316. The division, though more strictly hierarchical in the fourteenth than in the thirteenth century, might have seemed more familiar to a Muslim than to a northern European feudalistic theorist of society.

42 Arch. Crown, James I, Reg. Canc. 18, fols. 94v-95 (Dec. 1, 1272): "de tots los moros del bisbe e de les ordes e de les alqueries de les cavalers e de les homens de les viles e que lauraran jovades si no son castels de rics homens o de cavalers o de ciudadans ab termens"; "tots los moros de la eglesia e de cavalers e dordens e altres persones. . . ." *Furs*, lib. VIII, rub. VIII, c. 28: "quilibet homo civitatis et regni possit mittere sarracenos laboratores ad laborandum in hereditatibus suis ad certum tempus, vel imperpetuum, et ipsi sarraceni qui iam habitant in eisdem non teneantur dare domino regi . . . solidos."

43 Grau Monserrat, "Mudéjares castellonenses," p. 256: "sólo eran numerosos los mudéjares en las zonas de regadío alrededor de Játiva y Gandía."

the close of the crusade. The staples prove to have been oil, wine, vegetables, fruit, and grain. There were fourteen varieties of cereals, including alfalfa, barley, flax, millet, oats, blue vetch, and white wheat. Prominent fruits were apples, mulberries, peaches, pears, plums, pomegranates, quinces, sorb apples, grapes or raisins, and especially dried or fresh figs. Almonds stood out as the most valuable nuts. Vegetables included carrots, cabbage, garlic, onions, spinach, and turnips. Hemp and saffron belonged among special commercial crops. Domestic livestock consisted of cows, donkeys, horses, and, for Christians, pigs; fowl comprised chickens, geese, ducks, doves, and peacocks. Beeswax, cheese, and fleeces of wool rounded out the picture.[44]

The evidence from Christian tithes can be buttressed by incidental intelligence gleaned from the crusade and rebellion eras. Grain and wine recur as the agricultural staples. When King James determined to bring Valencia city to its knees, he repeated his favorite tactic employed "in other places of the [Valencian] kingdom, and in most of them and in the best of them": he laid waste "the grain and [vegetable] huerta" of the area. He then planned his siege of the city to start just before the harvesting of "the wheat and the barley." James similarly prepared his Murcian campaign to coincide with the opening of the Muslims' wheat harvest. The rebel leader al-Azraq supported his armies by means of his wheat crop. King James countered rebellion by amassing "wheat, wine, and barley" for his crusaders; he demanded that each Christian householder in Valencia surrender his family reserves except for one year's supply, and that professional "dealers" sell their stocks in return for a crown chit. Before abandoning an attack against the Muslims' Jérica, James resolved "to lay waste above the town, toward Viver," an area filled with "fine wheat fields"; the feat, involving coordinated infantry and cavalry tactics, devastated several districts, and was repeated again at Torres Torres.[45] King Peter organized a mass cutting of enemy wheat in 1277 to deny it to Muslim rebels. In this context the storage granaries of dealers,

[44] Burns, *Crusader Valencia*, I, ch. 9, esp. pp. 151-153. The Chivert Charter exempts from tax "bestiarium de tragino et arando." See also Dubler, *Wirtschaftsleben*, pp. 51-60.

[45] *Llibre dels feyts*, chs. 153-155 ("d'aquests blats tam bels"), 241 ("que ja forment ni ordi no proan haver segat"), 276 ("la pa e la orta"), 409 ("pa, e vi, e civada"). Muntaner, *Crònica*, ch. 14.

encountered in Valencian tax records, take on more meaning; farming was allied to commerce, supplying an abundance of marketable commodities.

Of direct interest to a study of Mudejar crops are the surrender charters of the Valencian aljamas; there the grapes, wheat, and vegetables appear clearly, sometimes with details. The crusaders' book of land division particularly clarifies the place of vineyards, cloaking other details of produce in ambiguous generalities. A man's nature forms itself to some extent according to the work he does; consequently this picture of a highly diversified crop, with a concentration on grains, vegetables, wine or raisins, and fruit, may tell something about the farmers, the bulk of the Mudejar people of Islamic and Christian Valencia. Many a farmer may have passed his life in immemorial isolation among his own people, especially in areas of slight Christian immigration, dismissing as comprehensible only to Allah the changes taking place at exalted levels of government. Even such a farmer made a valuable unit in the Christian order. His zealous protectors included not only the crown, but also the baronage and landlord class of Christians, to whom his cheerful good health was a matter of sincere if selfish concern.

Not all the Valencian landscape consisted of either gracious huertas or dry lands suitable for vineyards and grain. Much of the country was bleak and inhospitable; useful valleys sheltered in the lee of unproductive hills. Such marginal lands became the domain of the cattle and sheep industry, with its hides, wool, and meat profits. Traditional in Roman Valencia, the business continued through Islamic times. In a single obscure raid near Almenara King James netted "700 goats and 200 cows"; he mentioned these in his memoirs only because they chanced to come in handy as a present during negotiations for Almenara's surrender. As presents at Castro he promised "a quantity of sheep and goats"; at Uxó it was "1,500 sheep and goats, and 60 cows," and at Nules "1,000 sheep and goats and 50 cows." Both at Castro and Nules he added, besides outfits of clothing, two horses, and at Uxó three.[46] Needing 1,000 pack mules and 86 cavalry mounts as replacements during the crusade, King James

[46] *Llibre dels feyts*, chs. 245, 249, 250. On the livestock industry see my *Crusader Valencia*, I, 221-222, II, 480. More general information on the domestic animals of Islamic Spain is gathered in Dubler, *Wirtschaftsleben*, pp. 75-78.

turned to dealers in upland Aragon; Valencia seems to have been relatively poor in horses and mules.

When providing hospitality with a careful eye to the native customs of Valencian negotiators, James fed them mutton, chicken, and game. Learning that his supply train of 50 hogs for the Puig garrison was delayed at Tortosa, he bought from crusaders at Burriana enough "sheep, cows, and goats" raided from Muslims to last the little army "for a month." Muslim fugitives drove their "cows and other livestock" into their Moncada fortress in such numbers that eventually the stench of animals killed by artillery forced that stronghold's surrender. Similarly "all the Saracens from the villages, and the cows and asses and goats," had taken refuge within Cullera's walls, so that it "was filled up with people and livestock." At the siege of Burriana the crusaders at first grazed their sheep and animals too close to the walls, losing some to sallies from within. References of this kind could be multiplied; they not only clarify the extent and nature of stock raised in Islamic Valencia but show why the cattle tax became so important a revenue for the conquerors. Chickens were much in evidence, but hardly constituted a looter's prize; on a disappointing raid along "the banks of the Júcar" the king had to console himself with 60 prisoners, "a great deal of barley, and many fowls." At Peñíscola's surrender the Muslims fed the king's hungry party of seven knights, plus esquires and attendants, "a hundred loaves, two pitchers of wine, raisins, figs, and ten fowls."[47] In all, thirteenth-century evidence on Mudejar farms and stock anticipates the findings of a German traveler through Valencia in the eighteenth century; he reported "a superabundance of the productions of northern and southern climates which perhaps cannot be paralleled in any other country." He found three-fifths of the population in the south, supporting commerce, luxury crafts, the manufacture of fabrics, and most of the agriculture. In the north were stock, leather, hemp, distilleries, and the sort of livelihood which rugged labor could wrest from the soil.[48]

[47] *Llibre dels feyts*, chs. 156, 184, 187, 192, 194, 202, 215, 219-220, 250, and the meals cited below, p. 171.

[48] Fischer, *Picture of Valencia*, pp. 235-236. A fuller and more scientific exposition of eighteenth-century Valencia's products is Cavanilles, *Observaciones sobre Valencia.*

Slaves

The most fundamental social division, especially after the conquest, lay between slave and free man—the *sarracenus captivus* as against the *sarracenus liber* or *sarracenus alforre* (from *al-ḥurr*, freedman).[49] Slavery was an urban rather than rural phenomenon, though occasional helpers in the countryside may have been slaves. Mediterranean slavery differed widely from the image the term conveys to the modern mind. It was domestic or personal instead of agricultural or collective; the male slave was generally not a menial but a man of some status in a position of trust.[50] Like modern prisoners, slaves lacked a number of civil rights; unlike Roman or American slaves they retained human rights such as inseparability of family. They were not adult persons before the law, though responsible under it for serious crimes and protected by it in various ways; the Valencian *Furs* classified them as under domestic discipline like

[49] Robert Brunschvig, "'Abd," *EI*², I, 24-40. Editor, "Ḥurr," *ibid.*, III, 587-594. Franz Rosenthal, "Ḥurriyya," *ibid.*, III, 589. Dozy, *Glossaire*, pp. 52 (*ahorrar*), 287 (*horro*); see his *Supplément aux dictionnaires arabes*, 3d edn., 2 vols. (Leiden, 1967), I, 21. García de Valdeavellano, *Instituciones españolas*, pp. 356-358. The *sarracenus alforre* was sometimes also designated *liber; francus* simply means exempt from tax. *Captivus* corresponds to Arabic *asīr*, or in a more general way to *'abd.*

[50] Charles Verlinden's monumental *L'esclavage dans l'Europe médiévale* (Bruges, 1955) devotes to Spain and France the only volume to date. Furnishing excellent background, it is disappointing on thirteenth-century Valencia, doubtless owing to the paucity of materials. Still useful also as background are J. M. Ramos y Loscertales, *El cautiverio en la corona de Aragón durante los siglos xiii, xiv, y xv* (Zaragoza, 1915), and Miret, "La esclavitud en Cataluña en los ultimos tiempos de la edad media," pp. 1-109. Analogies with Majorca, though tempting and useful, should be handled with caution on this point; see Lourie, "Free Moslems in the Balearics," pp. 647-649. The distinction between the Moor *alfore* or *pacis* and the *captivus* runs through the Valencian documentation, as in the taxation on transported Moors in Valencia city's *Aureum opus* of privileges, and in the corresponding *Libro de privilegios* in the Alcira municipal archives; see, e.g., the document of March 10, 1249, published from the Alcira codex by Chabás in his *El archivo*, II (1887-1888), 400-403. See also *Fori*, duty lists of rub. CXLIV, nos. 4, 15; a Moor leaving by land or sea paid a besant, a Moor "de redemptione" paid 2½, and a Moor "de alfore qui exeat de regno" paid 2; apparently a Muslim brought in, and perhaps visiting Muslims, paid 4 pence. See also Goitein, *Mediterranean Society*, I, 130-147, and the thirteenth- and early fourteenth-century documents in Johannes Vincke, "Königtum und Sklaverei im aragonischen Staatenbund während des 14 Jahrhunderts," *Gesammelte Aufsätze zur Kulturgeschichte Spaniens*, XXV (1970), 19-112.

minors, women, and the mentally incompetent.[51] Technically they were not Mudejars, but those in Muslim employ formed part of Mudejar society, while those with Christian or Jewish masters shared many of Mudejarism's privileges and restrictions. Slaves not uncommonly worked out their freedom; Muslim alms ransomed others. Like free Christians, free Muslims often entered temporary debt-slavery to satisfy creditors or to acquire capital, but continued to pay the free Muslim's besant to the crown.

Muslim slaves were not uncommon in prosperous Christian households even of the artisan class; distinguished ecclesiastics, not excepting Bishop Arnold of Valencia in 1248, had their own.[52] Custom distinguished Muslim slaves on sale in Valencia as black or white. The practice probably derived less from color consciousness than from its usefulness in descriptive identification, though both Islamic and Christian society at the time did betray some color prejudice. Much later a brotherhood of converted black slaves formed at Valencia.[53] A typical sale of a Muslim slave during the postconquest years

[51] *Fori*, rub. LXXXIII, no. 9.

[52] Burns, *Crusader Valencia*, I, 22; for slaveholding bishops of James's realms, and for Canon Bertrand of Teruel's slave, see I, 35, II, 380.

[53] Miguel Gual Camarena, "Una cofradía de negros libertos en el siglo XV," *EEMCA*, V (1952), 457-463, a brotherhood "nacione nigrorum." See also the thirteenth-century Negro portraits in my illustrations, following p. 318. On the mixed attitudes of Muslims toward Negroes, see Bernard Lewis, "Raza y color en el Islam," *Al-Andalus*, XXXIII (1971), 1-51. Negro troops comprised the Islamic front lines in the international battle of Las Navas de Tolosa in 1212 (Desclot, *Crònica*, ch. 5). On Negro Moors see Verlinden, *L'esclavage*, 358-365, 530; Lévi-Provençal, *España musulmana*, V, 100; Cagigas, *Andalucía musulmana*, p. 42; G. E. von Grunebaum, *Medieval Islam: A Study in Cultural Orientation* (Chicago, 1947), pp. 209-211; and Goitein, *Mediterranean Society*, I, 131, 135, 137-139. Ibn 'Abdūn speaks of black slaves in his treatise, and of black soldiers (*Séville musulmane, le traité*, pp. 61, 62). By the next century at least, Negroes comprised the bulk of slaves in western Islam, according to Ibn Khaldūn. He takes pains to refute the idea, based on "misgivings" about the color black, that black skin marked descent from Ham, cursed by his father Noah; on the other hand, this otherwise enlightened sage insisted that "Negroes are in general characterized by levity, excitability, and great emotion . . . eager to dance whenever they hear a melody . . . [and] everywhere described as stupid." Like those Slavic peoples not Christianized, he concluded, the tribes beyond the Islamic Negro fringe "cannot be considered human beings" and make natural slaves, especially the Sudanese, captured and sold north by the more civilized Negro communities (*Muqaddimah*, I, 118-119, 169-170, 172-174, 301). At least by the end of our century and the beginning of the fourteenth, Europeans were receiving many Negro slaves (Verlinden, "L'esclavage en Sicile

took place at Valencia in 1283. The licensed broker Folchet had accepted from the Játiva resident Dominic Pérez, as security for a loan of fifty-five solidi, Dominic's "white slave woman, by name 'Ā'isha [Axa]," a transaction duly drawn by the Valencian notary James of Perpignan. To recover his loan, Folchet sold her for fifty-six solidi to the Jew Isaac (Açach), through another broker Ferrer and by a bill of sale drawn publicly according to Valencian laws regulating such transactions.[54]

King James did not think it strange to send presents of Muslim slaves from his victories to the pope, the cardinals, the Holy Roman emperor, the king of France, "and to counts and barons and friends of his own." He gave women slaves to the queen of France and to other noble ladies. Muntaner asserts that he disposed of two thousand captives in this fashion so that "the Holy Father and the cardinals and other powers of the Christian world were very joyous and content." Male and female Valencian slaves appear as customary booty in passages of the king's autobiography, as staples in lists of Valencian exports, and as an item of domestic commerce licensed and regulated by the crown. Valencian surrender treaties sometimes guaranteed that local Muslims might hide runaway slaves with impunity, indicating a natural and universal situation. This class of Valencian crops up in several contexts; converted slaves posed a special problem, for example, and the falling market in slaves brought on by postcrusade peace had repercussions on the Valencian economy and on relations between the two peoples.[55]

To what extent did Muslims own Muslim slaves? Christian documentation seldom concerned itself with such internal practices of the Mudejar community, but Valencian laws against Muslims owning either Christian or Jewish slaves suggest a larger context of slave-

---

sous Frédéric II d'Aragon [1296-1337]," *Homenaje a Vives,* I, 689). Perhaps this later influx among both Muslim and Christian helped identify Moor and dark color in the Spanish Christian mind, though in the thirteenth century the two peoples more usually looked alike.

[54] Roca Traver, "Vida mudéjar," doc. 14 (July 26, 1283): "una sarrahina blanca, per nom Axa." Goitein establishes the standard price for a slave girl at this time as twenty dinars, or lower if too young or inferior in quality (*Mediterranean Society,* I, 139). Isaac's name was Abengalell, perhaps Ben Hillel or Gilel.

[55] Muntaner, *Crònica,* ch. 13; he places the episode in 1266 but has Emperor Frederick II (d. 1250) as recipient. See the Játiva Charter's provision on runaways.

owning. Besides, slavery had been an integral part of Islamic Spanish society. Consequently the surrender pact of Chivert, in providing for emigration of any who might care to leave for Islamic lands, allowed a man to take along his family, livestock, wealth, and "slaves." Any decline in Mudejar landholding or commercial activity must have been reflected in this corresponding luxury of slaveholding; gradual shrinkage in the number of urban Moors undoubtedly had the same effect. Though slavery was a marked element among Christians in the realms of King James, it was not prominent as it was to become in the Renaissance; the best study of the subject concludes that "slaves are infinitely more numerous during the last two centuries of the Middle Ages than in the thirteenth."[56] Though Islamic Spain had been among the more active centers of the Islamic world's slave trade, information is scarce concerning Valencia's role; moreover, the recent decades of trouble had reduced the raids and victories over Christians that supplied the trade. King James lost many soldiers to slavery in Valencia, however, and made determined efforts to ransom them, a circumstance which suggests that slavery was as much a part of Valencia's Islamic and Mudejar social fabric as the ransomer orders were finding it in Granada and North Africa.

A final difference among Valencia's Mudejars, more administrative than social, distinguished free Muslims on royal lands from those on independently seignorial lands. Seignorial Moors may have been more numerous; they are certainly ill documented. To assert that "the large majority belonged to the nobility," however, is to project a later evolution backward into the postcrusade generation.[57] City Muslims, of course, like the cities themselves, mostly fell under the crown. In public matters, such as taxation or appointment of personnel, the crown archives tend to concern themselves with crown Muslims. Because they are easiest of access to the researcher, crown Mudejars tend to dominate the patterns of investigation; but pa-

[56] Verlinden, *L'esclavage,* p. 427. Piles Ros had believed slaves were forbidden to Mudejars, and consequently was surprised to encounter such cases; he gives a list of prices, of wide variation, for over a hundred fifteenth-century Moorish slaves on sale ("Moros de realengo en Valencia," pp. 246, 249).

[57] Grau Monserrat, "Mudéjares castellonenses," p. 256: "la inmensa mayoría." On the evolved, sixteenth-century situation, see Lapeyre, *Géographie de l'Espagne morisque,* pp. 26-27.

tience can uncover the essentials about their seignorial counterparts. All these divisions and distinctions sketch an ecology—the relationship of Mudejar groups among themselves and to their respective physical, economic, and social environments. The sketch remains preliminary and general, like the rough trail map which allows an explorer to penetrate some complicated wilderness. The greater task lies ahead.

THE JURIDICAL-RELIGIOUS MILIEU

CHAPTER VI

Surrender Terms: Universality and Pattern

THE ARMIES OF Aragon had marched south with two objectives in mind, to destroy Islamic Valencia as a political and military entity, and to reconstruct in its stead a Christian kingdom. Military necessity dictated a peculiar pattern of action designed to break the enemy's capacity to fight. This strategy in turn determined the later structure of political and personal relationships between victor and vanquished. The kingdom had fairly bristled with castles and towers, a checkerboard of fortifications to discourage the hardiest invader. There were "forty or fifty" major strongholds alone, scattered over a land "seven journeys long," each place designed to withstand long siege. The estimate comes from the baron Blasco of Alagón, who spent several years as a refugee at the court of Islamic Valencia just before the crusade and consequently "knows more about this than any man." Another contemporary, the Castilian historian and primate archbishop of Toledo Roderick Jiménez of Rada, tells of James acquiring "many" castles on the crusade, and explains that "the kingdom of Valencia was remarkable for multiplicity of defenses." A junior contemporary, the statesman Muntaner, added the total of castles or forts faced by King James's crusaders and was able to name three times the king's number; he located ten at one place, seven more in a small valley, and thirty in another cluster, while at Onda "there are as many castles as days in the year." Despite Muntaner's hyperbole, the defensive situation of the Islamic kingdom was obviously formidable. If taking key places was difficult, holding them by force in a hostile country was almost impossible. James had neither the financial resources nor willing garrisons. At the siege of Burriana the bishop of Lérida and the baron William of Cervera stressed this fact: "the king of Castile and you together could not hold Burriana."[1]

[1] *Llibre dels feyts*, chs. 128, 180. Desclot, *Crònica*, ch. 49. Muntaner, *Crònica*, ch. 9. Jiménez de Rada, *De rebus Hispaniae*, lib. VI, c. 5, p. 121: "regnum Valentiae, quod multis munitionibus praeeminebat."

King James consequently focused his strength against the key positions, forcing their surrender on terms. He bypassed the many defenses dependent upon such a point, trusting that problems of morale and supply would diminish the center's will to resist; meanwhile he subjected its countryside to a plague of unsettling raids. This general strategy, when carried to successful conclusion, resulted in a multiplicity of formal agreements as the outmaneuvered castles yielded conditionally. So brilliant and swift were the campaigns—despite intervening *longueurs* which drew the war out to a total of fifteen years—that it was adduced as "miraculous" in a seventeenth-century appeal for the king's canonization.[2]

Conditions and Concessions

Only a handful of these agreements survive in their original form, either from the crusade or from subsequent revolts. The earliest and most complete was drawn by the Templars, at King James's wish, for the castle and countryside of Chivert. The fall of Peñíscola had exposed this lesser castle. Since royal charters already allocated Chivert to the order, King James sent its knights to persuade surrender: there would be "no dishonor or shame" in the Muslims imitating their Peñíscola colleagues. The resultant instrument was signed at Chivert castle on April 28, 1234, in the name of the Templar master Raymond of Patot with his chapter; on the Muslim side the *faqīh*, a Koranic jurist or religious erudite named 'Abd Allāh, acted as spokesman with the ruling *qā'id* and fourteen of his local sheiks or notables. Apparently an Arabic original went to the Muslims, the Latin version being destined for the Templar archives.

The charter is precious also as representing a typical situation. Chivert was of middling importance, quite strong enough on its hilly perch to demand terms but not counting among the premier defenses of the realm; its fall was routine, occurring in the course of an unhurried general campaign. This compact spelled out in detail, therefore, concessions which might be expected by similar castles caught in equivalent situations. It recognized the local Islamic authorities and community, carefully naming their officials. It formally

[2] "Proyecto para la canonización de Don Jaime el Conquistador," in Tourtoulon, *Jaime I*, II, 414-415.

accepted the custom law as the basis upon which surrender rested. Above all, it changed nothing as to religion or social organization. It guaranteed houses, lands, and religious properties throughout the surrounding territory. It even waived a number of taxes—for example the fee on small sales or purchases, or on taking a wife or giving one to a nonresident. No one could suffer harm for past injuries to Christians, nor in the future for hiding Muslim fugitives. Legal problems likely to arise between Muslim and Christian were considered. Throughout the coming year natives might emigrate and fugitives return, each with property rights respected. All might cultivate whatever crops they chose.

An important concession was freedom from military duties against Christian or Muslim, except for defensive action in case of attack by Christian or Muslim upon the castle. Chivert Muslims got their own prison, butchery, free pasturage on wasteland, and the right to cut brush and branches for building or for other needs. Their tribute amounted to a sixth of the crops, plus a penny for each beehive or head of stock. A two-year interval of grace dispensed them from major taxes. The crusaders did requisition, without undue disturbance, a section of the town located at the castle's skirts; they compensated Muslims deprived of a house by this maneuver with abandoned houses of fugitives. Deprived fugitives in turn received the price of a new home if they returned within a year. The Christians obligated themselves to raise, without charge, a protective wall between the two peoples; no Christian or Jew could intrude beyond it. The terms were analogous to those awarded Christian communities by Muslim conquerors in similar circumstances. Schact traces their essential element—autonomous communal organization—to the Byzantine treatment of Jews, a model borrowed and generalized by the Muslims. Since the practice inherited by Mediterranean kings like James I probably owed as much to Islamic example as directly to the Byzantine, the problem of mutual causality in origins becomes complex.[3]

Another detailed treaty went to six districts centering upon Eslida,

[3] Arch. Nac. Madrid, Ords. militares, codex 542, Montesa (April 28, 1234), as copied by Manuel Ferrandis e Irles, "Carta puebla de Chivert," *Homenaje á Codera*, pp. 28-33, and recopied with slight differences as "Carta puebla de Xivert," "Colección de cartas pueblas," no. 76, *BSCC*, xxiv (1948), 226-230. *Llibre dels feyts*, ch. 185. Joseph Schact, "Droit byzantin et droit musulman," *Atti del convegno di scienze morali, storiche e filologiche* (Rome, 1957), pp. 205-206.

Ahín, Veo, Pelmes, Sueras, and Senquier, with their dependent villages and territories. The castles with their districts stood in the Sierra de Eslida, part of the Sierra de Espadán, later a favored place of refuge for rebel Muslims. Eslida itself ranged along a hillside amphitheatre, its small surrounding huerta blessed with natural springs. An eighteenth-century view reveals a diminished town of 170 inhabitants, its forty or more buildings clustering along the bottom slope of a conical hill. The ruins of a castle crown the top; carefully terraced, trimmed fields spread below and to the side of the town, in a countryside of steep hills. The 1242 treaty for the Eslida area and its neighboring castles restated a somewhat earlier agreement. It conceded full freedom of religion and assembly, together with retention of municipal organization and officials, laws and customs, houses and properties.

Again the formulas recur—"as was done in the time of the Saracens," or "according to their custom." Fields received water "according to immemorial custom"; flocks pastured freely "as was the custom in the time of the pagans"; children learned in school "according to their law"; culprits paid the fines dictated by "the law of the inhabitants"; the livestock tax fell "in the accustomed manner"; and a number of specified rents remained "what they used to be in the time of the pagans." The king assured safety to residents, promised not to allow Christians or Jews to dwell among them, allowed freedom of movement especially within their own districts, and guaranteed that fugitives might return and emigrants depart, both with property rights respected. All might sell or will properties, make valid contracts outside their own areas, and be free from a list of annoying feudal services.[4] Over thirty years later, a period of rebel-

[4] Eslida Charter, in "Colección de cartas pueblas," no. 63, *BSCC*, XVIII (1943), 159-160. It is also in *Colección diplomática*, doc. 241; Fernández y González, *Mudejares de Castilla*, appendix, doc. 17; Janer, *Moriscos de España*, doc. 15; and *Documentos inéditos de España*, XVIII, 55-58. The date must not be taken, as Escolano and the older historians took it, as the time of surrender; use of the perfect tense serves warning here. Senquier was given away by James in 1239 (*Repartimiento*, p. 370); the dependent village of Lauret was given as early as September 11, 1238; and Simon of Vallterra was rewarded in 1239 for having conquered the Sierra de Eslida (Honorio García, "El alcadiazgo de Eslida," *BSCC*, XVIII [1943], 163-164). The view of Eslida is by Cavanilles, *Observaciones*, II, 138.

lion having intervened, Prince Peter in June of 1276 negotiated a second settlement with Eslida. It reaffirmed property assurances, and carefully outlined freedom both of religion and teaching. The community retained its identity as well as a voice in choosing its Mudejar officials. Contracts were to be drawn according to Islamic law and by themselves. No one had to face legal action for his part in the rebellion. The community enjoyed the "special safeguard" of the prince. Exemption from several feudal dues, the usual freedom to emigrate, and a modest schedule of taxes completed the picture.[5]

In 1250 the Muslims of Uxó, north of Valencia city, received terms roughly the same as those of Chivert and Eslida. The Uxó valley and region comprised over a dozen villages with perhaps three thousand inhabitants. A strategic crossroads, it was defended by scattered towers and by a solid castle perched upon a peak. Its charter of 1250, relatively late, was not the special gift of "autonomy in gratitude for their loyalty" conjured up by some Valencian historians. It represented rather an administrative reorganization, confirming and reiterating original terms conceded by the crusaders some fifteen years before. The recent revolt of al-Azraq was reflected here in a siege of Uxó castle, possibly with King James himself penned inside.[6] When their cause went down in defeat, the rebel leaders fled, leaving their lands to be confiscated by the crown. The king's charter of 1250, severe against the activist faction, granted amnesty to the body of the populace; it spelled out anew the age-old customs under which local Moors had lived since the first surrender, referring back to "what is recounted in their old privileges" and to "what is recounted in the other privileges granted by us." King James makes it clear

[5] Arch. Crown, James I, Reg. Canc. 38, fol. 3v (June 27, 1276), referred to hereafter as the Second Eslida Charter.

[6] The transcription may be faulty; it reads either "e no foren assetjats" or "e no[s] foren assetjats." The first reading suggests a loyal faction of the social leadership penned in the castle, the second implies that James was inside. The king's memoirs say nothing on the point. The chronology of this period is unsatisfactory; Miret y Sans complains that he cannot relate it well to the events in the king's memoirs, but he loses sight of the king from March 10 to April 7, 1250 (*Itinerari*, pp. 201-203). Miret does not advert to the Uxó document. A standard popular text, by Frederic Moscardó Cervera, repeats the explanation "l'autonomia en regraciament a llur lleialtat"; see his *Breu compendi de la història del regne de València* (Valencia, 1953), p. 86.

that these "privilegis antichs" had been presented in a formal document—"the old charter, which is at this time in their hands."[7]

What is new about the 1250 instrument is not its content but its circumstantial framework. The Muslims turned over the castle; the king for his part renounced reprisals against the residents remaining; and the original charter was reissued formally. Even without the evidence of the 1250 charter with its repeated harking back to an original, King James's autobiography makes it clear that the Uxó region had surrendered on good terms during the crusade. These terms, as reproduced in the more detailed 1250 transaction, included freedom for religious teaching, retention of municipal and legal organization, a number of tax exemptions, a carefully stipulated set of dues, exclusion of Christian laws, and safety for merchants and emigrants. The charter defined Uxó's boundaries but decreed freedom to travel or buy anywhere outside their limits, "through all our land and jurisdiction to tend to all their affairs." This liberty of movement within James's realms and overseas to Islamic lands was a common concession, sometimes involving a small travel tax. The ease observable among Valencian Jews to remove or resettle, or to own property broadcast in the kingdom, appears also among Valencian Muslims; it reflects both the prosperity and the markedly commercial aspect of the population.[8]

Very similar to Uxó's charter was the agreement signed at Játiva on January 23 of 1251 or 1252. Here again a castle had previously delivered itself on terms to the crusaders. Játiva however was a mighty fortification, one of the strongest of the realm, and its dependent

[7] *Colección diplomática*, doc. 383 (Aug. 1250); also in Fernández y González, *Mudejares de Castilla*, appendix, doc. 23. Both the Catalan text and a Spanish translation are in *Documentos inéditos de España*, XVIII, 42-50. The pertinent phrases of 1250 are: "segons ques conte en los lurs privilegis antichs"; "segons ques conte in altre privilegi per nos a ells ortogat"; "segons que es contengut en la carta antiga, la cual de present es en la lur ma." Honorio García y García provides a sketch of the castle and a discussion of the defensive system in his *Notas para la historia de Vall de Uxó* (Vall de Uxó, 1962), p. 134.

[8] At Uxó, "pusquen anar per tota la terra et senyoria nostra a fer tots lurs afers, sens que nels sie vedat per alcuna persona"; the tax upon going abroad to Muslim lands was waived. At Játiva they were to go anywhere in the realm, untaxed. On similar movement by Jews see Abraham A. Neuman, *The Jews in Spain: Their Social, Political and Cultural Life During the Middle Ages*, 2 vols. (Philadelphia, 1942), I, 170. The original surrender of Uxó is described in *Llibre dels feyts*, chs. 249-251.

region formed a small principality. The involved story of its double surrender in 1240 and 1244, followed by conveyance to the crown in 1246 at the earliest, belongs to another context and will be taken up later. The four or five years' delay in its charter, renegotiated by reason of a transfer of fiefs, can be explained either by the general unrest of those years or as a consequence of Játiva's possible implication in the troubles. The charter is long and detailed. It treated the aljama as a political body, fifteen of its sheiks or eminent men receiving special mention. It confirmed the boundaries already arranged by the king's lieutenant, reserved a number of feudal revenues to the crown, defined the Islamic legal system with a few adjustments, and assured rights of property, commerce, sale, and purchase. A Muslim could hide fugitives with impunity. No official could forcibly enter a Muslim's home, nor any Christian take up residence without the community's consent. The king's protection covered everyone.[9]

The Knights Hospitaller drew up a pact providing similar conditions for the Mudejar community they imported under charter of safeguard from Silla, in the kingdom of Valencia, to Aldea just above its northern frontier. This incorporated Islamic customs and legal system, functionaries and communal organization, estates and slaves, pasture and passage for livestock, liberty of movement and of religion—all "according to the custom of the Saracens."[10] Peter of Castellnou granted another such document in 1260 to the Muslims in his lordship of Tales. Again the civil and much of the criminal law, along with the religion in which it was rooted, stayed intact, including the usual safeguards for Muslim defendants con-

[9] Miret y Sans dates the Játiva Charter January 23, 1252 (*Itinerari,* p. 219), departing from Fernández y González's 1251 date; the manuscript gives "Xative x calendas febroarii anno Domini MCCL primo." King James was in the kingdom of Valencia in January of both years. The charter is in Fernández y González, *Mudejares de Castilla,* appendix, doc. 24; *Colección diplomática,* doc. 412; *Documentos inéditos de España,* XVIII, 62; Janer, *Moriscos de España,* doc. 18. The assignment of properties in it had been made by Simon Pérez of Arenós as "tenens locum" of the king, an office he filled at various times from 1238 and actively held when Játiva fell in 1244 (*Itinerari,* pp. 137, 145, 167). On the sieges of Játiva and their dating problem, see below, Chapter XIV, section 3.

[10] "Carta puebla de Aldea" (Feb. 12, 1258), in "Colección de cartas pueblas," no. 60, *BSCC,* XVI (1935), 289-291: "secundum consuetudinem sarracenorum." For the safeguard, see *Colección diplomática,* doc. 766 (Feb. 19, 1258).

fronted by Christian plaintiffs. The Tales charter provided freedom of movement and residence in the area, arranged a schedule of fees and taxes, and absolved from past misdeeds any immigrants coming to settle. The motive and occasion for such a settlement charter differed radically from those behind documents of pacification. There is no indication here of previous rebellion or unrest.[11]

The seven treaties just examined fall regularly over a wide span of time: 1234, 1242, 1250, 1251, 1258, 1260, and 1276. In origin half of them are royal, deriving from James or Peter; one is seignorial; two come from military orders. Their circumstances are equally diverse; two are surrender pacts from the crusade, three are arrangements after the revolts of 1248 and 1275; two are settlement charters designed to attract Muslim immigration. The contents vary, but in each case the substance remains the same. This argues a customary or essential Mudejar pact, fitting all times and circumstances; variations according to the bargaining power of the aljama did not diminish the core concessions. Can this conclusion be sustained or must it remain, for lack of supporting evidence, an hypothesis?

Universality

Since few Valencian treaties survive fully in their original forms, the impression persists that they were seldom granted. The dramatic story of the capital city's fall can seduce even the careful scholar; surely the technique of conquest by surrender applied only to exceptional cases or was a maneuver confined to restricted areas? Some argue that King James expelled the Muslims from extensive districts, that he ejected them at least from the cities, that he seized the best lands so that Muslims were pushed back into the hills, or at least that he allowed them few and grudging concessions.

The seventeenth-century Muslim historian al-Maqqarī summed up the impression he received from Arabic sources: "not satisfied with the taking of Valencia city, the tyrant James prosecuted his conquests in those eastern districts, plundering and destroying whereever he went, and putting to the sword the unfortunate Muslims."[12]

[11] "Tales Charter," in "Colección de cartas pueblas," no. 84, *BSCC*, xxviii (1952), 437-438.

[12] Al-Maqqarī, *Mohammedan Dynasties*, ii, 235.

Modern Western historians tend to be equally unkind. Fernández y González, in his influential *Mudejares de Castilla*, contended that conciliatory pacts in Valencia were special exceptions; King James, despite his repugnance toward concessions to the Muslims, had "to conciliate and attach to his person the ill-tamed spirits of [some] warlike aljamas." Such groups consequently enjoyed a status different from that of most Valencian aljamas.[13] An authority as impressive as Menéndez Pidal berated James for his "spoliation" of the Muslims; in his celebrated *España del Cid*, even in its completely revised current edition, he contrasted the tolerance of the Cid's epoch to James's harshness. "Surrenders of spoliation" were to be "the norm which James I of Aragon and St. Ferdinand of Castile will follow in the thirteenth century"; the wretched Muslims of Valencia were allowed to survive only in rural areas and only because their Christian masters could not do without them.[14]

This remarkable misreading of James's policy is shared by Cagigas's widely read synthesis of current scholarship about the medieval Mudejars. He has the king impose harsh terms "on the poor, conquered Muslims" and exploit them mercilessly; driving them from their cities and fields, James dislocated the economy. In similar vein, Baer recently described how "in general the Muslims remained only in the country districts in a state of partial serfdom." Sobrequés Vidal has restated the thesis that crusaders drove the Muslims en masse from the north, the modern province of Castellón; this indeed seems to have become the received view. The elaborate statistical study of Morisco residence patterns recently published by Lapeyre likewise assumes that in the north "numerous localities were taken by storm" and their Muslims expelled; he cites as examples Albocá-

[13] Fernández y González, *Mudejares de Castilla*, pp. 264-265; see also Roca Traver, "Vida mudéjar," p. 179. Baltasar Rull Villar interprets the Eslida charter as extraordinary and an unusual lapse by King James which helps explain the later Morisco rising in the area; see his "La rebelión de los moriscos en la Sierra de Espadán y sus castillos," *ACCV*, xxi (1960), 62. The most devoted student of the Valencian *cartas pueblas*, Miguel Gual Camarena, can find no more than six Mudejar charters of the thirteenth century, with five others from the period 1316-1371 and five from the fifteenth and early sixteenth centuries ("Territorialidad de los fueros de Valencia," passim).

[14] Ramón Menéndez Pidal, *España del Cid*, i, 524 and n.; "la norma que respecto a las grandes ciudades reconquistadas seguirán, en el siglo xiii, Jaime I de Aragón y Fernando el Santo de Castilla"; "capitulaciones de despojo."

cer, Borriol, Benlloch, Cabanes, Cuevas de Vinromá, Salsadella, Serratella, Tírig, Villafamés and Villanueva de Alcolea. Authors like Grau Monserrat and Lloréns y Raga incorporate this thesis.[15]

The question is central to the whole subsequent history of Valencia. How far did the policy of liberal surrender extend? Was it widespread or for practical purposes universal, or was it limited in area or in scope? Did James begrudge concessions, so that Chivert was a shining exception? The answer can issue only from a mosaic of small evidences, multiplied even at cost of appearing to belabor the point. The detailed charter of Chivert, at first sight isolated, can in fact be projected so as to understand the surrender terms at least of its immediate neighbors. King James in his memoirs gives only passing reference to Chivert's surrender, while boasting of mighty Peñíscola's submission. He rode headlong through the night and exposed his person to death or capture in order to negotiate for Peñíscola. As desirable as it was impregnable, the great citadel *a fortiori* received terms at least equivalent to those given a lesser place like Chivert. When James sums the Peñíscola pact as simply granting the laws and liberties enjoyed under Islamic rule therefore, it is obvious he is abbreviating a treaty as broad as any of those surviving in detail.

A fair number of castles fell at the same time and under similar effortless circumstances. The king names Alcalatén, Ares, Borriol,

[15] Cagigas, *Mudejares*, I, 144, and II, 369, 395; James and Ferdinand "imponen a los pobres vencidos musulmanes capitulaciones de despojo"; "la dureza con los vencidos era síntoma de la época"; "Don Jaime llegó a concebir el extraño proyecto de lanzar fuera de España los moros que se habían quedado bajo la fe de los tratados. . . . Fatigábalos constantemente con nuevos impuestos desproporcionados, los vigilaba y celaba con medidas imprudentes," until they revolted. Baer, *Jews in Christian Spain*, I, 140. Sobrequés, "Patriciado urbano," pp. 30-31; see also Bayerri, *Historia de Tortosa*, VII, 202, 205. Lapeyre, *Géographie de l'Espagne morisque*, pp. 27-28. Grau Monserrat, "Mudéjares castellonenses," pp. 255-257, with some borrowing from Font y Rius; the Christians took by force Alcira, Gandía, Morella, Murviedro, Orihuela, Segorbe, and some lesser places, as well as Burriana and Valencia cities, the Muslims being left largely in the unirrigated uplands. The author allows for surrender prevailing in the center and south, but even here his opposing theses of removal and acceptance clash. Peregrín Lloréns y Raga, "Los sarracenos de la Sierra de Eslida y Vall d'Uxó a fines del siglo XV," *BSCC*, XLIII (1967), 56-57, where the thirteenth-century charters of special privilege excluded Christians and conferred a unique autonomy, "like independent cantons," which explains their subsequent turbulent history.

Castellón de Burriana, Cuevas de Vinromá, Cervera, Culla, Pulpis, and Villafamés as typical of "all those which would have to surrender" after Burriana's fall, because "they live on supplies from the Burriana plain." Chivert and Peñíscola were in this list; it is reasonable to conclude that the others, as well as their unspecified but multiple fellows, enjoyed the same liberal terms. The castle of Cervera certainly did, since its surrender was treated by James almost as a single action with that of Chivert and was preceded by parallel negotiations. To read the Chivert document, the sole remaining accord for this time and area, in the light of James's narrative—when Chivert was but one of a number of important, interrelated defenses—is to extend the area to which its main conditions are applicable.[16]

King James has casually recorded a number of surrenders. At the first agreement with Uxó, and again at those with Nules and Castro, "I granted them their law [religion] and their liberties, just as in their own time they used to have them from the Saracens." This included the stipulation "that they keep their law and all their customs as they used to do in the time of the Saracens, and that they give service faithfully as they had done to their king." Terms secured by the great castle of Almenara were no less advantageous—as is evident from the gratitude with which its people received the king, from his careful respect for their religious sensibilities during the bargaining, and from the circumstance that it was the key point whose surrender induced all three of the castles just mentioned to sue for peace. As for the castles of Paterna, Bétera, and Bulla, "I would respect their law and all their customs which they had in the time of the Saracens, and I would do them much good."

Silla, south of Valencia city, yielded after a bare week's siege; though the terms are unknown, no exodus ensued. Since the king's autobiography reports it as a routine surrender, routine terms may be supposed. "So great a castle" as Bairén was handed over reluctantly; after long preliminaries the Muslims "drew up their documents with me, according to the demands I had made on them, and I granted these insofar as they were reasonable, and a few things more, that I could enter into so good a place as that was." The episode in turn led to the submission of dependent castles in the Alfan-

16 *Llibre dels feyts*, chs. 130, 184-186; he includes Morella, which in the event may have followed an eccentric pattern. Chivert Charter.

dech and Bairén valleys. James was determined to have great Játiva at almost any price. Its capitulation allowed the defenders to retain for two years the largest citadel, and permanently to hold two flanking castles. Since the king had twice failed to reduce the place by siege and had allowed the greater concession of keeping the defenses, he certainly gave the usual privileges. This conclusion is further supported by a reading of the charter presented much later, after the revolt, in 1251. King Peter either confirmed or added to the Játiva charter shortly after his accession.[17]

At Alcira the Muslim governor fled and the citizens offered to deliver the city; actually the semi-independent ruler here resembled his counterpart at Játiva, so Alcira's fall involved a large entity comprising many towns. The surrender of a castle or town involved the area around it, and this could be extensive; Alcira and Játiva were very large regions, as were Denia, Cullera, and the bloc ceded by Zayyān from Valencia city down to the Júcar River. King James described the surrender of the Alcira region. "And they made a treaty with me by which they would stay in Alcira with those laws and customs [*furs e custumes*] which prevailed in Almohad times . . . and that every Saracen slave who might come to Alcira be free and I could not seize him, or any man for me." The last item went beyond the right of asylum accorded in surrender or settlement pacts. At Chivert and Játiva, for example, the local people could hide fugitive slaves without fear of punishment, and Christian searchers could not investigate a suspected asylum unless accompanied by a Muslim. At Alcira, however, as at Serra and Polop, the town air made the slave a freedman, who could thereafter travel the realm without hindrance. The conditions agreed upon at Alcira's surrender, which are syncopated in the king's book, "pleased me greatly." With some reluctance the Muslims allowed part of Alcira town to be walled off and set aside for Christians. A few years later, when the Muslims sued because immigrant Christians were encroaching on their privileges, they won their case by presenting to the crown this treaty (*instrumentum*).

[17] *Llibre dels feyts*, chs. 243, 244, 249-250, 254, 263, 314, 353. Arch. Crown, Peter III, Reg. Canc. 41, fol. 101 (July 3, 1279) warns the Játiva bailiff and justiciar not to harass the Muslims "contra tenorem instrumentorum a domino Iacobo etc. et a nobis eis concessorum"; Peter might have granted privileges as prince, but more plausibly he is here speaking as king.

At Biar too, after a long siege, James "kept the Saracens in the town," granting them his protection and all their religious customs. After that, when the disheartened remnant of the Islamic kingdom "saw that I had Játiva and Biar, they surrendered to me all the rest of the kingdom remaining, from the Júcar up to the land of Murcia, on the understanding which I had with them that I would keep them in the kingdom; and so I had everything." The equivalent phrase, "being left in the country," had been used to summarize the conditions required for the surrender of Alcira. The context, and the nature of the Alcira conditions, leaves little doubt that this whole area below the Júcar retained its organization and Islamic customs intact.[18]

As James penetrated into Murcia the whole pattern can be observed again—at Elche, Villena, and Murcia city where the Muslims gave up part of their fortifications, keeping property, religion, law, customs, and political framework. Below Murcia, in the stretch of territory less than thirty-six miles in length to Lorca, James accepted upon like conditions the surrender of twenty-eight castles, almost a castle per mile. These he mentions casually as he is leaving the subject of the Murcian crusade. Torres Fontes, in his excellent analysis of the Murcian campaign, rebukes James for betraying his promises to the Murcians and then shamefacedly concealing it in his autobiography. This interpretation rests upon a flat rejection of one out of two remaining sources, with full acceptance of the other; but allowing a margin of error to either of the post-factum commentators lends support rather to the account of King James. The later complaints of Murcia's Mudejars to Alfonso of Castile, of hoodlumism on the part of Christian immigrants, do not support the modern allegations against James.[19]

[18] *Llibre dels feyts*, chs. 330-332, 359-360. On asylum and freedom see also Gual, "Mudéjares valencianos," p. 171.

[19] Torres Fontes, *Reconquista de Murcia*, pp. 164-165, 178, 180-181. Desclot describes an expulsion, and wrote close to the events; his chapter 65 was done between early 1283 and early 1284. The Arabic tradition has the Murcians leave for Arrixaca suburb by the treaty terms, where they remained for ten years until expelled in 1284 or 1285. Allowing for inexactitude in both traditions, it is reasonable to believe James in reporting the Mudejars as removed to Arrixaca but maintained in the usual privileges, and later (1276, if a full ten years are granted, less if the span be taken loosely) partially expelled during the subsequent troubles. This means Desclot carelessly telescoped an event only seven to ten years old, placing it

The Alcalá Valley, stronghold of al-Azraq, yielded in an atmosphere so amicable, and presumably privileged, that King James sealed negotiations with an expensive gift.[20] James does not bother to record many other surrenders. Speaking of Altura, for instance, he qualifies it only in passing: "which they had surrendered to me."[21] The surrender of "a tower on the borders of the kingdom of Valencia" was the subject of at least two documents to his knights, yet the royal autobiography does not mention it. This is in keeping with his literary principle: "since this book is such that one ought not to put trivial things in it, I refrain from telling many things that happened and wish to tell only the more important, that the book may not be much lengthened."[22]

Random evidences nonetheless accumulate, constantly expanding the known number of aljamas with full Mudejar privileges. From later materials, for example, it is obvious that the Chulilla Muslims had preserved their community existence from the beginning, with the public worship which marked surrender on terms. This situation appears in a protest of 1340 by the bishop of Valencia; James had early given Chulilla to the diocese, and in view of the first bishop's opposition to public worship in Mudejar towns it is improbable that the privilege had been introduced meanwhile. The aljama does turn

back ten years further in 1266; knowing how strangely medieval authors juggled the concept of expulsion, it seems probable that the Murcian expulsion was both exaggerated and misdated by nearly a decade, an infelicity rendered easier by its being in reality a minor episode to contemporaries.

20 Arch. Crown, James I, Reg. Canc. 10, fol. 106v (Jan. 4, 1259) where James has contracted a debt of 300 solidi for a horse given as gift; the surrender was part of the revolt, so the manuscript year 1259 must be following the Florentine incarnational calendar. The place appears in *Llibre dels feyts*, chs. 371, 376; other areas discussed are in chs. 411-412, 416-421, 437, 440, 453.

21 *Llibre dels feyts*, ch. 317; the "Hoytura qu•ens haviens renduda," identified by Ramona Violant in the recent critical edition as a nonexistent "Oitura," may be Altura castle near Segorbe; Artana castle, where James drew up the surrender documents for nearby Eslida, does not fit the context.

22 *Ibid.*, ch. 270. Arch. Crown, James I, Reg. Canc. 10, fol. 61 (April 28, 1258): "quod si sarraceni vobis reddant turrem de Massa——s [*hole in MS*] que est in finibus regni Valencie vel vos ipsam ab eis . . . potuerit recuperare, quod vos eam cum terminis et pertinentiis suis habeatis et teneatis"; if the king "forte" receives it, he promises "omnino" to give it to the two men named. The document, which is a standard grant-cum-invitation to acquire by initiative, repeats an earlier grant and merely envisions surrender to these entrepreneurs as a probable alternative.

up in early documents, though with no details as to worship or privilege.[23] A similar tradition is in evidence at Cuart in 1279. Islamic political organization, religion, schools, property, and law had persisted. The document may represent late concessions but more probably reaffirms an early pact.[24]

An important but neglected evidence is the charter awarded to the valley of Alfandech de Marignén. A hilly area between Cullera and Gandía, Alfandech commanded the Júcar River passage along its north and the coastal road to Gandía along its east. It brought the huerta of Valencia to an abrupt halt, diverting the lower flatlands like a river inland and south past Alcira toward Játiva. As part of an interlocking chain of hill country it lent itself to guerrilla harassment. The crown introduced Christian settlement early but not too successfully; the eight major places of the valley were able to make do with a single church as late as 1298. Near the end of the century the valley's continuing wild state recommended it to the king as suitable for locating a contemplative Cistercian monastery, Valldigna. Yet Alfandech was well populated with Muslims, so that its aljama bore a large tax assessment in 1258, for example. Perhaps to help tame the area, King James included its *terminus* in 1249 within the wider regional *terminus* of Alcira city. As with so many surrender charters, that of Alfandech has been lost. The Moors here nevertheless did receive elaborate surrender privileges. The episode is recorded only in a complicated document from the turn of the century; in it James II reported on a charter of Peter III, which restored to the Mudejars after a rebellion the original conditions granted them by James I. The foundations of Islamic religious, political, and economic life were spelled out, much as in the Chivert charter. This reaffirmation included such details as holy books, mosque properties, and the right to bear arms anywhere in the realm —all "extensively contained in the present privilege."[25]

23 Arch. Cat., perg. 2,450 (Feb. 8, 1340). Arch. Crown, Peter III, Reg. Canc. 38, fol. 69v (Oct. 26, 1276), a protective charter confirming their accustomed status: "ad habitandum cum uxoribus et filiis vestris . . . salvi et securi sub fide et guidatico nostro cum omnibus bonis . . . que . . . consuevistis . . . possidere."

24 Arch. Crown, Peter III, Reg. Canc. 44, fol. 149v (July 16, 1279).

25 José Toledo Girau, *El monasterio de Valldigna, contribución al estudio de su historia durante el gobierno de sus abades perpetuos* (Valencia, 1944), pp. 11-12; and his *El castell i la vall d'Alfandech de Marinyèn des de sa reconquesta per Jaume I,*

Montesa castle had pacts and privileges too, as did Orcheta. Each place enters crown documentation only because it broke its part of the bargain.[26] Without this tardy documentation of 1277, Montesa's status would still be known through the chronicler Desclot's description of its surrender, when King James "leaves them there."[27] The Ayelo Moors were likewise granted the "law or Sunna of Montesa," at least as far as services and dues were concerned: Rafelbuñol apparently kept full privileges.[28] Among later statements of privilege is the 1277 surrender treaty for Serra.[29]

King James in his memoirs reveals a number of other charters. An example of those now lost was the "charter made for the Saracens" by which the districts of Tárbena, Algar, and Callosa were divided, each of the two parts falling under its own *qā'id*.[30] Another lost treaty was James's document regulating the status and revenues of the Mogente Muslims; they recalled it to King Peter's attention in 1279.[31] Both charters may have resulted from the first revolts, though nothing indicates this. A postrevolt charter, now lost, was the "peaceful settlement" by which al-Azraq got the villages around the castle of Altea; James cited this pact in a subsequent donation of 1258.[32] Nor was Eslida the only castle in its immediate neighborhood to win terms from the crown. In 1276, just after the death of King James, further negotiations in the Sierra de Eslida were under way. King Peter designated the commander of the Temple at Burriana to be his representative.[33]

fins la fundació del monestir de Valldigna per Jaume II (Castellón de la Plana, 1936), pp. 71-72; the document of April 15, 1277, from Arch. Reino Val., and of April 1, 1298, from Arch. Crown, Reg. Canc. 196, fols. 164 and 195v, given in translation, is hereafter cited as Alfandech Charter. On Alfandech, its 1257 tax, and the Valldigna foundation, see my *Crusader Valencia*, I, 61, 68, 82, 160, 223-224, 244.

[26] Arch. Crown, Peter III, Reg. Canc. 39, fol. 219v (July 3, 1277), on Montesa; fol. 172v (March 9, 1276-1277), on Orcheta.

[27] Desclot, *Crònica*, ch. 49: "e lleixa·ls estar."

[28] Arch. Crown, James I, Reg. Canc. 37, fol. 52v (Oct. 18, 1272): "ad forum sive çunam sarracenorum Muntesie." Peter III, Reg. Canc. 44, fol. 185 (July 15, 1280) has these customs of "Raffalbuynol" already in possession.

[29] *Ibid.*, Peter III, Reg. Canc. 39, fol. 162 (Feb. 15, 1277).

[30] *Ibid.*, James I, Reg. Canc. 13, fol. 188v (June 17, 1264): "carta sarracenis facta."

[31] *Ibid.*, Peter III, Reg. Canc. 42, fol. 163 (Nov. 3, 1279).

[32] *Ibid.*, James I, Reg. Canc. 9, fol. 59v (July 30, 1258): "pacem et composicionem."

[33] *Ibid.*, Peter III, Reg. Canc. 39, fol. 135 (Dec. 29, 1276).

Any number of places in the early records betray their privileged status by possession of a separate Sunna-based legal system, which implied the full complement of surrender privileges. Under this heading come areas like Alcalá, Cocentaina, Confrides, Gallinera, Guadalest, Penáguila, Planes, Polop, and Tárbena.[34] Muslim immigrants who answered the Christian call for settlers after the crusade kept the same privileges—for example those moving to Alaguar, Alcalá, Callosa, Castell, Confrides, Denia, Guadalest, Pop, Sagra, Tibi, and other places listed in a record of 1279.[35] Cocentaina appears as an organized political entity in a 1264 classification of jurisdiction over criminal cases. The tenor of the letter argues a previous pact, especially since a similar letter in almost the same words follows it in the registers, destined for Játiva, which did have such an understanding.[36]

Upstream from Valencia city, not on the Guadalaviar proper but on the banks of a feeder stream joining it from the north, lay a heart-shaped region called Chelva. It may have belonged to James's ally Abū Zayd throughout the crusade or have been recovered by Abū Zayd's forces, since the ex-Muslim soon awarded ecclesiastical rights there to the diocese of Segorbe by virtue of his *ius patronatus*.[37] Abū Zayd did the same with Uxó, however, and it is more likely that Chelva, like Uxó, surrendered upon terms to the king. Defended naturally by hilly environs, Chelva was vulnerable to forces operating up the Guadalaviar Valley. When the siege of Valencia isolated it on the downstream side, Chelva still commanded resources enough to demand a fair surrender. This was the pattern by which places like Uxó, Almenara, and Alfandech fell, and it fits the circumstances most plausibly.

Chelva appears some twenty years later as an aljama in its own right, troublesome to its neighbors and ambitious in local jurisdictional claims, with a crown castellan in charge of its defenses. It joined the revolt of 1275, apparently with enthusiasm. By early 1276 King Peter had notified Alfonso X of Castile that Chelva had sur-

[34] *Ibid.*, James I, Reg. Canc. 19, fol. 18 (June 14, 1273).

[35] *Ibid.*, Peter III, Reg. Canc. 44, fol. 160 (Nov. 14, 1279).

[36] *Ibid.*, James I, Reg. Canc. 13, fol. 236 (Nov. 6, 1264), two documents, where they appear as fully organized. The "ravallum sarracenorum Cocentanie" appears in an earlier land grant (Reg. Canc. 11, fol. 193 [Feb. 13, 1260]).

[37] Burns, *Crusader Valencia*, 1, 47, 52-53.

rendered. It received terms, as appears from a letter of Peter to his Valencian officials in 1279: "When we recovered Chelva it was sworn and agreed between us and the Saracens who were there that any Saracens wishing to cross over into Saracen lands could cross over with all their goods, safe and secure." At that late date still, "many of the aforesaid Saracens want to cross over," so the king ordered his officials to "desist from impeding and forbidding" the passage.[38] The bulk of the Muslims remained, a community of the Chelva River; they reappear in documentation as seignorial Mudejars under the lord of Jérica about 1350, their basic privileges intact, as an elaborate confirmation of 1370 demonstrates.[39]

During the times of trouble, when James was actively expelling Muslim rebels, he allowed them also to remain awhile with all their antecedent "customs." Though he took their castles, he permitted temporary possession of property. The letter describing this organized, privileged status was meant to cover quite generally "each and every Saracen town, castle, and place of any kind in the kingdom of Valencia which will surrender" to Prince Peter. This tends to confirm a wide extent for the basic state of being privileged, even though no details are revealed.[40] Muntaner, who as a youngster in his native Valencia had seen the elderly King James, has provided a descriptive catalogue of over eighty places conquered during the course of the crusade. The memoirist insists several times that his listing is partial, containing only important places. A half dozen of them are valleys; most represent some small region in addition to

[38] Arch. Crown, Peter III, Reg. Canc. 11, fol. 219v (1261?); Reg. Canc. 13, fol. 204v (1264); Reg. Canc. 39, fol. 151v (Jan. 24, 1276). Reg. Canc. 41, fol. 106 (July 12, 1279): "quando nos recuperavimus Chelvam fuit condictum et conventum inter nos et sarracenos qui ibi erant quod quicumque sarracenorum vellint transfretare ad partes sarracenorum possunt transfretare cum omnibus rebus eorum salve et secure"; "quod plures ex predictis sarracenis volunt transfretare quibus vos impeditis transitum supradictum et recessum de Chelva . . . dicimus vobis quatenus ab impedimento et contradiccione huiusmodi desistatis."

[39] The charter of Aug. 17, 1370, referring to privileges long held, is published in the *Documentos inéditos para la historia de España,* XVIII, 69-74, and in Fernández y González, *Mudejares de Castilla,* appendix, doc. 71.

[40] Arch. Crown, James I, Reg. Canc. 22, fol. 44r, v (June 26, 1276): "consuetudines quas habebant et sub quibus vivebant ante presentem guerram motam." They remained in "domibus suis propriis et tendis ac laborare suas hereditates"; it applies to "omnes et singulos sarracenos villarum et castrorum et locorum quorumlibet regni Valencie qui se vobis reddiderint."

its walled town or castle. Discussing points taken in the Valencian huerta and to its south, Muntaner inserts the general comment: "and so he made truces with many Saracen leaders that were in the said kingdom," each truce area surrendering under "a fixed annual tribute." Many places mentioned by Muntaner coincide with privileged areas already seen in this chapter; it is reasonable to assume that the remainder, except for the mixed list at the end briefly summarizing the whole crusade, also enjoyed terms. This conclusion alone makes the surrender status nearly universal.[41]

King James himself boasted of the universality of the Mudejar status in a speech of 1266, under circumstances which add weight to his words. He was besieging Murcia, capital city of the Islamic region just south of the crusader kingdom of Valencia. Hoping to persuade the Murcians to surrender, he reminded them how he had treated their northern neighbors in Valencia over the past three decades. "They knew very well that many Saracens lived in my country," he said; "my dynasty had kept them of old in Aragon and in Catalonia, and I in the kingdom of Majorca and of Valencia." All enjoyed the same status. "All kept their law just as well as if they were in the country of the Saracens; these were come at my mercy and had surrendered to me." All others, "who did not want to surrender, I had taken by force and had settled [their land] with Christians." King James assured his Muslim auditors: "I did not wish their death or destruction, but wished that they should live for all time." He desired them to keep "their mosques [and] their law, just as they had undertaken in their first treaties." Here the king speaks plainly. He allows for violent exceptions such as Valencia city, Burriana, and Majorca, and for the punitive expulsions after revolt; but he makes it clear that these represented undesired irregularities and that the numerous Valencian Muslims stayed on under a general, privileged rule.[42] Even in alienating a region's money or property rights to Christians, James preserved the immemorial life style of its resident Muslims. His successor King Peter, when granting the usual privileges in 1277 to Muslims he wished to attract as settlers, appealed like his father to a general policy—"all the liberties and Saracen

[41] *Crònica*, ch. 9: "e axi ab molts barons sarrahins que havia en lo dit regne ell feu treues."

[42] *Llibre dels feyts*, ch. 437.

customs which the Saracens have been accustomed to have in the kingdom of Valencia."[43] The same idea of a generalized Sunna for the Moors of the realm of Valencia recurs in a document of 1280. Peter's records in fact deal with a general situation in Valencia inaugurated by King James. His own surrender documents after the last Valencian revolt reiterate the theme of universality. He absolved the defeated rebels of Torres Torres, promising them in perpetuity that "you are free" and that "we will preserve you in your laws and customs as we preserved our other Saracens of the kingdom of Valencia, and we will also respect that charter which you hold on tax-exemption for a certain time, which the lord our father confirmed to you as is contained in the said confirmation."[44]

Peter required the Muslims of the Murviedro area in 1280 to comply with a feudal labor service, "just as is usual among the other Saracens of the kingdom of Valencia regarding such things"—thus assuming at this level a general status common to all.[45] A directive of 1279 to the castles and towns of Valencia reminded officials that the Muslim rebels had recently surrendered under treaties which included the familiar right to emigrate. "Since by the pacts and terms, under which the Saracens have remained in the kingdom of Valencia, all those Saracens who wish to cross the sea may do so," officials were to offer no hindrance.[46] Indirect confirmation also comes from the tithe documentation. One of the first tithe records, in 1240, classifying Mudejar properties as exempt, defined such lands as "subject to you under terms, as long as they remain this way."[47] As late as

[43] Arch. Crown, James I, Reg. Canc. 12, fol. 147v (Nov. 29, 1263), a lease of rights in Castellón, Calpe, and Játiva, "servantibus sarracenis eorum açunam prout tempore sarracenorum eisdem servabantur." *Ibid.*, Peter III, Reg. Canc. 40, fol. 74 (March 16, 1277-1278): "omnes franquitates et consuetudines sarracenicas quas sarraceni habere consueverunt in regno Valentie." This is an explanation of his term used immediately before, "ad Çunam sarracenorum."

[44] *Ibid.*, Reg. Canc. 48, fol. 20v (May 13, 1280); Reg. 39, fol. 151v (Jan. 24, 1277): "tenebimus vos in foris et consuetudinibus sicut tenebamus alios sarracenos nostros regni Valencie."

[45] *Ibid.*, Reg. Canc. 48, fol. 19 (May 12, 1280): "prout consuetum est circa aliis sarracenis regni Valencie super similibus."

[46] *Ibid.*, Reg. Canc. 41, fol. 106v (July 12, 1279): "cum secundum pacta et conditiones sub quibus sarraceni remanserunt in regno Valencie possint omnes ex ipsis sarracenis qui transfretare voluerint, in omnibus ut superius." This last has reference to a document of the same day for the Moors of Chelva (fol. 106).

[47] Arch. Cat., perg. 1,304 (an. 1240): "que sunt vobis cum conditione subiecta dum tali modo permaneant."

1314, very few Muslims were subject to tithes even by the reckoning of the Valencia bishop; yet any land which lost its immediate title to a Christian, however briefly, paid tithes thereafter.[48] In its small and indirect way the 1240 document confirms the impression of a general status retained from the beginning.

Further indications of common status turn up from time to time. James permitted Sa'd b. Ya'lā (Çaat Abeniali) at Pego in 1272 to dispose of his property as the "other Saracens of the same valley are allowed to do with their farms," noting that this obliged him to render the same taxes they gave.[49] Another instance of this appropriation of individual to group occurs in a grant of land at Benifayró in 1267, to be held under the same conditions as those observed by the other Muslims of the Alfandech Valley.[50] Peter referred to the surrender pacts of King James again when reinterpreting one of the most vital Mudejar privileges, the possession of their own laws and courts together with immunity from the ordinary courts of the realm; he described "a certain privilege which the lord James of happy memory, my father, conceded to all the Saracens of his realm" of Valencia.[51]

Conclusion

The evidence direct or indirect—by open statement, inference, implication, general color, or extrapolation—converges. King James faced two alternatives for his Muslim opponents. On the one hand he could expel or individually enslave them according to the laws of war, where feasible; or else he could permanently guarantee their religious, political, and legal survival as a self-contained community within the feudal framework of his Christian state. This held equally for north or south, and for lands which had been on either side of the precrusade civil war in Valencia. It was the same for surrender pacts and for settlement documents, for crown or for seignorial

[48] *Ibid.*, perg. 2,397 (July 28, 1314).

[49] Arch. Crown, James I, Reg. Canc. 37, fol. 48 (June 25, 1272), giving this right "sicut alii sarraceni eiusdem vallis possint facere de hereditatibus suis."

[50] *Ibid.*, Reg. Canc. 17, fol. 101v (March 2, 1267).

[51] *Ibid.*, Peter III, Reg. Canc. 50, fol. 124 (July 14, 1281): "pretextu cuiusdam privilegii quod dominus Iacobus felicis recordationis . . . concessit sarracenis omnibus regni sui [Valencie]."

grants, at the start, the middle, and the end of the conquest and reorganization. In short, it was a reflex automatic policy.

Whenever an organized aljama is encountered, therefore, a contract of the type already noted—whether oral, presumed, or formal—must be predicated. In the light of James's statement to the Murcians, the same must be assumed wherever Muslims can be found owning land, their status being assimilated to that of the nearest Mudejar community. A certain number of communities had acted as allies under Abū Zayd from the start; their privileges and guarantees could hardly have been inferior to those of the defeated enemy. Contemporary lists of aljamas, consequently, whatever their occasion, may be used to reconstruct the pattern of privileged status. Tax lists, even after allowance has been made for exempt places and for inclusion of rural into larger entities, show such communities to have been numerous. One catalogue, for Mudejar mintage tax in 1272, included some fifty places.[52] Charters of security and protection add other localities. A list of 1278 seems to represent a group of aljamas paying the new king for confirmation of privileges held formally by "documents from our chancellery."[53] The important centers of Mudejar semiautonomy can be estimated, therefore, not only by counting treaties for which evidence of any kind survives, but also in a number of indirect ways.

The same result can come from plotting the areas which probably surrendered. With proper reservations and a margin of error, James's victories might serve as a key; it is unlikely that fortified places capable of real resistance, and which did resist until overwhelmed, went unchronicled in the proud warrior's memoirs. If there really were half a hundred important castles forming the backbone of Valencian resistance, then almost all of them preserved the privileges and life style of their respective regions. An important methodological principle ultimately emerges. Any pact or fragmentary notice of a pact from the half-century crusade era can be used to reconstruct or to illumine the basic status common to Valencian Mudejar communities.

[52] *Ibid.*, James I, Reg. Canc. 18, fols. 94v-95 (Dec. 1, 1272).

[53] *Ibid.*, Peter III, Reg. Canc. 22, fols. 107v-108 (Sept. 25, 1278): "racione cartarum . . . de scribania nostra."

CHAPTER VII

Burriana, Valencia, and the Townsmen

TWO STRIKING deviations from this pattern of transition into Mudejarism were the cities of Burriana and Valencia. The same sad scenes transpired there as Castilian contemporaries witnessed at Cordova and Seville. Even so, compromise prevailed rather than ruthlessness. More important to the theme at issue, Valencia city and Burriana were not the kind of exceptions duplicated elsewhere during the Valencian crusade. Some historians do argue a wholesale subjection of northerly towns, especially Morella, but their conjectures cannot sustain close examination. Valencia and Burriana remain unique. Far from rendering the Mudejar norm dubious, they indicate how unusual was the set of circumstances required to justify such an aberration.

EXCEPTIONS: BURRIANA AND VALENCIA

At both cities King James saw an unusually valuable prize within reach. Of no other place except princely Játiva did he feel so strongly as about these two cities. Yet he preferred negotiated expulsion to storming and enslavement. At Burriana he apprehended "at the fall of the town a great wrangling between Catalans and Aragonese and many peoples from abroad"; at Valencia he feared that "if the town were taken by force, it would be difficult to avoid serious wrangling between factions of the army." Should uncontrolled factionalism prevail, James would be the loser. If the king feared chaos as his army dissolved during a sack, the barons equally shrank from a negotiated peace, rightly perceiving in peaceful conquests an augmentation of royal power to the consequent diminution of their own. At both Burriana and Valencia the king was determined to fight to the finish; at the same time, fears and hopes threatened this clear purpose.

Burriana, though no great capital like Valencia and Játiva, offered a special case. Al-Ḥimyarī had described it merely as an important city of Spain, "beautiful, well-populated, fertile, and with fruit trees and vines," master of the surrounding region. King James saw it as much more. He meant it to become the fulcrum for his conquest of the realm; with its fall would come all "those castles which are at the back of Valencia." Personal motives compounded strategic necessity. The king's pride rebelled against the "great shame to me" of having his crusade marred at its outset by failure. "The affairs I have begun I have pushed to a successful conclusion," he rebuked his reluctant barons; "I am within the kingdom of Valencia for the first time that I have ever entered here." Though the barons were counseling prudent withdrawal, "know for sure that I will not do so." On another day he told them: "This is the first place in the kingdom of Valencia that I have besieged, and retreat from here I certainly will not." After having conquered the Balearics, "an overseas kingdom," was he to be humiliated by "so inconsequential" a place, "no bigger than a corral"? He would "rather be struck by an arrow, provided that it was not fatal."

Though the king could raise an unpromising siege at places like Cullera without such torments of soul, at Burriana he meant to pay almost any price in order to avoid the appearance of defeat. "And believe me truly, twice I exposed my whole body so that those inside might wound me in order that, if I had to lift the siege, I could say I lifted it because of the blow I had sustained." His desperate need for victory did not exclude but rather counseled compromise. The shorter the siege, and the more orderly the conquest, the better were his prospects for the subsequent campaign. "Considering the outlay made here every day," he dared not extend the siege longer than absolutely necessary; and he coveted for his needy frontier garrisons the wheat harvest lately stored within the city. The besieged on their part realized the necessity of resisting precisely at this key place; they drew support from the expectation of help from the whole kingdom at their back; and they observed the deteriorating strength and morale of James's army. Thus the Muslims carried the fight to a point of no return, while the Christian ruler, anxious and impatient, lacked enough force to seize the city immediately. The stage was set for the classic compromise—negotiated expulsion.

A situation not dissimilar existed at the siege of Valencia city. Seriously wounded on the head, the king had been nervous lest some mischance rob him at this eleventh hour of a conquest he had dreamed upon since childhood. He was at odds with his barons and therefore anxious for a speedy, controlled conclusion. This was the culminating moment of his military career; he knew that "having won Valencia city I had won the whole kingdom." Accepting the queen's advice, that "if a man could have Valencia city he ought not to gamble with it from one day to the next," and cannily aware that among the knights "there were many whom it did not please that Valencia city be taken, who would prefer that it belong to the Saracens rather than come into my power," King James initiated secret negotiations with the Muslim king. His barons "lost color as if someone had stabbed them to the heart," when he openly announced the surrender thus slyly arranged; "not one gave praise, or thanked God for it, or took it well." As for the Muslims, their field reserves were scattered, their relief fleet from Tunis driven off, and their supplies running low.[1]

In addition to Burriana and Valencia cities, can the seizure of Morella in northwestern Valencia at the beginning of the crusade be adduced as a further example of assault and expulsion? Despite surface plausibility for the assumption, the most recent student of the northern campaign, Gual Camarena, rejects it.[2] The transfer of Morella seems rather to have been a completely negotiated affair. The point has remained moot, and recently Grau Monserrat, misled by Lapeyre, has again championed the thesis of violent subjection; his inability to find Mudejars in the local documentation for the second half of the century reinforces his conviction. A Mudejar community does appear subsequent to the crusade however; its disappearance seems to relate rather to the local expulsions following the earliest revolts.[3] Torres Fontes has raised the question of Murcia

[1] *Llibre dels feyts*, chs. 130, 164, 167, 169, 174, 178, 271, 278, 281, 292, 350; the Burriana terms are in chs. 177-178. Al-Ḥimyarī, *Kitāb ar-rawḍ al-miʿṭār*, pp. 95, 361.

[2] Gual Camarena, "Reconquista de la zona castellonense," p. 433.

[3] Grau Monserrat, "Mudéjares castellonenses," p. 255 and passim; aware of the document, he missed its significance. See it above in Chapter III, n. 20, with its long-time residents and the community's "cavaçala." The rhythm of Morella's Christian growth tends to confirm the suspicion of continuing Mudejar revolts there; see the careful account by Matías Pallarés Gil, "Don Blasco de Alagón, señor

as a similar exception, but on grounds not really convincing.[4] Among arguments in support of a thesis of violent expulsion, particularly dubious is the principle that confiscation and reassignment of properties—in other words a division or *repartimiento* of enemy lands—always denotes physical conquest. Many parcels of land belonging to refugees were available throughout the kingdom, their disposition falling naturally to the crown; elsewhere James amicably arranged, as at Chivert and Játiva, that special parts of town be vacated for Christian occupation. Resistance or rebellion was sometimes involved, but each area requires study on its own merits without intervening assumptions.

At Burriana and Valencia the Muslims let resistance go too far, until they could no longer command any form of terms. Yet circumstances so pressed the king that he was willing to settle for considerably less than the objective military situation offered. In the event, most townsmen at both places emigrated, though apparently some remained to form a Mudejar quarter in each. Villagers and rural farmers also seem to have stayed. These two episodes had been displays neither of brute force or tolerance, nor was either surrender typical.

Situating the Townsmen

Were the Muslims everywhere summarily required to evacuate the towns and take up rural residence? Menéndez Pidal has given this view wide currency, insisting that the city dwellers were exiled throughout the Valencian kingdom. He admits only that they remained in the countryside and in unimportant towns. This deliberate policy of James's he contrasts with the more liberal Mudejar system in the early twelfth century at Tudela, Zaragoza, and Tortosa. His view coincides with the opinion of Chabás, the distinguished Valencian archivist, that the crusaders systematically ex-

de Morella," *Congrés I*, 1, 219-231, including the 1233 arrangement for 500 settlers in town and countryside, the 1249 assumption of authority by the king, subsequent acceleration of development of the Christian city (50 shops provided, with a market in 1257, for example), and the tradition that Blasco was absent from the siege of Valencia city because he was busy subduing local rebels even as early as 1237-1238.

[4] See Chapter VI, n. 19.

pelled the enemy from the "cities and towns," suffering them to stay only in villages. Rull Villar has the Muslims thrust out, except for the rare case of a surrender treaty consigning them to an inner ghetto. Gual Camarena distinguishes the process as stemming from subsequent change of policy; the revolts forced King James away from his "benign and tolerant" practice, so that "gradually" the town Muslims were pushed into ghetto quarters.

Lapeyre, summing up current scholarly opinion on the question, states flatly: "In the cities, even if they surrendered to the conquerors, Muslims had to evacuate the area within the walls, though they could establish themselves in suburbs." In short, the Muslims were put into ghettos in accordance with the immemorial custom of both Muslims and Christians when dealing with an alien minority. The Mudejars lived at best much as Christians had lived in cities like Islamic Denia. These conclusions derive from the more basic thesis that, in the Valencian crusade, liberal terms were uncommon. With the overthrow of the basic thesis, this corollary might be dismissed; since it touches a fundamental of this book, however, it merits closer attention.[5]

There is no reason for believing that townsmen lost the universal surrender privilege of remaining where they were. An appearance of extrusion might arise, of course, from the very structure of larger Hispano-Islamic cities.[6] These centered on a nucleus called the medina, a kind of forum for religious, business, political, and social life, enveloped by any number of residential quarters. The quarter often amounted to a semiautonomous neighborhood, a mini-city with its lesser mosques, local baths, and necessary shops and services. No distinction was made between a street, a quarter, or a

[5] Menéndez Pidal, *España del Cid*, I, 524-525. Roque Chabás, "La carta puebla de Sueca y el P. Ribelles," *El archivo*, II (1887), 205-208: "ciudades y villas" as against "alquerías." Rull Villar, "Rebelión de los moriscos," p. 62. Gual Camarena, "Mudéjares valencianos en la época del Magnánimo," pp. 469-470. Lapeyre, *Géographie de l'Espagne morisque*, p. 27: "même si elles se livraient aux conquérants, les Musulmans devaient evacuer la zone comprise à l'interieur des murailles, mais ils pouvaient s'établir dans les faubourgs." See also Roca Traver, "Vida mudéjar," p. 131.

[6] See esp. Leopoldo Torres Balbás, "Estructura de las ciudades hispanomusulmanas: la medina, los arrabales y los barrios," *Al-Andalus*, XVIII (1953), 149-177; his "Aspectos de las ciudades hispanomusulmanas," *RIEEIM*, II (1954), esp. pp. 91-92; and above, Chapter IV, section 3.

closely adjacent suburb—each was, in all but size or accidentals of status, the honorable equivalent of the others. Any might seal itself off at night by heavy gates at the street entrances. If it stood just outside the massive city defenses, the suburb's walls usually connected with the main circle; the free-standing suburb which did not connect had a special name—not *ar-rabaḍ* (the Spanish *arrabal*) but *al-ḥāḍir*.[7] The populace, though unified to some extent by the common downtown medina, jealously grouped themselves away from all the other sectors, according to such norms as occupation, ethnic or geographic origin, shadings of religious belief, or factional persuasion. This peculiarity of Islamic cities may explain why Alfonso X, in theorizing about the very different European city, troubled to include under that designation all the interior segments plus the suburbs beyond the walls.[8] This phenomenon of fragmentation within the Islamic city reproduced itself on a lesser scale in secondary cities and small towns. Christians and Jews under Islam had their own quarters; in the same way, conquered Muslims expected and even demanded sectors of the city for their neighborhoods whenever an influx of Christian settlers took place.

The word *morería* consequently need not conjure up for this early date a picture of ghetto life but rather of parallel and independent communities continuing a familiar pattern. Nor should *morería* suggest a mean neighborhood enclaved in a hostile majority of Christians; it might be anything from a whole town or sizable segment of it to a street or an external or semi-internal suburb. One cannot assume, as Chabás does, for example, that the mere wording "ravallum Sarracenorum" at Cocentaina or Alcira denoted an outlying suburb and indicated dispossession. Just as the crown could establish a fully independent aljama for eight houses, so it could designate as a *morería* or *ravallum* the larger part of a town.[9] Even

[7] On *ar-rabaḍ*, translated by thirteenth-century Christians here as parish (*parochia*), see *Vocabulista in arabico*, p. 511, and Neuvonen, *Arabismos del español*, pp. 116-117; for the wider Islamic world, see Lapidus on the various names for a quarter (*Middle Eastern Cities*, pp. 63-64).

[8] *Las siete partidas*, ed. Gregorio López, 7 vols. in 3 (Salamanca, 1565), part. VI, tit. XXXIII, no. 6.

[9] Véronne, "La population musulmane de Valence," pp. 424-426. Rafael Esteban Abad, *Estudio histórico-político sobre la ciudad y comunidad de Daroca* (Teruel, 1959), pp. 215n., 217n. on the eight-house aljama decreed at (non-Valencian) Ba-

in the sixteenth century, after the Muslims had been thoroughly subordinated, a list of *morerías* gives Chiva 200 Muslim houses as against 26 Christian houses, and Turís 80 to 20; Segorbe, with a Christian majority of 261, contained a *morería* of 116 houses.[10] Muslims in Valencian towns seem at first to have kept a considerable part of the walled area. Far from being extruded, they shared the city with the Christian conquerors. The Muslim-controlled area, whether the whole city or a part, could nevertheless be called a *morería*. Though there were almost no Christians in 1270 at Alfandech, there was a "Saracen *morería*."[11] In places of mixed population, where one people did not grossly predominate, Muslims lived indiscriminately cheek by jowl with Christians, and their farms lay contiguous.[12]

In a few strategic centers the conquerors had to weigh the problem of security. Even at such places the Muslims seem to have kept their residence within the walls, at least at first. At Murcia city, after Aragon's definitive conquest of its kingdom, King James wrote into his charter of 1266 the unequivocal assurance that "I had to keep them in Murcia." Subsequently his barons complained that the Christian segment of the city "was so small that the Saracens could drive out" the Christian body after the army had gone. James then proposed to move the Islamic center into the suburb called the Rexaca, or Arrixaca, a booming adjunct which had served the growing Christian population during the twenty years since Castile acquired garrison control. James took care to support his action with the observation that, according to law, "the suburbs of a town were [in] the town." He also contended that the suburb in question "was a section [*barri*] of the city." The Muslims resisted these legalisms, stood firm against the scholastic Dominicans and experts whom James summoned to the fray, and finally yielded only to the threat of force.

---

guena by James II in 1296. The "ravallum sarracenorum Cocentanie" of 1260 is in Arch. Crown, James I, Reg. Canc. 11, fol. 193, dated more accurately by Miret as February 13 of the following year (*Itinerari*, p. 311).

10 "Sección de documentos," *El archivo*, IV (1890), doc. 70, pp. 373-388; description of 1567-1572, by Moorish quarters.

11 Arch. Crown, James I, Reg. Canc. 35, fol. 56v (March 19, 1270): "sarracenorum morerie."

12 Macho Ortega, "Mudéjares aragoneses," pp. 152-153; Halperín Donghi, "Recouvrements: Valence," pp. 157-159.

Even so, these Muslims in their "suburb" still lived hard by the neighboring Christians, too close indeed for comfort. King James arranged a protective wall; a property contract in February of 1266 describes "the wall recently built between the Christians and the Saracens," close to the cathedral and to two public roads. A similar contract describes a street in "the Christian part" going toward the wall, implying a psychological identity of Muslim and Christian "parts" within one town.[13] A few months later, despite their annoyance at King James's high-handed action, the Murcian aljama petitioned for greater separation; Alfonso allowed them to concentrate all Murcia's Muslims in Arrixaca, "because it is a separate place," and to throw up an excluding wall as well as to seal off present entrances, ejecting all Christians, in order to diminish the "dislike and discord" between the two peoples.[14] The exact relationship between these two walls is not directly pertinent; Torres Fontes has King James's wall, which separated Christians on the east and Muslims on the west within the mixed suburb, demolished and replaced by Alfonso's, which divided Arrixaca from the rest of the city.[15] It is not clear that Christian settlers could immediately have taken over the city in numbers; the suburb probably became the legal center for Mudejars, with final physical separation only effected by Alfonso, as his charter implies, so that James's wall may have attempted only a preliminary looser division.[16]

[13] *Llibre dels feyts*, chs. 446, 447. *Itinerari*, p. 383 (contracts of February 20 and 25, 1266): "et cum muro inter christianos et sarracenos de novo facto"; "in parte christianorum"; the date of eleventh kalends of March 1265 is 1266 in the modern calendar.

[14] Fernández y González, *Mudejares de Castilla*, appendix, doc. 46 (June 5, 1266).

[15] *Reconquista de Murcia*, pp. 68, 75-77.

[16] Since James's barons protested at the Christians having so small a section of town, the Arrixaca decision could hardly have altered the population balance immediately, especially if there were no drastic expulsion; on the other hand, Alfonso's charter of June 1266 reveals Muslims sharing the main city and Christians sharing the suburb, and orders each group to withdraw to its own side of a "muro nuevo" to be built, sealing off Arrixaca as wholly Mudejar. James may have meant the first wall as provisional, or partial. Muntaner's narrative has the Muslims keep half the city, then petition to retreat into Arrixaca suburb, but immediately after the conquest of the 1240's. A clue may come from Zaragoza's surrender in 1118, recognized by the Muslims as beneficent, where the conquered could remain within the city a year before moving just outside (Lacarra, "Repoblación de Zaragoza," p. 209); perhaps Murcia's Muslims, residing within town under a deadline, petitioned for earlier full withdrawal to Arrixaca.

The affair of Murcia's two walls underlines the attachment of the Muslims to their cities. In commenting on the fall of Valencia city they had displayed a strong sense of place as a dimension of self, to be surrendered finally as a despairing necessity. The quarrel at Murcia indicates that removal from the central part of the city, or beyond the walls, would have been resisted throughout the conquered regions. From the Christian viewpoint, too, emptying a town even partially made no sense except for those rare places which could count on a swift influx of Christians. In the greater part of the new realm Christian settlers were sparse even toward the end of James's life, and they seem to have concentrated in a few centers; there is no reason to think that Muslims elsewhere were living just outside of vacated, empty towns.

Some Town *Morerías*

At Valencia city the aljama may have been a new growth or a reconstituted entity; at any rate it represented an exception in its placement and evolution. King James might well have left this body within the walls, as his contemporaries were doing after the conquest of Seville.[17] As at Murcia, however, he preferred to have it just beyond the walls, though technically and legally within the city. A grant in 1245 located a public oven as "extra muros in moreria." This "Saracen street" or quarter (*vicus sarracenorum*) appears in the records from the start, with grants to friendly or useful Muslims. The captains of Aragon's ally Abū Zayd seem to have been represented there, along with civilian collaborators. One land-grant notation for Valencia city may refer to a group of these people: "twenty-seven Saracen [families] remain." Many others probably lived in the *morería* houses owned by Christians.[18] King James had reason to encourage former residents to remain—water-control experts, irrigation mechanics, skilled workmen, craftsmen, merchants useful for the continuance of the port's economy, specialists in the

[17] The position of the Moorish quarter in contemporary Seville is shown by Julio González in his *Repartimiento de Sevilla*, I, map facing p. 358. Though both high- and low-born Moors were expelled from the city (p. 308), a small group either remained or were immediately introduced (pp. 364-365).

[18] *Repartimiento de Valencia*, pp. 319, 568, 632; "remanent sarraceni xxvii." See also Véronne (34 householders) in "Population musulmane," p. 424.

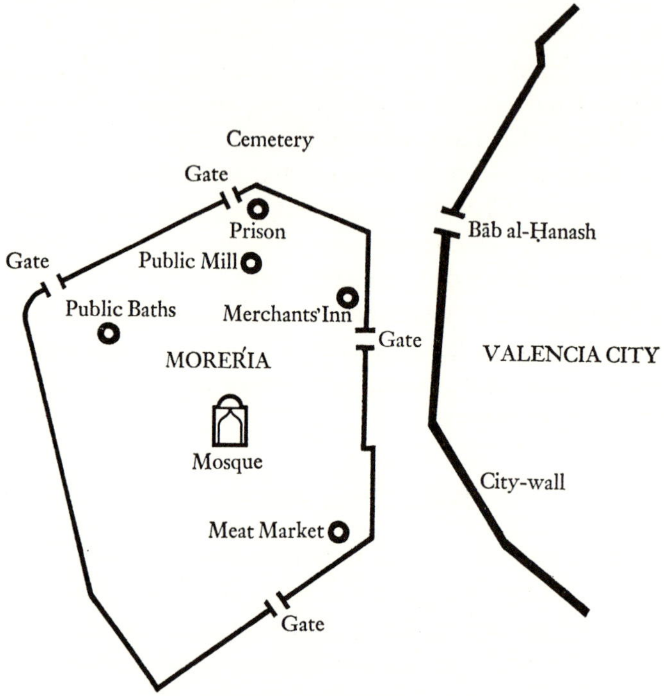

The Moorish Quarter of Crusader Valencia
outside the City's West Wall

local law, and the like. The full population of villages and farms around the city stayed in their houses under crown protection by the terms of surrender, though Christian masters assumed ownership and rents; some of these people, as was the custom, may have preferred to take up residence in the Valencia suburb. Whoever the inhabitants of the Moorish quarter may have been, they acquired during the initial division of conquered properties "a building for a mosque."[19]

[19] See Chapter IX, n. 69 and text. Retention of Muslims in the huerta still left a great deal of land free for personal settlement—as distinguished from grants entailing personal residence but already settled by tenant farmers or vassals. The inhabitants of the city who left their houses behind also abandoned the extra-mural estates, farms, and pleasure gardens commonly held by such citizens; Leopoldo Torres Balbás, "Los contornos de las ciudades hispanomusulmanas," *Al-Andalus*, xv (1950), 438; pp. 463-466 directly treats of Valencia.

A decade after Valencia city's surrender a bill of sale located a butcher's stall "near the gate of the *morería* of the Saracens at Roteros of Valencia."[20] In 1256 the crown leased the taxes on public ovens of the Moorish quarter to a revenue farmer.[21] Two years later the king allowed John of Borgia to build an oven "in the *morería* of Valencia," and licensed a debtor to recover 13,500 solidi from the quarter's crown rents.[22] Despite the mass emigration of 1238, then, a community persisted within the conquered city, and was enjoying a privileged, prosperous existence two decades later. It appears again in a routine tax document of 1263 along with "the new Jewry."[23] Five years later, in 1268, King James "conceded to you the aljama of Saracens of Valencia" the privilege of doing business as usual in their shops on most of the Christian feast days.[24] Toward the end of James's reign Valencia city's Christians attacked the aljama; shortly afterwards his successor King Peter confirmed to the "ravallum Valencie" the usual "Sunna and all those customs under which you were living there before the assault."[25] That these continuing customs and religious laws were not a grudging expedient but a legally established formality appears in 1290 when Peter's son referred back to the concession while renewing it.[26]

The capital's Moorish quarter lay adjacent to the western or left wall of the city, a good deal below the northwest gate, Bāb al-Qan-

[20] *Colección diplomática*, doc. 362 (Sept. 13, 1249): "prope portam morerie sarracenorum de Roteros de Valencia."

[21] *Itinerari*, p. 253 (Aug. 11, 1256).

[22] Arch. Crown, James I, Reg. Canc. 10, fol. 59 (April 8, 1258); fol. 58v (April 28, 1258). A grant of July 1 mentions the community's *qāḍī*, "tibi Çahat Avinjafia alcadio sarracenorum Valencie" (fol. 83v).

[23] *Ibid.*, Reg. Canc. 14, fol. 12v (Feb. 28, 1262 [for 1263]): "tintureria[,] moreria[,] judaria nova"; both the Martínez-Ferrando *Catálogo* (1, no. 435) and the *Itinerari* (p. 334) misunderstood *moreria* as an adjective, yielding only a Muslim's shop.

[24] *Ibid.*, Reg. Canc. 15, fol. 80v (Feb. 23, 1267 [for 1268]): "concedimus vobis aliame sarracenorum Valencie."

[25] *Ibid.*, Peter III, Reg. Canc. 40, fol. 69v (Feb. 16, 1277): "eam çunam et omnes eas consuetudines sub quibus ibi vivebant . . . ante barrigium." The sack was in 1275.

[26] Roca Traver, "Vida mudéjar," doc. 25 (Alfonso III): "confirmamus . . . sunnam vestram et consuetudines prout dictus rex, pater noster, eas vobis concessit . . . [et] continet." José Rodrigo y Pertegás has studied the capital's Moorish quarter closely in his "La morería de Valencia, ensayo de descripción topográficohistórica de la misma," pp. 229-251.

ṭara, and just outside the central Bāb al-Ḥanash exit. It lay immediately southeast of what became the red-light district, and far from the Jewry, which occupied a southeastern portion inside the city. Eventually both the prostitutes' quarter and the Jewry were to exceed the Moorish quarter in size. Its mosques, merchants' shelter, meat market, grinding mill, ovens, prison, and baths can all be located in relation to a modern map; in the present-day city, as the traveler moves east beyond the Botanical Gardens along the street of Cuart, entering the older city by passing under the imposing towers of Cuart (the fifteenth-century gate in the outer or fourteenth-century wall), the *morería* site appears along his left, roughly within the streets Cuart-Alta-Corona.[27] Exception though Valencia city's conquest may have been, its remaining Moors had obviously been assimilated to the general Mudejar status, either immediately or shortly after its fall. Its inhabitants had to be content with an adjoined suburb, but it is difficult to construe this circumstance as hardship or undue isolation.

Valencia and Burriana were special cases. Did towns which managed a more normal surrender extrude the *morería*? Alcira was a notable and strategic city, key defense of the Júcar River line. There if anywhere one could expect surrender terms to include abandonment of the walled town. Alcira's Muslims remained inside, however, and held the lion's share, so that only a section of wall and the alcazar or citadel came into Christian hands.[28] At what pace did Christian settlement gradually counterbalance Muslim presence in Alcira? Chabás, whose opinions always merit respect, believed that by 1279 the Muslims had been thrust outside the town. This was thirty-six years after the surrender, and subsequent to at least three Valencian rebellions, so it is not in itself an unreasonable conjecture; unfortunately it rests upon a reference to the ambiguous "moreria

[27] Manuel Danvila Collado, "Saco de la morería de Valencia," pp. 124-129. He puts it roughly on the site between the San Miguel plaza (Mayor de la Morería), Corona (dels Tints Mayors), Cuarte (Camí de Quart), and the Huerta de Tirador (de los Pelayres). The new city walls of Peter IV in 1354 enclosed the *morería* while leaving it within its own inner walls; the latter were breached, and the old gate destroyed too in 1401, thus effectively uniting the *morería* with the Christian part of the city. See also Teixidor's discussion of the Alcántara gate in *Antigüedades de Valencia*, I, 21-22, and Menéndez Pidal, *España del Cid*, I, 448, 470, 492.

[28] *Llibre dels feyts*, chs. 329-331.

sive ravallum"—that is, to the sector wherever it was and whatever its size.[29] There is no evidence in this phrase to suggest that the Muslims had been ejected, or that the situation was different at Alcira than in other major Valencian towns with large Christian communities. For what it is worth, a tradition among the Augustinian friars has them locate a priory at Alcira in 1274 because of its unusually large Mudejar quarter.[30]

At Chivert two areas, apparently comprising most of the town proper except for a section quite close to the castle, went to the Muslims in perpetuity.[31] At Villena, a subject for discussion on the last day of negotiations was "how I would divide the town"; the king's partition "pleased them much, and I set a day by which they would have evacuated that part." At Biar, a strategic place, "I kept the Saracens in the town and drew up the treaties [guaranteeing] their Sunna."[32] As late as 1258 James can be seen appointing Mudejar authorities here for farming taxes due from resident Christians, an incident which hardly suggests a Christian community of any size.[33]

At Segorbe, seat of the abortive diocese of that name, Christians were at first very few in number and had to be content with worshiping in a commandeered house. The ringing of church bells, a practice exceedingly irritating to pious Muslim ears, raised a tumult in the town in 1245 during which the Christians were roughly handled. The incident reveals that the Muslims lived within the town and were far superior in numbers.[34] As decades passed, the growing Christian community may progressively have dispossessed the Muslims, or rather confined them more straitly within a section of Segorbe. By 1265 the Christians had already taken over the Mude-

[29] "Sección de documentos," *El archivo*, II (1887-1888), p. 271; see also his "El libro de las ordenanzas municipales de Alcira," *ibid.*, VII (1893), p. 314, on the Moorish quarter later, off the island.

[30] Arch. Mun., Pedro Sucías MS, "Los conventos del reino de Valencia," 3 vols. (1906), III, 31 (1274). On the house, see Burns, *Crusader Valencia*, I, 211, II, 474.

[31] Chivert Charter.

[32] *Llibre dels feyts*, chs. 359, 442.

[33] Arch. Crown, James I, Reg. Canc. 10, fol. 103v (June 16, 1258): "tam a christianis quam a sarracenis."

[34] Francisco de Asís Aguilar y Serrat, from manuscript by J. B. Pérez (1537-1597), *Noticias de Segorbe y de su obispado*, 2 vols. (Segorbe, 1890), I, 83. *Viage literario*, III, 45 and n. For the date see my *Crusader Valencia*, II, 393.

jar marketplace.[35] By at least 1275 the Muslims were established either just outside the main walls or else inside but as a distinct sector; in the "wall of the town of Segorbe" was a town portal, flanked by two towers and a barbican, "which leads toward the Moorish quarter of that town."[36]

At important Murviedro, on the other hand, mid-century property deeds can still refer to the Christian "suburb"[37] or quarter and even to "Murviedro, in the [part of] town of the Christians." Muslims may therefore have predominated and must have been within the city. In all towns the Christian population grew very slowly. Many places had no Christians or else none to speak of. At Carlet in 1241 the bishop compromised with the local lord over future tithes "if the said stronghold [town] ever chances to be populated by Christians."[38] The records not infrequently place Muslims "in" a town—though such language can prove ambiguous; thus Muḥammad b. Muḥammad b. Zabr (Mahomet Abemahomet Abenzabro) was allowed to erect buildings "in our town of Chella," with an added gift of land "in its countryside."[39] Evidence of a more diffuse nature is also at hand. King James describes a general situation in his memoirs, when speaking of his anxiety at the time of al-Azraq's rebellion; if African help ever came, he feared that "the communities [*pobles*] of Saracens of each one of the towns" would revolt and capture many Valencian alcazars. Worried because of the king's concern, "the Saracens of some notable places" like Játiva sent envoys to him; soon afterwards local rebellions broke out. The king's fear of losing cities by internal rebellion suggests a situation in which Muslims outnumbered Christians in many of them. His high indig-

[35] *Itinerari*, pp. 378 (Sept. 23, 1265), 380 (Oct. 26, 1265).

[36] Arch. Crown, James I, Reg. Canc. 20, fol. 307; *Itinerari*, pp. 526-527 (Dec. 19, 1275): to Peter of Palau a gift of "illas ii turres que sunt in muro ville de Segorbio supra illud portale ville predicte quo itur versus morariam ville eiusdem et barbacanam eciam eiusdem muri contiguam."

[37] Arch. Crown, James I, Reg. Canc. 9, fol. 28; *Itinerari*, p. 274 (May 1, 1258): "in ravali Muriveteris"; "quoddam cimiterium quod habemus apud castrum Muriveteris in villa christianorum."

[38] Arch. Cat., perg. 2,341 (Feb. 7, 1241): "si unquam contigerit predictum castrum popularetur de christianis."

[39] Arch. Crown, James I, Reg. Canc. 16, fol. 208 (July 26, 1270): "in villa nostra de Xielsa"; "in termino eiusdem." The manuscript seems to read "Xielsa"; my identification of this unknown town as Chella is conjectural, assuming a miscopy or ambiguously shaped s for l.

nation over the rebellions can be better understood, therefore, since he "had kept them" there, allowing them "to live in plenty with me and with my dynasty," and "did not drive them from their homes [*alberchs*]."[40]

This balance did shift with every increase of Christian immigration and with each successive expulsion of Muslims. The Christian growth of an area as reflected in the land-division documents may be a partial index to the process; but here a mere change of title, an unclaimed grant, or repeated references to a single property can mislead. If the Muslims of some towns are later found only in outlying or isolated pockets, and if their removal must be postulated this early, the change may have taken place as a result of the several rebellions, a convenient pretext and urgent motive for imposing this condition upon certain places. Since the Muslims were not really driven out en masse on the occasion of al-Azraq's first rebellion, the choice of exile or of more easily supervised external quarters may help explain what James meant by "expulsion." Townsmen being more mobile, with portable skills, they undoubtedly responded to the lure of emigration more readily than could the farmer. They also bore the brunt of the oppressive Christian presence, ever more so as Christian settlement to the larger towns increased. Those remaining probably withdrew from the urban agglomerations, preferring smaller places in the countryside where they could enjoy their own life style with greater psychological freedom.[41] The process may have advanced far by the end of King James's life. Certainly the anti-Muslim riots in the last year of James's reign indicate—at least for a number of towns—a somewhat diminished Muslim population, in an awkward posture for defense. The problem of withdrawal and expulsion is too complicated to be included in this book; but

[40] *Llibre dels feyts*, chs. 364, 366, 368. Did the Alcoy Christians receive a privilege in 1256 not to have a *morería* in any town of the *terminus*? The assertion rests only on the dubious authority of the sixteenth-century chronicler Francisco Diago, citing a lost document; see José Vilaplana Gisbert, *Historia religiosa de Alcoy* (Alcoy, 1892), p. 20.

[41] Juan Vernet found this true for Moriscos, and it would seem to apply equally to the Mudejar in times of stress; see his "Antropónimos musulmanes," p. 126. By the sixteenth century Moriscos were mostly tenant farmers on seignorial lands, and consequently protected by the lords; Reglá compares their status to that of Negroes in the antebellum South ("La cuestión morisca y la conyuntura internacional en tiempos de Felipe II," *Estudios de historia moderna*, III [1953], p. 221).

its relevance to the crusaders' policy on Muslims within towns requires notice. Muslims were probably more visible in towns, as Ballesteros believes, immediately after a conquest than in later decades. The crusaders tended to go back home; grantees frequently failed to take up residence; Muslim fugitives cautiously returned after their first fear, relying on the king's promise of security and restoration of property; and Muslim allies received houses within the city.[42]

The distribution of Valencian Muslims deserves to be carefully remarked. Townsmen, villagers, and bumpkins all kept their places of residence. The privileged permanence of this active and intelligent people—their morale unbroken on the battlefield and their politico-social integrity persisting—must have exerted an influence upon incoming Christian settlers. There is reason to suspect some Arabization and perhaps a threat to the immigrant's identity. Such continuity of status and so widespread a placement conversely must have influenced the attitudes of postcrusade Muslims. King James expected gratitude and loyalty. He should have prepared instead for the inevitable resentment and revolt.

[42] Antonio Ballesteros y Beretta, *Sevilla en el siglo xiii* (Madrid, 1913), p. 102; ch. 8 studies "La aljama."

CHAPTER VIII

Incorporation: Motives and Mechanisms

VALENCIAN MUSLIMS remained a community intact, enjoying extensive privileges. Why did King James yield so much? The early thirteenth century was not distinguished for tolerance; this was the generation of the Albigensian wars and the medieval Inquisition. Nor was Aragon so strong a kingdom that it could welcome the incorporation of new power blocs; it was a fragmented, half-formed feudal sovereignty in tenuous balance. Besides, James needed every scrap of income he could cajole from his subjects and every advantage he could wring. Surely it was possible to concede far less to conquered Muslims, to impose obligations more burdensome—in a word, to exploit these people?

MOTIVES OF THE PLANNERS

The immediate answer might be that calculation or far-sighted wisdom induced the king to grant maximum liberties in order to win the war and insure a contented subject population. Was King James so wise above his generation? Was he so Machiavellian as to concede everything, determined to withdraw it with cynical brutality at the earliest moment? Neither solution plausibly fits the man. A clue does come from his speech to the Murcians: his predecessors had done the same as he, from "olden times."[1] That is to say, James solved this problem, as he solved so many others, by applying inherited patterns, filling in the outlines drawn by his forebears.

Mudejar populations, as a specialist on Spanish medieval cities reminds us, had appeared "from earliest times in the cities newly created" by Christians and "in perfect harmony with the Christian settlers." The Muslim population of Aragon proper was copious in King James's lifetime, a static element of the normal scene. A region

[1] *Llibre dels feyts*, ch. 437.

like Daroca had long displayed Mudejar aljamas in a form its historian calls "true communes," enclaved among the Christian towns.[2] Similarly the Tortosa region, along the northern border of the Islamic kingdom of Valencia, exhibited the same system at work. Surrender conditions at Tortosa had been advantageous, subsequent Christian immigration light, and the Mudejar communities well treated, a happy example on the Valencian flank which surely influenced its Muslims when pressure to surrender became strong.[3] Precedents ran far back into history. The conquest of the Ebro Valley down to Tortosa was largely the work of surrender treaties. The terms for Tortosa (1148) seem modeled on those for Zaragoza (1118) and Tudela (1115); all three resemble and probably reflect the conditions upon which the Cid founded his small principality of Valencia near the end of the preceding century.[4] Early in the twelfth century Alfonso the Battler of Aragon so widely extended his realm that seventy out of a hundred subjects were Muslims.[5] King James was not only conscious of the antecedent incorporation of Mudejars by "my dynasty" in both "Aragon and Catalonia" but publicly boasted of it to the Muslims.[6]

[2] Torres Balbás, *Resumen del urbanismo*, p. 303. Esteban Abad, *Daroca*, part 2, ch. 8, on Moors, esp. pp. 215-216. Martínez-Ferrando also makes the point in his "Estado actual," p. 153.

[3] Bayerri, *Historia de Tortosa*, VII, 202ff., 205. He rejects the popular theory that the Muslims fled in strength from Tortosa to Valencia and other Islamic lands.

[4] J. M. Lacarra in Font y Rius *et alii, Reconquista y repoblación*, pp. 66-72; like Menéndez Pidal, Lacarra suggests that Alfonso's visit to Valencia, as an adventuresome prince helping the Cid in 1097, influenced his own Mudejar pacts twenty years later ("La conquista de Zaragoza por Alfonso I [18 Diciembre 1118]," *Al-Andalus*, XII [1947], 95n.). See also the Mudejar materials scattered in his "Documentos para el estudio de la reconquista y repoblación del valle de Ebro," 2d series, *EEMCA*, III (1947-1948), 499-727; and the normative use of the Sunna in the materials assembled by Ramón García de Linares, "Escrituras árabes pertenecientes al archivo de Ntra. Sra. del Pilar de Zaragoza," *Homenaje á Codera*, esp. p. 172n. For the Tudela and Tortosa treaties, see below, Chapter XI, nn. 3, 39. The Cid agreement is studied by Menéndez Pidal, *España del Cid*, I, 488-493, 520-522; cf. Bayerri, *Historia de Tortosa*, VII, 5, 620. On legal precedents, especially the Cuenca *fuero* of 1089 or 1090 so widely influential, see Mobarec Asfura, "Condición jurídica de los moros," pp. 38ff.

[5] Eduardo Ibarra, "Cristianos y moros, documentos aragoneses y navarros," *Homenaje á Codera*, p. 81.

[6] *Llibre dels feyts*, ch. 437.

Behind the Christian precedents in Spain a sharp eye might discern the Islamic tradition of the *dhimmī* or protected nonbelievers; without pressing the comparison too strictly or positing more than a measure of osmotic borrowing, one can admit that the resemblances between Muslim and Christian provision for minorities were remarkable.[7] Below this tradition, in turn, and continuing alongside it in parallel, was Byzantium's separation of noncitizen groups. The mentality upon which Mudejarism rested had become universal; it had entered the very air the Mediterranean people breathed. In the crusader East, where interpenetration and understanding between Christian and Muslim were small,[8] the same *laissez faire* or pluralism prevailed. Ibn Jubayr, as a tourist or even polemicist, may have exaggerated grossly in his observations about subject Muslims in 1284. Under the Christian ruler of Syria ("the hog of Acre—may Allah destroy him"), Muslims "live in great comfort," "govern themselves as they wish," and are better off than Muslims in Islamic lands. This celebrated passage, current in a truncated form which obscures the author's more general assessment of peasant life here as being much the same under Christian or Muslim absentee landlords, does reveal at the very minimum the Mediterranean expedient of separated-subject status. Ibn Jubayr also reported on the surprising penetration of Sicily's court by Muslims; this Christian kingdom had long organized its subjected Islamic population in autonomous communities paralleling Spain's Mudejarism.[9]

To see King James's tactic as a hasty expedient or as a clumsy solution which was, in the words of one authority, "politically the

[7] Claude Cahen, "Dhimma," *EI*², II, 227-231. Leopoldo Torres Balbás explores Spanish applications in "Mozarabías y juderías de las ciudades hispanomusulmanas," *Al-Andalus*, XIX (1954), 172-199, citing, for example, the retention of native law, religious freedom, a measure of autonomy, and a special tax structure. However, the situation varied in different times and places. For a summary view of a specific area see Reyna Pastor de Togneri and Marta Bonaudo, "Problèmes d'assimilation d'une minorité: les mozarabes de Tolède (de 1085 à la fin du xiiie siècle)," *Annales, économies, sociétés, civilisations*, XXV (1970), 351-390.

[8] See Preface, n. 3, with reference to Cahen, Smail, and their opponents.

[9] See the revisionist interpretation of Ibn Jubayr by Claude Cahen, "Indigènes et croisés," passim, esp. the additional text on p. 358. The *Travels* of the Valencian Ibn Jubayr are cited above in Chapter I, n. 6. On Sicily's subject Muslims, see Michele Amari, *Storia dei musulmani di Sicilia*, 4 vols. (Florence, 1854-1872), III, 269-270, 291, 334, 531-534.

worst" possible,[10] is to miss the point. In the king's surrender activities an element of cynical expediency or anyway of pragmatism did indeed manifest itself, as did an element of open-handed tolerance. At bottom, however, King James had no policy of his own; he executed a policy of his people and times. This normalcy of procedure may account for the fact that only two original surrender charters survive; such an instrument, though cherished by its holder at the time, was of little interest to others to preserve. Explanation by past crown policy may diminish the praise due to James as an organizer and administrator. Yet he did face a problem peculiar to his own reign—the immense extent of the various conquests to which the prepared system had to be applied, with the consequent necessity of applying it well or suffering for the failure. Here was no inching forward as with his predecessors, nor the gaining of a province, but rather a near doubling of territory, the addition of a small Islamic world in communities too numerous, compact, and prosperous for the comfort of a Christian king. The affirmation of an underlying pattern, however adapted to exceptional circumstances, carries full circle to the original question. Need the pattern have been applied? What elements of the situation recommended or compelled this solution?

Tolerance and kindness were not at issue. The laws of war allowed King James to be quite ruthless by modern standards, and he generally showed himself disinclined to alter those laws. When a handful of Muslims fought "well and skillfully" at Valencia city until their tower was aflame, and then called for mercy, "I said I would not give them quarter, because they had not surrendered at the beginning, and I burned them there." When James cornered two thousand Moors in a Majorca cave he refused any terms and insisted they become slaves. He could slaughter men, women, and children wholesale, as at Moncada and Cullera in Valencia or at the sack of Majorca, and report the deed without compunction. He writes with equanimity about the mass expulsions at Burriana and Valencia city. When expulsion substituted for massacre, it was owing to military or economic advantage. Of one group spared, the king confessed that "I wanted them alive rather than dead" because

10 Rull Villar, "Rebelión de los moriscos," p. 62.

of the profits of the slave trade. (He got seventeen thousand besants for his hundred selected prisoners, and felt he could have sold them at twice the price if he had not been in a hurry.)[11] This is not to say that James, according to his lights and times, was a cruel man. Cruelty and ruthlessness are not characteristics of the self-portrait in his memoirs. James was aware that gratuitous cruelty was wrong. He realized too that application of the Golden Rule would bear fruit for Christendom in Islamic lands; Pope Gregory IX had just appealed to this common insight when urging tolerance for the Jews in France: "Christians must show the kindness which we want shown to Christians living in pagan lands."[12] Once the surrender pacts in Valencia were down on parchment James did feel bound by their policy of tolerance.

Some affect to see in the expulsions which occurred after al-Azraq's revolts a malign clerical influence; others suggest an increasing intolerance in James's declining and presumably more pious years. Inverting these interpretations, an historian recently lamented that "the new, pacifying doctrine" of the mendicant orders "had not yet reached the royal chancelleries," and that the tolerant teaching of Catalan public figures like Nolasco and Penyafort "do not illumine the sad [second] half of the thirteenth century"; pride prevented this "new conception" from bearing fruit.[13] Neither interpretation fits the known data. The king's moral life did not become less irregular as he advanced in years, nor did he show himself more amenable to clerical pressure. The mendicants, on the other hand, visibly influenced the king in his larger policies toward the Valencian Muslims.[14] Neither tolerance nor intolerance stood out as distinguishing elements in his personality. Judging by character and by military conventions of the era, there is no reason to suppose that he could not have expelled or enslaved all the Muslims of the Valencian kingdom, as the Muslims of the Holy Land seem to have done with

[11] *Llibre dels feyts*, chs. 78, 102, 203, 205, 268, 369.

[12] Arch. Vat., Reg. Vat. 17 (Gregory IX), fol. 5r, v (April 6, 1233): "est autem iudeis a christianis exhibenda benignitas, quam christianis in paganismo existentibus cupimus exhiberi."

[13] Cagigas, *Mudejares*, II, 395-396.

[14] See my *Crusader Valencia*, ch. XI, on "The Mendicant Orders," and my "Christian-Islamic Confrontation," passim.

the smaller population of Christians after the fall of Acre later in the century.[15] For a complex of reasons this did not seem desirable or feasible during the crusade.

To begin with, the Moors of Valencia had remained powerful despite civil wars and the decline of their military machine. They withstood King James so sturdily at his precrusade invasion at Peñíscola that he refused to mention the dismal failure in his autobiography. At Cullera, on account of military limitations forcefully outlined by his uncle Ferdinand, James had to raise the siege and depart humiliated, complaining that "the Saracens will hold us in little worth and so will the Christians." When the tower of Moncada was the king's objective, the master of the Templars warned James: "I will do whatever you want; but you already know how the Moors defend their fortresses; it will not be proper for you to undertake anything unless you can bring it off." The stronghold of Bairén would have cost so heavily to take by force that its Muslim castellan was ashamed to surrender without a show of struggle, demanding seven months' interval for the sake of appearances. At Játiva, wearying of the siege, James "bethought him, being the wise man that he was, that since he could not prevail by force, he might gain his ends by stratagem and wiles." Valencia city, though isolated by the greatest army King James ever commanded and put under long siege, was capable of further resistance at the time of its surrender. Famine, the key weapon of its besiegers, works slowly. As the *Chronicles of St. Denis* put it, "the king realized that the town could hold out and that he might wait a long time before it could be taken," so he settled for terms.[16]

The taking of Burriana had been a close affair. Even after James had conquered and garrisoned it, his barons warned that he would not be able to hold the town against Muslim counterattack. Here the effective force of perhaps five hundred crusaders made forays but "did not dare to penetrate far into the zone of the Saracens." When Almenara had surrendered and Christian troops already held the

[15] Richard, *Royaume latin de Jérusalem*, pp. 346-348.

[16] "Chroniques de Saint-Denis," *Recueil des historiens des Gaules et de la France*, XXI, 108: "Le roy regarda que la ville estoit deffensable, et qu'il i porroit longuemont séjorner avant qu'elle peust estre prise; si s'accorda de tenir les convenances fermement." *Llibre dels feyts*, chs. 195, 196, 199, 308, 310; on famine, chs. 241, 269, 278. Desclot, *Crònica*, ch. 49.

town, the central citadel continued holding out, though manned by only twenty Muslim knights who had already eaten their horses to survive. Very many of the strong points throughout Valencia succumbed only to skillful negotiations. James consoled himself for his concessions in the several surrenders by recalling "the old saying, 'who does not give what it hurts to give, does not get what he wants.'" This philosophy the king once spelled out to a military colleague: "Sir William, cleverness is worth more than force!" In short, simple necessity made some surrender scheme inevitable.[17]

Other factors helped. Sheer expense made alternatives to siege operations welcome. "We incur great expense here," the bishop of Barcelona remonstrated after the Murcia siege; "and if we add to it, we only lose it"; to this observation "the other high barons agreed." At Burriana the financial embarrassment of the crown reached such a pitch that James found it impossible to raise loans, until the master of the Hospitallers stood surety in exchange for wide confirmation of his order's privileges. On another occasion the king was forced to sell his Moncada prisoners cheaply: "I had to let them go for so little because the merchants were pressing me for what I had borrowed from them for the army." At Játiva he proposed the exorbitant expenditure on both sides as a compelling motive for the *qā'id* to submit, because "while he would have made it costly for me, he too would not escape expense," so that "there would be two losses, one to me and the other to him."[18]

Greed for estates served as counselor to the knights; visions of a conqueror's fame, extensive revenues, and counterbaronial power available in Valencia inspired the king. Delay in accepting conditional surrender might see a Christian army melt away as feudal obligations lapsed; thus the baron Peter Cornel absolutely refused to garrison conquered Burriana for a few months, because in "so very important a matter" he must first return to his home estates for consultation with his vassals. On the other hand, offering good terms might win active allies, as when a Majorcan sheik surrendered and then supplied the Christian army with food and "made known to the king all the devices that the Saracens within the city were

[17] *Llibre dels feyts*, chs. 180, 189, 244, 264; the remark, "mes val giny que força," in ch. 43 occurred in the context of a feudal war.

[18] *Ibid.*, chs. 165, 205, 350, 452.

desirous to attempt."[19] Concern for the economic stability of his new realm, for its productivity, and for effective administration and tax-gathering, made it prudent to concede privileges in such form as would keep the native population content within a familiar framework. In the same context, the conquerors had to conciliate the kingdom's skilled labor force, unless they were willing to chance the financial loss involved in replacement or the discontent of natives enslaved.

Cynical expediency could hope for subsequent pretexts by which to lessen the privileges, should such an eventuality seem advisable. This note the king sounded when his barons complained that Murcia city's surrender still left almost everything in Muslim hands. James's reply, in the context of a capitulation already accepted, rings ominously: "When a man can have from his enemy—I do not say it only of Saracens—one measure of land, he ought always to wait until he can have ten or one hundred." Common sense had a role also, arguing against damaging buildings, toppling trees, or smashing irrigation canals one hoped soon to own. "Cutting down wheat and trees was not good," James told the *qā'id* of Bairén, whom he was preparing to siege, "since the Moors would stay on, under me." This was the same reproach by which the Muslim *qā'id* of Calatrava had once tempered the tactics of Alfonso VI of Castile: "It is unworthy of a powerful [king] to destroy and sow ruin; if you manage to become master of the region, your realm will be damaged as a result."[20] Add to all these considerations the practical situation expected to result from the crusade—a sea of Muslims surrounding islands of Christian settlers—and it becomes obvious that terms had to guarantee religion, property, and a measure of freedom. The unusual extent of territory being acquired, together with the pressures counseling generous privileges, led to a maximum Mudejarism. Valencia became a unique subspecies of the Mudejar experience, something closer to a tributary province and closer yet to modern colonial status.

The overriding, practical reasons for liberal terms were rendered more acceptable by the psychological conditioning; that such a

[19] *Ibid.*, chs. 179, 366 (financial loss). Desclot, *Crònica*, ch. 39.

[20] *Llibre dels feyts*, chs. 308, 446. Torres Balbás, "Contornos de las ciudades hispanomusulmanas," p. 449, quoting Ḥarīz b. 'Ukasha, governor of Calatrava.

pattern had already been prepared by predecessors, was usefully employed elsewhere in the realm on a smaller scale, was an accepted practice toward Jewish populations in both Christian and Islamic cultures, and had a model of sorts in *mozarabías* of Christians falling under Muslim rulers. Finally, an important theologico-juridical context framed all this. Only a Christian could properly come under the legal system of the day or share in the intertwined political and religious forms of governing, unless important adjustments were first made. It involved less dislocation of the forms if Muslims came in as a subsistent entity, sharply defined from their Christian fellows. To isolate non-Christian religious groups was thus the recommendation of canon law.

A formidable tangle of motives and circumstance! Yet all seem to have been present, as well as others more subtle. It is not necessary to deny James a modicum of humane feeling, for example, toward a group with whom he was so often in friendly contact. He had expectations also of converting many. He may, as Cagigas has suggested, have been moved by the imperial ideal of presiding over two religions.[21] At any rate, enough has been seen of the complex situation to forestall attributing the king's actions merely to economic or religious motives, or seeing them as measured by military necessity, or simplifying them as "compromises of day-to-day politics" in opposition to deeper theory "in the church."[22]

It is difficult to sort out a man's motives, arranging them in a neat hierarchy of values. Can a priority of motives be assigned here? Viewed from one angle, James seems to have acted by habit, granting the usual privileges his father might have granted—more when he had to, less or none at all when he could—tailoring the pattern to the present circumstance. In this he did what was expected of a king satisfying his religious and military, not to mention imperial, ambitions. Concomitantly and subordinately, as James's words reveal, he shrewdly realized the economic and administrative advantages of the resultant system, and he gambled on the chance that this system would keep his new realm at peace. Uneasiness is evident from the very beginning of the conquest, however, over

[21] See Chapter IX, n. 4.

[22] Norman Daniel, *Islam and the West, The Making of an Image* (Edinburgh, 1962), p. 116.

this fellowship with the "enemies of Christ," later becoming focused into anger by what he considered the treachery of the rebels.

These motives contained contradictory elements. Religious zeal (or perhaps spiritual self-interest), economic benefits, and weight of custom could not always be reconciled. As James became increasingly able to expel more Moors and increasingly possessed of suitable pretexts, for example, he discovered such a course to be less to his own or to his barons' financial advantage and less suitable to his African diplomacy. King James's personal life, and by the same token perhaps his public life, exhibited a welter of conflicting motives. He was not a man who felt compelled to choose between them when he could postpone the unhappy decision by tolerating a juxtaposition. It was directly upon such intertwined attitudes, motivation, and principles that the relationship between victors and vanquished, in its formal structure, had been reared.

Practical Procedures: The Parleys

"I had stayed in more of their [Islamic] towns than they had," King James admonished his barons, "and knew better the customs of the Saracens than they did."[23] The barons were fortunate in having so well qualified a leader to apply traditional solutions to the problem of large-scale surrender. Courage, experience, shrewd boldness, a certain tolerance, kingly generosity (marred by occasional meanness), and a sense of drama informed his techniques for arranging capitulations. A general picture of the process may be assembled by gleaning details from the king's personal narrative.

The Christian forces had to contend with several heavily defended strong points, such as Morella, Peñíscola, Murviedro, Burriana, and Valencia city. There were many lesser castles, varying in strength but of considerable power, scattered over the land at every sort of place awkward for adversaries. Dependent upon these stood innumerable supporting towers or forts, usually providing defense for a rural settlement. Such a tower often loomed grim and solitary, a few buildings at its skirts, in a sweep of fields. It was usually square,

[23] *Llibre dels feyts,* ch. 446. On practical procedures, see my "How to End a Crusade: Techniques for Making Peace in the Thirteenth-Century Kingdom of Valencia," *Military Affairs,* XXXV (1971), 142-148.

with a moat or outer palisade perhaps encircling an area of refuge for cattle and peasants. It is not easy to distinguish between unimportant castles and important towers; James sometimes dignified as "castles" defenses which were more properly towers, and at least once he used the term "tower" for a great edifice housing within its works over a thousand people. These monuments were evidence of a land constantly at war—not only against deep-piercing Christian expeditions or pirates raiding from the sea, but among a succession of rival Islamic factions within and without its borders.

The huerta of Gandía can serve to illustrate local defenses. Here, in an amphitheater of productive farmland ringed by mountains and stretching to the sea, James encountered five castles, strategically installed at five gateways through the rocky periphery. Three had small towns in their shadows. Scattered below them—especially along the coastal road, waterways, and the foot of the mountains—lay twenty-six small settlements, ranging from primitive hamlets to considerable complexes with tower defenses. No city yet existed in the area, only market centers; the urban influence was distant Denia. The dominating castle was Bairān (Bairén), three miles northwest of Gandía. Before the castles could surrender, they had to consult and associate in their action the heads of the settlements, many of whom had fled with their people at the danger signal to the nearest fortification. The alarm probably spread here as at Játiva; King James describes how "those in the castle ordered the trumpet sounded and smoke signals made to those in the villages, that they should come in." A chain of signal fires leaped from hill to hill and from tower to tower, warning the whole region of an approaching army. Terrain and military difficulties varied throughout the kingdom, of course, but Gandía shows the rural disposition as well as any place.[24]

King James might formally summon a fortress to surrender, as at

[24] Vicente Fontavella González, *La huerta de Gandía* (Zaragoza, 1950), studies the region with a geographer's eye but with an historical and evolutionary method; his maps, charts, plans, and air photographs contribute to an understanding of thirteenth-century situations here. The five castles are located and named (p. 309), with the twenty-six settlements (p. 130); the picture on p. 305 gives some idea of what the thirteenth-century village and tower were like, evolving from a Roman villa (p. 310). On Denia see p. 344; on the danger signals see p. 65 and *Llibre dels feyts*, chs. 287, 313.

Chivert, Cervera, and Enguera; if reaction was in doubt, as at Elche, he had to consider "whether to march by or besiege it." Alfandech castle "surrendered immediately on the day after" receiving such a challenge. As the crusaders entered a neighborhood in force, the Muslims of an imperiled point commonly dispatched messengers to initiate negotiations. Pairs of agents turn up several times in James's memoirs—as at Biar, Almazora, Peñíscola, and Villena. In one case a single Moor "came for himself and for others." From Nules, Uxó, and Castro castles the king asked ten envoys each, "from among the more important and powerful notables there"; the initial messengers from these places, however, were the usual pair. Close reading of the context in the Biar account reveals that the pair of envoys first contacted the king's executive officers (*porters*), as was only natural; subsequently James asked them "to come before me." The delegates took along, at least sometimes, a small body of retainers; one such group prepared a meal during the parley. James respected the diplomatic status of the agents. When the *qā'id* of Játiva paled, fearing a trap, the king reassured him by reminding him of this policy. "You are just as safe as if you were in the castle of Játiva," he said, "for my policy [*cort*] is such that I never arrest any man who comes to me, whatever his offense." The Elche negotiators enjoyed formal safeguard throughout.[25]

The king might put off an answer while he consulted his barons —though at times he could be careful to avoid involving them—or perhaps the queen alone.[26] If indicated, he prayed for guidance. He might already have prepared for this visit by maneuvers designed to unsettle the negotiators—by mounting a series of raids or the preliminaries to a siege, or by sophistically urging the example of larger castles which had already sought safety in surrender, or by grimly invoking the possibility of a massacre like the Majorca holocaust.[27] James was not above hustling a reluctant leader into precipitate action, as when he reminded the Almenara agents "that other

[25] *Llibre dels feyts*, chs. 182, 185, 189, 199, 249, 253, 335, 355, 411, 420, 439. The Biar episode has: "vengren nos ii sarrains," but "dixeren als nostres porters" and only later "faem los entrar denant nos" (ch. 355). At Peñíscola two messengers came, then at the town a team of four appeared, and for the negotiations more (chs. 182, 184).

[26] *Llibre dels feyts*, chs. 113, 419, 278 (queen).

[27] *Ibid.*, chs. 183 (prayer), 185, 278 (massacre), 315.

castles were conducting negotiations to surrender," and that if Almenara anticipated the others "they would thus win greater favor from me for the good beginning they had made with me." Though he used the technique of bluffing during the Valencian crusade, James's most brilliant use of effrontery had been the capture of Minorca island, a matter of lighting over three hundred false campfires and then demanding surrender with as much aplomb as he could muster. A sudden flash of ruthlessness could be effective. Seventeen corpses headless and hanging did not shake Enguera; but at Murcia tardy resistance to James's interpretation of their treaty collapsed when he fiercely prepared to storm the town.[28] The king handled negotiations personally, if he was in the field. Where convenient, he might occasionally designate a substitute. Very shortly after James's death, his son Peter similarly commissioned a Knight Templar to deal with the Sierra de Eslida rebels. Peter made him "specific and special procurator for negotiating and effecting treaties in my place and name with castellans and sheiks of Saracen aljamas, concerning agreements and treaties to be drawn between me and them." Unless a single strong man dominated a local region, King James dealt with the whole aljama of a town, valley, or district. He therefore addressed the sheiks who had come to surrender Murcia as though he were dealing with the representatives of a Catalan commune. The same spirit informs his mode of address at places so diverse as Chivert, Pego, and Játiva.[29]

To effect a surrender, King James would cheerfully stoop to bribery, to buying off a powerful autocrat, or to encouraging the traitor within. At Elche he dropped 300 besants into the sleeve of the counselor Muḥammad, who "was pleased with me, and promised me on his law that he would do all he could for my advantage." To an influential counselor at Játiva James promised "wealth, more than you ever owned," if he would act for the king's interest. To the Játiva *qā'id* James offered: "I will give him ten times more than his dynasty [*linyatge*] ever had." On Majorca James had used both spies and traitors, a practice he continued in Valencia. At Biar the

[28] *Ibid.*, chs. 120, 121 (Minorca), 243 (Almenara), 342 (Enguera), 449 (Murcia).

[29] Arch. Crown, James I, Reg. Canc. 37, fol. 57v (Dec. 22, 1272): "vobis aliame et toti universitati sarracenorum vallis de Pego." *Llibre dels feyts*, ch. 439 (Murcia). Chivert Charter; Játiva Charter. Peter's document is in Soldevila, *Pere el Gran*, part 2, I, appendix, doc. 82 (Dec. 29, 1276).

people tried to stone a townsman for betraying them to James. At Almazora the traitor proved to be a double agent, so that the Christians fell into an ambush. Turncoats could arrange to receive coveted posts and properties. The Elche counselor got not only his 300 besants but riches for his family and custody of "the town with all its revenues." Each of the Almenara messengers, besides keeping their estates, asked for themselves and their relatives thirty-three jovates from among the best lands abandoned by Muslim fugitives, together with forty sets of clothing, two horses, two hundred cows, and a thousand sheep and goats.[30]

Where the enemy agent seemed ill at ease, sensitive to public opinion, or fearful of intrigue, King James did not hesitate to clear his tent of other people, setting the stage for a discreet tête-à-tête. Occasionally he took hostages from some castle commander as surety for a preliminary agreement. At Bairén he demanded the eldest son and two nephews of the *qā'id*, though in the event he satisfied himself instead with a sworn pledge from twenty elders. At Majorca the enemy *wālī* or king sent out his young son as hostage; James gave him good care. One of the most powerful lords of the Majorcan countryside, Ibn 'Abīd (Ben Aabet), offered his sons and daughters as hostages. The lord of Játiva, while retaining semi-independence, "left his son in my care." During the surrenders following the Valencian revolt which disturbed James's last years, King Peter continued his father's technique of taking hostages; arranging to delay acceptance of Serra castle until a month and a half after signatures were put to its treaty, he took ten hostages "of the better Saracens" as surety, and released his own prisoners as "a pledge" of good faith.[31] Within the framework of the liberal Mudejar system he was offering, James delighted in haggling and driving the best bargain possible. His principle was that a king should "look well first" when signing a grant, to be sure whether he really wanted "to do this

[30] *Llibre dels feyts*, chs. 189 (Almazora), 243 (Almenara), 351 (Játiva), 356 (Biar), 417 (Elche); on Majorca there was the spy 'Alī (59), the chieftain Shu'ayb (113), and the lord Ibn 'Abīd (see n. 31), who undertook to win over the other lordships (71).

[31] *Llibre dels feyts*, chs. 308-309, 354; the Majorcan lord reads as Ben Aabet and, in another manuscript, Bean Abet, elements suggesting Ibn 'Abīd rather than Ibn 'Abbād. Desclot, *Crònica*, chs. 39 and 41, on Majorca. Soldevila, *Pere el Gran*, part 2, 1, appendix, doc. 57 (Feb. 15, 1277): "x raenes dels malors sarrains."

or not." In preparing these smaller details, he could be devious. When Uxó, Castro, and Nules arranged to make terms on the same day, he set a different time for each interview, "for I did not want one [castle] to know the treaty of another." Previously on the island of Minorca, after he had won by ruse from the "hard pressed" delegates a generous share of revenues plus control of defenses, James was not ashamed to boast of inserting into the pact at the eleventh hour a levy on butter and on cattle transport.[32]

Preliminary negotiations could become protracted. At Murcia the two envoys sent to parley carried their notes of the meeting back to town, where the notables and learned men assembled in council to discuss the king's conditions. The messengers then returned to James with full power to accept his terms, bringing not only a document of authorization but also a written set of counterproposals. Still another council followed, further problems, agreement on the third day, and surrender on the fourth. To arrange the capitulation of Almenara, the king met secretly with two messengers on the roadside. Then these two, a *faqīh* and his influential friend, returned to consult the council. Summoned next day by the king as he rode past town, the messengers requested a week's extension to "speak with their friends privately first," after which they sent for James by letter and opened the gates, though for a day the inner alcazar refused to submit. Paterna sent a courier "secretly, with documents from the whole aljama," as did Bétera and Bulla in their turn. James dealt directly with the *qā'id* alone at Bairén, though "twenty sheiks from among the notables" supported the leader's oath.[33]

At Elche the king summoned by letter "two or three Saracens from the substantial men" from the aljama of Elche, a group "some fifty in number." Eventually the delegates left to inform this assembly of James's terms, and then brought back its counterproposals. Next day the aljama sent another set of terms, offering upon acceptance to surrender a tower of the defenses and to sign a formal pact. For the castle of Castro, as similarly for Nules and Uxó castles, James conducted parleys with ten of its leaders. He arranged the surrender of Villanueva de Castellón with the Játiva *qā'id* and a hundred

[32] *Llibre dels feyts*, chs. 121 (Minorca), 243, 249 (Uxó, etc.), 498.

[33] *Ibid.*, chs. 243-244 (Almenara), 254 (Paterna, etc.), 439-441 (Murcia); see also 410 (Villena).

chief men. At talks preceding the capitulation of Játiva itself the *qā'id* got a period of grace in order to let the notables "meet in the mosque on Friday and deliberate there until Saturday." At Eslida, Ahín, Veo, Senquier, Pelmes, and Sueras he addressed the treaties to the "entire aljama of the Saracens."[34]

James prepared the capitulation of Valencia city by no less than three separate meetings at dawn secretly with the diplomat 'Alī, fetched through the lines to his siege camp by a knight. He accomplished the main negotiations, still secretly, in two formal but private sessions with a nephew of the Muslim ruler, escorted with his entourage into the Christian camp before dawn by two Christian nobles. Only the Muslim, an interpreter, James, and the queen (who played an active advisory role) engaged in these central talks, since the king feared his barons would object to allowing surrender. After these protracted talks, James publicly announced the agreement to a concourse of his camp's notables. He neglects to say anything about the ceremonial signing, which so impressed Ibn al-Abbār, the poet-secretary of Zayyān: the Christian king came out from his camp at ar-Ruṣāfa "decked in his finest outfit and surrounded by the magnates of his court," to formalize the treaty in full sight of both armies.[35]

King James showed impressive energy and dynamism throughout these maneuvers, as well as experience and deftness in handling individual cases. Contact was personal wherever possible, and opportunity swiftly grasped, but the transaction then went forward with detachment, at a leisurely pace. At Játiva the talks dragged on so long, he writes, that "it would be a tedious lengthening of the book" to supply details. As circumstances dictated, the king might appear for negotiations with an adequate troop of men—about a hundred at Paterna, Biar, and Elche, for example—or in his anxiety he might present himself almost alone, as when he rode a day's journey into enemy land with a handful of retainers to appear at nightfall under the walls of Peñíscola.[36]

[34] *Ibid.*, chs. 249 (Castro, etc.), 327 (Villanueva), 352 (Játiva), 416-420 (Elche). Chivert Charter: "toti aliame sarracenorum." Eslida Charter (including Ahín, etc.). On such terms as "notables" (here *meylors*), "sheiks," "elders," and "good men," as well as the communal government of the aljama, see below, Chapter XVI, section 2.

[35] Ibn al-Abbār, "Un traité inédit," p. 33; *Llibre dels feyts*, chs. 271-281.

[36] *Llibre dels feyts*, chs. 183 (Peñíscola), 254 (Paterna), 352 (Játiva), 355 (Biar), 420 (Elche).

He made practical demonstration of sympathy for Islamic religious susceptibilities on occasion, preparing food for the diplomats "according to their law." Twice he offered this service at Murcia, taking care to prescribe "new pots" for cooking; he ordered "live chickens and sheep and kids prepared," ready to be killed fresh for the negotiators. After conversations with the Almenara envoys "in front of the castle," James set his falcon upon a passing heron and presented the captured bird alive to the envoys, telling them that "I knew their custom, and that they would not take it dead"—a politic deed which "delighted" them. At his overnight stay before Peñíscola castle, he did not allow his men to build even a brush shelter for him, lest destructive cutting of branches offend the Muslims. King James preferred not to proceed with bargaining until he had rendered the Muslims benevolent—"merry with food and with the wine they drank." For the Uxó envoys he cooked "two sheep and five hens," freshly killed. At Nules "I did not want to treat with them until they were warmed with food and wine." His familiarity with their susceptibilities was not merely theoretical but practical, allowing him to exploit the Valencian Moors' tolerance of wine.[37] More was implied in this feasting than fellowship or gestures of kindly hospitality, though these and pragmatic motives were obviously at work. The medieval Muslim, probably because of distant nomadic antecedents, possessed a mystique of dining. To offer food to an enemy, or to accept it, implied a relationship. The contemporary historian Abu 'l-Maḥāsin (d. 1234) praised "the admirable and generous custom of the Arabs, who grant life to the captive who has eaten or drunk of their viands"; he cited the recent example given by Saladin after the battle of Hattin (1187).[38] King James emphasized these preparley dinners, aware of their special impact upon the community preparing to surrender.

At all times King James paid attention to the Arabic love of rhetoric, a tradition in which mere words take on a strange reality. James's negotiations consequently became a kind of celebration, an almost liturgical ritual of pronounced formality. The structure was ceremonial, arranged in crescendo: polite overtures, protracted prac-

[37] *Ibid.*, chs. 184 (brush), 244 (heron), 250 (Uxó), 252 (Nules), 436-439 (Murcia).

[38] In Philip K. Hitti, *Islam and the West: An Historical Cultural Survey* (Princeton, 1962), p. 183.

tical negotiations, formalities of submission and seizure, presentation of homage, ultimate festivities, and gifts. At each step rhetoric played its role, joined to solemn courtesies. At Minorca the king's party dressed in their best finery, furbished and decorated their dwelling, and dispatched a train of horses and baggage-mules to bring in the delegates. Upon arrival these dignitaries "saluted me with great reverence, bent their knees before me, and announced that they saluted me for the *qā'id* a hundred thousand times." King James responded with his own rhetoric of mannered happiness, invoking on them God's benevolence. The Muslims returned thanks to God and to the king for these sentiments. Preliminaries over, both parties proceeded to the bargaining phase.

Similarly, when James arranged a private interview with the defeated Zayyān in 1242 he did so in style, with mutual professions of respect and "love"; Zayyān proffered his arguments, returning at Vespers time to receive James's leisured answering address. At another such interview the secretary to the ruler of Játiva "saluted" James in the name of his principal, "commending him to your favor as to the very man he has most at heart to serve, and love, and honor." For the talks on Valencia city's capitulation, the Muslim dignitary made a fine entrance, then in an access of courtesy "refused to kiss my hand but rather prostrated himself, and proceeded to embrace [my knees]." Sitting down, he "saluted" James, professing himself "most honored" to visit him. The king rejoined that he was equally pleased, wished God's blessings, and promised him "honor and good." After further complicated interchanges of compliments and pleasantries, James offered to empty his tent for greater privacy, and the talks began in earnest.

The use of rhetorical flourish and structured formal address, conveyed in brief snatches in the king's memoirs, can be examined more closely in his encounter with al-Mufawwiz (Almofois), Játiva's prime minister sent as envoy, who was "the most learned man of Játiva and one of the highest." His name and eminence identify him as belonging to the Banū Mufawwiz, the Játiva representatives of the Yemenite Banū Ma'āfir. James describes the scene—the Muslim and his aide sitting in the presence of the monarch's court, then rising in response to an invitation to speak. He began with direct address, "My Lord, my Lord!" then went on to convey "many greetings" from his *qā'id* and the notables, and presented their response to complaints. The body of his argument was sober, clear, and descriptive, in contrast to exordium and peroration. In the second half of his discourse he declaimed on the glories of Játiva: "You know well what the castle of Játiva is, that there is no other better in the whole of Spanish Islam [*Endeluzia*]." To surrender it to James would occasion scorn from Christian and Moor alike. The Muslim played on this clever appeal to knightly honor. "And although the *qā'id* is not of your religion, nor his Moors, they would make you ashamed of them if they did what dishonored them." Dropping from emotion to concluding statement, he petitioned the king not to wish his enemy to be base. "And on that note he sat down."

The eloquence of al-Mufawwiz moved James to spontaneous reply. He makes it clear that he spoke without retiring to consult or prepare an answer. First he applauded the Moor's learning, holding it to be demonstrated not only "by the fame you derive from it" but also because "you expose your reasoning so well." James steered clear of the points at issue; taking care not to tangle with a formidable debater, he contented himself with the observation that if both sides of every controversy were debated nothing would ever get settled. He proposed an arbitrator in place of further argument. Al-Mufawwiz returned a noncommittal answer, then talks for the day were broken off. The process had been stately, the address of Játiva's ambassador obviously impressive and well received. Rhetoric had clothed the brutal nakedness of the Muslim-Christian confrontation with a touching, human dignity.[39]

Drafting the Treaties

The procedures for actually drafting the treaty proved time-consuming. Even at Elche, where the Christian barons "marveled greatly

[39] *Llibre dels feyts*, chs. 122, 274, 307, 387. On al-Mufawwiz, see below, p. 408. The Zayyān interview is hard to date; it occurred during the summer, after he had fled from the Murcian revolt into Alicante, shortly before the surrender of Bairén and Villena, and with James traveling afterwards to Catalonia and Aragon. Examination of place-names in manuscripts signed by the king makes 1241 impossible and points to mid-1242 as the only open date before the siege of Játiva (see the manuscripts in *Itinerari*, pp. 147-165 passim).

that I had dispatched the affair so quickly," it had been complicated. James had come to the town, where the sheiks had presented him with a copy of the agreement between him and the envoys. This he signed, receiving their oath of fealty. After a night spent outside the walls, "the capitulation was drawn up, and by the hour of tierce [nine in the morning] all agreements and the rest of the deeds had been signed." There still remained mysterious copyings to be done. James had to hurry away to another surrender, leaving the final paperwork in the hands of his secretary for Arabic, the Jew Astruc of Bonsenyor.

Similar stages in drafting, preparing final copies, and attending to signatures and seals are discernible in the earlier Minorcan crusade. "In this treaty—that is, in drawing up the documents and having an oath sworn on the Koran by all the principal and leading men of the island—three days had to pass before all could be accomplished." The king had absented himself here as part of a ruse; putting in his appearance now, "I caused charters to be drawn with my seal, which I gave them," accepting them as subjects so long as they obeyed the conditions of the treaty. The several steps involved in a treaty-drawing process were often syncopated in the king's narrative into a single action. "I had my charters drawn" at Nules, again at Uxó, and at Biar. At Bairén, "when the charters had been drawn up, I caused them to be handed over to them," arranging to receive the castle formally next morning. At Murcia the aljama sent written instructions telling the king "in what manner I should draw up the charter." At Peñíscola the king could not sign the treaty until after he had entered into possession of the castle, the notaries from his itinerant secretariat not yet having caught up with him, "because I had come so hastily." Later, when "the notaries arrived, I had the papers drawn up."[40]

The Mudejar community preserved its own record, their new obligations and rights soon passing into the oral custom-law of the region concerned. The community could present its charter to new sovereigns for confirmation or for replacement in case of accident or disrepair. The Uxó people came to the drafting of their postrebellion charter in 1250 bearing the original surrender treaty "in their

[40] *Llibre dels feyts*, chs. 121-123 (Minorca), 184 (Peñíscola), 250 (Uxó), 252 (Nules), 310, 314 (Bairén), 359 (Biar), 420-422 (Elche), 439 (Murcia).

hands." To repel land-grabbers at Alcira four years after its surrender, the aljama presented its guarantees in "the treaty document [*instrumentum*] of the Saracens." Such versions, kept by aljama and by crown, were probably a chirograph, from the same a-b-c sheet. The medieval scribe prepared duplicate texts upon a single parchment, in bilingual interlinear form, separating these twin exemplars by letters of the alphabet across the page, then tearing the sheet apart along the line of letters, so that either party could later prove the authenticity of his version by fitting it to that of the other signatory. When King James rebuked the *qā'id* of Játiva for breaking his treaty, he reminded him "that the treaties were divided by a-b-c [and] that I held one of them and you the other." Though the seal had largely replaced the chirograph as a guarantee in most of continental Europe by this time, the natural wariness between enemies on the Christian-Islamic frontier must have encouraged the retention of comfortably old-fashioned modes of drafting. The charters were done on parchment, despite the vicinity of paper mills in Catalonia and at Játiva. Paper was misprized as fragile, an attitude reflected, for example, in Emperor Frederick II's prohibition in 1231 of its use for public acts; in the realms of Aragon, too, though the collection of notarial notes known as the Valencia *Repartimiento* was written on paper, parchment was preferred for solemn affairs. Consequently the original of the 1234 Chivert charter was described, by the notary who copied the surviving 1325 transcript, as a "carta pergamenea."[41] Originals of later agreements might be on parch-

[41] Uxó Charter: "en la carta antiga lo cual de present es en la lur ma"—more broadly, "in their possession." Alcira trial record (as in Chapter XI, n. 46): "viso etiam instrumento sarracenorum"; though actual possession is ambiguous, the context favors it and Chabás so interprets it. *Llibre dels feyts*, ch. 334: "que les cartes partides son per a.b.c. que nos ne tenim les unes e vos ne tenits les altres." This practice began in the eleventh century; Francisco Carreras y Candi discusses it in his "Desenrotllament de la institució notarial a Catalunya en lo segle xiii," *Congrés I*, pp. 762-763; on attitudes toward paper, and on its spread here, see pp. 761-762. An illustration of the nonregistered document, torn so that each party might keep half, is the episcopal constitution transferring income to the Valencian sacristan, in Arch. Cat., perg. 4,616 (June 4, 1247); see also Boix, *Historia de Valencia*, I, 506n. The surrender pact of Tudela in 1115 on parchment in Latin and Arabic survived in the ducal archives at Pedrola until destroyed in an eighteenth-century war (Fernández y González, *Mudejares de Castilla*, II, 287n.). On the other hand a Játiva document of August 18, 1250, had to be presented for renewed drafting as early as 1317 "propter vetustatem" involving wear and tear (*corrosum*) and a

ment or paper; a 1279 confirmation of Mudejar privileges for Guadalest was done on "parchment," while a similar Arabic constitution for Carbonera's aljama was "redacted on paper."[42]

Did the crown preserve its copy? It seems to have done so only for its current files. After signing the surrender agreements at Elche, King James left behind notaries "who would bring me the charters drawn between me and the Saracens."[43] Such current, immediate documentation traveled with the king; a great deal of it was lost in a celebrated conflagration shortly after the fall of Valencia city when some knights, angry over the substitution of Catalan legal forms for Aragonese, burned down an inn housing both records and secretarial personnel. The secretaries sometimes deposited very important agreements at local religious establishments, or better at Barcelona or Sigena. Thus the treaties with Abū Zayd eventually went in 1260 into a locked box kept by the Hospitallers at Sigena in the Huesca area, where the crown had established its main documentary depot. King James was already conducting a lesser "public archives" at the palace of the counts in Barcelona. He also cached sealed boxes of important documentation in other odd corners of the realm for safekeeping.[44] Originals of the many surrender treaties,

---

badly damaged seal (Arch. Crown, Real Patrimonio, Real Casa, extra series, James I, perg. no. 90).

[42] Arch. Crown, Peter III, Reg. Canc. 41, fol. 97 (March 27, 1279): "sarracenica et redacta in papiru." Reg. Canc. 44, fol. 142v (June 22, 1279): "cartam pergamini sarracenicam." Romano, who copies both documents in his "Abenmenassé" (p. 256), rebukes Martínez-Ferrando for seeing the royal donor of these privileges as James; examination of the originals, however, leaves the matter in doubt, with first and third persons apparently opposed ("tradidimus" the document, "quam dominus rex conficiebat").

[43] *Llibre dels feyts*, ch. 422.

[44] On the disposition of royal documents and the rudimentary archives, see J. E. Martínez-Ferrando, *El archivo de la corona de Aragón* (Barcelona, 1944), ch. 2. Eduardo González Hurtebise in an earlier account erroneously supposed that the Barcelona collection was more important than Sigena's, because of King James's phrase "nostro publico archivo Barcinone"; see his *Guía histórico-descriptiva del archivo de la corona de Aragón* (Madrid, 1920), p. 8 and passim. The bailiff of Barcelona kept a box of crown correspondence with King Louis IX of France from Egypt, handing it over through his notary on demand in 1253 (*Itinerari*, p. 232). See also the examples gathered in my *Crusader Valencia*, I, 293-294, II, 311. An order of 1286 shows King Alfonso turning over nine registers of James I and twenty-one of the recently deceased Peter III to a crown notary.

except that for Valencia city, seem not to have been registered by the crown or permanently preserved. Community charters of like nature often went unregistered, as appears from an episode of 1285, when the Jewish communities of Valencia submitted their charters for confirmation; since the crown possessed no copies of its own, King Peter ordered transcripts made for the record.[45] Baronial and religious order charters for Mudejars have largely disappeared with the years; the Mudejars' own copies would have lost their practical use as circumstances changed and the Morisco era began.

Whether or not there was a separate statement of surrender, the multiple papers prepared by the notaries always included an allied feudal contract specifying the obligations and exemptions of the holders, perhaps in shortened form to stress the privileges, while leaving details to local custom. The distinction may help solve a difficulty of terminology involved in calling surviving surrender arrangements *cartas pueblas*, or settlement charters. The Chivert charter, for example, which Sá Vall insists is not a surrender treaty but a *carta puebla*, may have been the one as much as the other; the surviving text may be either the elaborate charter or a brief treaty comprising a summary of the charter.[46] In any case, a constitution or settlement charter issued in the context of formal surrender and incorporating the terms and exemptions agreed during negotiations amounts in effect to a surrender treaty. Whether one charter or two, the instrument provided legal recognition of corporate existence, assigned a set of laws, regulated community life, and defined the community's place in the feudal state. In general shape these charters have the form of feudal collective agrarian contracts and settlement charters; undoubtedly they assumed that familiar aspect, above others, in the eyes of contemporaries.

The contemporary *carta puebla* often comprised a collective contract with force of juridical ordination, by which one entered both an agrarian situation and a community of public law. Despite its corporate nature, the settler held individual right to his share, usually as an hereditary tenant but with his property alienable and

[45] Arch. Crown, Peter III, Reg. Canc. 56, fol. 96 (May 8, 1285).

[46] Guillem de Sá Vall, "Rendición del castillo de Xivert," *BSCC*, XXIV (1948), 231-233; "faem los cartes," and "faem nostres cartes ab ells"; the Muslim commitment is in "the charters."

owing rent. Agricultural stipulations were as important as commercial, legal, political, or other aspects of the charter in an economy where townsmen either owned external farms or felt involved with their prosperity. Owing to the ubiquitous, progressive tribe of Catalan lawyers, the trends represented by the *carta puebla* here differed from those in contemporary Castile. Comparison of Christian with Mudejar charters reveals a basic similarity, the divergences being such as one might expect; in the case of Muslims, however, James or his barons were not merely settling local law, upon condition of residence with homage, but also admitting an alien body into the Christian scene as a semi-independent enclave. Both Christian and Muslim communities over the years could accumulate further privileges or legal decisions, slowly building up a corpus of local liberties.[47] A century later the crown processed a routine request from "delegates of the aljama" of Fraga in Aragon, granting confirmation of their "privileges, good usages and customs, freedoms, liberties, and exemptions of the said aljama and of its individuals"—in short, a local constitution.[48]

James had arranged the treaties in any convenient spot: on the wet strand before Peñíscola, on empty roads or open hillsides, in a fig garden, at a country house, or in his capacious field tent.[49] This tent was an elaborate affair capable of holding a full war council, as at Silla, and furnished with "good couches" and luxurious hang-

[47] Font y Rius in his "Régimen municipal," part 2, pp. 231-234, explains the kinds of *cartas pueblas*. Rafael Gibert and Sánchez de la Vega review the whole subject for medieval Spain in their "Los contratos agrarios en el derecho medieval," *Boletín de la universidad de Granada*, XXII [1950], pp. 305-330. The *Documentos inéditos de España*, XVIII, 50-51, has a formula, applicable to the Valencian scene, by which such charters were usually given. A definitive collection of *cartas pueblas*, as yet unpublished, has been assembled for the kingdom of Valencia by Miguel Gual Camarena. See also the monumental collection by J. M. Font y Rius, *Cartas de población y franquicia de Cataluña*, confined to Catalonia proper, 1 vol. in 2 to date (Madrid, 1969), passim.

[48] In Macho Ortega's example, the "nuncios aliame" requested from the crown reconfirmation of their "privilegia, bonos usus et consuetudines, franquitates, libertates, ac immunitates dicte aliame et singularium eiusdem concessas" ("Documentos de los mudéjares aragoneses," pp. 157-158).

[49] *Llibre dels feyts*, chs. 184, 249, 360. Arch. Cat., Liber de bisbalía, fol. 8r (an. 1249), for country house. On the Minorcan shore "mattresses, mats, and cushions" were hastily arranged on short notice; for the 1242 interview with Zayyān, two ceremonial tents were raised on shore (*Llibre dels feyts*, chs. 119, 307).

ings. The king preferred tents, as at the siege of Valencia where he set up his tent hard by "some houses," though certain knights there did take up quarters in houses. He was in a tent before Cullera and before Murcia. His memoirs put him in a house once, but this seems a slip of the pen. He conducted high-level diplomatic talks on the Bairén shore in a tent set up for the purpose. The surrender ceremony outside Castellón de Játiva took place in a prized tent James later presented to the bishop of Valencia. On such occasions, mats and cushions for the visitors were supplied in a twinkling.[50]

A final ritual remained. This provided a spirited scene, as the townsfolk poured out to view their conqueror, to offer and receive gifts, and to swear allegiance on the Koran. The central characters were "the *qā'id*, with the principal hundred men of the town"; or "all the notables of the town and the rest of the people" assembled outside the town. For Villena James offers details: "all the people in Villena, from twenty years and up, swore to me that they would observe what they had agreed in this treaty." At Peñíscola "the Saracens when they saw me arrive all came out to meet me—men, women, and children in the castle," amounting to "a good two hundred." The community oath on the Koran was a standard fixture of these meetings. On Minorca "all the principal and best men in the island swore to it on the Koran"; at Alcira in Valencia "all the notables came out and swore on their Koran." At Elche, after "they had taken their oath of allegiance to me," James stayed overnight so that "all the Saracens of the town might then come out to me" to receive conditions formally and to surrender the strongest tower of the wall.

This was a form of fealty not unlike the standard ceremony of homage (*bay'a*) for a new caliph in Spain where, after the notables had sworn directly, the people pledged submission through agents, the hand of each person successively being placed on the agent's palm. The word used by King James, *sagrament*, had both a religio-mystical and a feudal usage, so that it conveyed overtones of holiness; the use of the Koran emphasized its religious nature. At Valencia the ceremony was staged outside, apparently just beyond the walls on the esplanade which served for certain religious func-

[50] *Llibre dels feyts*, chs. 193 (Cullera), 198 (Silla), 256 (Valencia), 307 (Bairén), 327 (Castellón), 436 (Murcia house, cf. ch. 434).

tions. Sometimes allegiance or confirmation was sworn in a mosque. Perhaps religious ground added another touch of the sacred. Muslims commonly introduced public and tax activities into their religious edifices, however, as did contemporary Christians, despite the scandal this gave to pious men like Ibn 'Abdūn.[51]

On such a happy occasion gifts were distributed to the Muslims; if necessary the king's party organized a committee to fetch them. At Peñíscola James presented "clothing, stores, and cattle," and at Castro "a quantity of sheep and goats, and clothing for five of the notables besides two horses." As part of the agreed gift at Almenara, James brought along "700 goats and 200 cows," meanwhile engaging several goods merchants to prepare cloth in quantity. The king purchased a steed to put with the gifts for the Alcalá Muslims "when they surrendered the castle to us"; the bill remained in his accounts unpaid for years afterward.[52]

The transfer of defenses almost formed a ceremony apart. During negotiations the enemy tried to reserve some defenses, where circumstances gave them sufficient bargaining leverage, or to arrange for a compensatory equivalent. At this stage of the crusade the king often contented himself with possession of the alcazar or of one strategic tower. For Bairén he designated the Albarrana, apparently

[51] *Ibid.*, chs. 121, 184, 327, 330, 331, 412, 420. At Castellón de Játiva the hundred notables "foren tots a aquel sagrament." On the pledge to the caliph see Lévi-Provençal, *España musulmana*, v, 11. On *bay'a* see below, Chapter XII, n. 27. The new settlement at Chelva in Valencia in 1370 had the oaths "en la mezquita del raval de Chelva appellado Benaxuay, sabado"; the swearing after the surrender of Argel in Bougie to Aragon in 1510 was done by "vosotros todos juntos en vuestra mezquita," though the document was drawn at Zaragoza (Fernández y González, *Mudejares de Castilla*, appendix, docs. 71, 94). A fifteenth-century loan involving the Uxó and Eslida districts was drawn in the mosque of Adzaneta and ratified by assemblies in the mosques of other towns but sometimes in a plaza or a portico (Lloréns, "Sarracenos de Eslida y Uxó," p. 60). Ibn 'Abdūn deplored the use of mosques for discussion of taxes, lawsuits, and worldly business (*Séville musulmane, le traité*, p. 53). On the mosque and public life see below, Chapter IX, section 2. On the use of Christian churches for extraordinary community business involving public assembly, see Burns, *Crusader Valencia*, I, 19. There is some mystery as to James's actual presence at the Uxó signing of 1250, perhaps a confusion of dates or a later solemnization by his agents of a hurried earlier surrender to the king in person (see Miret y Sans's discussion, *Itinerari*, esp. pp. 201-203).

[52] *Llibre dels feyts*, chs. 184, 245, 249. Arch. Crown, Reg. Canc. 10, fol. 106v (Jan. 4, 1258). *Itinerari*, pp. 283-284: "quando ipsum castrum [Alcalá] nobis reddiderunt."

a detached citadel tower; at Elche he took the Calahorra, judging it "the strongest"; at Alcira he preferred the double tower or gate complex looking toward Valencia city. The critical moment of transfer understandably raised apprehensions. The *qā'id* of Bairén on the day of surrender was at the point of renewing hostilities. The capitulation of Almácera turned into an ambush. The glowing prospects painted by Biar's envoys dissolved upon James's arriving into a town full of armed Muslims in ugly mood. At this critical moment in the peace transactions the king would warily sit his horse, waiting while an advance guard climbed to the parapets of the town. At Murcia he sent in "fifty knights with their usual squires," along with "one hundred and twenty Tortosan crossbowmen." At Peñíscola he had only seven knights to send, due to his haste in accepting negotiation. At Valencia, where the surrender program was progressive, the Muslims undertook to run up the king's banner themselves. The ceremony conveyed much more to contemporaries than meets the modern eye. In their surrender treaty of 1231 the Minorcans gave James the alcazar, "in such wise that your ensign or standard be positioned by the hands of five of your agents [*personae*] on the castle summit, and that your name and sovereignty be proclaimed in a loud voice by these agents of yours." This solemn liturgy was to unfold every year thereafter, according to the treaty, the agents proceeding from proclamation to formal possession; the king could restage this ceremony at any season but only once in the year, and each time he must "immediately repatriate" to his loyal Moors all he had symbolically taken.

Seeing his standard unfurled, and hearing his men call "Aragon! Aragon!" James sometimes dismounted to kiss the ground, in public gratitude to God. At Peñíscola as he waited tensely, surrounded by Muslims: "I took care that none of them could grasp the reins of my horse." At Murcia he uneasily gave himself to prayer, because "my people were so long about it"; but after being "a good piece there, I at last saw my banner fluttering in the wind on top of the alcazar and I saw the towers well manned with footmen and crossbowmen."[53] Now followed the division of the town, where called

[53] *Llibre dels feyts,* chs. 184, 189, 282, 312-313, 356; on flag-raising, chs. 443-444, and see 282, 314, 443; on the towers taken, chs. 282, 309, 330-331, 417-420. On reluctance to give up defenses see esp. the cases of Bairén, Játiva, and Minorca; the

for by treaty; the assignment of military police or a garrison contingent; consultations on implementing or interpreting the treaty—a wall or road to build, a mosque to take, or occasionally some nonconforming bands to pacify; then finally, back at base, "great and brilliant rejoicings." Of the hundred knights in his entourage at Paterna, James left behind ten plus his queen.

What of the grand entry into the city to the chant of the Te Deum, the consecration of mosques designated to serve as churches, the distribution of promised properties, and the preparation of statutes incident to the forming of a Christian commune? These scenes do not really belong to the essential surrender; in any case they probably occurred only at more important towns.[54] One such major city, Murcia, required at least thirteen days for the process of negotiation, surrender, transfer of defenses, and solemn entry. On January 2, 1266, King James left Orihuela to besiege Murcia, whose defenders by that time knew themselves to be in an untenable military position. On January 20 he held the first formal interview looking toward surrender, and on January 23 the second, concluding with an agreement on the twenty-sixth. He allowed three days—to January 29—for arranging evacuation of the inner alcazar, held by a third force of Granadan allies or masters. James sent his troops in to garrison the defenses on the thirtieth, appeared at the alcazar on the thirty-first to divide and organize the city, and made his ceremonial entry as conqueror only on February 2.[55]

Where a castle fell to a lord other than the king, as at Chivert,

---

Uxó Charter puts this as the king's first and central demand. *Traités de paix et de commerce et documents divers concernant les relations des chrétiens avec les arabes de l'Afrique septentrionale au moyen âge*, ed. Louis (comte de) Mas Latrie, 2 vols. (New York, [1886] 1963), II, 182-185 (June 17, 1231): "ita quod signum vestrum sive vexillum ponatur per manus quinque personarum vestrarum in sumitate castri, et clametur alta voce ab ipsis personis vestris nomen et dominium vestrum, et hoc facto reddatur castrum." The editor confuses this document with Majorca's fall.

[54] *Llibre dels feyts*, chs. 253 (rejoicing), 254 (Paterna), 331, 445 (implementing), 421 (garrison), 442, 444 (division, police). For the solemn entry and subsequent activities, see my *Crusader Valencia*, II, 370.

[55] Torres Fontes reconstructed this time table for his *Reconquista de Murcia*, ch. 9, especially pp. 145-154. The Granadans were an extrinsic element, allies who had come to dominate, some 800 light horse and 2,000 foot, and who stayed aloof in the alcazar.

no details of the process survive; the similarity of the treaties themselves, however, suggests that it was much the same. By far the largest number of important places surrendered to the king, though he might leave arrangement of charter details for lesser castles to the lords who had secured them by arms or grant. At Alaguar Valley James handled the ordinary financial arrangements; Tales, on the contrary, went to the baron Peter of Castellnou, who then drew up a seignorial charter. The capitulation to the crown at Valencia city provided that rental arrangements be worked out between the Muslims of the countryside and incoming Christian landowners.[56]

To watch King James at his negotiations is to comprehend better both the underlying pattern of Mudejarism and the king's personal attitude toward it. What charters, laws, and privileges reveal in an abstract way, these very human scenes illustrate graphically. In his autobiography the king is at pains to proclaim himself an enemy of Islam, a bloody expeller of pagans, a Christian champion repelled by the vileness of Mudejar Islam's encumbrance of his realms. Merely in telling where he went and what he did, however, he unwittingly betrays his real self as possessing a shrewder humanity and a deeper Christianity.

[56] Arch. Crown, Peter III, Reg. Canc. 42, fol. 187 (Dec. 10, 1279): "prout cum eo composuerint" (Alaguar). Tales Charter. Valencia Capitulation (see Chapter I, n. 3): "quod component cum dominis qui hereditates tenuerint."

CHAPTER IX

Islam: An Established Religion

THE WORLD OF Islam was marked by diversity of people and local cultures. Schism, sects, and schools sundered its religious unity. Bickering factionalism could suddenly shatter its monolithic political units, or set one against its neighbor. Below all differences, however, every faction shared at least a religio-cultural tropism; the discords were family quarrels. Each party saw itself as keeper of the sacred Book, sons of the Prophet, whose face was to the holy city, whose destiny was paradise. Freedom of religion, therefore, was the most important privilege to be wrung from the infidel conqueror. The resolutely pious saw this need clearly, but even the backslider or relatively indifferent could not escape it. Ibn Khaldūn astutely grasped the paradox. Only "special people who take a particular interest in their religion" experience sustained concern for its services; "the common people have no compelling need for them" except from time to time. Though religious institutions and vocation are "nobler" than the political or economic, the religious demands of most individuals tend to remain potential and occasional. The relative neglect of religion in daily life therefore contrasts with the indispensability of religion to society.[1]

Freedom of religion for the Mudejar did not mean merely the right to worship as he chose. Contemporary Christian law and theology condemned enforced conversion, so that the lowliest Muslim, whatever burden of prejudice and religious disorientation he suffered, could anticipate a measure of religious freedom. In the Valencian surrender pacts the Christians conceded something quite different, something more than the "entire liberty of conscience" stressed by older authors.[2] This was public worship as a community, under the committed judicial protection of the sovereign and with

[1] *Muqaddimah*, II, 335-336; see also I, 305, 319. Alfred Bel's work on North African religious life, *La religion musulmane en Berbérie, esquisse d'histoire et de sociologie religieuses*, provides some background but is disappointing for the present investigation (2 vols. [Paris, 1938], I, bk. 3, ch. I on the thirteenth century).

[2] Janer, *Moriscos de España*, p. 13: "entera libertad de conciencia."

sociopolitical effects. The Muslim's public acts of religion defined his faith much more than did his private conscience. Moreover, his prime religious institution was not a separate church incarnated into social forms, as in Christendom, but the indivisible society itself. The Aragonese crown was according formal recognition to a religious entity, the local aljama, as a legal personality with specific rights and as an alien society in its entirety. Socially and as a barrier to acculturation this recognition of public structure was much more important in its effect on the Muslim than was individual liberty of conscience.

The King's Other Religion

Islam was not a church, then, nor even the religious function of the Muslim, but rather his social, civil, intellectual, and religious life as viewed in its most important single aspect. There could be little separation of church and state, and for that matter no clergy and no laity, since these clear categories did not reflect the complex reality. Civil operations were religious in root and rationale, the state being an executive function of the religious community and wielding a law theological in origin and outline. Allah was all—and government or society, caliph or humanist were evanescent phenomena useful only in their capacity to direct man's energies toward Him. This was more than a denial of the church-versus-state dilemma; it was the antithesis of the European tradition of Christian humanism, and a repudiation of the tension between sacral and secular, not just at the political but at all levels. Compared to this position the medieval theocracy of the Christian West appears modern, a radical separation of Caesar from Christ. In practice the situation was not simple; religions tend to assume forms sociologically analogous. One can overstress the theoretical unity of Islam, failing to notice that practical adaptations qualified and compromised it. On the other hand, so central was this orientation and so effective its controlling factors that it is difficult to exaggerate the underlying tropism of the community.

Modern political categories, often meaningless in the context of medieval Christendom or Islam, are of little use in probing the Valencian situation. Since religion could not be disengaged from the community's social, political, and legal forms, however, and since independence for Muslims in these secondary areas posited as its condition a semiautonomous theocracy, it may help to describe what emerged in Valencia as a double confessional state. In becoming an independent society in the kingdom of Valencia, Islam became in effect an established religion, enjoying favored status officially recognized, with privileges and properties conceded by the crown for the service of religion, and with an assured religious role in the legal, social, and educational public life of its communities, all under official protection. To meet specific need, crown protection sometimes took the form of a special *guidaticum* or flag of safeguard, like that applying to mosques and religious books at Eslida in 1276.[3]

This structural reality explains the title assumed by an earlier hero of the Reconquest, Alfonso VI of Castile, who recaptured Toledo and presided over the Cid's exploits in Valencia; borrowing the *ṣāḥib dhu 'l-millatayn* from his Spanish Muslim colleagues, Alfonso became "ruler of the two religions."[4] St. Ferdinand III, contemporary of James the Conqueror, in similar vein displayed upon his royal tomb an inscription in Latin, Castilian, Hebrew, and Arabic. King James seems to have conceived his relation to the Mudejars of Valencia in these same expansive terms. The arrangement seems reasonable enough to the modern mind, which no longer sees religion as the central value or controlling principle of society. The shock of confrontation might better be conveyed today by analogies involving ideologico-political systems like capitalism, fascism, and communism. Under a kind of diplomatic immunity in Valencia the essential enemy controlled his own mini-commonwealth—the aljama's customs, morals, beliefs, values, manners, intellectual and artistic expression, business modes and ethics, and all the daily life and psychology of its people. It may be argued that tolerance at this extreme is not easily distinguishable from intolerance, or from the ghetto and colonial reservations. The perception is not altogether unjust. The Valencian reality, though by no means so malevolent, in many ways closed the antipathetic communities away from each other, despite the eroding forces of acculturation that seeped through.

[3] Arch. Crown, James I, Reg. Canc. 38, fol. 3v (June 27, 1276).

[4] Cagigas, *Mozárabes*, II, 466-467, 481, with examples from Toledo, Lérida, and Valencia; and his *Mudejares*, I, 241.

Where two exclusive systems closely exist, this dilemma is native to the concept of tolerance, no matter how sympathetic its framers may be toward the minority; the tolerance that fully preserves an alien group's existence also condemns that group to a life apart, inverted, and undernourished, so strange to the other community as to seem repugnant and even inimical. Examining the consequences of this structural fault would require a separate book; here the edifice itself commands attention. It is enough to know that the Mudejar edifice was flawed in its foundations.

The Valencian poet Ibn ʿAmīra, fleeing his native land after the crusaders had seized it, lamented that "the infidel has caused the faith to vanish; the bell has replaced the cry of the muezzin."[5] Ibn ʿAmīra was framing his regret in rhetorical conventions. The reality proved more bizarre. In this Christian land far more muezzins could be heard calling from minarets than bells clanging in steeples. The ubiquitous clamor of the muezzin, raised five times daily, served as perpetual reminder of solidarity for the vanquished Valencians and a public profession of the faith in which their unity stood rooted. The situation continued into the fourteenth century, occasioning restrictive legislation, itself an index of abiding practice; the ecumenical council at Vienne in Provence in 1311 deplored the way "the priests of these people in their temples or mosques at certain hours every day invoke and cry out from some high place" the name of the Prophet "in the ears of Saracens and Christians." The council's admonition found its way into the permanent corpus of canon law.[6] That the Vienne statement applied to the realms of Aragon is apparent from a decree of excommunication seventeen years later at the metropolitan council of Tarragona; "certain" Christian "temporal lords of the Saracens" had ignored the Vienne ordinance out of self-interest, thus falling into "the sin of pagan-

[5] Ibn ʿAmīra, in al-Ḥimyarī, *Kitāb ar-rawḍ al-miʿṭār*, p. 106. He reflects the contemporary hatred of Christian bells; Ibn ʿAbdūn had inveighed against them in the previous century—perhaps with reference to Mozarabic churches—relegating them "to the lands of the infidels" (*Séville musulmane, le traité*, p. 123).

[6] *Corpus iuris canonici*, ed. Emil Friedberg and E. L. Richter, 2d edn. rev., 2 vols. (Leipzig, 1879-1881), *Clementinae*, lib. V, tit. II, c. 1: "sacerdotes eorum . . . in templis seu mesquitis suis . . . diebus singulis, certis horis in loco aliquo eminenti eiusdem Machometi nomen, christianis et sarracenis audientibus, alta voce invocant et extollunt."

ism."[7] James II supported Vienne by a law of 1313 forbidding the common practice among Spanish Muslims of praying publicly in streets and plazas.[8] The *corts* or parliament for the kingdom of Valencia in 1303 prohibited the sounding of trumpets from mosques and minarets "according to the damnable Mohammedan sect."[9] Even on estates governed by the bishop of Valencia, that prelate unhappily reported as late as 1331 that "the praises of the unbeliever" were "regularly raised."[10] Despite the bishop, the muezzin's call was to endure there for another decade.[11] Late evidence thus discloses a continuing pattern of public prayer throughout the thirteenth century and into the fourteenth, reinforcing the materials from the crusade generation. Thirteenth-century materials are more specific.

At the surrender of Villena James the Conqueror specifically safeguarded the muezzin's call, allowing the people "to keep their law as to crying out." At Elche he stipulated "that they might observe their law in crying out in their mosques." In refusing the Murcians possession of the main mosque, located hard by the gate of the king's alcazar, he exclaimed that the cry of the muezzin "close to my head while I am sleeping, though you may think it good, is not a pleasant thing."[12] However soothing to the royal ear, such noise abatement was no factor elsewhere in the city. Muezzins vigorously plied their vocation in every town. Surrender agreements incorporated them as a routine proviso. At Uxó in 1250 "the imams can proclaim in the mosque." At Chivert the muezzin could "proclaim without any impediment." At Eslida he could not be "forbidden to proclaim in the mosque."[13] To proclaim (*preconizare* or *preconitzar*) meant to

[7] Fernández y González, *Mudejares de Castilla*, appendix, doc. 75.

[8] Janer, *Moriscos de España*, p. 14.

[9] Roca Traver, "Vida mudéjar," p. 141: "segons la damnada secta mahometica."

[10] Arch. Cat., perg. 2,404 (Jan. 19, 1331): "ubi perfidi Mahometi consueverunt laudes extolli." Here and in the following note compare *perfidus* or unbeliever to the expression "perfidious Jews"; at that period it seems to have been the Christian counterpart for the Jewish use of "gentiles," expressing a similar danger of distaste for the outsider and with an added danger of assimilation to the feudal "faithless" betrayer.

[11] *Ibid.*, perg. 2,450 (Feb. 8, 1340): "invocatur inibi nomen perfidi Mahometi."

[12] *Llibre dels feyts*, chs. 418, 440, 445. Ibn 'Abdūn recommended as many muezzins for a mosque as the number of its doors plus two, a formula he related to their role in the Friday liturgy (*Séville musulmane, le traité*, p. 46).

[13] Chivert Charter: "sine aliquo impedimento pregonare." Aldea Charter: "et possint preconizare." Eslida Charter: "nec prohibent preconizare in mezquitis."

publish or make announcement, and here refers rather to the muezzin's "announcement" (*adhān*) or five-times-daily call than to preaching the Friday preliminary address in the mosque.[14] In his Murcian plaint, James reproduced the offending cry as "ala lo sabba, o alla." King James prided himself on being knowledgeable in things Islamic, and he does not seem to be indulging here in a deliberately insulting garble, so the phrase ought to fit one of the seven formulas or substitute phrases of the *adhān*. Can it be the "[ḥayya] 'alā 'ṣ-ṣalāt" or "[come] to prayer," distorted by a scribe? More probably the currently preferred reading of the king's words should be replaced by a discarded but older and simpler manuscript variant, "lo sabacala," meaning the muezzin himself. Later confirmation of the prayer-call privilege at Uxó does catch the phrase properly: "call ala zala as the custom has been"; this represents, as perhaps James had meant to, "[ḥayya] 'alā 'ṣ-ṣalāh" or "[come] to prayer," involving the pausal form of *ṣalāt*.[15]

The sermon gets no specific mention in early Valencian documents, though Valencia city's *qāḍī* Abu 'r-Rabī', who died fighting King James's crusaders at Puig, was celebrated for his treatise on the art of preaching.[16] Lull alludes to the effectiveness of the contemporary Islamic sermon, contrasting in his *Blanquerna* the de-

---

Uxó Charter: "concedentes . . . cabazallanos qui . . . possint preconizare in mezquitis."

14 The word is used in the *Aureum opus* meaning to "publish" a penalty assigned to a crime, and in the *Furs* to describe the action of town criers. On the other hand *prehicar* or *preïcar*, related to *predicare* or preach, was used by King James for summoning a parliament (*Llibre dels feyts*, ch. 504), so perhaps *preconizare* might be stretched to cover preaching.

15 In his edition of the *Llibre dels feyts*, used in these notes, Miguel Coll i Alentorn prefers the first reading, from the Biblioteca de Catalunya manuscript of 1380, over the simpler variant from the Poblet manuscript in the Bibl. Univ. Barc. The Uxó confirmation is in Fernández y González, *Mudejares de Castilla*, appendix, doc. 71 (Aug. 17, 1370): "vuestros alfaquines criden Ala Zala segun era acostumbrado." For the *faqīh* (pl. *fuqahā'*), see below, p. 221; for the *sabaçala*, see p. 190. On the cry, see T. W. Juynboll, "Adhān," *EI*², I, 187-188; A. J. Wensinck, "Ṣalāt," *EI*¹, IV, part I, 96-105; and Carra de Vaux, "Shahāda," *EI*¹, IV, part I, 259. On the pausal form see August Fischer, "Zur Syntax der muslimischen Bekenntnisformel," *Islamica* (Leipzig), IV (1931), pp. 518-519n. Enrico Cerulli gives the full *adhān* as copied with explanations for Alfonso X of Castile in "Transcriptions françaises de mots arabes dans un manuscrit du xiiie siècle," *Groupe linguistique d'études chamito-sémitiques, Comptes rendus*, IV (1945-1948), 27-28.

16 Al-Maqqarī, *Mohammedan Dynasties in Spain*, II, 336.

voutly weeping Muslim auditors with the sleepers at a cardinal's sermon.[17] In his capacity as courtier Lull was earlier able to observe the postconquest Mudejars of King James in both Valencia and Majorca, an experience strengthened during his subsequent apostolate over several decades to the Muslims of Catalan lands including Valencia. He was impressed by the possibilities of music and verse as an apostolic tool, "as the Saracens chant the Koran in their mosques." The chant was that arrangement of "sounds in certain harmonious cadences" which Ibn Khaldūn contrasted with the "forbidden" use of "melodious music" in reciting the Koran; some authorities permitted the former, a production which at least the musically knowledgeable "perceive as music."[18]

Valencian charters usually named the muezzin (*mu'adhdhin*) only by his function, or as though included in the more generic office of the locality's imams. The Alfandech treaty spoke openly of a "*çabaçalano* or muezzin." The *çabaçalanus* (*ṣāḥib aṣ-ṣalāt*) was the imam or leader, a respected member of the community who acted as main functionary at a mosque, leading the congregational prayers and often delivering the Friday sermon. During the ritual daily *ṣalāt* the worshipers lined up behind an imam, official or temporary, to go through prescribed Koranic expressions in varying positions of the body, at early morning, late noon, midafternoon, sunset, and evening. The trumpets and similar wind instruments forbidden by the 1303 law were used to summon "to the *ṣalāt* [*çala*]" as well as to "other public acts" of worship.[19] *Çabaçaloni* figure in the Chivert and Alfandech

[17] Lull, *Blanquerna*, ch. 93. On sermons see also Ibn Khaldūn, *Muqaddimah*, II, 70-73, as well as the description both of the official Friday sermon and of the homiletic or informal preaching witnessed by the traveler Ibn Baṭṭūṭa, including his account of a fiery preacher on hell (*Travels*, I, 222, 227, 231-232, II, 286, 450, 451).

[18] Lull, "Tractatus de modo convertendi infideles," ed. Ramón Sugranyes de Franch, in *Raymond Lulle, docteur des missions* (Schöneck-Beckenried, 1954), p. 18. His *Libre d'amich e amat*, no. 154, in the *Blanquerna* rebuked Christians for not prefacing their correspondence with Christ's name to do him the honor Muslims thus gave to Muḥammad or Allah. See also Ibn Khaldūn, *Muqaddimah*, II, 399-401. The Sufis of the tenth century had spread the use of chant and music, earlier rejected for worship as profane (Aly Mazahéri, *La vie quotidienne des musulmans au moyen âge, xe au xiiie siècle* [Paris, 1951], p. 12).

[19] *Corts* of Valencia as cited in n. 9: "per fer la cala o altre acte publich"; "nafill o altre instrument o trompeta." Roca Traver, "Vida mudéjar," pp. 141-142, has the angry complaints of James II and the persistence of the practice in 1329. Ibn 'Abdūn prescribed six imams for proper alternating in directing Friday prayers (*Séville musulmane, le traité*, p. 47).

charters, and *cabazallanos* in the Aldea, Uxó, and Játiva pacts. The plural relates to the multiplicity of mosques in a given area. It also fits the picture drawn by Lévi-Provençal for an earlier era in Spain, when the main mosque supported a number of imams and muezzins by turn during the week, and all took their posts on Friday to relay the word of the main *ṣāhib aṣ-ṣalāt* to the overflow crowd.[20] The smaller mosques in a Spanish town normally had little minarets of their own, each with a caretaker who was simultaneously schoolmaster and muezzin. The minaret was seldom the Persian or Turkish cylinder but a square structure, incorporating rooms suitable for living quarters; more modest than the Christian bell tower, it often stood in two storeys, one set back like a small box upon a larger, and was separated by a patio from the mosque. Prayer leaders, muezzins, and similar religious personnel received salaries; Ibn Khaldūn supported the opinion that in general they were very cheaply recompensed.[21]

Valencian surrender records refer often to Islam's public liturgy. Besides the formal prayer five times daily, good Muslims frequented mosques and gathered on Friday for midday worship at the main mosque. At Eslida they might "make their prayers on Fridays and at their festival times and on other days, but let them do so according to their law." The wording could cover canonical festivities as well as more informal observances or even such purely local aberrations as the Sunday day of rest.[22] At Seta, Muslims "may adore and read [aloud] in their mosques."[23] At Uxó they could "proclaim their Sunna in prayers."[24] At Denia and several other places "they may

[20] Alfandech, Aldea, Chivert, and Játiva Charters. Lévi-Provençal, *España musulmana*, v, 298-300. On the political function of the *ṣāḥib aṣ-ṣalāt*, see below, p. 386. Ibn Baṭṭūṭa describes the corps of mosque servitors and of muezzins, each under its sheik, at Mecca (*Travels*, I, 175, 222).

[21] Torres Balbás, "Los edificios hispanomusulmanes," *RIEEI*, I (1953), p. 99; his "El ŷāmūr de Alcolea y otras de varias alminares," with an inventory of survivals and discussion of tip-endings (*Al-Andalus*, XXIII [1958], 192-202); and his *Artes almoravide y almohade* (Madrid, 1955), pp. 14ff. Ibn Khaldūn, *Muqaddimah*, II, 335.

[22] Eslida Charter: "nec [prohibent] fieri orationem in illis diebus veneris et festivis suis, et aliis diebus, sed faciant secundum eorum legem." Second Eslida Charter: "et faciatis orationes vestras in meschitis vestris." On this second charter see Chapter VI, n. 5.

[23] Arch. Crown, Peter III, Reg. Canc. 44, fol. 149 (July 20, 1279): "possint adorare et legere in meçquitis eorum."

[24] Uxó Charter: "e que pusquen publicar lur çuna en oracions."

read their books and Sunna, and make prayers, in their mosques."[25] At Aldea they were "to pray according to the custom of the Saracens."[26] At Cuart "they may read their books and pray in their mosques."[27] At Alfandech mosques, books, and prayer life came under the guarantees.[28] At Alcira "they could conduct their services [*fer lur offici*] in the mosques just as they were accustomed."[29] At Rafelbuñol they could "keep the books of your law."[30] The Eslida charter in 1242 protected both Koran and Hadith.[31] The Sunna and Hadith, transmitting the Prophet's words and example, will recur for more direct examination later, in the context of Valencian law.

His "books" were more sacred to the Muslim than was the Bible to the Christian, so it is no surprise to find them expressly mentioned. The Koran, which King James always treated with respect, was for Muslims the word of God spoken directly by Him in a sacred language; some theologians explained it as His uncreated Logos or subsisting Word. Daniel consequently calls the Koran "very nearly what Christ is in Christianity," while Hitti compares it to the Eucharistic Host.[32] Such comparisons can mislead, since there exists in Islam no parallel for the further meaning of Christ; but they do underline the belief that the Koran was no mere holy

[25] Arch. Crown, Peter III, Reg. Canc. 44, fol. 160 (Nov. 14, 1279): "et quod possint legere libros et açunam eorum et faciant orationes in mesquitis suis."

[26] Aldea Charter: "et orare secundum consuetudinem sarracenorum."

[27] Arch. Crown, Peter III, Reg. Canc. 44, fol. 149v (July 16, 1279): "quod possint [legere] libros legis sue et orare . . . in mecquitis eorum."

[28] Alfandech Charter.

[29] *Llibre dels feyts*, ch. 330.

[30] Arch. Crown, Peter III, Reg. Canc. 44, fol. 184 (July 15, 1280): "et tenere etiam libros legis vestre."

[31] Eslida Charter: "Alcora et libros omnes de Alhadet secundum legem suam et Alcopzi sint de mezquitis suis"; for how conflicting versions turn on punctuation, see n. 52. *Alcopzi* in this context might represent the Arabic plural for books, if derived from an eastern dialect; but the Spanish colloquial form displaced the stress accent to the second syllable, while the classical form has one syllable too many. Moreover, external evidence points to a very different meaning (see p. 212). Arnald Steiger includes *alhadet* and *alcursi*, but with meanings inapplicable here (*Contribución a la fonética del hispano-árabe y de los arabismos en el ibero-románico y el siciliano* [Madrid, 1932], pp. 129n., 204).

[32] Daniel, *Islam and the West*, p. 33. Arthur Stanley Tritton has a chapter on the books used in medieval Islamic schooling; see his *Materials on Muslim Education in the Middle Ages* (London, 1957), ch. 12. Philip K. Hitti, *Islam: A Way of Life* (Minneapolis, 1970), p. 26.

book of revelation, capable of being translated or in the ordinary commercial sense sold, but a unique phenomenon and a bond of union. Muslims would even ransom their books of religion. As part of a peace treaty with Castile in 1285, Abū Yūsuf of Morocco demanded thirteen mule-loads of books from territories recently conquered by Castilian crusaders, especially from Cordova; over twelve hundred volumes of Spanish learning on the Koran, the Hadith, religious jurisprudence, and the like (but not on the more secular subjects such as medicine, geography, and history) found their way to a Fez college favored by the sultan and eventually into the mainstream of North African thought.[33] This remarkable demonstration of Muslim veneration for books on sacred subjects had an echo, four hundred years later, when in 1689 a victorious sultan of Morocco offered to exchange a captured Spanish garrison for five hundred Muslim prisoners plus five thousand Arabic manuscripts preserved at the Escorial.[34] The books in the surrender treaties made by King James with Valencian towns must have included many local treasures; Valencia had been particularly famed for the production of fine books. Looking back from the fourteenth century, when North African bookmaking had already declined into "such a bad handwriting and with so much corruption and so many clerical errors that they cannot be understood," Ibn Khaldūn recorded how the art of copying and binding books, together with techniques of textual transmission, "formerly reached tremendous proportions in Iraq and in Spain." In his lifetime "some slight remnant of this institution" persisted at Granada.[35]

The Chivert charter exempted from taxation the pool of ablutions used for ceremonial cleansing before prayer—"the pool which is in the major mosque"—together with conduits and allied necessities. An emissary of King James observed with detached eye the *qā'id* of Bairén at his religious ablutions; he relayed his impressions to the king, who committed them to his memoirs. The *qā'id* went apart to a fountain or pool near his castle, put aside his tunic (*almexia*)

[33] Ibn Khaldūn, *Histoire des Berbères*, IV, 118. The description of contents comes from Ibn Abī Zar', with the reckoning of some hundred volumes per pack-mule added as editor's comment.

[34] Henri Pérès, *L'Espagne vue par les voyageurs musulmans de 1610 à 1930* (Paris, 1937), pp. 5-6.

[35] Ibn Khaldūn, *Muqaddimah*, II, 391-394.

"and sat in the pool, and bathed himself and then splashed the water up over himself." Normally it was unnecessary for a treaty to specify the pool attached to each mosque or its water sources, since they were included in the concession of mosques and "Saracen customs."[36]

The act of granting religious freedom in its institutionalized expressions did not require descriptive elaboration. Some charters nonetheless provided one or two representative details. Fasting, the poor tax, and the Mecca pilgrimage, together with the fivefold daily prayer and the profession of faith, formed the basic public obligations or five pillars of Islam. The Chivert charter specifically guaranteed fasting. This referred to the community's dawn-to-sunset fast during the month of Ramaḍān, culminating in a joyous celebration. Important to the spiritual discipline of the community, Ramaḍān was a mass experience throughout the kingdom of Valencia and beyond it to the ends of the Islamic world. So accustomed were Christians to this and other activities of the parallel society in their kingdom that they rarely paid attention to them, and then only in passing in connection with some other affair. The arrest of the transient Muḥammad in 1287 at Silla occasioned the information that he was on his way to Játiva "to keep and fast the Lent of the Moors in the *morería*."[37] (The assimilation of Ramaḍān to Lent echoes a similar infelicity in Muntaner's memoir, where he had the North Africans offer "indulgences" for a holy war.)[38] The survival of the community fast can be seen as late as 1515 in an Arabic accounting of money collected in the Moorish quarter of Valencia city for its observance.[39]

Almsgiving turns up among the pieties recognized for the Alfandech Valley, and obviously refers less to sporadic voluntary chari-

[36] Chivert Charter: "et aliupum quod est in mesquida maiori," together with the *cabaçasonos* of the mosque and *terminus* by which the water comes in. *Llibre dels feyts*, ch. 312. The Catalan *jub*, for a pool or bath, is directly borrowed from the Arabic. On *almexia* see Dozy, *Glossaire*, p. 163.

[37] Roca Traver, "Vida mudéjar," doc. 20 (1287): "tenir e dejunar la quaresma dels moros en la moreria." Chivert Charter: "ieiunare."

[38] *Crònica*, ch. 51: "els maleyts moabits anaren preycant ecridant per tota la Barbaria, e donar perdons a llur mala lig."

[39] Fernández y González, *Mudejares de Castilla*, appendix, doc. 97. All classes of Valencian Moriscos, whether rural or urban, persevered in observing Ramaḍān up to the year of expulsion (Halperín Donghi, "Moriscos y cristianos viejos en Valencia," p. 82).

ties than to the obligatory tax or *zakāt*. The *azaque* which Eslida's charter discusses was the *zakāt* insofar as it fell on livestock; the charter's restricted application of the term may reflect the pastoral nature of the region. A fraction of the theoretical tenth of a man's income, it was the only tax the Koran imposed upon the believer.[40] Ibn Khaldūn says it amounted only to "small assessments because, as everyone knows," the charity tax on property, grain, and cattle was "low." The Arabist Pascual de Gayangos flatly affirms that the *peytes* waived by King James when demanding tribute from Abū Zayd's Valencia were the *zakāt*; but the apposite phrase in the king's memoirs refers rather to indirect levies beyond rental.[41]

The Chivert charter guaranteed the right "to make pilgrimages."[42] Pilgrimage to Mecca was a basic obligation, once in a lifetime, for every Muslim able to perform it. The geography of mandatory pilgrimage linked Valencian society, at least at its vital and influential levels, to the farther reaches of the Islamic world. After the crusade it continued to do so. Trips abroad were also covered by a privilege wider than any local guarantees in the name of pilgrimage. Freedom of foreign journeys, including commercial, literary-educational, and social voyages, was normal for Mudejar society in its early period, although it was strictly conditional on the payment of a small fee for a travel license. The Christian laws eventually restated or incorporated the policy of liberty of movement in peacetime for "any Saracen man or woman to the country of the Saracens for reasons of commerce or pilgrimage."[43]

[40] Alfandech and Eslida Charters. On *zakāt* see Joseph Schact, "Zakāt," *EI*[1], IV, part 2, 1202-1205. See also Qudāmah b. Ja'far, *Kitāb al-kharāj*, in *Taxation in Islam*, ed. and trans. Aharon Ben-Shemesh, 2d edn. rev., 3 vols. to date (Leiden, 1965-1969), II, chs. 9, 13.

[41] Ibn Khaldūn, *Muqaddimah*, II, 89; see p. 150 for the religious land tax and p. 153 for charity expenses of the ruler. *Llibre dels feyts*, ch. 25; Gayangos's interpretation is attached to Forster's translation, *Chronicle*, I, 49, II, 709.

[42] Chivert Charter: "facere romerias."

[43] *Aureum opus*, appendix *In extravaganti*, doc. 8, fol. 236 (1348): "quicumque sarracenus vel sarracena ad terram sarracenorum, causa mercandi aut romerie." Leopoldo Torres Balbás reviews the origins and nature of these pilgrimages in his "Rábitas hispanomusulmanas," *Al-Andalus*, XIII (1948), 475-491. He distinguishes the different kinds of holy places, all of which I refer to simply as oratories; some of these had become elaborate centers for defense or for hospitality, prayer, and the study of the Koran, while others were little mosques or chapels. Piles Ros studied the fifteenth-century counterpart of the voyaging in his "Moros de realengo

While the Mecca pilgrimage was undoubtedly one of the basic religious freedoms granted in the charter, it was probably not the only object of the Chivert concession. More troublesome to the Christians and incessantly practiced were local pilgrimages. A cult of holy men and sanctuaries flourished at the time in Spanish Islam; it persisted into the next century, so that the ecumenical council of Vienne denounced it to the Christian lords of Muslim communities. Besides "adoring" the vile Prophet in their temples and publicly praying at the call of the muezzin, the council fathers noted, "a great multitude of local and even distant Saracens converge at a [given] place where some Saracen was once buried, whom the other Saracens venerate with devotions"; this kind of "peregrination" unsettled the Christian populace and had to cease. As with Ramaḍān, there was question of a mass movement, this time amounting to demonstration of social solidarity so obtrusively turbulent as to disquiet the Christian inhabitants.[44] Lull remarked on the "religious men" revered as saints, including the many mystics who increased the people's devotion. The Sufi mystical movement, strong in Valencia at the moment of crusade, provided a number of these saints, especially the octogenarian Abū Aḥmad Ja'far b. Sīd-bono

en Valencia," pp. 258-260. Laws by then prohibited foreign travel in theory but not in practice; one paid a fee to change domicile from seignorial to crown lands or vice versa, and protesting lords were rebuked; the author found foreign travel permits in "abundance" and "so numerous" that obviously anyone could get one. Mudejars left from all over Valencia, most often by sea and usually on Venetian ships, stayed abroad as long as five years, and gave reasons as general as wanting "to see the world" or more commonly to trade; each left a pledge, usually a hundred florins, against his return; conversely, Muslims visited Valencia from places like Oran, Tunis, Tlemcen, and Granada, sometimes bringing along their households. Émile Dermenghem supplies background on feasts and pilgrimages from the medieval North African scene in *Le culte des saints dans l'Islam maghrébin*, 6th edn. (Paris, 1954), part 4; the role of the saint as the embodiment of Moroccan history and its major moving force in the past is a theme of Clifford Geertz's study in contrasts, *Islam Observed: Religious Development in Morocco and Indonesia* (New Haven, 1968), pp. 43-55. See also the reference of Ibn 'Abdūn to "pilgrimage to holy places" in his *Séville musulmane, le traité*, p. 16.

[44] *Corpus iuris canonici, Clementinae*, lib. V, tit. II, c. I: "ad locum insuper ubi olim quidam sepultus extitit sarracenus, quem ut sanctum sarraceni alii venerantur et colunt, magna sarracenorum earundem partium, et etiam aliarum, confluit publice multitudo; . . . peregrinatio praelibata."

al-Khuzāʿī, who died in 1227 at a village near Cocentaina and whose tomb was venerated even by non-Muslim Valencians during the subsequent century.[45]

A celebrated Valencian holy place at this time was Bairén near Gandía, an area remaining in Muslim hands by the surrender pacts. Another appeared in the book recording land divisions, near Valencia city. An important shrine drew pilgrims to Denia. Several more could be found at Burriana, Játiva, and the cemeteries of the capital. Chivert's privileges covered not only mosques but "all the oratories [*oratoriis*] which are in that town." Perhaps the mosques in towers, deliberately excluded from the crown gift of mosques to the church of Valencia, were really oratories or shrines of this kind.[46] The name *rābiṭa*, from which so many Spanish places acquired the name Rápita or Rábida, indicated a settlement around a hermitage as a place of pious retreat. This differed from the *ribāṭ* or fortified monastery, which often guarded frontiers; al-Ḥimyarī defined Spain itself as a kind of *ribāṭ* "where one fights for the faith," and the Almoravids had derived their name (*murābiṭūn*) from that institution. Sometimes the religious character of a document's Latin *rabat* or *rapita* is obvious; at other times an ambiguous Latinate form merely indicates a city ward or suburb, from the equivalent Arabic *ar-rabaḍ*.[47]

[45] *Blanquerna*, ch. 99. This Valencian Sufi group, especially of the Banū Sīdbono who later emigrated to Granada, is discussed by Évariste Lévi-Provençal in "Le voyage d'Ibn Baṭṭūṭa dans le royaume de Granada (1350)," *Mélanges offerts à William Marçais* (Paris, 1951), pp. 216-217. See also Ribera y Tarragó, "El santón de Almusafes," *Opúsculos dispersos*, pp. 19-22.

[46] *Repartimiento de Valencia*, pp. 195-196, 203, 224, 367; one of these was a "turrim sive rapitam sitam iuxta mare et Guadalaviar et dicitur rapita orationis." Julián Ribera y Tarragó, "Monasterio musulmán en Denia," *El archivo*, I (1886), 67-68; "Enterramientos moros en Valencia," *ibid.*, 209-212, 217-219; both reprinted in his *Disertaciones*, II, 202-204 and 257-266. Torres Balbás, "Rábitas hispanomusulmanas," p. 484. Chivert Charter: "cum omnibus oratoriis que sunt in castro illo." *Aureum opus*, doc. 2, fol. IV, and *Colección diplomática*, doc. 185 (Oct. 22, 1238) for tower mosques.

[47] See the "rapita minor" and "rabat Anaxat" listed under mosques in n. 65; contrast the word for *barrio* occurring in the *Repartimiento de Valencia*, above, p. 86n. Al-Ḥimyarī, *Kitāb ar-rawḍ al-miʿṭār*, p. 17. See also Dubler, *Wirtschaftsleben*, pp. 112-114, with place names. See also Lucien Golvin, "Note sur le mot ribât (terme d'architecture) et son interprétation en occident musulman," *Revue de l'occident musulman et de la Mediterranée*, VI (1969), 95-101.

Schooling was a common function of the mosque. The Valencia-Murcia region had long been a home for learning and literature; before the Christian conquest a number of even the lesser Valencian towns, including Eslida, had been noted for their schools. During the campaign against Valencia city, when the diplomat-poet Ibn al-Abbār sailed to Tunis to beg military aid, the poem in which he couched his plea before the sultan Abū Zakarīyā' Yaḥyā included a lament for the harried kingdom's "schools in which the sacred texts" were being destroyed.[48] The year before Valencia city fell, a great calligrapher and teacher died at the secondary mosque which soon became St. Catherine's parish, Abū Ḥāmid b. Abī Ẓāhir (Abuhamid Benabizaher).[49] Lull, in encouraging missionary schools, re-

[48] On the intellectual life of Valencia see Chapter XVII, section 3. Julián Ribera y Tarragó, "Moros célebres valencianos en literatura y viages," in *El archivo*, I (1886), 137, 140, and in *Disertaciones* with altered title, II, 205-210; and his separately printed *La enseñanza entre los musulmanes españoles* (Zaragoza, 1893). Bayerri found nothing on Tortosan twelfth- or thirteenth-century schools, though an organized school system flourished in the eleventh century (*Tortosa*, VI, 49). Arthur Tritton affords a good introduction to every aspect of medieval education in his *Muslim Education in the Middle Ages*; he includes Spain on his horizon; ch. 6 discusses "Institutions" large and small, down to the thirteenth-century numbers of schools in various cities. Bayard Dodge briefly reviews educational institutions and curricula in his *Muslim Education in Medieval Times* (Washington, D.C., 1962); more amply, see Mehdi Nakosteen, *History of Islamic Origins of Western Education A.D. 800-1350, with an Introduction to Medieval Muslim Education* (Boulder, Colo., 1964), esp. ch. 3 on primary schooling in tutors' homes or shops, secondary and college instruction in the mosque or *madrasa*, and the savant circles at mosques, salons, bookstores, libraries, and research centers. See also Mazahéri, *La vie quotidienne des musulmans au moyen âge*, ch. 5; he reckons that half the population in major centers of civilized Islamic countries were literate by our century, with ten per cent boasting a solid general education and with at least one savant per hundred people (p. 136). Ribera insists on the private and therefore varied character of Spain's education from primary through highest level, in contrast with that in the East; primary education was free for the poor and normal for all; higher learning began with the Hadith, sometimes offered a mixed-subject curriculum like the American college, conferred status and public notice on the professor, and often continued overseas after the degree. See his *Enseñanza*, with sections on primary and higher learning (chs. 3-4), on teachers and students (chs. 5-6), and some attention given to women, libraries, titles, methods, and the Mudejar college at Zaragoza; his explanation of the European university as deriving from or relating to these schools is based on a misunderstanding of the latter's noncorporate nature.

[49] On Abū Ḥāmid, see Julián Ribera y Tarragó, "La plaza del alcalde (ráhbatolcádi)," *Disertaciones*, II, 323. See also his "Escuela valenciana de calígrafos árabes," *ibid.*, 304-308.

luctantly praised the way Muslims schooled their children well, though of course for satanic ends.[50]

Provision for public instruction appears in the Valencia surrender treaties. The Cuart Muslims "may teach their children in schools." Those at Seta "may teach their children the book of their law." At Uxó, the Koran was "publicly" taught as the basis of "letters" for the young.[51] The Eslida Muslims "may teach students" the Koran and the Hadith "according to their law." The second Eslida charter simplifies this: "you may teach your children from your Koran and your other books."[52] At Rafelbuñol the Muslims might "teach your children in schools."[53] At Játiva the official "who may teach your children and boys" was named: the *ṣāḥib aṣ-ṣalāt.*[54] From evidence so sketchy, one cannot say whether these were local schools of modest pretensions, largely of the elementary grade, or serious centers of Koranic study, drawing scholars from other places and preparing missionaries for the religious education of the people. Teaching of all kinds was of a private character in Spanish Islam, and literacy was widespread; the schools in the treaty documents were either controlled by officials of the community, or else they were public in the sense that their support was informally a community concern. Ibn 'Abdūn felt that his twelfth-century Sevillian mosques suffered a certain lack of decorum when study was permitted indiscriminately. He recommended confining instruction in the naves to the Koran and tradition, relegating more secular branches of

[50] Lull, "Tractatus de modo convertendi infideles," p. 135.

[51] Cuart doc. in n. 27: "possint . . . docere filios suos in scolis." Seta doc. in n. 23: "possint . . . filios suos docere libros legis sue." Uxó Charter: "que pusquen . . . en amostrar de letra a lurs fills in Alcora publicament, sens nengu perjudici de aquells fer."

[52] Second Eslida Charter: "possitis docere filios vestros de vestro alchorram et aliis libris vestris." The first Eslida Charter had phrased it: "et possint docere scholares Alcora et libros omnes de Alhadet secundum legem suum et Alcopzi sint de mezquitis suis"; the *BSCC* version supplies a comma before "et Alcopzi," while Janer puts it after "Alcora," thus providing conflicting readings: "let *alcopzi* be in their mosques," and "let all the books of the Hadith and of the Alcopzum be in their mosques." The meaning of *alcopzi* is discussed below, p. 212. The Eslida area, though known for its schools, did not have a kind of university, as some believe; see García y García, "Alcadiazgo de Eslida," pp. 161-165.

[53] Arch. Crown, Peter III, Reg. Canc. 44, fol. 184 (July 15, 1280): "et docere filios vestros in scolis."

[54] Játiva Charter: "et cabazallanos, qui doceant filios et pueros vestros."

learning to the galleries. He also provided a profile of the good teacher; a syllabus of reading, writing, and reckoning; a philosophy of teaching; and administrative admonitions, such as how to whip the student and how to keep the teacher hard at work.[55] Ibn Baṭṭūṭa furnished fascinating glimpses into the great colleges of Islam, but unfortunately they are inapplicable to the Valencian scene because the *madrasa* came late to Spain. More pertinently, he described the various "circles" of instruction at the Damascus mosque: the teachers of the Koran leaning against pillars as they dictated, the teachers of tradition sitting on high chairs to read aloud, and the calligraphy class practicing on poetry.[56]

Ibn Khaldūn described the Spanish curriculum as culminating in rather than beginning with the Koran. Whereas the North Africans severely restricted text and subject matter to the Koran until the pupil had mastered it, Spaniards taught "reading and writing as such," using as texts secular materials, such as poetry, as well as the Koran, and laying special stress on calligraphy. Ibn Khaldūn felt that higher learning had largely died in Spain by his time, leaving only this foundation. Educated Spaniards he characterized as excellent in literary skills but deficient in deeper knowledge of the Koran and religious sciences. A curiosity of the Spanish tradition, besides its distinctive script and fine calligraphy, was the method of learning to spell by ingesting whole words at once rather than by single letters.[57]

Lévi-Provençal, familiar with an earlier stage of Spanish Islamic schooling, described a primary education consisting of training in the Koran together with grammar, either at the teacher's shop or from a tutor brought into the affluent home. Higher education in letters and theological jurisprudence followed, under masters at the mosque.[58] The Uxó phrase "amostrar de letra en Alcorá" lends itself to either interpretation. "Filii et pueri" suggests youngsters, but "scholares" studying the Hadith does not. The treaty privileges in

[55] Ibn 'Abdūn, *Séville musulmane, le traité,* pp. 49, 53-56.

[56] Ibn Baṭṭūṭa, *Travels,* I, 133-134; II, 272, a Tigris *madrasa* with 300 cells for lodging students, provision for clothing and expenses by the learned founder, and description of curriculum. On the late advent of the *madrasa* in Spain, see Tritton, *Muslim Education,* p. 107.

[57] *Muqaddimah,* III, 300-303; see also II, 430; on script and spelling, II, 377-378.

[58] Lévi-Provençal, *España musulmana,* v, 263-266.

Valencia had to concern themselves directly with specifics; they extended their protection, consequently, to formal schooling, apparently at both primary and secondary levels. By implication, these same enactments supported higher Islamic intellectual activity, though this was equally offensive to contemporary Christians because of its alien religious orientation. Learning at its highest level became a relatively unstructured and complicated affair, however, a kind of social function. Since it was only slightly institutionalized, it did not require the careful guarantees sought by the schools. King James and King Peter displayed an active patronal interest in the local Islamic intellectual scene only when pragmatic ends dictated it, for instance when they promoted the conversion of Mudejar savants by means of mendicant centers of Arabic learning. The Aragonese never went so far as King Alfonso of Castile, who established at Seville in 1254 his "university or general schools of Latin and Arabic" (with three Muslim kings cosigning) and who is said to have lent his patronage to the school of the great Muḥammad b. Abī Bakr al-Riqūṭī in conquered Murcia.[59]

Mosques

The Valencian crusader used "mosque" as a blanket term covering a variety of buildings, ranging from private oratories through neighborhood places of worship to grand establishments.[60] Actually

[59] See my "Christian-Islamic Confrontation," pp. 1305, 1308, and 1313.

[60] On the kinds of mosques and their administration, see Ibn Khaldūn, *Muqaddimah*, I, 450. A sound introduction to the mosque is J. Pedersen, "Masdjid," *EI*[1], III, 362-428. There was precedent in church law for a non-Christian group (the Jews) having a place of worship: "sicut legalis diffinitio iudaeos novas non patitur erigere synogogas, ita eos sine inquietudine veteres habere permittit" (*Decretales Gregorii IX*, in the *Corpus iuris canonici*, lib. V, tit. VI, c. 3). The *Siete partidas* of Alfonso X echoed this ruling as applied to Mudejars. In theory new places could not be built nor the permitted one amplified (*Corpus*, c. 7), but practical circumstances nullified the provision. In Valencia, of course, the situation had advanced beyond that in which this legislation had originated. No mosque or minaret ruins survive in Valencia, though earlier writers mistook the remains of the Pinohermoso palace for one at Játiva; in the sixteenth century Viciana described the ex-mosque, in use at Játiva as a main church, as nearly quadrangular with seven naves. On the relation of Valencia city's cathedral to the mosque structure, see my *Crusader Valencia*, I, 19-20. Torres Balbás has a survey on mosques in his *Artes almoravide y almohade*, pp. 10ff.

a special place of worship might be merely a bare plot of ground; the most formal of these was the open-air esplanade or *muṣallā* for large-scale communal religious actions just outside Valencia city's aptly named eastern gate Bāb ash-Sharī'a.[61] The most important actual building was the major mosque, found not only in big towns like Alcira but in small places like Lombar near Calpe.[62] A peculiarity of the Spanish mosque was a tree-shaded garden area, sometimes bright with oranges. The class of secondary mosque, like the ten confiscated for use as Christian parishes in Valencia city, seems to have been impressive both in size and aspect. Below this level, surplus mosques abounded. Examination of property-distribution lists in conquered Seville discloses a minimum of seventy, not counting possible repetitions.[63] Muslim writers exaggerated the number of mosques of Cordova as almost five hundred, a few authors outdistancing this total with unabashedly absurd figures.

The communal mosque was more than a church. It served not only as a religious sign but as a center for community life, forum for deliberations and the expression of public opinion, and symbol of unity. This was truer for the mosque than for the church or synagogue. In no other religion were the lives of the people centered so much on the religious edifice as in Islam. Social, political, educational, military, and religious life were all connected closely with it.

By his crusade promises, confirmed by formal proclamations of 1238, King James committed himself to transferring mosques and

[61] Évariste Lévi-Provençal, "Notes de toponomastique hispano-maġribine: les noms des portes, le *bāb aš-šarī'a* et la *šarī'a* dans les villes d'occident musulmane au moyen-âge," *Annales de l'institut d'études orientales*, II (1936), 210-234, esp. pp. 226, 230-231, including comments on Valencia. Leopoldo Torres Balbás, "Edificios hispanomusulmanes," esp. pp. 74-102; "Muṣallā y sharī'a en las ciudades hispanomusulmanas," *Al-Andalus*, XIII (1948), 167-180; Ribera Tarragó, "La xarea de Valencia musulmana," *Disertaciones*, II, 326-329. The Valencian *Repartimiento* mentions the city's *muṣallā* (p. 155). Ibn Juzayy (d. 1355), the editor of Ibn Baṭṭūṭa, supplies an account by his teacher Abu 'l-Barakāt Balfīqī (1266-1369) about the semiannual festival prayers on the *muṣallā* of Velez (Ballash) in Spain (*Travels*, I, 13).

[62] Arch. Cat., perg. 4,624 (Dec. 31, 1251) rents the confiscated "mezquitam maiorem . . . in alcaria de Lomber." Al-Ḥimyarī singles out for notice at Alcira its "major mosque" and "other mosques" (*Kitāb ar-rawḍ al-mi'ṭār*, p. 213). A proper Friday community service required forty male residents and a main mosque (Von Grunebaum, *Islam, Essays*, p. 142).

[63] *Repartimiento de Sevilla*, II, 534-542. On the neighborhood mosques, see Ibn 'Abdūn, *Séville musulmane, le traité*, pp. 53-57.

cemeteries into Christian hands. An interpretative decree reserved to the crown those that were either in the form of towers or involved in fortifications. Many barons invoked the crusader's patronage over churches to reserve ownership of local mosques. Besides the eleven mosques taken for cathedral and parishes within the walls of Valencia city, others went to various orders and individuals. One became a stable, another a municipal building; the king owned one, a troop of soldiers another, and a woman a third, while two citizens shared a fourth, and authorities converted ten to public housing. Scattered, incomplete records for Valencia city alone reveal three dozen mosques and suggest more.

So thick were mosques in Valencia city that half the Christian mosque-parishes contained at least one extra belonging to the parish. This is not surprising, since any Muslim could build a mosque, many of which amounted to little more than prayer rooms or tumbledown wayside stations.[64] One respectably established surplus mosque at Valencia city fronted immediately upon "a similar mosque," both with cemeteries. The rental of a site left by dismantling an unimportant mosque reveals its measurements as fifty feet by fifteen. The conquerors' lists sometimes describe a mosque as "tiny" (*parvula*), or drop a clue to its size by stating the function to which it was being converted—residence, stable, hospital, or church. In renting a mosque at Fortaleny in 1256 the Christian owners referred to its "minaret [*turris*], walls, doors, windows, [and] roof"; a similar description was recorded for Murviedro in 1255. At Alcoy in 1273 the patio (*platea*) of a mosque was leased on condition that "a roofed building" be constructed over it; presumably this patio was the courtyard, like those the Chivert charter guaranteed to all mosques ("cum plateis"), rather than a plaza of

[64] Ibn Shaddād (1216-1285), who compiled a statistical list of public buildings at Aleppo, counted 216 mosques (Ziadeh, *Urban Life in Syria under the Early Mamlūks*, p. 153). In the early fourteenth century the North African traveler Ibn Baṭṭūṭa reported Bagdad as having eleven mosques for Friday services, with others "very numerous," while Sarai had thirteen for Friday prayers, with others "exceedingly numerous" (*Travels*, II, 329, 515-516). For a comparison of the synagogue's role as community nerve center and its relation to governmental, educational, and social activity, see Isidore Epstein, *The "Responsa" of Rabbi Solomon Ben Adreth of Barcelona (1235-1310) as a Source of the History of Spain* (New York, [1925] 1968), pp. 57-63. On the analogous role of the cathedral and parish, see my *Crusader Valencia*, I, 18-19, 54-59, 100, 107-108, and passim.

the sort that opened in front of some city mosques or infrequently at the confluence of several streets or at gates. A very small mosque in the Muslims' quarter of Liria in 1255 embraced a fig garden. At Valencia city a suppressed mosque included a fig tree and probably a garden. Another mosque "in the sector near the bridge" was substantial enough to exchange in 1241 for a fonduk. Varying rentals—a yearly gold piece, eight solidi—afford some index to the contrasting worth of different mosques. To rent out its own nonparochial, surplus mosques the diocese had to create an office—"administrator and governor of the mosques and cemeteries formerly belonging to the Saracens in the whole diocese of Valencia." By sifting through rental records—adding data from such sources as land-distribution lists, real estate transactions, and local histories—one can gather some idea of the bewildering number of mosques both in city and kingdom.[65]

To reassemble here the mosaic of evidence on mosques set forth in my introductory book would involve needless repetition; suffice it to say that their number in the kingdom was great. Where a community went into exile, as at Valencia and Burriana, sweeping confiscation of religious buildings ensued. Where Christian immigration gradually nudged aside the Muslim populace, the process involved a certain assimilation of mosques. To construct its network of rural parishes, each of the three dioceses in Valencia took over a large number almost immediately. Parish distribution, as reconstructed from thirteenth-century evidence, provides a map of these

[65] The mosque documentation, gleaned from many archival remnants, has been gathered in my *Crusader Valencia*, esp. I, 62-64, 136-142; see also the index; the mosque administrator is found in the cathedral manuscripts and in the crusade-tax *Rationes decimarum*. The Arch. Cat. MSS include items like "quoddam oratorium in suburbio civitatis Valencie"; "unam meschitam in exerea Valencie"; "aliam mezquitam parvulam in qua est ficulnea et est in ralaya [ravallo?] Lirie"; a mosque at Murviedro rented "cum parietibus, ianuis, fenestris, suppositis, introitibus," and at Fortaleny "cum turre que in dicta mezquita est . . . cum parietibus, ianuis, fenestris, tectis." The *Repartimiento* lists a number of Valencia city mosques: Abenhamiz (p. 251); Açaquem (p. 205); Amet Abinbaceyla (p. 551); Dalabida in the Jewish section (p. 300; Alabedi on pp. 202, 203, 299); Dalgalchi (p. 240); Delponti (Metalponti; pp. 240, 300); Magi Celili (p. 300); Boatella (not suburban; pp. 189, 271, 299, 308, 516); Xepolella (Chepolella, Xupollella, Xopollea; pp. 214, 301, and cf. spellings on pp. 231, 304, 536, 620); rabat Anaxat (p. 532); rapita minor (p. 203); and one near the baths of Algacir (p. 308); see also pp. 241, 272, 290, 291, 541, 548, 564, 572, 578, 597, 605, 606, 609, 649. Besides those cited above in the text, the *Repartimiento* names a few plazas at Valencia city (pp. 258, 284, 306, 311, 313).

confiscated mosques. Despite the turnover, the evidence surprisingly indicates that most mosques remained for at least some time in Muslim hands. A single mosque was adequate to the needs of the small group of Christians found in the average early settlement. In the city of Alcira only two mosques were confiscated at first. At Játiva likewise they did not pass in any number into Christian hands. In Murcia city the crusaders took only the major mosque, leaving ten others to the Muslims. The hamlets around Uxó each boasted its own mosque. Murviedro had a number of them within town. Segorbe long retained its mosques.[66]

Where Muslims kept possession of much of their town, they held on to the mosques in that part. Thus the Chivert pact awarded them all "mosques" and "oratories" of the district. Valencian documentation usually has the Muslims retaining mosques in the plural—as at the Alfandech Valley, Eslida, Játiva, Murcia, and Uxó; the Aldea charter speaks in the singular. More general or indirect evidence on this topic betrays continued possession of some mosques as normal for all localities. Where a Christian lord legally held possession, the mosque may actually have remained in Muslim hands. At Carlet and Alfarp castles, for example, the diocese wrested from the local lord "the mosque and cemetery establishments," vindicating its overlordship and adjusting an important juridical position without necessarily disturbing the Muslim community in its claim and possession.[67] The impression that Valencia's Muslims kept the bulk of the kingdom's mosques and that they still clung to most at the end of the period under discussion finds confirmation in a complaint filed by the bishop of Valencia. Bishop Deçpont publicly notified his metropolitan, who reported it to Pope Benedict XII, that mosques were more numerous in his diocese than churches.[68]

[66] See the multiple evidences on the mosques in my *Crusader Valencia*, I, 64ff., and ch. 3 with parish maps on pp. 45, 83, 89. *Llibre dels feyts*, chs. 437 ("que haguessen lurs mesquites," in Murcia), 445, 430. García, *Historia de Uxó*, p. 81. Al-Ḥimyarī, *Kitāb ar-rawḍ al-mi'ṭār*, pp. 213-215 and 361. (Murviedro).

[67] Arch. Cat., perg. 2,341 (Feb. 7, 1241): "insuper retinemus corpora mezchitarum et cimiteria." Aldea, Alfandech, Chivert, Eslida, Játiva, and Uxó Charters.

[68] *Collectio maxima conciliorum omnis Hispaniae et novi orbis*, ed. José Sáenz de Aguirre and Giuseppe Catalani, 6 vols. (Rome, 1753-1755), v, 286-287; see H. C. Lea, *A History of the Inquisition of Spain*, 4 vols. (New York, 1907), I, 76. Deçpont made his complaint during his tenure of 1289 to 1312, as an argument for expelling the Moors, but it passed on to Rome only in 1332.

In conquered Valencia city, despite the mass expulsion at surrender, the distribution of properties provided "a building for a mosque, which belonged to 'Alī al-Gadaslī [Ali Algadasli]."[69] The crusaders may have meant this to serve as an additional place of worship in compensation for those confiscated, and to provide for the heavier traffic anticipated in a congested *morería*. The item stresses "one" building, however, and its recipients already retained the auxiliary neighborhood places of worship; it is therefore likely that this was a considerable and dignified edifice, fit to function as the aljama's central mosque. Within this quarter, at least one surplus mosque soon fell into disuse or was replaced; the cathedral disposed of it. The canon Bernard of Vilar, "in the name of the Valencian church," gave at rent "a certain mosque in the Muslim quarter of Valencia, which the Saracens of the same quarter used to possess."[70]

The Valencian crusaders, including the king in his memoirs, spoke of mosques without disrespect. As memory of the realities faded, later chroniclers of Valencia assumed that the crusaders had abused mosques; they recounted with lively imagination how James's knights had gleefully smashed the Arabic carvings and otherwise displayed their contempt.[71] Absurd as these fables are, there is no hint at Valencia of the other extreme, the unusual tolerance of mosques evinced in the contemporary kingdom of Jerusalem, where Christian overlords and subject Muslims at times shared a mosque, somewhat like Protestants and Catholics in certain post-Reformation churches.[72]

[69] *Repartimiento de Valencia*, p. 568: "et una domus pro mezchita que fuit de Ali Algadasli." Roca Traver assumes this was their only mosque ("Vida mudéjar," p. 133).

[70] Arch. Cat., perg. 2,872 (June 1, 1277): "sit omnibus notum quod ego Bernardus de Vilario . . . nomine ecclesie valentine dono et stabilio . . . quandam mesquitam in moreria Valencie quam sarraceni eiusdem morerie tenere solebant." The imperfect tense indicated continued possession.

[71] Burns, *Crusader Valencia*, II, 370.

[72] Richard, *Royaume latin de Jérusalem*, p. 131; see also *An Arab-Syrian Gentleman and Warrior in the Period of the Crusades, Memoirs of Usāmah ibn-Munqidh (Kitāb al-I'tibār)*, trans. Philip K. Hitti (New York, 1929), pp. 163-164. In fourteenth-century Valencia, at least some mosques brought a revenue to the crown; all those below the Júcar, excluding Aspe, Elda, and Novelda, yielded 333 solidi yearly: "lalahbeç de les mesquites cascun any." See the *Rentas de la antigua corona de Aragón*, pp. 111, 126; the "lalahbeç de les oliveres," however, surpassed it at 500 solidi (p. 110).

Religious Properties

The communities also kept many cemeteries, despite an impression created to the contrary.[73] A solution to the contradictory evidence again lies in the surprising number involved throughout the kingdom, and in the drastic scale of confiscation at the capital. Cemeteries normally stood outside the main gates of a town; from Arabic records, Ribera located one each east and west of Islamic Valencia city and two to the south.[74] Like the mosques, these cemeteries served a social function. Commercial and recreational life spilled over into them from the nearby town; hermitages of the devout clustered around tombs where pilgrims came; and sometimes settlement edged in close.[75] Isolated burial places also existed, like the hill above a hamlet on the country road, south of Murcia, where King James noted the tombs of the Murcian kings, including that of the recently deceased hero Ibn Hūd.[76] Many small plots must have existed, either adjoined to larger grounds or standing in isolation, since the crown retained for itself the class of cemeteries holding twelve bodies or less, surrendering others to church authorities or to Mudejar aljamas.[77]

Within an Islamic city one expects the tomb of a holy man but not a proper cemetery; something between the two, at the heart of Valencia city, was the Moorish pantheon in which its rulers rested. They must have enjoyed an imposing edifice, because King James

[73] Roca Traver feels that the Muslims usually lost their cemeteries ("Vida mudéjar," p. 134). On burial customs see Julián Ribera y Tarragó, "Ceremonias funebres de los árabes españoles, estudio litúrgico" (*Disertaciones y opúsculos*, II, 248-257); and on their survival in sixteenth-century Valencia, Halperín Donghi, "Moriscos y cristianos viejos," p. 87.

[74] Ribera Tarragó, "Enterramientos moros en Valencia," *Disertaciones y opúsculos*, II, 257-266. See also Torres Balbás, "Aspectos de las ciudades hispanomusulmanas," pp. 88-89; Lévi-Provençal, *España musulmana*, V, 225; Von Grunebaum, *Islam, Essays*, p. 147.

[75] Ibn 'Abdūn inveighs against using cemeteries as picnic grounds; he comments on the restless young frequenting them, strolling players and tale-tellers at work there, and the encroachment of houses, shops, and merchants; he proposes boarding up windows opening on a cemetery view (*Séville musulmane, le traité*, pp. 57-61, and on funerals p. 50).

[76] *Llibre dels feyts*, ch. 423.

[77] *Aureum opus*, doc. 12, fol. 4r,v (1261): "ciminteria ultra duodecim vasa continentia"; see my *Crusader Valencia*, I, 62, with the documentation of its n. 44.

immediately confiscated it for public use, assigning as the capital's town hall "the building which formerly was the burial place of the Saracen kings."[78] The Christians called this building both "sepultura" and "ciminterium." It held more than twelve bodies, since King James wrote it down as the single exception to his legal surrender of such larger cemeteries;[79] perhaps it included the relatives of Valencia's governors within the same structure. Besides this pantheon and the inner-city tomb shrines, several public burial grounds appear in the Christian records for the capital. One stood to the south just outside the Bāb Baiṭāla on the highroad toward Ruzafa.[80] Another lay to the northwest, outside the Bāb al-Ḥanash.[81] A third formed part of the esplanade complex outside the Bāb ash-Sharī'a on the east.[82] A cemetery stood farther down the Ruzafa road as well, and a very small one in the northwest at Roteros.[83]

Other cemeteries named seem to coincide with these either literally or, as contiguous plots, effectively.[84] For example, city authorities

[78] *Fori antiqui Valentiae*, rub. III, no. 6: "in domo que condam sepultura erat sarracenorum regum."

[79] *Aureum opus*, doc. 12: "excepto ciminterio in quo assignavimus generale forum Valencie fieri."

[80] *Repartimiento de Valencia*, pp. 230, 231. This is the same cemetery as on p. 250, before the Taulat gate toward St. Vincent's. Its name is Romance and ultimately Roman, perhaps relating to a cattle market; as a place name it appears as early as the ninth century (Buchatella). Roca Traver locates this cemetery at the juncture of modern San Vicente and San Fernando streets, where the old highway bent east toward Ruzafa.

[81] *Repartimiento*, p. 188, Bebalhaix; cf. p. 172.

[82] See n. 61.

[83] *Repartimiento*, p. 229, for Roteros; the Daroca road cemetery may be the same (*ibid.*). Ruzafa is on p. 244 and may be Ribera's more southerly grounds, below the Boatella cemetery. The Roteros cemetery, not the same as the large northwestern place, held only a dozen bodies or less, since the king took it to build a hospice, later granting it to the church; see Arch. Cat., perg. 1,324 (Feb. 25, 1245): "in qua platea . . . fuit . . . quondam fossarium sarracenicum." See also Burns, *Crusader Valencia*, I, 140, with notes.

[84] Thus Arch. Cat., perg. 2,327 (May 15, 1242), has "fossarium sarracenicum . . . in civitate Valencie," and "in alio fossario"; these were probably at, rather than in, the town. The documents speak often enough of a mosque with its cemetery, as though of a parish church; these were probably cemeteries which had acquired small mosques. Roca Traver found a cemetery, which the passage of time had absorbed, "in the very center of the city," in a 1267 document describing "aquel fosser morisch que es de la cequia denant l'alfondech d'en R. Castela, entro les cases que foren d'en J. de les Celes" ("Vida mudéjar," p. 134). However, the houses of the knight John Lasceyles, acquired close to the cathedral in 1238, had been given

sued St. Martin's parish in 1266 over title to a Moorish cemetery at the Boatella gate—the old Bāb Baiṭāla—on the grounds that this had held less than twelve corpses; hardly the extensive main cemetery, it must have been an adjunct or separated portion. The same plot, or one close by, turns up in a diocesan rental contract of 1270, "the ancient Saracen burial place which I have and hold in the Boatella of Valencia"; it measured 23 royal *braciae* in length, or some 115 feet.[85] Similarly, a benefactress of the Valencian church acquired a mosque with its buildings and cemetery on the road outside Valencia city leading to the Dominican church; possibly this was the great cemetery at the east, but more plausibly it was an adjacent smaller plot.[86] The removed Mudejars retained or acquired a cemetery for the aljama, located just outside the Bāb al-Ḥanash and above the northern wall of their external quarter; was this the main northwestern grounds, an adjunct, or a new area?[87] Christian Valencia's later chroniclers ineptly located a Moorish cemetery within the city, where the main Christian market spread.

The abundance of cemeteries taken over by the diocese throughout the new kingdom made it necessary to include these properties under the revenue bureau which leased mosques. Cemeteries consequently appear in diocesan rental contracts. Lucy, widow of William of Agramunt, rented one outside the city wall of Murviedro in 1252. Berengar Arbesa rented another in 1254 near a village in the Castellón countryside. The rural cemetery at Nacla near Corbera, rented out in 1260, measured a mere fanecate in extent or about 830 square meters. The Poliñá del Júcar cemetery was somewhat larger; a section of it measuring a fanecate and a half was leased in 1254. At

---

to the diocese in 1242 in exchange for a mosque and cemetery "near the burnt tower" in Roteros (see my explanation and documentation in *Crusader Valencia*, I, 136, 137, and II, 433, 435); if the pre-1242 houses still bore his name, this plot had to be hard by the main mosque; more probably the fonduk, canal, houses, and cemetery were at or near Roteros, identified with that cemetery or else an adjunct of it.

85 Arch. Cat., perg. 1,210 (April 30, 1244); perg. 1,343 (Feb. 5, 1270); perg. 1,348 (May 5, 1271); and perg. 4,617 (Feb. 9, 1248); partially copied and studied in my *Crusader Valencia*, I, 140, II, 437. The *braça* was 1.67 meters.

86 Arch. Cat., perg. 1,308 (Oct. 21, 1240): "mesquitam cum cimiterio eidem pertinenti."

87 See the site as established by Rodrigo y Pertegás, "La morería de Valencia," p. 236 and map.

Andarella their counterpart was furnished with trees and irrigated by canals, as perhaps were most such burial grounds.[88] At Espioca no less than three cemeteries went to the Christians, amounting to nine fanecates of land.[89] Others turn up for towns like Alcoy.[90] Valencian surrender charters single out cemeteries for mention only in connection with tax exemption. Presumably the Mudejars retained some cemeteries, lost others to crown and dioceses, or arranged for replacements, as local circumstances warranted. At Eslida "the dead are buried in their cemeteries without obstacle or fee." At Aldea "they may have a cemetery frank and free." At Chivert "all cemeteries" were tax exempt. At Játiva "cemeteries" fell under the religious privileges.[91]

More crucial to the question of tolerance was the disposition of mosque properties. These provided essential financial support for the alien religion. Mosques were not maintained directly by the state but by a foundation or endowment set up by a wealthy founder. This supplied not only ministerial and administrative but humbler personnel like cleaners and porters; it maintained the building, effected repairs, renewed furnishings, and cared for all the charitable, educational, and other communal concerns. An oratory or a small mosque required at least a caretaker *ṣāḥib aṣ-ṣalāt*, though this decency might be neglected in the multitudinous chapel-mosques scattered in hidden corners of town. In an established wealthy region like Valencia the dead hand of accumulated legacies and foundations tended, as with Christian churches of the time, to concentrate re-

[88] Arch. Cat., perg. 2,355 (Aug. 29, 1252; Murviedro). Perg. 4,628 (April 22, 1254): "fossarium in termino de Castello in alcaria que vocatur Ereco" (Creco?). Perg. 1,527 (April 9, 1260): "unum fossarium sarracenicum . . . unius fanecate terre" (Nacla). Perg. 1,524 (April 7, 1254): "quoddam fossarium usque ad fanecatum et plus" (Poliñá). Perg. 1,811 (Aug. 27, 1249): "cum arboribus cuiuslibet generis . . . aquis, cequiis ad rigendum." Perg. 1,521 (June 21, 1243). See Burns, *Crusader Valencia*, II, 436-437.

[89] Arch. Cat., perg. 1,595 (June 16, 1279): "tres petias terre in dicto loco de Spiocha in quibus fuerunt fossaria tempore sarracenorum quas extimo [aestimo] tenere in sum[m]a usque ad novem fanechatas terre."

[90] Arch. Cat., perg. 4,638 (Sept. 18, 1256): "fossarium quod est in Alcoy"; I have copied this with a translation in *Crusader Valencia*, I, 141, and II, 439.

[91] Eslida Charter, section on revenues: "et mortui sepeliuntur in eorum ciminteriis sine contrario et missione." Aldea Charter: "habeant . . . cimiterium franchum et liberum." Chivert Charter: "et omnia cimiteria," "omnibus cimiteriis." Játiva Charter: "habeatis cimiteria."

ligious riches unhealthily. What was the fate of such tempting targets in crusader Valencia? The king's public position again seems clear: "all the buildings and estates" belonging to the kingdom's mosques went to the diocese. During a property controversy in 1241 Bishop Ferrer of Valencia irresponsibly waived in favor of the crown and landlords this claim to "all the estates, buildings, and farms which in Saracen times belonged, or ought to have belonged, to any of their mosques in the entire kingdom of Valencia." Succeeding bishops refused to acquiesce. Confirming this picture of property seizure are the documents listing mosque properties in the hands of Christians—"the mosque and the houses of the said mosque" going to a layman, for example, or "all the holdings formerly belonging to the mosques" held by the Chiva lord. Though the editor of the Seville *Repartimiento* doubts that mosque properties were given away there, at Valencia the juridical confiscation and a measure of actual seizure is undeniable.[92]

An equal number of references, both in charters and the king's narrative, suggest on the contrary that properties normally remained with the mosques. This evidence is at least as detailed and universal. Incidental items surviving in the Chivert charter show the aljama retaining the "honors" or estates belonging to mosques, "frank and free" and "in the control and custody" of *faqīh* and *qā'id*. At Uxó the king ordered "Let the rents of the mosques go to the support of the said mosques, just as they did of old."[93] A crown privilege to

[92] Arch. Cat., leg. XXII, no. 3, perg. of Nov. 9, 1241. *Collectio conciliorum Hispaniae*, v, 189-190. The *Repartimiento* of Valencia assigns to the diocese both mosques and "omnes domos et hereditates." For mosque properties in both the Tortosan and Valencian dioceses see the documentation assembled in Burns, *Crusader Valencia*, I, 65-66, II, 398-400, including phrases like "cum omnibus alodiis et possessionibus suis" and "pro omnibus possessionibus quondam ad mezquitas pertinentibus." González, in *Repartimiento de Sevilla*, I, 351.

[93] Chivert Charter: "dicta mezquita cum oratoriis suis omnibus, cimiteriis . . . et honoribus sit franca et libera"; they are "in comanda et custodia" of the *faqīh* and the *qā'id*. Uxó Charter: "e que sien les rendes de les mezquites a ops de les dites mezquites, axi com ere antigament." Even in the harsher era of the late fifteenth century, the surrendering Granadans kept by treaty both the mosques and their pious foundations (Fernández y González, *Mudejares de Castilla*, appendix, doc. 87). An ambiguous item in Lacarra's "Documentos" for the Ebro Valley repopulation includes among taxes on Muslims a return from "ii furnos qui fuerunt de las mesquitas, et alteras hereditates qui fuerunt de las mesquitas"; perhaps these were the crown's share of *waqf* property taken with one or other mosque for Christian use (doc. 400).

Játiva discloses a set of shops as part of the financial base for the local mosque and as sharing in the mosque's exemption. This concedes to the aljama in perpetuity "for the support of your mosque those eight shops which you have just built"; it insists that "you the aljama, and your successors, may have forever the eight shops with their revenues, for the support of the said mosque frank and free."[94] The word translated as "support" is the ambiguous *opus*, commonly used in Valencian documents about Christian churches to signify construction, substantial improvement, upkeep, and material requirements.[95] The Eslida charter decreed: "Let *alcopzi* of the mosques remain," a phrase guaranteeing the various *waqf* foundations or pious endowments. Taken by the letter, *copz* might seem rather to relate to *qabḍ* or *qābiḍ*, respectively the collecting and collector of rents, which would reductively imply the mosque endowments for maintenance, salaries, charitable purposes, education, and other intentions of the donors. A twelfth-century document from the conquered Tortosa area clarifies the strange word, however; it defines "the *alhobz* of the mosques" as including the bakeries, shops, and landholdings (*honores*) which pertained to the resources (*facultates*) of those mosques. Both forms approximate to *al-ḥabus* (properly *ḥubus*), a Spanish and North African synonym for *waqf*, which later yielded the Castilian *habiz*. The second Eslida charter supports this interpretation of the first charter's *alcopzi*, by declaring explicitly that "the estates of the mosques or belonging to

[94] Arch. Crown, James I, Reg. Canc. 21, fol. 151v (June 7, 1273): "concedimus vobis aliame sarracenorum Xative . . . imperpetuum ad opus mezquite vestre illa octo operatoria que modo construistis . . . que octo operatoria cum introitibus et exitibus . . . habeatis vos aliama et successores vestri imperpetuum ad opus dicte mezquite vestre francha et libera." "Support" is an apt translation, because it is improbable that the Muslims were building a new mosque in 1273. There was an effort to promote the paper and dye industries here but not, it seems, on a scale to increase the Muslim population very much. There had been much war damage in the area, however, so the possibility that rebuilding was meant cannot be ruled out; see Reg. 13, fol. 285 (Nov. 8, 1265). Alienation of rents would be a more likely reason for registering this document than destruction of shops to build a mosque, though the latter required royal permission.

[95] Burns, *Crusader Valencia*, 1, 98, and index under *opus*. Lapidus has arranged a schematic list of the eastern foundations, though largely for the next two centuries, by type of property, donor, and institution benefited (*Muslim Cities in the Middle Ages*, pp. 195-198, and see index under *waqf*).

the mosques are to be as they customarily were in the time of the Saracens."[96] The generous context of the charters makes it probable that the concession in each case included not only rents used to staff and support the mosques but all other philanthropic foundations administered by the *qāḍī* under the generic title of *waqf*.

As with mosques and cemeteries, some middle ground must be sought between conflicting evidence in resolving the dilemma of seizure versus concession. Far-flung properties owned by the confiscated Valencia city establishments can create a false impression of general seizure. It is reasonable to suppose that when the crown assigned a single mosque or a percentage of mosques to Christians in a given locality, the supporting properties of each followed. Thus the early web of parishes throughout the kingdom—"all the parochial mosques" as the metropolitan called them—may comprise a map of places which suffered partial seizure of their foundations.[97] In most of the kingdom the loss to Muslims was therefore trivial. In a few cities, however, and in a few more areas later as the rhythm of Christian immigration increased, it must have been traumatic.

Supportive Adjuncts

Many aspects of life that were affected by Islamic beliefs do not properly pertain to a discussion of essential religious freedom. Sam-

[96] Eslida Charter; on variant readings for this sentence, see above, nn. 31 and 52. "Documentos del valle del Ebro," part 3, doc. 86: "alhobz que fuerunt illarum mezquitarum." Second Eslida Charter: "et hereditates meschitarum sive de meschitis sic[ut] consueverunt esse tempore sarracenorum." See also Dozy, *Glossaire*, p. 282 (*habices*); and editor, "Ḥabus," *EI*[1], II, part 1, 187. In Murcia, a lawsuit, in which the church sought to recover from various laymen "los heredamientos que eran alhobçes en tiempo de moros," only hints at the problem, which is more visible in Valencia (Juan Torres Fontes, *Repartimiento de la huerta y campo de Murcia en el siglo xiii* [Murcia, 1971], p. 83). Two and a half centuries later, when the properties in conquered Granada stayed with each mosque-become-parish, meticulous lists were prepared; María del Carmen Villanueva Rico has edited these as *Libros de habices del reino de Granada*, 2 vols. (Madrid, 1961-1966).

[97] "Ordinatio ecclesiae valentinae," in José Sanchis Sivera, *La diócesis valentina, nuevos estudios históricos* (Valencia, 1921), p. 233: "omnes parroquiales meçquitas episcopatus Valentie." For the manuscript and published versions of the "Ordinatio" and a full-dress discussion of the trial for which it is the transcript see Burns, *Crusader Valencia*, I, ch. 14, and II, esp. pp. 494-495.

ple borderline areas of the wider freedom, however, ought to be indicated. The separate legal code based upon the Mudejars' ethical and doctrinal presuppositions receives separate treatment in the next chapter, where its implications for religious freedom can be studied. Circumcision was a religious sign, though hardly a matter of legislation or documentary notice by Christians. The Valencian *Furs* do advert to it, nonetheless, in connection with apostasy; since apostasy to Islam became a formal crime when sealed by circumcision, Mudejars must have circumcised as a usual practice. The later Moriscos of Valencia certainly did. Circumcision applied to both sexes in Islam, but at that time was not observed everywhere in the Islamic world.[98]

In a medieval Christian country, one touchstone of freedom for Muslims could be the continuing practice of polygamy. No direct evidence survives for Valencia to illustrate this common Islamic custom. That Christians were not disconcerted by the practice and could tolerate it, however, appears from King James's attitude toward Jewish polygamy. He did not hesitate to recognize it as legal in Barcelona, decreeing in 1267 "that according to the laws of the Jews it is permissible for any Jew to have at the same time several wives." In 1259, overruling a Jewish faction which protested polygamy, he found it allowed "by the law and rite of the Jews."[99]

That the crown was not just indulging in isolated eccentricity is clear from the testimony of the Barcelona rabbi Solomon b. Abraham b. Adret (1233-1310), a figure of international renown esteemed by James I and Peter III, who counseled thousands by formal *responsa*. Answering a correspondent puzzled over the Franco-German insistence on monogamy, he bore witness that this was not the rule for the realms of Aragon: in fact "there are a number of men

[98] *Furs*, lib. VI, rub. IX, c. 2: "e per ço sera circumsis"; cf. *Fori*, rub. CXIX, no. 29. Halperín Dhongi, "Moriscos y cristianos viejos en Valencia," p. 84. Mazahéri, *Vie quotidienne des musulmans au moyen âge*, pp. 47ff.

[99] Francisco de Borfarull y Sans, "Jaime I y los judíos" (amplified as *Los judíos en el territorio de Barcelona, siglos x al xiii, reinado de Jaime I, 1213-1277*), in *Congrés I*, p. 887, doc. 62 (April 1, 1267): "attendentes quod secundum legem iudeorum licitum est unicuique iudeo habere eodem tempore plures uxores"; pp. 47-48, doc. 18 (Jan. 20, 1259): "secundum ius et ritum iudeorum istud facere non deberemus."

in our community, among them scholars and communal leaders, who married a second wife while wedded to the first," without anyone questioning their right.[100] Thus there was no aprioristic obstacle either in practice or theory to the toleration of Islamic polygamy.

The editor of Alfonso X's Castilian code, the *Siete partidas*, interpreted its approval of marriage "according to the law" of Muslims to include polygamy, as did Fernández y González.[101] During the era of the Spanish caliphate, Lévi-Provençal thought, polygamy was probably rare among middle and poor classes because of its expense.[102] At the crusade period in Valencia, the Eslida charter referred to marriage, but only in connection with legal decisions involving it. But it is significant that when the Uxó charter decreed the continuance of Islamic customs, it paused to single out marriage as an illustration. The Chivert charter considered marriage within the range of guaranteed ancient custom, busying itself merely with the question of tax on foreign brides and husbands.[103] The single marriage contract from a Valencian aljama in this century sheds no light on the practice of polygamy.[104] It is disappointing not to be able to clarify the point. Unlike the Jewish cases, no controversy came into Christian courts to leave its documentary trace. In 1287 crown officials did lease a sturdy building at Valencia city to accommodate "safely and securely" the harem of the last Almohads, political refugees under Aragonese protection; a harem can comprise a single wife, of course, and the plural wives of the ex-caliph's sons in

[100] Baer, *Jews in Christian Spain*, I, 254; Ben Adret later modified his theoretical position without affecting his testimony to the practice; he was rabbi for half a century and important also in state finance. He reported bigamy as having become rare in Aragon by 1300, occurring only in very special circumstances (Epstein, *"Responsa" of Ben Adreth*, p. 87). In *The Responsa of Rabbi Simon B[en] Ẓemah Duran as a Source of the History of the Jews of North Africa* (New York, [1930] 1968, pp. 88-89), Epstein concludes that "a plurality of wives was quite common" among Spanish Jews until closer contact with the traditionally monogamous Barbary Jews induced a reaction.

[101] Fernández y González, *Mudejares de Castilla*, p. 129n. (including Gregorio López).

[102] Lévi-Provençal, *España musulmana*, v, 258. Mazahéri sees polygamy as limited largely by expense, so that better-off burghers, for example, practiced it (*Vie quotidienne des musulmans au moyen âge*, pp. 62-63). Goitein concludes that polygamy tends to be rare in a progressive middle class (*Mediterranean Society*, I, 74).

[103] See Chapter X, nn. 15-16. [104] See p. 225.

this document just might have added up to one apiece.[105] Though the average Valencian Muslim may have been monogamous, it seems probable that polygamy did exist; if so, it was guaranteed routinely under the rubric of religious freedom. After the first decades of Mudejar existence, acculturative pressures from increasing immigration may have radically diminished the practice, while the classes most given to it may well have shrunk in numbers and prosperity. Even so, the later Valencian Moriscos, clinging to Mudejar traditions and surely unable to innovate in the direction of sexual freedom during their less tolerant era, divorced and remarried with ease, an inexpensive form of serial monogamy equivalent to polygamy.[106]

Regular use of the Koran in Christian courtrooms and for taking feudal oaths notably illustrates the extension of religious freedom into public life. Islamic law was far more religious than Christian civil law, less secularized indeed than Christian canon law, so that reliance on the oath in court was correspondingly more important. If the medieval Valencian Christian seemed extravagantly dependent upon oaths, without further sanctions beyond the wrath of God, the medieval Muslim equaled his zeal.[107] The Koran therefore became an important furnishing in the Valencian or other Arago-Catalan Christian court. In a typical case, the ecclesiastical trial over ownership of the Valencian diocese between the primate of Toledo and King James's metropolitan of Tarragona in 1239, a Moor called as Arabic expert was sworn by special ceremony, taking oath "by his own law."[108] Another litigation, filed in the cathedral archives at Valencia, concerned disputed boundaries of two Valencian vil-

[105] F. D. Gazulla, "Las compañías de zenetes en el reino de Aragón (1284-1291)," *BRAH*, xc (1927), doc. on p. 180: "conducat aliquam domum idoneam in Valencia uxoribus filiorum Miramani et quod esse possunt in ea salvum et secure."

[106] Halperín Donghi, "Moriscos y cristianos viejos en Valencia," p. 86.

[107] On a false oath as its own terrible penalty without further sanctions, see the *Furs*, lib. II, rub. xvii, c. 13. On the oath in Islamic life, see N. J. Coulson, *A History of Islamic Law* (Edinburgh, 1964), p. 126. James exempted the Jewish communities of Valencia from the use of the maledictions or cursing oath, so that they swore only on the Law of Moses or the Decalogue (Neuman, *Jews in Spain*, i, 158).

[108] "Ordinatio ecclesiae valentinae," p. 284: "qui nobis per leges suas adiurati," referring to a Moor and a Jew called as experts on four Arabic books. The trial comprises ch. 14 of my *Crusader Valencia*, this episode occurring on p. 268.

lages; the Muslim witnesses "brought with us a book which is called the Koran, namely the book by which Saracens swear and take oath according to their law."

The court scribe recorded the ceremony itself with the words as they fell upon his puzzled Christian ear. "And the said Saracens swore . . . and holding the said book in their hands they made this oath and said 'Bille assedi le illeha illehu valcorane alladinz.'"[109] What is one to make of this nonsense verse? The eye is tempted to reconstruct the broken fragments as *Bi 'l-lāhi ashhadu* [*an*] *lā ilāha illa huwa wā 'l-Qur'ān 'alā 'd-dīn*, or "By God, I witness [that] there is no God but He: by the Koran, by the Faith!" The Latin *bille* may be rather *billāh*; and Latin *illehu* may be *illa 'llāhu*. The Valencian *Furs* incorporated an oath as "Ille ille alledi lla illehu huma hamel çusma hua misach." This resembles the oath in Aragon's *Fuero*: "Bille y lledie y llen huahat hedel amble tomo ham mediah nabi mecal y çahach aleybnec minath buamar bitayich." The first part of both forms combined seems to yield *allāh alladhi lā ilāha illa huwa* or "God except whom there is no God." The phrase "hedel amble tomo ham mediah" is clarified by a fourteenth-century version "edal quilbe, romoan media" or *al-qibla al-muḥammadīya*. Later in the century, under King Peter's successor Alfonso, the oath on a solemn truce read: "We swear to you by Allah, and by the law of Muḥammad, and by the *qibla*, and on the Koran touched by our own hands." A strangely bilingual oath for taking land in fifteenth-century Aragon ran: "By God, except whom there is no God, and by the *qibla*, and by the fast of the month of Ramaḍān and by the words of the Koran." The *qibla* in these oaths meant the direction toward which Muslims prayed.[110]

[109] Arch. Cat., perg. 2,372 (an. 1240): "deduximus nobiscum unum librum qui dicitur alcoran videlicet quo sarraceni secundum legem illorum iurant et faciunt sacramentum." "Et dicti sarraceni iuraverunt . . . et tenendo dictum librum in manibus hanc iuram fecerunt et dixerunt [etc.]."

[110] The fourteenth-century oath ran: "Bille ylledi ylle ylauhua bat edal quilbe romoan media huali micael aleybuet unabet hunau bicayt"; the land oath was: "Bille ille alladi illehua et por la alquibla mahomadia et por el ayuno del mes del Ramadan et por las palabras del alcoran" (Macho Ortega, "Mudéjares aragoneses," pp. 195, 207, 209). The charter of Alfonso the Battler in 1131 provided: "et mauro qui voluerit iurare ad christiano et dicat: Alamin catzamo [*qasamū*?] ettalat teleta," contrasting this with the Christian's oath "super cruce" and the Jew's "in carta

Chivert included among the many details of its charter the stipulation that "no Moor is to be compelled to swear by another creature or thing except by almighty God," and not of course by God understood as Trinitarian. Muslims commonly took oaths in their dealings with King James, as when twenty sheiks "swore" and gave "their oath" during preliminary negotiations for surrender. After yielding a town to the king, normal procedure required the townsmen to swear fidelity "on the Koran." At Bairén twenty sheiks "swore" and took "their oath" during preliminary negotiations. The rebels at Villena broke "the agreement and oath [*sagrament*] of their law." Information given to the king's agent by some Játivans was certified "by the law they observed."[111] Christian authorities often accomplished inquiries of a paralegal sort among Muslim subjects under oath (*per sacramentum*), as in a case of 1246 involving "the Saracens of Tárbena and Dos Aguas."[112] In the next century a Valencian settlement charter, presented in the local mosque, was sworn to "by the *qibla*."[113] Oaths might also be administered in connection with contracts or official business between Christian and Muslim.[114]

The Christian community of a maritime region like Valencia was familiar with a plethora of calendars, domestic and foreign, so that it easily bore with an Islamic variant. Nevertheless, this peculiarly

sua atora" or Torah (Fernández y González, *Mudejares de Castilla*, appendix, doc. 4). The truce oath of Alfonso III read: "iuramus vobis per deum et per legem Mafumeti et per lalquible et super alcorano nostris propriis manibus tactis" (Arch. Crown, Alfonso III, perg. 150).

111 Chivert Charter: "non compellatur [maurus] facere ipsum [iuramentum] per aliam creaturam vel rem nisi per Deum omnipotentem." *Llibre dels feyts*, chs. 309 (Bairén), 325 (Játiva), 433 (Villena).

112 *Itinerari*, p. 181 (Aug. 11, 1246); the case opened at Valencia city, the "sarraceni de Disagues et Terrabona" to solve an issue "per sacramentum."

113 Chelva Charter (1370): "cumplir todo lo dicho por el Alquibla." The *Siete partidas* provided that this be done by facing south before a mosque entry (part. 3, tit. 11, no. 21); see the analogous Christian custom of an oath before a church door in I. A. Agus, *Urban Civilization in Pre-Crusade Europe: A Study of Organized Town-Life in Northwestern Europe During the Tenth and Eleventh Centuries Based on the Responsa Literature*, 2 vols. to date (New York, 1965ff.), 11, 794, where a Christian embarrassed a Jewish business colleague with the practice.

114 During the land disputes around Alcira at the close of the Valencian crusade, the crown arranged for the appointment of four adjudicators, two from each people, to be sworn on oath (document in Chapter XI, n. 46): "a duobus christianis et duobus sarracenis ydoneys et legalibus, prestito tamen ab eis iuramento."

alien calendar, employed for local contracts, surrender treaties, and official documents, held overtones of public recognition for Valencian Islam. The Uxó charter exhibited the careful dating, "in the month of Jumāda II [Jumet Alahir] according to the reckoning of the Moors in the year 648, the said calendar coinciding with the month of August in the year 1250 according to the calendar of the Christians." Similarly a contract between Muslims at Murviedro was dated "in the last decade of the month Shawwāl of the year 696."[115]

Inquiry into religious freedom might extend to such aspects as the relationships between the crown monopoly on butcher shops and the religious dietary laws governing butcheries of Saracen communities; but the central point has been adequately made. There is danger perhaps of falling into the opposite fault, and failing to see the restriction on Islamic freedom and the real element of persecution. But taking all the evidence together, the religious effects of detailed recognition of the Islamic religion stand clear. The daily prayer in the streets; the pervasive, reiterated call of the muezzins; the thronging to mosques for Friday services; the tight complex of religious customs and courts; the tax exemption for properties supporting religion and for mosque water rights; the activity of the imams; the continuance of religious schools even in smaller towns; the respect shown for the Koran, for pilgrimages, and for moral and dogmatic teachings; the public recognition of Islamic marriage and burial; and the crown protection guaranteeing Valencian Islam's way of community life—all modify decisively the image of the fanatic crusader inherited from eighteenth-century *philosophes.*

[115] Uxó Charter. The Islamic year 648 opened on the modern Christian date April 5; August of the Christian thirteenth century ran from our July 16 (xvii kalends of August) to August 13 (ides of August). The Murviedro contract is in Chapter X, n. 18. Normally the Christians dated their Latin copies of such agreements with Muslims by one of the Christian calendars.

CHAPTER X

The Law and Its Interpreters

MAN LIVES BY LAW. More than just frame and guide, it is a manner in which life flows. It incorporates and passes on into the community more substance, more basic attitudes, values, and presuppositions, than its unwitting subject realizes. Especially was this true for the medieval Muslim. To a superficial observer, accustomed to the impersonal professionalism of the law devised by the West, it might seem that the Islamic moral-religious system usurped the role of true law. The clear-cut categories and jurisdictions were absent, the rational procedure from principle, and the psychology proper to the kind of civil society connected only extrinsically to religious values. Though it did embrace content unconnected with religious values, Islamic law at its most characteristic loomed as theology in practice, representing religious morality as much as law and operating at times by procedures so pragmatic, casuistic, and informal as to appear vague. Students of Mudejar society understandably find law "the most thorny" of its aspects, irritatingly devoid of "legislative unity."[1]

[1] Roca Traver, "Vida mudéjar," p. 179: "más espinosa," "unidad legislativa." For background see Ibn Khaldūn, *Muqaddimah,* III, 1-34, esp. p. 12 on why the Malikite school prevailed in Spain of the crusade era. Useful background surveys, often stressing the origins and caliphate era, include the topical handbook of José López Ortiz, *Derecho musulmán* (Barcelona, 1932), with the older bibliography; Coulson, *History of Islamic Law,* esp. part 2, "Legal Doctrine and Practice in Medieval Islam"; G. H. Bousquet, *L'Islam maghrébin, introduction à l'étude générale de l'Islâm* (Algiers, 1954), chs. 6, 12; Lévi-Provençal, *España musulmana,* v, ch. 3; Von Grunebaum, *Medieval Islam,* ch. 5; Rafael Castejón Calderón's study of the early era, *Los juristas hispano-musulmanes* (Madrid, 1948); and Joseph Schact, "The Law," in *Unity and Variety in Muslim Civilization,* ed. Gustave von Grunebaum (Chicago, 1963), pp. 65-86; or Schact's more ample *Introduction to Islamic Law* (Oxford, 1964) which supersedes his *The Origins of Muhammadan Jurisprudence* (Oxford, 1950). Useful in understanding the evolution of legal offices are Émile Tyan, *Institutions du droit public musulman,* 2 vols. (Paris, 1954-1956), and especially his *Histoire de l'organisation judiciaire en pays d'Islam,* 2d edn. rev. (Leiden, 1960). See also his brief *La notariat et le régime de la preuve par écrit dans la pratique du droit musulman* (Lyons, 1945), and for Spain José López Ortiz, "La jurisprudencia y el estilo de los tribunales musulmanes de España," *AHDE,* IX (1932), 213-248.

Islamic law derived directly from God's revelation and indirectly from its living interpretation in the life of Muḥammad. The Koran, Sunna, and Hadith provided its triple but unified source. The Koran was God's word, down to the language and very letters uttered. The Sunna was the Prophet's practice, rendering one's understanding of the Koran more ample and exact. Hadith comprised the living example of the Prophet as conveyed in a statement by and about him, orally transmitted, authenticated by Islam's legal scholars, and eventually compiled in writing. Some jurists made Sunna and Hadith identical; but a hadith, which may contain several sunnas, embodies the sunna without formally identifying with it. The jurist or *al-faqīh*, something of a combined theologian-canonist-moralist, drew upon divinely guided community consensus (*ijmāʿ*) and often upon logical or analogical reasoning to evolve disparate methodologies and to amass for Islam its *fiqh* or religio-social jurisprudence and practical law. The jurists became in effect "the guardians of the Islamic conscience."[2]

Of the four great rites or legal traditions which divided orthodox Sunnite Muslims, the Malikite school—supplementing tradition very generously with interpretations from community custom, consensus, and common good—"reigned supreme up to the end" in Islamic Spain, "scarcely affected by Almohad propaganda" against it. Valencia was famed for the purity of its Malikite rite. During the Berber centuries preceding the Valencian crusade the power of the Spanish jurist class grew until "they frequently formed the most influential and active section of the population," with the Malikite tenets acting as a unifying factor in divisive Spanish Islam.[3] Lévi-Provençal's observation that Spanish jurists neglected the Hadith does not seem to hold true of Almohad Valencia; the Eslida charter of 1242 particularly protected "all the books of the Hadith [*de alhadet*]."[4]

By the inflationary process that devalues many an honorific, the title of jurist may already have attached as well to persons educated at a college-mosque in a smattering of religious law, especially if popular perception affiliated him somehow into the ranks of reli-

[2] Coulson, *History of Islamic Law*, p. 73.

[3] Lévi-Provençal, "Al-Andalus," *EI*², I, 497 (quotations).

[4] Eslida Charter. Lévi-Provençal, *España musulmana*, v, 307-308n.

gious teachers.[5] The second ruler of Granada, a contemporary of Kings James and Peter, styled himself Muḥammad al-Faqīh, Ibn Khaldūn explains, "because he had studied law as a royal prince." The subgovernors of Minorca in the crusade era affected the title *faqīh* as their main form of address, as did a ruler of Ceuta, thus anticipating a Mudejar usage of later centuries.[6] By the fifteenth century in Aragon proper the title *faqīh* would come to cover the local minister of cult, primary school pedagogue, prayer leader, preacher, or salaried custodian of extensive mosque properties.[7] In Morisco Valencia the importance of the *faqīh* became extraordinary.[8] Either rich Moriscos rather automatically assumed the role of *faqīh* or, as Ribera Tarragó concluded, the function fell to the rich; physician, legist, or Koranic expert, this later *faqīh* might enjoy a reputation either in his village or over the kingdom.[9] By that period the term probably concealed several correlative functions. Al-Maqqarī tells us that *faqīh* remained an elevated title in Spain from the Almoravid to the late Granadan period, as honorable "as that of *qāḍī* in the East"; it did suffer from imprecision, applying "to any man learned in grammar, rhetoric, metaphysics, theology, or jurisprudence."[10] The prime analogue must have remained the Islamic jurist. The *faqīh* should not be confused with the detested class of lawyers or advocates, who appealed for petitioners at a price, or with the antithetical *faqīr* or holy mendicant, much less with the Jewish *alfaquín* (Catalan *alfaquim*) in the service of the crown of Aragon, whose title derived from a different Arabic term.[11]

[5] Gibb, note to Ibn Baṭṭūṭa, *Travels*, I, II; see also the correspondence between *mawlānā* of the Persians and *faqīh* explained by the traveler (II, 293). Soldevila improperly makes *faqīh* merely a title of respect among Muslims of the Valencian crusade era (*Pere el Gran*, part I, II, 249n.), while Tourtoulon sees it as designating any literate figure (*Jaime I*, II, 300n.). The usual Latin form was *alfachinus*, but the Tortosa Charter had *alfachus*. In 1284 King Peter conferred the dignity with an annual salary in gold; here it was obviously an official post (Dufourcq, *L'Espagne catalane et le Maghrib*, p. 183).

[6] Ibn Khaldūn, *Histoire des Berbères*, III, 363, IV, 75, 159.

[7] Macho Ortega, "Mudéjares aragoneses," p. 197.

[8] Halperín Donghi, "Moriscos y cristianos viejos en Valencia," pp. 91-93.

[9] Halperín Donghi, "Recouvrements: Valence," p. 172.

[10] Al-Maqqarī, *Mohammedan Dynasties in Spain*, I, 141-142.

[11] Ibn 'Abdūn damns the advocates as evil, lying, expensive, and too numerous in twelfth-century Seville (*Séville musulmane, le traité*, p. 26). On the Jewish *alfaquín*, see below, p. 253.

Law as it emerged from the pens of the jurists in opinions and treatises was ideal, designed to shape the community rather than to evolve from its needs. It left whole areas of human interaction untouched. This *sharī'a* had settled into rigid classical molds long before the Almohad era; its scope and procedural rules severely limited the canonical courts. The gap intervening between doctrinaire theory and historical practice, or between human need and the silence of the law, had to be filled by retaining antecedent customs of a given region and by contriving jurisdictions of more pragmatic non-*sharī'a* courts. The latter—whether special, administrative, or understood as political power in action—came under the religious rubric in their own fashion, though they can give the appearance of parallel lay courts. Two main factors underlay the Islamic judiciary. Justice was the personal task of the ruler, not an independent branch of government; its distinct organism amounted to a series of personal delegations, subordinate to the political executive and recoverable by him. On the other hand, since Islam lacked true legislative power, the judiciary masked legislative evolution, both creative and adaptive. Given these qualities, detailed legal content and current legal administration for a given region or time becomes a very difficult problem for the student of the history of Islamic law.

Sunna and Custom in Valencia

What specific content did Valencian law offer as distinguished from that of other Islamic communities? No codes have survived, nor sufficient indirect evidence to encourage legal experts toward serious conjecture about local peculiarities. An exception is the work of Honorio García. He suggests that the mass of Islamized native Valencians lived under the Koran and Sunna rather more in theory than in practice. Where religion did not enter directly—as in details of economic life, administration, and other practical matters—custom law survived until, in the interplay of influences, both Mozarab and Hispano-Islamic laws had evolved, bearing a strong resemblance to each other. García, who devoted many years to the origins of Valencia's Christian law, built this theory upon specific technical points; the dowry legislation and its peculiar countergift, for example, betrayed Islamic elements and apparently Mozarabic influences. García's death terminated these broadly ranging investigations, but his tentative basic conclusion helps illumine the legal structure behind the Koranic facade.[12]

The actual laws remain in darkness. Some light might be cast on them by isolating those Islamic usages that the conquerors continued. Additional information might accrue from examining analogous Mudejar laws like a Castilian code of the thirteenth or early fourteenth century whose 308 titles cover such fundamentals as marriage, sales, crimes, and inheritance as nuanced by local custom.[13] A student of Valencia's Christian law, Miguel Gual Camarena, sees the important growth or expression of such Islamic law as coming after the death of King James; this impression may derive from the author's devotion to a special kind of document, the formal charter of settlement, whose extant examples are rare for the early period but become more numerous afterwards.[14] From settlement charters one can glean a certain amount of information not only on regulatory laws of daily life and the constitution of courts but on procedure—as at Játiva where not all witnesses were allowed to testify as equals.

Contracts were very important in Islamic Spain, serving a multiplicity of occasions from marriage to the employment of a servant. When the Eslida charter granted comprehensive jurisdiction to the local *qāḍī,* the specific items it enumerated to illustrate his power were contractual; he was to judge "in marriages and inheritances and purchases and all other cases." The Uxó charter satisfied itself with the single item of "their marriages"; marriage cases were very important and could require a separate *qāḍī*, especially in the Malikite rite. The Chivert charter devoted much attention to marriage, but rather in connection with waiving fees.[15] The later or second

[12] Honorio García y García, "Posibilidad de un elemento consuetudinario en el código de Jaime I," *BSCC,* XXIII (1947), p. 447. See also his "Los elementos germánico y musulmán en los 'Furs,'" *BSCC,* XXXI (1955), p. 81; for a listing of García's articles on Valencian law see my *Crusader Valencia,* II, 348-349.

[13] "Leyes de moros del siglo xiv," *Tratados de legislación musulmán,* ed. Pascual de Gayangos, in the *Memorial histórico español, colección de documentos, opúsculos y antigüedades,* 48 vols. (Madrid, 1851-1918), V, 428-448; with it is a much later work (1462) summing the principal obligations of the Sunna.

[14] "Territorialidad de los fueros de Valencia," p. 286; his prize-winning "Las cartas pueblas del reino de Valencia (siglos xiii a xviii)," awaiting publication, is schematized on a chart facing p. 272.

[15] Eslida Charter: "in casamentis et divisionibus et emptionibus et aliis omnibus." Uxó Charter: "en lurs matrimonis." Chivert Charter: "si aliquis serracenus de alio loco voluerit ducere uxorem in castro illo vel serracena maritum hec liceat eis

Eslida charter, however, specified that "you may draw up your deeds of marriage, of sale, and of all other contracts by the authority of your *qāḍī*."[16] Such contracts were innumerable. At the close of the crusade, the crown had licensed Christians to purchase properties from Alcira Muslims, but only if done directly "with the Saracen owners of those [lands], by Arabic charters" or contracts drawn by the Mudejars; in a resultant dispute, King James instructed each recent buyer to show his "Saracen instrument."[17]

Unfortunately only one marriage contract has survived for the thirteenth-century kingdom of Valencia, an elaborate document in Arabic from Murviedro, just north of Valencia city. It is dated 1297, not so late as to allow it to represent innovation, yet late enough to demonstrate continuing freedom of marriage customs. The contract itself, a declaration of intent, effected the marriage. Drawn up by the local notary with aljama officials, it joined Yūsuf b. Yaḥyā to the maid Maryam bint ʿAlī b. Madyān. The bride's mother, the widowed Maḥabba bint Farrāj b. Shākir, endowed the couple with an impressive list of local properties on both banks of the Palancia, including houses, fields, vineyards, and farmland. As dowry or bride-price Yūsuf handed over a hundred gold pieces (the Islamic Valencian *mithqāl* was specified), promising a balance of two hundred more within two years. The contract as a whole illustrates the continuity of Islamic institutions rather than local differences.[18] Evidence from

facere sine aliquo dono et missione." See Tyan, *Organisation judiciaire*, pp. 372-374 and 559-561. Out of thirteen contracts from Aragon-Navarre in the thirteenth century, published by Jacinto Bosch Vilá, only four are posterior to 1238; they are mainly bills of exchange, purchase, or loan; see his "Los documentos árabes y hebreos de Aragón y Navarra," *EEMCA*, v (1952), 407-416, and "Los documentos árabes del archivo catedral de Huesca" of 1145-1269, *RIEEIM*, v (1957), 1-48. H. R. Idris has drawn up a chart on marriage information compiled at the end of the fourteenth century from North Africa and Spain in his "Le mariage en occident musulman d'après un choix de Fatwās médiévales extraites du Miʿyār d'al-Wanšarīšī," *Studia islamica*, xxxii (1970), 157-167.

[16] Second Eslida Charter: "et possitis facere instrumenta vestra matrimonialia, vendicium, et omnium aliarum contractuum in posse vestri alcaydi."

[17] Document and episode below in Chapter XI, n. 46: "nisi christiani emissent eas [terras] a sarracenis dominis cum cartis sarracenicis"; "viso etiam instrumento sarracenorum" in each case.

[18] Arch. Crown, talón 567, caja 4; published in *Spanisch-islamische Urkunden aus der Zeit der Naṣriden und Moriscos*, ed. Wilhelm Hoenerbach (Berkeley, 1965), doc. 4 (Aug. 21, 1297). On marriage proceedings see Maurice Gaudefroy-Demombynes, *Muslim Institutions* (London, 1961), ch. 8.

later generations of Valencian Mudejars confirms the continuing control of the aljama over marriages.[19]

As in any culture, inheritance was a solemn subject. The Alfandech charter insured the ancient customs of property inheritance.[20] Cuart's privileges, confirmed after revolt, allowed Mudejars to "will and leave their goods according to their Sunna and law."[21] Though the Chivert charter provided clearly that "the heir inherits according to their law and Sunna," the Eslida charter merely stated that the *qāḍī* was to judge "in the divisions [*in divisionibus*]." The directive is not so mystifying as it sounds. Ibn Khaldūn discusses this "subdivision of arithmetic [which] is inheritance laws." Dividing an estate among many relatives by properly proportionate shares required "a good deal of calculation" and readjustments by "whole numbers, fractions, roots, knowns, and unknowns" through the elaborate "chapters and problems of inheritance law." He cites the extensive bibliography that accumulated on this "discipline in its own right"; the Spanish Malikites were eminent among commentators in juridical mathematics.[22] Sometimes a special judge, called the *ṣāḥib al-mawārīth*, whose jurisdiction flourished especially in Spain, handled inheritance cases.[23] Notices from Valencian charters offer sufficient assurance

19 Piles Ros, "Moros de realengo en Valencia," p. 238; Muḥammad Farrāj (Mahomet Faraig) disinherited his son for marrying against his will, an action supported by crown courts against the son's appeal; another Muḥammad disputed the validity of the marriage of his daughter 'Ā'ishah (Axa) to Muḥammad of Burgos, an artisan of Valencia city, but was forced to relinquish her dowry lands or perhaps inheritance when the husband submitted to the appeals court an Arabic contract from a *qāḍī*. See also the cases of violently bearing away one's inamorata (pp. 237-238). Vincke publishes a document of 1338 in which a Mudejar couple married "contra ritum sarracenorum" and incurred the death penalty, later reduced to a hundred lashes ("Königtum und Sklaverei," doc. 38).

20 Alfandech Charter.

21 Arch. Crown, Peter III, Reg. Canc. 44, fol. 149v (July 16, 1279): "possit legare et dimit[t]ere bona sua secundum çunam et legem eorum."

22 Eslida Charter. Chivert Charter: "heredes suas hereditet bona sua . . . secundum legem et çunam suam"; it also provides that Islamic custom be followed both in life and "in morte," probably a reference rather to inheritance than to burial practice. Ibn Khaldūn, *Muqaddimah*, III, 20-23, 127-129. Inheritance interested the crown also by reason of inheritance tax, the size of which is unknown; eventually a separate official, "collector of inheritances belonging to the king," supervised this Mudejar tax; for Eslida in the fifteenth century this was not the *amīn*, Sa'd Abū Wakī (Çaat Abogi), but one Abu 'l-'Azīz (Abulazis); Piles Ros, "Moros de realengo en Valencia," pp. 271-272.

23 Tyan, *Organisation judiciaire*, pp. 545-550; see also pp. 374-375.

that the substantial Islamic law remained operative in its social applications. Allowance must be made as well for different local usages surviving from the former Islamic kingdom. The Christian understanding of the term Sunna undoubtedly embraced a variety of roughly analogous legal codes or custom patterns, anchored not only in the Koran and Sunna but also in local needs and native traditions. Chivert's charter, for example, specified that "your law and Sunna" was to be applied according to the "usage by which the people were accustomed to live in the time of the Saracens."[24] James was concerned to continue local law on specific points; his policy seems to have been to make allowance, wherever possible, for those Islamic customs which differed from place to place in the kingdom of Valencia.

The king does not bother to specify *sharīʿa* as opposed to Sunna, and he was given to loose phrases like "the law code [*forum*] or Sunna." Mudejar charters of the twelfth and thirteenth centuries commonly summed up religious, legal, and civil freedoms—that is, the immemorial local way of life in areas surrendering—as *açuna et exarea* or *xara*. Valencian documents rarely used *sharīʿa*, however, preferring "law [*lex*] and Sunna" or either word alone.[25] Each form included or assumed the others. The settlement of Denia, advertised as "according to the Sunna of the Saracens," was explained as involving governance by a *qāḍī* as well as all the usual "privileges and customs [*consuetudines*] which the Saracens were accustomed to have in the kingdom of Valencia."[26] Muslims of Aldea were "to give judgment in formal or in extralegal cases according to the Sunna of the Saracens," and to conduct further appeals "always by the Sunna."[27] How carelessly King James employed Sunna to cover in

[24] Chivert Charter: "consuetudines iuxta quod facere consueverunt in tempore sarracenorum."

[25] In Arch. Crown, James I, Reg. Canc. 37, fol. 52v (Oct. 18, 1272), Prince Peter equates the "law code" of Ayelo with the Sunna, regulating its provisions "ad forum sive çunam sarracenorum Muntesie." The Eslida Charter refers to religion several times as "lex." The Chivert Charter sums the Islamic order as "legem et çunam." Daniel comments on Christian writers' use of the word "Law" (*Islam and the West*, p. 33).

[26] Arch. Crown, Peter III, Reg. Canc. 40, fol. 74 (March 16, 1277-1278): "ad çunam sarracenorum, ita scilicet quod habeatis alcadiam . . . et omnes franquitates et consuetudines sarracenicas quas sarraceni habere consueverunt in regno Valentie."

[27] *Ibid.*, fol. 33 (Oct. 25, 1277): "iudicent secundum zunam sarracenorum in causis et extra causas"; "per zunam omni tempore."

a comprehensive way the laws of a community can be seen from his application of the term to the Lérida Jews in 1270; the *nasi* Hasdai was to be rabbi and judge of the city's Jews for "crimes and cases which one Jew will have or bring against another according to the Sunna [*azuna*] of the Jews."[28]

Some important conclusions emerge. An autonomous legal system functioned, with its own code, judges, courts, tradition, precedents, and mode of procedure. It did not represent a rare privilege designed to placate a few powerful strongholds, but was the ordinary lot of those surrendering—in short, of all Muslim residents who were not slaves. Moreover, a general notion of the Mudejar legal system can be pieced together. The uneven bargaining power of the several communities at the time of surrender did not, as some historians assume, confuse and variegate the essentials conceded to all.[29]

Of the two spheres of law—public and private, not distinguished as such by the *fiqh*—the former was more susceptible to change, because it dealt with questions of sovereignty, politics, administration, public finance, and general relations with the Christian ruling class. Mudejar communities had perforce to adapt themselves to the methods and mentality of the new sovereign's curia, or to the traditions and vagaries of their immediate overlord. It was on matters which the conquerors thought of as public law that the two peoples probably concentrated their haggling during the surrender negotiations. As to the inner sphere of private law—the regulating customs conferring cohesion and pattern on a community—the crown would tend to permit whatever insured contentment and stability, especially where Christian sensibilities were not offended or the king's interests touched. James was already conditioned to a patchwork feudal kingdom of local customary laws, including Mudejar systems. Alfonso I in 1115 had allowed the conquered Muslims of Tudela their legal functionaries and laws, as he did also with Zaragoza in 1118. Raymond Berengar gave similar privileges at the fall of Tortosa in 1148

[28] Bofarull, "Jaime I y los judíos," doc. 95, and *Itinerari*, pp. 441-442 (July 28, 1270): "quod tu sis rabbi super iudeis Ilerde in mandatis legis veteris et sis iudex aliame . . . de crimines et causas . . . secundum azunam iudeorum." Though there was a prominent family of James's realms called Nasi, as a prefix it is a title; on the title and on "Naçi Acdai" himself see Neuman, *Jews in Spain*, II, 130, 217, 224, 229; Baer, *Jews in Christian Spain*, I, 216.

[29] Roca Traver, "Vida mudéjar," p. 178.

and of Lérida in 1149. At Tortosa the Muslims kept "their usages [*usaticos*] and their codes [*fueros*]" and were to "remain honored in their usages just as they were in the time of their other kings."[30]

Most Valencian records take for granted that the surrendered territories retained their law in specifics as in substance. The question fell into a category very like that of religion, with which the documents sometimes coupled it. The king's remarkably detailed memoirs find little place for particulars of his religious concessions, which he treats inclusively as part of their "law." At Elche the Muslims asked for their property, their religion, and "that they might be judged by the custom of the Saracens, and not be cited into court by any Christian, but that the Saracens be their judges as in the time of the Miramamoli." *Custum* here has the sense of established usages incumbent upon the community; the title Miramamoli (*Amīr al-Mu'minīn*) or Commander of the Believers, though dating back to the early Umayyad caliphs, refers to the Almohads. These requests James granted without difficulty; indeed, they had been his own suggestions for a fair treaty. At Paterna, Bétera, and Bulla, "I would let them keep their law and all the customs which they had in the time of the Saracens." At Chivert, "law and Sunna" were to be applied by "the customs according to which they were accustomed to act in Saracen times"; a single sentence yokes the words law, Sunna, code, and customs.[31]

For the capital city and its dependent district, the Sunna served as basis of the legal system.[32] King Peter harked back to "that Sunna and all those customs" allowed at the city in the day of his father King James.[33] In a postrebellion document James spoke of "those same customs [*consuetudines*] which they possessed and under

[30] Fernández y González, *Mudejares de Castilla*, appendix, doc. 2 (1115); and doc. 5 (1148): "Iures usaticos et suos fueros . . . et quod sedeant honoratos in Iures usaticos, sicut fuerunt in tempus de suos alios reges." See also Menéndez Pidal, *España del Cid*, II, 487-488.

[31] *Llibre dels feyts*, ch. 254: "lur ley e totes les costumes que havien en temps de sarrains" at Paterna, Bétera, Bulla [Bufila]; chs. 416, 418: "que fossen jutjats a custum de sarrains, e que no fossen forçats per negun chrestia, mas qu·els sarrains los jutgassen segons que era usat en temps de Miramamoli." Chivert Charter.

[32] Arch. Crown, James I, Reg. Canc. 15, fol. 81v (Feb. 26, 1267), a clarification.

[33] *Ibid.*, Peter III, Reg. Canc. 40, fol. 69v (Feb. 16, 1277-1278): "eam çunam et omnes eas consuetudines."

which they lived before the waging of the present war."[34] The city's aljama was to retain its own courts, Peter admonished the Christian authorities, "just as had been customary."[35] At Rafelbuñol, a settlement held by a Muslim secretary of King Peter, "you may use the Sunna of the Saracens . . . and you may have an *amīn*, whomever you wish, who may judge among you according to the aforesaid Sunna."[36] All at Alcalá, Cocentaina, Confrides, Gallinera, Guadalest, Penáguila, Planes, Polop, Tárbena, and in their districts or dependent villages, brought their legal cases before the *qāḍī* to be judged "according to the Saracen Sunna."[37] This information involved no new privilege but was conveyed by King James during a routine appointment. In the next century the Chelva Muslims were still living under the "Sunna or *sharī'a* of the Moors and according to their customs."[38]

The Chivert charter of 1234 acknowledged four sources of law for the aljama. The "law and Sunna" provided the essential system, but as supplemented or interpreted "according to the *Fuero juzgo* and the customs" prevalent locally before the crusade.[39] More commonly,

[34] *Ibid.*, James I, Reg. Canc. 22, fol. 44 (June 6, 1276): "sub eisdem consuetudinibus quas habebant et sub quibus vivebant ante presentem guerram motam."

[35] *Ibid.*, Peter III, Reg. Canc. 43, fol. 96v (Jan. 4, 1285): "prout est fieri consuetum."

[36] *Ibid.*, Reg. Canc. 44, fol. 185 (July 15, 1280): "quod utamini çuna sarracenorum . . . et quod habeatis alaminum quemcumque volueritis qui inter vos iudicet iuxta çunam predictam."

[37] *Ibid.*, James I, Reg. Canc. 19, fol. 18 (June 14, 1273): "secundum çunam sarracenicam."

[38] Chelva Charter: "sunna o xara de moros e segun se acostumbraba"; this evidence is ambiguous, since the "customs" could be the tax structure prevailing under the Christian lord.

[39] Chivert Charter: "suam legem et çunam secundum forum iudicium [iudicum] suasque consuetudines iuxta quod facere consueverunt in tempore sarracenorum." The *Fuero juzgo* was the *Lex Visigothorum* as revised by Reccaswinth, later supplanted by Frankish law in places or supplemented by local custom-codes. A fifteenth-century Mudejar judge was commissioned to settle Valencian cases according to "çuna e xara" together with the *Furs* and good reason. The fourteenth-century Chelva Charter says that the local Moors "fueron siempre e son" of the *fueros* of Aragon, in a context involving Moors and Christians. Roca Traver believes that the ideal law of the Koran was directly supplemented by the *Fuero juzgo* ("Vida mudéjar," p. 180), but account must be taken of the intervening custom law, especially in the private sphere, and of a variety of Christian laws. Though special caution must be exercised in making analogies from Jewish legal experience, in Valencia city the Jews received the "customs and laws" of the Zara-

the extrinsic Christian law was the *Furs* of Valencia; but Chivert fell long before the preparation of the *Furs*, and anyway the Templars exercised their seignorial right in designating their preferred usage. This element of Christian law was rarely mentioned and seems to have played a minor role in Mudejar affairs, probably nuancing only the public law, as in the control of minor taxes; it did furnish a larger framework, helping to mesh the parallel Christian and Muslim communities, occasionally resolving a perplexity not covered by Moorish custom and clarifying those privileges and duties affecting all Valencians, including Moors and Jews.

Jurisdictions and Personnel

The *qāḍī* was at once the spokesman for divine law and the prestigious embodiment of the ruler's judicial powers. His spiritual nature retained its priority in Spain, and under the Almohads his activities normally went free from interference by the ruler. The most exalted member of the judiciary, he also tended to be the central figure in a town's religious, social, and intellectual establishment. He headed the local association or school of law, organized the professional witnesses, and sometimes appointed delegate judges. He found himself serving as executor for minors, manager of philanthropic properties, bureaucrat in the civil government, and cultic functionary at the mosque. He often rose to his post via an academic, religious, or civil service career, and in turn could mount from it to other eminences. Because war had religious overtones, he was occasionally a warrior. He could cut a princely figure as *bon vivant* or Maecenas. In Spain he easily acquired a measure of direct political control over towns, a role in which he reenters the Mudejar story in a later chapter.[40]

goza Jews, and had their own courts and judges "secundum vestram legem" (*Itinerari*, pp. 138-139 [March 6, 1239]). For the relative prevalence of the Lérida, Barcelona, Tortosa, Aragon, Daroca, Zaragoza, and Valencia Christian codes in the kingdom of Valencia, see Gual Camarena, "Territorialidad de los fueros de Valencia," esp. table facing p. 272. See also below, Chapter XI, n. 1; J. Cerdá Ruiz Funes, "Fuero juzgo," *Nueva enciclopedia jurídica*, x, 326-346; José Font y Rius, "Furs de Valencia," *ibid.*, x, 528-532; and the other codes treated *ibid.*, passim.

[40] Tyan, *Organisation judiciaire*, pp. 100-119, 275ff., 342ff., and passim; on his military origins and attributes in Spain, pp. 414-416; on his control of state funds,

Ibn Khaldūn explains the evolution of the *qāḍī* as a delegation of the caliph's competence to settle "suits between litigants," which soon widened, as the ruler preoccupied himself with high policy, until it came to include "certain general concerns of the Muslims, such as supervision of the property of insane persons, orphans, bankrupts, and incompetents under the care of guardians, supervision of wills and mortmain donations," giving away in marriage women who lacked guardians, "supervision of [public] roads and buildings, and examination [and appointment] of witnesses, attorneys, and court substitutes, to acquire complete knowledge and full acquaintance relative to their reliability or unreliability." The more secular jurisdiction over complaints outside the religious law fell to a lesser (*maẓālim*) jurisdiction. The *qāḍī* had no supervision over torts, a field which required "much authority" and aggressive action, and which "is concerned with the examination of evidence, with punishments not foreseen by the religious law, with the use of indirect and circumstantial evidence, with the postponement of judgment until the legal situation has been clarified, with attempts to bring about reconciliation between litigants, and with the swearing in of witnesses."[41] In Spain however the office of *qāḍī* displayed a number of quirks. The title lost its exclusiveness and was often applied indiscriminately to anyone judging a case, even in a non-Koranic court. More important, the correlative non-*sharī'a* jurisdiction called *maẓālim* evolved only feebly and in ways essentially different than elsewhere in Islam, while the Koranic *qāḍī* acquired much of its alien scope, integrating it into his ordinary jurisdiction.[42]

In theory the chief *qāḍī* of a caliph or local independent princeling appointed in turn the lesser *qāḍī* for each outlying town, and in a large city for each neighborhood. The *qāḍī* of a major center like Valencia city, installed at the secondary mosque which became the

p. 409. See also Tyan's *Droit public musulman*, I, 215-216; López Ortiz, *Derecho musulmán*, pp. 68-79; Lapidus, *Muslim Cities*, pp. 136-138. Ibn 'Abdūn devotes much space to the Spanish *qāḍī*, his adjutants (no more than ten for a city the size of Seville), his treasurer, relations to the prince, and so on (*Séville musulmane, le traité*, pp. 14-23). On the *qāḍī* in North Africa, see H. R. Idris, *Berbérie orientale sous les zīrīdes, xe-xiie siècles*, 2 vols. (Paris, 1962), II, 554ff.; Hopkins, *Medieval Muslim Government in Barbary*, ch. 8, with ch. 9 on the other jurisdictions, into which the *qāḍī* might intrude; Brunschvig, *Berbérie orientale*, II, 133-138.

[41] *Muqaddimah*, I, 455-456.

[42] Tyan, *Organisation judiciaire*, pp. 111, 343, 446ff., 521-525.

crusaders' church of St. Catherine[43] and surrounded by a complex of personnel and formalities, contrasted with his rural counterpart informally dispensing justice at the local mosque or gateway, and with his delegate *qāḍī* in the city presiding modestly over some lesser category of cases. Necessarily supplementing the *qāḍī* was a range of informal, summary non-*sharī'a* courts, set up either for special purposes or as adjuncts to some administrative function. Operating flexibly outside the theologically restricted boundaries of the *qāḍī*, these jurisdictions covered such areas as commercial life and repressive police activity. Such ancillary magistracies overlapped each other's own jurisdictions as well as that of the *qāḍī*; custom served as guide against confusion, depending upon the complexity of a given community, so that the court of the *qāḍī* tended to confine itself to the more important litigation of a private or civil nature. The *qāḍī* appears frequently in Valencian records, both in his judicial and political capacities. By the Eslida charter he "judges their cases" in contracts, marriages, "and all other cases"—a universal mandate limited only by the modifier "according to their law."

The *amīn*, despite his generic name ("trustworthy") and indeterminate office when considered aprioristically, was a specific functionary in Valencia. Roca Traver makes him main administrator of the aljama, with a generalized legal jurisdiction along the lines of the Christians' municipal justiciar, presiding over the local council, governing the daily life of the aljama, and conducting a court of first instance in lighter cases, or in smaller towns a more considerable court.[44] This description owes too much to the evolution of the office in the fourteenth and fifteenth centuries. The real nature of the *amīn*, like that of the *qāḍī*, must await final definition until after his political duties have been examined; at that time he may seem a likely tenant of the underdeveloped *maẓālim* jurisdiction.[45] It will

43 Ribera, "La plaza del alcalde," pp. 319-325.

44 Eslida Charter. Roca Traver, "Vida mudéjar," pp. 127-128. 'Ibn Abdūn has no judicial office corresponding to Valencia's *amīn*, discussing only the *amīn* who headed each craft and the *amīn* who checked meat and measures as *muḥtasib* (*Séville musulmane, le traité*, pp. 86-88, 98-99, 119). See also Claude Cahen, "*Amīn*," *EI*², I, 147; and in Spain, Dozy, *Glossaire*, p. 56.

45 During feudal or fragmenting periods, local authorities often showed themselves zealous in exercising *maẓālim* audiences, as a device to hold political power (Tyan, *Organisation judiciaire*, p. 476); as the *amīn* acquired political power ever more in Mudejar Valencia, it is plausible that he followed this precedent.

suffice for the moment to remark that he had a jurisdiction and also a subordinate role in the court of the *qāḍī*.[46]

The Játiva charter, in setting the *qāḍī* as the aljama's judge, mentions "judgments issued by the said *qāḍī* with the counsel of the *ṣāḥib al-madīna* and the *amīn* and of other notables [*probi homines*]";[47] here the role of the *amīn* must be assessory. In the city and huerta of Valencia, on the other hand, charges of a noncapital kind brought by Christians and Jews against Muslims came under "the jurisdiction [*posse*] of the *qāḍī* and the *amīn* and other Saracens of the said city," according to a clarification of 1267; the same letter ordered defendants in noncapital criminal cases involving only Muslims to be bound over to the *amīn*.[48] On the basis of this document it has been argued that the *amīn* handled civil cases between Muslims and non-Muslims; actually the letter assigns to Islamic courts the civil and most of the criminal cases brought by non-Muslims, and it implies—but annoyingly does not state clearly—that the *amīn* judged such cases. Aside from the ambiguity that would allow the *amīn* to have been an officer of the court here rather than a judge, the further problem arises that he certainly did not judge such cases elsewhere. At Játiva, "if any Christian brings a complaint against a Saracen, he is to take legal satisfaction in the court of your *ṣāḥib al-madīna* [and] according to the Sunna of the Saracens."[49] At Chivert, "if at any time a dispute or quarrel shall have arisen between Christians and Saracens or Jews, let the *faqīh-qāḍī* judge the Saracens according to their law, and the Templars' Christian bailiff judge the Christians and the Jews."[50] The *amīn* nevertheless

[46] See Chapter XVI, section 1.

[47] Játiva Charter. A normal procedure was that described by Ibn Baṭṭūṭa in 1325, where the *qāḍī* of Tunis sat by a pillar in the main mosque after Friday service and delivered forty opinions (*Travels*, 1, 14). Ibn 'Abdūn describes the sitting of Seville's *qāḍī* somewhat more formally (*Séville musulmane, le traité*, p. 18).

[48] Arch. Crown, Reg. Canc. 15, fol. 81v (Feb. 26, 1267), also in Roca Traver, "Vida mudéjar," doc. 3, with comment on p. 188: "non teneantur facere ius . . . nisi posse alcadii et alamini et . . . sarracenorum dicte morerie secundum açunam."

[49] Játiva Charter: "si aliquis christianus conqueratur de sarraceno, recipiat iustitiae complementum in posse zalmedinae vestri, secundum zunam sarracenorum."

[50] Chivert Charter: "si aliquo tempore orta fuerit contencio sive querela inter christianos et sarracenos vel iudeos alfachinus alcaydus iudicet sarracenos secundum legem suam et christianus baiulus Templi iudicet christianos et iudeos." I have amended the transcription from "christianos baiulis"; the bailiff was often a Jew.

possessed judicial powers and probably extended his jurisdictional presence as his political office assumed centrality in subsequent generations.[51]

The *ṣāḥib al-madīna* (Catalan *salmedina* and Castilian *zalmedina*) or city prefect represented a special form of non-*sharī'a* justice—the repressive or police function. As Ibn Khaldūn explains it, the "religious function" of the police—prosecuting suspects, exercising "preventive punishment," reckoning compensation, and executing legal penalties—had eventually divided, the *qāḍī* assuming some of the imposition of punishment while a state official investigated suspects and executed sentence. "In Spain he is called the *ṣāḥib al-madīna*," the police chief or director of public order; under the Umayyads he had "acquired great celebrity"—a high chief exercising general jurisdiction even over government dignitaries, while a lesser chief controlled "the common people." In his days of glory the high chief had sometimes conducted a court with monopoly over capital offenses and over most criminal cases involving legal punishment. Under the Almohads the post lost its general jurisdiction but retained "a certain reputation"; in North Africa it fell "only to important Almohad personalities." By the late fourteenth century in North Africa "its importance has greatly decreased"; if no longer the preserve of Almohad personalities, however, it still went to competent followers of the incumbent dynasty.[52] To judge from Valencian documentation, the *ṣāḥib al-madīna* remained a prominent personage during the turbulent postcrusade years, perpetuating some of the former prestige.

[51] Piles Ros, "Moros de realengo en Valencia," pp. 273-274, commission of *amīn* for Eslida (Feb. 5, 1425): "e facats juhis e tingues raho e justic[ia] a totes les gents e p[er]sones que denant tu juhi faran esclamaron."

[52] Ibn Khaldūn, *Muqaddimah*, I, 456-459, II, 35-37. See also Lévi-Provençal, *España musulmana*, V, 87-90. See also Tyan, *Organisation judiciaire*, pp. 576-595; as a religious figure in Spain the *ṣāḥib al-madīna* acquired cultic functions like preaching and directing the Friday prayers; yet he belonged more to the administrative or civil aspect of society; a *qāḍī* might be promoted to the office; as collaborator with the ruling authority in maintaining order, he sometimes swallowed the superior office and emerged as town governor in the Almohad era; more than a police chief, he was almost a military figure (see esp. pp. 583, 584-586, 588-589). On this confusing office, see also Abdelkrim Aluch, "Organización administrativa de las ciudades en el Islam español," *Miscelánea de estudios árabes y hebraicos*, X (1961), 44-45. He discusses as well the principal religious and juridical offices, though summarily.

If early Valencian documents explicitly name the *amīn* less often than the *qāḍī*, they find even fewer occasions to advert to the *ṣāḥib al-madīna.* Details do survive for a large city, Játiva. There the *qāḍī* was to "judge and decide your cases"; his office, treated first, was obviously preeminent. Less significant, the *ṣāḥib al-madīna* conducted the prison, arrested the accused, handled cases brought by Christians, executed [*faciat*] "justice and punishment among you" in noncapital criminal charges, and retained "a tenth of the fines for his labor."[53] The Muslims of Cocentaina town and countryside maintained their own *ṣāḥib al-madīna.*[54] It is unwise to institute comparison with the Christian version of the same office, which had already gone through long evolution since its borrowing from the Muslims; the *çavalmedinat* was an alternate title for the *cort* or Christian municipal government at Valencia city.[55]

The *ṣāḥib al-madīna* could appoint functionaries called *exortivi* in the crusaders' Latin—as many as necessary to help him "exercise justice." This is a rare Valencian reference to the *ṣāḥib ash-shurṭa,* sometimes called in Christian documents the *zabaxorta* or *savasorta.* He can be understood as assistant or delegate, or even as a lesser *ṣāḥib al-madīna*; the plural form may indicate survival of the time-honored practice of providing a separate *ṣāḥib* for different social strata of delinquents. Ibn Khaldūn seems to identify the *ṣāḥib al-madīna* with the *ṣāḥib ash-shurṭa,* and as erudite an Arabist as Lévi-Provençal found difficulty in distinguishing the two. Tyan saw the first as at times the chief officer in the police system. Dozy concluded that *zavalmedina* was merely a popular name for the Spanish *ṣāḥib ash-shurṭa,* and noted

[53] Játiva Charter: "zalmedina faciat iustitias et districtus inter vos, excepta tamen morte hominum." It seems less probable that the last phrase refers only to murder and manslaughter. 'Ibn Abdūn discusses the twelfth-century Spanish *ṣāḥib al-madīna,* his assistants, and his manner of punishing; he urged that this functionary, like the *qāḍī* and other judicial officers, be Spanish rather than Berber, as being more familiar with the various social classes and popular dispositions (*Séville musulmane, le traité,* pp. 33-34).

[54] *Itinerari,* p. 521 (July 14, 1275).

[55] *Colección diplomática,* doc. 160 (Oct. 2, 1237) mentions the secretariat of the "çavalmedinat" or *curia* having a monopoly on all its writings, seals, testimonies, judgments, and sentences. See also the *Repartimiento de Valencia,* p. 157, and Chabás, "Libro del repartimiento de la ciudad y reino de Valencia," p. 245, on the "çalmedinatum" of Valencia city. In 1275 Alfandech lands were given to the *salmedina* of the Christians of Zaragoza (*Itinerari,* p. 521).

that the authority governing a thirteenth-century Hispano-Islamic town sometimes adopted the title.[56] A much lesser figure, the court officer, called in Catalan *saig* or *saio* (Latin *sagio*), finds a place in the Chivert charter. In Christian administration the *saig* detected, arrested, confiscated, punished, and in general acted the part of agent or of police arm; presumably he enjoyed an analogous role in the aljama's courts. In the aljamas of fifteenth-century Aragon he was in fact a constable or peace officer.[57]

Játiva's charter exposes to view an institution peculiar to the Islamic West and especially to Spain—the council of the *qāḍī.* Where Eastern lands, and especially non-Malikite schools, encouraged recourse to a consultative council of jurists, Spain made such recourse obligatory and "a fundamental rule of the judicial organization." The role was collaborative rather than collegial, involving one to four consultants, who sometimes doubled also as notarial-secretarial staff. Conversely, Spain's *maẓālim* courts never developed the assembly and notables prominent in the East.[58] The "other respectable men"[59] or notables serving as auxiliary assessors at Játiva came from a sociopolitical category of citizens difficult to define with precision, a task relegated to its proper chapter.[60] The central figure in a Valencian aljama's court system always remained the *qāḍī.* As King Peter in 1284 reminded the justiciar and jurates at Valencia city, "Saracens

[56] Lévi-Provençal, *España musulmana*, v, 88-91. Dozy, *Glossaire*, p. 367. Baer has found a Jew of Huesca in 1190 named Abraham Çavi Xorta, whom he identifies with a property owner named Zavaxorta and with the Islamic title *ṣāḥib ash-shurṭa* (*Jews in Christian Spain*, I, 94, 394).

[57] Chivert Charter: "saionem," the Catalan *saig* (*sag*, etc.) and Castilian *sayón*, from Low Latin *sagio*. This is a Christian office mentioned several times by Lull; it represents either a borrowing by Christian or Muslim or else application by the Christians of their own terminology to the analogous Islamic institution. Lévi-Provençal speaks in passing of *sayones* under the *ṣāḥib ash-shurṭa* in the caliphate era (*España musulmana*, v, 90). See also below, p. 400n., and his duties in *Fori*, rub. CXXXVIII, "de sagionibus." For later Aragon, see Macho Ortega, "Mudéjares aragoneses," p. 162.

[58] Tyan, *Organisation judiciaire*, p. 230; pp. 230-236 explore "le consilium du magistrat en Espagne"; see pp. 522-523 on why the *maẓālim* jurisdiction lacked its assembly, contrasting the system on pp. 494-495.

[59] Játiva Charter: "cum consilio zalmedinae et alamini, et aliorum proborum hominum aliamae."

[60] The *prohom* or *probus homo* is discussed in Chapter XVI, section 2.

ought to fall under the jurisdiction of their *qāḍī* for charges elaborated among themselves."[61]

Qāḍī, amīn, and *ṣāḥib al-madīna* comprised the main judiciary in a Valencian aljama. Since the duties of an office could be divided, or two offices combined into one, possibilities of confusion multiply. One *qāḍī* might handle only certain kinds of cases; a notable might function both as *qāḍī* and as *ṣāḥib al-madīna*; officials might subdelegate powers or, where personnel was scarce, contrive to assimilate various powers from one court to another. Since any administrative office in Christian or Islamic Spain tended to appropriate some judicial powers convenient to its operation, jerry-built lesser jurisdictions could emerge by the side of the major courts. The accumulating or combining of coordinate jurisdictions in a single person was especially common in Islamic Spain. A clear example, from outside Valencia, was King James's appointment of Mūsā of Morocco (Muça de Marrochs) in 1263 as both *amīn* and *qāḍī* for life over the Muslims of Lérida with its region. The king limited his description of the combined functions to their legal aspect: "You are to hear all cases among the said Saracens and others who normally plead at Lérida before the *amīn* or the *qāḍī* of Lérida, and you are to draw and fashion Saracen public documents [*publica instrumenta*]."[62] Mūsā was to pay the crown five morabatins a year. Did Mūsā exercise these three offices, including that of regional notary, in person, or was it assumed that he would delegate his powers?

A fascinating subsidiary court, and among the most important, was the *ḥisba* jurisdiction of the *muḥtasib*. Eastern theorists derived his office from the private obligation in piety to hinder evil and pro-

[61] Arch. Crown, Peter III, Reg. Canc. 43, fol. 96v (Jan. 4, 1284-1285): "sarracenos Valencie debere respondere in posse alcadi eorum super querimoniis que exponentur inter ipsos."

[62] *Itinerari*, p. 339 (May 17, 1263): "diebus omnibus vite tue alaminatum et alcadiam sarracenorum Ilerde, ita quod tu sis alaminus et alcadi dicte morerie et tu audias omnes causas que erunt inter dictos sarracenos et alios qui consueverunt in Ilerda causiditare coram alamino vel alcadi Ilerde et conficias ac facias publica instrumenta sarracenica." On one man's accumulating offices in Spain, see Tyan, *Organisation judiciaire*, pp. 608 (*qāḍī* and *ṣāḥib al-madīna*), 627 (*muḥtasib* and *ṣāḥib al-madīna*, with *qāḍī* in control). In the late fourteenth century, the Eslida Moor Ṭalḥah (Talba), comprehensively waiving all rights in law to privileged jurisdiction under Muslim or Christian judges in favor of the Morella justiciar, summed them as: "renunciam al for del iusticia, alcayt, çalmedina, alami, e çuna del dit loch de Eslida, e sotsmet ami e mos bens al for e jurisdiccio del justicia de Morella" (Grau Monserrat, "Mudéjares castellonenses," doc. 19 [Sept. 18, 1385]).

mote good, as generalized or transferred into a public mandate; more practically, the absence of autonomous municipalities in the centralized Islamic state made some such office inevitable for controlling the necessities of urban life. A censor or supervisor of community morality ranging over a miscellany of concerns from liturgy to bad example, his main function was regulating commercial and industrial activity, professional ethics, public morals, and community utilities or amenities. He combined the jobs of building inspector, health officer, policeman, and watchdog of the public interest. Strangely enough, though he reached his highest status in the West, almost equaling the *qāḍī* at one time in prestige, Spanish theory and practice tended to restrict his competence to pragmatic realities of commerce, viewing him largely as market controller with peripheral concerns. A jurist and a religious man, he fell under the indirect control of the *qāḍī*, who conferred and revoked the office and used it at times for his own purposes.[63] In the crusader East the *muḥtasib* translated into the Christian *mathesep* at Jerusalem; in the cities of Christian Spain an imitative form evolved under the Catalan name *mostassaf* and the Castilian *almotacén* and *almutazaf*. So useful was the office that Christian armies adopted a version, as in King James's crusading host of 1266 against Murcia.[64]

[63] Tyan has a long discussion, contrasting the office in the West and in Spain with the East, in his *Organisation judiciaire*, pp. 617-650; see esp. pp. 621, 626-627, and on its administrative nature, pp. 645-648. Brief descriptions are in Von Grunebaum, *Medieval Islam*, pp. 165-167; Lévi-Provençal, *España musulmana*, v, 84-86; Ibn Khaldūn, *Muqaddimah*, i, 462-463. Lévi-Provençal has edited three manuals discovered for this office in medieval Spain. From the twelfth century, see his Ibn 'Abdūn, *Séville musulmane, le traité*, with explicit discussion of the *muḥtasib* on pp. 42-45; Ibn 'Abdūn remarks that this functionary relieved the *qāḍī* of "distasteful contact" with the lowest classes, including "ignorant workmen" (p. 44). See also the two treatises by Ibn 'Abd ar-Ra'ūf and by 'Umar al-Garsīfī, "Traduction annotée et commentée des traités de *ḥisba*," *Hespéris-Tamuda*, i (1960), 5-38, 199-214, 349-386. Perhaps the Byzantine market inspector or *agronomos* relates to the origins of this office. On the contemporary Mamluk officer in the Islamic East, see Lapidus, *Muslim Cities*, pp. 98-100, 146-147. Pedro Chalmeta Gendron's doctoral thesis, "Estudio sobre la ḥisbat al-sūq en al-Andalus" (Madrid University, 1967) is as yet unpublished, except for an article on the resemblance between the Islamic and Christian officials; Thomas Glick explores the "cultural diffusion" implicit in this resemblance, in "*Muḥtasib* and *Mustasaf*: A Case Study of Institutional Diffusion," *Viator*, ii (1971), 59-81.

[64] Munro, *Kingdom of the Crusaders*, p. 101, where he has charge of policing the city. The "almudacefia" of the crusading army invading Murcia in 1266 was held by Bertrand of Claret, over "tocius nostri exercitus presentis et eciam civitatis

The *muḥtasib* could prevent or detect delinquencies, and he acted as a summary court. Using simple, flexible procedures and drawing heavily upon custom, he rather upheld the common usages than issued judicial opinions, and he confined himself to lesser and relatively straightforward cases within his peculiar competence. In Spain his status had declined badly by the eleventh century, but in Mudejar Valencia he either retained considerable power, or else regained it owing to a kind of osmosis with his Christian counterpart. A decree by King James in 1267 reviewed the duties of the Valencia city *muḥtasib* while warning away the intrusions of the Christian "almudaçafus." The Christian officer must not "enter the Moorish quarter of Valencia nor impose any coercion on its Saracens nor for any reason pass judgment on those inside or outside the quarter." Every year the aljama was to "establish and create as *muḥtasib* one of the Saracens of that quarter, which *muḥtasib* may administer justice over those Saracens and coerce them in matters requiring coercion, except for affairs or charges admitting the death penalty."[65] There is no reason for regarding this action as the introduction of the office; in the context of other items granted here, and of the case precipitating the decree, it is more likely that it confirms the custom previous to 1267, embodying it in a formal privilege.

Gual Camarena suspects that the *amīn* in documents of the Valen-

---

Murcie cum ipsam adquisierimus et dum fuerimus cum exercitu nostro in regno Murcie, ita quod vos, et quos volueritis loco vestri, teneatis dictum officium almudacefie tam panis vini quam mensurarum quam eciam omnium aliarum rerum que pertineant vel pertinere debeant ad officium antedictum tam dicte civitatis quam predicti exercitus nostri . . . et habeatis racione dicti officii totum illud quod almudaçafus debet percipere" (*Itinerari*, p. 382 [Jan. 5, 1266]). Later details of this office, which became especially important in the armies of Arago-Catalonia, are in Jill Webster, "Francesc Eiximenis on Royal Officials: A View of Fourteenth-Century Aragon," *Medieval Studies*, XXXI (1969), 242-243. The Christian municipal officer in the realms of Aragon has his own bibliography; see esp. the *Libre de mostaçaf de la ciutat de Valencia*, ed. Francisco Sevillano Colom as *Valencia urbana medieval a través del officio de mustaçaf* (Valencia, 1957). The *Aureum opus* for Valencia city has a provision of Dec. 29, 1239, "De offitio almudaçafie," and of Jan. 19, 1251, on the oath of office by the "mostaçaffi"; the laws of the Valencian kingdom describe some of his duties (*Fori antiqui Valentiae*, rub. CXXXVI, no. 7; see the *Aureum opus* docs. gathered on pp. 297, 299).

[65] Arch. Crown, James I, Reg. Canc. 15, fol. 81v (Feb. 26, 1267): "qui almudaçafus super ipsis sarracenis iudicet et eos distringet in quibus distringendi exceptis factis et querimoniis pene mortis."

cian kingdom, far from being the equivalent of the Christians' head jurate or executive, was in fact the *muḥtasib*. Lending color to this theory is a petition from the fifteenth century in which the Muslims of Monforte asked the king to name annually "one *amīn* who is called a *muḥtasib*."[66] Considering the ambiguity of the title *amīn* when out of specific context, the evidence is not decisive. Ibn 'Abdūn's treatise on the officials of Seville in the twelfth century brushed past the *amīn*, not even considering him as a holder of political-juridical authority, but it devoted space to the *muḥtasib*. It is clear, though, that the two offices were distinct. Time may have given the *amīn* the functions of other personnel, several of which are otherwise absent from the local Valencian scene; and in one or other place the *amīn* and *muḥtasib* might easily have combined.

A celebrated local jurisdiction was the custom court over irrigation affairs. The administration and repair of canals, the timing and apportionment of water, and the related disputes connected with a given network of canals fell under the water community itself, supervised by its own functionary and subofficials. Immemorial custom, familiar to every farmer along the system's banks, regulated minute details. Who declared and enforced these consecrated neighborhood usages? Historians point to the tribunal of waters, a nonprofessional but official panel of farmers sitting as informal courts.[67] Though most of these assemblies have disappeared in Valencia, tourists are familiar with the solemn sessions in Valencia city today, in which arguments are heard out in a side doorway of the cathedral—formerly the entrance to the main mosque—and irreversible judgments handed down for the surrounding huerta. Valencians celebrated the millennium of this surviving tribunal of waters in 1960. Recent historical inquiry inclined to root this patently non-Islamic, collegial institution in late Roman times; so parochial and nonprofessional a court was hardly expected to leave records of its continuing activities through the Islamic centuries. Glick, a specialist in Valencian irrigation records, dismisses this history of the tribunal as improbable and as a theory that evolved from dubious premises. In its

[66] "Mudéjares valencianos," p. 176.

[67] For example, Martínez-Ferrando, in "La dominació aràbiga a la Catalunya nova, València i les illes," in his *Baixa edat mitjana*, pp. 1062-1063; and Sanchis Guarner, "Època musulmana," pp. 343-344.

place, a summary custom jurisdiction did of course exist for the functioning of a crisis-ridden water system; its judge undoubtedly was the superintendent or subordinate *cequiarius*, who might take advice from such assessors as his own inspectors or a council of farmer-elders serving like a jury.[68]

Intersystem irrigation controversies often had to go before an outside judge or even the ruler; two cases resolved in the days of Abū Zayd have left documentary traces, especially the dispute between Torres Torres and Carcer, settled after twenty years by the Murviedro *qāḍī* in 1223.[69] A more intractable quarrel between Uxó and Eslida perdured through the last two Islamic rulers and came finally before King James; its meandering course is traced in the next chapter. A similar dispute between Christian settlers at Bairén and Benietos caused the authorities to marshal the Mudejar ex-superintendents and *cequiarii*.[70]

In the postcrusade period the crown appointed a number of "masters" or supervisors, though it relaxed to local control many canals with their elective or appointive offices; Bonfil appears in this capacity at Alcira in 1259, Bortaco of Montornés in 1269, and William of Puigalt in 1276. They included among their functions the collection of the crown rents and imposition of fines upon delinquents, receiving the considerable salary of 500 solidi annually.[71] Presumably the crown patterned this office on the Islamic precedent. The crown intervened also, on appeal, to assist Mudejar plaintiffs in irrigation quarrels, as at Segorbe in 1267, Aldaya in 1268, and Murviedro in

[68] Glick, *Irrigation in Medieval Valencia*, ch. 3, with bibliographical orientation. Vicente Vicent Cortina has compiled an annotated bibliography on the less recent works about Valencian water and water courts, as part of his *Bibliografía geográfica del reino de Valencia* (Zaragoza, 1954), pp. 52-55, 67-70, 99-111, 147-151. Tyan was unable to discover more about "the *qāḍī* of water" beyond his existence (*Organisation judiciaire*, p. 559n.; see also pp. 110-111).

[69] Glick, *Irrigation in Medieval Valencia*, esp. citing J. M. Cueco Adrián, "Un documento árabe inédito," *Levante* (Aug. 1, 1965), and Sarthou Carreres, *Provincia de Castellón*, p. 165.

[70] Roque Chabás, *Distribución de las aguas en 1244 y donaciones del termino de Gandía por D. Jaime I* (Valencia, 1898), pp. 3-6, document from the Gandía municipal archives, *Privilegis*, fol. 73 (July 16, 1244), testimony of "los moros cequieros"; the signatories are analyzed below on p. 411.

[71] Arch. Crown, James I, Reg. Canc. 10, fol. 131v (March 14, 1259); Reg. Canc. 16, fol. 185 (June 27, 1269); Reg. Canc. 19, fol. 12 (April 9, 1276).

1282.[72] The earliest surviving reference to postcrusade parochial water courts, aside from the Eslida charter's generic directive to continue its water practice as "in Saracen times," comes from Uxó with its valley and small huerta. Uxó's surrender agreement and its charter after the revolt both provided that the aljama "can pass judgment among themselves as to the waters, just as the custom was in the time of the Moors."[73]

Appointments and Appeals

Not illogically, the designation or confirmation of aljama officials rested with the civil authorities, or more properly was transferred from the Muslim overlord to the Christian king or seignior. At the Tortosa surrender in 1148, which left a Muslim "alguaçir" or vizier still in control, justice went to him and to any judge he chose; the aljama at large could select its own "alcaides" (surely coordinate judges, despite the spelling), according to their usages.[74] After the surrender of Seville, the Castilian king named the *qāḍī-faqīh*.[75] Probably the *qāḍī* in Valencian towns named his own auxiliaries, much as Valencia city's *qāḍī* had done in the pre-Cid province even for places as considerable as Alcira and Murviedro.[76] A number of appointments or arrangements have survived for crusader Valencia. In 1275 King James "granted to you 'Abd Allāh Ḥabīb Ḥibbān [Aduluhabeb Abin], Saracen, that you be *ṣāḥib al-madīna* of the Muslims in the Cocentaina Moorish quarter and in the countryside for all your life as long as you conduct yourself well and faithfully in that office."[77] An element of popular election, or at least of nomination by

[72] *Ibid.*, Reg. Canc. 15, fol. 83v (March 2, 1267), fol. 90 (April 10, 1268); Peter III, Reg. Canc. 46, fol. 77v (April 8, 1282); the first and last were mixed cases, involving Christian landlords on the Mudejars' side.

[73] Eslida Charter: "et explectent aquas suas sicut fuit consuetum tempore sarracenorum." Uxó Charter: "et que pusquen jutgar les aygues entre si, axi com era acostumat en temps de moros, segons ques conte en los lurs privilegis antichs."

[74] Fernández y González, *Mudejares de Castilla*, appendix, doc. 5.

[75] *Repartimiento de Sevilla*, pp. 364-365.

[76] Menéndez Pidal, *España del Cid*, II, 514.

[77] Arch. Crown, James I, Reg. Canc. 200, fol. 270v (July 14, 1275): "concedimus vobis Abduluhabeb Abin sarraceno quod sis zalmedina sarracenorum ravalli Concentanie et terminorum suorum in tota vita dum bene et fideliter in ipso officio te habebis." Miret y Sans notes the document in passing but reads the name as Albiri (*Itinerari*, p. 521).

local notables, can be discerned; at the Eslida aljama the *qāḍī* "may be chosen at the cognizance [*ad cognitionem*] of your Saracens." The phrasing may be clarified by comparison with some Christian elections in Valencia, in which a panel of candidates was presented to the crown for final selection; whatever the method, participation or approval of the community is implied.[78] The crown paid a salary of 180 solidi annually to each *qāḍī* from local Mudejar revenues.[79] This was a necessity in a system where justice was gratuitous, but it tied the *qāḍī* to the Christian authorities.

At Játiva the crown retained appointment of both *amīn* and *ṣāḥib al-madīna*, but surrendered election of the *qāḍī* to the people; they could remove the latter if he proved incompetent.[80] The Perpunchent system was much the same.[81] At Uxó the people elected *qāḍī* and *amīn*. In the seignorial situation at Chivert the Knights Templar chose the *amīn*.[82] Only in 1359 did Chivert's people acquire the right to present three names from which the choice was made. In each crown aljama beyond the Júcar River the people elected the local *amīn* either from the beginning or at least from 1290.[83] On the seignorial domain of Carrícola and Montes the lord named the *amīn* responsible for both townships. Carbonera had a similar arrangement.[84]

Contemporary records hint at an appeals system, incompatible

[78] The Second Eslida Charter speaks of contracts being "in posse vestri alcaydi et alcaldi et dominus sit de aliama vestra et eligatur ad cognicionem sarracenorum vestrorum." At Tortosa in 1207 'Alī b. al-'Alā' (Ali Abinahole) was named *qāḍī* by a delegate of the queen, with the lord Raymond of Moncada and the aljama both joining in consent (Font Rius, "Tortosa a raíz de la reconquista," p. 123).

[79] Valencian accounts with this figure survive only for the region below the Júcar in 1315: "item prenen cascun any los alcaldes moros per salari de la alcaldia lur—CLXXX solidos" (*Rentas*, p. 115). At Játiva the *qāḍī* got far less than the aljama chief: "item hi pren lalcayt de la moreria de Xativa—CC solidos," as against "item hi pren lalcadi—L solidos," and "item el Satl el Çahat medina [*ṣāḥib al-madīna*]—XXX solidos," and "item hi pren lo saig de Xativa—solidos" (p. 104).

[80] Játiva Charter: "possitis eligere et ponere alcadi inter vos, quem volueritis."

[81] Gual Camarena, "Mudéjares valencianos," pp. 175-176.

[82] Uxó Charter. Chivert Charter.

[83] Gual Camarena, "Mudéjares valencianos," p. 176, including Chivert 1359 data.

[84] "Repàs d'un manual notarial del temps del rey en Jaume I," ed. Joan Segura, *Congrés I*, pp. 302, 310 (Sept. 27, 1259): "quod nos G. de Valclara et Bg. de Timor damus vobis Mafomet Huarat Ganim quod sitis alami de tota honore que fuit de Ri. de Timor, scilicet de Carricola et de Muntis, et dicimus et mandamus omnibus mauris sive sarracenis presentibus et futuris quod recipiant vos per alami." He got the same recompense (*iura*) from the aljama as did the Carbonera *amīn*. The appointment was done by the dead baron's executors in his name, perhaps by way of an inheritance gift.

with the medieval Islamic judicial system. Since the *qāḍī* or other judge held delegation from the ruler and gave his vicarial judgment alone, an appeals court above was as incongruous as a court of first instance below or a collegial rendering of judgment in parallel. Jurisdiction could divide between several judges, either according to rite and therefore over different subjects, or by competence conferred for a single category, or by full control over a portion of territory. However divided, jurisdictions remained coordinate, functioning in parallel rather than in the hierarchical mode of an appeals system.[85] In some cases a judge might "reform" a decision handed down by himself or his predecessor, thus opening the door to action resembling appeal; and a suitor might appeal occasionally to the civil power.[86] None of this altered the basic non-appeal structure of the judiciary. The Valencian evidence, recorded by Christians, falls naturally into the vocabulary of appeals; solving the paradox recommends logically a prior sampling of that evidence.

Nine important aljamas, including the villages and scattered populations of their districts, shared a single *qāḍī* holding the widest possible jurisdiction. This implied subordinate minor courts in the areas. More interesting still, a notice concerning these places affords a glimpse of an appeals system, with a sort of superior court at Játiva. In the pertinent document, King James "wished and confirmed" that Muḥammad "be *qāḍī* of all the aljamas, namely of Cocentaina and of Planes and of Alcalá and of Gallinera and of Penáguila [and] of Guadalest [and] of Confrides and of Polop and of Tárbena." The post included "all Saracens in the villages and districts of the said places." James specified for all these places "that you judge and conclude according to the Saracen Sunna all cases"; on the other hand, "if any feel themselves wronged they may appeal to the *qāḍī* of our Moorish quarter of Játiva." The term employed is *appellare*; its context of grievance and appeal seems clear. Since this was a routine appointment and supposed a settled judiciary, it summons visions of similar courts of appeal in the realm.[87]

[85] Tyan, *Organisation judiciaire*, p. 108.

[86] Brunschvig, *Berbérie orientale*, II, 129-130, where the civil appeal went from *qāḍī* to the Tunis council.

[87] Arch. Crown, James I, Reg. Canc. 19, fol. 18 (June 14, 1273): "per nos et nostros volumus et confirmamus tibi Mahomat Abenhalyr sarraceno quod . . . sis alcadi omnium aliamarum videlicet de Concentaina et . . . de Planis et de Alcalano et de Galinera et de Benaguila [et] de Guadilest [et] de Confridas et de Polop et

The same arrangement turns up in the Játiva charter where, after judgment by the *qāḍī* and other officials, a man could carry appeal either to the king "or to another *qāḍī* of the Saracens according to your law." At Aldea the charter from the Hospitallers left justice to the *amīn*, with appeal to the Muslim *qāḍī* of Tortosa. The *ṣāḥib al-madīna* of Cocentaina, one of the towns with appeal to Játiva, was to "exercise that office just as is the custom to exercise it well at Játiva, and you may have from it, for your office and work, those revenues which the *ṣāḥib al-madīna* of Játiva gets there for his office and work." Játiva was the principal town for the southern part of the kingdom of Valencia, and the Christian administration divided at the Júcar River; was this division, like so many other administrative usages and divisions, echoed in the preexisting Mudejar legal patterns? If so, the appeals system to Játiva would be matched at the kingdom's center by a system related to Valencia city. The Tortosa region, down through much of the extreme northern part of the Valencia kingdom, had once been a unity, part of its own Islamic kingdom; if northern Valencia enjoyed its own appeals network, Tortosa would be its natural center.[88] No evidence survives for an appeals system centered on politically important regional centers like Denia or Alcira, though a later record suggests a subsystem at Jérica with appeal to Játiva.[89] In the conservative way of legal affairs and

---

de Tarbana et omnium sarracenorum habitancium . . . in alqueriis et terminis secundum çunam sarracenicam omnes causas . . . et si quis vel si qui senserint se gravari, possint appellare ad alcadum ravalli nostri Xative. Mandantes etc." *Appellare* earlier carried the meaning of demanding one's right, going to court, accusing, and the like; see *Glossarium mediae latinitatis Cataloniae, voces latinas y romances documentadas en fuentes catalanes del año 800 al 1100*, ed. Mariano Bassols de Climent *et alii*, 1 vol. to date (Barcelona, 1960), I, 112; and Rodón Binué, *El lenguaje técnico,* p. 207. In thirteenth-century legal usage in Spain *appellare* bore the normal meaning of appeal (see, e.g., the trial record, "Ordinatio ecclesiae valentinae," pp. 329-330).

[88] Játiva Charter: "vel ad alium alcadi [*sic*] sarracenorum, secundum legem vestram." Aldea Charter. The Cocentaina document of 1275 is in n. 54. Arch. Crown, James I, Reg. Canc. 20, fols. 270v-271r (July 14, 1275): "exerceas ipsum officium sicut . . . in Xativa melius exercere consuevit et habeas pro officio et labore tuo ea iura que zalmedina Xative inde recipit pro suo officio et labore." On the Tortosa unity see my *Crusader Valencia,* I, 43.

[89] Gual Camarena, "Mudéjares valencianos," p. 176, citing a document beyond our period in which a chief *qāḍī*, from whom an appeal could be made only to the crown or to the *qāḍī* at Játiva, was named for the whole Jérica region; does this represent an efficient novelty or a conservative survival?

in the light of permissive Mudejarism, arrangement for appeals may represent a usage of more antiquity and continuity than do the changeable political units of the Islamic past. The phrase in the Játiva charter "according to your law" indicates that this appeals system is of long-standing precrusade origin, especially in the context, which is for the most part an *ad hoc* document of simple concessions or retentions. Have we finally found in this appeals system the elusive *alcadí general* proposed by Macho Ortega, for whom Valencian historians have searched in vain?[90] If so, does he represent a compromise between naive acceptance of a single hierarchical system in the kingdom and local juridical autonomy?

A way lies open toward resolving the conundrum of Islamic appeal. Recourse to the delegator, though by no means the same as appeal, may have seemed so to the Christian jurist; under the acculturative pressure of the conquerors' own system, into which the Islamic system meshed at several points, it may have bent in this direction. Fifty years after the death of James the Conqueror his successor Alfonso had to caution against permitting development of a complex system of Mudejar appeals; recourse could be had from any one *qāḍī* to only one further *qāḍī*. Another factor in the puzzle is the relative standing of the several judges who gloried in the name

[90] Macho Ortega concluded that every large aljama of fifteenth-century Aragon had its own *zavalaquen* (see below, n. 92), and that there existed a "tribunal del alcadí general de los reinos de Aragón y Valencia y principado de Cataluña," named for life by the crown ("Mudéjares aragoneses," pp. 177-178). The 1318 charter of Urzante allowed appeal to the "alfaque de Tudela, segund uuestra açunna"; see P. León Tello, "Carta de población a los moros de Urzante," *Primer congreso de estudios árabes e islámicos* (Madrid, 1964), p. 337. Torres Fontes, who sees an ambiguous and passing reference to an appeals judge in the *Siete partidas* of Alfonso X (see, e.g., part. III, tit. xx, no. 8), has found an "alcalle mayor de los moros de todos los mis rregnos" of Castile in 1369, whom he sees as a late evolution from the main "*qāḍī* of the aljama" in pre-Mudejar towns; see his "El alcalde mayor de las aljamas de moros en Castilla," *AHDE*, XXXII (1962), pp. 143-145, 163; this is not the Castilian frontier functionary called the "alcalde mayor," in his "El alcalde entre moros y cristianos del reino de Murcia," *Hispania*, LXXXVIII (1960), 255-280. See also Roca Traver, "Vida mudéjar," p. 187, and Gual Camarena, "Mudéjares valencianos," p. 181. No analogy can be drawn on this point from the legal structure of the Jewish aljamas, which seem generally independent of each other in jurisdiction; in 1257 James did make Solomon *alfaquí* chief rabbi for all Jews of Aragon proper, though the claim of his nephew Moses Alconstantini to enjoy the same privilege for the kingdom of Valencia was rejected (Neuman, *Jews in Spain*, I, 145-146).

qāḍī. In Spain the term properly applied to the judge in "an important town," according to al-Maqqarī, while the incumbent at a smaller town was a *musaddid* or *ḥākim*; medieval biographies reveal that this subaltern or vicar-judge was appointed by the *qāḍī*, depended on him, acted in his name, and in fact formed part of his magistrature.[91] In a large city like Valencia, Lévi-Provençal suggests, each segment or neighborhood had its own *ḥākim*. The term itself is uncommon in the records of early Valencia, but it does appear. Confirmation in 1279 of the surrender constitution for the Guadalest Valley reveals that its Mudejars "use their Sunna under the jurisdiction of their *ṣāḥib al-'aḥkām*"—that is, under their *ḥākim*.[92] Since common or careless usage in Spain inclined to designate any kind of judge a *qāḍī*, and since recourse within such a magistrature or the reference of weightier cases from an incompetent subaltern court took on the look of appeal, the otherwise inexplicable spectacle of a case passing from one *qāḍī* to another makes some sense. Beyond this closed apparatus stood the ruler, as residual tenant of all delegated justice. Recourse to him was not so difficult as one might imagine, and larger quarrels such as those between communities especially engaged his interest. The ruler was now the Christian king, a circumstance opening new perspectives to the Mudejar.

[91] Tyan, *Organisation judiciaire*, pp. 561-564. Ibn 'Abdūn, *Séville musulmane, le traité*, pp. 17-18, 23-25 (including relation of his office to the *qāḍī*), 33-34.

[92] Arch. Crown, Peter III, Reg. Canc. 44, fol. 142v (June 22, 1279): "et uterentur eorum açuna in posse cavalaq[e]mi eorum." On the term as *ḥākim*, see Lévi-Provençal, *España musulmana*, v, 73-74. It confused Dozy in its forms *zavalchen* and *zavalachen* (see *Glossaire*, pp. 366-367). The Spanish Muslim commonly substituted *al-'aḥkām*.

CHAPTER XI

Christians and the Islamic Judiciary

THE RULER IN Islam was theoretically the unique lawmaker and judge; in practice his delegates, especially the *qāḍī*, administered justice within a framework of juridical theology and of custom. Ironically, this tradition of regarding the sovereign as the source of all justice facilitated the substitution of a Christian king, or his local or feudal counterpart. On the Christian side, the feudal suzerain had always been primarily custodian of justice; in his emerging role of sovereign he was emperor-legislator and head of the judicial hierarchy. Islamic and Christian trends converged now, in a world of judicial diversity which tolerated throughout the realms of Aragon a confusion of feudal courts, town courts, church courts, seamen's courts, Jewish courts, and even Genoese private courts, not to mention a diversity of law codes and preferential treatment within the same code for middle and upper classes.[1]

CROWN INTERVENTION

King James easily, if illogically in the Islamic context, stepped into the judicial shoes of Valencia's Abū Zayd; the aljamas without further ado took their more intractable cases to him on appeal. At the end of the eleventh century the Cid had unabashedly essayed this

[1] The major themes and theories on law in the realms of Aragon are surveyed by J. M. Font y Rius, "El desarrollo general del derecho en los territorios de la corona de Aragón (siglos xii-xiv)," *Congrés VII*, 1, 289-328; for Valencia and its seven dominant Christian codes particularly, see the detailed work of Gual Camarena, "Territorialidad de los fueros de Valencia," passim. On the right of the Genoese to civil courts in all cities of James's realms, see *Itinerari*, p. 102 (1233). For his Jewish aljamas James devoted an astonishing amount of time to individual complaints, domestic relations, and a range of cases. Royal officials, solving appeals by Jewish law, often supervised from afar the work of professional rabbinic jurists commissioned for the occasion (Neuman, *The Jews in Spain*, pp. 145-146, 152-153, 262-263), affording us a key perhaps to procedure with Mudejars.

role of supreme judge for his Islamic community: "I want to be both *qāḍī* giving judgment and vizier executing it." He set his court days as every Monday and Thursday, or in emergencies any day, proclaiming that he did not intend to seclude himself from the people, with wine and women, like their previous rulers.[2] The wording of the 1148 Tortosa surrender, by which Muslim officials dispensed justice "as in the time of their *other* kings" suggests the assimilation of Christian ruler to his Islamic predecessors.[3] Though seignorial jurisdiction intervened in many places to block easy appeal, seignorial Moors too belonged in the last analysis to the king. Slaves fell rather under domestic discipline, as when Raymond Lull punished his educated slave with a beating; but they came into the orbit of crown appeals when involved in various crimes. Preeminently "the persons or bodies" of Muslim freemen "belong to the king."[4] A lone fourteenth-century jurist was to protest that this put the Muslim peasant in a juridical position more advantageous than that of his Christian counterpart. Intervention by the king was not uncommon in Valencia, especially for Moors who came directly under the crown.

The crown especially reserved to its bailiff all capital crimes. In the city and immediate district of Valencia, non-*sharīʿa* criminal cases involving only Muslims came before the "*amīn* of that Moorish quarter."[5] Charges invoking the death penalty went to the king's representative.[6] Játiva and Cocentaina had a similar reservation, perhaps wider in scope, until 1264, when both places were allowed to transfer such trials from the justiciar to the bailiff.[7] This conformed

[2] Menéndez Pidal, *España del Cid*, I, 489: "a la vez cadí que juzque y visir que ejecute"; "con mujeres a beber y a cantar."

[3] Tortosa Charter, in Fernández y González, *Mudejares de Castilla*, appendix, doc. 5 (Dec. 1148 misdated as 1143); also in *Colección de documentos inéditos del archivo general de la corona de Aragón*, IV, 130-134: "usaticos sicut fuerunt in tempus de suos alios reges"; "per direito et per iusticia sic est fuero in lure lege"; "stent in lures fueros et in lures iusticias . . . cum suos castigamentos" (italics added to translation).

[4] "Corpus ipsius sarraceni sit domini regis" (1247) and "secundum forum persone seu corpora sunt domini regis"; this position of the Aragon *fuero* was generalized by the jurists (Hinojosa, "Mezquinos y exáricos," pp. 529, 530n.).

[5] Arch. Crown, James I, Reg. Canc. 15, fol. 81v (Feb. 26, 1267): "ab alamino [e]iusdem morerie."

[6] The justiciar, since the bailiff general replaced a bailiff at the capital (Roca Traver, "Vida mudéjar," p. 188).

[7] Arch. Crown, James I, Reg. Canc. 13, fol. 236 (Nov. 6, 1264), for both documents, in similar terms, and granted as a privilege.

in spirit to the restraint on capital cases in Islam, where the death penalty required the ruler's confirmation. Islamic Valencia, accustomed to the death penalty, had reserved a special place at the capital for executions. The beheading of the Franciscan "martyrs of Teruel" at Valencia city four years before the crusade illustrates both a common form of the punishment and a common motive—abusing the faith of Islam.[8] Had another form of capital punishment, private retribution, either survived locally or been revived during the recent troubled decades? It is improbable that formal family revenge, carried out in the tribal spirit of feuding, had been able to continue in any part of Spain, but the Chivert charter does address itself to a generalized situation of spontaneous revenge. "If any Saracen of that castle at any time causes a homicide, wound, or any other injury, he is bound to answer for it personally [in court], but his friends must not suffer any impediment or unpleasantness on this account, whether he flees or remains."[9] The Játiva charter may echo this provision faintly when reserving to the crown the trial of any Muslim arrested for killing another, in that it forbade concomitant seizure of the arrested man's property. At this time in Christian society Roman law was popularizing the death penalty, as against the more tribal concept of fines or banishment. This tension affected the custom law of Jews and Mudejars as well;[10] its impact in Valencia would have derived from the extraordinary influence of Roman lawyers in this experimental frontier kingdom (they gave it the first generally applicable, fully Romanized code in Europe) and from the conver-

[8] On the Franciscans John of Perugia and Peter of Sassoferrato (near Ancona), a priest and a lay brother publicly decapitated for preaching at Valencia city a decade before its fall, see León Amorós Payá, "Los santos mártires franciscanos B. Juan de Perusa y B. Pedro de Saxoferrato en la historia de Teruel," *Teruel*, xv (1956), 5-142, and my *Crusader Valencia*, I, 198-199, II, 467. See also Lévi-Provençal, *España musulmana*, v, 91, on this crime and its punishment; and Tyan, *Organisation judiciaire*, pp. 610-611 on capital punishment. The *fuero* of Cordova has a section on homicide, providing a fine for manslaughter by or of Moors or Christians, and for murder a fine, exile, or death; the editor Orti Belmonte compares the section with the passage from Toledo's laws which influenced it, and discusses its relevance to Mudejars ("Fuero de Córdoba: mudéjares," pp. 14-15, 91).

[9] Chivert Charter: "item si aliquis serracenus eiusdem castri faceret aliquo tempore homicidium vulnus vel aliqua alia iniuria in persona sua teneatur in hoc respondere sensui [= sed sui?] amici propter hec nullum sustinea[n]t impedimentum vel gravamen sive fugiat sive restet."

[10] Salo W. Baron, *A Social and Religious History of the Jews*, 2d edn. rev., 12 vols. to date (New York, 1952ff.), XI, 27, 35, citing the Tortosa custom-code of 1279.

gence of Islamic law and Christian administration of that law precisely at the point of capital punishment.

A number of murder cases reached the king. When the Muslims of Picasent condemned to death the killer Ḥasan b. Sulaym (Açan, son of Çulem), the crown intervened to commute the penalty to slavery, ordering Simon of Arnet to sell the unfortunate Ḥasan.[11] King James took up the case of another Valencian Mudejar accused of murder. Though only a relatively minor affair of one slave accidentally causing the death of another, he demonstrated the royal concern for a humble Mudejar and perhaps for the economic interests of his Christian lord or owner. "Know that we have acquitted Aḥmad [Azmet], the Saracen of Berengar Andrew, citizen of Valencia of the parish of St. Catherine, from all civil and criminal penalties" in connection with "the death of Sa'īd [Zahit], Saracen of Berengar a resident of Valencia." King James had found, "by trustworthy men, that he did not kill him deliberately but by a chance blow with a javelin while throwing it with other Saracens." The king's decree offers a rare glimpse of the lower orders of Mudejar society at leisure, at the moment when horseplay or bravado turned to tragedy. "The said Aḥmad threw the said javelin, and the said Sa'īd [attempted] to catch it in his hand before it hit the ground," with the result that "the aforesaid javelin struck him through the throat and killed him."[12]

It is probable that James maintained experts in Islamic Valencian law in his traveling household, much as he kept Muslim retainers.

[11] Arch. Crown, Peter III, Reg. Canc. 42, fol. 191 (Dec. 16, 1279). Ibn 'Abdūn explains the customary triple recourse by the *qāḍī* to the Islamic ruler before he could sentence a malefactor to crucifixion; he also discusses the amputation of hands, beating, imprisonment, consideration for people of quality already shamed by arrest, sobering of a drunkard before inflicting punishment, restraining of public indecency, and proper handling of juvenile hoodlumism (*Séville musulmane, le traité*, pp. 37-42, 113, 121-122).

[12] *Ibid.*, James I, Reg. 20, fol. 322v (Feb. 14, 1275): "noveritis nos absolvisse Azmet sarracenum Berengarii Andree civis Valencie parochie Sancte Katherine ab omni . . . pena civili et criminali quam . . . facere vel imponere possemus ratione mortis de Zehit sarraceno Berengarii vicini Valencie de qua idem Azmet exstiterat inculpatus, pro eo quod invenimus per homines fidedignos quod non interfecit eum scienter sed ictu fortuito cum uno dardo quando cum aliis sarracenis ipsum iactando, et quod dictus Azmet iactavit dictum dardum, et dictus Zahit [*sic*] illud recipere in manu antequam venisset ad terram . . . et dardus predictus dedit ei per gulam et interfecit eundem."

Speaking in another context, he enunciated a principle that points in this direction. "In any king's court canonists, civil legists, and experts in the [various] custom-laws ought to travel with him," because cases in each of these categories will come before him. "I have three or four kingdoms, and different lawsuits of every sort come up." A modern king, he said, resolved to carry off affairs properly, dared not dispense with this cumbersome legal staff. "If I did not have in my court men [of each law] with whom I could deliberate, it would shame me and my court, for neither I nor any nonprofessional can be learned in the writings about law everywhere." For this reason, James concluded, "I carry these [legal experts] with me."[13]

King James did maintain in his service men professionally familiar with Arabic ways—Jews like the brothers Solomon and Bahye from Zaragoza or Astruc Bonsenyor of Barcelona. They held the post of Arabic secretary or operated as diplomats. During the African and Granadan invasions of Valencia, when the king sent Bernard Porter as "our envoy to the illustrious king Ibn Yūsuf the lord of Morocco, and to the king of Tlemcen," the accompanying retinue or household included both Muslims and Jews.[14] The crown employed Jews also as royal physicians under the honorific *alfaquí* (Catalan *alfaquim*)—a position many observers confuse with those of Arabic secretary and diplomat, partly because the title gives the appearance of deriving from *faqīh* and partly because a single man occasionally exercised the three functions together.[15] Many a Jew moved comfort-

[13] *Llibre dels feyts*, ch. 396: "car en tota cort de rey devia esser que decretalistes e legistes e furistes hi anassen, car de totes maneres hi venen pleyts; e nos, la merce de Deu qu•ens ho ha donat, havem iii o iiii regnes, e venen nos pleyts de moltes maneres e diverses, e si no haguessem en nostra cort ab qui•u poguessem deliurar, seria vergonya de nos e de nostra cort, e car nos, ni•ls homens lechs, no sabrien en les escriptures que son de dret pel mon; e per ço que•ns en poguessem ajudar quant mester fos, los haviem a menar ab nos . . . e per aquesta rao los menam nos."

[14] Soldevila, *Pere el Gran*, part 2, I, doc. 38 (Oct. 27, 1276). The Genoa commune at this time (1247) also had an official *scriba litterarum sarracenicarum*, while its archbishop kept a dragoman familiar with the dialects both of Egypt and the Maghrib. For the role of Jews as Islamic experts see King James's *Llibre dels feyts*, chs. 74, 76ff., 120, and 325. See also the works of Baer, Romano, Shneidman, and Wieruszowski in my Bibliography.

[15] Authorities as diverse as Amador de los Ríos, Gayangos, Neuman, Soldevila, Tourtoulon, and Wieruszowski apply the term to interpreters or experts in Mus-

ably in both Christian and Muslim worlds, understanding the niceties and forms of each, enjoying homes away from home among his relatives and business contacts in the Jewries of North Africa and Spain. An inventory of personal possessions, confiscated by the crown in 1286 from one such Valencian Jewish diplomat, physician, and Arabic secretary, suggests how assimilated a man could become to the Islamic life style; his accouterments of war included "a Barbary saddle, oval [Moorish] shield, one sword, one assagai, and one Turkish bow."[16] Men like these proved invaluable as advisers, agents, and interpreters, and as a means of liaison with the Valencian Mudejar world. In handling appeals from Islamic courts, however, the king was able to draw from a pool of Muslim jurists for judges delegate, as episodes from later Mudejar history demonstrate,[17] though these

lim affairs. See, e.g., Neuman, *The Jews in Spain*, II, 222-223, 345; or José Amador de los Ríos, *Historia social, política y religiosa de los judíos de España y Portugal*, 2 vols. (Buenos Aires, [1875] 1943), I, 405. Most derive it from *faqīh*. From *al-ḥakīm* or physician, the term really applied to the official doctor but by extension of courtesy to erudite men, especially in Hebraic learning; see Neuvonen, *Los arabismos del Español en el siglo xiii*, pp. 148, 150; and Steiger, *Contribución a la fonética del hispano-árabe*, p. 112n., but cf. pp. 273-274, 344, 346n. See also David Romano, "Los hermanos Abenmenassé," pp. 252-253, which distinguishes all three offices and notes that the Romance version of *ḥakīm* was rather *alhaquín*. Pope Honorius III, extending his protection to King James's physician Sheshet b. Isaac Benveniste (the last name is Romance, not a mangled Semitic form), calls him "Azzacho iudeo barchinonensi alfakimo tuo"; see Solomon Grayzel, *The Church and the Jews in the XIIIth Century: A Study of Their Relations during the Years 1198-1254, Based on the Papal Letters and the Conciliar Decrees of the Period*, 2d edn. rev. (New York, 1966), doc. 42 (Aug. 27, 1220). Peter III appointed Samuel, son of Abraham b. Nahmias (Bonnemaiz), to two posts for life—"alfaquimatum nostrum et scribaniam nostram de Arabico." Baer refers to a number of these officials, including David b. Aldaian (Abnadayan), physician to the king's uncle Prince Ferdinand, abbot of Montearagón (*Jews in Christian Spain*, I, 405); Abraham, astronomer to Alfonso X of Castile (p. 126); Abraham, physician to Raymond Berengar IV (p. 55); Abenbenist *alhachim* of Aragon in 1141 (p. 388); Çac Alfaquim or Isaac b. Wakar (pp. 136-137 and passim); "Samuel Abenvenist iudeus, noster alfaquimus" of James I (p. 404); and the brothers Bahye and Solomon Alconstantini (pp. 404-405).

[16] Romano, "Los hermanos Abenmenassé," p. 280 (March 21, 1286) on Samuel the *alfaquim*: "sellam janetam et adargam et unum ensem et unam atçagayam et unum archum turquesium." The jennet saddle takes its name from the Berber Zanātah tribe. On *atçagaya*, see Chapter XIII, n. 15.

[17] Piles Ros, "Moros de realengo en Valencia," p. 237, where the bailiff general assigned ʿAlī Shuʿbah (? Xupio) of Valencia city as king's judge-delegate to hear and judge various disputes among Muslims of Seta Valley and to pronounce sentence, according to the "çuna e xara" plus the *Furs* and good reason; see also the

professionals may not have traveled with the king's court on such a permanent basis as did the Jewish intermediaries. Among the various Muslim falconers, trumpeters, craftsmen, soldiers, servants, musicians, and entertainers encountered in the king's or prince's household, aristocrats or dignitaries rarely figure. Perhaps this is because no salary had to be entered for them in the account books, or because their signatures as witnesses were entered in a class of Arabic documents that has long since disappeared. An exception was Muḥammad of Salā, who appears in King Peter's "household" and who won appointment later as Valencia city's *qāḍī*.[18]

A legal donnybrook of impressive proportions, both chronologically and in substance, was the contest between the Mudejar communities of Eslida and Uxó. Appropriately enough it concerned irrigation canals; beginning perhaps at local water tribunals, it terminated before the person of the king. The dispute became complicated and long-standing while Valencia was still an Islamic country. A group controlling the regional water system, either as entrepreneurs or as spokesmen for their aljama, sold both water and appurtenances to Eslida, drafting the customary contract of sale. When Eslida fought against the usurper Zayyān, probably in support of Abū Zayd during those tumultuous days just before he called on Aragon for help, Zayyān vindictively "took away that water from them and awarded it to the Saracens of Uxó"; later his lieutenant officially sold them the same rights in perpetuity, again with the necessary show of paperwork. Eslida eventually "made its peace" with Zayyān. Perhaps as price for their support, "he restored the same dominion which they had exercised over the aforesaid water"—not neglecting

---

case here of the judge-delegate Ibrāhīm over a Christian-Muslim quarrel in Cheldo. At least in the later period the crown might delegate an appeals-hearing to Jews, as in the case of Fāṭimah, daughter of Muḥammad of Zaragoza, against Ibrāhīm b. Mufarrij Marwān (Mofferig Margan) of Huesca, concerning marriage promises; the crown withdrew the appeal from the Jews hearing it, and ordered a summary hearing and judgment from two Jews of the Cavallería family "segun çunia e xara e juxta lo que derecho y razon quisieren"; see Macho Ortega, "Documentos de los mudéjares aragoneses," pp. 144-145 (Oct. 29, 1495).

18 See document in Chapter XVI, n. 75. Muslim servitors were fairly numerous. Soldevila's "Saracen who served as an interpreter" in Prince Peter's entourage in 1268 was rather a Jewish *alfaquim* (*Pere el Gran*, part I, II, 249n.).

to fortify them with the usual written contract. Uxó refused to concede defeat and persisted in withdrawing water.

Probably at this stage the rival aljamas went to court, Eslida bringing action to enjoin return of the system, and Uxó tabling a defense of its ownership. Meanwhile the crusaders swept across this northern area of Valencia, destroying Zayyān's rule in the early 1230's. Years of turmoil followed, Uxó especially getting caught up in the revolt of the late 1240's. Eventually the case was continued. Progressing by stages now unknown, it reached the person of the king almost a quarter-century after the principal litigants had surrendered to the Christians. Eslida as suitor pleaded its case "in my [royal] presence," displaying the original contract of purchase; it "charged and deposed that the water or irrigation system of Uxó belongs and ought to belong to them [of Eslida], and that the Saracens of Uxó ought not to irrigate without their consent and permission." Uxó rebutted these arguments, presenting before the king its own dossier of contracts, especially "showing me the charters drawn for them by the aforesaid Zayyān and by the man who acted as his lieutenant." Eslida countered with its own "letters of the same Zayyān in which he ordered the Saracens of Uxó to restore that water to the Saracens of Eslida."

King James studied the portfolio of claims, undoubtedly with the close advice of experts. If he did not work his leisurely way through the legal maze during his long sojourns in a northern city like Barcelona, then he managed it by intensive bursts of work during two weeks on the road. Leaving Barcelona on October 18, 1260, and Tortosa on October 26, the king was at Chivert on the last day of the month, at Castellón by November 2, at Onda on the fifth, and at Valencia city with his verdict delivered on the twelfth; he may have detoured through Eslida and Uxó after leaving Onda, but more probably he met the waiting litigants at Valencia city. On November 12 he "gave sentence" there. In it the final formula of Zayyān took precedence, so Uxó had to surrender the water rights. "The aforesaid Saracens of Eslida," in accordance with "the letters of the said Zayyān," were to "have and hold it in the fullest way they previously had and held it." In adjudicating the cause King James showed full respect for the legal claims of the preconquest area, acting rather as successor to the Islamic ruler than as conqueror imposing a novel authority. It did not occur to James to repudiate Zayyān as a usurper in revolt against

Abū Zayd, or to set himself up as supplanting both Islamic rulers root and branch.[19]

These cases represented direct intrusions by the king. He exercised another sort of control—by the sharper delineation of Christian jurisdictions over certain Mudejar cases, and by the rebukes issued to local Christian officers trespassing on the jurisdiction of crown bailiffs. Such incidents, which belong to the following section on criminal authority, also demonstrate that local magistrates tended to encroach upon Mudejar rights. Even when the king was making no direct interference in Mudejar courts, he was implicated in aljama legal affairs from the economic side. He received a fourth of the fines from all cases. This aspect of the Mudejar judicial system occasionally reveals itself in the royal registers during arrangements for tax collecting. Sometimes the crown included Mudejar fines in farming a collection; sometimes it reserved them totally or partially.

Fines could mount to an impressive total. Some crimes paid better than others. At Játiva, whenever a paternity suit was successfully prosecuted, the delinquent father had to forfeit twenty solidi to the

[19] Arch. Crown, James I, Reg. Canc. 11, fol. 185 (Nov. 12, 1260). So important a document deserves full transcription. "[Cognoscant omnes quod] nos Iacobus dei gratia et cetera vidimus sarracenos de Eslida ante nostram presentiam conquerentes [et] asserentes quod aqua sive cequia de Uxo erat et esse debebat eorum, et sarraceni de Uxo sine eorum voluntate et licentia de ipsa rigare non debebat, hostendentes nobis cartam emptionis ab ipsis factam de aqua predicta de quibusdam sarracenis de Uxo quorum ipsa aqua erat. Vidimus similiter ante nostram presentiam sarracenos de Uxo asserentes quod dicta aqua erat et esse debebat eorum ideoque quia quando ipsi sarraceni de Eslida alzaverunt se contra Zahen, ipse Zahen abstulit eisdem aquam et eam diffinivit eisdem sarracenis de Uxo, et postea quidem tenens locum ipsius Zahen ipsam aquam vendidit ipsis sarracenis de Uxo[;] hostendentes nobis cartas de predicto Zahen et de illo qui locum eius tenebat inde eis factas. Et econverso dicti sarraceni de Eslida . . . dixerunt quod postea postquam ipsi alzaverunt se contra ipsum Zahen composuerunt se cum eodem et ipse Zahen restituit eundem dominium quod in aquam predictam habebant, hostendentes nobis quasdam litteras ipsius Zahen in quibus mandavit sarracenis de Uxo ut desempararent ipsam aquam sarracenis de Eslida. Unde nos visis et auditis rationibus supradictis et cartis et visa [carta] . . . predicta facta a predicto Zahen dictis sarracenis de Uxo ut ipsam aquam desempararet sarracenis de Eslida, sententiendo mandamus quod dicti sarraceni de Uxo desemparent dictam aquam dictis sarracenis de Eslida ut littera dicti Zahen continet. Et predicti sarraceni de Eslida habeant et teneant ipsam prout melius et plenius eam hactenus habuerunt et tenuerunt. Datum Valencie ii idus Novembris anno domini mcclx." Roque Chabás gives a Spanish translation with a few comments, "Zahen y los moros de Uxó y Eslida," *El archivo*, 1 (1886-1887), 262-263.

crown; single girls "found pregnant" had to pay five solidi. Such laws may represent pre-Christian penalties paid to the ruler as a curb on immorality. The wording implies that if the father publicly recognized his offspring he paid no fine, while a woman was free of her fine only if she could produce a husband. Again, in waiving the crown share for a two-year grace period at Játiva, the king cannily reserved for himself fines connected "with a person's death, with theft, or with rapine."[20] Even without such special cases justice was great profit, as the contemporary saying went. The "civil and criminal fees" accruing to the crown from Valencian Mudejar courts sufficiently guaranteed the unabated interest of the Christian king in the courtroom and codes of his Mudejar subjects.

Criminal Jurisdiction

A most perplexing question connected with Valencian Mudejar courts concerns the extent and siting of criminal jurisdiction. Even for Islamic countries this can be a tangled subject. Tyan eventually concluded that the *qāḍī* did exercise a repressive jurisdiction where the Koran formally dictated such concern, but that this proved neither characteristic nor extensive, and in Spain diminished to the vanishing point.[21] The non-*sharīʿa* courts handled a range of peccadillos, sins, intermediate transgressions, and crimes, according to a procedure more rational and efficient. In reserving control of "crimes," which of these did the crusaders really have in mind? Roca Traver denies any criminal jurisdiction to Valencia kingdom's Mudejars, holding that the bailiff, lord, or king exercised it all, merely taking counsel from the *qāḍī* of the local aljama.[22] If so, that arrangement

[20] Játiva Charter: "si aliqua sarracena fuerit inventa pregnans, quae maritum non habeat, solvat nobis quinque solidos; et quod omnis sarracenus qui negaverit filium vel filiam, quem vel quam habuerit ab aliqua, solvat viginti solidos nobis, si mater probare poterit . . ."; "nisi pro morte hominum, vel pro furto aut rapina."

[21] Tyan, *Organisation judiciaire*, pp. 600-603; the *qāḍī* had only one procedure for civil or criminal cases, the accused assuming a posture analogous to the defendant in a civil case (p. 571).

[22] "Vida mudéjar," pp. 181-186. Among the most serious crimes were the capital offenses of counterfeiting, homosexuality, and treason, adultery between Moors, and sexual relations with a Christian woman (see Piles Ros, "Moros de realengo en Valencia," pp. 269-270, for fifteenth-century cases). For Koranic crimes and fixed punishment, such as crucifixion of highway robbers or amputation of hand for theft, see Tyan, *Organisation judiciaire*, pp. 567-568.

evolved much later in the century. The general situation in King James's day was described by his successor in 1281, who took note of the "privilege which the lord James of happy memory our father conceded to all the Saracens of this realm [of Valencia], namely that in criminal cases they may not be cited before a Christian judge but that they are to be judged for their crimes according to their Sunna and that they are to be cited by Saracen judges [*iudices*]."[23] The letter was sent as a rebuke to the justiciars of Valencia city and other towns of its kingdom. Against this general rule stood exceptions and privileges. In April 1277 the king allowed Muslims of the Alfandech Valley to plead civil and criminal cases before the bailiff of Valencia. The privilege was confirmed near the end of the century and extended to cover Muslims coming under the seignorial rule of Valldigna monastery.[24]

The charter of Chivert, though the most detailed of the Valencian agreements, did not reserve to Templars or crown any civil or criminal jurisdiction. A prison can be understood as a concomitant to criminal authority at least in initial or petty manifestations, and the charter did include among its minutiae the provision that the Muslims "may have a prison in their quarter, in which criminals, debtors, and other men may be confined." Though this sounds like a detention center, used for holding culprits before trial, it may well have been a true prison; in Islamic lands a true prison, for punishing malefactors, came under the care of the *ṣāḥīb al-madīna* or his police agents, though the debtors' prison belonged to the *qāḍī*.[25] The Játiva charter

[23] Arch. Crown, Peter III, Reg. Canc. 50, fol. 124 (July 14, 1281): "cuiusdam privilegii quod dominus Iacobus felicis recordationis pater noster concessit sarracenis omnibus regni sui videlicet quod in causis criminalibus non possint coram christiano iudice preveniri [?] sed quod pro suis culpis secundum suas zunas iudicentur tantum ac quod preveniantur [?] a iudicibus sarracenis."

[24] Alfandech Charter (see Chapter VI, n. 25), with elaborations cited. Though the 1148 Tortosa pact gave the aljama all inter-Moor delicts, in criminal matters the officials of the local lord Moncada intervened (Font Rius, "Tortosa a raíz de la reconquista," p. 123). Some analogy with the Mudejar situation, or at least some insight into the mentality of the Christian rulers, may be derived from a comparison with criminal jurisdiction in the Jewish aljamas. It was possible to acquire the right of capital punishment, as the Calatayud Jews did in 1229 and the Barbastro Jews in 1273; in 1280 all Jewish aljamas got sweeping criminal jurisdiction, the death penalty excepted (Neuman, *The Jews in Spain*, pp. 138, 145-146).

[25] Chivert Charter: "insuper habeant dicti mauri carcerem in suo arravallo in quo malefactores debitores et ali[i] homines distringantur." On the double prisons

seems to provide for a prison within the Moorish sector of town under custody of a *ṣāḥib al-madīna.* At the Valencia city *morería,* a prison stood just inside the quarter's wall, next to the main or northeast gate, apparently housing both the keeper and his wards; so important a concession, though revealed by documentation of much later date, must represent a thirteenth-century privilege. A Valencian law of 1273 required separate prisons for Jews and Moors, revealing a mentality which undoubtedly preferred separate Mudejar prisons wherever feasible.[26]

At Cocentaina "all criminal cases" came under the Christian justiciar for twenty years after the crusade; then they were transferred to the king's bailiff. Under the bailiff, these cases continued to be tried by the Sunna. The document of transference granted "to each and every Saracen of the Moorish quarter of Cocentaina, present and future forever" that from 1264 onward they did not have "to answer in anything to the jurisdiction of our justiciar but to the jurisdiction of whoever is bailiff of Cocentaina." The order further specified these words as applying "in such wise that he will hear and decide, according to your Sunna, all criminal cases arising between you,"

---

see Tyan, *Organisation judiciaire,* p. 385; on the prison not as a detention center but as implying criminal jurisdiction, see pp. 612-614. Ibn 'Abdūn devoted a section of his treatise to prisons, distinguishing the real prisoners destined for punitive detention of varied duration from the run-of-the-mill accused who should normally have either been brought to trial in a short time or else freed. He recommends a separate jail for women under a matron, and reports that an imam was available for spiritual needs (*Séville musulmane, le traité,* pp. 39-42). Compare the section of Valencia's *Furs* on the Christian prisons (*Fori,* rub. CXXXVIII).

[26] Játiva Charter: "alhapz et captiones hominum sint in ravallo praedicto et quod zalmedina teneat alapz supradictum." *Alhapz* may refer to *al-ḥisbah* jurisdiction (see Lévi-Provençal, *España musulmana,* v, 85); as the complement of *captiones* under the zalmedin's "charge" it may mean a prison, as Torres Fontes has it; in any case *captiones* required a place of detention. On the Valencia city prison see Rodrigo y Pertegás, "La morería de Valencia," p. 243, and Roca Traver, "Vida mudéjar," pp. 135-136. Gayangos's translation, in the English edition of the *Llibre dels feyts,* which has the Murcians surrendering on condition that they continue to "sentence both civil and criminal cases according to their laws," is an unwarranted interpretation (ch. 440). A fifteenth-century order to the lord of Sot shows a prison or place of detention at so small a place, where the Mudejar woman Maryam had been unduly detained for three months and had to be released or tried by the *qāḍī* (Piles Ros, "Moros de realengo en Valencia," p. 240).

while the *qāḍī* was "to hear all civil cases."[27] Gómez of Soria was bailiff there in 1260, the castellan being Andrew of Odena.[28] In 1264, the date on the document, Cocentaina castle had just come into the power of Peter Ferdinand, son of King James, who was maintaining a garrison of thirty in it.[29]

This privilege of answering to the bailiff can either be understood as a wise delegation of powers to a lower level or as an administrative dodge releasing to the crown a larger share of the criminal fines. It also insured the accused more objective treatment than locals might mete out. Where a justiciar did cite Muslim criminals to court, the king might interpose his bailiff as protector. A number of such incidents survive in the records. When the Valencia city justiciar and his agents arrested Ibrāhīm "my [crown] Saracen" in 1284, the king ordered his release to "the lieutenant of the procurator of the kingdom of Valencia beyond the Júcar, who holds [this] jurisdiction." Ibrāhīm was a wealthy man, already exculpated by the king on allied charges; whether he were innocent or guilty this time, the king insisted, arrest and trial belonged solely to the king's officer.[30]

The crown also warned the Valencia city justiciar in a confused case about a Muslim slave, who was in the process of buying his freedom when he fled. Overzealous justiciars had provoked the

[27] Arch. Crown, James I, Reg. Canc. 13, fol. 236 (Nov. 6, 1264). "Concedimus vobis universis et singulis sarracenis ravalli Concentanie presentibus et futuris in perpetuum quod de cetero non teneamini de aliquibus in posse iustitie nostre Concentanie respondere sed in posse illius qui baiulus noster Concentanie fuerit. Ita quod ipse audiat et determinet omnes causas criminales, que inter vos fuerint secundum açunam vestram, et ille sarracenus qui cadit [*sic*] vester fuerit audiat omnes causas civiles que inter vos fuerint et eas determinet secundum açunam vestram." See also Roca Traver, "Vida mudéjar," pp. 185-186. Only the *ravallum* is specified, the *orta* and *termini* appearing later to share a tax privilege, though probably also involved in the judicial privileges of their focal city.

[28] Arch. Crown, James I, Reg. Canc. 11, fol. 193 (Feb. 13, 1260).

[29] *Ibid.*, Reg. Canc. 13, fol. 193v (July 1, 1264).

[30] Roca Traver, "Vida mudéjar," doc. 16 (Nov. 22, 1284): "Abraphim Abensumada sarracenum nostrum"; Bernard de Belvis "tenenti locum procuratoris regni Valencie ultra Xucharum ad quem spectat iurisdiccio." Abraham Abensumada, Abençamadi, Abencuda, and Abenzumayr in the run of crown documents may all be the same man; if so, he was a noble who farmed the collection of Mudejar taxes at Denia, then at Pop and elsewhere, and acted as liaison agent for returning some prisoners to Granada, appearing from about 1276 to 1285.

crown by pursuing Muslim culprits in the mountain regions, which probably provided refuge for the harried. Finally in 1290 the king ordered all Valencia's justiciars, present and future, to desist from imposing fines in the uplands; they were to proceed only by permission and special license of "the bailiff of the mountains."[31] In 1284 instructions to the bailiff of Murviedro on the coast show him active in the criminal jurisdiction of Gilet in an obscure episode of violence: "we are informed as to how you acted in the matter of those two Saracens of Gilet in the district of Murviedro who forced an entrance and broke down the door of a certain Saracen and inflicted other hurt on him."[32]

The Játiva charter of 1252, by reserving only capital cases, seems to concede all other criminal jurisdiction sweepingly to the aljama. A privilege of 1264, however, makes it obvious that the same arrangement prevailed here as at Cocentaina.[33] Had James perhaps recaptured criminal jurisdiction at Játiva for the crown after 1252? Closer examination of the situation suggests that at least the *amīn* retained criminal jurisdiction proper to his own court. A 1267 clarification for Valencia city appears to acknowledge full jurisdiction for the courts of *qāḍī*, *amīn*, and *ṣāḥib al-madīna*; its reservation of capital cases to the crown explicitly in the case of these three functionaries, as well as for the *muḥtasib*, implies criminal jurisdiction of some kind for each of them. On the other hand, a law of 1342 in the Christian code for the Valencian kingdom was to claim that the bailiff of the capital, Valencia city, had always exercised civil and criminal ordinary jurisdiction over all the Muslims of the kingdom.[34]

[31] *Ibid.*, doc. 13 (May 29, 1283); doc. 22 (March 24, 1290): "in dampnum nostri et sarracenorum montanearum nostrarum"; "licencia baiuli [aliamarum] dictarum montanearum."

[32] Arch. Crown, Peter III, Reg. Canc. 46, fol. 182 (April 16, 1284): "intelleximus ea que fecistis super facto illorum duorum sarracenorum de Xilet termino Muriveteris qui invaderant et fregerunt portas cuiusdam sarraceni et alia dampna intulerunt eidem; propter quod eorum corpora et bona sint nobis confiscata per sententiam alcaldi."

[33] *Ibid.*, James I, Reg. Canc. 13, fol. 236 (Nov. 6, 1264), following a similar document to Cocentaina.

[34] *Ibid.*, Reg. Canc. 15, fol. 81v (Feb. 26, 1267): "exceptis factis seu querimoniis pene mortis," "querimonia pene mortis." Vicente Branchát, *Tratado de los derechos y regalías que corresponden al real patrimonio en el reyno de Valencia y de la jurisdicción del intendente como subrogado en lugar del antiguo bayle general,* 3 vols. (Valencia, 1784-1786), II, ch. 2, doc. 1, on law no. 65.

Can the problem of the existence and extent of criminal jurisdictions be dismissed by postulating divergences due to greater or less bargaining power at surrender? This easy solution is patently wrong for Játiva, a main exception despite maximum bargaining power. Nor can it be reconciled with King Peter's declaration recognizing a universal criminal jurisdiction which he found distasteful and was modifying. Several resolutions may be suggested. It is reasonable to assume a range of misdemeanors and petty crimes falling under Mudejar courts, and a category of quite serious crimes received into the court of sovereign or lord, to be judged by Islamic standards. If all were loosely spoken of as in the "criminal" domain—as for instance was the relatively minor crime of blasphemy in the key document by Peter above—and if the same term was more strictly applied to serious crimes over which no local community expected control or even a mention in its charter, then the issue is resolved. The death penalty may have stood in a class apart, if it were as rare as in the *Furs* of the Christians; this would explain its being singled out by documents which remain silent on other criminal reservations. More plausibly, the crown may have removed criminal jurisdiction from Muslims in a few places, and eventually everywhere, by expansion of the reservation clause.

A more satisfactory solution is at hand, however, which takes into account the general concession by the crown, the general reservation to the bailiff, specific cases like Valencia and Cocentaina, and the decidedly concessionary transfer of jurisdiction from justiciar to bailiff. Criminal cases, heard at first by a Mudejar court under the eye of the Christian representative, came soon to be in danger of domination by this agent. Transfer of such a bizarre double court from the explicitly judicial justiciar to the management of the more ambiguously judicial fiscal agent, the bailiff, would have conciliated the ruffled Muslims. It would also have proved more profitable to the crown; the mutually advantageous concession would understandably have spread everywhere in a short time. Without any real change in the court, it would naturally have come to be viewed and described inversely as a function of the bailiff's court, contrived with the cooperation of Muslim assistants. This new angle of vision, proper to the stronger position of the Christians toward the century's end, inevitably though subtly would have transformed the nature of the court.

Christian versus Muslim

Muslims and Christians had occasion to confront each other in court. The Begís aljama was cited, along with the commander of the Hospitallers for that area, to plead before James in 1262 in their dispute with Blasco Simon.[35] Three Mudejars of Almonacid, with their Christian castellan, similarly appeared before the king in 1276 to answer charges brought by the bailiff of Daroca.[36] The Almonacid community later appeared against Bonat, a merchant of Murla.[37] Christian courts could require Muslims to attend as witnesses, as frequently happened in district boundary disputes. On some occasions the courts cited both peoples together to advance an inquiry. An example convenient to hand, though outside the Valencian kingdom, was the hidden treasure discovered at Daroca in 1257; the crown had empowered its judge "to compel to court all those, Christains as well as Jews and Saracens, who in this affair have knowledge or possession of that treasure or money, to speak up and to restore it."[38]

A Moor haled into court by a Christian appeared before his own judge—the *qāḍī* at Chivert, *ṣāḥib al-madīna* at Játiva, and the *amīn* at Valencia city;[39] in criminal cases he retained his own law. Nor

[35] Arch. Crown, James I, Reg. Canc. 12, fol. 5v (Jan. 3, 1262).

[36] *Ibid.*, Peter III, Reg. Canc. 39, fol. 231v (Dec. 26, 1276).

[37] *Ibid.*, Reg. Canc. 59, fol. 100 (Sept. 18, 1282): "Bonatum mercatorem de Morlanis"; there was a market at Murla (Reg. Canc. 48, fol. 163; Oct. 10, 1280).

[38] *Colección diplomática*, doc. 617 (Oct. 29, 1257): "distringendi omnes illos, tam christianos quam iudeos et sarracenos, qui in facto isto sciunt vel tenent de isto thesauro vel peccunia aliquid, a[d] dicendum . . . et ad restituendum."

[39] Aldea Charter (*alamin*). Chivert Charter—where, however, a Jew went before the Templar official; it was a general rule in the kingdom that Jews accused by Christians went before a Christian judge, no privilege being admitted (*Furs*, lib. III, rub. v, c. 48). The Tudela Charter of Alfonso of Aragon had also allowed the Moor in such a case his own judge; in Fernández y González, *Mudejares de Castilla*, appendix, doc. 2 (March 1115); also in *Colección de fueros municipales y cartas pueblas de los reinos de Castilla, León, Corona de Aragón y Navarra coordinada y anotada*, ed. Tomás Muñoz y Romero (Madrid, 1847), p. 415. Roca Traver cites cases, though from a later period, of Valencian Moors bringing Christians before a Christian court ("Vida mudéjar," p. 181). For his interpretation of Christian-Mudejar procedure, which differs from my own, see p. 187, and the clumsy wording of the Chivert Charter. Earlier, in Castile, a tendency had developed to favor the Christian side in mixed cases, and at Toledo in 1118 Alfonso gave such cases to the Christian judge; though blood cases brought the same law on Moor

could the testimony of Christians or Jews condemn him. The requirement of a witness from one's own religious group had become normal in Europe by the twelfth century. Thus at Chivert a Moor cited for "crime, delinquency, or default" would not be sentenced unless good Muslim witnesses supplied evidence, and the charter laid down the principle that "no Christian or Jew [alone] can give testimony against a Saracen."[40] In much the same spirit the Jews of Majorca acquired a privilege in 1269 by which Muslims could not bear witness against Jews, though the Chivert charter must mean decisive witness.[41] After the turn of the century James II was to modify the general privilege; in any criminal suit initiated by Christian against Muslim, two Christians of good reputation sufficed as witnesses, a small but significant erosion of the principle.[42] As late as 1285, however, the Muslims were clinging to the full privilege; in that year the crown ordered the justiciar and the people of Valencia city to verify their claim to the privilege and then "release" the Muslims accused by Christians "to their judge according to what the custom has been."[43]

Muslims and Christians each kept their penalties. The respective laws being different, criminal offenses met with punishments of varying severity, occasioning dissatisfaction when the vanquished enjoyed leniency denied to the victors. The inequality persisted until

and Christian at Toledo and other places, the Sepulveda *fuero* executed a Muslim murderer of a Christian while merely fining his Christian counterpart (Mobarec Asfura, "Condición jurídica de los moros en la alta edad media," pp. 44-46).

40 Chivert Charter: "crimine maleficio vel demanda"; "verum nullus christianus vel iudeus possit facere testimonium contra sarracenum"; *demandare* in Catalan legal terminology had come to mean "claim as due" or else "interrogate" (Rodón Binué, *El lenguaje técnico*, pp. 76-77). See also the Aldea Charter; Roca Traver, "Vida mudéjar," p. 188. The more usual thing was for two Muslims or a Muslim and Christian to be required, while for a Christian charged by a Muslim the reverse was in order; see, e.g., the *Fori*, rub. LXVII, no. 24.

41 *Itinerari*, p. 428 (July 21, 1269).

42 Roca Traver, "Vida mudéjar," p. 188n., citing *Aureum opus*, priv. 12 (1301).

43 *Ibid.*, doc. 15 (Jan. 4, 1285): "remittant eos ad eorum iudicem prout est fieri consuetum." Doc. 21 (Jan. 3, 1290) concerns Muḥammad al-Jumaḥī (? Mahomet Aliumani, perhaps al-Hammānī) of Calpe, who came to Valencia city at the request of Yūsuf Zīrī (Juceffum Xerri), the ambassador (*nuncius*) of Granada's king, to answer charges of involvement in the kidnapping of a Valencian citizen's son; the crown is ordering an investigation of the charges and, if indicated, the release of Muḥammad.

the early fourteenth century when James II in unjudicial mood decreed that in such contrasts the harsher of the two laws was to be applied to the hapless Moor.[44] "Many Saracens" who blasphemed or mocked Christianity were arraigned before Muslim judges, for example, until King Peter stopped the practice in 1281. Peter ordered judgment to be given "by a Christian judge and our Christian officials, and according to the laws and codes of the Christians, notwithstanding any privilege or statute; for it seems disgraceful and quite improper that the judgments protecting the Faith be turned to the disadvantage of the faithful."[45]

Just as litigation between Muslims could rise to the king's person on appeal, so could confrontations between members of the parallel legal communities. In seven villages around Alcira, during the confused years immediately after that city's surrender, disparate squabbles erupted over farms purchased without clear title or entered nefariously by Christian land-grabbers. These were lumped as an intertangled problem and set before the king. Carefully preserved, James's decision of July 18, 1245, is the oldest extant privilege in the Alcira municipal archives. His settlement ordered Christian owners to restore lands for which they could not display "Saracen" deeds of purchase. The record affords a precious glimpse into procedure. King James had convened his court at Játiva, the major center of his new kingdom after Valencia city and, since the expulsion of 1238, the focus for Mudejar life and loyalty; if Valencia served as Christian capital, Játiva at this date provided a nonpolitical, shadow capital for the Moorish counterculture. Játiva was also readily accessible to witnesses from the Alcira area, but removed from the pressure of Alciran passions. In recognition of the occasion's solemnity King James surrounded himself with a complement of seven distinguished barons. He examined "each and every document" of grant issued for the area, and "read also the treaty of the Saracens." He had

[44] *Aureum opus*, priv. 52, fol. 52r, v (May 7, 1311). This applied only to crown Muslims ("in locis nostris"), to corporal punishment, and to crimes committed by Muslims against Christians. The Tortosa Charter had provided for "suos castigamentos, sicut est in lure lege."

[45] Arch. Crown, Peter III, Reg. Canc. 50, fol. 124 (July 14, 1281). "Iudicetur per iudicem et officiales nostros christianos et secundum leges et foros christianorum . . . non obstante privilegio aliquo vel statuto. Indignans [*hole obscures*] enim ac nimis inconveniens videtur quod iudicia fidei in fidelibus commutantur."

"taken counsel in diligent conversation" with local Muslims. Finally he delivered sentence "with the will and consent of the sheiks [*senum*] and Saracen people of Alcira."[46]

Seignorial Areas

Did any basic difference exist between royal lands and the regalian or nonregalian seignorial holdings in operations of the intra-Mudejar legal system? Probably not. Where lords can be observed making their own legal arrangements, as at Chivert, Aldea, and Tales, no important distinction emerges. As we have seen, the tradition of Mudejar surrender in the evolved contemporary form would have influenced lords as well as king. Besides, King James boasted in general terms about the privilege of law for all Moors who had surrendered rather than resisted. It was the lords—against James, the churchmen, and the townsfolk—who favored the retention and even further immigration of Moors in Valencia, a circumstance indicating an indulgent attitude by barons toward the Islamic way of life. Nor does one expect barons and knights to have been more rigid than the lords ecclesiastical, yet liberal charters survive from religious orders.

It may be well to allow that lords clung more zealously to fines from their aljama courts, since this was characteristic of their class. They were also able to encroach upon Mudejar privileges more easily than was done on crown lands, where the king discouraged predatory officials. Such allowances are nevertheless marginal, closely limited by the preceding arguments.[47] A major difference on baronial

[46] "Sección de documentos," *El archivo*, II (1887-1888), doc. 56, pp. 403-406 (July 18, 1245), from Alcira archives; see Chabás, "El archivo municipal de Alcira," *ibid.*, p. 37: "visis omnibus et singulis instrumentis a nobis confectis christianis"; "viso etiam instrumento sarracenorum"; "habito consilio et diligenti tractatu, voluntate et consensu senium et sarracenorum Algezire." Under the heading of interlaw adjudication might come the king's detention of a Muslim in Valencia in 1277 as a rebel against the Hospitaller grand master; see *Cartulaire général de l'ordre des hospitaliers de S. Jean de Jérusalem (1100-1310)*, ed. Joseph Delaville Le Roulx, 4 vols. (Paris, 1894-1901), III, doc. 3,629 (Aug. 4, 1277), a notice.

[47] It is safer to draw analogies from Christian settlement charters on points of economic or social life; in law as in religion the Islamic problem was very different from that of the Christian settler. Thus, at Borriol the charter to Christians by the bishop of Tortosa reserved both civil and criminal cases; the law, at least public,

lands was substitution of the lord or his bailiff in place of the king. At Chivert, Moors could appeal disputes with the Templars or their bailiff to the order's *preceptor riparie*, who signed the charter immediately after the master and above a large number of other commanders; he had to take counsel of prudent men before handing down his verdict.[48] In a contretemps at Cuart just after the turn of the century, the privileges of its Mudejars, granted by James the Conqueror and Peter and recently confirmed, conflicted with the privileges of Cuart's overlord, St. Vincent's hospital. Without specifying either set of privileges, the crown resolved the issue by declaring that the Mudejar charters were not to diminish those of the hospital. The nature of the controversy suggests jurisdictional—that is, legal—rather than rental claims.[49] Muslims of this time and place were familiar with justice given by a local lordling, and would hardly have adverted to the substitution; Lull has a Moor explain, in the *Book of the Gentile*, how "the custom prevails among us that kings and princes and important lords hold court [*corts*] and deliver justice to their people," as a function of their status.[50]

Outside crown lands many barons in Valencia, perhaps most, lacked that juridical quasi-sovereignty designated as *merum et mixtum imperium*.[51] Their Muslims therefore fell under the king's bailiff in criminal matters, and specifically under the bailiff general from 1282 when that functionary appeared in the Valencian administrative structure. At the turn of the century and in the early fourteenth,

---

was the *Furs* of Valencia; see the "Carta puebla de Borriol," in "Colección de cartas pueblas," no. 6 (Sept. 15, 1250), *BSCC*, XXII [1946], 15-16. James made the same reservations here at the beginning of this year (no. 22, pp. 13-14); in 1254 he granted the place to his lieutenant in the realm of Valencia, with full civil and criminal jurisdiction.

48 Chivert Charter; on Hospitaller organization in the realms of James, and especially in Valencia, see my *Crusader Valencia*, I, 183-190.

49 Arch. Nac. Madrid, Clero, St. Vincent's, leg. 2,079, arm. 45, fab. I, unnumbered (1306).

50 *Libre del gentil e los tres savis*, in *Obras de Ramón Lull*, ed. Mateo Obrador y Bennassar *et alii*, 21 vols. to date (Palma de Mallorca, 1906ff.), I, 271: "custuma es enfre nos que·ls reys e·ls princeps e·ls grans senyors tenen corts, e fan ajustar les gents, e demostren lur tresor, a maniffestar lur granea."

51 *Mixt imperi* from a king or lord allowed the judge to inflict lesser punishments and to handle civil cases; *mer imperi* was the higher power, commonly reserved to the sovereign but sometimes alienated, of imposing severe (including capital) punishment.

the crown made determined efforts to clarify criminal jurisdiction over Muslims, as part of a more general reorganization of Valencian bureaucracy. This applied not only to royal lands, including most towns of any size, but to fiefs of barons lacking *merum et mixtum* dominion; that relatively minor portion of the realm given over to feudatories with near-sovereign powers was consequently excluded from the reorganization.

A series of decrees beginning in 1298 established that, while the bailiff general had held "all jurisdiction civil and criminal over all the Moors of the realm of Valencia resident in crown places, or in other places over which the lord king had *merum imperium*," he would keep from now on only "the jurisdiction of the Moors of royal places and of the orders and of the delinquents in those places," transferring to the agent of the king's procurator general "jurisdiction over the Muslims of high barons [*richhomens*] and knights." This reorganization lay in the future, however, beyond the period of crusader Valencia proper.[52] Alfonso IV, in a privilege of 1329, recalled his concession to "the lords of villages and places in the countrysides of the city and regalian towns of the kingdom of Valencia" of criminal jurisdiction over their Moors. "They ought to act with the counsel of the judges of the Saracens, who are called in [our] common speech 'alcadis,'" but "with recourse to one 'alcadi' only." The crown helped supply the local *qāḍī*; to implement his plan effectively Alfonso had his bailiff general provide "a suitable number" of these Mudejar judges for installation. The decree

[52] Roca Traver, "Gobernación foral," p. 188, quoting *Furs*, Cortes of Valencia in 1342, rub. VIII: "com lo batle general . . . hagues tota iuredictio civil e criminal en tots los moros del regne de Valencia domiciliats en los lochs reals o altres, en los quals lo senyor rey hagues merimperi, lo senyor rey En Jacme . . . atorga . . . que'l portantveus de procurador hagues iuredictio en los moros dels richhomens e dels cavallers e que al dit Batle, que tota la iuredictio solia haver, romangues la iuredictio dels moros dels lochs reals e dels ordens e dels delinquents en aquells lochs. . . ." See also Roca Traver, "Vida mudéjar," doc. 23 (March 15, 1290), where the lord of Ixar had jurisdiction over the Saracens of the realm of Valencia as procurator for the absent king. Fernández y González, *Mudejares de Castilla*, p. 272 (1328). Lalinde Abadía, *Gobernación*, p. 397 (April 13, 1299); on the jurisdiction of crown agents by this reorganization, see pp. 376ff. See also the discussion of the bailiff general's later role by Piles Ros, "Moros de realengo en Valencia," pp. 235-245, and the law of James II ("sarrahins de llochs reals son del for del batle y los altres del for del gobernador").

changed little, merely substituting at the local level the regalian lord for regalian bailiff or the justiciar.[53]

The Muslim generation who surrendered to King James, and their sons who followed them in the thirteenth century, retained their civil courts and most of the jurisdictions affecting their lives; even in criminal matters the common run of offenses still entered the court of *qāḍī, amīn, ṣāḥib al-madīna*, or *muḥtasib*. The new ruler presided over the system of civil and lesser-criminal tribunals normally through his bailiff general and local bailiffs, intruding in person only to handle appeals or to regulate procedural organization. On non-crown lands the local lord or his bailiff played the same role only if he held the rare powers of *merum et mixtum* dominion, though he certainly enjoyed influence of a minor kind along these lines. In the sphere of serious crime, and especially where capital punishment or accusations of killing were involved, an ambiguous situation resulted. Such cases seem to have come before the local justiciar and to have been reductively in the control of the king's bailiff general, or on *imperium* lands in the lord's hands; in fact, however, they followed Islamic law, procedures, and penalties, implemented by Muslim judges acting under the immediate control of, and in the name of, the Christian officer.

The average free Muslim, unless he had to bring charges against a Christian or serve as witness against one, never entered a Christian court. His legal furniture remained in place, though the occasional serious criminal found himself answering to the agent of the new Cid. Framing this picture, to be sure, was the intrusive regulatory activity of king or baron, but even their intervention substituted for the lively personal interest demonstrated by the authoritarian *wālī* and supplied as well the arbitral function proper to that Islamic personage. During the thirteenth century the frame served less to shadow than to protect the Islamic legal system. Within that system, held erect as by a strong skeleton, the social and religious body of Islam lived on, in surface appearance as hale and hearty as under the Almohads.

[53] Roca Traver copies the *Aureum opus* privilege but applies it too widely ("Vida mudéjar," pp. 184-185): "procedere debent cum consilio iudicum sarracenorum qui alcadis nuncupantur vulgariter [et] ad unum tantum alcadi recursum habere"; "plures statuantur alcadis, cum quorum consilio in premissis per alcarearum et locorum dominos procedantur."

THE POLITICAL-MILITARY MILIEU

CHAPTER XII

The Muslim in the Feudal Order

In their political organization, the Mudejars formed self-contained legal communities, which constituted a species of state within a state. This alien body related to its Arago-Catalan host, at the administrative and governing levels, only in the most tenuous fashion. Were they merely guests and wards of the Christian state, or had they a function within the feudal order? The question may be put more precisely if the phrase "feudal order" gives way to the more satisfactory description "the evolved feudal or even postfeudal situation." The realms of Aragon comprised a rather complicated form of transitional or feudal monarchy; under the influence of ubiquitous Roman law experts, the king was beginning to conceive of himself not as first among equals but as sovereign ruler and legislator, even as a kind of emperor over his subjects. Though a king could implement this dream only irregularly in one or other aspect of his government, the logic implicit in the law movement continued to inspire new energies and to direct their thrust. The feudalistic way of life meshed with, and adjusted itself to, the antipathetic orientation of political life toward Roman sovereignty. The result was less a hybrid than a dynamic process, an accommodation partly resisted and partly welcomed but nowhere static. This dialogue between sociopolitical forms characterized a number of contemporary kingdoms. King James's realm differed from these not only in the intensity of its legal renaissance, but in the nature of its feudal forms and in the ambient nonfeudal society modifying them.

The Muslim as Vassal

The classic textbook feudalism of northern Europe was organized around serfdom on communal manorial estates and rooted in an immemorial array of military magnates, interlinked with their vassals by a psychology of personal loyalties and possessed of a range of governmental powers over their territories—a system recently disturbed by the intrusion of burghers and by a series of ambitious kings. The textbook picture, though too neat to fit the complexities of life, is not unjust as a general or introductory description. This arrangement did not prevail in the Arago-Catalan kingdom. An approximation might have been found in the rural hinterland, especially in the more backward province of Aragon proper—and by reflection later in the northwest uplands of Valencia where Aragonese settlement waxed strongest. A class of landed magnates and lords was indeed abroad, preoccupied with military adventure and land, owing armed service to the crown, high-handed, family-proud, conservatively clinging to special interests, defending themselves readily by rebellion, indignant against taxation or interfering kings, and inclining to demand onerous burdens from their tenants. Does their presence denote a feudal society?

Reacting against an earlier view that feudalism had largely bypassed the specifically Catalan area, historians like Soldevila insist on its presence "neither more or less" than in the other European countries that once formed part of the Carolingian empire; they point to servile classes, heavy seignorial taxes, a hierarchy from king through high nobles down through the multiplicity of small nobles including knights, and the varied forms of homage, contract society, and feudal technical terms. Catalonia was wholly "of feudal formation."[1] This is at once correct, yet subtly wrong. Catalan feudalism

[1] Ferran Soldevila, *Historia de España,* 8 vols. (Barcelona, 1952-1954), I, 185-191: "ni más ni menos"; "nacionalidad de formación feudal," quoting Calmette. Luis García de Valdeavellano has the best general review of Spanish feudalism, "Les liens de vassalité et les immunités en Espagne," pp. 222-255, in the symposium *Les liens de vassalité et les immunités,* 2d edn. rev. (Brussels, 1958), published as *Recueils de la Société Jean Bodin pour l'histoire comparative des institutions,* I (1958); the author attacks the moot problem of to what extent feudalism was native to the peninsula, but rather neglects Catalonia, where he is willing to admit "un vrai système féodal" (p. 240). See also his *Historia de España,* 3d edn., 2 vols. (Madrid, 1963), I, 308ff. on Catalonia before 1212; his "Las instituciones feudales en España," appended to the Spanish translation of F. L. Ganshof, *El feudalismo* (Barcelona, 1963), 229-305; and apposite sections of his topical *Instituciones españolas,* esp. lib. 4, sec. 1, chs. 9-16, on the "Catalan feudal regime," pp. 394ff., and on the "feudal state," pp. 406ff. J. M. Font Rius, J. M. Lacarra, and P. Bonnassie have recently clarified a number of details in the symposium *Les structures sociales de l'Aquitaine, du Languedoc et de l'Espagne au premier âge féodal* (Paris, 1969); see esp. the evolution of castle feudalism, pp. 63-72.

as it existed by James's day was of relatively recent growth and was countered by a remarkable exterior ambience as well as by several balancing interior factors. It reflected the instincts and historical development of the Mediterranean-Provençal medieval man. Catalonia was undeniably feudal in much of its structure, and Aragon even more so; but a most imperfectly feudal soul inhabited this body.

Feudalism in the realms of King James differed from its northern counterpart in several essentials. Its agrarian organization was by owner-renter and landlord classes, the tenants holding individual farms even when in a commonalty, with a tendency at all levels toward nearly independent holdings. The landlord class viewed its homage less in terms of loyalties than of land-contract obligations; the vassal-lord structure was shallow and acted rather as extrinsic formality than dynamic essence. The role of women, both socially and economically, was rooted in a history far different from that of northern Europe. The dominant Catalan partner, when it had federated with Aragon about a hundred years before, had been "a society which contained feudalistic elements but which in essence was not feudal at all";[2] since that time a new feudalism of fragmented castle territories had largely replaced the old villa estates in Catalonia, affording a more enlightened landlord society than in Aragon.

When King James set up a separate kingdom of Valencia, the stage was set for a further emptying of feudal forms. Landlord, lord, and alodial farmer assimilated to each other. "The term lord stood equally for landlord, farmer-owner, and feudal lords"; this contrasts with the French situation, for example, especially in the simplification of the rental and tax patterns.[3] The revenue picture was not a neat arrangement of alodial baronies practically independent of the crown, followed by a linked series of levels of vassal estates relatively dependent either on a lord or on the king-as-lord, then by a set of crown estates managed by employee-bailiffs or castellans, and finally, among the mass of tenantry sustaining all these estates,

[2] A. R. Lewis, *The Development of Southern French and Catalan Society, 718-1050* (Austin, Tex., 1965), p. 387. In connection with Arago-Catalan feudalism, see also the discussion of agrarian organization above, in Chapter V, section 3.

[3] Tourtoulon, *Jaime I*, II, 198-201.

by a sprinkling of alodial small farmers or knights. Valencian lords did not form such a hierarchy, nor was the status of their land or the nature of their rents sharply distinct from those of burghers or nonnobles, aside from tax exemptions enjoyed. A few barons did display great estates, with courts, armed retainers, and subholdings; the mass of knights, including 380 created especially for Valencia by King James, had lesser fiefs or rather small holdings. Where vassalage existed, its structure remained shallow and weak, rather like a landlord-tenant relationship.

The more usual situation was of large and small landlords holding farms relatively independent of each other and differing little from the neighboring farm of nonnoble connections. A farmer could subdivide, or a lord cut up his property for vassals, but neither could make ties toward a higher lord except to the king, and the resultant tenants or vassals could leave simply by returning the property-portion to landlord or lord. This weakened the feudal orientation both at top and bottom, reinforcing the assimilative pressures. Further diluting the feudal status was the circumstance that nonnoble landlords kept rights to justice inherent in the estates they held, as much as feudal lords did, having the court of first instance, with appeal to the justiciar. Barons and knights did refuse to pay most crown or local taxes, a position James tried vainly to undermine. When they or ecclesiastics bought crown lands, the king tried to insist they pay taxes, but by 1271 he had abandoned this attempt.

The crown owned the largest bloc of land in Valencia, retaining all territories that it had not expressly given away. The king might alienate lands to a vassal or to a nonnoble tenant, receiving feudal services from him as would any lord, plus regalian taxes from the nonnoble. In the case of direct sale or grant the land became equivalently an alod, economically a free property beyond rent or recovery, despite King James's early attempts to claim at least ten solidi per jovate of land. Purchased land, like awarded land, still paid regalian taxes if its buyer were nonnoble. There is a strangely democratic air about all these holdings, whether feudal or alodial, high or low; each owner, lord or mere landlord, stood in relation to his holdings and to his renters, if any, in much the same way. Each could cut up his lands ad infinitum and dispose of them as he wished. Only the personal status of the owner made a real difference, in the freedom of knight and cleric from taxes to crown and to local administrative bodies; when these privileged men bought lands from nonnobles they insisted on extending this right.

Clearly this was feudalism with a difference, displaying a concomitant, countervailing trend toward assimilation of status among lords, landlords, and farmer-proprietors. Especially pertinent were the judicial rights, which accrued even on nonnoble lands; the ceiling that flattened growth toward any feudal pyramid; the ease with which tenant and vassal alike broke relations and departed; and the insidiously and increasingly pervasive effects in Valencia of the Romanized *Furs*. Though society was somewhat hierarchical, it consisted more of open levels with flow between them than of closed castes, as well as of osmosis of status between the magnate merchant and the privileged city-patriciate groups. A knight might be a relatively impoverished fief-holder, a noble of the second rank, or a privileged person of family who lacked socioeconomic power; a townsman-commoner who could afford to appear on the battlefield with his own horse and equipment need not have felt himself the social inferior of many a knight. If the knight put on airs, as King James complained, these seem in large part to have been a matter of snobbery and social fashion.[4]

The major difference between the realms of Aragon and northern Europe with respect to feudalism derived from the city-state ambience in which these realms functioned. An urban-commercial world set the dominant rhythms; barons often engaged in business, while townsmen frequently held some land; salaried soldiery and town militia complicated the military scene, and feudalistic styles glossed urban existence as much as rural. Kingship made its presence effective by a variety of administrative or representational mechanisms. Through the busy Mediterranean ports, international influences blew steadily. Following the lead of great communes like Barcelona and Montpellier, along with numerous second-ranking towns, the semiautonomous city-states with their republican patriotism already comprised a force counterbalancing feudalism. King

[4] On knights, Christian and Islamic, see Chapter XIII, section 2.

James advised the king of Castile to retain the loyalties not of the feudal barons but of the communes and church, "for with these he could destroy the others."[5]

The realms of Aragon had more in common with their Islamic neighbors' society of commercial cities and castles than might at first appear. Islamic Valencia knew nothing of communes, but it enjoyed a vigorous city life. Though its society was not properly feudal except in superficials or external patterns, its castle lords and regional rulers displayed a nobiliary life-style not too dissimilar. Spanish Islamic agrarian organization paralleled that of the Christians in many ways. The social system both in its parts and in their arrangement also showed resemblances. Moreover it is possible to think in terms of a matching "feudalism" in Islamic society at large. Poliak sees its distinguishing trait as a city-dwelling landlord stratum, linked by homage and a warrior destiny. Unlike their ruralized European counterparts, the Muslim lords formed an urbanized feudal society, controlling the economic life of a city, with the bourgeois as humble subjects. Absentee landlords, they practiced a dominantly money feudalism, seeing even land-holdings as money income and accepting indifferently a place in the state's tax-farming hierarchy or direct rents. The Muslim's homage was personal, not territorial, and his payment derived not from his lord but from the central state. Nor did his warrior role inhibit him from living a secondary life as merchant or bureaucrat. Perhaps Poliak's attempt to isolate general lineaments of an Islamic feudalism forces a quite different society into an alien conceptual frame. It is enough to note a number of points at which the two societies displayed strong analogies. These points were more numerous in thirteenth-century Spain,[6] and they multiplied in ratio to the waning power of feudal forms in the European society that Spanish Islam confronted. These points of analogy

[5] *Llibre dels feyts,* ch. 498: "car ab aquests destruyria los altres." F. Elías de Tejada explores the evolution of the tension between royal and feudal power in his *Las doctrinas políticas en la Cataluña medieval* (Barcelona, 1950), remarking on pp. 25-26 how "a esta estructura se va a sobreponer a lo largo del siglo xiii un aparato político representativo que transforma la vieja máquina feudal en una monarquía constitucional, aun dejando subsistente el armazón feudal de los señoríos."

[6] A. N. Poliak, "La féodalite islamique," *Revue des études islamiques,* x (1936), 248-265.

pertain to the respective social structures of each people. A more colorfully "feudal" quality shared by both was the knightly or chivalric psychology, in itself a subjective matter not necessarily characterizing a vassalized or feudal society. This belongs properly to the next chapter, where Muslim knights will enter the scene.

Islamic Valencia had become a society shaken and rearranged at the level of military-governmental order. It now had to cope with a conqueror group that was itself in the process of change. The Christian kingdom of Valencia, separately established and representing a break from the evolutionary processes shaping either Christian or Islamic parent society, was bound to feel the forward push of new forces most strongly. The border kingdom, welcoming immigrants from all the provinces of Languedoc and Aragon-Catalonia while at the same time throwing the factionalized Islamic regions into a unity of the conquered, effected a confrontation of rare promise. Standing against the promise was the religio-political ideology of either community, which tended to preserve itself segregated from the infidel. At this ideological level the Muslim did constitute an illogical, alien element within Christendom; some historians consequently deny that Mudejars of the time enjoyed any place within Aragon's society or swore homage.[7] In the order of practical politics, however, a more ambiguous status evolved, not always consistent with contemporary Christian theory. Valencian Mudejarism was at once a separate confessional state and a part meshed into the larger feudal-monarchical whole. How did the Christians contrive this?

James was not a modern king, controlling affairs from a fixed capital, but a wandering and often distracted military ruler, relying perforce on strong local governments. Into this scheme Valencia's Muslims easily fitted both as lords and as stable municipalities or communities. Conveniently enough, this accorded with the pattern of Spanish Islam, where the fragments of empire were tough, cohesive units prepared to survive disintegration of the larger mass. James regarded his conquered Muslims as "vassals" and "subjects"—

[7] Janer, for example, distinguishes sharply between the Muslim in the semi-independent tributary protectorate and the Mudejar who merely preserved some privileges; his view is perhaps unduly influenced by Castilian sources (*Moriscos de España*, pp. 10-11).

words nearly synonymous though haunted with a feudal air. Muslim townsmen, like their Christian counterparts,[8] swore homage to the king, and the rural hinterland was associated expressly though indirectly in their allegiance. The functioning of Muslims as organized communities, even where population was scattered, had analogies among James's Christians. The communal evolution of his people had been peaceful, rather than the outcome of tension and of leagues of armed unions as it had so often been elsewhere in Europe; experience thus favored natural grouping by Mudejars in the same spirit.[9] As with the Jews, however, such organization within the Christian realm provided only a foundation for viewing the Muslim as something less alien. Had such a view evolved? King James's choice of words on this subject reveals the contemporary mind.

Muslims of the Uxó community held their charter upon condition "that they be docile and loyal vassals to us, and after us to all our line." Those of Eslida, Veo, Ahín, and other districts of the Eslida charter "have bound themselves into his [the king's] service and have become his vassals."[10] James had similarly promised Minorca's Muslims that he would "keep and defend them as my men and vassals," so that the island's Muslim governor became his "man and vassal."[11] James employed the same language when referring to Mudejar subjects of his Christian vassals. In 1271 he directed a tax instruction to all vassals of the Calatrava knights in Valencia, Mus-

[8] The Christian obligation is in *Fori*, rub. cxxxii, no. 16: "omnes nobiles, milites, cives, et alii habitatores regni Valentie firment directum in regno Valentie, et debent facere sacramentum et fidelitatem nobis vel nostris successoribus in Valentia rite succedentibus"; and in no. 18, all these classes do so "quandocumque et quotienscumque a nobis fuerint requisiti, licet a nobis feudum non tenuerint." Thus both fief-holders and common citizens had to fulfill their obligations—*firmare directum*, a feudal phrase—and swear *fidelitatem* as often as required, even if they held no fief or property from the king; this prescription was paradoxically entered under the heading "de feudis."

[9] José M. Font y Rius, "Orígenes del régimen municipal de Cataluña," *AHDE*, xvii (1946), p. 300.

[10] Uxó Charter: "que ells sien sotmeses é leals vasalls a nos, é á qui aprés de nos será de tota la generatio." Eslida Charter: "qui miserunt se in servitutem suam, et devenerunt vasallos suos."

[11] *Llibre dels feyts*, ch. 121: "homens nostres e vasals." Muntaner, *Crònica*, ch. 8: "lo moxerif de Manorques sen feu son hom e son vassall," a situation prevailing also on the island of Ibiza.

lim as well as Christian.[12] An exemption of 1246 embraced the Valencian Templars' "men"—in feudal terminology indentical with vassals—"Christians as also Jews and Muslims."[13] At Chivert the Muslims swore before their Templar lords to observe the obligations in their charter "as good and faithful men ought to do to their good and legal lord."[14] The many Templar documents show this manner of conceiving Mudejar-Templar relations as normal and widespread. At the end of the century, despite all the revolts and after definitive subordination of Valencian Islam to Christian power, the king in transferring Culla to the Templars "orders Christians as also Saracens and Jews that henceforth they are always to hold you as their lords, and make homage and fidelity to you, and obey you loyally as their lords."[15]

The words vassal and man were ambiguous. They bore a formal feudal meaning in one context,[16] and stood for any freeman in another. The lowest tenants of an estate might occasionally be dignified as *vassalli servitutis*;[17] a serf or even a slave could appear as a

[12] Arch. Crown, James I, Reg. Canc. 16, fol. 248 (July 18, 1271).

[13] *Colección diplomática*, doc. 292 (Jan. 12, 1246): "hominibus . . . iudeis, christianis, seu sarracenis."

[14] Chivert Charter: "sicut boni homines et fideles debent facere suo bono domino et legali."

[15] "Colección de cartas pueblas," no. 32 (March 27, 1303), *BSCC*, XII (1931), 134-138: "mandantes . . . tam christianis quam sarracenis et iudeis quod de cetero vos pro dominis suis semper habeant et homagium et fidelitatem vobis faciant et vobis obediant fideliter tanquam dominis suis." See the similar practices among seignorial Mudejars in fifteenth-century Aragon; an aljama in plenary session swore to the new lord of the area "homenage et fieldat, segun vasallos son tenidos a senyor natural," doing homage "de manos e de boca," solemnizing it by an oath taken on the Koran, and handing over to the lord through its *amīn* a symbolic bit of grain and money. One farmer of that time, taking over his farm from the Christian lord, kissed the latter's hand and made a written "carta de vasallaje" in which "fago et constituezco me vasallo de vos . . . me obligo seyer vos bueno e leal vasallo" (Macho Ortega, "Mudéjares aragoneses," docs. on pp. 194-195). The Urzante Charter of 1318 has the aljama "recebimos por sennor a uos . . . et deuenimos uasallos . . . et besamos uuestras manos como a sennor natural al qual deuemos aguardar e obedir en todas cosas" (p. 338).

[16] Rodón Binué, *El lenguaje técnico*, pp. 38-39 (*baron*), 116-117 (*fidelis*), 136-138 (*hominaticum*), 138-141 (*homo*), 228-229 (*sacramentum*), 235 (*solidus*), 254 (*vassallus*), with the commentary from Catalonia's feudal theorist of the thirteenth century, Pere Albert (235-236). See also *Fori*, rub. CXXXI.

[17] Hinojosa, "Mezquinos y exáricos," p. 527.

lord's *homo*, though under his domestic rather than seignorial jurisdiction; a *fidelis* was often merely a town jurate; *vassallus* sometimes substituted for "subject."[18] Strangely enough, a Catalan might become a lord's *homo proprius et solidus*, or *homo*, secure his protection, do homage, and declare himself a vassal, yet not be a noble; he could break the bond by paying a redemption.[19] Landlords in Valencia called their ordinary Christian settlers *homines et vassalli*, or *homines nostri*, or *vassalli et supditi mei*, with reference to their owed *fidelitas*.[20] The technical meaning of these terms nonetheless remained feudal, however much contemporaries bandied them in looser modes. García, relating the contractual realities in northern Valencia to the wording, concluded that Valencian settlers "rather display the character of [true] vassals and *homines solidi* of Aragon and Catalonia," and that Valencians consequently "began their social evolution at the point where it ended in other regions," a development designed to lure immigrants.[21] Reviewing the history of these words in Catalan feudal usage, it is obvious that law and ideology were alike unsympathetic to such an evolution, but that appropriation of forms encouraged it. However limited or ambiguous, the assimilation was a sociological reality.

The word lord offers an analogous parallel, including by extension nonnoble landlords holding Valencian alods or independent properties. Beneath the verbal form, and perhaps because of it, there occurred a certain assimilation or equalizing of the two kinds of lord; the status, though twofold, at a number of points became identical. In the same way the use of "vassal" and "man," sometimes in conjunction with the technical "fidelis," not only betrayed a mentality but exercised causal activity. Thirteenth-century people of the Catalan-Provençal regions were becoming more conscious of hierarchies and definitions in status, perhaps as a reflection of a certain decline in the reality; if they used feudal words loosely, they did not do so in the naive way of earlier generations. An immemorial weight of tradition bore down on such a term, identifying its possessor as

[18] García de Valdeavellano, *Instituciones españolas*, pp. 331, 383-384, 413, 545.

[19] *Ibid.*, p. 344, treating of Catalonia-Aragon, and of a phenomenon not common but frequent enough.

[20] García y García, *Estado económico-social*, pp. 26-27.

[21] *Ibid.*, pp. 28-29.

at some level not outside feudal society. The context of synonyms substituted, of activities like homage, of expectations on the lord's part, and of the very times, helped freight the words with meaning from the past. This was particularly true in the case of Mudejar lords. Some may prefer to minimize or dismiss the feudalistic style of these words, taking them as bald variants for subject or citizen and refusing to credit the tyranny exercised by the residual original meaning of words in shaping reality; even at that extreme, however, the terminology still reveals that Muslims high and low entered the Christian political order, becoming an accepted, integral element equal in some way with the other components of the Arago-Catalan feudal state. In a number of elaborated specific contexts, on the other hand, a proper Mudejar feudalism appears.

The Valencian leader al-Azraq did homage in 1244 for his eight castles. "I make myself your vassal of you [*sic*], the lord Alfonso, eldest son of the king of Aragon." Prince Alfonso accepted him: "And I the lord Alfonso receive you for my beloved and very noble and very honored faithful vassal." When King James quarreled with the *qā'id* of Játiva, he spoke as he would of any other lord. "The *qā'id* is my vassal; he became my vassal when he made the agreement with me in the camp near the city, that he would protect and defend me and my interests." Vassalage had its traditional obligations. "Since he is my vassal, he ought to take justice at my hands, and I should give him a judge." For judge the king chose his uncle, Ferdinand, "one of the great men of Spain by family and by nobility." He did so, James said, in response to the feudal problem arising when "a lord makes demands on his vassal" and the vassal rejects the claim.[22] What the irritating ambiguities of terminology hint at breaks into the open here; analysis of technical words becomes especially persuasive in the context of such actual episodes.

[22] Arch. Crown, "Liber patrimonii regni Valentiae," fol. 227v (April 16, 1244); and in "Sección de documentos," ed. Roque Chabás, *El archivo*, I (1886), pp. 204-205, dated "xvi die Aprilis, era mcclxxxii" or 1244: "me fago uuestro uassallo de uos senor don Alfonsso primero fijo de rey daragon"; "et yo don Alfonso recibo uos . . . por mio amado et mucho alto et muy onrrado et mio fiel uassallo." On the conflict of Christian with Islamic dating of this homage, see below, p. 325. *Llibre dels feyts*, ch. 337-338: "e l·alcayt es nostre vassayl, que . . . se feu nostre vassayl . . . e pus nostre vassayl es, deu fer dret en nostre poder, e nos devem li dar jutge"; "que demanda faça senyor a vassayl."

In all these undertakings, the Christocentric ceremonies of northern Europe are absent, though Christian subjects of a Mudejar vassal fell under the Muslim's overlordship. Salo Baron remarks how the similarly alien Jews, who had enjoyed an "evolving new feudal relationship" in the Carolingian north, later found the Christological terminology of feudal position "a major obstacle"; consequently "Jews fitted badly into this hierarchical system" in the north, which rested on land, overtly Christological allegiance, and the exercise of authority over Christian subjects or even nobles. He cites exceptions for thirteenth-century England, nonetheless, and the *terra hebraeorum* near Narbonne where between the tenth and twelfth centuries "Jewish feudal lords held sway over Christian as well as Jewish vassals."[23] The Valencian experience must have been more liberal for Jews; since Jewish holders of land and villages were not uncommon, feudalism was far more ambiguous, and the Christological element had given way in adaptation to Islamic sensibilities.

Christians conveyed the equivalence of aristocratic classes in their own and Islamic societies not only by words which involved feudal structure, such as vassal and homage, or which implied a chivalric warrior status, such as knight and baron, but also by terms denoting nobiliary family lines. In predicating high "lineage" of Muslims sharing some honored name, Christians imported their own categories into a familial society differently organized; but by the same token they recognized a basic parity of status. When a contemporary man of affairs observed that Minorca and Ibiza islands were "thickly peopled with Moors of good lineage," or when King James adverted to the "lineage" of some Valencian urban notable, each betrayed this recognition of social parity.[24]

Communal and Tributary Vassalage

The application of the word vassal to Mudejar military figures, though surprising, was at least analogous to its usage in Christian feudal societies, and there were precedents for the relationship it expressed. More unexpected was the application of technical terms like man and vassal to aljama community leaders or sheiks, and by a

[23] *Social and Religious History of the Jews*, IV, 49-51, 161-164.

[24] Muntaner, *Crònica*, ch. 8.

kind of extension even to the humblest subject insofar as he belonged to the aljama. This practice comes to seem less strange when examined in the context of King James's imperfectly feudal society. A commune was often more important than many magnates together; by a transfer of forms King James treated each commune as though it were a corporate vassal. Negotiating with Montpellier in 1269, he convoked a meeting of the elected consuls, together with "five or six of the better men" or leaders, addressing them as "men" under him as their "lord." Similarly the people of Huesca promised to act towards him as "a man [vassal] ought to act towards his natural lord"; James in turn handled the assembled Huescans "as your natural lord." The men of Pertusa were his "vassals," while the besieged townsfolk of Balaguer were his "natural [vassals]" under the "lordship" of the countess. This wider usage, even in the case of Christians, should not be read too literally; nevertheless the gloss of a feudal relationship did somehow apply to the towns. More precisely, the relationship of king to town was understood and translated by relatively feudal minds according to feudal patterns, and therefore expressed in feudal terms. The Mudejar aljamas fitted nicely within this framework.[25]

King James restricted the ceremonial of doing homage; he required it only from the local Muslim leaders of importance in a given area, though these acted for their people. At Játiva it was the *qā'id* with "the hundred chief men of the town" who formally took James as their "lord." At Alcira the leaders or sheiks swore "to guard me life and limb," coming to "swear fealty to me and promise to be loyal to me and mine." At Chivert the charter carefully named the main leaders assembled for homage.[26] It is hard to say when the authorities were treating such men as a kind of group lord over their people or when they regarded them rather as communal jurates, since much naturally depended on the nature of the particular community

[25] *Llibre dels feyts*, chs. 30-32, 38, 42: "nos som vostre se[n]yor natural"; "vostra dona natural . . . mes val la nostra senyoria que d·om del mon." Though [*h*]*om*[*e*] bears the usual English meanings for man, its feudal use is as synonym for vassal. *Naturals* might be translated "liege men," the *se*[*n*]*yor natural* being the direct, hereditary lord, and the *vassal*[*l*]*s naturals* his lieges. See also Rodón Binué, *El lenguaje técnico*, pp. 138-141.

[26] *Llibre dels feyts*, chs. 327, 330-331; "los meylors c homens de la vila, e que·ens reebes per senyor." Chivert Charter.

and kind of leadership exercised. Though these realities must have assumed in Mudejar eyes the appearance of the Islamic homage (*bay'a*), the Christians clothed them with feudalistic meaning.[27]

Feudal relationships also existed on a more exalted level. Fictional subordination, represented by payment of tribute as a bribe or truce subsidy, differed from the status of true ally. As ruler of Islamic Valencia, Abū Zayd became a truce-tributary to Castile in 1225 and to Aragon in 1226; he angered his people and began to lose power only when in 1229 he became a vassal-ally.[28] Even the earliest of these agreements, a fully extrinsic tributary understanding, showed feudal trappings; King St. Ferdinand of Castile described how in 1225 "the *sayyid* Abū Zayd, king of Valencia, coming up to me at Moya, became my vassal and kissed my hands."[29] Kissing the foot, hand, hem, or earth had become the common Islamic form for expressing "the oath of allegiance," as Ibn Khaldūn explains, "since such an abject form of greeting and politeness is one of the consequences and concomitants of obedience."[30] For centuries in Spain this kind of kiss had displaced the egalitarian handclasp between ruler and aristocrats. In Spanish feudal usage also, kissing the hand was the central act in becoming a vassal.[31] A decade after the Moya episode, in 1236, Abū Zayd made himself and his faction of the civil war more deeply subordinate vassals of the Christian King James: "We will be your feudal allies (*legales amici*), and our sons one after the other are your vassals." With his sons and successors he promised "to make war and peace for you"; to seal the words, "we do homage of the hands to you." King James in return pledged that "we will be to you a good and legal lord," defending Abū Zayd against intruders upon the Muslim's *conquesta* or share of the Valencian

[27] See M. M. Bravmann, "*Bay'ah* 'homage': a Proto-Arab (South-Semitic) Concept," *Der Islam*, XLV (1969), 301-305. Émile Tyan, "Bay'a," *EI*², I, 1113-1114.

[28] Chabás, "Çeid Abu Çeid," doc. on pp. 147-151 (April 20, 1229).

[29] Fernández y González, *Mudejares de Castilla*, appendix, doc. 13 (May, 1225): "eo videlicet anno, quo Zeyt Abuzeyt, rex Valentiae, accedens ad me apud Moyam, devenit vasallus meus et osculatus est manus meas." See also doc. 14 (May 21, 1225): "el anno que el rey don Ferrando entró en tierra de moros y ganó por vasallos al rey de Valencia, e su hermano el rey de Baeza."

[30] *Muqaddimah*, I, 429. Around the year 1000 the poet Ibn Darrāj al-Qasṭallī wrote how the kings of León and Castile, tributaries to the Muslim ruler of Zaragoza, "glory in the land for having kissed your hand."

[31] García de Valdeavellano, *Instituciones españolas*, p. 384.

kingdom. Christian knights holding key castles as guarantees for the treaty "are vassals of you, the *sayyid*"; Abū Zayd and James together were to select the successors of these castellans.[32]

From 1243 until the 1264 revolt, the Murcian king made himself a vassal of the Christians in much the same way, to stay the flood of Castilian crusaders into his land. Authorities differ as to whether this amounted to nominal vassalage, without internal change or loss of autonomy, or rather an effective Christian suzerainty. In either case, the Castilians introduced garrisons, took over key castles, demanded taxes, and settled a scattered Christian population; in short, they effected a military occupation.[33] After the fall of Valencia city, the defeated ruler Zayyān offered to surrender the rest of his kingdom if James would grant him some important feudal holding, and suggested as suitable fief the island of Minorca. Around 1265 the Murcian Muslims sent an embassy to Rome under the leadership of the learned Abū Ṭālib b. Sabīn, brother of the celebrated philosopher who corresponded with the Emperor Frederick II, to seek the pope's help in making the king of Castile honor his religiously sworn promises of the Alcaraz treaty as feudal lord. The pope, apparently Alexander IV, showed himself sympathetic and praised the religious sentiments of Abū Ṭālib to the papal court.[34] At least once during James's reign the pope intervened in a like case. An ally or truce partner, the Hafsid ruler of Tunis, sued for damages done him by

[32] Arch. Crown, James I, perg. 678; published in Chabás, "Çeid Abu Çeid," pp. 155-156 (May 28, 1236): "erimus vobis legales amici, et filii nostri unus post alium sint vassalli vestri"; "facere g[u]erram, et pacem pro vobis"; "facimus vobis homagium manuale"; "erimus vobis domini boni et legales"; "sint vassalli vestri Aceyd." *Amicitia* in the context of Catalan feudalism meant a pact of alliance, often involving a feudal relationship (Rodón Binué, *El lenguaje técnico*, pp. xx, 21-22); *legales amici* might be "sworn allies," but the homage and vassalage expressed make "feudal allies" a better translation. North African rulers offered a remote tributary vassalage to Aragon, as when the Tunis tribute was to be promised under oath and confirmed by the "oath and homage" of notables, or when the king of Bougie offered to become King Peter's "man and vassal" to gain aid against the king of Constantine (Muntaner, *Crònica*, chs. 31, 44).

[33] Antonio Ballesteros, "La reconquista de Murcia (1243-1943)," *BRAH* (1942), 133-150; see also his *Alfonso X*, ch. 9, and the corrective comments of Torres Fontes in his *Reconquista de Murcia*, passim.

[34] *Llibre dels feyts*, ch. 307. Cagigas, *Mudejares*, II, 372-373. Fernández y González, *Mudejares de Castilla*, p. 104. Al-Maqqarī describes the papal interview from Arabic sources; see also Torres Fontes, *Reconquista de Murcia*, pp. 73-74.

the crusading fleet of King James's metropolitan archbishop of Tarragona, Benedict Rocaberti, "acting as pirates";[35] in 1259 papal arbitration settled the affair.

A contemporary Castilian version of tributary vassalage was the relationship between King St. Ferdinand and Ibn al-Aḥmar, founder of Nasrid Granada (1232-1273). The Muslim remained a sovereign but for a time paid tribute to Ferdinand; he could attend the *cortes* or parliament at the side of Castilian nobles, and he was expected to send armed forces to help the Christians against Muslim enemies. Ibn al-Aḥmar led five hundred elite horsemen to Ferdinand's siege of Islamic Seville, helped at the seige of Jaén, and in 1254 sent a hundred horsemen with tapers to stand ceremonial guard over the corpse of his Christian lord.[36] Such extrinsic vassalage, of a tributary or alliance nature, was not uncommon; it had operated in reverse also, through a long history of Christians serving Muslims. Analogies existed in Christian and Islamic areas elsewhere in the Mediterranean world, notably in Byzantium and the crusader states of the Near East. Christian Trebizond and Lesser Armenia were vassal states to Seljuk Rūm, whose sultan on the other hand relied on his domestic Christian armies to control Muslim enemies.

Muslims in the Christian Armies

Christian contingents and knight-adventurers fought for Islam, particularly in North Africa, respectably and without taint of defection.[37] Conversely Islamic forces did battle for the Hohenstaufens in Italy in this century, invaded France under Alfonso X in 1253, and at one point were reported as helping to prepare an attack against England and Ireland. Mutual military aid had too long a history in

[35] *Itinerari*, p. 263 (Oct. 1, 1257): "piraticam tirannidem exercendo."

[36] Cagigas, *Mudejares*, II, 388-389.

[37] See the standard study by Giménez Soler, below, n. 49. Unlike Christian service under Muslims, the role of Muslim armies under the Cross is a neglected subject. Even Luis Querol y Roso, in his *Las milicias valencianas desde el siglo xiii al xv, contribución al estudio de la organización militar del antiguo reino de Valencia* (Castellón, 1935), includes no reference to the contribution of the Mudejar aljamas; he does mention, for a much later period than ours, that Valencian Moriscos served as light infantry with arrows or lance, a topic he does not develop (pp. 50-51). See also the contribution of Gazulla, below, n. 49.

Spain to be disregarded as frontier bumptiousness or rare wartime expediency. It is especially pertinent here in illustrating the compatibility of crescent and cross in military enterprise, and in relating the military factor to the feudalistic forms of government. As trappings and terminology appropriated reality at the feudal political level, so experience in the field prepared its reshaping on the feudal military plane.

Over many generations, military practice had helped prepare the way for acceptance of Muslims into a Christian scheme, until massive conquest with its attempted colonial absorption produced the Valencian paradox. None of this would have seemed strange, for example, to the Cid. From Mudejar leaders of status equivalently baronial in the new kingdom, King James now expected military service in times of local danger. He became incensed, during the rebellion of al-Azraq, because the *qā'id* of Játiva and other leaders did not spontaneously offer him troops; he expressed his anger vehemently, and from that critical moment began considering expulsion.[38] At the level of popular help too, in defensive action against attacking Muslims, the king expected the appropriate, loyal response from the rank-and-file of Mudejars. During the Islamic invasion and revolt that agitated Valencia in the last years of King James's and the first of Peter's rule, the crown ordered Aragon's Muslim communities to send their army contingents to aid the Christians. By the time such units were ready to march, however, the crisis in the war had passed, so King Peter revoked the obligation, commuting it to payments by each aljama averaging nearly three thousand solidi, plus large quantities of weapons.[39]

The very Muslims who had to surrender Peñíscola fortress in 1234 transformed themselves into stout crusaders against Islam's rally during the second stage of the Christian conquest. The Hafsid ruler of Tunis had committed himself to the relief of Valencia city; but his fleet of eighteen vessels under Ibn ash-Shahīd, driven off the capital's port in 1238, ran north to disembark its troops at Peñíscola. Al-Ḥimyarī devotes a section to Peñíscola as an important stronghold of Islamic Spain, "with a numerous population" and a jurisdictional territory embracing towns, farms, and "abundant water." Conscious

[38] *Llibre dels feyts*, ch. 362.
[39] Soldevila, *Pere el Gran*, part 2, I, appendix, doc. 83 (July 25, 1277).

of its strategic siting, he locates it in terms of the North African coast—"six days of navigation" from Argel. The town was almost impregnable, a semi-island of rock and fortification; it had outlasted one crusade under King James in 1225 and had surrendered on terms a decade later owing only to a combination of maneuver and bluff. Peñíscola's garrison of ten Christian knights rode out of the castle to engage the Hafsid expeditionary force, which was already disembarking supplies on the strand. Here was Valencian Islam's golden opportunity. The local Muslims could have set upon the Christian band in the open, welcomed their belated ally, and raised a counter-crusade. Instead "the Saracens of the town" marched into battle alongside the Christians "and helped them powerfully" so that "they overcame the men from the galleys, and killed a good seventeen of them."[40] This enthusiastic collaboration would have gone unremarked, as similar joint efforts undoubtedly did, had the action not constituted a turning-point in the crusade's military development.

When Chivert castle surrendered, its exemption from military service was neither general nor aimed at preventing its inhabitants from fighting against Muslims. The charter dispensed only with offensive campaigns "against other Saracens or Christians" beyond the region belonging to Chivert castle. The Muslims agreed on the other hand to fight "any Saracens and Christians making any damage or attack or hurt to their castle or property." In such an event "the Moors of Chivert would defend themselves and their property according to their power, along with the Brothers" of the Temple.[41] The picture of recently surrendered Mudejars battling alongside Templars to drive off Muslims startles the modern eye. Yet Islamic forces did serve in the ranks of Christendom's military orders in

[40] *Llibre dels feyts*, ch. 265: "que·ls ajudaven fort be"; the surrender had been in late 1233 or early 1234 (cf. *Itinerari*, p. 150). For this episode seen from the Tunisian vantage, see Brunschvig, *Berbérie orientale*, I, 32-34. Al-Ḥimyarī, *Kitāb ar-rawḍ al-mi'ṭār*, p. 120. On the very different use of Muslim townsmen as infantry mobs in the Islamic East, for example in 1260 and 1281, especially to defend cities, see Lapidus, *Muslim Cities*, pp. 163ff.

[41] Chivert Charter: "contra sarracenos alios aut christianos nisi forte aliqui sarraceni aut christiani facerent aliquid maleficium vel forciam vel gravamen castro suo et rebus; et tunc mauri Exiverti una cum fratribus deffenderent se suaque secundum posse suo." The Mudejars kept the castle oratory, there being no chapel and apparently little or no Christian garrison; the Moors had to move their residences from the castle or alcazar area.

any case; contemporary troops of Mudejar archers, for example, were led by a commander of Santiago against the bishops of Cuenca and Sigüenza.[42]

Uxó's warriors, though barred from distant zones of revolt, were committed to fight local actions; "they must defend all my land."[43] Alfandech's charter allowed the surrendering Muslims of its valley to keep their weapons, presumably including the ubiquitous crossbow. Mudejars commonly kept their weapons at surrender. This had been traditional, appearing, for example, in a line of the 1115 Tudela capitulation: "no man is to forbid arms to these Moors."[44] The custom can be witnessed on a large scale when Mudejar crossbowmen of Valencia marched off to the French wars by the hundreds for King Peter; it appears by indirection in the manslaughter case at Valencia city resulting from a javelin practice or game among Mudejars.[45] As a courtesy even the population defeated and expelled from Valencia city in 1238 were permitted to carry their weapons on the trek into exile.[46]

One testimony to Mudejar military participation has survived by merest chance. It represents the kind of small fief easily overlooked. A notarial formulary or textbook, by incorporating the pertinent document as an illustration of notarial practice, rescued from oblivion the defense dispositions of Montes and Carrícola. In 1259, after the crusader-owner had died, King James restored the town and its defenses to the local Muslims as a group, stipulating that they were to man its tower or fort themselves. The Mudejars here undertook in writing "to defend and garrison" the fortification protecting the area.[47] During the crusade James left only token garrisons to control strategic castles that had surrendered; at Alcira, for instance, he sent a small troop to take over a portion of the defenses, leaving walls and towers largely in Muslim hands. Less important places and especially the average rural town had to contribute to their own protec-

[42] D. W. Lomax, *La orden de Santiago (1170-1275)* (Madrid, 1965), p. 127.

[43] Uxó Charter: "dejen guardar tota la nostra terra."

[44] Alfandech Charter. Tudela Charter: "non devetet nullus homo ad illos moros lures armas."

[45] See above, p. 252.

[46] Valencia Capitulation: "cum suis armis."

[47] "Repàs d'un manual notarial," p. 310, doc. 1 (1259): "teneamini nobis guardare et custodire turrim sine missione nostra."

tion. Mudejar castles proper, on the other hand, formed an element in military feudalism distinct from the military obligation falling upon the general Mudejar populace.

An international episode during King Peter's reign illustrates both the defensive role and the retention of arms. As part of the War of the Sicilian Vespers, France in 1285 mounted a massive invasion of Aragon. A Franco-papal alliance elevated the enterprise into a formal crusade. At the council of Narbonne the cardinal-legate, preaching the crusade to the notables of France, excoriated Peter of Aragon for employing Muslim troops. "He has joined himself with Saracens to destroy the Christian faith, and with their aid he strives to withstand us, for by his own strength which is naught he could not stand alone."[48] King Peter had really refused more Islamic help than he had accepted; the Granadan sultan, intrigued by mysterious preparations for the Sicilian war, in 1282 had already declared his willingness to fight as ally "with all my forces, whether it be against Christians or against Saracens."[49]

Peter did not refuse such help in 1285, though this time forces came from deeper Islam—North Africa. A combined army from Morocco and Tlemcen came up and kept their promise to fight well against the French; in 1286 the Moroccan caliph negotiated to help Aragon against "all the Christians of the world"; the Christians in

[48] Desclot, *Crònica*, II, ch. 136 (1285). On the French invasion, see J. R. Strayer, "The Crusade Against Aragon," *Speculum*, XXVIII (1953), 102-113, with materials cited there.

[49] Muntaner, *Crònica*, ch. 47. See esp. F. D. Gazulla, "Las compañías de zenetes en el reino de Aragón," e.g., the document of April 15, 1284 ("scribimus genetis nostris qui sunt in Tirasona quod veniant ad nos ad exercitum nostrum"), arrangements for more jennets on October 28 ("con los cabos de los genetes et con los otros sobre fecho de lur venida"), payment of November 4 to three leaders ("sarraceni janeti qui in nostro servicio venerant"), the arrival of Çahim's troop in 1285 ("filius Iahit Abennaquen habeat venire ad dominum regem cum genetis et familia sarracenorum"), and a letter of King Alfonso in 1286 recalling to Morocco's sultan the arrangements with Peter III for Moroccan troops to fight against the French invasion. Over these Muslims was a "genet de casa de senyor rey." See also Andrés Giménez Soler, "Caballeros españoles en África y africanos en España" (*Revue hispanique*, XII [1905], p. 355) where Abenraho and his troop signed an agreement at Valencia in 1303, taking service under James II, and received the castle of Negra plus the rents from two towns. On Sicilian service by subject aljama armies, see Amari, *Musulmani di Sicilia*, III, 334, 537-538.

turn undertook to aid Morocco against "all the Muslims of the world."[50] This kind of military assistance, though not the result of vassalage, reveals something of the traditional attitude in Christian Aragon. The inclusion of military service among the Valencian Mudejars' duties, therefore, was neither an innovation nor an eccentricity. The Muslim vassal, like the Christian, expected in times of invasion to rally at least to the defense of his locality for the king. Though prudence might modify wider obligations, as in the case of a Valencian rebellion, in the thirteenth century the expectation of some service underlay such nervous exceptions.[51]

An incident during the French war illuminates the wider use of Valencian Mudejar commoners in battle. The exploits of these Valencians would not have entered history had they not proved central to the climactic siege of Gerona. The town stood athwart the French invasion route in 1285; locked into it were 110 knights or esquires with 2,500 foot. The backbone of the defense, however, was a large contingent of crossbow specialists—"600 Saracen archers from the kingdom of Valencia, all bearing strong and mighty crossbows." This army of Valencian Mudejars broke the main storming of Gerona. With good reason "the French feared greatly the Saracen bowmen, much more even than any other soldiers within the city of Gerona." Valencian marksmanship was extraordinary. One Mudejar defender "swore by his religion" to hit a French count lying wounded in a church outside the walls; aiming through its distant window, the bowman killed both count and attending esquire with a single missile. The contingent's *esprit* was legendary. Forbidden to expose themselves beyond the protection of the walls, threescore of the zealous Muslims bored an exit hole one midnight, silently invaded the French camp, crept up on the tent where a party of Norman knights was celebrating, and in a commando onslaught, unseen and unheard by the camp, killed five knights and bore back thirty-eight prisoners.[52]

[50] Dufourcq, *L'Espagne catalane et le Maghrib*, pp. 205-206, 213.

[51] Muntaner, commander at Djerba island off North Africa, describes how his captains decided it was more prudent not to let their own Muslims fight in a critical battle against Muslims (*Crònica*, ch. 255).

[52] Desclot, *Crònica*, chs. 153, 156, 163.

These Valencian crossbowmen probably formed part of the body of Mudejars drafted in 1283. Throughout the new kingdom, only recently subdued after the rebellion of the late 1270's, King Peter sent the Jew Samuel b. Manasseh from aljama to aljama, assigning contingents of lancers and crossbowmen. "Each aljama" so assessed had to dispatch these troops "well equipped and well trained."[53] It is important to stress that these were levies drawn from the general Mudejar population by reason of customary loyalty. They were not mercenaries sent by Islamic rulers, such as King Alfonso of Aragon used in 1286 against Christian rebels in Valencia, nor the celebrated *almogàver* (*al-mughāwir*) irregulars hired locally by Kings James and Peter, "who are Catalans and Aragonese and Saracens" mixed, such as held lands also in Valencia.[54] Underlining the distinction, a crown directive of late 1285 cautioned the Valencian procurator not to exact war taxes from Mudejar veterans of the Gerona campaign. This instruction reveals that the Valencian aljamas contributed a money levy as well as men; and that during the collection at the lowest levels the property of recusant veterans had been confiscated pending payment. The crown ordered "the procurator of the kingdom of Valencia" and his lieutenants "that you do not oblige the Saracens of the kingdom of Valencia who were in our service at Gerona" to join in contributing "anything toward the expenses or salary paid to these Saracens by the other Saracens of the realm of Valencia"; in case the procurator had "taken pledges from them for this reason, you are to restore these to them."[55]

[53] *Colección de documentos inéditos . . . de Aragón*, VI, 196 (Aug. 12, 1283): "que aquels de cascune de les vostres aliames, quel dit alphaquim nostre elegira a asso nos tremetau, ab companya de balester et de lancers de cascuna daqueles aliames, e be aparelats, e be adobats, et nos darem a aquels bona soldada."

[54] Arch. Crown, James I, Reg. Canc. 12, fol. 18v (March 20, 1262) records, for example, the *hereditas* owned in Les Alcuces among his Christian neighbors by Sa'īd al-Mughāwir (Çahat Almogabar). The quotation is from Desclot, *Crònica*, ch. 79. On Alfonso's use of Granadan mercenaries see Soldevila, *Història de Catalunya*, I, 381, and his *Vida de Pere el Gran* (Barcelona, 1963), p. 333.

[55] Arch. Crown, Peter III, Reg. Canc. 57, fol. 203 (Sept. 13, 1285). "Procuratori regni Valencie vel eius locum tenentibus. Mandamus vobis quatenus non compellatis sarracenos regni Valencie qui fuerunt in servitio nostro in stabilimento Gerunde ad solvendum vel contribuendum aliquid in expensis sive solido soluto ipsis sarracenis per alios sarracenos regni Valencie et siquidem pignora ipsis facta super racionem predictam restituatis eas sibi." *Stabilire* in feudal terminology meant

The episode shows something further. The 1283 draft law had promised the specialists that "I will give them a good salary [*bona soldada*]"; the 1285 intervention concerned precisely this salary, which the crown drew from the money contribution of the aljamas. The authorities apparently allocated such salaries also to Muslims on castle guard duty.[56] Occasions for defensive warfare, especially convulsions demanding a kingdom-wide levy, were not common. Military activities of Muslim loyalists during the recurrent rebellions of the thirteenth century are almost undocumented, except for rewards given in landholdings. Enough can be seen at places like Uxó, however, to explain why the consequent "expelling" of Muslims left so many fighters and leaders in the areas of expulsion. Without the larger history of the French invasion, the military obligation of the ordinary aljama-vassal might have remained obscure.

At the turn of the century, when Christian Valencia faced invasion from Granada by "a great crowd of knights on horse, and footmen," and when the enemy was able to besiege and burn Cocentaina, the vassal *ra'īs* of Crevillente, Muḥammad b. Hudhayl (Abenhudell), served Aragon well, especially in an intelligence capacity.[57] The work of the Crevillente people recalls the use of Muslim spies during the Valencian crusade and rebellions. As early as the conquest of Majorca the agent 'Alī spied for James on the eve of the crusaders' assault. In the last Mudejar revolt Peter gathered the intentions of the rebel forces and their disposition around Montesa "from spies he had among them."[58] Defectors contributed both intelligence and active service; Abū Zayd and his faction might unkindly be considered in this category, but a more apt example was the Muslim officer

---

to garrison with troops or to appoint a castellan; *stabilitos* or *locatos* are soldiers enrolled, though *stabilimentum* can bear the meaning of treaty or order (Rodón Binué, *El lenguaje técnico*, pp. 164-165, 238-239).

[56] A late example, probably not an innovation, comes from a charter of 1359 arranging Chivert revenues and constitution; the Templars promised fourpence to each Mudejar for each night's castle guard: "guaytar al castell" (Gual Camarena, "Mudéjares valencianos, aportaciones," p. 194).

[57] J. E. Martínez-Ferrando, *Els descendents de Pere el Gran, Alfons el Franc, Jaume II, Alfons el Benigne* (Barcelona, 1954), p. 106; quotation from letter of James II to Ferdinand IV (Sept. 1, 1304).

[58] *Llibre dels feyts*, ch. 59. Muntaner, *Crònica*, ch. 10: "per espies que tenia entre ells." The kings also gathered intelligence through their Jewish diplomats and agents.

who came over to the Christian side with his prisoners after the battle of Luchente just before James's death.[59]

The evidence thus far has centered on public defense or royal armies. Paralleling this, with only slight documentation surviving, was Mudejar military service to Christian as well as Mudejar lords. Seignorial retinues or armed bands were a paramilitary factor in the Valencian kingdom. A noisy episode involving such a group of retainers entered the crown records in 1281. An official party of Christians, including members from the household of the king's brother, rode off to rescue "a certain Saracen woman slave" who had been stolen. The local power took umbrage at their intrusion. That power chanced to be the Lady Alda Simon of Arenós, converted daughter of ex-king Abū Zayd and now wife of the high baron Blasco Simon of Arenós. She sent a great band of armed Muslims, who routed the Christian troop. The invading posse had to take refuge in a nearby building. Here, as they later complained to authorities, they sustained siege, peril of death, and the ultimate humiliation of having their weapons taken from them by the Muslims.[60] Such private bands of retainers contributed to general disorder in the new kingdom. When King James, out of patience with the enthusiastic private brawling disturbing the Valencian kingdom, caused all residents "from fourteen years up" to swear to an elaborate program of law and order, he expressly included the Mudejars, prescribing an oath upon their law.[61]

Just as Valencia's military accommodation was the continuation of a long history, so it served to link the past with an equally storied future of Muslim-Christian armies fighting under Christian banners. A quarter-century after King Peter's death, the roaming band of military adventurers called the Catalan Grand Company enlisted Turkish cavalry under one Mālik to conquer Seljuk towns, going on

[59] *Llibre dels feyts*, ch. 559. Each contingent of the irregulars called *almogàvers*, who included Muslims and fought for James and Peter, served under a leader called an *almocadèn* or *almocatán*, which was the title King James describes the Luchente defector as holding; see Dozy, *Glossaire*, p. 167, 172.

[60] Arch. Crown, Peter III, Reg. Canc. 44, fol. 212v (Feb. 26, 1281): "qua[n]dam sarracenam captivam."

[61] *Aureum opus*, doc. 88 ("De pace"), fol. 27v (ca. 1271): "mandamus denique quod omnes et singuli habitantes in regno Valencie tam christiani quam sarraceni de pace, quilibet secundum legem suam, a xiiii annis ultra iuret dictam pacem fideliter observare."

to devastate Byzantium with the help of "loyal and true" Muslims under "oath and homage to us."[62] Later still, in 1347, the crown called upon Valencian Mudejars again, to put down the rebellious Christian nobles of the kingdom of Valencia.[63] Thus in Valencia the wheel of fortune had come full circle, in an ironical way, almost exactly a century after the end of the crusade, with the sons of the vanquished supporting the regime against the sons of the crusaders. Twenty years afterward, according to the scandalized contemporary Froissart, Peter of Castile "collected from the kings of Portugal and Granada an army of 40,000 composed of Jews and Saracens as well as Christians" for the battle of Montiel; the French captain Du Guesclin refused to take prisoners, killing fiercely "because of the great number of Jews and infidels" in Peter's army, mostly "Saracens from Granada and Benmarin [Morocco]" who fought to the death with bows and lances.[64] A tax exemption in 1413, connected with a collection designed to support the Mudejar archers' contingent in the army of the king of Aragon, reveals that "the greater part of the Moors of the aljama [of Zaragoza] are at present in this siege [of Balaguer] in our service, and fight for us here"; exempting their aljama from the tax, the king confessed, "pleases us much."[65]

The presence of Jews on the Christian battlefield reflects the operative principle behind the Islamic role in Spanish Christian armies, as well as the parallelism and shared fate that linked the two alien communities in Christendom over the centuries. The twelfth-century German rabbi Eleazar b. Joel Halevi had observed how "it is still customary in Spain for Jews to accompany their king into war." Muslim historians speak of Jews fighting in the Spanish crusade on the Christian side. Jews went out in a body to defend Toledo against the Almohads in 1197. It comes as no surprise then to find Jewish bow-

[62] Muntaner, *Crònica*, esp. chs. 215, 228. On the complex feudal relationships of the company, see my "The Catalan Company and the European Powers, 1305-1311," *Speculum*, XXIX (1954), 751-771.

[63] Jerónimo de Zurita y Castro, *Anales de la corona de Aragón*, 7 vols. (Zaragoza, 1610-1621), lib. VIII, c. 19.

[64] *Chronicles*, chs. 242, 245. On Jews as soldiers in Christian armies, see Baer, *Jews in Christian Spain*, I, 80, 89, 113, 114, and notes.

[65] Macho y Ortega, "Documentos de los mudéjares," pp. 158-159 (Oct. 5, 1413): "la mayor partida de los moros de la dita aljama sean de present en aqueste sitio en servicio nuestro . . . [e] aqui nos sirven"; "muyto nos plazeredes."

men receiving lands at Jérez in the apportionment of 1266, a Jew as combat casualty at Orihuela, or the bellicose armament with which King James's secretary Samuel b. Manasseh of Játiva outfitted himself.[66] Valencian records are silent as to Jews in battle, and perhaps it is unreasonable to look for any in so gratuitously aggressive an undertaking as the Valencian crusade. Moorish participation in Christian military affairs was understandably more widespread, and its perduration lends more meaning to the lesser military duties, clearly visible in the Mudejar tax documentation in Valencia, such as local garrisoning, providing guard dogs, laboring on fortifications, and supplying mules for army transport.

Mudejar nobles and castellans of Valencia, though never merely the equivalent of their Christian counterparts, were by no means a despised group alien to the Aragonese feudal system or normally mistrusted on its battlefields. The concept of political society under King James allowed for a spread of loyal differences. Ideology or religion was no absolute obstacle to participation. The association nonetheless contained seeds of discontent for both parties. Its product was less a fusion than a juxtaposition. The Muslim was indeed subject or vassal; but from the beginning he was also a man of another people and creed, set somewhat apart. His communities and castles formed separate entities.[67] His nobles did not travel as part of

[66] Baer, *Jews in Christian Spain*, I, 59-60, 88, 396-397; he suggests that such warfare was normally defensive and rare, the Jews more often remaining neutrals between two warring camps. Samuel belonged to the Valencia city Jewry, but Romano believes he came from the south and probably from Játiva ("Los hermanos Abenmenassé," p. 250; cf. p. 280). Baron discusses the military and paramilitary role of the Jews in Spain against the background of similar activities elsewhere (*Social and Religious History of the Jews*, x, 123, 355, with cross-references to pages on Jews in earlier Spanish wars, and xi, 110-116, 335-338). Alfonso XI, among the arguments with which he defended Seville's Jews, remarked that "not infrequently they go out with the Christians against the Saracens, not fearing to expose themselves to death" (xi, 111); Jewish absence from battlefields had antecedents in prohibitions by laws of Christian Rome, and repercussions in pacifist theory and practice (pp. 110, 116); note also the Jewish wing at the Uclés battle of 1109, and at Zalaqa in 1086 on both sides (x, 123). See the bellicose equipment of a Valencian Jewish official above, Chapter XI, n. 16.

[67] An apparent exception, from the last area conquered before the Valencian crusade, showed Mudejars participating in the Tortosa *cort*, but decreed that they must sit on the lowest benches, below the Christian delegates. Was this attendance a survival from an early era when Mudejars dominated the mixed government,

the monarch's entourage. His potential for rebellious mischief was not forgotten. In short, there were sharp limits to Muslim participation in the Christian political order; participation itself diminished, especially on the nobiliary and urban levels, as the century wore on amid a welter of revolts. Nevertheless the Mudejars, from nobles to townsmen, had their moment of stability as an element intermeshed with the Valencian feudal order.

---

or a provision dealing with relatively rare occasions when both peoples necessarily conferred, as for common taxes?

CHAPTER XIII

The Military Aristocracy

THOUGH ISLAMIC Valencia boasted a stratum of aristocrats analogous to Christian barons and knights, its individual members come into view largely by indirection. To gain a clearer idea of this class, each fortuitous appearance of a Mudejar lord or knight in the records must be isolated for examination.[1] Before the conquest, larger cities like Játiva and Alcira displayed strong local rulers, almost little princes, each surrounded by his noble bodyguards, knights, advisory intellectuals, and council of notables. Smaller towns mustered a less imposing aristocracy. Fairly rural environments such as Jérica or Alpuente had inherited a proud nobiliary past that they were unlikely to forget. Over the length of the Valencian kingdom each castellan *qā'id* thought himself a center of authority; on occasion he ruled his area with unabashed independence. As with every upper class, snobbery created strata beyond those of power or wealth. Ibn Khaldūn, treating of the precrusade troubles in Spain, distinguished the *arriviste* Berber faction from the "ancient" Spanish upper classes. He divided the latter into notables more involved with city life, as distinct from "houses who had to some degree kept away from urban

[1] On this class see also Julián Ribera y Tarragó, "La nobleza musulmana en Valencia," *El archivo*, I (1886), 349-350, 355-357, II (1887-1888), 49-53, 200-205, IV (1890), 86-91, republished as "La nobleza árabe valenciana," *Disertaciones*, II, 214-243. See also his "Tribus árabes en Valencia" (Chapter IV, n. 4); "Moros célebres valencianos" (Chapter IX, n. 48); "Los Benigaslón de Uxó," *BSCC*, XI (1930), 65-67; "Tribu de Maáfar: los Benimofauaz de Játiva," *El archivo*, II (1887), no. 3, and in his *Disertaciones*, II, 236-243; "Tribu de Jazrach: los Jarifes de Jérica," *El archivo*, II (1888), no. 4, and in his *Disertaciones*, II, 229-235. For the upper classes in Almohad North Africa, see Brunschvig, *Berbérie orientale*, II, 116-168, and Hopkins, *Medieval Muslim Government in Barbary*, ch. 7 on "The Almohad Hierarchy"; on "fiefs," see George Marçais, *Les arabes en Berbérie du xie au xive siècle* (Paris, 1913), pp. 245-253. On later Granadan lordships, see Caro Baroja, *Moriscos*, pp. 82-83. Amari concluded that there was a nobility in the European sense among Christian Sicily's aljamas (*Musulmani di Sicilia*, III, 265). On Spain's long tradition of praising Moorish leaders and arguing for the nobility of "moros onrados," see K. R. Scholberg, "Minorities in Medieval Castilian Literature," *Hispania* (Baltimore), XXXVII (1954), esp. 206ff.

civilization and the cities and who were firmly rooted in military life." His three examples of members of these old Spanish military families in action were Ibn Hūd seizing Murcia, Ibn al-Aḥmar setting up Granada "with the help of a group of relatives called the chiefs," and Ibn Mardanīsh or Zayyān of Valencia.[2] What were all these fractious dynasts like? What power did they retain as Mudejar lords?

Muslim Nobles

The *sayyid* Abū Zayd, supplanted ruler of Valencia, was not a typical Mudejar lord, since his conversion in mid-crusade placed him rather in the Christian camp. He can serve nonetheless as a convenient door through which to enter the aristocratic order of Valencian Islam. Conversion brought him control over Christian population, patronal disposal of local churches, and alliance by marriage to noble Christian families. He compromised this status somewhat by clinging to Islamic externals, remaining in dress and mode of life the perfect model of an Almohad gentleman. With a foot in both worlds, he retained his eagle seal and Arabic signature; in particular, he wielded his grand Almohad title with its religious connotations in preference to his baptismal name, Vincent. Repetition of the name by everyone from sons and intimates to official crown records confused later historians as to the genuineness of his conversion. Abū Zayd, Christian feudal lord but outsider, can therefore tell us something from his style of life about the Mudejar nobiliary scene.[3]

His political history up to his simultaneous conversion and loss of royal title in 1236 has already been related. Here the feudal seignior, dean of Mudejars despite his Christian taint, takes up the story.

[2] *Muqaddimah*, I, 335.

[3] Chabás, "Çeid Abu Çeid," in five installments (see above, Chapter II, n. 10). His first Latin signature comes only in 1247. The *Llibre dels feyts* has him as Çeit, Seyt, Azeyt, and Aceyt, with the remainder as Abuzeit, Abuçeit, and Abuceyt (chs. 25, 136, 276, 360). Latin documents give his further title as "nepos almiramamolin" or "almiramomenum," or variants like "nepos regis Almomeleni" (1246), and "ego Açeyt Abuçeyt vel potius Vincentius . . . nepos almiramomenim" (1247). His eagle seal was not necessarily, as many conclude, a sign of his drift from Islam. On his political career, see Huici and others as cited above in Chapter II, nn. 10, 12, and 13.

By a waiver of April 22, 1236, Abū Zayd recognized the bishop of Segorbe as proper church authority over his central fief—Segorbe town, plus all the castles, towns, and districts of Almenara, Alpuente, Andilla, Arenoso, Artas, Ayodar, Bueynegro, Cardelles, Castielmontán, Chelva, Chulilla, Cirat, Domeño, Fuentes, Liria, Montán, Nules, Onda, Terdelas, Tormo, Tuéjar, Uxó, Villamalefa, and Villamalur; later substitutions amended the list. He contributed to the rebuilding of St. Felix church at Játiva, reduced the death duties of Christian tenants foresighted enough to die fortified with the sacraments, and kept a proprietary eye on his crusader's *ius patronatus* over local churches and especially on his share of the tithe. A conscientious squire, he improved his land by bringing in Christian settlement, though the area stayed predominantly Muslim for another century. As with a number of lords, his first estates served merely as a base for land exchange and dispersal of holdings; this subsequent history, with its disposition via inheritance to Christian in-laws, is obscure.[4]

Abū Zayd received a large number of Valencian castles, especially Castalla, Ibi, Tibi, Onil, Orcheta, Villahermosa, and Villamalefa. Eight of these he transferred on the occasion of his son's marriage.[5] The crown attached a significant condition to his strategic castle of Ganalur: "in such wise that the castle and defenses be destroyed." His holdings tended to center on Segorbe in the north, Castalla in the south, and Murcia beyond the border. Though James gives the impression that Abū Zayd lost the great castle of Castalla shortly, what happened was that the king gained its co-lordship; in 1262 James directed García Pérez to make "homage of fidelity to the *sayyid* Abū Zayd for the castle of Castalla" in such wise as to hold it for both men, just as Berengar of Entenza held Roda castle for Abū Zayd and for James.[6]

[4] Aguilar y Serrat, *Noticias de Segorbe*, II, 76, document of April 22, 1236. Background on this region, with its bibliography, is in Burns, *Crusader Valencia*, I, 42-53, and II, esp. 392; for the ex-king's Villahermosa settlement see I, 167 (March 1243), and for other aspects of his religious history see pp. 90, 124, 167, 199-200.

[5] Arch. Crown, Peter III, Reg. Canc. 41, fol. 58v (April 9, 1279): "ius domino regi competit in octo castris que Açeyt Abuçeyt olim rex Valencie dedit pro contrahendis nuptiis."

[6] "Sección de documentos," ed. Roque Chabás, *El archivo*, IV (1890), doc. 17 (Oct. 13, 1262): "fecistis homagium fidelitatis Ceido Abuzeit de castro de Castaylla." Chabás, "Çeid Abu Çeid" (part 5), p. 298; in a document of May 19, 1251, here, the Latin notary of his household appears, but this Peter López had at least one

The supporters of the Almohad in the civil war that became absorbed into the crusade received rewards of land and position in Christian Valencia. A gift of 136 jovates in two villages, "for the support of fifty-two men of the *sayyid* Abū Zayd," seems to concern his special retainers and household.[7] His relatives turn up in both the Valencian and Murcian divisions.[8] Some of his Murcian lands went to a son and to a cousin. He himself received his parents' valuable properties in Valencia. Benefits would have accrued to Abū Zayd even had he not been a Christian; at Murcia "cavallerias" or knightly holdings went to the puppet "rey moro," still a Muslim, while two Christians were inscribed as his "vassals."[9] Even the definitive conquest of rebel Murcia left its king at least in possession of the castle of Yusor, which was retained by his family for some decades and eventually sold.[10]

If Abū Zayd illustrates the Mudejar nobiliary class by his extensive holdings in property and castles, he also fitted the role by his dress, retinue, bearing, and manners. He had an imposing presence; a Castilian contemporary described him as a tall man of majestic mien and brilliant eye who went about turbaned in silk, clothed in scarlet, the favored color among military men in Islamic Spain, and sur-

predecessor, mentioned in a 1242 letter. On the king's exchange of Cheste and Villamarchante for Castalla see *Llibre dels feyts*, ch. 360, where the context suggests a date of 1245; the exchange document, dated Sept. 10, 1251, reveals that Castalla and Onil castles, given to the ex-king's son and daughter as a wedding gift when both married into the family of Simon Pérez of Arenós, were exchanged for Cheste and Villamarchante by the latter baron in 1251 (*Colección diplomática*, doc. 403). The 1262 homage shows that other castles like Castalla that appear in documents, as though only the king and a beneficed castellan were involved, may have sustained a coordinate or intermediate lord even after being taken over by the crown. *Repartimiento de Valencia*, p. 257: "ita quod dirruatur castrum et forcia que est ibi per quod alicui de regno sive aliis malum non adveniat."

[7] *Repartimiento de Valencia*, p. 195: "ad opus lii hominum de Aceyt Aboceyt."

[8] *Ibid.*, pp. 195, 225, 257, 446, 525, 578, 592. "Furtadus de Aceyt miles" and "Furtadus Petriz del Azeyt" appear on pp. 223 and 225, "Toda del Aceyt" on p. 599. In the *Repartimiento de Murcia*, pp. 3, 190, 221, "Sancho Ferrandez fijo de Açeyt" and "Simon Alffonso sobrino del Açeyt" received lands.

[9] *Repartimiento de Murcia*, p. 22: "omes del rey de Murçia"; pp. 109-110.

[10] *Ibid.*, p. viii. Cagigas, *Mudejares*, II, 374 and note. Al-Maqqarī, *Mohammedan Dynasties in Spain*, II, 338, castle "Yozar" of the Murcia district, which this last ruler of the Banū Hūd held until his death. See also Torres Fontes, *Reconquista de Murcia*, p. 87.

rounded by his sons, with a great retinue.[11] Al-Azraq, lord of Alcalá in conquered Valencia, cut no less a princely figure. King James devoted a passage of his autobiography to describing an informal encounter between this aristocrat and the lord of Castile. King Alfonso was out hunting when the Mudejar's escort of ten "Moorish knights" (*cavallers de moros*) rode up, together with his bodyguard, followed by the great man himself. After making an entrance and kissing the king's hand, al-Azraq indulged in a witticism against his overlord the king of Aragon that still rankled years later in James's memory.[12] More striking yet was Ibn 'Īsā, lord of Játiva and subsequently lord of Montesa. A Catalan writing in the early 1280's drew a word-portrait of this Mudejar grandee. "And he looked in truth to be a noble, for he came riding upon a splendid horse and his saddle and breast leather were inlaid with foil of gold." His bridle and reins "were of silken cord and wrought with bosses of silver and garnished with broidery and studded with precious stones and pearls." Ibn 'Īsā himself "was clad in scarlet embellished with golden fringe, and bore no arms save only a sword that hung about his neck, and this was of great price and richly jewelled." As befitted his status, "he brought with him four hundred Saracen horsemen."[13] This apparition from the Mudejar beau monde affords a sudden insight into an extensive class of men, whose representatives continued to grace the Valencian political scene for years after the crusade.

An entourage such as those described usually carried banners. Ibn Khaldūn, going into the subject at length, remarks that "flags have been the insignia of war since the creation of the world"; just as martial music serves to intoxicate "the souls of brave men emotionally and cause them to be willing to die," so "the great number of flags, their manifold colors, and their length" are meant to overawe the enemy. He says the Almohads restricted the massed unit of drums and banners "to the ruler," placing it immediately behind him. In Spain, however, such ruling devices tended to devolve upon local dynasts like the Játiva *qā'id*. A scene from the Majorcan crusade

[11] Chabás, "Çeid Abu Çeid," part 5, p. 363, quoting the primate of Spain, Jiménez de Rada, *De rebus Hispaniae*.

[12] *Llibre dels feyts*, ch. 377.

[13] *Crònica*, I, ch. 49, on the Játiva *qā'id*: "honrat hom." Desclot probably died in 1289; he was an important functionary of the king's curia.

in the king's memoirs indicates that even lesser military lords displayed their personal standards; James describes a body of Muslim infantry huddled on a hill, under a prominent "standard of bright red and white, divided lengthwise, with a man's head or one of wood on the spike." Ibn al-Aḥmar or The Red, founder of thirteenth-century Nasrid Granada, flew a red flag; probably al-Azraq, or The Blue, carried blue. The king of Castile wrote to James, probably in the late 1250's, telling how al-Azraq had sent his streamer ensign or pennant ("son peno") as a proxy when offering tributary alliance; Alfonso responded by sending back his own, thus taking the Mudejar "under his protection." Since al-Azraq rode into battle "with a great din of woodwinds and trumpets," similar stirring accompaniment undoubtedly enlived his formal appearances.[14]

Such a noble's escort included as well an inner circle of honored bodyguards called *exortins*. Gayangos related the term to *ash-shurṭah*, the military official who also evolved as a city police functionary; but Dozy rejected this, proposing instead a word for a ruler's guard as pronounced locally. Riding with al-Azraq to visit the Castilian king were ten of his knights plus "his *exortins*." A Muslim ruler at a parley with James brought a royal guard of three *exortins* bearing spears.[15] A Mudejar lord's resources also included troops, like the four hundred around the Játiva *qā'id*.[16] Sometimes an eminent lord stood out among his followers by reason of contrasting simplicity. The powerful *qā'id* of Bairén eschewed the gaudy plumage of aristocrats, and opted for the severity of a linen shift.[17] Majorca's ruler, during his interview with King James, contrived to convey splendor through stark simplicity.[18] The nephew of Zayyān, who conducted

[14] *Muqaddimah*, II, 48. *Llibre dels feyts*, ch. 64: "una senyera de vermeyl e de blanch per lonch meytadada, e una testa d•ome o de fust al ferre"; ch. 372: "son pena," "en sa comanda"; ch. 375: "ab gran brugit de corns e d•anafils," a *corn* being a kind of hautbois or oboe. Flags were commonplace even in civilian life; pilgrim companies raised them on the march (Ibn Baṭṭūṭa, *Travels*, I, 17).

[15] *Llibre dels feyts*, chs. 87, 377: "iii exortiquins denant ab ses atzegayes"; "e sos exortins." Dozy, *Glossaire*, p. 258; see also p. 223 on *azagaya*. *Atzegay* was the Berber javelin (Catalan *atzagaia*, English "assagai"); the twelfth-century treatise by Ibn 'Abdūn noted the weapon to be carried in town by mercenary soldiers—"an *akzal*, that is to say a short lance" (*Séville musulmane, le traité*, p. 63). See also above, Chapter XI, n. 16.

[16] *Llibre dels feyts*, ch. 559.

[17] *Ibid.*, ch. 312.

[18] *Ibid.*, ch. 87.

preliminary negotiations for his uncle at the surrender of Valencia city, affords yet another example of the Muslim aristocrat's retinue. King James, no stranger to ceremonial, was impressed by his honor guard of "ten knights, well equipped and well dressed, and on good horses and good new saddles, who might go into any good court as men well appointed." This nephew, the *ra'īs* Abu 'l-Ḥamlāt (Abulphamalet) was "the most powerful man in Valencia after Zayyān, and the son of the king's sister, and his most trusted counsellor."[19] Contemporaries must have stood in awe of him; but that single sentence from his Christian enemy is the sole record of his glory; it is biography and epitaph combined. A lesser personage, though important in his own right, 'Alī al-Baqā' (Ali Albaca) of Peñíscola, issued from the stricken capital twice to hold talks. Zayyān had dispatched him to James two years earlier on a similar mission, offering to surrender the bulk of the kingdom in return for the region south of the Guadalaviar.[20]

King James left many Muslim leaders in anonymity under designations like "the *qā'id*" or the "Saracens" of a defense. Other leaders he casually dismissed under their given names. The few who impressed themselves sufficiently on his mind to win description or a proper name in his memoirs must have been men of consequence within their respective nobiliary, functionary, or other class. When Ibn Lūb (Aven Lop) ambushed and captured the Hospitaller commander of Oropesa during the Valencian crusade, scattering the Christian contingent into panic, the king's preservation of his name suggests a *qā'id* of more than usual importance; the name itself may link Ibn Lūb to the regal Banū Mardanīsh clan of Zayyān.[21] Similarly the Mūsā bearing the epithet al-Murābiṭ (Muça Almoravit), who surrendered the key southern stronghold of Biar, was obviously a *qā'id* of note, his family a relict perhaps from Almoravid times.

[19] *Ibid.*, ch. 272. The name illustrates the pitfalls involved in reconstruction. Gayangos, despairing of the Catalan form, conjured up the variant Abnalmalec or Ibn Mālik. Such latitude, though reasonable, might yield more restrained choices like 'Abd al-Malik or Abu 'l-Malik. Alas for such analogies, however; the name is obviously related to that of Zayyān, whom both Ibn Khaldūn and Yaḥyā b. Khaldūn give as the son of Abū Ḥamlāt; Ibn al-Khaṭīb and an-Nāṣirī offer the variant Abu 'l-Ḥamalāt.

[20] *Llibre dels feyts,* chs. 242, 271-272.

[21] *Ibid.*, ch. 229: "e dix que Aven Lop avia dat salt al comenador d·Orpesa al pinar desa·l grau, e que havia pres lo comenador."

Biar's emissaries boasted to King James that "it was the best castle which stood on that [southern] frontier, and that if I held it I would have the whole frontier." After surrendering, Mūsā apparently stayed on as Mudejar regional chief.[22]

In fleshing out the portrait of the Valencian aristocrat, analogies are available from neighboring Majorca. Ibn 'Abīd (Ben Aabet), a notable ruling over one of the island's twelve districts, was able to influence other districts to surrender; as Mudejar lord he retained control of his area along with the two Christian bailiffs he requested.[23] An equally imposing Majorcan was Ifant Allāh (Ifantilla), a warrior aristocrat who led the hosts of Islam at the battle of Inca and then rallied the castles of the mountainous hinterland until he fell in battle. His stature as a foe is indicated by the distinctive end reserved for him: King James detached his head and flung it by catapult into the besieged city of Majorca.[24] Yet another islander illustrative of the nobiliary class was the *ra'īs* entrusted by King James with the governance of conquered Minorca.[25] Sometimes the impressive nature of a property confiscated by the crusaders hints of nobiliary status in its otherwise unknown master. When King James wanted to reward Poblet monastery for its help at the abortive precrusade siege of Peñíscola in 1225, he gave the monks the persons and properties of two Muslims, the *faqīh* Ibn 'Abd Allāh (Abdinabdela) of Peñíscola and Aḥmad (Azmet) of Cervera; as a prize under

22 *Ibid.*, chs. 355, 359: "lo castell . . . era lo meylor castell que fos d·aquela frontera e que si nos l·aviem, que hauriem tota aquela frontera." Almoravid and its root is reflected in a number of place names such as Miravete, formerly in the north of Valencia kingdom, and Almoravit near Orihuela (for others see Dubler, *Wirtschaftsleben*, pp. 112-113). Almoravid was also a Christian name, possibly with a different origin.

23 *Llibre dels feyts*, chs. 71-72; the Christians reorganized the twelve into fifteen. On the name, see above, Chapter VIII, n. 31.

24 *Ibid.*, ch. 70. Gayangos and recently Soldevila read the name as Infantilla, reconstructing it as a bastard mixture of Catalan En (Sir) with the Arabic for Conqueror by the Grace of God; *a priori* the mixture is not improbable, since Desclot calls him En Fatilla (*Crònica*, ch. 40), and Muntaner calls an African notable En Bugron (*Crònica*, ch. 44), but the Spanish mixture Ifant Allāh is more acceptable both phonetically and in view of local vagaries. Ilfant or Ihant was an Arabic borrowing from Spanish Infante; see Diego Catalan, "Sobre el 'Ihante' que quemó la mezquita de Elvira y la crisis de Navarra en el siglo xi," *Al-Andalus*, XXXI (1966), 209-235. Of less probable Arabic alternatives, al-Fāḍilah is unfortunately a feminine name, while names like Faḍl Allāh (Faḍlallāh) or al-Fāḍil do not quite jibe.

25 *Llibre dels feyts*, chs. 377, 119: "faem raiz."

these circumstances, they must have been wealthy aristocrats, at least of the urban patriciate. Since the gift does not indicate any military connections, the two may belong to the more resolutely civilian aristocracy described by Ibn Khaldūn.[26]

Some notables were rooted in Valencian families with impressive genealogies or proud antecedents. These are not always easy to verify because *arrivistes* in a family line tended to appropriate suitable genealogies, concealing less exalted origins, while enemies maliciously attributed plebeian beginnings to hated political figures. Islamic chronicles can portray the same man both as a scion of aristocracy and as a petty adventurer grasping power by pure audacity. An example of Valencian rustic nobility with ancient roots was the tribe that gave Jérica its nickname "castle of the nobles." They traced their genealogy back to a friend of the prophet, and had contributed to Islam a pretender to the caliphate, a governor of Egypt, a Damascus intellectual, governors of Denia, Játiva, and Jérica, a *qāḍī* of Murviedro, and assorted counselors and learned men of the Valencian kingdom. This family also gave Játiva its last ruling dynasty.[27]

Knights and Castles

How numerous was the Islamic knightly class in the Valencian kingdom? The mosaic of evidence, though not sufficient to assemble into a complete picture, suggests that it was large. The "forty or fifty" castles in Islamic Valencia assessed by King James as formidable strongholds point to many of *qā'id* status and a multitude of "knights"; their performance against their Christian counterparts in sallies, ambushes, open battle, successful siege, and defensive action —all seen through the eyes of the crusading enemy—betrays military skill, equipment, courage, organization, and aristocratic outlook equal to those of their Christian counterparts. Zayyān, distracted by civil war and stripped of most of his domains, was able to gather for the last battle at Puig an impressive number of such equivalent knights just from the area between Játiva and Onda—"full 600 knights" plus a mass of infantry.[28] Allowing for many floating ad-

[26] *Itinerari*, p. 56 (Sept. 5, 1225).

[27] Ribera y Tarragó, "Tribu de Jazrach: los Jarifes de Jérica," pp. 229-235. See also Évariste Lévi-Provençal, "Shorfā'," *EI*[1], IV, part 1, 385-388.

[28] *Llibre dels feyts*, ch. 217: "dc cavallers e be xi milia homens de peu."

venturers or nonaristocratic cavalry, the implication is that the towns and castles of central Valencia during an emergency fielded a considerable body of men equal to the Christian *cavaller*. How to classify these men, from the landlord class down to the impecunious proud hillsman, is a more difficult question, as is the assessment of progressive loss from their ranks by expulsion or especially by flight during the decades after the crusade.

Though the aristocratic status of such Muslims is often obvious, the import of the wider term knight as applied by Christians appears more dubious. To a Christian it carried feudal overtones, especially in the growing class consciousness of the mid-thirteenth century, but it retained as well its simpler meaning of cavalryman. King Peter in 1281 spoke of the "milites sarraceni" and the "multitude of armed soldiery both cavalry and infantry" about to invade Valencia from Granada and North Africa; *milites* here does not have the ring of *cavallers* encountered above in the brave entourage of al-Azraq. As with the more shifty term baron, context often brings out its nobiliary or patrician connotation. The repetition of "knight" in so many documents, and its assimilation to the Christian class of the same name, is striking.[29] Despite the ambiguity latent in the terms, and the deeper ambiguity rooted in the differing cultural situation into which such terms were imported, examples of plainly aristocratic "knights" and "barons" appear in Christian sources.[30] King James "made peace with many Saracen barons" in the kingdom of Valencia. In North Africa the expeditionary force of King Peter faced "Saracen kings and sons of kings and barons."[31]

[29] Arch. Crown, Peter III, perg. 266 (Aug. 23, 1281): "milites sarracenos ad terram Valencie"; "multitudo armatorum quam militum quam peditum."

[30] "Barons" in Catalan can bear the generic meaning of worthies, from the German for freeman; King James uses it thus in his memoirs as a term of respect when addressing urban patricians at places like Montpellier, Huesca, and Balaguer. Elsewhere he employs it in strictly nobiliary context, denoting nobles below the count-viscount rank (see his "nobles barons" in *Llibre dels feyts*, ch. 58). Christians applied the word in both senses to Muslims. Muntaner speaks of truces with their "kings and barons" (*Crònica*, ch. 52), and King James has the *wālī* of Majorca address the council notables as "barons" (*Llibre dels feyts*, ch. 70).

[31] Muntaner, *Crònica*, ch. 9: "e axi mateix ab molts barons sarrahins que havia en lo dit regne ell feu treues"; ch. 52: "eren reys e fills de reys e barons e moaps de sarrahins, qui eren la flor de tots lo sarrahins del mon." See also ch. 44: two wise Saracen knights as envoys from Bougie; ch. 50: "a tots aquells de la ciutat, e als cavallers sarrahins de la ciutat"; ch. 75: four Saracen knights; ch. 85: 195 knights; ch. 247: "tota la cavalleria"; ch. 249: "meteren cavalleria de Tunis."

In Spain these knights often affected the externals of the Christian knight. According to the contemporary Spaniard Ibn Saʿīd al-Andalusī or al-Maghribī (1214-1274), the Muslim knight of his country differed in this respect from his North African counterpart. The Spaniard preferred the heavy lance and shield of the Christians, wore a coat of mail, required a second horse to carry his equipment, and flourished an emblem with his own arms and blazon. Tallying with this is the description of an unhorsed knight King James helped kill on Majorca, outfitted with "coat of mail," long European lance, belted sword, and shield, with "his Zaragoza helmet on his head." When the Catalan Lull, himself of knightly status, composed his story about a knight traveling to a Muslim king's court to joust on behalf of the Virgin Mary, context makes Christian and Muslim knights counterparts. Their relationship was the natural affinity and assimilation of aristocratic classes in societies otherwise mutually alienated.[32]

On occasion Christians formally dubbed Muslims as European-style knights; King James received an embassy from Murcia, consisting of "the vizier and one knight [*cavaller*] from among the most powerful of the town—King Don Alfonso of Castile had made both knights." The son of the *qāʾid* of Villanueva de Castellón received an expensive horse from James "when I made him a knight." The conferring of Christian knighthood on Muslims was not unprecedented. In 1229 the Emperor Frederick II knighted the son of al-Kāmil; facing this son in battle around 1245, Joinville described how "he bore on his banner the arms of the Emperor who had made him

[32] Sánchez-Albornoz, *La España musulmana*, II, 344-345. Ibn Saʿīd, born near Granada in 1208 or 1214, studied at Seville, and toured the Near East in 1241, 1250, and 1267; he served the ruler of Tunis, dying at Damascus in 1274 or Tunis in 1286. His emblem description applied to Granadan beginnings; only powerful personages in North Africa wore mail. *Llibre dels feyts*, ch. 60: "i cavaller a peu, e tench son escut abraçat, e sa lança en sa ma, e sa espaa cinta, e son elm saragoça en son cap, e i perpunt vestit"; according to Soldevila, the Zaragozan helmet came from "Saragossa de Sicilia," a Catalan name for Syracuse; his further conjecture in favor of an Islamic origin seems less well founded. The king's party in the episode, though it outnumbered this warrior four to one and was mounted besides, stayed wary; the Moor still managed to sink his long lance deeply into a charging horse, bringing it down ("mes mija braça," a *braça* being the distance between outstretched hands; see Chapter IX, n. 85). Ramón Lull, *Blanquerna*, ch. 64.

knight," quartered with the insignia of Muslim sultans. Richard the Lion Heart had knighted Saladin's nephew and was erroneously believed to have dubbed Saladin himself.[33]

The socioeconomic structure of Islamic aristocratic society displayed points of analogy with the lightly feudalized, city-state society of the Catalan Valencians, as the preceding chapter demonstrated. Far more important in terms of human relations and postcrusade assimilation of the Muslim aristocrat was the inner structuring of character or at least of self-image that the modern ineptly thinks of as feudal—the allied phenomenon of chivalry. Chivalric ideals and modes of action spell "knight" today much more than do the mechanisms of landholding and hierarchical vassalage. The prejudice may be more just than it seems to the historian, since it concerns a grounding of spirit more basic to the whole personality of the knight than his admittedly important outer structure. The Islamic world of course had no institution comparable to chivalry; but the aristocratic warrior's subculture inculcated a pattern of attitude and chivalrous practices (*murūwa*) so similar "that the translation of *fāris* by 'knight' is not in itself an error."[34] The *fāris*, like his Christian counterpart the *miles*, transliterates as "horseman." He was sensible of a high standard of dignity, self-sacrifice, and honor; he protected the weak, showed himself courteous and correct to his conquered enemy, wrote courtly poems, and displayed cool valor in battle, especially offering himself as champion in single combat and setting an example for other fighters. Since all this remained merely personal

[33] *Itinerari*, p. 283 (Jan. 4, 1259), on the debt of 900 solidi for the horse, "quando ipsum fecimus militem"; the Castellón of this document centered upon a supporting castle for Játiva. *Llibre dels feyts*, ch. 436: "e vench l·algutzir e i cavaller dels pus apoderats que eren en la vila, e·l rey Don Alfonso de Castella havia·ls feyts cavallers abdos." Jean de Joinville, *Histoire de St. Louis*, ed. Natalis de Wailly (Paris, 1874), ch. 64; in the René Hague translation, *Life of St. Louis* (New York, 1955), pp. 73, 273-274.

[34] Editor, "Fāris," *EI*², II, 800. The idea of soldiers' guild or pact of honor (*futūwa*) as a kind of chivalric order is now discredited, despite the influential articles under that term in *EI*¹, (II, part I, 123-124; supplement vol., pp. 79-80) and in *EI*² (II, 961-969). In any case the data on which it rests had nothing to do with western Islam. See the comments of Stern and Cahen in *The Islamic City: A Colloquium*, ch. 3 and pp. 37ff.; and Gerard Salinger, "Was the *Futūwa* an Oriental Form of Chivalry?" *Proceedings of the American Philosophical Society*, XCIV (1950), 481-493, including the bibliography; reviewed by Claude Cahen, *Revue historique*, CCVII (1952), 142-143. See also Bichr Farès, "'Irḍ," *EI*¹, supplement vol., pp. 96-97.

and uncodified, without formalities or initiation, it resembled rather a set of manners or self-image adopted out of individual choice by more affluent men of sensibility, or a mentality abroad which influenced the conduct of a certain stratum in Islamic society. Something not dissimilar existed among the merchant class in Christian towns, where an imitative posture of gallantry and warrior manliness was assumed in a context divorced from fiefs, nobility, or investiture; one thinks of the young Francis of Assisi riding off to battle clothed in fine armor and illusions.[35]

The Christians acknowledged the Muslim practice of those virtues that both accepted as chivalric. King James could say in 1244: "no Saracen ever broke his word to me, in what he had promised as to surrendering a castle," except for the unique case of al-Azraq. Like the Christians, Muslims practiced the custom of single combat before a battle, frequently sending out their champions; King James described one such contest under the walls of Valencia city, in which the Christian champion lost. A vignette some thirty years after the death of King Peter, when the Aragonese were stemming an attack from Granada, conveys both the sense of chivalry and the single-combat code. On the battlefield the son of the Muslim ruler of Guadix, "a skilled knight and one of the ideal knights of the world," charged directly at the prince of Aragon, shouting repeatedly: "ani be ha soltan" or "I am a king's son." This approximates the classical *anā bnu 's-sulṭāni*, or *anā ibn as-sulṭān*, preferably in its colloquial form *anī ben as-sulṭān*. The more closely corresponding *anā bi-hā sulṭān* would alter the meaning to "I am here ruler." Before being

35 Allied to this phenomenon of the manneristically feudalized patriciate was the widespread commoner knight of Castile discussed by García de Valdeavellano; unbeneficed and nonnoble, the *caballeros ciudadanos* kept privileges as long as they could maintain horse and equipment. In the early thirteenth century in Castile these men became the equivalent of the urban patriciate; their numbers swelled during the first half of the thirteenth century, and Alfonso IV of León (d. 1230) legislated that all above a certain income had to serve with a horse in this class (*Instituciones españolas*, pp. 320, 324-328); see also p. 338 on the assimilation of Valencian and Barcelonan patriciate by analogously nobiliary privileges, though the Catalan and Valencian patriciate was not at all the equivalent of Castile's *caballeros villanos*. Carmela Pescador offers an extensive discussion, "La caballería popular en León y Castilla," *Cuadernos de historia de España*, XXXIII-XXXIV (1961), 101-238, and XXXV-XXXVI (1962), 59-201. Elena Lourie pulls together the Hispanist writings on the topic in "A Society Organized for War: Medieval Spain," *Past and Present*, XXXV (1966), 54-76.

cut down, this paragon managed to shatter the prince's shield with "a most marvelous blow."[36]

A castle or tower, the central protection for a Christian district, was at this time both a symbol of feudal power and a key point in its functioning; normally the king granted them.[37] Though the term *castrum* can be ambiguous, reference here is to a defensive fortification of at least local importance. Contemporary accounts describe some, as when outlying forts dependent upon the strategic castle of Bairén were themselves "castles of stone, large and strong." Others, such as Uxó, are available for examination *in situ* today by the archeologist-historian. Each "castle" in the literary sources ought to be studied on its own merits, to be sure it meant a military stronghold rather than a town; in Valencia however *castrum* invariably involved at least a tower.[38]

On Minorca the Muslim negotiators had pressed hard to retain their castles and forts, but the Christians "at last" forced the issue against the indignant Moors. On the other hand, the *qā'id* or Játiva, in return for relinquishing his main alcazar and territory in 1244, received for himself and his kin in perpetuity the castles of Montesa and Vallada—the queen having advised King James during the negotiations "not to delay for a castle or two."[39] It must not be thought that the Conqueror foisted off an inconsiderable fort on the *qā'id* as a form of dismissal; "the awesome stronghold" of Montesa will appear shortly in episodes demonstrative of Mudejar nobiliary strength.

[36] *Llibre dels feyts*, chs. 273, 356 (al-Azraq, champions). Muntaner, *Crònica*, ch. 247: "aquell fill del rey moro era bon cavaller e era hu[n] dels bells cavallers del mon"; "yo axi mateix so fill de rey"; "molt maravellos colp." On Islamic chivalry see the *Lámpara de los príncipes* [*Sirāj al-Mulūk*] of Abū Bakr aṭ-Ṭurṭūshī (Abubequer of Tortosa), ed. Maximiliano Alarcón, 2 vols. (Madrid, 1930-1931). Dante reflected Christian respect for Islamic chivalric qualities in placing Saladin (d. 1193) among the virtuous pagans (*Inferno*, IV, 127); contrast his Muḥammad among the sowers of discord in a later horrible scene (XXVIII, 22-23). A bizarre case of single combat in 1245 pitted a Marinid emir against the Christian serving as champion for the emir's Muslim foe; wounded badly in the first charge, the emir killed the Christian here too (José Alemany, "Milicias cristianas al servicio de los sultanes musulmanes del Almagreb," *Homenaje á Codera*, p. 139).

[37] Antonio Ballesteros y Beretta, *Historia de España y su influencia en la historia universal*, 2d edn., 9 vols. (Barcelona, 1942-1944), III, 510, 541.

[38] *Llibre dels feyts*, ch. 307: negotiations with the *qā'id* of Bairén and "ab aquels de Villalongua, e de Borro, e de Villela e de Palma [de Gandía], qui eren castells de rocha grans e forts"; the Muslims lost control of these.

[39] *Ibid.*, chs. 121, 353: "per i castell ni per ii."

Orcheta, Tárbena, Tous, and Carmogente Fiefs

Specific Mudejar fiefdoms can be pinpointed, their brief histories traced, and their incumbents named in sequence. The task is not easy. The researcher must pick away like a magpie at a rubble of documentation, then fit his bright bits of information into a pattern. Since most Mudejar fief-holders drifted eventually into one or other revolt, it is arbitrary to discuss a few here rather than in the next chapter on patriot rebel-lords. The generalities thus far elaborated require some concrete illustration, however; and this selection may serve simultaneously as exemplars and as a bridge to the more exciting figures who inhabit the following chapter. Perversely, one of the most valuable fiefs appears only by the light of a few documentary flashes. In 1258 King James granted to a certain at-Tīfāshī (Tevecin) and his son Sa'd (Çahat) forever "the castles and towns of Orcheta, of Finestrat, and of Torres with their fortifications and villages, with buildings, houses, farms, gardens, vineyards, ovens, mills, waters, grass, meadows, hunting, fishing, wood"—a feudal grant comparable in its expression to those being conceded to Christians.[40] This Mudejar had to wife (surely from before the crusade?)

[40] Arch. Crown, James I, Reg. Canc. 10, fol. 77 (June 16, 1258): "per nos et nostros damus concedimus et assignamus per hereditatem propriam francham et liberam tibi Teuiçino et filio tuo Cahat et vestris imperpetuum castra et villas de Orchita, de Fonestrat, et de Turribus cum suis fortaliciis et alquariis cum casis casalibus ortis ortalibus vineis furnis molendinis aquis herbis pratis peciis venacionibus et piscacionibus lignis silvis garriciis nemoribus planis montibus terris cultis et incultis heremis et plantatis cum introitibus exitibus dominiis et pertinenciis suis omnibus a celo in abissum ad habendum tenendum. . . ." The form of his grant, though conventional, is unusually sweeping. His name Cahat becomes Çaat and Azeth in other documents, making Sa'd probable. Teviçinus (elsewhere Tovicinus) may well derive from Tivis(s)a, with a Latin suffix indicating it was the man's place of origin. Tivisa was a fief north of Tortosa on the coast; its root was the same as Valencia's town Tibi plus an Iberian suffix denoting city (-issa). In 1317 a Bertrand Teviça, a pirate or privateer from this area, ran afoul of the king's law by seizing friendly Tunisians at sea; see Ángeles Masiá de Ros, *La corona de Aragón y los estados del norte de África, política de Jaime II y Alfonso IV en Egipto, Ifriquía y Tremecén* (Barcelona, 1951), p. 179. The famous Tunisian encyclopedist Aḥmad b. Yūsuf (d. 1253) bore the name at-Tīfāshī, since his forbears came from Tīfāsh, thus suggesting a plausible form for this Valencian. Other options remain open. If the Tovicinus reading is preferred, it may relate to Tous as Tovos (see n. 51). The common Spanish name Tashfīn might be distorted into either form. Aṭ-Ṭabasī would mean "(from a family) from Ṭabas."

a Christian named Mascarosa, the mother of Sa'd. Her son's services to the crown a decade later won Mascarosa a pension of 100 solidi from the king.[41] The date of the castle grant deserves noticing. The second Mudejar revolt, still in full progress in May of that year, had ended at about this time—"recently," according to a crown letter of July 30.[42] The king may have been buying support near the end of the war; if so, the price was a continuing position in the military-feudal structure of Valencia.

Somehow this family lost control of the fiefs by 1270, perhaps because of involvement in the obscure troubles of the 1260's. King James dismantled Finestrat castle so that it could never be turned against him, but rebels were to rebuild it toward the end of his reign. All three fiefs went in free alod to Berengaria Alfonso, the king's current mistress, on August 21, 1270. How highly James valued them appears from his provision that they constitute the inheritance of any male bastards resulting from his arrangement with Berengaria, but that otherwise they were to revert to the crown. Transfer of Orcheta, along with Serra and Mola, to the Knights of Santiago before a year was out underlined the military importance of these castles, as the substitution of Mogente castle to Berengaria showed their equivalent economic value. The transfer document reveals previous ownership of all three by Sa'd from the defunct at-Tīfāshī. Yet the family retained some royal favor. In July 1270 the king gave a large land grant of thirty cafizes, plus a town plaza for building-projects at Xielsa, to Muḥammad b. Zabr "nephew of at-Tīfāshī."[43] We can leave Muḥammad here on his peaceful estates. Seven years later he will be ruling his castles once more, an independent rebel around whom the failing Great Revolt will rally. By that time his name and documentation will be linked with those of another hero, Ibrāhīm, to whose story in the next chapter we must defer this final episode of Muḥammad's life.

41 Arch. Crown, James I, Reg. Canc. 16, fol. 208 (Aug. 26, 1270).

42 *Itinerari*, pp. 274-275, 278.

43 Arch. Crown, James I, Reg. Canc. 16, fol. 258 (April 9, 1271): "que quidem castra et villas . . . adquisivimus ab Azeth filio Timçi[n] [Tivitin?] quondam et a quibusdam aliis Sarracenis." Martínez-Ferrando's catalogue gives "ab Azeth" incorrectly as Ali Azech; the dead father's name, the Tevicino above, is difficult to make out here. Azeth is the Çahat above. The grant to "Abenzabre . . . nepoti Tovicini" is on fol. 208 (July 26, 1270). The original grant to Berengaria is on fol. 205 (Aug. 21, 1270).

Farther north, in its own range of hills, stood another fiefdom. This was Tárbena, which had formed part of a more complex domain under the mountain princeling al-Azraq until 1244. Detached then during a general settlement or pacification of the most southerly part of Valencia kingdom, it fell under the overlordship of King James's heir Alfonso but probably retained its ruling *qā'id*. Involved in the decade of guerrilla wars ending in 1258, Tárbena castle was bestowed by the crown in 1259, along with its valley, dependent castles, towns, and district, to Muḥammad 'Amr b. Isḥāq (Emnebenezach). During the previous two years the crown had administered the castle through bailiffs, a circumstance suggesting connection with the 1258 revolt.[44] The wide holdings of the *qā'id* Muḥammad, and his brother the *qā'id* of Castell, emerge from a number of documents. In 1264 a division was made between Muḥammad and his nephew Bakrūn (Bocharon) for the castles and places of Tárbena, Algar, and Alenz.[45] Soon afterward the crown reconfirmed the castle's command to Muḥammad, half the revenues going to the crown. The grant included "the whole castle completely of Tárbena, with the settlements, countryside, and appurtenances, and with all rights belonging to the same." It was qualified "in such wise that of all the revenues and profits of this castle (a proper fee having been deducted for guarding the said castle) we are to get half, and you and yours to get the other half, without any opposition."[46] At the

[44] *Ibid.*, Reg. Canc. 10, fol. 109v (April 4, 1259). "Emnebenezach" is quite clear in the documents; the element Emn- is difficult to reckon with, though equivalents may be suggested, like 'Amr, 'Āmir, Amīn, or Amān. The crown porter Bonanat served as administrator and tax-farmer here from early 1257, and a successor from April of 1258. On the 1244 transfer, see below, pp. 325-326.

[45] *Ibid.*, Reg. Canc. 13, fol. 188v (June 17, 1264): a long contract "prout in carta sarracenis facta" to "Mahomet Emnebenezach alcaydum de Tarbana fratrem alcaydi de Castielo olim defuncti," concerning the castle, a village with its mills, a place, three more villages, "et aliis bonis . . . possessionibus quas tu . . . et frater tuus quondam habebatis in regno Valencie." Some towns belonging to him in the Calpe district appear in Reg. 10, fol. 109v (April 8, 1259). There is also a charter of protection for the *qā'id* accompanying the first document (June 17, 1264). Castiel was probably Castell, west of Tárbena and until recently a stronghold of al-Azraq; Castalla, far to the west, seems a less likely choice.

[46] *Ibid.*, fol. 236 (Nov. 5, 1264). "Damus et concedimus vobis alcaydo Mahomat et vestris totum castrum integriter de Tarbana cum alqueriis terminis et pertinentiis suis et cum omnibus iuribus eiusdem. Ita tamen quod de omnibus redditibus et exitibus ipsius castri deducta competenti missione ad opus custodie dicti castri de communi, habeamus nos medietatem et vos et vestri aliam medietatem libere et sine aliqua contradiccione."

same time Muḥammad received as a present the village of Ayot near Castell and a formal dispensation from any civil or criminal proceedings the crown could initiate for past transgressions. This aristocrat survived Valencian alarums and rebellions for some years yet.[47]

After the rebel al-Azraq had come and gone, one might have expected to see Muḥammad and Bakrūn enter upon length of days as the king's good soldiers; but they apparently implicated themselves in a Valencian extension of the Murcian revolt, along with other Mudejar feudatories, and had to leave the country under safe-conduct.[48] King James gave their fief of Tárbena in 1268 to Berengaria Alfonso and her potential issue, a gift paralleling her acquisition of the at-Tīfāshī fiefs two years later. Taken with the expulsion of Tárbena's owners, the episode points to local troubles connected with the Murcian revolt of 1265-1266.[49] The Tárbena aljama persisted, though no longer as a Mudejar fief; another Muḥammad became its leader around 1273, but as a subordinate to Christian administrators of the region. Probably it was Muḥammad who raised this region in revolt in 1276 and then held it against Kings James and Peter in turn. Peter determined to bring Tárbena down by ravaging the countryside; when his forces proved unequal to the task, he had to draft 1,700 militia with axes from a dozen Valencian cities like Burriana, Castellón, and Liria, "so as to subjugate them to our mind and will."[50]

47 *Ibid.*, fols. 236-236v (both of same date).

48 A safeguard-passport of 1268 for the ex-*qā'id* of Tárbena and his kin is *ibid.*, Reg. Canc. 15, fol. 99v.

49 *Ibid.*, fol. 105v (May 4, 1268). A previous instruction shows that Muḥammad had lost it somewhat earlier (Reg. 14, fol. 95, April 5). James may have purchased the castle or made compensation; an accounting for three years' expenses up to May 1268 lists 12,000 solidi paid for it in the king's name to Muḥammad, either as full or partial payment (fol. 97 [May 1, 1268]). A document referring to the flight of Muḥammad and Bakrūn lists the villages of the Jalón Valley in their holding as Albayreni, Albinyen, Alibayt, Algar, Alquellelm, Atrayello, Arrahal, Azahut, Benixaloni, Cotar, Duran, Rahal Abencurbulin, Rahal Alhanegin, Muscayra, and Sata (fol. 105v, May 4).

50 Arch. Crown, James I, Reg. Canc. 19, fol. 18 (June 14, 1273); this new Muḥammad was "Abenhalair." The *qā'id* or *qāḍī* Muḥammad, who recurs in a dozen documents, is not always the same man. During the war-scare leading to the 1275 revolt, King James ordered the castle of Tárbena, along with those of Alcalá, Gallinera, Penacadell, and Penáguila, to be provisioned by their Christian castellans for two months; see the "Sección de documentos," ed. Roque Chabás, *El archivo*, IV (1890), 311, doc. 41 (March 4, 1275). The final quotation is from Soldevila,

The castle of Tous apparently remained in Mudejar hands at first; a raiding party from Tous, Tárbena, and Carcer, by defeating a Christian patrol around 1243, broke the feudal homage sworn by their overlord of Játiva and gave King James his pretext for reducing the military power of Játiva's *qā'id*.[51] James took Tous either then or after one of the subsequent rebellions, since he disposed of it to Peter Zapata of Alcira in 1265 as part of a land exchange. Zapata continued to hold it through King Peter's reign, except for a stormy hiatus during the final revolts.[52] In 1275 the last Mudejar revolt found its center for a time at Tous; local Muslims seized Tous castle, refused the king's summons to disgorge it, and used ten days' feudal grace to prepare for siege until invaders from abroad could arrive. Perhaps the seizure was nominal—a reversal of allegiance by a Mudejar garrison only formally under the control of a Christian castellan—since James says only that "the Saracens of Tous had revolted, and [its] castle."[53] The subsequent fate of Tous appears as an echo in a revenue instruction of 1279, when King Peter rebuked a collector who made "the Saracens of Tous pay more than the amount for which they were assessed for the castles, which I granted them at the time they restored the castle of Tous." They had surrendered on terms, and were holding unnamed castles, plural but presumably less strategic.[54]

The history of Carmogente castle is a puzzle. With its greater neighbor Mogente it acknowledged the overlordship of Játiva, itself a vassal of King James. Like Mogente it stood further southwest

Pere el Gran, part 2, I, appendix, doc. 63 (April 26, 1277): "ut reduceremus eos ad nostrum intellectum et voluntatem."

[51] *Llibre dels feyts*, ch. 333. The text gives Terrabona, uncorrected by the editors; Tárbena appears nowhere else in the king's memoirs. Terrabona recurs in archival records, and Tous appears under variants like Thoves or Tovos, so that medieval Valencia gains two nonexistent towns. These formed separate enclaves of early Mudejar power, merely cooperating with Játiva in the raid—"ab los moros que eren de Tous, e de Terrabona e de Carcel."

[52] Arch. Crown, James I, Reg. Canc. 14, fol. 75v (July 20, 1265); Peter III, Reg. Canc. 71, fol. 141v (June 21, 1283). Its lord was a relative of the Agnes Zapata who subsequently became mistress of King Peter.

[53] *Llibre dels feyts*, ch. 54.

[54] Arch. Crown, Peter III, Reg. Canc. 41, fol. 62v (April 23, 1279): "intelleximus quod Iacobus Panicerii compellit sarracenos de Tous ad solvendum pro castris que ipsis sarracenis concessimus tempore quo restituerunt castrum de Tous ultra quantitatem pro qua taxati fuerunt."

THE KINGDOM OF VALENCIA

The Antonio Cavanilles Map of 1795

First sections: the north

Second sections: the south

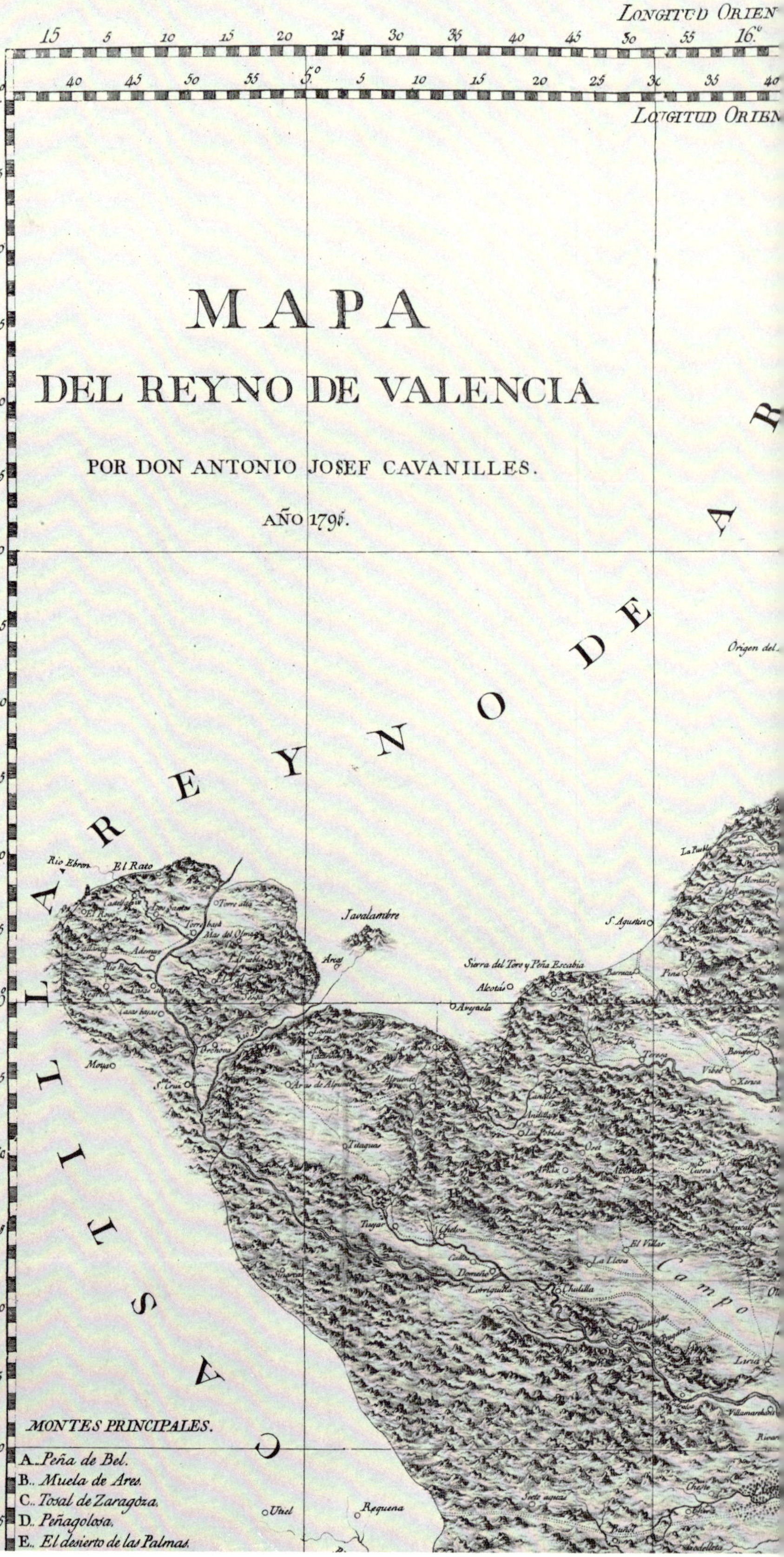
LONGITUD ORIEN
MAPA
DEL REYNO DE VALENCIA
POR DON ANTONIO JOSEF CAVANILLES.
AÑO 1795.
REYNO DE AR
CASTILLA
Javalambre
Sierra del Toro y Peña Escabia
Origen del
El Rato
Rio Ebron
Campo
MONTES PRINCIPALES.
A.. Peña de Bel.
B.. Muela de Ares.
C.. Tosal de Zaragoza.
D.. Peñagolosa.
E.. El desierto de las Palmas.
Utiel
Requena
Chelva
Chulilla
Liria
Villamarchant
Chiva
S. Agustin
Pina
Arcos
Alcotás
Titaguas
La Losa
Moya

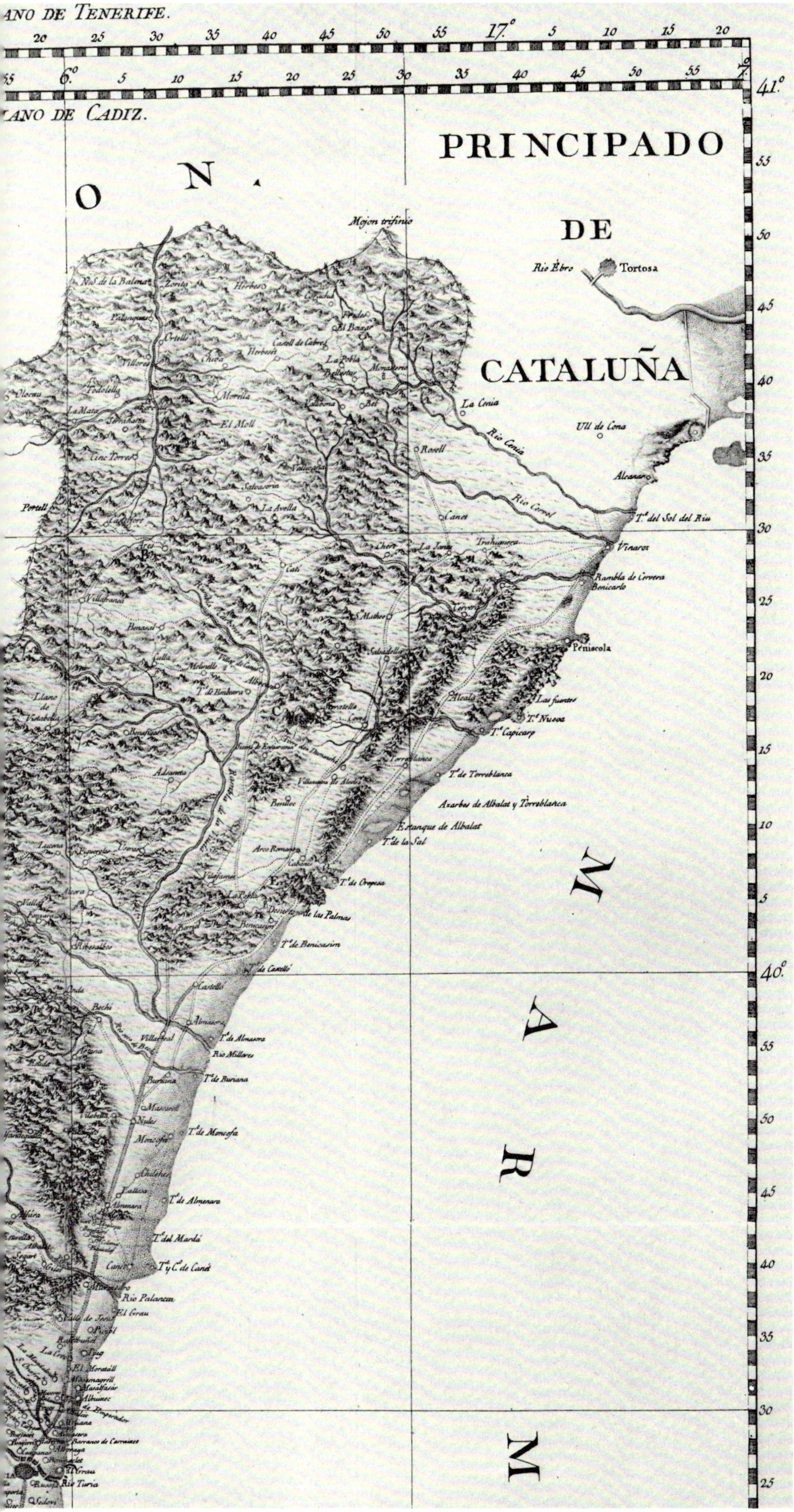
ANO DE TENERIFE.
LANO DE CADIZ.
O N
PRINCIPADO
DE
CATALUÑA
Mojon trifinio
Rio Ebro
Tortosa
La Cenia
Rio Cenia
Ull de Cona
Rosell
Alcanar
Rio Cervol
Canet
T.e del Sol del Riu
Vinaroz
Rambla de Cervera
Benicarlo
Peñiscola
Morella
El Moll
La Avella
Cati
Chert
Traiguera
Villafranca
Alcala
Las fuentes
T.e Nueva
T.e Capicorp
T.e de Torreblanca
Azarbes de Albalat y Torreblanca
Estanque de Albalat
T.e de la Sal
T.e de Oropesa
de las Palmas
T.e de Benicasim
de Castelló
Castelló
Almasora
T.e de Almasora
Rio Millares
Villareal
Buriana
T.e de Buriana
T.e de Moncofa
Moncofa
T.e de Almenara
Almenara
T.e del Mardá
T. y C.e de Canet
Canet
Rio Palancia
El Grau
Rio Turia
M A R M

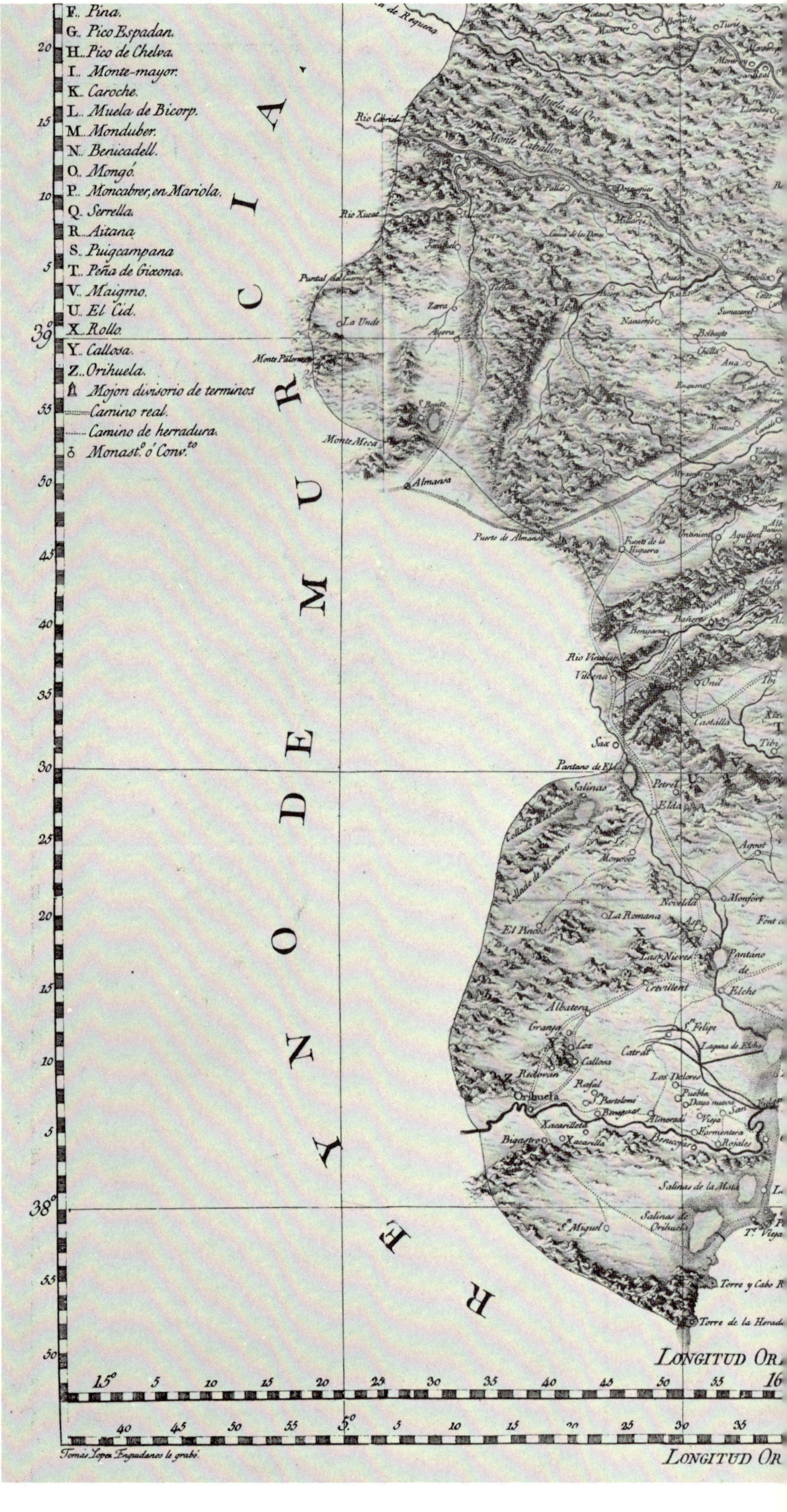
F.. Pina.
G.. Pico Espadan.
H.. Pico de Chelva.
I.. Monte-mayor.
K.. Caroche.
L.. Muela de Bicorp.
M.. Monduber.
N.. Benicadell.
O.. Mongó.
P.. Moncabrer, en Mariola.
Q.. Serrella.
R.. Aitana.
S.. Puigcampana
T.. Peña de Gixona.
V.. Maigmo.
U.. El Cid.
X.. Rollo.
Y.. Callosa.
Z.. Orihuela.
Mojon divisorio de terminos
Camino real.
Camino de herradura.
Monast.o ó Conv.to
REYNO DE MURCIA.
Rio Cabriel
Muela del Oro
Monte Caballon
Rio Xucar
Puntal del Cuervo
La Unde
Zarra
Ayora
Monte Palomera
S. Benito
Monte Meca
Almansa
Puerto de Almansa
Fuente de la Higuera
Ontinient
Aguillent
Bolbayte
Chella
Ana
Enguera
Benejama
Bañeres
Rio Vinalop
Villena
Onil
Castalla
Sax
Pantano de Elda
Salinas
Petrel
Elda
Monover
Agost
Novelda
Monfort
La Romana
Asp
El Pinoso
Las Nieves
Pantano de Elche
Crevillent
Elche
Albatera
S.n Felipe
Granja
Cox
Callosa
Catral
Laguna de Elche
Redovan
Los Dolores
Orihuela
Rafal
S. Bartolomé
Benejuzar
Almoradi
Xacarilleta
Bigastro
Xacarilla
Benicofar
Formentera
Rojales
Salinas de la Mata
S.n Miguel
Salinas de Orihuela
T.e Vieja
Torre y Cabo
Torre de la Horada
LONGITUD OR
Tomás Lopez Enguidanos le grabó.
LONGITUD OR

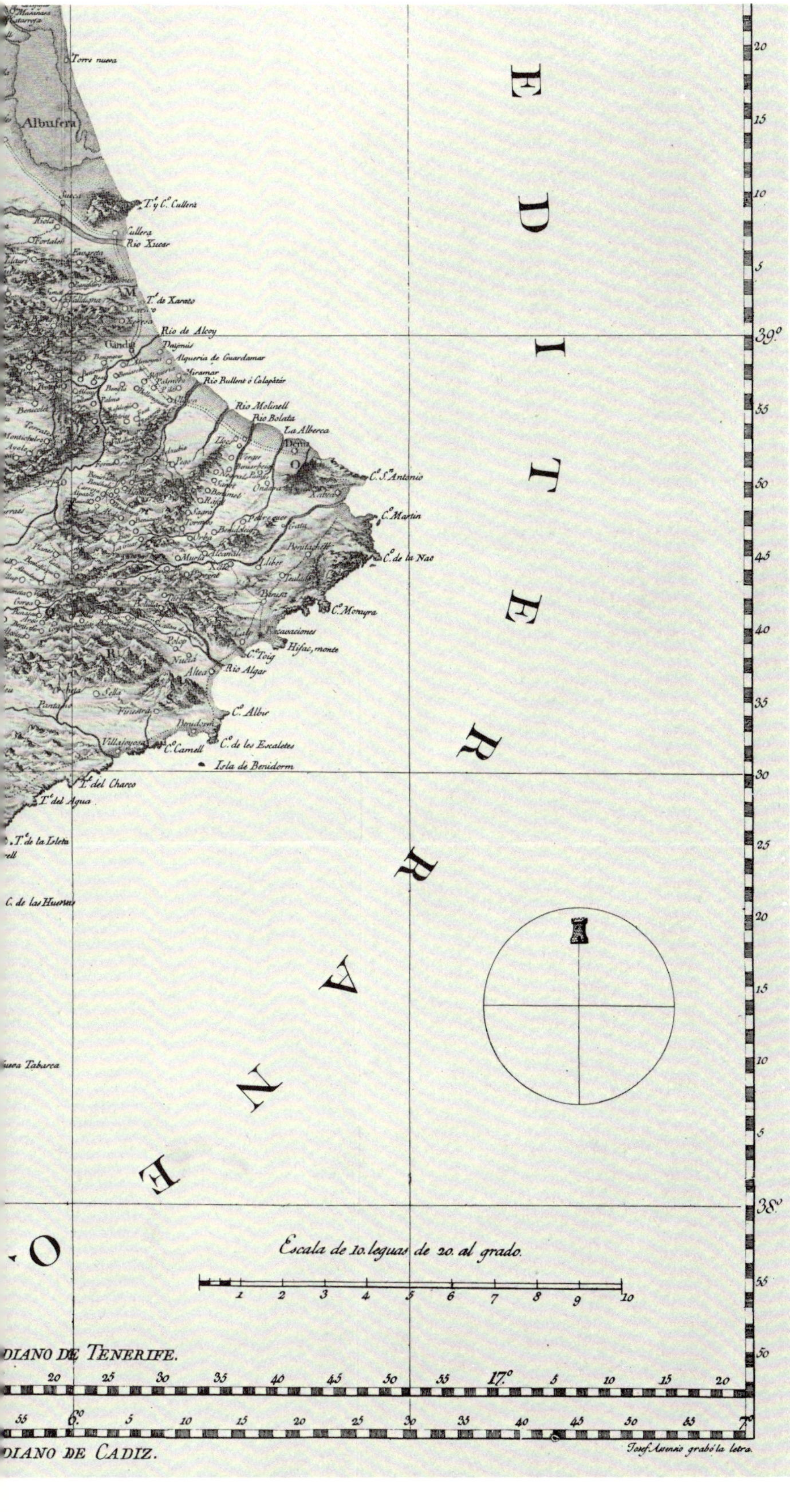

Torre nueva
Albufera
Sueca
T. y C.o Cullera
Cullera
Rio Xucar
Fortaleni
T. de Xarato
Rio de Alcoy
Gandia
Alqueria de Guardamar
Miramar
Rio Bullent ó Calapàtàr
Rio Molinell
Rio Bolata
La Alberca
Denia
C.o S.n Antonio
Xabea
C.o Martin
C.o de la Nao
C.o Morayra
Excavaciones
Hifac, monte
C.o Toig
Rio Algar
Altea
Sella
C.o Albir
Benidorm
Villajoyosa
C.o Camell
C.o de les Escaletes
Isla de Benidorm
T.e del Charco
T.e del Agua
T.e de la Isleta
C. de las Huertas
Nueva Tabarca
M E D I T E R R A N E O
Escala de 10. leguas de 20. al grado.
1 2 3 4 5 6 7 8 9 10
39.o
38.o
17.o
6.o
7.o
DIANO DE TENERIFE.
DIANO DE CADIZ.
Josef Asensio grabó la letra.

PORTFOLIO OF

THIRTEENTH-CENTURY SPANISH MUSLIMS

The *Cántigas*, or "Songs in Praise of St. Mary," constructed under the personal direction of King Alfonso X, the Learned, of Castile, ranks with the contemporary masterpieces of Aquinas and Dante. Like a Gothic cathedral it interweaves a corpus of troubadour poetry to Our Lady, centering upon immemorial Miracle legends common to Christendom, with a corpus of troubadour music, including Arabic airs and rhythms—all illustrated by a heroic prodigality of 1,262 miniatures. The earliest edition dates from "after 1255"; ours is from "after 1259."

Done by various artists at cities like Murcia, Seville, and Toledo, each episode of six panels (followed left to right like a comic strip) blazes with color. A mirror held up to daily life in the thirteenth century, the pictures comprise as well "an esthetic Bible, encyclopedically condensing all the elements of medieval art" (Marcelino Menéndez-Pelayo). The present portfolio isolates the principal Moorish and Mudejar episodes, reflecting the costumes, weaponry, attitudes, mores, and acculturative details abundantly visible around the artists. Realism overrides convention, so that scholars are able to document medieval artifacts and architecture from these miniatures. The paintings also convey the juxtaposition of two cultures, in its climate of violence.

The miniatures here are reproduced from the manuscript collection of the monastery library at the Escorial, north of Madrid. For the explanations provided on the next pages, the panel sequence within each episode has been identified alphabetically, A through F; for double panels, the sequence in part 2 continues then from G through L.

Cántiga 46. *Muslim Raiders and Virgin's Picture.* Muslim raiders overrun Christians, seizing cattle (A), returning joyfully (B) to divide the loot, including arms, vessels, and cloth (C). The leader chooses a painting of the Virgin, visiting it daily in his home with reverence (D). The image feeds the child; milk flows from both breasts (E), thus converting the entire region (F). Note four Negroes (A, C), turbans for dignitaries (C), flocks of goats, sheep, and cows (B), the medieval nude and the baptismal form (F), the European armament favored by many Spanish Moors (A), and the Arabic inscription on the left-hand curtain (D).

Cántiga 63. *Battle between Christians and Muslims.* The local lord, Count García, welcomes a pious but absent-minded knight (with zebra-striped contingent), come to help defeat al-Manṣūr (A). Missing the battle because of his custom of hearing three Masses (B), he is saved from embarrassment by a miraculous counterpart who leads the action (C, D), and is hailed as hero by the returning count (E), so all thank the Virgin (F). Note how the action "crosses" to make one picture of C and D, and the fine Negro head (D).

Cántiga 83. *Muslims Capture and Mistreat a Christian.* Raiders snatch a Christian from Lucena into captivity (A), mistreating him (B). His prayers to the Virgin (C) strike the irons from his neck and hypnotize the guards, and he walks out carrying his chains (D) as an ex-voto to leave at Mary's shrine, where he dictates an account to a scribe (E), offering a Mass of thanksgiving as church bells ring (F). Note costume detail and two Moors without the usual beards (A), the "double action" where the protagonist appears twice, and the Negroes as relief guards (D).

Cántiga 99. *Invaders Flee Supernatural Vengeance.* Muslims siege a Spanish city (A), raising their tents and encircling the defenders (B), attacking fiercely (C), until they break in, destroying altars and images (D). While attempting to harm the Virgin's image some conquerors drop dead (E); the rest flee the town fearfully (F). Note the Negro heads, one with white beard (D, F), infantry forces and banners (A), shield positions and the crossbow contingents for which Spanish Islam was noted (C), the Moorish gate on the Christian town and other architectural details (A, D), pickaxes (D), portable tents (F), and Arabic inscription on the banner (C, F).

Cántiga 95. *Hermit Foils Islamic Raiding Fleet.* A rare double set of twelve panels shows a German count settling at a seaside shrine in Portugal (A) to serve the Virgin as a holy hermit (B), generously feeding her pilgrims (C) until captured while fishing (D). With the hermit below decks (E), the raiding fleet is constantly blown back to the same spot (F). The Muslims bring him up (G); offer gold and gifts; he accepts a crystal goblet (H); they restore him to the shrine, never afterwards daring to molest him (I). They go home (J); the hermit spreads the story (K); and crowds increase at the shrine (L). Note eating utensils (C), Negro portraits (D, F, J), details of galley construction, and the theme of sea peril.

Cántiga 126. *Moorish Crossbowman Wounds Elche Citizen.* At Elche in Murcia, at the frontier of the Valencia kingdom, a Muslim crossbowman pierces a citizen's neck (A). Physicians prove unable to remove the quarrel or arrow-bullet by forceps (B), nor can they shoot it out with a crossbow reversed (C). Carried to a Marian shrine (D) the victim repents and prays (E) until the Virgin appears with two angels to cure him (F). Note the banner with Arabic and the characteristic palms designating Elche.

Cántiga 167. *Death of a Mudejar Baby in Aragon.* A Mudejar family at Borgia in Aragon sees its infant son die (A), but has recourse to the Virgin, fashioning a wax image of their child as ex-voto (B). Father and mother transport the coffin on muleback (C) to put the corpse and ex-voto at the Virgin's shrine, where they spend the night (D). On the third day the Virgin revives the child (E), which results in the family's conversion (F). Note the women's dress and hair (A, F), the Europeanized Mudejar styles in the north (C), and the manner of baptizing (F).

Cántiga 169. *Murcian Mudejars Attack a Church.* A Marian church in the Arrixaca quarter of Islamic Murcia attracts Genoese, Pisan, and Sicilian merchants (A). Prince Alfonso of Castile masters Murcia and protects the church

(B). King James of Aragon, after subduing a revolt (for Castile), and as recompense for making the major mosque the cathedral, yields to the Muslims' plea to have this church destroyed (C). Unable, they later win this privilege from Alfonso, now Castile's king (D), but their puppet-king Ibn Hūd refuses confirmation, reverencing Mary (E). During a revolt they labor to harm the church and again cannot (F). Note the contemporary portraits and costume of James, Alfonso, and Ibn Hūd (B, C, D, E) and the puppet's throne or Hispano-Islamic chair and curled shoes (E).

Cántiga 176. *Prisoner Escapes Islamic Majorca.* A Christian languishing in prison on this Balearic island promises a pilgrimage if freed (A). The Virgin appears (B) and leads him safely through the Islamic city and away (C, D). Bearing a wax image of himself as ex-voto, the pilgrim fulfills his vow (E, F). Note light boats (*batel* type as in *Cántiga* 183) (A to D), unveiled women (A to C), types of headdress (C), and city battlements.

Cántiga 181. *Muslims Battle Muslims in Morocco.* Opposing forces preparing for battle in Morocco are encamped (A) under their respective Muslim leaders (B). One faction fights under the Virgin's banner (C, D) and, of course, wins (E, F). Note the setting up of tents (A), the heraldry and armament (E, F), the ruler's pillow unlike the Murcian Muslim's throne in *Cántiga* 169 (B), and the two examples of crossover action shared by neighboring panels (C-D, E-F).

Cántiga 183. *Muslim Fishermen Suffer Disaster.* A stone statue of the Virgin at the seashore near the Islamic town of Faro (A) is contemptuously thrown into the sea by Muslims (B). The town's fishermen can make no catch (C), until the culprits recover the statue and display it honorably on the town wall (D). The fish return immediately (E), in greater abundance than ever (F). Note fishing boats, nets, costume, and technique (C, E, F) and architectural details.

Cántiga 185. *Granada King Driven from a Jaén Castle.* This double set of panels is sited at Chincoya castle in Jaén (A), whose castellan is a friend of the Moorish castellan of Belmez (B). The Belmez lord can therefore inform Granada's king that only fifteen men garrison Chincoya, low on rations (C). Granada's king sallies to seize this prize (D, E). Meanwhile the Belmez Moor rides out with two of his knights (F) to meet his Christian friend (G), but kidnaps him (H). Granadan armies siege Chincoya (I), but the Virgin's image brought to the battlements routs them (J), defending the castle like a good castellan (K), until the Granadan king ignominiously flees (L). The song's refrain has an oddly modern ring: "Power to St. Mary!" Note the king's pillow-throne, the Arabic on Granada's banner, and the heraldic flags.

Cántiga 192. *Negro Mudejar Wrestles with the Devil.* A good Christian lord unflaggingly attempts to convert his unbelieving captive from Almeria (A). In prison the Muslim wrestles with and bites the devil (B). An apparition of the Virgin rescues the Moor, urging conversion (C). The grateful Negro tells the lord, who adds his own pleas (D), until the captive seeks baptism (E), becoming a fervent Christian (F). Note the Negro portrait, especially in D, and compare the baptismal scene with previous baptisms.

Cántiga 46. Muslim Raiders and Virgin's Picture

Cántiga 63. Battle between Christians and Muslims

Cántiga 83. Muslims Capture and Mistreat a Christian

Cántiga 99. Invaders Flee Supernatural Vengeance

Cántiga 95. Hermit Foils Islamic Raiding Fleet (pt. 1)

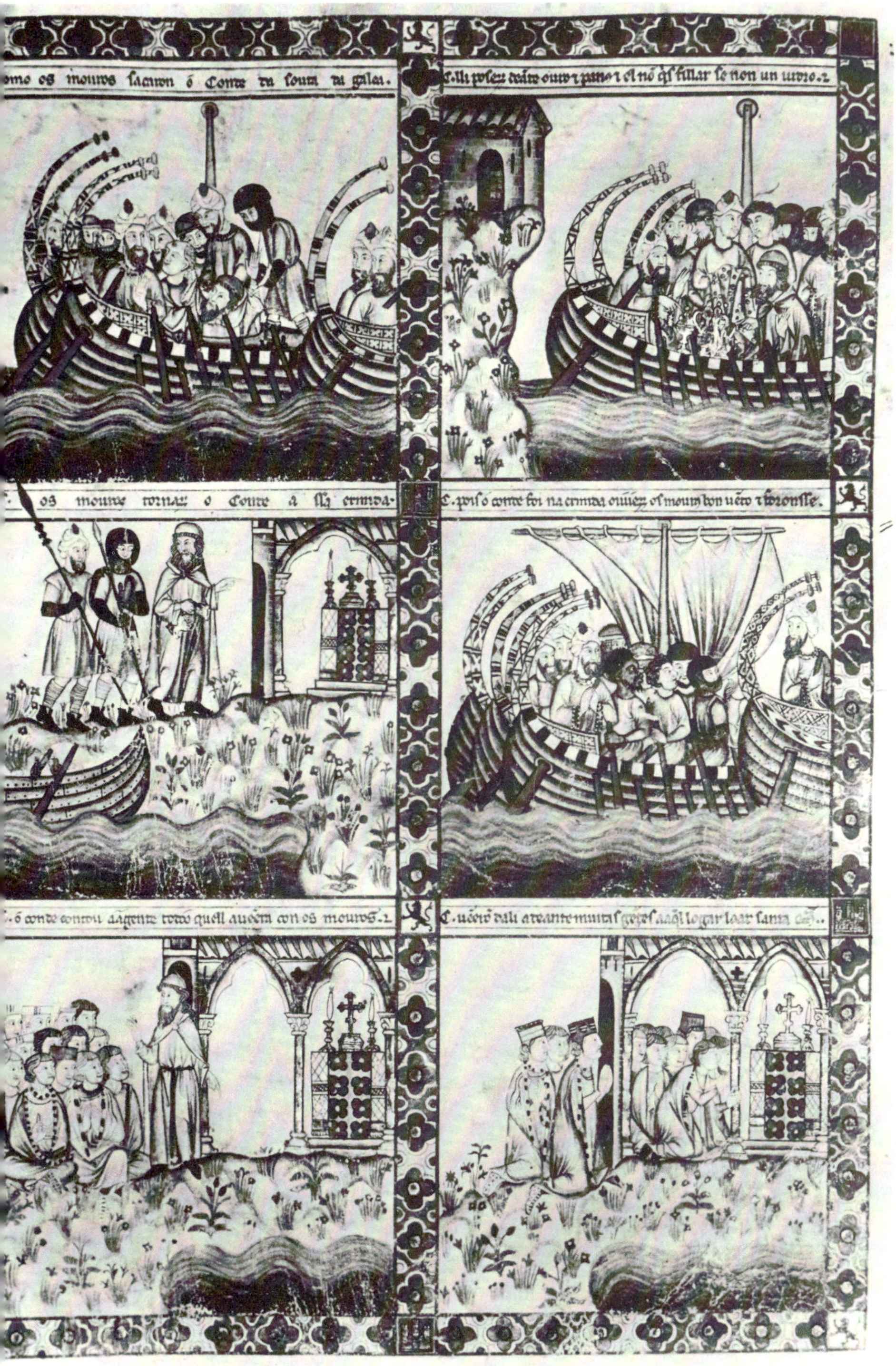

Cántiga 95 (pt. 2)

Cántiga 126. Moorish Crossbowman Wounds Elche Citizen

Cántiga 167. Death of a Mudejar Baby in Aragon

Cántiga 169. Murcian Mudejars Attack a Church

Cántiga 176. Prisoner Escapes Islamic Majorca

Cántiga 181. Muslims Battle Muslims in Morocco

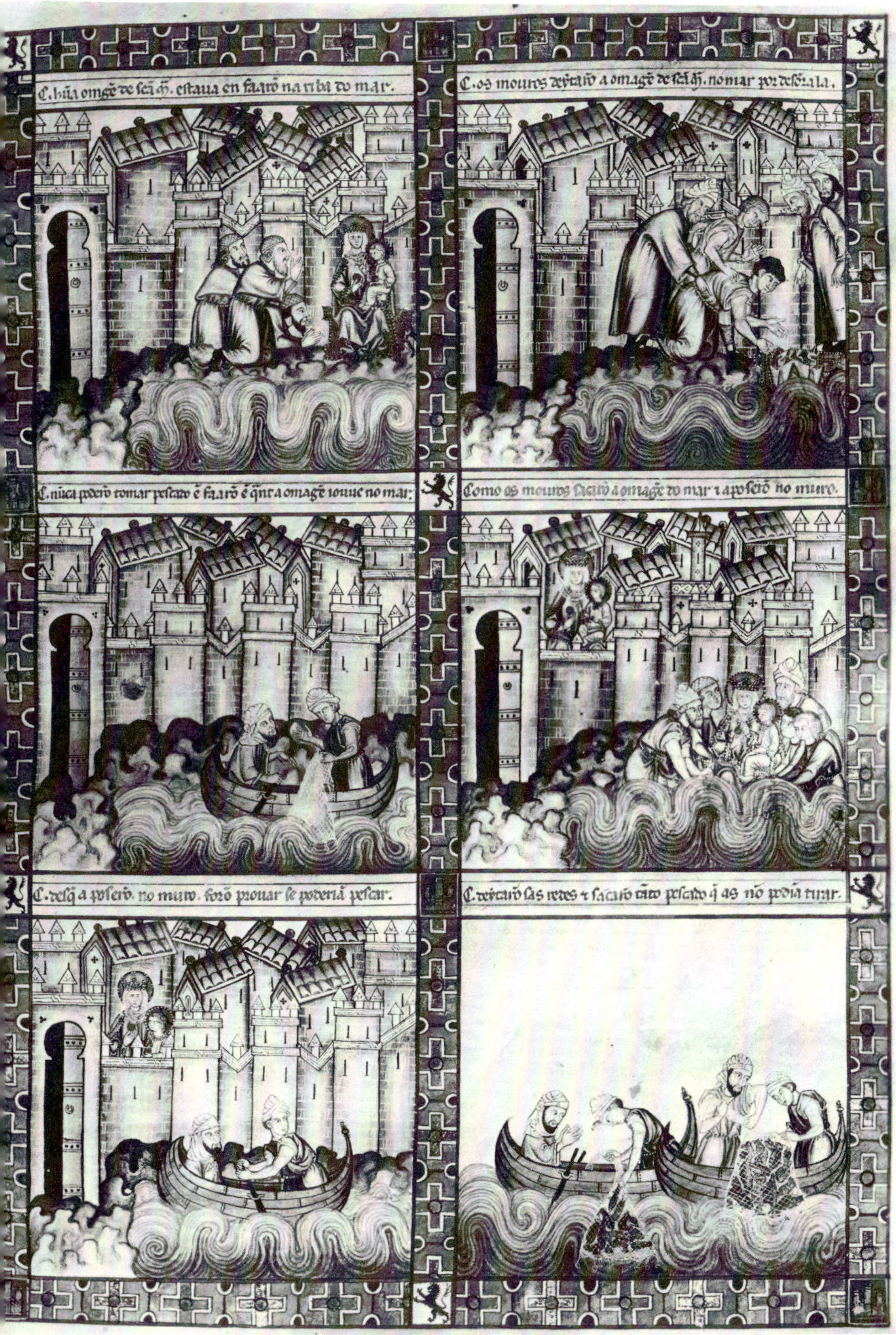

Cántiga 183. Muslim Fishermen Suffer Disaster

Cántiga 185. Granada King Driven from a Jaén Castle (pt. 1)

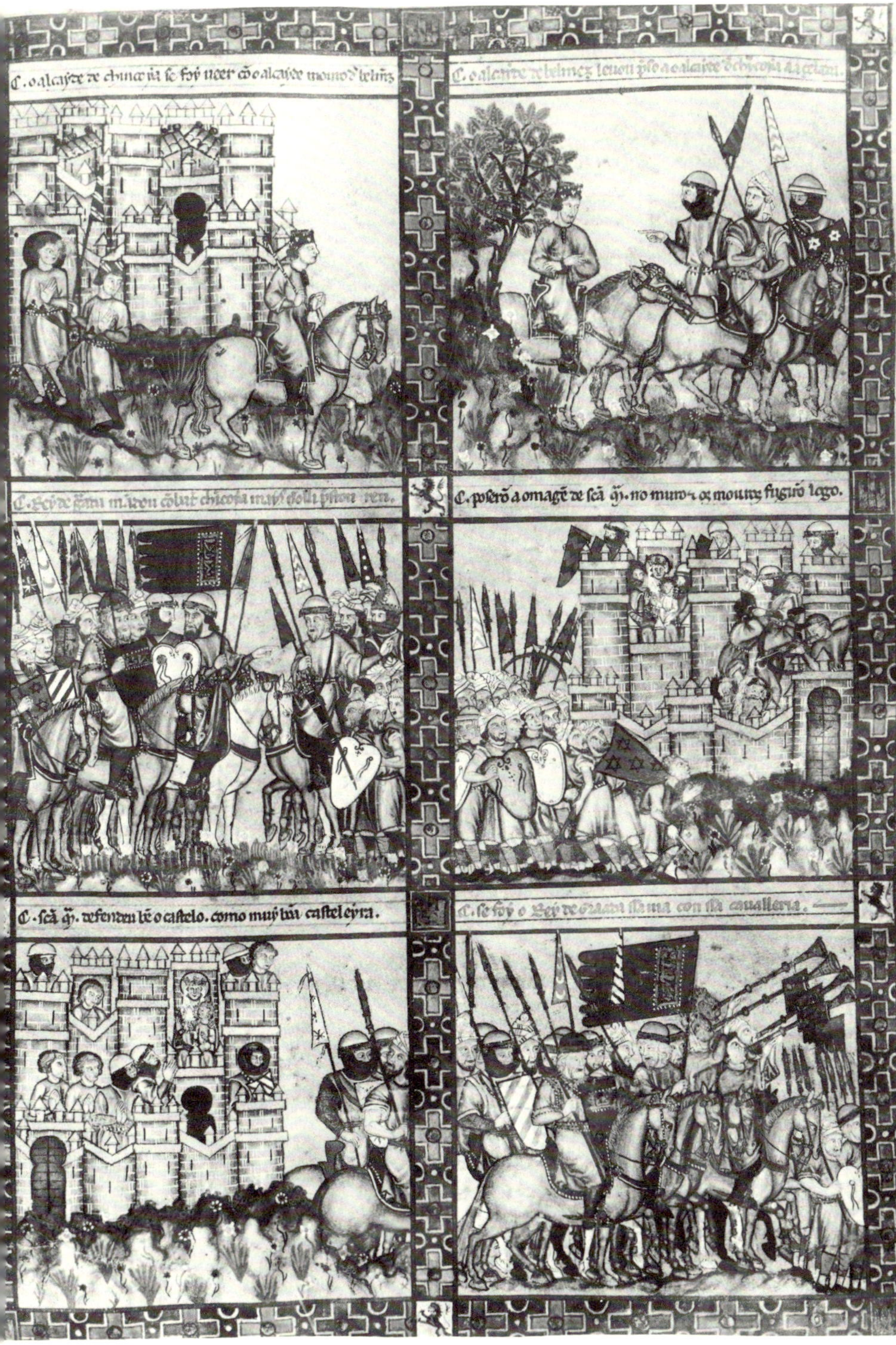

Cántiga 185 (pt. 2)

Cántiga 192. Negro Mudejar Wrestles with the Devil

MISCELLANY OF CHESS MINIATURES

Three miniatures, illustrating chess moves, from the *Libro de Ajedrez* codex, a game-book produced for Alfonso X, the Learned, at Seville in 1283. Its 150 miniatures, remarkably realistic, reflect the Muslims seen by the Christian artist(s) in southern and eastern Spain, especially at Seville and Murcia. Illustrations from the manuscript collection of the monastery library at the Escorial.

Mudejars explaining a chess move. Note details of the turbans and robes, which in Spain suggested men of importance, the curled shoes, and the full beards that custom and Castilian law alike imposed on Mudejars.

Three women at chess. Note hair styles, jewelry, clothing, and musical instrument.

Negro gentlemen at chess. Rachel Arié rightly dismisses Julián Ribera's suggestion that they are conventional symbols for "Moor." Most Moors in these pictures are white, and the prevailing tone of the artist is realistic; furthermore, by this time there were Christian Negroes. Note domestic utensils, veils, and musical instrument.

down the valley commanded by Montesa, and supported that center. During the king's siege of Játiva in 1244, the Mogente region preferred to become tributary to Castile. James fiercely blocked the move, and by the general settlement of Almizra took over Mogente-Carmogente.[55] Perhaps Carmogente remained a Mudejar castle; perhaps it went to Berengaria Alfonso along with Mogente in 1271; or perhaps the Knights of Santiago briefly acquired it.[56] Whether as a Mudejar survival or a rebel's nest, Carmogente surfaces in the documentation at the end of King James's reign, controlled by Abū Sa'īd b. Qābīl (Abucezit Abencablia), a man whose previous appearance in the Christian records had been as recipient of gifts. This *qā'id* eventually surrendered, on the promise of estates, sometime before November 1276, by which time the Santiago Knights were provisioning the castle for war.[57] True to his word, King Peter in 1279 ordered his "faithful subjects the castellan and bailiff of Mogente" to give Abū Sa'īd "the estate which belonged to Faḍl 'Abd as-Salām [Hadel Assalom] and his wife," because the ex-*qā'id* "surrendered to us the castle of Carmogente which he held at the time of the past war."[58] The castle's days of glory ended with the *qā'id* Abū Sa'īd.

[55] *Llibre dels feyts,* chs. 341, 349.

[56] As early as April 1257 Santiago had rights in the Carmogente countryside ("in quacumque parte volueritis infra terminos castri de Carmuxen"); a general shuffling of Santiago castles in southern Valencia around 1270 may have involved Carmogente too; see the documents cited in Burns, *Crusader Valencia,* I, 178, and II, 455.

[57] Arch. Crown, Peter III, Reg. Canc. 38, fol. 95v (Nov. 30, 1276). The name also recalls Spanish antecedents like al-Kalbī, borne by two of the first emirs, and the Banū Hābīl, originally of Jaén, as well as al-Habalī and distortions of initial Galb-.

[58] *Ibid.,* Reg. Canc. 42, fol. 122 (July 31, 1279). "Fidelibus suis alcaydo et baiulo de Moxen salutem et gratiam. Cum nos dederimus et assignaverimus Abucezit Abencablia tenenti tunc castrum de Carmoxen hereditatem que fuit Hadel Assalom et uxoris eius situm in termino de Moxen cum domibus et aliis ad ipsam hereditatem pertinentibus, eo quod nobis reddidit dictum castrum de Carmoxen quod tenebet tempore guerre . . . preterite, mandamus vobis quatenus visis presentibus tradatis dicto Abuçeyt hereditatem et domos predictas ac ipsum faciatis easdem habere et tenere et pacifice possidere." The contradictory spellings Abucezit and Abuçeyt (Abū Zayd) represent the manuscript versions; *tenenti tunc* is a dubious reading. In Reg. Canc. 48, fol. 145v (Sept. 10, 1280), Peter began a letter of protection: "mandamus vobis quatenus Abceyt Abincablia sarracenus." In James I, Reg. Canc. 10, fol. 79v (June 1, 1258), King James gave "per hereditatem propriam francham et liberam vobis Abzeit Avencablia . . . unicuique . . . domos et ii iovatas" of dry-farming land at Alcudia; given to this castellan while the king was besieging Alcalá, it may have been a bribe for good conduct or services.

The order kept it only briefly, then dismantled its defenses; in February 1301 James II allowed that they need not restore these.[59]

Though castles serve as a prime index of feudal status, many Mudejar aristocrats pursued an existence equally aristocratic on nonmilitary estates. Whether or not they fitted into the Christian feudalistic arrangement, they added solidarity to the nobiliary castellan group. In return for surrendering his region, Ibn Shu'ayb (Xuaip), the sheik who led the enemy at the battle of Inca and then rallied the mountain castles of Majorca, received such lands for himself and four kinsmen as would let him continue to "live as an aristocrat" ("onradament viure").[60] In Valencia likewise, the brother of the *qā'id* surrendered Játiva's lesser defenses for generous estates, "albeit in the plain."[61] King James did not stint in this kind of grant to Muslim beneficiaries; the status of these men shaded off into that of landowner-squire, but many might reasonably be aggregated to the higher classes.

Treatment of Mudejar castles requires reassessment of the influential memoir writer Desclot, whose interpretations have blocked off a clear view of the evidence. During the decade or two before the first al-Azraq revolt, Mudejars more commonly held castles than they subsequently did. King James "stripped all of the castles and tore down the defenses thereof and placed therein garrisons of Christian horsemen and footsoldiers, but the Saracens who tilled the soil remained." These skeleton garrisons facilitated a later take-over in the 1275 revolt.[62] Desclot describes his Saracens contemptuously as peasants who sheltered under the walls of Christian castles during a time

[59] Burns, *Crusader Valencia*, II, 455: "quod si Fratres ordinis Uclesii destruxerint seu destrui fecerint, castrum seu opus, quod est constructum in castro vocato Carmuxen sito in regno Valencie, quod non compellantur ad construendum seu reparandum castrum predictum."

[60] *Llibre dels feyts*, ch. 98: "e era lur cap Xuaip, qui era natural de Xurert"; ch. 113: "aquel que havien feyt cap e seyor, e havia nom Xuaip, e era estat de Xiver, de tots sarrains de les montayes e dels castells . . . ; iiii d·altres qui eren de son linyatge." Shu'ayb, a common name, is the Jethro of the Old Testament and Koran. In the Casacuberta edition the Old Catalan Xurert confronts the modern Catalan Xurest; a note on the map introducing vol. II confesses failure to identify it. Later in the text both become Xiver; can it be Chivert? For *onradament*, compare *honrat*, Chapter XIV, n. 9, and see Rodón Binué, *El lenguaje técnico*, pp. 141-142, where the word *honor*, commonly used for "fief," carries the connotation of worthy—land as a dignity or nobiliary gift.

[61] Desclot, *Crònica*, ch. 49.

[62] *Ibid.*, chs. 49, 67.

of marauding, discovered these to be lightly garrisoned, and seized "ten castles or more," besides besieging "a good two score castles." He confesses that King Peter had to regain "a great number of castles and towns." Montesa particularly was wrested from these tillers of the soil with difficulty; then all "who held castles in despite of the king," Desclot concludes, "surrendered these castles to the king and departed from the land."[63]

Desclot's careful narrative has influenced thinking on Mudejar history. Unfortunately, an unfair interpretation of the enemy's character distorted his view at this point; moreover he was generalizing from traumatic early episodes of the war, such as the seizure of Finestrat and Tous. When he wrote the early chapters, Valencia still rang with echoes of the war; rebel surrender lay only six years in the past, and the kingdom's reconstruction was in progress. When he finished the full work, the last stage of the rebellion was hardly more than a decade old. Desclot wrote as a participant shaken by this treason and far more shaken by its near success. Like King James in his autobiographical account of the first revolts, Desclot confected a justification and even propagandistic summary of the last revolt, his selection and coloring of the data reflecting equally his shock and outrage. Fortunately, as with the king's account of the first troubles, Desclot can be balanced by the addition of numerous bits of evidence. The result vindicates a monk-historian writing seventy years later, in the 1350's, as more objective on this point. The latter concluded that, "after the winning of the kingdom of Valencia from the Saracens by James, there remained many Saracens holding castles in the kingdom." In the rebellion at the end of the reign and the beginning of the next, "Peter with his vigorous campaigning took the aforesaid castles away from the Saracens."[64] All the evidence

[63] *Ibid.*, chs. 67, 74.

[64] *Crónica de San Juan de la Peña*, ch. 36. The Latin text edited by Antonio Ubieto Arteta (Valencia, 1961) reads: "remansissent plurimi sarraceni tenentes in eo castra et sibi post aliqua tempora rebellassent, capiendo et interficiendo christianos plurimos dicti regni, et demum in ipsa rebellatione christiani plurimi obiuissent." The edition by Tomás Ximénez de Embún, entitled *Historia de la corona de Aragón* (Zaragoza, 1876), ends: "christiani plurimum amisissent," with the parallel Romance: "muytos moros tenientes castiellos en aquell . . . se leuantoron et se alçoron . . . prendiendo muytos christianos del dito regno . . . e muytos christianos . . . hi fuessen muertos." See also the edition of the old Catalan text by A. J. Soberans Lleó, *Crònica general de Pere III el Cerimoniós* (Barcelona, 1961). A

shows Mudejar castles to have been surprisingly numerous. Their recovery by Christian authorities was neither inevitable nor precipitate. Transfer came only as a consequence of their repeatedly turning into a mortal danger, and then only at the cost of four decades of diplomatic and military toil.

Latin text was in circulation at least by 1359; the Catalan version existed by 1366, the Aragonese a few years later; our present Latin text, retranslated from a Romance version, may have been done by Guillem Nicolau. Desclot began his work in 1283, and after interruption took it up again in 1285, finishing it in 1288.

CHAPTER XIV

Patriot Mudejar Lords

STALKING THE elusive Mudejar lord through the thickets of alien Christian documentation is a thankless task. By the long view of history, the life-span of this class was brief; the most promising specimens fell soonest, victims of their patriot ideals or lust for power. Individual nobles become most visible at moments of crisis—toppling under the impact of the crusade, changing into tributaries, or yielding castles after a revolt. The average *qā'id* of the early Mudejar period, a power in his real world, enters history without name or personality. A whole range of nobiliary figures can be salvaged from the records, however, and fitted into their respective political scenes. These were, in modern terms, the patriot leaders, men who stood forth as natural champions, rallying their people against the Christian yoke. Some were fiery instigators of revolt, like al-Azraq. Others, like the Játiva dynasty, served as natural focus for dissident forces, magnetic presences reluctantly assuming the rebel role. Still others, outmaneuvered by King James's strategy, bided their time, ready to respond to the cry of revolt.

AL-AZRAQ, LORD OF ALCALÁ

The most famous Mudejar lord was al-Azraq, or The Blue.[1] The descriptive title meant "of light-blue eyes," but al-Azraq and its vari-

[1] On al-Azraq see *Llibre dels feyts*, chs. 334, 356, 361-364, 368-369, 371-374, 556. See also the brief studies by Roque Chabás, "Don Jaime el Conquistador y Alazrach," *El archivo*, IV (1890), 280-282; Julián Ribera y Tarragó, "El Blau?" *El archivo*, II (1887-1888), 19-20, and "Alazrach," *Disertaciones*, II, 298-300; Carmelo Giner Bolufer, "Valles de Pego," 46-74; and F. de P. Momblanch y Gonzálbez, "El rey D. Jaime y las guerras de Alazrach," repaged offprint, *VII Asamblea de cronistas del reino de Valencia* (Valencia, 1970). Salvador Sanpere y Miquel advanced the eccentric notion that al-Azraq was a Jew, entrusted by the papal legate in 1216 to make a truce with the Valencian Muslims, thus gaining the royal favor and castles from King James ("Minoría de Jaime I," *Congrés I*, pp. 604-605). He bases the argument on the Jew's name Azach (really Isaac), and on al-Azraq's name Yuan (explained below in text).

ant Zarqūn had likewise become both an ordinary name and a sobriquet like that borne by such contemporaries as The White and The Red.[2] Holder of a dozen castles with their subcastles and surrounding countrysides, al-Azraq was a charismatic figure, rallying Valencian Mudejars in a series of countercrusades. Like the Játiva *qā'id* who "kept a power of horse at salary," he could field a mercenary army; when his cash reserves ran low he was able to pay them by selling off his surplus wheat.[3] His status as military landowner might have remained hidden except for the accident of rebellion. Islamic sources ignore him, and he played no known role in the multiple incidents of Almohad fragmentation and Valencian civil war. A princeling of the mountains, he may well have stayed aloof, consolidating his own power. In the bare details of his military career he tends to leave the same impression as in the king's autobiography—that of a mere troublemaker, one of any number of landlords of no distinguished antecedents or claims. The great al-Azraq was much more.

[2] Ribera's understanding of the term as a personal attribute owed something to the Castilian derivative *zarco*; cf. *azarcon* in Dozy, *Glossaire*, pp. 225-226, and also Neuvonen, *Arabismos*, p. 226, on *zarco* from *zarqā*, and its feminine *azraq*. However, the historian of Mecca Muḥammad b. 'Abd Allāh al-Azraqī (d. ca. 860) came by his name because his ancestor, a Byzantine slave called al-Azraq, had blue eyes. Cagigas, who describes al-Azraq as "emigrado de Játiva," reconstructs the name as "al-Yazrayî" (*Mudejares*, II, 416), perhaps confusing him with Conde's governor of Játiva in the early days of the Valencian crusade "Ahmed ben Izá el Chazragi" (Aḥmad b. 'Īsā al-Khazrajī); see José Antonio Conde, *Historia de la dominación de los árabes en España, sacada de varios manuscritos y memorias arábigas* (Madrid, 1874), p. 263. Two other medieval historians bore the name Ibn al-Azraq, as did a *qāḍī* poet of Granada, the great Spanish astronomer Azarquiel (Azraq plus Latin -ellus), the founder of an important sect of radical puritans called the Azraqites who overran Iraq and southern Persia in the Umayyad era, and even the river Kārūn in the *Travels* of Ibn Baṭṭūṭa (II, 284). A boon companion of the twelfth-century governor of Murcia-Valencia and also a *qā'id* under him had the name Ibn al-Azraq; see Évariste Lévi-Provençal, *Inscriptions arabes d'Espagne* (Leiden, 1931), pp. 92, 100. A Valencian al-Azraq of the fifteenth century lived at Eslida. Just before Valencia city's fall, a grant transferred one of its buildings, owned by Muḥammad "Alazradi Azabach"; the property was valuable, since it went to a member of the queen's entourage in a document witnessed by four notables (*Itinerari*, p. 133 [July 11, 1238]). Buried in King James's accounts for 1265 at Gandía is a carpenter, "Aladrach fuster" (Arch. Crown, James I, Reg. Canc. 17, fol. 37-38). Besides the famous "Red" ruling at Granada, see the "Mahometus el Ruvio de Vilena sarracenus," whose Valencian estate King James freed from taxes (Arch. Crown, Reg. Canc. 11, fol. 192v [Feb. 5, 1260]).

[3] *Llibre dels feyts*, ch. 334: "vostre poder de cavallers que vos tenits a soldada"; ch. 374: "e dones soldades a peons."

He first turns up in a homage document arranging tributary status under Prince Alfonso, the heir of King James. The Christian year affixed was 1244; the year given by the interlinear Arabic version was reductively 1245. The first date suggests that al-Azraq had found his lands exposed to danger by the Almizra treaty in March between Castile and Aragon, which assigned his region to Aragon, and also by James's siege of neighboring Játiva. Under such circumstances, prudence would have suggested a timely shift to the winner's side. The less likely date 1245 would fit his surrender into the mopping-up stage of the crusade during the months following the fall of Biar. In recording the homage, the Christian scribe reduced his name Abū 'Abd Allāh Muḥammad b. Hudhayl al-Azraq to a garbled Habuabdele Yuan Fudayl; "Yuan," perpetuated by historians and sometimes taken for Juan, miscopies Aven, a version of the Spanish Aben, for ibn.[4] He appears in a letter of 1250 to the queen of Aragon as "Muḥammad b. Hudhayl, known as Alazrach."[5] Styling himself lord (*senor*) of Alcalá, he dominated a substantial segment of the Valencian kingdom, most of it just below the present Alicante-Valencia border, a mountainous country adjoining the Alcoy massif. His domain centered upon the *comarca* or territory of Pego, stretching west to encompass most of Alcoy, northwest into the Albaida country, and deeply to the south and east around Altea, Callosa, and Jalón. This was a kingly domain, sown with castles under their local lords.

The wider Pego territory formed an interrelated jumble of eight major valleys, a wilderness secreting cultivated patches, its hilly spines riddled with caves and springs, its 246 square kilometers holding eighty population centers ranging from hilltop castles to tiny hamlets. Each of the eight valleys displayed its river, a castle or two, and scattered settlements. Al-Azraq held court in the Alcalá Valley, where remnants of his palace can still be seen along with fragments of the fortified eyrie of Benisilim. His holdings to the west domi-

[4] Document in Chapter XII, n. 22. The Muslim says: "yo habuabdele yuan fudayl Alguazil y senor dalcala"; and the prince replies: "recibo uos Abuadele yuan fudayl alguazil et senor dalcala." King James's Castilianized heir, who knew no Catalan yet preferred to follow the Castilian vogue for the vernacular rather than Aragon's usual Latin, had the transaction drawn in Castilian with interlinear Arabic. The name Ibn Hudhayl was not uncommon, a distinguished namesake, for example, being a blind poet of the Cordova caliphate era.

[5] Chabás, "Alazrach," p. 281 (March 9, 1250).

nated the inland road threading down through the massif from Játiva; to the east he could threaten the security of the coastal highway. Pego, whose name derives from the Latin *pagu(m)*, boasted a civilized history stretching back past the Romans into the prehistoric era; in its Islamic phase it had produced celebrated intellectuals and, in more recent times, had coagulated into a powerful seigniory. An ancestor of al-Azraq, the *qā'id* of Gallinera 'Abd ar-Raḥmān, left his name on a valley town he founded, as did at least one other warrior forbear named, like al-Azraq, Abū 'Abd Allāh b. Hudhayl.[6]

During Islamic Valencia's civil war, this proud family had acquired independence. As long as the similar seigniory of Játiva stood to the north of his domain, al-Azraq must have been accorded by the crusaders a status analogous to that of Játiva's *qā'id*—tributary fiefdom with maximum autonomy. By spring of 1244, with renewed crusade in the wind, the lord of Alcalá relinquished some castles and renegotiated others as formal fiefs. Only the homage document survives from this time, making it difficult to say whether al-Azraq had previously lost some outlying key castles by defection of their local castellans, as the context of James's memoirs suggests. In April al-Azraq signed his act of homage transferring Tárbena and Pop to Prince Alfonso of Aragon; each castle apparently kept its local *qā'id* and probably continued to some extent under the influence of Alcalá. The Mudejar kept two castles—Alcalá and Perpunchent—as direct fief (*eredat*) for himself and his dynasty, free of all rents, "to do with completely as I like." In so genial a contract, with the prince accepting "the lord of Alcalá for my beloved and very exalted and very honored and my loyal vassal," these valleys undoubtedly included a sweep of adjoining territories not explicitly mentioned. Al-Azraq did lose Ebo with its castles of Serra and Castellot, as well as the heartland castle of Pego. The latter was really the low-slung castle called Hambra (al-Ḥamrā'), a long-walled construction of the eighth and ninth centuries whose ruins still run along a flat hillside south of Pego town.[7]

[6] Giner Bolufer, "Valles de Pego," pp. 46, 49, 51, 61, 66-67, and passim. His chronology of the revolts, with al-Azraq exiled after a 1252 rising, is inexact. Alcalá corresponded to modern Alcalá de la Jovada, or Boronat castle.

[7] See document, Chapter XII, n. 22. Alfonso also got "dos alcarias de Hebo et de tollo . . . con los otros castielos"; if "tollo" is Castellot, the two forts of this valley seem to have been included. Since al-Azraq had to seize, for his 1258 revolt,

Al-Azraq kept four other castles "free and quit," but promised half their revenues to Prince Alfonso for three years—Margarida and Cairola in the northwest part of Alcalá Valley, Castell de Castells beyond the valley to the south, and the great castle and valley of Gallinera protecting Alcalá at the north. Besides providing for vassal tenure of these castles, the contract envisioned al-Azraq gaining an indefinite number of others during the next three years, presumably as fighting ally in the closing mop-up of the crusade. The lord of Alcalá must have kept other fiefs, probably as liege to the crown. Rugat castle was his, as well as strongholds like Altea, Jalón, and Polop. These wider holdings probably amounted to subfiefs, however, each *qā'id* being vaguely responsible to Alcalá, much as the Mudejar *qā'id* of Tous answered to Játiva's lord. Before the 1257 revolt, Desclot assures us, al-Azraq remained in possession "of ten strong castles."[8]

From this base Alcalá's lord revolted in 1247, having apparently bided his time until the three-year grace period of his surrender treaty had passed, when he was due to turn over four of his six principal castles. Swiftly he developed his action into a countercrusade; by late 1248 he had attracted the wider attention of Christendom. This revolt and what seemed a subsequent revolt of 1258 have been the subject of endless dispute among local historians, owing to chronological data difficult to reconcile. It now seems clear that both formed part of a decade's unrest and disjointed guerrilla action in the Valencian kingdom, erupting as full-scale war in its initial (1247-1248) and culminating (1258) stages. Through phases of success and stalemate al-Azraq maintained the initiative, until in Easter of 1257 he was able to impose a year's truce by threatening alliance with Castile. During his revolt, he was able to retake his lost castles of Gallinera,

the castles of Pego and Serra as well as Gallinera (Benirrama), he must have lost them now. The Hambra name recalls Granada's Alhambra or "Red" castle. Pop should not be confused with the more considerable castle of Polop to its south; al-Azraq had claims on both. Pop, sequestered in the wild Sierra de Laguart, was exceptionally strong as a place of retreat; the Valencian Moriscos made their last stand here in November 1609 under Aḥmad, a native of Laguart Valley's village of Camp(f)iel.

[8] Desclot, *Crònica*, ch. 49. On the Rugat holding see *Llibre dels feyts*, ch. 375. The Jalón, Polop, and Altea castles were in the hands of al-Azraq at the end of his 1258 revolt, either by seizure or by continued control.

Serra, Pego, and even "so considerable and so estimable" a defense as Penáguila. He sustained long, hard campaigns against the crown forces over several years, capturing another dozen castles, nearly killing King James by an ambush, and with only one thousand men defeating a Christian host of three thousand. Strategic Penacadell barely resisted his onslaught. Pushed back upon his Alcalá fiefs, he was able to hold out there for three or four years, eventually surrendering on good terms. During the war al-Azraq negotiated several times with the king of Castile, securing protective, tributary overlordship. Treachery by his chief counselor, rather than military action, finally brought him low. In the final campaign against his central fief, he lost sixteen castles around Alcalá and Gallinera in a single week.[9] The tangled course of these wars is less relevant here than their substance.

The very terms on which this Mudejar lord ceased his revolt echo his politico-military importance. "Al-Azraq himself returned to us all the castles which he held in the kingdom of Valencia," and some time in late 1258 or afterwards betook himself into voluntary exile. For twenty years after the fall of Valencia city, he had ruled his "ten strong castles," along with their outlying defenses and dependent castles. Even as an exile he remained a considerable landlord in the home kingdom, especially through his close relatives. Besides his nonmilitary estates, he retained or acquired from the crown as recompense for his castles all villages under the jurisdiction of Altea castle. A property transaction of July 1258 involved these villages given "to Alazrach recently when [the king] made peace with Alazrach." A letter of August 1258 shows the Alcalan or his agents in possession.[10] The value of the villages appears from the equivalent properties with which King James recompensed their previous owner, when acquiring them for the treaty: "warehouses and buildings and workshops which we have in the city of Barcelona along the sea-

[9] *Llibre dels feyts*, ch. 363: "de tan bon loch et de tan honrat"; ch. 377 on sixteen castles. The most recent reconstruction of the double revolt is Momblanch, "D. Jaime y Alazrach," pp. 10-31.

[10] Arch. Crown, James I, Reg. Canc. 9, fol. 59v (July 30, 1258), at length also in *Itinerari*, p. 278: "alquariarum castri de Altea quas a vobis habuimus et accepimus et easdem dedimus Aladracho quando nuper fecimus pacem et composicionem cum eo et ipse Aladrachus reddidit nobis omnia castra que tenebat in regno Valencie." Fol. 65 (Aug. 14, 1258) licenses Berengar to recover the towns.

shore, with an oven," tax exemptions, and privileges.[11] The surrendered castles formed only part of the Mudejar lord's military holdings. He had previously conferred "the castles of Polop, Altea, and Jalón" on his brother Bāsim (Bacem) and his nephew Abū Ja'far (miscopied by one medieval scribe as Aliafar). Abū Ja'far continued the title previously cherished by al-Azraq, vizier (*al-wazīr*). Subsequent documents leave no doubt that Abū Ja'far was the senior partner, unless Bāsim soon died. By a formal charter of 1261, King James confirmed the transfer. The crown had assigned these castles during the previous war to Carroz, Christian lord of Rebollet; consequently, if al-Azraq did not hold them for all or part of the war, he regained them at the negotiating table.[12]

In 1263 King James returned to the subject of this Mudejar fief, clarifying the status of two out of the three castles as under the vizier's control; he granted "the castle and town of Polop, and the tower called Altea, with their villages," to "Abū Ja'far Ḥamīd [here as Abuliafar Hamet], son of the deceased Abū Sa'd b. Hudhayl [Acet Abinhudey]," frank and free, with all revenues and appurtenances, to keep, sell, give, or pledge.[13] This was the same vizier-nephew rather than an intruder or a new name such as 'Abd al-Jabbār, since a clarification seven years later assigned to the vizier Abū Ja'far (Abiafer) "the castle and town of Polop with its districts," together with three towns of the Jalón district, "as is more fully

[11] *Itinerari* (July 30): "omnia illa alfundica et domos et operatoria que nos habemus in civitate Barchinone iuxta litus maris."

[12] Arch. Crown, James I, Reg. Canc. 11, fol. 199 (April 9, 1261): "vobis Bacem et alguazir Aliafar sarracenis donacionem quam Alazrac frater tui Bacem et avunculus tui alguacir Aliafar tibi fecit de castris de Polop de A[l]tea et de Xalo." Chabás published a transcription in *El archivo*, IV (1890), doc. 19, but misread Aliafar as Aliajar, though it twice appears clearly. As the next note strongly suggests, the scribe read Abū as 'Alī. The castle here is written clearly as Polop; Giner Bolufer read it as Pop, and ran the names together into a single owner, "Hacen Aliatjar aben Bazel ben al-Alazdrach" ("Valles de Pego," p. 54). King James wrote that one condition for getting the final "truce" with al-Azraq was giving "Polop a un seu nebot" (*Llibre dels feyts*, ch. 97). Bacem might be Bassām or a variant of Abū Ḥasan, but Bāsim is the better choice.

[13] Arch. Crown, James I, Reg. Canc. 12, fol. 118v (Sept. 30, 1263): "castrum et villam de Polop et torrem que dicitur de Altea cum eorum alqueriis"; "Abuliafar Hamet, filio quondam de Acet Abinhudey." Martínez-Ferrando entered the first name in his catalogue as Abenhafar Hamez, son of Aceit, but the Abū of the original is clear. Hamet may be Aḥmad, far more common as a Spanish name.

contained in our charter"; generously, "the Saracens resident in the said places are frank and free" of taxes by the payment of 300 solidi twice a year.[14] The run of documents allows reconstruction of the rebel lord's family circle. His father Ibn Hudhayl had three sons—Abū Sa'd, dead by 1263, Bāsim, and Muḥammad al-Azraq. Nothing further is heard from Muḥammad's son 'Abd Allāh, possibly fallen in the interminable warfare. The son of Abū Sa'd was Abū Ja'far, eventually sole heir in Valencia to al-Azraq.

As al-Azraq rode into exile, he could console himself that a brother and an uncle still presided from Banū Hudhayl strongholds, and that many a friendly *qā'id* clung to his rural castle ready for the next revolt. Yet much had changed. In his Alcalá Valley, the guardian castles of Alcalá and Benisilim were occupied by Arnold of Valeriola, lord of Tormos. The next valley to the south, Benichembla, harbored Christian lordships of Murla and Parcent. Ebo Valley was lost; so was Gallinera Valley, the former bulwark of the family's seigniory; both went to Prince Peter. Pego castle and valley fell under the administration of Arnold of Romaní, and a decade later divided into a lordship of Adsubia under the Roca family and a barony of Pego under Prince Peter. Forna Valley constituted a separate barony. Towns redolent of Spanish Islam's past came under infidel settlers. Beniganim, founded by the poet Ibn Ghālib, now belonged to a company led by Dominic of Puigvert. Benumea, recalling a refugee prince at the close of the Umayyad rule, admitted Peter of Cabrera and his colleagues. The village of Benizuleyma, named for a son of the eleventh-century king of Denia-Zaragoza, Aḥmad b. Sulaymān b. Hūd al-Muqtadir, went to the Sanchis and Siscar clans. The Mur family took over one town, the Corts, Escrivá, and Torres another. Settlement was exiguous, to be sure; but the infidel had planted his foot in the pleasant valleys.[15]

[14] *Ibid.*, Reg. Canc. 16, fol. 156 (April 22, 1269): "volumus et concedimus tibi algaziro Abiafer quod tu et successores tui habeatis castrum et villam de Polop cum terminis suis . . . et illas alquerias . . . ut in dicta carta nostra plenius continetur"; "et concedimus tibi quod sarraceni habitantes in dictis locis sint franchi et liberi." Martínez-Ferrando gives the name as Abiaf in his catalogue, but the manuscript supplies an *er* symbol. The three settlements of Jalón were Almacerof, Benibrahim, and Murta; local Muslims had to use the Játiva saltworks.

[15] Giner Bolufer collects the *Repartimiento* data in "Valles de Pego," pp. 50, 53, 55-56, 58, 66-67, 70, 72-73.

Al-Azraq lived to ride the mountains again, threatening "not only the kingdom itself but also the whole of Spain."[16] Leading a relief force toward Tous castle in April 1276, during the Morocco-Granadan invasion and last Valencian revolt, he was cut down ignominiously on a diversion under the walls of Alcoy on a late April day of 1276. His demise shed an aura of romantic martyrdom around his memory, as easily happens with a hero fortunate enough to fall on the field before a patriotic war can sour into a lost cause. The sober contemporary account in the royal memoirs contents itself with noting that he led an invasion in support of a rebellion which was already successfully under way, only to perish promptly at Alcoy; a lifetime later this scene had evolved into the account of the San Juan de la Peña history, where al-Azraq became the presiding captain (*capitaneus*) "to whom the entirety [*universi*] of the Saracens gave allegiance"; nothing must do except that "King Peter killed him and his followers," though in fact Peter had not yet arrived in Valencia when the Muslim hero fell.[17]

Though not strictly correct in assigning al-Azraq as instigator and head of the revolt, the chronicler preserved a poetic truth by awarding him preeminence. The ex-Mudejar lord had obviously been a magic figure, a rallying point for the Valencian imagination. When the armies of Granada surged over this area on damaging raids a quarter-century later, burning Cocentaina to the ground, the memory of al-Azraq rode with them and lent unwonted savagery to their attacks.[18] His reputation as an ogre lives on in the local idiom inher-

[16] *Crónica de San Juan de la Peña*, ch. 36 (Ubieto edn., p. 161; Ximénez edn., p. 165): "nedum regnum ipsum, quin etiam tota Ispania, evidenti erat exposita periculo."

[17] *Ibid.*, "cui universi sarraceni adherebant"; "iste Petrus rex interfecit eum et adherentes sibi." Soldevila compares the several accounts and demonstrates the evolution (*Pere el Gran*, part 1, III, 412-414). Momblanch makes him leader of the rising, even isolating him by positing a truce between the Morocco-Granada invaders and the Christian kings ("D. Jaime y Alazrach," p. 40). The traditional account of his death has him lead 250 horse against the city's San Marcos gate; the overconfident Christians pursued the remnant and were ambushed on the Barranco de la Batalla.

[18] Martínez-Ferrando's interpretation in *Descendents de Pere el Gran*, pp. 106-107, summer of 1304. The identification of this later period with the dead rebel's spirit occasionally leads an able historian to resurrect him: Aurea L. Javierre Mur has "al-Adzach" lead "los moros sublevados en Valencia" to conquer Montesa in 1314, in *Privilegios reales de la orden de Montesa en la edad media* (Madrid, 1956), p. 68.

ited by modern Christians, the playful threat to naughty children, "El Drach will get you!" ("Que vindrá el Drach!").[19] The word *aladrach* for wild animal also preserves his memory. The patriot's death provides the occasion for colorful festivities every April 23 at Alcoy, featuring the *Moros y cristianos* parade, mock battle, and general gala.[20]

Parallel with this late invasion, the clan of al-Azraq had rebelled in the valleys, constituting one of three major nuclei for the long war. Among the fifteen districts that the new king Peter resolutely excluded from a general truce were their castles of Pop, Serra, and the ambiguously spelled A(l)tea and Alarch (Alarp?).[21] Peter soon simplified all the districts into three generic classifications, one being summed as "Alcalá castle."[22] Having contended so publicly and Homerically with the legendary al-Azraq, King James could hardly omit this counterego from his autobiography; but he did condense his role drastically, denied him any title, and maliciously blackened his memory by labeling him dishonest. Al-Azraq, seeping back from fragmentary notices like ectoplasm gathering into ghostly facsimile, refuses to accept the rebuff and emerges as a considerable patriot-figure in the history of Mudejar Valencia.

Rebel Sheiks

If the crown records discreetly credited the rebels of early 1276 with the seizure of "many" castles (*plurima*), the contemporary Desclot did not hesitate to specify them as forty.[23] The capacity for dealing such stunning blows to the occupation forces indicates strong leadership at the several levels of Mudejar society. A factor in the strength of this leadership structure was the enthusiasm with which

[19] Francisco Martínez y Martínez, *Còses de la meua tèrra* (Valencia, 1920), pp. 170-173; sometimes "y te s'emportará" is added; here the name al-Azraq assimilates to a dragon image, though that is not this word's etymology. At the other end of the Mediterranean, Muslim mothers silenced crying children in this century: "Quiet, King Richard is coming for you!" (Joinville, on crusade with Louis IX, *Histoire de St. Louis*, chs. 17, 108; William of Tyre also tells of this).

[20] Rafael Coloma, *Libro de la fiesta de moros y cristianos de Alcoy* (Alcoy, 1962), with general background briefly in Joan Amades, *Las danzas de moros y cristianos* (Valencia, 1966).

[21] Document below in n. 31.

[22] Soldevila, *Pere el Gran*, part 2, 1, appendix, doc. 15 (Sept. 6, 1276).

[23] *Crònica*, ch. 67.

Spanish Muslims rallied around revolutionary heroes or shifted allegiance to a new dynasty. The contemporary Ibn Sa'īd contrasted Spain of this period with the East, where people were slow to elevate the warrior on horseback or to change dynasties.[24] In restive Mudejar Valencia, though al-Azraq was the most celebrated of such castellan-princes, he was by no means the only one. The 1276 war began around another hero altogether, the *qā'id* Ibrāhīm who rebelled and converted the dismantled castle of Finestrat on the southeast coast into his stronghold. King James was at Valencia city at the time, and had two Christian armies operating in the realm to quell civil disturbances; yet when he "considered helping that region where the castle was," he soon had to abort the expedition.[25]

Ibrāhīm appears only in Christian sources. King Peter excluded him from the general truce of 1276—"the castles and places and whatever else the *qā'id* Ibrāhīm holds." The crown forces eventually ran him to earth in late February of 1277 at one of his castles, Garg on the Jalón River. Peter was later to link the surrender of Ibrāhīm with the fall of Montesa and Biar almost as coordinate centers of resistance. The stately notice of capitulation reveals this adversary's full name and something of his status. On Sunday night, the twenty-third of Ramaḍān, "the noble *qā'id* Abū Isḥāq [Ibrāhīm] al-Asqarī" bound himself to deliver his castle within five days "to our lord the sultan" Peter. The king in turn promised to establish "a retinue of Muslim freemen" for the rebel, to present him with two horses and two mules, to outfit not only "him and his son" but also "forty of his men," to permit free departure to Islamic lands for all who so chose, and to take the *qā'id* under crown protection. This treaty seemed particularly important to the Christians; it remains one of the few still preserved at the royal archives and one of the rare Valencian Arabic documents.[26]

[24] Al-Maqqarī, *Mohammedan Dynasties in Spain*, I, 101-102.

[25] *Llibre dels feyts*, ch. 555: "vench nos ardit que·l alcait Abrafim s·era alçat, e que havia bastit i castell que nos haviem enderrocat ja peça havia, lo qual ha nom Serra de Finestrat; e nos . . . pensam d·acorrer enves aquela part on lo castell era."

[26] Arch. Crown, Peter III, Reg. Canc. 39, fol. 169v (Feb. 25, 1277), five lines of large, clear script; context clarifies any ambiguity of date. See also Soldevila, *Pere el Gran*, part 2, I, appendix, doc. 58 (Feb. 28, 1277); doc. 59 (March 10); doc. 95 (Sept. 8); doc. 111 (July 18, 1278). Juan Vernet supplies a translation of doc. 58. Soldevila interprets his castle of Garach as Garig or Gartx, but it may rather be Garg near Jalón; he also gives the *qā'id* as al-Ashrī. The original manuscript shows that the explanatory notation that provides our only identification of this *qā'id*

The mantle of the fallen leader soon graced his colleague Muḥammad, who ruled Finestrat, Orcheta, and other castles of the rebel territory. This was apparently the same dynast, forcibly retired by the crown from these castles onto more peaceful estates, whom we left rusticating in the previous chapter. Operating out of Orcheta, his riverine and coastal navy harassed the Christians. King Peter authorized the outfitting of a defensive fleet and counterattacks by land and sea, announcing at the same time his plans for a more ambitious campaign against the area. His proclamation of March 1277 specified "some castles which the *qā'id* Ibrāhīm held and which the *qā'id* Muḥammad or another holds now" as the hub of this outlawry.[27] Six months later he had pacified the area. Peter announced final "peace with the *qā'id* Ibrāhīm and the *qā'id* Muḥammad and with the Saracens of the districts which these men hold and with the Saracens of the district of Biar."[28] Both rebels remained in place for nearly a year, under crown protection.

Peter then expelled them, in late July of 1278, either by tacit provision of the earlier treaties, or on some legalistic pretext, or because they had broken the peace by involving themselves in final episodes of the war. Peter's document merely declares that he had chartered the vessel of two Genoese merchants "to transport the *qā'id* Ibrāhīm and the *qā'id* Muḥammad to Tlemcen with a large multitude of Saracens, whom we expelled from the kingdom of Valencia."[29] Since the ship operated under this crown charter until Christmas but moved cargoes of rebel property along with their owners, it is difficult to say how many castellans went into exile with their households and retinues or how many commoners followed them. The

---

as Ibrāhīm was fitted in as an afterthought by a contemporary—"carta de la co[n]-vinença / q[ue·]l alcaid Abrahim feu ab lo / del senor rey," with *del* deleted and the crucial portion between my vertical lines inserted by the same or a similar hand. The truce document is below, n. 31.

27 Soldevila, *Pere el Gran*, part 2, 1, appendix, doc. 59 (March 10, 1277): "aliqua castra que Alcaçdus Abraym tenuerit et modo teneat alcaydus Mahomet vel alius." In the original manuscript, I read the fourth word as *alcaydus.*

28 *Ibid.*, doc. 95, a form letter sent broadcast, with special copies for seven southern districts including Murcia and Alicante: "noveritis nos fecisse pacem cum alcaydis Abrahim et Mahomet et cum sarracenis locorum que ipsi tenent et cum sarracenis loci de Biar."

29 *Ibid.*, doc. 111 (July 18, 1278): "transferre alcaydum Abrafim et alcaydum Mafumet apud Tirimçe cum magna multitudine sarracenorum, quos eyicimus de regno Valencie."

orders significantly single out only the two leaders by name, though this single expulsion apparently included all those hard-core dissidents throughout the kingdom who suffered the penalty of exile. An echo of these leaders comes in a document some ten months later. Various Moors were still making their way to friendlier lands, notable among them "Saracens of the *qā'id* Muḥammad"; this time the king licensed only one ship as carrier, a monopoly for the Italian Ser Francesco drawn in May 1279.[30]

There were any number of rebel lords who remain as nameless as the many knights encountered in the preceding chapter. The crusaders preserved the names of Islam's heroes only in contexts of practical use to themselves, or when some individual impressed himself repeatedly upon their warrior lives. When Peter granted his truce in the fall of 1276 from one end of Valencia kingdom to the other, the rebel leaders honored to negotiate for all their colleagues were men now unknown to history, mentioned in no other document or memoir, and surfacing in a list so garbled as to conceal even their number —"the noble sheik [*veillo*] Abrurdriz Hyale Abenayeth and the noble knight Abenzumayr Abenzaquimaran and the vizier Abulfaratx Asbac." The sixteenth-century archivist Zurita found four nobles in this list, the twentieth-century archivist Martínez-Ferrando discerned five, while the dean of Catalan historians, Soldevila, recently insisted on "only three." Martínez-Ferrando read the first man as "Abrurchiz Hyale" and the second as "Abeneyech"; Zurita saw a "Halen Abu Hayet." Alteration of name-forms later in the manuscript (Hale or Byale for example becomes Yhale or Ybale) and ruinous spots blighting lower names contribute to the difficulty. Numbers aside, the names appear to be Abū Idrīs Ya'lā b. 'Ā'idh or Nāhid, then Ibn Sumayr b. Zakī Marwān, and finally Abu 'l-Faraj Yashbak. These bare and perhaps dubious names, perceived through a screen of shifting syllables, are all that survive of the "noble sheiks" who represented both native rebels and foreign invaders, and whose signatures effected a pause in the general fighting.[31]

30 Arch. Crown, Peter III, Reg. Canc. 41, fol. 71v (May 10, 1279): "quod non permittatis sarracenos tam alcaydi Mahometi quam alios de terra nostra transfretari ad partes sarracenorum nisi in navi Ser Francisci."

31 *Ibid.*, Reg. Canc. 38, fol. 27 (Sept. 3, 1276): "del muy noble don Jayme rey darago, a que deus perdone, e entrel veillo noble Abrurdriz Hyale Abenayeth Ay [?] el cavallero [cavero ?] noble Abenzumayr Abenzaquimaran el alguazir Abulfaratx Asbac aixi quel dito Senyor Iffant atregua a todos los castellos que son alçados."

The Muslim commander who held off the royal forces in the protracted siege of Alfandech remains faceless today, though his area ranked with the domains of Ibrāhīm and of al-Azraq's relatives as one of the three centers of revolt with which no truce was possible.[32] Anonymous too are the men who served as lieutenants in the seventeen castles to which King Peter refused mercy, or who defended those sixteen inner castles of al-Azraq which fell to King James during earlier fighting, or who surrendered the various castles which returned to Peter's control by 1279. The paths of patriot glory have become too overgrown to reveal the least clue. Two unusual rebels do emerge from the mist, each rescued from oblivion by the careless comment of a Christian chronicler. Ibn Baṣṣāl in his own day must have been a man more outstanding than al-Azraq, though cast in a supporting role by the accidents of history. King James described him as "the best Saracen al-Azraq had [on his side], and [politically] the most powerful, and distinguished besides in worth more than he." The higher *valor* or "worth" of Ibn Baṣṣāl could refer to social rank, battlefield bravery, knightly character, or all three. His death in battle disconcerted the rebel army entrenched before Penacadell and routed their siege. Though the war dragged on for years yet, the fall of Ibn Baṣṣāl marked its turning point, the Christians going on the offensive and the Muslims losing heart.[33]

Another hero of the resistance was Albacor or Albocar, described

---

In repeating the names below, the manuscript omits Abenzaquimaran, inserts Abulfaratx as an afterthought between lines, and spells one name Aben Zumer. See also Zurita, *Anales de la corona de Aragón*, lib. IV, c. 1. Soldevila argues that "el titol que precedeix cadascun precisa prou bé que són solament tres" (*Pere el Gran*, part 2, 1, 11n. with doc. 12), but other documents list a title for one name of a series, leaving the other(s) plain, while James's documents usually shy away from this aben-aben combination; perhaps Soldevila should rather have stressed the use of only three connectives. Whether three names, four, five, or seven, all are equally unknowns. Soldevila dates the document August 29.

[32] See document of September 6, 1276, in n. 22: "exceptis tamen castris . . . [de] Abrahim, et excepto castro de Alcalano, [et] vallis de Alfandec de Marynnen, et sarracenis dictorum castrorum et rebus eorumdem."

[33] *Llibre dels feyts*, ch. 371: "e aqui mori Abenbazol, que era lo meylor sarray que Alazarc havia, e·l pus poderos, e encara de valor valia plus que ell." Variants in the *Llibre* manuscripts are Abenbaçol, Abetibassol, and Almaçarich. Ibn Baṣṣāl was an honored name in Spain, borne, for example, by an eleventh-century writer on agriculture.

by Desclot as "a shepherd and black."[34] Though the name suggests a confusion of the common Abū Bakr or even Bakkār, it may rather be al-Baqqār with its drover-cowboy implications. Desclot tended to have a low regard for the social origins of Valencian Muslims; if he meant to convey this bucolic title, he may well have missed the meaning it could have had for Mudejars. Such a "shepherd" could belong to the proud tribal groups that kept to the Valencian highland with their flocks. Did Albocar's sobriquet "the king" represent claims to leadership as distorted by Christians fearful of a restoration, or was it his name converted into a slogan (Mālik)?[35] Aristocrat, rustic scion, or plebeian adventurer, this patriot did great damage to the Christians and held "many strong castles in the mountains about Alcoy and Albaida." Despite all efforts, Desclot recounts, the forces of Aragon could not subdue him. Eventually "the king" mounted a serious attack against Alcira, fell into the hands of the Christians, and was triumphantly paraded before being executed. He seems to have preceded al-Azraq; but for his untimely death he might eventually have surpassed in fame the lord of Alcalá. He presages a much later hero, either rustic aristocrat or demagogue, the Algar Moor named Garbau, who styled himself Sālim al-Manṣūr as "king" of the Sierra Espadán during the 1525 Valencian rebellion.[36]

The Banū 'Īsā of Játiva-Montesa

The castle of Játiva, along with its network of supporting castles, had come to assume unique importance for the Islamic kingdom of Valencia. Its domain spread to the north and west of the al-Azraq regions. The Alcoy massif ended there in the rock wall of the Sierra del Castillo, along whose crown sprawled the white battlements of Játiva's castle. Astride converging roads, it particularly commanded the approaches south into the massif as well as the main invasion

[34] Desclot, *Crònica*, ch. 49. The influential chronicler P. A. Beuter called him "Ali Bocor"; see his *La coronica general de toda España y especialmente del reyno de Valencia*, 2 vols. (Valencia, [1538-1551] 1604), part 2, ch. 47, esp. fols. 132-133.

[35] Ibn Baṭṭūṭa met such a case during his travels in Egypt seventy-five years later, a captain in the sultan's bodyguard whose name gained him the popular title of "the king"; though Ibn Baṭṭūṭa pedantically corrected the etymology, he himself was wrong and the man's name was a form of *al-malik* (*Travels*, I, 30-31).

[36] *Crònica*, ch. 49. García, *Historia de Vall de Uxó*, p. 70.

routes north toward Valencia city. The first sight of this splendid citadel overwhelmed King James; "a castle so noble and fine, with a fine huerta," roused "great joy and great happiness in my heart," together with determination "to have the castle for Christendom." James also described the beauties of the surrounding countryside and the strength of "the castles which were around Játiva"; he recognized the wide "lordship" (*senyoria*) and "holdings" (*pertinencia*) of its *qā'id*. His queen and advisers called Játiva "the finest castle in the world and the wealthiest ever seen"; the *qā'id* boasted there was "no better in all Spanish Islam." King James was brutally candid about his need to control the region. He told the *qā'id* that "God wanted me to be king of the kingdom of Valencia, and Játiva was the noblest place there outside of Valencia city." He saw it as "the key to the kingdom, and I could not be king of the kingdom of Valencia if Játiva were not mine."[37]

As befitted such a domain, it was ruled by a princely house, kin to the Banū Mardanīsh. The young king James had correctly assessed this dynasty's relative autonomy during the months following the Murcian revolt of Ibn Hūd. He dispatched one of his closest friends, a baron of his household named Peter López of Pomar, on an embassy to the ruling *qā'id* of Játiva.[38] He may well have detached the *qā'id* from Abū Zayd at a period when Valencia still stood strong and unaffected by the turmoil in Spanish Islam; probably, too, this

[37] *Llibre dels feyts*, ch. 318: "lo castell tan noble e tant bell, e tan bela orta, e haguem ne gran gog e gran alegre en nostra cor"; "haver lo castell per crestianisme, e que Deu hi fos servit"; ch. 322: "castells qui eren entorn de nos e de [*or*: nos a] Xativa"; ch. 336: "no•n a altre meylor en toda la Endeluzia"; ch. 333: "en sa senyoria"; ch. 341: "de la pertinencia de Xativa"; "nenguns dels castells de Xativa"; ch. 350: "Deus volia que nos fossem rey del regne de Valencia, e que Xativa era lo pus noble loch que•y fos, de Valencia enfora, . . . era clau del regne, e nos no serien rey del regne de Valencia si Xativa no era nostra"; another manuscript reads "clau del altre regne de Valencia si Xativa"; ch. 353: "el pus bell castell es del mon e•l pus rich que jo anch vees." See also Cagigas, *Mudejares*, II, 369-370.

[38] *Llibre dels feyts*, ch. 129: "Pero Lopis de Pomar, qui havia estat por missatgeria nostra al alcayt d•Ixativa." The time had to be before 1229, and the stay both important and sufficiently long to be able now to encourage the king to undertake the conquest of Valencia. Peter "era cavaller antich e era de nostra meynada"; he was an intimate companion-in-arms throughout the king's wars, and headed his own *companya* as well (chs. 29, 41, 63-64). *Antich* here bears the less usual meaning of "experienced." One relative became the first castellan of conquered Játiva; another received from the king a dowry of 13,500 solidi for his daughter (*Itinerari*, p. 427).

detachment on Valencia's flank related to the abortive crusade of 1229 which King James was then preparing. The *qā'id*, Abu 'l-Ḥusayn b. 'Īsā, king in all but name, did swing over to the cause of Ibn Hūd; a decade later, after the Murcian's death, the *qā'id* formally declared Játiva's independence. When the Christian crusade overwhelmed Valencia, its current ruler Zayyān had long lost any control over Játiva, or for that matter over Alcira and all the territory from the Júcar River south. Thus Játiva and the south did not fall within the terms of Valencia's surrender. Until his success at Valencia city, King James seems to have entertained no serious plans to attack this formidable region. He ambitioned merely that, with the fall of Valencia city, "all that kingdom will be conquered, down to Játiva." To protect his flank he did maintain a spoiling force in the neighborhood of Játiva during Valencia's siege.[39]

As his conquest succeeded, however, the king's appetite grew. His autobiography relates the circumstances that fired his covetousness.[40]

[39] *Llibre dels feyts*, ch. 206: "tot aquel regne sera pres, tro a Xativa." Al-Maqqarī, who chooses Játiva as the only subdivision of the Valencia region requiring extended comment, puts one of James's seven armies at Játiva early in the crusade; probably only the two at Valencia city and the spoiler forces near Alcira and Játiva were Aragon's, the other three belonging to Castile and perhaps carelessly placed (*Mohammedan Dynasties in Spain*, I, ch. 4).

[40] That James had not meant to attempt Játiva's absorption is based not only on his narrative of how the idea first came to him, but also on his repetitive insistence at this point that Játiva was part of the Valencian kingdom and essential to its survival; he was obviously groping for legalities to justify himself. Perhaps a contrary case, at least in terms of impractical dream, can be devised from a careful study of the king's previous grants of places he hoped to conquer. The king left to his younger son Peter by a will of 1241 (often misdated 1242): "totum regnum Valencie a Biar usque ad rivum de Huldecona [Ulldecona]"; see Soldevila, *Pere el Gran*, part I, I, 8n., and contrast p. 17, where the previous espousal agreement of 1235 assigned to any future son (Peter) only "quidquid iam adquisivimus diebus nostris et acquisituri sumus a sarracenis in regno de Valencia." Was James acting merely as master over tributary Játiva and therefore as vaguely an indirect lord over the scattered mountain castles down to Murcia, or had he slyly resolved on full conquest of Játiva as well as Biar as early as January of 1241? The treaty of Cazola, sometimes incorrectly called Cazorla, had reserved Játiva by name in 1179 for conquest by Aragon, though its arrangements dealt rather with velleities. Al-Maqqarī, speaking of the principalities emerging from the eleventh-century chaos, ranked Játiva as important but of second rank, with "the kings of Ronda, Huesca, Játiva, and other cities . . . ; as all these petty sovereigns were more or less dependent on the more powerful states [like Seville, Valencia, and Zaragoza] with which their own dominions became in time incorporated, we shall not stop to give account of them" (*Mohammedan Dynasties in Spain*, II, 259; see also p. 327,

To recover six knights captured during a venturesome border raid, James allowed himself to get involved in a pseudo-siege designed to bluff Játiva. After several weeks in the siegeworks, he abandoned the pretense and went to Montpellier. Characteristically he blended this episode into his subsequent real siege, thus minimizing his failure to free the prisoners. This first "siege" took place in May 1239, at which time the Valencian crusade to all appearances had run its course. Precisely a year later the enterprise took on new life, as the dismayed *qā'id* watched a flood of crusaders settle around his stronghold. The armies of Arago-Catalonia proved almost, but not quite, equal to the challenge. By a compromise around June of 1240 the dynast was able to enter the Christian feudal system on terms so minimal that historians commonly assign a later date to the conquest of Játiva. King James had a feudal pact drawn up, with the usual delineation of obligations, rights, and taxes, and the *qā'id* swore homage.

Ibn 'Īsā kept his lordship, castles, and military control, agreeing only that he would not "hand over this place to any man ever, if you surrender it, except" to King James. The situation had become stabilized again; the southern regions, including the independent principality of al-Azraq, might well have shielded for long lifetimes behind the buffer fief of Játiva, all locked into their mountain fastness like an enclaved, miniature Granada. Aragon, Castile, and Murcia were not ready to acquiesce in this form of equilibrium. Ibn 'Īsā must have had premonition of the coming struggle; on his deathbed he enjoined his son and heir to respect the central provision of Játiva's feudal charter—"that, if he did come to lose it, he should not surrender the castle to any Christian at all, nor to a Saracen, but only to him," James of Aragon. The king for his part took occasion to remind the new *qā'id* "that I loved his father the *qā'id* very much, and very much loved his son whom he had left to me in my custody"; the word custody (*comanda*) bore not only this loose popular meaning but the technical sense of infeudation, specifically the state of contract vassalage.[41]

where Denia and Játiva join the revolt of Ibn Hūd). Al-Idrīsī, writing in 1154, described Játiva as "a handsome town with castles whose strength and beauty have become proverbial" (*Description de l'Afrique et de l'Espagne*, p. 37).

[41] *Llibre dels feyts*, ch. 318, first siege, and ch. 319 for the origin of his covetous resolve; a grant that year, "in bastita Xativa xii kalendas Iunii anno domini

The new *qā'id* was Yaḥyā b. Muḥammad b. 'Īsā (Iahia Abenmafomat Abenaisa[42]); like many an heir of a strong father, he may have been unequal to a situation the patriarch founder of the principality had managed for years. King James seized upon the opportunity presented by a border scuffle to claim technical breach of feudal contract. Marshaling the crown resources, he again invested the city. Yaḥyā countered with diplomacy designed to shift allegiance to Cas-

---

mccxxx nono," places him in the siegeworks (*bastida*) on May 21, while others locate him at Valencia city on April 13 and at Montpellier on June 2 (*Itinerari*, p. 139; see discussion of the Chabás dates of May and June 1240 on p. 576). On June 17, 1240, he was again "in bastita Xative," though he was at Valencia on May 16 and July 15; according to Soldevila the second date signaled Peter's birth at that city (*Pere el Gran*, part I, I, II). See *Llibre dels feyts*, ch. 327 for homage and the condition "que aquel loch no liuras a nuyl hom, pus s·en desisques, si a nos no, per negun temps"; ch. 334 for written pact; ch. 350: "son pare li havia manat que a negun chrestia del mon, no a sarray, non lliuras aquel castell si a nos no, si ell lo havia a perdre"; ch. 354: "tant amavem nos son pare del alcayt, e tant amavem son fiyl qu·ens havia lexat en nostra comanda"; on *comanda* see Rodón Binué, *El lenguaje técnico*, pp. 55-56 with pp. 58-60. This last quotation indicates that the unnamed *qā'id* in the various chapters on Játiva was two people and that the first surrender was by the father; the repetition, in pact and deathbed warning, about surrendering to James confirms this. The alternative is to make Yaḥyā the single *qā'id* throughout, supposing some special arrangement with the father at the time of the siege of Valencia city or earlier, an unsatisfactory hypothesis. Conde, whose pioneer gleanings from the Arabic sources are liable to error, gives only two of the family at Játiva; he has Ibn Hūd appoint Aḥmad b. 'Īsā al-Khazrajī as Játiva's *wālī* because of his service, wealth, and eminent family; on his death in mid-1241 (Sha'bān, 639), his son Yaḥyā Abu 'l-Ḥusayn succeeded until his surrender in 1246 and 1248, when he and his vizier Abū Bakr Muḥammad became penniless wanderers. Besides the problem of date, with Játiva falling during the siege of Seville (1248) but King James making his triumphal entry at the end of Ṣafar 644 (early December 1246), Conde elsewhere puts Yaḥyā b. Muḥammad b. 'Īsā Abu 'l-Ḥusayn, father of Ḥusayn b. Yaḥyā the ruler of Denia, as the first of Játiva's two rulers, a man he also makes ruler of Denia (*Dominación de los árabes en España*, pp. 262-263, 266-267, 269). See also Cagigas, *Mudejares*, II, 369. Perhaps the added name of Játiva's *qā'id* Dhu 'n-Nūn, related him to the Berber clan of the Banū Zennun (Dhi 'n-Nūn, or Dhu 'n-Nūn), one of whom was lord of Santaver, with a son Yaḥyā, lord of Huélamo (d. 937), another son named al-Fatḥ, lord of Uclés (d. 916), and a third named Muṭarrif, lord of Huete and later governor of Guadalajara (d. 945).

42 Spellings in the manuscripts vary. "Iafia Abenmafomat Abenaxa" appears in Arch. Crown, Reg. Canc. 9, fol. 24; "tibi Iahie Abenmahomet Abenaysa" is in Reg. II, fol. 192. The odd form Aboyahia Abolhaxen appears in Reg. II, fol. 192, but the Abū is an intrusion, while Abolhaxen (misread by Martínez-Ferrando in his catalogue as Aldehacen) is a garble for Aben Aysa or Haxa, rather than Abu 'l-Ḥasan.

tile. This belated intrusion James met with passionate resistance; he warned Castile that "whoever enters Játiva, passes over my dead body."[43] By bullying the Castilian king into a treaty of partition at Almizra, James isolated not only the *qā'id* but all that mountain region down into Murcia. Even so, he could not quite encompass the defeat of Játiva, until he had promised Yaḥyā and his dynasty an equivalently honorable fief plus personal revenues surpassing his Játiva rents ten times over. In early 1244 the *qā'id* undertook to hand over the lesser castle, reserving transfer of the main castle until 1246. In recompense the Mudejar prince could name any "honored" place to hold as substitute—the adjective denoting feudal dignity. James writes: "I asked what suitable fief I could give, and he requested Montesa and Vallada, which are good castles and near Játiva."[44] After

[43] *Llibre dels feyts*, ch. 347, a free version of "qui en Xativa vol entrar, sobre nos haura a passar." Miret y Sans, who counts three sieges of Játiva (*Itinerari*, p. 577) but describes a fourth (see p. 171), has the main siege begin at least by December 30, 1243; this is probably an error. Documents locate him "in obsidione Xative" at least by January 7, 1244 (actually 1243 but in copy as 1244), on February 11, 1244, and again on February 8, 1245; see the datings and explanations in *Itinerari*, pp. 165, 171, and 551n. Miret y Sans here has James return to besiege (continue to besiege?) Játiva after the fall of Biar, against the testimony of the king's memoirs. In a question confused by incarnational and nativity calendars, with siege documents rare and with corroborating evidence ambiguous, I read the 1245 date as meaning 1244 and the chronology as reconstructed here. Though the archivist Zurita put a first siege in 1240, a second in April-May 1244 (lifted), and a third in (February-)April 1248 (*Anales de Aragón* [1562], book 3, chs. 38, 42, 44)—a chronology repeated by Ballesteros in 1963—subsequent authors preferred to place the final surrender in 1244, relatively modern ones choosing 1249. The city's historian Sarthou Carreres accepted 1244 (*Geografía de Valencia*, II, 484), but a decade later allowed 1249 as well or even 1248 (*Castillos de España* [Madrid, 1932], pp. 251-259, and *Datos para la historia de Játiva*, I, 73). Only in 1948 did Ventura Pascual y Beltrán publish his 1922 attack, "La conquista de Játiva por Jaime I no pudo ser en 1249" (*ACCV*, XVII [1948], 41-50), positing four serious sieges in 1239, 1240, 1244, and—only because of *Repartimiento* grants and holdings—1248. Muḥammad b. Shanab listed the Arab historians' dating as between December 30, 1247, and January 1248 ("Notes chronologiques," p. 76). Torres Balbás, last in line, concluded that there was a long siege from 1239 into June 1240, then the main siege in 1248; he based the latter on the near concurrence of Zurita with the biographical encyclopedist Ibn Khallikān (d. 1282), who gives the date of surrender as between January 18 and 28, 1248; this brought transfer of the second castle into 1250 ("Játiva y los restos de Pinohermoso," pp. 145-147). The data for 1248 should be placed rather in the context of the revolts.

[44] *Llibre dels feyts*, chs. 327, 334 (first surrender, homage, charter), 333ff. (raid, problem of Castile), 351 (endow, "heretar l·em"), 353ff. (later surrender, expulsion). Compare "loch honrat," "heretat covinent," and "castells bons," as well

taking counsel and weighing the chances of losing the siege, James assented. The lord of Játiva's secondary castle, a brother of Yaḥyā, also received rich estates, as did the prime minister negotiating the surrender.[45] From at least 1246, therefore, Játiva ranked as a crown aljama rather than a fief, its nonmilitary *qā'id* over the Mudejar segment of the community being an appointee of the king. The first of these civil administrators was Muḥammad of Morella; the Abenetos who erroneously seems to have been his predecessor was instead Abenecos or Abenocos, a distortion of Ibn 'Īsā himself (Abeneça).[46]

Older historians spoke of a definitive fourth siege in 1249, but no documents support this; besides, a spate of property grants to Christian settlers on and before 1248 suggests crown control. The evidence requires revision of current historical teaching about the time and process of Játiva's absorption. Játiva castle at some point contributed to the episodes of rebellion that agitated Valencia widely from about 1246 into 1252. In the light of documentation now available, it would be more surprising had the region remained calmly loyal than that she sustained both turmoil and repression. In his survey of the revolt, King James singled out one district by name—"those of Játiva, who had forfeited" (*forfeit*) or defaulted in essential feudal obligation.[47] Unlike even the more affluent rebels of the realm, this entity was able to offer the crown as amends an immense increase of annual revenue; the king refused the bribe. General pacification of disturbed towns included either a reissue in 1252 of Játiva's previous charter, or else conveyance then of the usual though adapted charter that had been

as the phrase in ch. 350, "el e son linatge ne porien viure honradament," with the implication of feudal dignity discussed above. The first siege can be dated by the terminal phrase of a 1240 document, "in bastita Xative" (*Itinerari*, p. 143 [June 17, 1240]).

[45] Desclot, *Crònica*, ch. 49. *Llibre dels feyts*, ch. 51.

[46] Arch. Crown, James I, Reg. Canc. 11, fol. 199 (April 9, 1261): confirmation of a grant formerly given in Arabic by "alcaydus Xative quondam nomine Abenecos [Abovetos ?]"; Martínez-Ferrando read it as Abenetos. The *qā'id* Muḥammad of Játiva referred to in expenses of the Murcian campaign is probably this same Muḥammad of Morella (Reg. 15, fol. 99, March 1267).

[47] *Llibre dels feyts*, ch. 368: "aquella de Xativa, qui havien forfeit." See Rodón Binué, *El lenguaje técnico*, pp. 122-124, on *forisfacere* and variants. The thirteenth-century use of Catalan *forfer* also accommodated the general meaning of crime, but the feudal usage resonated in this form, especially in the context of a vassal's delict or of a "castel forfeu."

delayed until the crown could attempt an administrative overhaul of its uneasy southern acquisitions.[48]

The central castle of the Banū ʿĪsā now became Montesa, described by a contemporary historian as "an awesome stronghold, which had not been conquered in the winning of the kingdom of Valencia; in fact the Saracens had held it since olden times."[49] Standing as it did in a valley west of Játiva which could serve as direct invasion route from Granada to Valencia city, Montesa in its status as an independent fief offers a striking example of Mudejar nobiliary power. King James admitted that he would rather have conceded less; in bowing to necessity he incorporated this reduced principate, this shadow of Játiva which remained a potential enemy, as an element in his feudal kingdom. He must soon have regretted his concession. During the range of revolts around 1255, Montesa seems to have involved itself at least peripherally. King James narrates how all malcontents unable to seize castles "went out of the land [and] all betook themselves to Montesa"; with medieval carelessness for numbers, he sets them at "60,000 men-at-arms, not counting women and children."[50] Significantly, the dispossessed "all" had instinctively sought the leadership of the Játiva dynasty. There is no suggestion that Montesa joined the rebellion, but the episode implies condonation. Did the *qāʾid* at some time flee to avoid personal complicity, or briefly suffer exile due to fortunes of war? The contemporary Ibn al-Abbār al-Quḍāʿī, encountering him, grieved to see "the *wālī* Yaḥyā and his *raʾīs* Abū Bakr" wandering in poverty, dependent upon the largesse of friends.[51] If the episode fits here chronologically, opportune diplomacy arranged some compromise restoration.

Subsequent events suggest that a grim condition henceforth en-

[48] See Chapter VI, including n. 9 on the charter's dating.

[49] *Crónica de San Juan de la Peña*, ch. 36: "unum castrum vocatum de Montesia mirabilis fortitudinis quod non fuit captum in adquisitione regni Valentiae, quinimo sarraceni id ab antiquis temporibus tenuerant."

[50] *Llibre dels feyts*, ch. 368: "exien se de la terra, e anaven se·n a Montesa tots." Desclot counts the defenders at the 1277 siege of Montesa with similar exaggeration as 30,000 (*Crònica*, ch. 74: "trenta millia homens d·armes").

[51] Conde, *Dominación de los árabes en España*, p. 269, drawing on the eyewitness account of al-Abbār al-Quḍāʿī (Alabar Alcoday) of Valencia. Not only did Yaḥyā survive as ruler, but Abū Bakr Muḥammad succeeded him.

cumbered the title to Montesa—reversion of the castle to the crown, either permanently at some future date or temporarily in times of military crisis. Yaḥyā meanwhile enjoyed the king's favor, marked by a spate of gifts: in 1257 the concession of regalian herbage on flocks from Aragon and Castile, plus mill wheels and water rights at Yocor near Játiva; in 1259 a tax-free jovate in Yocor; and in 1260 the king's country estate at Játiva.[52] These may have formed part of a continuing stream of such benefactions, but their enregistering at this time of unrest in Valencia has the look of a conciliatory bribe. When Yaḥyā died some time after this rain of gifts, his vizier and relative succeeded. Abū Bakr (Muḥammad) b. Yaḥyā b. ʿĪsā (Abubequer Abenaisa, or Mahomet Benayhe Abenayça) faced a difficult time. Perhaps the original agreement expired at his predecessor's death; perhaps either Yaḥyā or Abū Bakr had compromised himself during a revolt, opening the door to legal challenge; or perhaps King James became uneasy at the accession of the zealous Nasrid, Muḥammad II, to the throne of Granada. Whatever the reason, Abū Bakr abruptly appears in the Christian records of 1273 in possession of Montesa but being asked to surrender it. Vallada was already gone, its town and revenues in the hands of Hugh of Baux, its castle and defenses by April 1274 securely under Jazpert of Barberá.

Loss of the key castle, Montesa, while neither dismantling nor disarming the reduced principality of the Banū ʿĪsā, would have reduced it from a semiautonomous military presence to a more domesticated barony, manageable by the crown and incapable of real mischief. Unwilling to resist, its masters evaded and procrastinated. Familiar with the recuperative processes at work in the wider Arabic world, they could anticipate the countercrusade soon to surge over Spain. That same year, the dying founder of Nasrid Granada counseled his son to detach from Castile and cleave to Morocco; the Marinids, masters of Marrakesh from 1269, were ready to recover their Spanish empire so recently lost. By surviving until that imminent day, Montesa could play a vital role. Before the year was over,

[52] Arch. Crown, James I, Reg. Canc. 9, fol. 24v (Feb. 27, 1257), "casalia . . . dirutta . . . ita quod rehedificetis"; Reg. 11, fol. 152 (Sept. 29, 1259); fol. 192 (Jan. 24, 1260), a *rahal*, an open estate in the countryside, "cum domibus, terminis, et pertinentiis suis"; see a Gandía gift in James I, perg. 1,112 (Feb. 17, 1247).

in December 1273, King James conceded a year's moratorium on relinquishing the stronghold.[53] When time ran out, the diplomatic *qā'id* contrived to avoid delivery for several months, until served with a decisive order at the end of March 1275. "By the present instrument we and ours desire and command you—the *qā'id* of Montesa, and Ibn Fārim—that you hand over the castle of Montesa to our faithful Arnold Escrivá, bailiff and our procurator for Valencia in our stead." The vizier or perhaps *ḥājib* of Abū Bakr has suffered at the hands of Christian scribes; he appears in manuscripts variously as Abenfarrin, Abenfejim (though differing from the first only by an ambiguous stroke), Abinfen, and Ben Farim.[54]

Undismayed, the *qā'id* opened a new diplomatic front. Through the offices of the vizier of Castile's Mudejar kingdom, Murcia, King James granted a further, generous reprieve of two years, not omitting a mild reproof: "You, *qā'id* Abū Bakr b. 'Īsā, the *qā'id* of Montesa ought to have returned to us the castle of Montesa."[55] Who was the influential luminary from Murcia? Christian documents provide an embarrassment of spellings. He is Abubecha Abenhuarda in this letter, but elsewhere Abubacre Abuadah, Aben Hudab, Aben Huadach, Abenuhatza, Abuadan Abenutzali, and Aben Uadah, a mixture of sounds which can accommodate reconstructions as varied as Ibn Waḍḍāh and Ibn Hudhayl. King James took the precaution of sending Escrivá to Montesa to secure a binding document as guarantee

[53] *Ibid.*, James I, Reg. Canc. 19, fol. 82v (Dec. 17, 1273). James was following the wider crisis, so that a confrontation with Montesa would have been untimely. On March 20 he had urged reluctant feudatories to march behind him to the aid of Castile, just as their fathers did "in facto Ubede, Almerie, Provincie et nobis in Navarra, Maiorica, Valencia, Murcia, et pluribus aliis locis . . . nos sequi in Yspaniam" (*Itinerari*, p. 478).

[54] Arch. Crown, Reg. Canc. 20, fol. 233v (March 28, 1275): "cum presenti carta volumus et mandamus vobis alcaydo de Montesa et Abenfarrino quod tradatis castrum de Montesa fideli nostro Arnaldo Scribe baiulo et procuratori nostro Valencie loco nostro." The conjectural reconstruction Fārim may be preferable to choices like Faris, Farḥūn, or Hārūn. If one prefers to relate it to some tribal name prominent in Valencia, nearby Rugat was one of several ancestral strongholds of the Valencian branch of the Banū Fihr.

[55] *Ibid.*, fol. 257v (May 17, 1275): "tu alcaydus Abubaqr Abenayça alcaydus [*sic*] Montese debebas reddere castrum de Montesa." *Alcaydus* precedes the name as vocative title and follows it as descriptive title—an unusual procedure, possibly a scribal error, which can be seen again in n. 56 with *alguazirus*.

for delivery in 1277.[56] James could not afford a domestic quarrel at the time, since Abū Yūsuf of Morocco had put himself at the head of "all the forces of his empire" in mid-1275 and was preparing to move a coalition army against Christendom.[57] Islam's hosts soon rolled back the Castilian defenders, exposing all Spain. The kingdom of Valencia fell into disorder, until James found himself battling to keep from being swept back to his old borders. Montesa remained aloof from these excitements, sustaining only an episode of fighting during a confused period in early 1276.[58] Her trial was to come in the next reign. King James's autobiography, after the manner of such selective revelations, glosses over the triumphs of the Banū 'Īsā. He leaves the impression that he brusquely expelled all Muslims of the Játiva-Montesa region during the mid-century revolts, some going to Murcia or Granada, others to Castile.[59] He draws the curtain of silence over Montesa and its dynasty. Actually the Banū 'Īsā had survived for a third of a century under his crown and were still ruling their extensive fief from Montesa castle when James died in mid-1276. They had weathered the long years of rebellion, without compromising their status as military vassals.

Though the Montesa barony's behavior remained technically correct under King Peter, its rock-like presence at the neo-Christian heartland constituted a menace for Aragon and a heartening banner for the forces of Islam. Before the Escrivá note fell due, the new king anticipated the crisis it posed. He was slowly bringing the Valencian

[56] *Ibid.*, fol. 297 (May 19, 1275). The Murcian vizier appears in the *Repartimiento de Murcia* (pp. 192-193) under several forms, but most fully as Alguazil Aboadille Abn Abilcaçim Abn Abilhatab Aben Uadah. He is Abubecre Abuadan in *Itinerari*, p. 385. In Arch. Crown, James I, Reg. Canc. 20, fol. 329v (March 6, 1276) he is "tibi alguaziro Abuquequero Abenutzali alguaziro [*sic*] olim civitatis Murcie." See, too, the forms for his name in Fernández y González, *Mudejares de Castilla*, appendix, doc. 47 (1266).

[57] Ibn Khaldūn, *Histoire des Berbères*, IV, 74-81, 361-464.

[58] Reflections of these spring troubles can be seen in the flight of "sarraceni de Muntesia vel aliorum locorum regni Valencie" to various Islamic lands, facilitated by the crown in October 1276; and in the prohibition against "arma, victualia, seu alias res prohibitas" being imported "apud Muntesiam vel alias partes seu loca sarracenorum," a canonical device applicable only to Islamic areas at war with or militarily dangerous to Christendom. Soldevila publishes both documents in *Pere el Gran*, part 2, I, appendix, docs. 33, 41.

[59] *Llibre dels feyts*, ch. 369.

revolt under control, but every success threw Montesa into bolder relief as the primary threat. Peter expressed his nervousness when sending out draft calls over Aragon in early January of 1277. Postponing the levies due from Zaragoza and other places, he cautioned that "if the *qā'id* and Saracens of Montesa broke the pacts and agreements they have with us, they ought to surrender to us the said castle"; or, if new waves of foreign invaders arrived, he would have to activate this call-up.[60] With al-Azraq, Muḥammad, Ibrāhīm, and the Eslida rebels expunged from the scene, the king could now afford to confront Montesa under feudal as well as crusading guise. On April 17 Peter moved his headquarters permanently down to Játiva. Except for two weeks' logistical negotiations at Valencia city, and brief excursions to nearby centers, the king would leave his Játiva base during the next half-year only to conduct his siege of Montesa.

A month after Peter's arrival, on Pentecost Sunday, May 17, the *qā'id* faced the day of decision. The king waited in vain for compliance. That day he sent a warning to Catalan officials against commercial passage of horses toward Montesa, in view of its threatened disaffection and of raids in the area.[61] On May 20 Peter dispatched Simon Zapata as his plenipotentiary to require immediate delivery of Montesa "from the *qā'id* Abū Bakr b. 'Īsā and 'Abd Allāh b. Fārim and from others whom it concerns," furnishing Simon with a "letter of credence" and recalling the Muslims' documentary promise given to King James. The two leaders returned a written response justifying their delay. Peter rejected this: "I do not accept the reply as sufficient [*bastant*]." He sent Simon back on May 22 with a peremptory notice "to his loyal [*feels*]" adversaries.[62] When the next

[60] Soldevila, *Pere el Gran*, part 2, I, appendix, doc. 67 (May 27, 1277), referring back to conditions attached to the January 13 draft (given, without these conditions, in doc. 52). For the progress of the war, but with focus on Peter and without the extra documentation and background in our article, see part I, III, ch. 16, and part 2, I, chs. 2, 3. See also his shorter *Vida de Pere el Gran*, chs. 6, 11.

[61] Arch. Crown, Peter III, Reg. Canc. 39, fol. 201v (May 17, 1277).

[62] Soldevila, *Pere el Gran*, part 2, I, appendix, doc. 65 (May 20, 1277): "ad petendum et recipiendum nomine nostro castrum et villam de Montesa ab alcaydo Abu ben Abenayca et Abdela Abinfen et ab aliis ad quos ad quos [*sic*] pertinent et quorum interest"; and doc. 66 (May 22, 1277), a Latin explanation of the mission and "credencia," the king's discontent "de responsione quam dictus alcaydus sibi fecit ad predicta per dictum Eximinum," and the renewed warning "per alias litteras sarracenicas" registered here in a Catalan original in full ("nos no tenim per bastant").

few days brought no satisfactory answer, he convoked the first elements of a massive siege army, setting July 8 as target date for rendezvous; over 150 draft notices went to prelates or knights holding Valencian fiefs under military service, not to mention vassals without Valencian holdings. Montesa's ruler, forced to abandon the revolution or lead it, had crossed his Rubicon. The drift of events for some time had carried him toward that decision. Fugitive warriors from areas surrendering under Peter's blows or rendered vulnerable by the defeat of men like the *qā'id* Ibrāhīm had been falling back upon Montesa, streaming in to man its walls and outposts. The Morocco-Granada axis had mounted a fresh invasion, apparently timed to hit Valencia at the moment of Montesa's rebellion.

Peter moved deliberately. He was about to attempt what James the Conqueror had never quite brought off—the conquest of the Játiva region—not merely by possession of its capital city but by breaking the military power of its dynasty. As late as June 12, in an embargo on wheat export from Tortosa, Peter spoke in moderate tone of Montesa's disloyal disposition. A week later, when licensing some merchants who doubled as negotiators for captives, he referred openly to "the war we are waging with Montesa."[63] Meanwhile he raised funds by every expedient possible, even wringing the aljamas of his northern Jews and Mudejars. Pope Gregory X on April 12 conceded to the beleaguered king the general crusade tithe for the Holy Land, voted by the recent ecumenical council of Lyons. Its executors, the metropolitans of Arles and Narbonne, later explained to Pope Nicholas III that this eventually amounted to 15,000 pounds in the money of Tours "because the untimely fury of the Muslims was invading his realm most powerfully and perilously."

The peril, however, lay in Montesa rather than in the wider war that was now becoming quiescent. Peter forestalled "an inquisition into Valencian parts" by the two metropolitans about the real need for deflecting Holy Land funds in such great quantity; he argued that the sixteen-day journey by the investigators would prove unsuitably expensive, while his "nobles and prelates, who were present at the siege of Montesa and knew fully the necessity and truth of the matter" could not be spared to give testimony. On July 30, 1279,

[63] *Ibid.*, docs. 67 (May 28, 1277), 68 (*idem*), 71 (June 20, 1277): "guerra quam habemus cum Muntesia."

Peter instructed his envoy to Rome about this anti-investigatory maneuver, and stressed that the pope must realize "the need which the lord king had, on account of the war he waged against the Saracens, especially in the affair of Montesa," so that no repayment should be exacted. The wars of al-Azraq some twenty years earlier had attracted the attention of Christendom; the convulsive effort to destroy the power of the Banū ʿĪsā of Montesa, disguised under the rubric of the generalized Valencian revolts now coming to an end, won more substantial attention and financial aid.[64]

On July 3 a final draft call, convoking Catalan feudatories from the Pyrenees to Tarragona, recapitulated by way of propaganda the crown's legal grievance against the Banū ʿĪsā. Tone and content differ from the many expressions employed to describe the wider revolt; Montesa was treated as a clear case of feudal law, though the underlying menace of Islam was implicit in the context of parallel revolt and foreign invasion. Details of the hardy siege, curtailed by a clever stratagem of the crusaders, fill the pages of the contemporary Desclot. It is sufficient to note that the stronghold fell on September 29, after a death struggle of two and a half months. Confident of victory by August 21, the king had terminated a call to many feudatories for September 1, remarking that "we have now learned for certain that Abū Yūsuf, king of Morocco," and other invaders were not on their way, and that the crown hoped "soon to conclude the affair of Montesa."[65]

[64] Arch. Vat., Reg. Vat. 38, fol. 33-33v, ep. 143 (April 12, 1277); also fols. 31v-32, ep. 138 (*idem*), and fols. 33v-34r, ep. 144 (*idem*). The later accounting for the tithe is appended to *Rationes decimarum Hispaniae*, docs. 3, 10, 12, 14, and 15; see esp. doc. 3 (1280): "tempore quo sarraceni regnum ipsum hostiliter impugnabant, quando idem dominus rex 15,000 libras [turonenses] accepit mutuo de pecunia decimali"; report of December 2, 1279 enclosed: "ad defensionem sui regni . . . propter necessitatem que sibi et regno suo imminebat, pro eo quod Agarenorum rabies importuna regnum ipsum potentissime et periculos[is]sime invadebat." Doc. 15 (July 30, 1279) contains Peter's instructions: "satis possit constare domino pape, per famam de necessitate quam habebat dominus rex . . . propter guerram quam habuit cum sarracenis, specialiter in facto Muntesie"; "multi episcopi et prelati et nobiles ac barones et etiam religiosi, qui fuerunt presentes et noverunt plenarie necessitatem et negocii veritatem in obsidione Muntesie."

[65] Soldevila publishes the documents of July 3 and August 21 (part 2, 1, appendix, docs. 75, 93); "negotium Muntesie credamus in brevi ad laudabilem finem deducere." His itinerary of descriptive royal addresses on p. 115 shows that Montesa probably fell on September 29; the siege continued on the twenty-eighth but the king was in the town on the thirtieth. Desclot, *Crònica*, ch. 74.

Though the castle flew the crimson and gold standard of Aragon when Peter left the battleground in the first days of October, the defenders had been able to win terms. As late as June of the following year, after a decent interval allowing Ibn ʿĪsā to arrange his affairs, the crown was making provision for the peaceful conveyance of the *qāʾid* and his household to Islamic lands. A safeguard specified that "the former *qāʾid* of Montesa with seven persons, and Ibn Fārim with four persons, [may] leave the kingdom of Valencia and go to any lands they choose."[66] Custody of the central castle had gone to Bernard of Bellvis, procurator or co-governor of all Valencia south of the Júcar River. It would soon know days of glory again. Just after the turn of the century, when Christendom suppressed the Knights Templar, James II reorganized their assets around a substitute order, to hold the Valencian frontier. He called them Knights of Montesa and installed their headquarters in the great castle of the fallen *qāʾid*. Meanwhile, in the wake of Peter's victory, slavers continued for at least a year and a half their purchases among the multiple prisoners of war at Montesa.

Montesa's fall disconcerted the other rebel groups; abandoning hope, according to Desclot, they surrendered the remaining castles in the kingdom. A good portion of the Muslim populace around Montesa, shaken by the descent of armies, had hemorrhaged away into other areas of Valencia. Peter's successor would strive to coax them back and to replace the economic loss by new Muslim settlement. The last princely dynasty of Valencia, hope of the Mudejars and fulcrum for countercrusading invaders, had disappeared as though it had never existed. History would barely remember the *qāʾid*, viewing him as a minor Mudejar rebel, at best a castellan like the *qāʾid* Ibrāhīm. The tragic downfall of the Banū ʿĪsā, when seen in detail, underscores the power of the Mudejar nobiliary caste. Its erosion at Montesa did not begin until a generation after the crusade; for over thirty years this Mudejar fief had been a star in the Christian feudal firmament. It

[66] Arch. Crown, Peter III, Reg. Canc. 40, fol. 114v (June 4, 1278): "quod permittatis alcaydum qui fuit Muntesie cum septem personis et Abenfejim cum quattuor personis exire de regno Valencie et ire ad quascumque partes voluerint absque solucione. . . ." This is the Abenfarrinus of n. 54, differing only by an ambiguous stroke; he is Ben Farim in a document of May 22. Soldevila is misled, by Desclot's careless exaggeration of the king's manner of entry, into believing Montesa fell without terms (*Pere el Gran*, part 2, I, p. 51).

fell as the result of determined rebellion, more the victim of its own hubris than of antagonism from outside.

Had more time elapsed before the revolts, or had the power of Granada and North Africa not supported the rebels, the assimilation of this aristocratic class might have proved a notable social experiment. Previous efforts in this direction had been ambiguous, as with tributary allies not really within the Christian polity, or else they had occurred on a scale too small and feeble, as with ephemeral pre-Valencian frontiers like Tortosa. Ironically the large scope of the Valencian experiment, which provided solid base for a continuing mutual respect and a promising evolution, also offered the Muslims the chance of a last, desperate gamble for independence. King James, whose every instinct drove him toward keeping his word and whose memoirs are never more noisy and implausible than when he is rationalizing some instance of breaking his promise, was thus handed an occasion for destroying the Mudejar power basis. It took him and his sons many years to encompass this; but the advantages of justification and propaganda were his, and time was on his side.

CHAPTER XV

Horizontal Power: The Rulers

PREVIOUS CHAPTERS have penetrated aljama life at points as varied as religion, ethics, law, population distribution, ethnic strains, and social strata. Now that the Mudejar has been fitted into his background, it is time to organize into an understandable pattern the structure of political authority that framed his life. Since this project breaks new ground, caution decreed its postponement until explanatory data had been presented. Historians have hitherto assumed a multiplicity of unrelated rural or town-ghetto communities, each under its *amīn* assisted by one to four officers (*adelantados*) and advised by a council of wise elders.[1] The picture, appealingly logical though it may be, reflects other centuries or places. It does not correspond to the Valencian evidence, nor does it begin to suggest the complex organization of authority among early Valencian Mudejars.

A complicating factor in reconstructing the situation was the tendency in Islamic public life for authority and influence to hide behind a shifting screen of titles that were imprecise, modestly ambiguous, or generic; these require clarification for a given time and place. The few Arabic writers who advert to the Valencian rulers do so by titles conventionally correct but remote; in the rush of their larger stories, they were not interested in nuancing the terms to fit the local scene or to discern the changing reality beneath a preferred mode of address. The Christian observer may innocently have caught something of this underlying meaning, however, and recorded some clues about the relationship of power to bland title. Comparison with usage else-

[1] Roca Traver, "Vida mudéjar," p. 158. Andrés Giménez Soler, a knowledgeable specialist, makes this generalization of Mudejar communities in his *La edad media en la corona de Aragón*, 2d edn. rev. (Barcelona, 1944), p. 293. Ernesto Mayer places the aljama under its *qāḍī*, assisted by *faqīh* advisers, and contrasts its structure with that of the Jewish conciliar organization; see his *Historia de las instituciones sociales y políticas de España y Portugal durante los siglos v a xiv*, 2 vols. (Madrid, 1925-1926), I, 321. Esteban Abad reports the Daroca aljamas as "muy simple" in governance, led by an *amīn* with two elected *adelantados* as assistants (*Ciudad y comunidad de Daroca*, p. 216).

where, an exercise that must always be undertaken with caution when dealing with so variegated a world as Islam, can be particularly misleading in the present case. However it does provide a historical and introductory frame. Whatever can be elicited from Valencian titles, it is the reality of the rule behind them that can best illumine the Mudejar transition. The following three chapters will analyze the mechanism of that rule—first in the hierarchy of regional dignitaries; then as localized in the town; and finally in the pervading but informal influences wielded vertically throughout these structures, unifying and relating them. Attention naturally turns first to the visible depositories of larger power. Some of these continued in Mudejar times as dynasts like the Játiva family, succeeding each other by processes established before the crusade; others were semireligious figures, rising to political office by varied combinations of election, confirmation, or appointment; finally others smack less of the seignior, the *qāḍī*, or the tax administrator, appearing more in the guise of elected community leaders, whatever other posts they controlled.[2]

The King

Like all political phenomena in the Middle Ages, the Mudejar civil order undoubtedly displayed wide variations. Large cities, royal towns, and seignorial hamlets differed in their complications. Early organization contrasted with later, as when revolts ended in the exiling of some lords and the fragmenting of their seignorial units. Valencia had endured centuries of civil mutations, moreover, so that its social-governmental apparatus retained fossilized remnants of previous hierarchies within its strata. Ribera has done valuable work

[2] The Minorca surrender treaty has an elaborate proviso for election plus confirmation of the combined "alfaqui et alcayd et alcadi et almoxeriff"; it keeps "pro alfaqui super vos, in loco nostro, venerabilem et legalem alfaqui qui modo est ibi . . . ut sit alfaqui in tota vita sua, et post obitum eius, liceat vobis eligere alfaqui de vobis alium quem volueritis, et sit semper alfaqui"; "et quando elegeritis alfaqui, faciatis nobis scire per vestrum nuncium et litteras, causa ut confirmemus ipsum; et nos debere mittere nuncium nostrum tunc, qui accipiat iuramentum ab illo ut serviet vobis omnia supradicta; et si forte inter vos non concordabitis de eleccione, nos possimus eligere pro alcayd [-alfaqui] unum de vobis et constituere cum consilio senium vestrorum."

in identifying some of the tribes or clans surviving from the kingdom's past, for instance, while Gayangos suspected that an Almohad faction still clung to a little power under Zayyān at the time of the crusade.[3] Whatever the local variations, unifying outlines can be discerned.

At the apex of power in both precrusade and Mudejar society sat the "king." A semantic difficulty tends to obscure his role. The ruler of Islamic Valencia had acted as governor (*wālī*) for the Almohad caliph at Marrakesh; the technical title *sayyid*, innocuous in an earlier context, identified Abū Zayd and his dynasty as princes of the blood, the chosen few whom these caliphs preferred as rulers and military commanders; this explains why Abū Zayd as the convert Vincent pathetically continued to flaunt this remnant of imperial status. During the collapse of Almohad power throughout Spain, Valencia's "king" had remained aware of his connection with Marrakesh and at least once referred a problem to the caliph.[4] Like Ibn Hūd's pretense of ruling Murcia as emir for the Abbasid caliphs of Bagdad, such gestures were mainly expedient trappings of legitimacy; the Christian neighbors saw through them, describing Ibn Hūd as "practically a monarch" ("fere monarchus").[5] After the same fashion, the Majorca ruler heartened his fighters when the crusade went against them: "the Amīr al-Mu'minīn has held this land over a hundred years, and wishes me to be lord over you."[6] Such links were tenuous. In practice Abū Zayd governed Valencia autonomously.

Muslim and Christian each understood kingship differently. The European institution had evolved by eccentric paths from elements as divergent as the Roman military *rex*, the Germanic tribal chieftain, and the Old Testament's anointed rulers, but especially from

[3] Gayangos's comment is in Forster's translation of James's *Chronicle*, II, 444.

[4] On the Almohad technical *sayyid* rank and the reigns of Abū Zayd and Ibn Hūd, see Chapter II, especially Huici, *Imperio almohade*, as cited in n. 3. The original title *sayyid*, dating from pre-Islamic Arabia, meant the preeminent leader of a tribe or cluster of tribes, not an authoritative ruler but a chief respected for a composite of personal qualities, family, and prestige (Tyan, *Droit public musulman*, I, 72-73, 84; Von Grunebaum, *Medieval Islam*, pp. 154-155).

[5] Jiménez de Rada, *De rebus Hispaniae*, lib. IX, c. 13.

[6] *Llibre dels feyts*, ch. 79: "miramoli."

ideas of imperial sovereignty in Roman law. The Islamic term was simply attached to forms of rule proper to Islam; for the pious, the word itself (*malik*) sometimes held a secular ring, though various dynasties did adopt it. As a word, it had suffered an evolution of its own, which had detached it from any necessary connection with autonomous rule. It had declined from meaning at least an imperial governor, and within a century of the Valencian crusade would frequently attach to court dignitaries and persons of similar low rank.[7] No semantic complications arise for an analysis of the Valencian situation. King James did not employ *malik* or translate it, nor is there any evidence suggesting that Abū Zayd adopted it. Both used king (*rex*) in the ordinary European sense, without equivalence of value. Independent rule, under any name, had common denominators in both cultures.

Kingship, as Ibn Khaldūn shrewdly observed, is not a matter of title. He defined royal power as existing in any locality where a usurper or provincial governor ruled his subjects, collected taxes, dispatched military expeditions, protected the frontiers, and was not controlled by a stronger power—"this is generally accepted as the real meaning of royal authority," whatever the formalities. Elsewhere he described the spectacle of Spanish Islam after the Las Navas disaster in 1212 and the fall of Cordova in 1236 as a condition in which kings sprouted on all sides. "Every *qā'id* and man of influence, who could command a score of followers or possessed a castle to retire to in case of need, styled himself sultan and assumed the insignia of royalty," so that Islamic Spain "afforded the very singular aspect of as many kings as there were castellated towns in the country."[8] In the similar fragmentation of Islamic Spain two hundred years previously, each neighborhood ruler studiously avoided terms of sovereignty like king (*malik*) or sultan, but nonetheless adopted "royal surnames and trappings." The poet Ibn Rashīq mocked these sovereign pussycats "who by inflating themselves imitate the lion." The chronicle of Alfonso X at our period reflected further disinte-

[7] Ibn Baṭṭūṭa, *Travels*, I, 226 and n.; see also pp. 112-114.

[8] *Muqaddimah*, I, 315-316, 380-382, 470. See also Gayangos's translation, appendix to Forster's version of the *Chronicle*, II, 696. On sultan and *malik* see Tyan, *Droit public musulman*, I, 82, 85-86, 380-384, and II, 36; see also T. W. Arnold, *The Caliphate* (Oxford, 1924), ch. 11 on independent princes; Sanchis Guarner, "Època musulmana," p. 350; and M. Plessner, "Malik," *EI*[1], III, part 1, 204.

gration from the situation Ibn Khaldūn described: "after the death of Ibn Hūd, the land split up under many small kings."[9]

The essential autonomy of these entities facilitated not only the crusade but the subsequent substitution of James as overlord. At every level—judicial, financial, legislative, ceremonial, psychological, and administrative—the new king slipped into the place vacated by the old. Even his direct control of so much of the kingdom accorded with the pattern by which Islamic kinglets had held much of the area's property like the caliph before them.[10] In resolving the Eslida-Uxó irrigation quarrel, a regional litigation extending back through two Islamic reigns, King James conducted himself as inheritor of the last *wālī*, succeeding to his civil powers.[11] When negotiating surrender charters, James's policy was to demand taxes "exactly as they had paid to their king." He entertained an exalted concept of kingship, reserving the title "lo rey" to the independent Muslim rulers of Majorca, Murcia, Valencia, and of alien blocs like Granada or Tunis, but refusing it to relatively autonomous regions like Játiva and Minorca.[12]

One expects the term *sulṭān* to have been popular as a noncommit-

[9] *Muqaddimah*, I, 316; the poem of Ḥasan b. Rashīq (d. 1071) at Almeria is erroneously ascribed by Ibn Khaldūn to the vizier Ibn Sharaf. *Primera crónica general de España quę mandó componer Alfonso el Sabio y se continuaba bajo Sancho IV en 1289*, ed. Ramón Menéndez Pidal *et al.*, 2 vols. (Madrid, 1955), II, ch. 1037: "et despues de la muerte de Abenhut, partiose aquella tierra en muchos pequennos reys." Compare the Christian use of *reges* for Tudela and Tortosa in their twelfth-century charters. Ibn Khaldūn gives a general explanation of the fragmenting process later in the *Muqaddimah*, telling how in Tunisia at such times "every castle was in the possession of an independent rebel": as factions emerge, a gap widens between higher and lower classes, with the notables vying among each other, grasping at clients and allies, spending their fortunes to win the rabble, until one manages to dominate and then to persecute his rivals (II, 303, 305). From an earlier context, the Valencian Ibn Jubayr during his eastern travels of the 1180's compared the princes sharing a divided land—especially a ruler over four cities—to the kings "of the regions of Andalusia" (*Voyages*, III, 277). Muntaner's reference to North African "kings and sons of kings" is above, Chapter XIII, n. 31.

[10] Lévi-Provençal, *España musulmana*, v, 114.

[11] See Chapter XI, n. 19.

[12] *Llibre dels feyts*, ch. 250: "aixi con fayen al rey lur." A romantically remote area, useful for propaganda purposes, could become a "kingdom," as with the rumored conversion of a "king of Africa" who was really governor for the Tunisian town of Mahdia, or the "kingdom of Zala," probably Moroccan Salé, claimed by a son of Abū Zayd who converted (see my "Christian-Islamic Confrontation," p. 1393).

tal indication of *de facto* power-holding, and indeed the *qā'id* Ibrāhīm, when surrendering his castle to Peter III during the last Valencian revolt, naturally addressed the Christian king this way. Arabic authors like Ibn al-Khaṭīb or Ibn Khaldūn who treat of this period have the "sheik" Ibn al-Aḥmar proclaim himself "sultan" of al-Andalus, while paying lip-service to the sultan of Tunis; earlier Arabic writers translated the Christians' *rex parvus*, Alfonso VIII of Castile, as "the little sultan." Sultan and king ought to have interchanged admirably, but Europeans had not yet domesticated the word sultan. It was to enter the Castilian language, for example, only from the last third of the thirteenth century, and then from Provençal or French rather than directly from the Arabic. In his autobiography King James employed sultan ("lo souda") only for the ruler of the "Turc" against whom he planned to crusade in the Near East. Muntaner, reporting that the Granadan lord of Guadix at the beginning of the next century called himself sultan ("soltan"), equated the term with king ("rey") and specifically with kingship as in Aragon.[13] Since the Christian attribution of "king" to Muslims did not translate a title but a reality of power, Abū Zayd as ruler had no difficulty in applying the term *rex* to himself when addressing Christians. An oddity of this usage is that for a few years both James and his ally Abū Zayd employed it simultaneously. The crusader had begun calling himself "king of Valencia" at least by 1236; yet as late as 1238 the convert Abū Zayd continued his own title "king of Valencia, descendant of the *amīr* 'Abd al-Mu'min," though by 1247 he saw himself as "former king" and "sometime king of Valencia."[14] The *wālī*-turned-king had metamorphosed into puppet-king

[13] *Llibre dels feyts*, ch. 533. Muntaner, *Crònica*, ch. 247. Lull uses the term both for "el Solda" in the East and for any local "solda." Muntaner records that, at the definitive subjugation of Minorca just after Peter's death, the presence of mercenary Turkish troops made the battle "molt cruel"; "havia hi turche bons homens . . . a sou" (ch. 172). Ibn Baṭṭūṭa uses sultan indiscriminately for Muslim and non-Muslim rulers, big and small, except for the caliph, in his *Travels* (see p. 3, note by Gibb). On sultan entering Castilian, see Neuvonen, *Arabismos del español*, p. 264.

[14] Chabás, "Çeid Abu Çeid," part 5, doc. on p. 147 (1229): "nos Ceyd Abuceyd rex Valencie"; pp. 152-153 (1232, 1237), same; p. 160 (1238): "Vincentius rex Valencie"; p. 166 (1247): "nos Aceyt Abuceyt quondam rex Valentie," and "olim rex Valentie"; p. 372 (1264), Pope Urban: "regi quondam Valentie." The first document in which James styled himself "king of Valencia" was an arbitration at

and then into convert-king, while James at every surrender of a castle ensconced himself more firmly in his stead. Title, palaces, and prerogatives shifted easily to the king of Mudejars, James the Conqueror.

A feature of precrusade governance that persisted in at least some places was the ruler's council. The major innovation of the Almohads at the imperial level—aside from their peculiar religious orientation—had been the elaboration of this council; consisting of a handful of men available for advice and collaboration, it had expanded greatly for consultation during crises.[15] This council must have differed, at least in formality, from "the household, functionaries, and officials" described by the eyewitness Ibn al-Abbār as following Zayyān when he went into exile from conquered Valencia. It was more exalted in function than the aljama council of the ruler's city, too, though it may have been identical in some personnel.[16] Though Christian documents had no occasion to mention the council used by Abū Zayd or his successor Zayyān, analogies may be drawn from the autonomous feudal enclaves of the kingdom and from neighboring kingdoms. James described the "conseyl general" of the Majorcan king-*wālī* and how the Minorcan lord similarly gathered his notables, later expanding their number into a more general council.[17] The Játiva dynasty consulted an inner "council of the *qā'id*," which either swelled into a larger council on occasion or

Tarazona signed by "nos Don Jayme por la gracia de Deus rey Daragon et de Mayorchas et de Valencia, comte de Barçalona et de Urgel et sennor de Montpeller" in *Itinerari*, p. 124 (Sept. 30, 1236). The situation in neighboring Murcia, tributary to Castile from 1243 and subject to it from 1266, involved a puppet King Muḥammad from that latter date; Alfonso X retained him because he was childishly pleased "de aver reyes por vasallos." Within twenty years Muḥammad was progressively stripped of rents and position. See Torres Fontes, "Mudéjares murcianos" (repaged offprint), pp. 7ff., 15.

[15] Tyan, *Droit public musulman*, II, 584-586. Hopkins segregates the cabinet of ten or twelve men from a chamber of fifty representatives of tribes, believing the ten not included in the fifty (*Medieval Muslim Government in Barbary*, p. 89). According to Huici, Almohad Spain developed no administrative novelties beyond what the new theology demanded, and the only difference between it and the Almoravid administration lay in a certain exclusiveness in appointing its own supporters (*Imperio almohade*, II, 576).

[16] "Traité d'Ibn al-Abbār," p. 33. For a town council, see *Llibre dels feyts*, chs. 438-440: "conseyl d·aquels de la vila"; "en lur conseyl"; "de lur conseyl."

[17] *Llibre dels feyts*, chs. 79, 121.

was displaced by the municipal council.[18] The lord of Alcalá was betrayed by a member of his inner "council"; James bribed this man who "was very close to al-Azraq and went around with him," serving as his confidant "more than anyone else in his entourage."[19] When King James, who never established a council of Muslims for his new kingdom, "convoked a great council in the buildings of King Lobo" or Lūb a few weeks after Valencia fell, Mudejars easily appreciated what he was about.[20] Probably the procurator, the bailiff, and similar administrative furniture did not strike them as very different from the previous ministerial bureaucracy; the *ḥājib* or prime minister, for example, appears in the person of Zayyān's nephew during the last days of Valencia city, and in the figure of the *algutzir* or vizier of the king of Murcia.[21]

Correlative Rulers: *Ra'īs* and *Wazīr*

Below the royal level, local organization was deceptive. It appeared to consist of smaller units with their respective countrysides, organized as components of larger units such as a town or a city with its more extensive surrounding territory. Each region thus had a mechanical kind of unity, like a hollow block holding several smaller blocks, each of which contained yet more blocks. The reality was less simple. Superimposed on this tidy map were innumerable enclaves of local power, affiliated or alienated according to a complex of motives now obscure, including such factors as family, tribe, sect, pre-Islamic or pre-Berber arrangements, ancient feuds, present heroes, and current circumstance. Just as the Játiva and Pego-Alcoy regions found it possible to act like independent kingdoms, the Alcira district at the time of the crusade made at least a recognizable subor-

[18] *Ibid.*, chs. 322, 335: "del conseyl del alcayt"; the larger contained many elders, while it was a mark of honor for the eminent Setxi that he belonged as well to the inner council.

[19] *Ibid.*, ch. 373: "era molt privat d•Alaçrach e anava ab ell"; "era de conseyl d•Alaçrach . . . pus que altre que fos en sa companya." Council or counsel can translate *conseyl*, but the more obvious meaning here is the first.

[20] *Ibid.*, ch. 402: "faem fer gran conseyl en les cases del rey Lop"; on Lūb or Ibn Mardanīsh, see above, Chapter II, n. 10. Thirty years later James held a "conseyl" of barons, knights, and citizens in "lo palau nostre de Valencia"; the palace was so crowded that a deliberative group had to meet apart (chs. 514-515).

[21] *Ibid.*, ch. 436.

dinate sphere of its own, as did Bairén-Gandía, while Segorbe had recently risen to become a similar center of control. Valencia city enjoyed a geographical *tinença* so large as to comprise an almost separate power bloc, and cities like Morella and Burriana probably found themselves in the same position. Majorca offers helpful analogies; its king had not only ruled over the other semiautonomous island blocs, but had presided over the main island through a governance of twelve districts, each under its own lord. Sharing a similar background, the Valencia kingdom must have developed some such system of regional districts; some do manifest themselves, but their overall number and placing remains elusive.

From the evidence thus far analyzed, the precrusade kingdom contained materials for parallel pyramids of power. These are best understood in the context of the geographical and historical divisions explained at length in Chapter III. Of the three zones laid out there, each unified by its history and the socioeconomic differences rooted in its economy, the north reveals no dynasts. Possibly the strength of Abū Zayd and the decisive conquests of the crusaders conceals them from view; the sprawling nature of the country, too, and its exposure to Christian attack, had thrown it back upon the Valencia *wālī* for defense. The interlocking sets of greater and lesser castellans, together with natural town-and-countryside *termini*, seem to define its local government. At the center, the capital city's bloc easily dominated the rest, though points like Liria and Burriana were obviously secondary nuclei of authority. Along this zone's northern border, the Segorbe-Jérica region, which had remained particularly loyal to Abū Zayd after his fall and dreamed perhaps of restoring the ancient Alpuente principality, provided a possible dynastic base. Similarly the segment at and just below the Júcar, with a riverine unity of its own along the Alcira-Cullera line, offered the fugitive Zayyān both a reservoir of troops and, after the surrender of Valencia city, an alternate kingdom. A dynastic figure, already prominent there before 1238, presided at Alcira. Throughout the center, too, each greater and lesser *qā'id* disposed his jurisdiction in terms of the dominant powers.

The southernmost unity, turned in upon itself by the dictates of its central massif and memories of a proud past as kingdom of Denia, survived the crusade more easily, leaving intact independent dynasts like the lords of Játiva, Pego, and Bairén. The *qā'id* controlling Gandía's huerta from Bairén could look north to Valencia or west to Játiva or south to Alcalá for support. In times of trouble, his colleagues could polarize around the nearest dynast. All three provinces fell into a unity by reason of their north-south orientation by road and shipping. The south was the least tractable of the three; while it blocked Murcia away as a separate kingdom to its south, it offered no exact boundaries to keep the two regions from mutual political encroachment.

The units were generally neither rural-feudal nor urban-communal, but a mixture. A powerful city like Alcira, Játiva, or Morella served as stronghold for some overlord; his subcastles, whether town alcazars or more isolated rural establishments, supported him more than he controlled them. That the complex of castellans and city notables cooperated so smoothly may have been due to a peculiarity of the social structure to which the final chapter will give its full attention. Both castellan and city notable, in any case, often represented a branching family continuity more cohesive for society than that of spectacular dynasts thrown up by circumstance. The crusaders dismantled the larger units of the kingdom, or replaced their governors with Christians; nevertheless sizable units remained, especially at the *qā'id* level, with a few great dynasts in the south. Islamic government thus survived the wreck of the system, as component boulders survive the collapse of a wall, each isolated castle or town entity retaining a measure of political self-sufficiency. These Mudejar units cooperated in a number of ways, as shown by their tax, legal, and military history, and could coalesce into rebellious unity with stunning suddenness. Conquest did not necessarily spell dissolution.

Two distinguished titles require notice before descending to the complicated local scene of the castellan. *Ra'īs* was a relatively uncommon term in the crusading world of King James. He used it only for exalted lords or rulers, though its generic meaning of chief applies equally well in the Islamic world to military captain, local politico, school superintendent, city mayor, or head of some artisan grouping.[22] Since James dignified the ruler of Alcira with this title,

[22] Ibn Khaldūn, in explaining that each ship in the fleet of 'Abd ar-Raḥmān an-Nāṣir had a *qā'id* captain, adds that a *ra'īs* acted as executive officer who di-

context may afford some clue to the reason why. The crusaders had left Alcira independent and unbothered after the fall of Valencia city, apparently fearing to try their overextended strength against a major city wrapped in its defenses on a mid-river island. Twice James bypassed the region to attack Játiva (1239-1240). Only after the crusade seemed to have ended, with Játiva securely established as a fief and the king long gone on business outside his new kingdom, did an opportunity arise for taking Alcira.

Whether this happened at the end of 1241 as Miret y Sans seems to say, or in 1242 as Chabás and many historians more plausibly argue, or even in 1243 as is not improbable, chance delivered the city.[23]

---

rected the mechanics of moving the ship (*Muqaddimah*, II, 40-41). Lapidus, in his *Muslim Cities*, passim, cites examples of a *ra'īs* of a corporation, of Koran readers, of law schools, of a village, of various merchant groups, and of the Jews. The vizier of Granada (d. 1271-1272) was also *ra'īs* of the city, or "mayor" as Gibb translates him (Ibn Baṭṭūṭa, *Travels*, I, 176n.). See also Neuvonen, *Arabismos del español*, pp. 163-164.

[23] The question is a mare's nest of calendar conjecture, starting from a fifteenth-century note that the city fell on the vespers of St. Sylvester (December 31) of 1243, continuing with the debate on whether the original or the fifteenth-century dates referred to the incarnational or the nativity calendars, further complicated by a document which removed James to Barcelona in 1242, and reopening when Miret y Sans and later Soldevila showed that Chabás had erred on the latter date by following a mistake of Tourtoulon and Villanueva. Miret seems to have accepted 1241, but the sense of his argument indicates that a misprint is involved and that he really favored 1242. He believed he had excluded 1243 by putting James already at the Játiva siege on December 30; but the subscription "apud castilio nostro Xative" may only indicate a diplomatic or reconnoitering visit and perhaps only to Villanueva de Castellón. Correlation of the *Llibre* with the documents revealing the king's itineraries suggests 1242 as the better date but does not exclude 1243. Assuming a reasonable confusion of dates, however—with the king spending sixteen months in the north in 1242, and misremembering it as 1243—then, by the itinerary of 1243, he could have hurried south in September of 1243, made a reconnaissance around Bairén and Villanueva (Castellón de Játiva), arranged for Alcira's sudden and peaceful surrender after his stay at Corbera, prepared the siege of Játiva which began by January 7, and thus have had time to celebrate the peaceful take-over of Alcira on December 31 as he passed by to join his army preparing that siege. In sum, despite the weighty authority of Miret y Sans and recently Soldevila, the date of December 31, 1243 still seems inviting when considered in relation to the king's movements as seen in the dating of his documents. (A minor annoyance is the fluctuating dates of the siege documents, indifferently 1243 or 1244.) See as a beginning the discussion and references in the notes of *Itinerari*, pp. 576-577, with p. 165. A complicating factor in the Alcira story may have been the provision for a truce at the surrender of Valencia city "quod hinc ad septem annos . . . guerram non faciemus . . . in Deniam nec in

James had descended with his armies, resolved to press a feudal legalism against his Játiva vassal; ironically, the secure ruler of Alcira, long surrounded by crusader territory, judged the thrust to be aimed at himself. "The *ra'īs* of Alcira" fled to Murcia "for fear of me," accompanied by "a good thirty knights." Since this left "the power" (*lo poder*) in the hands "of the Saracens and the lords" (*lo senyoriu*), they nervously approached the Christian king with a view to surrender. James confessed himself "much pleased" to accept so "fine and notable a place, among the best in the kingdom of Valencia."[24]

Culleram nec in suis terminis," leaving Zayyān with "illis duobus castris, Denia scilicet et Cullera" (Valencia Capitulation). Ibn Khaldūn includes a siege of Alcira by James I (*Histoire des Berbères*, II, 306), and later laments its loss, but gives no useful detail; he recounts how Alcira broke away from Zayyān to ally with Ibn Hūd until his death, then supported Zayyān against King James. Ibn Shanab, collating some of the dates from Islamic historians, puts the fall of Alcira (incorrectly given as modern Algesiras) as June 30, 1242 ("Notes chronologiques," p. 70). See the Eslida Charter date with comments above in Chapter VI, n. 4, and the dates in Chapter I, n. 3. A celebrated literary-political Alciran, al-Makhzūmī, fled to North Africa in 1242 at the fall of "Valencia," according to his biographers, who may have been referring to the collapse of the rump kingdom of Alcira left to Zayyān, if not to James's later seizure.

[24] *Llibre dels feyts*, ch. 329: "lo rayz d·Algezira era exit de Algezira per paor que havia de nos . . . e romas lo poder de la vila en los sarrains e en lo senyoriu"; "era bon loch e honrat e dels meylors que fossen en lo regne de Valencia . . . e a nos plach nos molt"; ch. 332: "l·arais d·Algezira, ço es lo seyor." Aside from other testimony, the king's actions demonstrate how important Alcira was to his rule and, by implication, to its previous *ra'īs*. He had a palace there from the start, where he received the Játiva *qā'id* ("en les nostres cases del reyal"), which appears to have been the palace of the former *ra'īs* (*Llibre dels feyts*, ch. 334). The subscriptions to James's documents reveal that he subsequently attended to important business at Alcira in 1247, 1249, 1261, 1268 (twice), 1269, 1270 (twice), 1271 (twice), 1273 (four times), 1274, and 1276 (twice, dying as he directed the war from there). Presumably he visited it from nearby Valencia as well, and paused here on his many trips to Játiva. A count of the places where he signed documents after 1244, disregarding length of stay, shows he favored three towns when in Valencia, staying at Valencia city something under fifty times, at Játiva twenty-two times, and at Alcira eighteen times; the nearest rivals were Denia and Murviedro (each six times), Biar, Burriana, and Gandía (five each), Cocentaina (four), Chivert, Cullera, Luchente, Murcia, and Onteniente (two), with fifteen other places showing one stop apiece. The brief description of the Valencian crusade in a contemporary letter by Ibn 'Amīra leaves no doubt that Alcira was a central loss—whose circumvallating blue waters met their match in the fierce blue-eyed Christian hosts with their shining lances. Ibn al-Abbār in more sober lament records how the evil swallowed Valencia city, then advanced on Alcira, with Denia going soon and Játiva (both letters in al-Ḥimyarī, *Kitāb ar-rawḍ al-mi'ṭār*, pp. 105, 113, 215).

He thus acquired the prerogatives and rents of "the *ra'īs*—that is, the lord." Why did James call him *ra'īs*? Possibly the choice reflected the governor's own title, conferred by some now obscure whim of history, though James mentions no other *ra'īs* ruling within the Valencian kingdom. Since he belonged to the Banū Mardanīsh, perhaps a predilection for the title had survived the half-century from the time Almohads had supplanted that clan as rulers of all Valencia. More probably its status briefly as the capital of Zayyān, protected by treaty after the fall of Valencia city, made its now subordinate overlord adopt the style used by Zayyān's second-in-command previously. The latter, who appears in the king's memoirs as "raiç" at Valencia city, was the nephew of King Zayyān, an imposing figure and effectively the realm's prime minister. Beyond Valencian borders the king did not refuse the title to a number of semi-independent rulers beneath the status for which he reserved the term king. He called the governor of Crevillente, in revolt against Castile, "the *ra'īs*." On one occasion he proffered advice to the Castilian king about the *ra'īs* of Guadix and the *ra'īs* of Málaga, rebels against Granada. Having appointed a governor over the semiautonomous fief of Minorca island, James wrote: "I made him *ra'īs*."[25] The designation, more common perhaps south of Valencia kingdom, appears in the books of land division both for Murcia and Valencia. The adjutant for Játiva's Yaḥyā b. 'Īsā also bore the title.[26]

Another name recognized as seemly for a lesser ruler was *wazīr* or vizier. In the East a vizier was an exalted personage, a kind of prime minister; in the West the *ḥājib* or chamberlain had usurped this role, becoming the power behind the throne and sometimes

The rebellions and sieges from Alcira's past, and information from geographers and others, also point to its political and military importance. On *ra'īs* as the older title common to local Banū Mardanīsh, see Ibn al-Khaṭīb, *A'māl*, p. 481.

25 *Llibre dels feyts*, chs. 272, 274, 277, 279, 282 ("raiç Abulphamalet"); ch. 422: "lo fyl de Banud [Ibn Hūd] el Arrais" at Crevillente; ch. 506: "los raeçes"; ch. 119: "faem raiz" at Minorca. Erwin Rosenthal elaborates a theory of *ra'īs* by Ibn Khaldūn as *primus inter pares* over a nonurban principate, with other ideal uses by al-Fārābī and Ibn Bājja; see his *Political Thought in Medieval Islam: An Introductory Outline* (Cambridge, 1958), pp. 87, 127, 160.

26 *Repartimiento de Murcia*, pp. 229-230: "el arraz Abubacre, fijo de Amir Amuzlemin," "el arraez Aboabdille, fijo del arraez de Malaga." *Repartimiento de Valencia*, p. 167, a country estate "quam vendidit ad Rayç Aboabdile Abuceqri." On Játiva's *ra'īs* Abū Bakr, see al-Quḍā'ī above, p. 344n.

during periods of decadence and disintegration an independent princeling. The Almohads ignored the institution; though the Hafsids later revived and developed it, no trace was left for the crusade epoch in Valencia.[27] Its apparent coordinate, vizier, amounted in the West to an honorific title indiscriminately awarded, along with an allowance, to favorites of the ruler. It carried no specific office; consequently its bearer might be a general, a governor, a minor official, or a courtier without any post. Immoderate use of the title in Spain had devalued it long ago. Casting about for a suitably vague yet dignified appellation, upstarts sometimes adopted either emir or vizier.[28] By the twelfth century, Mudejar surrender treaties at Tudela and Tortosa spoke of "viziers in their vizierates," and "all those viziers."[29] In the Valencian crusade era, the term might be used indifferently of a class of minor officials in a district, a town or regional governor, a prime minister of some kinglet, or a feudal lord.

The vizier dealing with King James at the surrender of Murcia—the same plenipotentiary sent by the king of Murcia to the king of Castile that year—was obviously the prime minister; on a similar mission this Abū 'Amrūs b. Ghālib (Abuambre Abengalip) brought along as associate a second vizier, Abū Bakr b. Waḍḍāḥ (Abubecre Abuadah).[30] At the height of his power, when swearing

[27] Popular with eleventh-century Andalusian kinglets like the lord of Alpuente (see Lévi-Provençal, *Inscriptions arabes d'Espagne*, p. 54), *ḥājib* finds no direct reflection in Valencia's Christian documents.

[28] D. Sourdel, " 'Wazīr' et 'Ḥāğib' en occident," *Études d'orientalisme*, II, 749-755. Tyan, *Organisation judiciaire*, pp. 258-259, 537-544. Ibn Khaldūn, *Muqaddimah*, I, 464; II, 6-14. Dozy, *Glossaire*, pp. 129-130 (*alguacil*).

[29] Tudela Charter (1115): "illos alguaziles lures alguazilias"; "de lure alcadi et de lures alguaziles sicut in tempus de illos moros." Tortosa Charter (1148): "alguaçir," "alguaciles," "cum alguaziris," "totos illos alguaçiros." Ibn 'Abdūn includes the twelfth-century vizier as the local ruler's right-hand man or at least a kind of secretary-adjutant (*Séville musulman, le traité*, pp. 29-33). At Valencia the Cid made Mūsā his vizier, and the *qāḍī* was to appoint his own vizier (Menéndez Pidal, *España del Cid*, I, 487, and II, 554). See also Lévi-Provençal, *España musulmana*, v, 13; Imamuddin, *Socio-Economic and Cultural History of Muslim Spain*, ch. 3. In the *Repartimiento de Valencia* a vineyard went to "Ali filio Jucefi alguazir" at Murviedro, previously "obligata Axe filie sue" (p. 497).

[30] Fernández y González, *Mudejares de Castilla*, appendix, docs. 46-47 (1266). On the Romance shift from 'Amrūs to Ambre, see Chapter XVII, n. 19. *Llibre dels feyts*, ch. 439. In the court of Peter III an *alguazir* was a police functionary (Karl Schwarz, *Aragonische Hofordnungen in 13. und 14. Jahrhundert* [Berlin,

conditional homage to Aragon in 1244, al-Azraq styled himself "vizier and lord of Alcalá"; Prince Alfonso carefully applied the same form in addressing his acceptance to the Mudejar. When al-Azraq later went into exile, his nephew continued the dynastic pretensions under that same title; in conferring castles on the nephew, James several times called him vizier. Eminences like these, on the other hand, would hardly have acknowledged the social existence of a town peace officer like the vizier at Murviedro in 1290, Faraj b. Aḥmad b. Sa'd b. Muḥammad.[31] As with *ra'īs* at Alcira, no instance of the title vizier for a living ruler or subruler, except the case of Alcalá's lords, survives from the crusade era in Valencia.

Abū 'Uthmān Sa'īd of Minorca, nominally under Islamic Majorca and then a subject of King James, gloried in the titles *faqīh* and *mushrif*. The second title, *almoixerif* to the Christians, bore connotations of customs controller or treasurer; the contemporary Arabic word list attributed to Martí equates it with "bailiff."[32] *Faqīh* as a ruler's title had contemporary parallels, though in all cases it seems to have been designed to shore up actual power with the adventitious prestige of religious scholarship; Minorca's administrator defined his office more fully by a cumulus of four titles combining the main

1914], p. 14); see also Webster, "Francesc Eiximenis on Royal Officials," p. 242. In Islamic and Christian Granada two centuries later the *alguacil* administered smaller places, unlike the more important *qā'id* (Caro Baroja, *Moriscos*, p. 81).

[31] *Spanisch-islamische Urkunden*, doc. 4.

[32] Martí, *Vocabulista*, p. 265. Neuvonen, *Arabismos del español*, pp. 157-158. Abū 'Uthmān Sa'īd apparently benefited from the same process operative in late Almohad Valencia, where a city *qāḍī* could drift into independence and then gain preeminence over neighboring cities; see Guillem Rosselló Bordoy, *L'Islam a les illes balears* (Palma de Mallorca, 1968), pp. 108-110. Lévi-Provençal makes the *mushrif* an aide and liaison between the Berber—in this case Almohad—town ruler and the local aristocracy, one of their own ("Villes et institutions urbaines en occident musulman," p. 81). It was nevertheless commonly a fiscal title. See also *Llibre dels feyts*, chs. 47, 50, 119, 122; "Maylorcha era cap de les altres yles e fayen ço que·l seyor de Maylorques los manava . . . subiugades al rey de Maylorques"; "la yla de Maylorques ab les senyories de les altres yles que son entorn, de Manorques e de Yvissa"; "l'alcayt" of Minorca. James replaced him with a *ra'īs*. On *senior* here, see Rodón Binué, *El lenguaje técnico*, pp. 231-234; the Játiva lordship ("en sa senyoria") is in *Llibre dels feyts*, ch. 319. The Minorca *qā'id* is in the surrender treaty as Aboabdil Mafomat (Abū 'Abd Allāh Muḥammad); see *Itinerari*, p. 94 (June 17, 1231).

religious and secular roles of a subruler—"alfaqui et alcayd et alcadi et almoxariff."[33]

Qā'id: A Flexible Title

Qā'id was a term elastic enough to designate alike a princely ruler and a grubby castellan in some rural backland. In origin an important military commander or even ship captain, the *qā'id* had evolved in western Islam in the direction of military governor or counterpart of the *wālī* in a frontier province. In thirteenth-century Spain he was normally commander of a fortress.[34] In crusader Valencia the term equates best with castellan, ranging from subordinate captain defending a rural outpost to autonomous princeling in his city alcazar. After the crusade the title persisted, sometimes strangely inherited by the civilian successor of a demoted military master. Wherever a *qā'id* crops up in the royal memoirs, he has a castle or is a military leader with rule implied.

When the Murcian vizier offered to surrender that region's capital city to James in 1266, its alcazar was completely controlled by the king of Granada's *qā'id*, a governor or diplomatic presence as much as a castellan, "who was their head [*cap*]."[35] Ibn Sīdrāy (Avenced-

[33] He calls himself "ego alfaqui Aboabdille Mafomet, filius domini alfaqui Abolança Aly Abineixem, alcady et alcaid insule"; the document confirms "pro alfaqui super vos" the same "alfaqui . . . Ababdille Abenixem ut sit alfaqui in tota vita sua"; that the title is not personal appears from arrangements for future election of a successor with all four of his titles (given above in n. 2). Four others in the treaty bear the title *alfaqui* in its more usual sense; see the *Traités de paix et de commerce*, II, part 6, doc. 1, 182-185 (June 17, 1231), though the editor erroneously makes this client of Majorca that larger island; see also the "alfaquinus magnus"—or, in the Arabic, "most distinguished *faqīh*"—in his Genoa-Majorca treaty of 1181, and the "rex" and "elmir sublimus" as Majorca's ruler in 1188, part 3, doc. 3, pp. 109-113 (June 1, 1181) and doc. 4, pp. 113-115 (Aug. 1188). For two other contemporary rulers affecting the title *faqīh*, see above, p. 222.

[34] Dozy, *Glossaire*, p. 79. G. Kampfmeyer, "Al-Ḳā'id," *EI*[1], II, part 1, 635-636. Lévi-Provençal, *España musulmana*, v, 32-33. At the fall of Lisbon in the twelfth century the Christians saw the *qā'id* as ruler (*princeps*), distinguished from the city's notables (*primicerii*); see *De expugnatione lyxbonensi, the Conquest of Lisbon*, ed. and trans. C. W. Davis (New York, 1936), p. 94: "ab eorum alchaie, id est principe"; p. 114: "ipso civitatis alcaie" with "et primiceriis civitatis"; p. 172n.: "alchaida princeps eorum." See Neuvonen, *Arabismos del español*, pp. 89-90; Steiger, *Fonética del hispano-árabe*, pp. 134-135; *Vocabulista in arabico*, p. 358 ("ductor").

[35] *Llibre dels feyts*, ch. 439: "l·algutzir"; "aquel qui tenia l·alcacer por lo rey de Granada . . . e qui era cap lur."

rell), the *qā'id* of Bairén, who testily insisted in the midst of his relatives upon a decent interval before surrendering his castle, was a princely lord.[36] The more considerable ruler of Játiva, king in all but name, received no other title throughout James's memoirs but "the *qā'id* of Játiva." When Ibn 'Īsā transferred to become *qā'id* of Montesa, his nonmilitary successor at Játiva directed the Mudejar segment of town as *qā'id*. Lesser castellan-governors abounded under the same title, like the commanders of the "large and strong" stone castles at Borro, Palma, Villela, and Villalonga, which could no longer hold out after Bairén collapsed. The *qā'id* Mūsā al-Murābiṭ surrendered Biar. At Almenara, when the townsmen gave up, its *qā'id* hung on for a time with his twenty knights in the alcazar. In this case all the garrison were strangers including the *qā'id*, who proclaimed himself representative for Zayyān; the townsmen showed themselves unsympathetic to these intruders and prepared to help drive them out. The relatively small castles of Nules, Castro, and Uxó each boasted its *qā'id*. King James held a meeting with similar local castellans of Planes, Pego, and Castell, each of whom bore the title *qā'id*. Others appear in Valencian documentation, like the *qā'id* Muḥammad of Tárbena and the *qā'id* of Villanueva de Castellón, and the list might easily be extended.[37]

On the other hand, James resolutely refused any form of address to the proud magnate al-Azraq, who had so long humiliated the king. James dismissed the successful traitor in his memoirs as "head" (*cap*) of the rebels.[38] A valley like Uxó contained several defensive works to guard the several hamlets; its charter reveals that "all the places and the villages of the valley of Uxó" were to remain "under the service of the castle of the said valley of Uxó, according as was the custom from the first." The *qā'id* there had his jurisdiction, kept by the succeeding Christian *alcayt*. Precrusade Uxó had in turn depended for survival upon a strategic larger castle or two, each under its respective *qā'id*; the latter may have been soldier intruders sent from Valencia city as at Almenara, or powerful dynasts as at Bairén

[36] *Ibid.*, ch. 314: "l•alcayt"; the name baffled Gayangos but may relate to Sīdrāy, well known in Spanish politics in the mid-twelfth century.

[37] *Ibid.*, ch. 245 (Almenara); ch. 249 (Uxó, etc.); ch. 307 (Palma, etc.); ch. 359 ("Muça Almoravit"); ch. 376 (Planes, etc., ambiguously one or three men).

[38] *Ibid.*, ch. 370. *Cap* was used by contemporaries for chief, leader, head of family clan, directing agent, and the like.

and Játiva. During the 1276 rebellion, King Peter negotiated with each *qā'id* and council of the aljamas of Eslida and its mountains.[39] Wherever the crusaders did not replace a *qā'id*, he retained both his castle and what James called its seigniory. By the late 1250's such men persisted mostly in the southern third of the conquered kingdom, from above Játiva down to Finestrat.

A major problem in interpreting the Valencian scene is the confusion between *qā'id* and *qāḍī* in Christian documents, arising partly from the parallel military and civilian structure glimpsed in a garrison town like Almenara, but mostly from a language difficulty. In Latin more than in the Romance tongues, the word for *qā'id* is easily confounded with *qāḍī*—*alcadus* (Catalan *alcalde*) for *alcaydus* (Catalan *alcayt*). The Chivert charter, for instance, applies both forms alternatively to the same functionary. An inherent ambiguity compounds this mechanical difficulty confronting medieval and modern transcribers. *Alcalde*, the Romance derivative from *qāḍī*, mirrors the element of rule that the religious judge had acquired in Islamic Spain—a metamorphosis whose complexities are deferred to the study of the city functionaries in the next chapter. When the crusaders usurped the alcazar of a local *qā'id*, leaving civil administration to either a *qāḍī* or a demilitarized *qā'id* while designating the Christian castellan as *alcayt*, each representative of local government tended to assimilate roughly to any of the others, aside from the disposal of military force. Happily the Christians used bailiff often for an *alcalde*, thus contracting the area of confusion.[40]

At mid-century, Játiva had a Christian *alcayt* in control of its castle, a bailiff (*baiulus* rather than *alcalde*), a *qā'id* (*alcayt*) directing the civil affairs of the Moorish quarter, and a *qāḍī* who in this case lacked high civil power. Potential confusion in word structure found echo in a certain assimilation of offices in the Mudejar situation. The fact that the governing *qā'id* of an Islamic castle had enjoyed juridical functions, as did his replacement the bailiff (*alcalde*) and certain feudal castellans (*alcayt*), could only contribute to erosion of precision about all four offices. The *qā'id* moreover was often as much a

[39] Uxó Charter: "sien tots los lochs e les alcheries de la vall de Uxó a servitut del castell de la dita vall de Uxó segons que de primer ere acostumat." Soldevila, *Pere el Gran*, part 2, I, p. 82, doc. 50.

[40] See Chapter III, n. 4 on *alcalde*, its derivation and relation to bailiff.

governor or feudal lord as the *qāḍī* was rallier of local defense; after all, the *qāḍī* was not the "bishop" contemporary Europeans sometimes thought him to be—not even a warrior-bishop or prince-bishop—but an intellectual-theologian-official-judge who could turn as readily to war as to commerce. Something sacral may have inhibited this versatility elsewhere, but in Spain the logic of the Islamic unitary society easily made the *qāḍī* a ruler or a fighter. A final observation may clarify the Christian attribution of *alcayt* to a position of civil authority. Christian militia in Islamic lands, or a Christian community enclaved there for commerce, obeyed an *alcayt* at its head; this powerful figure was really a colonial governor, and in Tlemcen he had become ruler, judge, financial officer, and military head for Christians of all origins. Below him every captain of a Christian troop also used the title, these underlings bearing little resemblance, however, to their magnificent *alcayt mayor*.[41]

However careless the adscriptions of *qā'id* and *qāḍī* in Christian documents, or their transcriptions by later copyists, and whatever the osmosis of the two functions at their touching peripheries, Muslim contemporaries undoubtedly distinguished the two in life as they did in language. The problem rather affects the researcher trying to decide whether a given community operated under the direction of a warrior-castellan or of a judge-intellectual, or some combination of the two. Eslida's charter twice referred to the tax office of the "alchaydus castri," but it also applied an order to the various "alcadi castrorum" and bailiffs of the region! The confusion here was worse than that of Chivert's usage. The second Eslida charter submitted all contracts "to the jurisdiction of the *alcaydus* and the *alcaldus*"; it did not make clear which of the two was to be the elected "lord" of the aljama.[42]

The leader of any aljama, whether aristocrat or warrior or politically powerful *qāḍī*, may have seemed a *qā'id* to Christians by analogy with their broad understanding of the word as governor or captain. Some leaders would have fit both titles without incongruity. Just across the border from Valencia in the older, more secure fron-

41 Dufourcq, *L'Espagne catalane et le Maghrib*, pp. 151-152, 516-517.

42 Second Eslida Charter: "in posse vestri alcaydi et alcaldi, et dominus sit de aliama vestra et eligatur ad cognicionem sarracenorum vestrorum." Here the form *alcaldus*, so similar to the Spanish and Catalan spellings, is clear in the manuscript.

tier of Tortosa, the master of the Templars caused a notice to be drafted in 1279: "We constitute, make, ordain, concede and choose you, Muḥammad al-Gabaretī (Gavarretç) our Saracen, *alcayt* of the Saracens in Tortosa and its countryside" for a compulsory period of ten years, at an annual salary of one and a half cafizes of grain. Muḥammad, who in turn presented a document accepting the terms, received a free hand—"free and general administration."[43] Was Muḥammad merely a leader or was he the community's *qāḍī*? One is tempted to opt for the interpretation of leader; but the contemporary *Costums* of Tortosa call the judge and community leader, exercising court jurisdiction, an *alcayt*.[44] Wherever a warrior figure held an Islamic castle, the king called him a *qā'id* in his memoirs; whenever James replaced him, it was with "our *alcaits* and our men." Though such a *qā'id* seems often to have been a species of feudal or local lord, responsible to the Valencian ruler only after a tenuous fashion, he does not really fit the classic notion of military governor or marcher lord responsible for a frontier area; perhaps Islamic Valencia as a whole had long disintegrated into a neo-frontier exploited by local families and castle-holding adventurers.

The basic pattern visible everywhere reveals a multiplicity of relatively self-contained communities, each controlling its hamlets and countryside, and each related to its *qā'id*. These men did not govern in isolated splendor; there is evidence of hierarchy, or at least of preeminence, and of a preeminence or vigilance which recalls the Christian feudal system. The manner of surrendering castles in Valencia by central blocs of territory argues in favor of this idea of hierarchical interdependence, as does the natural division of the Islamic Valencian kingdom into immemorial *termini* around specific towns, each of which itself belonged to a wider *terminus*. This pattern explains why the term *qā'id* was so imprecise, with the incon-

[43] Arch. Crown, James I, perg. 170 (Nov. 6, 1279): "cum testimonio huius publici instrumenti constituimus, facimus, ordinamus, concedimus, et eligimus te Mahomet Gavarretç sarracenum nostrum alcayt sarracenorum in Dertusa et terminis eiusdem"; "liberam et generalem administrationem." A document by Muḥammad follows, within this document, accepting the terms; he could not resign the office, once taken, but must serve the ten years. Though the surname recalls Spanish names like the Banū Savarico or Sabarico of Seville, Ibn Ja'far, or al-Jabbar, it is more likely a toponymical indication deriving from one of the many rural places called Gavarret, itself derived from the not uncommon Catalan place-name Gavarra.

[44] Bayerri, *Historia de Tortosa*, VIII, 209.

sequential village tower boasting its own as much as did the formidable regional castle. The social quality of Spanish Islamic sovereignty suggests that these military notables belonged to the same groupings and perhaps the same families as the urban notables. The evidence does not allow more than a sensing of this relationship, except in the case of some very important urban center like Játiva where the roles of civil and military notable coalesced. Decades of fragmentation before the crusade undoubtedly fostered the Játiva and Alcira pattern in the truly urban environments, and the Bairén pattern of castellan over a countryside wherever no principal town focused the relatively dispersed population. What remains unclear is not so much the hierarchical relation within each pattern according to which the multiple lesser castles served the authority of their given region, as the cross-relationship between what seem to be relative autonomies. Perhaps a loose alliance of cities and regions best describes the political scene, as against the network of social and family ties, and provides as well a key to Valencia's lack of organized resistance to the crusade. After the crusade, and especially after each revolt, this *qā'id* class progressively gave way to Christian castellans. The deceptive surface appearance of a fragmented Mudejar community in Christian Valencia during the later decades of King James's reign may owe something to the fact that these local aristocrats and headmen, especially the more powerful key figures, had been removed. The probing of Mudejar Valencia's authoritarian levels in terms of titles in crusader documentation can yield rewarding insights. It can reveal something of Islamic Valencia on the vigil of defeat, and something of how the Christians perceived in their own terms the institutions of the fallen enemy. In the absence of more satisfactory materials, these titles can also contribute to our understanding of early Mudejarism's political and social organization, during those brief decades before the failed gamble of revolt began to destroy the structure of power.

CHAPTER XVI

The City-State Polities

MUSLIM LORDS, however strong, did not comprise their kingdom's essential power. They were but one element in a complex construction. The weightiest single entity was not the lord but the ubiquitous town, considered as at once a political alliance of families and a territorial unit. Was the mighty lord of Alcalá therefore a lesser man than the Muslim castellan of Peñíscola? As an individual the castellan was a weaker figure, but the diffused urban power in which he participated made him greater. Town and community did not always jibe. The Mudejar aljama was not just the Moors of a given place. A single city might hold several aljamas, though nothing like this developed in Valencia;[1] conversely, an aljama might comprise a number of towns and hamlets as well as scattered individuals. The Eslida aljama consisted of the six towns named in its charter, each of which had its castle or fortification and villages. The Játiva charter, conferring privileges on the city Moors, discloses the participation of its whole huerta. Uxó's charter embraced "all the Moors of the valley," organized around their several settlements and towers.[2] Administrative life therefore betrayed a markedly local and coalescive character. Between very large divisions like Alcira that might aspire to independent rule and small ones like Uxó that could not survive long alone, the kingdom amounted to an agglomeration of city units and town units; even the mountain or pastoral areas organized themselves around rural villages.

In adding this final data to the geographical and political information already assembled, we have reached the limits of evidence available concerning the horizontal structure of power. What then gave life to the whole? Since Islam had no communes, did each city

[1] Fifteenth-century Avila held three aljamas, each under its own *faqīh* (Fernández y González, *Mudejares de Castilla,* appendix, doc. 74).

[2] Uxó Charter. Játiva Charter, directly for the judicial scene and by implication for other privileges.

or military unit muddle along, occasionally harassed by the bureaucracy of a distant king? Such a situation would have represented a vacuum of power, hindered united military action, and spelled the end of prosperity. Before turning to the solution of this mystery, a final administrative complexity requires attention. Who were the functionaries administering the urban political life at the center of a given aljama?

Qāḍī, Amīn, Faqīh

Qāḍī, amīn, and *faqīh* have already been discussed at length as officials in the religio-judicial scene,[3] but their intrusion into the political context demands separate examination. The *qāḍī*, despite his potential for confusion with the *qā'id*, belonged to the local, civil milieu rather than to the military chivalry. He smacks of the intellectual, not the bellicose. Given the undifferentiated nature of Islamic society, however, where a man might simultaneously inhabit several strata, it is inadvisable to make sharp distinctions. Not only were roles interchangeable and capable of bizarre combinations, but at the local, relatively understaffed level any major office tended to assimilate to others, especially in Spain with its less precisely articulated bureaucracies. As the most visible representative of Islam's mystique, as trustee for philanthropic foundations, as prestigious intellectual and theologian, as influential judicial officer and friend of the mighty, and often as a man endowed with literary gifts, holiness, and family connections, the *qāḍī* inevitably emerged as a local power during crises. In a word, he did not belong merely to the judicial and religio-moral furniture but to the wider world of public affairs.

Behind his special prominence in Spain, however, lay a long historical development. His military attributes had come to the fore more than once there, and the dominant Malikite theory had consecrated this role. When the Cordova caliphate dissolved, many a *qāḍī* took over his region as head of state. The East at the time of the crusades saw a like phenomenon, but Spain gave fullest scope to its development. Some judges "founded veritable dynasties," as in eleventh-century Seville; and at the decline of the Almoravids,

[3] See Chapter X, section 2.

according to Ibn al-Abbār, "they seized power in all parts of the state," and twice at Valencia.[4] So reflexive had this political role become, and so tenacious the residual political power of the *qāḍī* in the council of the aljama, that the Valencian Arabist Ribera Tarragó deliberately refrained from translating him as judge, preferring to convey his "political and ruling functions" by the Romance term *alcalde* and even governor. Among notable figures who had played this role in the past had been Valencia city's own Ja'far b. Jaḥḥāf, whom the Cid had retained in office.[5] During the crusade of James I the celebrated preacher serving as *qāḍī* to the besieged capital, Abu 'r-Rabī' b. Sālim, had won martyrdom and undying fame by a warrior's death at the battle of Puig in 1237.[6]

This background prepares us for the central role of the *qāḍī* in postcrusade Valencia. How is this compatible with the dominance of the *amīn* within the aljama, which has led most authorities to designate the latter as true governor of its affairs? The contradiction may amount to an optical illusion. The *amīn* held the center of the stage in his tax-collecting role; this made him the go-between for the two peoples, brought him and him alone into constant official contact with the colonial authorities, and by a natural parallelism transformed him into a Muslim counterpart of the bailiff.[7] An evo-

[4] Tyan, *Organisation judiciaire*, pp. 413-416 on military attributes, especially in Spain; pp. 416-429 on heads of state; p. 418 for quotations by Tyan and Ibn al-Abbār. On the analogous tendency in North Africa, where the local *qāḍī* briefly became a civil chief, for example, in the early eleventh-century crises, see Idris, *Berbérie orientale*, II, 562; and for the Balearics, Rosselló Bordoy, *Islam a les illes balears*, p. 108.

[5] Ribera Tarragó, "La plaza del alcalde (ráhbatolcádi)," pp. 319-325: "funciones políticas y gubernativas." Menéndez Pidal, *España del Cid*, I, 435, 482, 487. Cagigas, *Sevilla almohade*, p. 21.

[6] Ibn Khaldūn considered him the most learned traditional savant of his time in Spain, and his death a martyrdom (*Histoire des Berbères*, II, 306-307).

[7] On the *amīn* see above, p. 233 and note. Some parallel may exist between the evolution of the Valencian *amīn* and that of the crusader Holy Land's *ra'īs* over his *raisagium*, a native overseer-accountant who served as liaison to the absentee Frankish landlord (Cahen, "Régime rurale," pp. 306-309). The *amīn* kept his connection with the gathering of taxes even after he had developed administrative preeminence. Macho y Ortega found that the differing governmental structures of fifteenth-century aljamas in Aragon proper had in common a ruling *amīn* and his aides the *adelantados*; both were elected for terms, the lord or crown often naming or intervening in the case of the *amīn*. The *amīn* both governed and had charge of

lution of this kind would explain the appearance of the ruling *amīn* in older Mudejar aljamas and in Valencian aljamas of the fourteenth and fifteenth centuries; scholars working with a range of materials wider in time or place than thirteenth-century Valencia naturally read the terminal result back into the postcrusade period of Valencia.

What became of the *qāḍī* in such cases? While it is easy to think that he subsided into his judicial place in the aljama, it is equally likely that sometimes the main *qāḍī* absorbed the role of *amīn*, appearing in Christian documents under the latter name as more relevant to Christian interests. Taken in wider perspective the subject is obscure. Macho Ortega fancied this later *amīn* as analogous to the head jurate of a Christian municipality; Gual Camarena preferred a parallel with the bailiff or even with the Christian *almotacén*; Roca Traver and Grau Monserrat made the *amīn* principal official of the aljama, president of its council, and roughly equivalent to the *cap de jurats*, with a varying set of powers but always holding "the personal governance of the aljama in every sense of the word."[8] Dealing only with fifteenth-century Valencia, Piles Ros found the *amīn* the governing power within the aljama, central to much of its business as reflected in Christian documents. A letter of appointment by the crown in 1425 commissioned the *amīn* of the Sierra de Eslida as "holder, administrator, and exerciser" faithfully of "the office of alaminate," conferring an unspecified legal jurisdiction and ordering him "to defend and maintain the rights and regalian claims

---

revenues; he also convoked and chaired the weekly aljama meeting, defended the common good, kept revenue records, and rendered some justice; in backward areas lacking judges, he widened the latter role. Some places had two, for two lords, doubtless an expedient for collecting revenues; a few had none; and Zaragoza substituted a *merino*. See his *Mudéjares aragoneses*, pp. 155-159.

[8] Gual Camarena, "Mudéjares valencianos, aportaciones," p. 176. Roca Traver, "Vida mudéjar," p. 127. Grau Monserrat, "Mudéjares castellonenses," p. 261. A standard history, Giménez Soler's *Corona de Aragón*, has each *morería* ruled by an *amīn* assisted by two lieutenants or *adelantados*, with a *merino* representing the crown in each (p. 293). This conclusion is reflected in any number of works, for example in M. T. Oliveros de Castro, *Historia de Monzón* (Zaragoza, 1964), p. 200. The Castilian *almotacén* or Catalan *mostassaf* derived from the office and name of *muhtasib*. The Christian jurate sometimes went under the title *fidel*, Castilian *fiel* (García de Valdeavellano, *Instituciones españolas*, p. 545), which has the same meaning as Arabic *amīn*.

of the lord king" in the same fashion as his predecessors "in times past were well accustomed to maintain and direct." The commission assigned the usual salary, and imposed the new official upon "the jurates [*jurats*] and elders and Moors resident or inhabiting the said Sierra"; ironically, it specifically denied him any role in tax-collecting.[9]

An elaborate fifteenth-century instrument of debt, signed by a concourse of notables gathered at each participating aljama in turn, reveals the outline of government as it had become, very much later, in the Uxó-Eslida region; characteristically, however, the affair concerned both money and Christian-Muslim interaction rather than aljama life. Here the alaminate of Uxó put forward as signers the local *amīn*, his lieutenant, ten jurates (two from each of five subtowns), and a great list of "notables, natives, and residents of the said Uxó Valley," including five holding the title *faqīh* plus one sheik—over 150 in all. The Eslida alaminate mustered an *amīn*, two jurates, "the town *muḥtasib*," thirty notables (*proceres*), two men titled *faqīh*, and someone bearing the storied name al-Azraq. The Ahín alaminate boasted its own *amīn*, lieutenant, two jurates, another jurate from a subtown, and notables. Alcudia de Veo had a similar roster but with two jurates from Veo and two from Alcudia. Sueras varied this by gathering three jurates from as many subtowns and by having two notables with the title *faqīh*. Fanzara, besides the usual *amīn* and one jurate, listed a jurate each from two subtowns, and notables. Some of these places were small in themselves, the subtowns presumably amounting to rural representation; the relentless replication of the master pattern, on a descending scale of size, is

[9] Piles Ros, "Moros de realengo en Valencia," pp. 273-274, document from the bailiff general (Feb. 5, 1425): "lo offici d[e] alaminat en tota la serra deslida tenidor regidor ex[e]rcidor be e lealment . . . e facats juhis e tingues raho e justic[ia] . . . e com alami dessus dit mantingues e defenes los drets e regalies del dit senyor rey segons los altres alamis en temps passat be han acostumat tenir e regir . . . ; no donam ni atorgam a tu poder q[ue] rebes les rendes ni pecu[n]ies de la dita s[er]ra . . . ; als jurats e vells e moros vehins e h[ab]itadors de la dita s[er]ra." See also p. 236 for his governing role. Eslida's *amīn* was 'Abd as-Salām al-Ahwānī (Abducalem Alahuen), a local man; when the *amīn* elsewhere fell ill, the crown appointed his interim substitute, Muḥammad b. 'Uthmān (Mahomet Ozmen, p. 236); the *amīn* and *qāḍī* at this time were still normally different individuals (p. 243).

the main feature of this political structure.[10] Macho Ortega's documents, dating from about 1400, seem to confer the same centrality on the *amīn*.[11]

The thirteenth-century *amīn* was at least a prominent figure, even in relatively small communities. Perhaps Almohad chaos or post-crusade necessities expanded the importance of a previously minor official; the treatise of Ibn 'Abdūn on the functionaries of twelfth-century Seville had dismissed him with a passing notice. In the institutional history of Islam, *amīn*—one who is trustworthy, or overseer or trustee—commonly denoted someone administering a position of trust, especially of an economic nature or requiring financial responsibilities; he appears as legal representative for orphaned minors, customs officer, estate steward, treasurer, and in western Islam the head of a trade group. The Cordova caliphs had appointed an *amīn* as representative over a craft or industry, at once responsible delegate of the workers and subtly a civil administrator.[12] In Valencia the *amīn* was ubiquitous. Towns ranking in size from Valencia city through Liria to places as small as Aldea, Carbonera, and Carrícola boasted one in the thirteenth century. The charters of Alfandech, Játiva, and Uxó list him just after the *qāḍī*; Chivert's charter presents him tardily as a secondary official. No trace appears of his

[10] Lloréns, "Sarracenos de la Sierra de Eslida," pp. 56-57: "omnes sarraceni proceres vicini et habitatores dicte vallis d'Uxo"; "mustaçafus dicte ville"; "Çahat Alazrach."

[11] Macho Ortega, "Documentos de los mudéjares," p. 153 (Sept. 11, 1400): "alamino, veteribus, et rectoribus aliame sarracenorum" of Arandiga; p. 154 (Jan. 18, 1402): "al alami e vells de la aliama de los moros de la val l'Almonetzir"; p. 156 (March 4, 1404): "todos e qualesquiere clavarios, adelantados, jurados, alamines, e biellos . . . de las aljamas." See pp. 159-160, however (June 23, 1414): the *alguatzirus* of the king for Zaragoza's aljama; p. 144 (Dec. 22, 1394): "vos alfaquinus, iurati, et aliama sarracena" of Burgia; cf. p. 147 (March 4, 1399): "Abdulaziz moro alamin d'Arandiga"; pp. 147-148 (March 11, 1339 [for 1399?]), the Albarracín *amīn*; and p. 152 (July 8, 1400), where the crown seeks to extradite for severe punishment the three Christians who waylaid and murdered "Hamet alamin del lugar nuestro de Benaguasir." At Borgia in 1294 the *amīn* is last on a list of functionaries: "los officios del alfaquinado et de çabçala et de escrivania et de alaminatge de los moros son et se tiennen por el sennor rey" (*Rentas*, p. 232).

[12] Lévi-Provençal, *España musulmana*, v, 178; see also Cahen, "Amīn," i, 147. Near Mecca the first hill created by God, repository of the Black Stone during the deluge, was called *al-Amīn*, "the trustworthy" (Ibn Baṭṭūṭa, *Travels*, p. 210).

namesake, the *amīn* who helped administer irrigation systems. The latter was characteristic of Yemenite or Saharan practice more common below the Valencian kingdom's border; if he operated under this name within the kingdom at this time, he must have played a very humble role in aljama affairs.[13]

Documentation presented in previous chapters showed the social status of the *amīn* to range from village artisan to city property holder, and described the conditions and salary attached to the office. Individual representatives have appeared—Yūsuf at Játiva, Muḥammad b. Hawwāra b. Ghānim and his associates at Montes-Carrícola, Muḥammad b. al-Bulay and later Muḥammad b. Sālim at Biar, Muḥammad at Elche, yet another Muḥammad at Chelva, and specific though nameless officeholders elsewhere. Others can be added—Ibn Sulaymān (Abençulama) at Alcudia in 1273, Zayd b. Taram (Aceit Abentaram) at Ibi from 1261, Aḥmad an-Najjār (Azmet Anajar) at Cuart from 1262, and the anonymous official addressed at Beniopa in 1282.

King, religious order, and lord appointed the *amīn* respectively at Játiva, Chivert, and Carrícola; at Uxó the people elected him. All the aljamas below the Júcar had election rights at least by 1290.[14] Whether elective or appointive, the office ran for a specified period, sometimes for life, and paid an annual salary. One man might hold the separately labeled posts of *qāḍī* and *amīn*, though this was uncommon.[15] At Ibi in 1261 King James appointed the *amīn* for life;[16] at Chelva in 1269 "we give and concede to you Muḥammad of Morocco that you be *amīn* of the Muslims."[17]

13 On the *amīn al-mā'*, usually subordinate to the supervisor of waters called the *ṣāḥib as-sāqiyah*, see Glick, *Irrigation in Medieval Valencia*, pp. 203-205. Unlike the *amīn* under discussion he had no criminal jurisdiction but was merely an administrative officer. In 1435 Abū Bakr Ismā'īl (Obaquer Ismael) appears as divider of waters or *alamín* at Elche (p. 205).

14 Gual Camarena, "Mudéjares valencianos, aportaciones," p. 176, document of March 24, 1290: "mas allá del Júcar."

15 Mūsā of Morocco (Muça de Marrochs) in 1263 became both *amīn* and *qāḍī* at Lérida (*Itinerari*, p. 339).

16 *Ibid.*, p. 311 (April 9, 1261). See also the non-Valencian appointment of the Muslim Fawz b. al-'Aysh (? Foz d'Halaço) as *amīn* for life at Pina in 1267 (p. 400).

17 *Ibid.*, p. 419n. (Jan. 14, 1269): "damus et concedimus tibi Mahumeto marroquitano quod sis alaminus et scriptor sarracenorum." In identifying a landholding in Valencia's huerta, James says only that it is held "by the nephew of the *amīn* of

His judicial role formed the subject of uneasy inquiry in Chapter X; his activities as tax-collector require separate treatment.[18] The two functions, with whatever administrative duties may logically have accompanied them, sum the *amīn* insofar as he is visible in the thirteenth-century Valencian kingdom. At Játiva he (or an officer similarly named) accompanied any Christian official sent to confiscate goods in a Muslim's home, and at Valencia city (but not at Játiva or Chivert) he received Christian and Jewish noncapital charges against criminous Muslims—both functions hinting that he represented the aljama to the outside world in ways other than fiscal.[19] King Peter drafted Mudejar militia in 1283 through their "alemins et veyls," probably because for most Mudejar households this crisis-activity amounted to a form of tax; on the other hand the *amīn*, by virtue of his position as bridge between Christian and Mudejar communities, may already have been shading off into the main administrator he later became.[20]

The *qāḍī* stands out as a more eminent personage within the aljama; insofar as a single man can be designated principal administrator in the postcrusade years, it was more usually this judge. As late as 1252, in the reorganization of the Játiva aljama, "all the Saracens are to be governed by your *qāḍī* and assessors."[21] At Chivert the

Uxó," indicating that this *amīn* or his class in general had an elevated status (Arch. Crown, James I, Reg. Canc. 12, fol. 55 [June 10, 1262]). The crown "condemned the *amīn* of Castalla" to pay two thousand solidi, perhaps a tax default by his aljama (Reg. 12, fol. 40 [May 4, 1262]). At the non-Valencian aljama of Borgia in Aragon, the *amīn* Ismā'īl (Ismaeli) succeeded his father in 1271 in the combined offices "de alfaqimatu, alaminatu, et scribania sarracenorum" (Reg. 21, fols. 10v-11 [Aug. 25, 1271]).

18 Typical examples include Biar's *amīn*, who submitted the annual accounts in 1275 (Arch. Crown, James I, Reg. Canc. 20, fol. 237: "computavisti . . . de omnibus redditibus"); Mogente's *amīn*, who received instructions about the household tax in 1279 (*ibid.*, Peter III, Reg. Canc. 42, fol. 163); and the Játiva charter's directive that the *amīn* "colligat et recipiat iura nostra raballi predicti." See my sequel to the present book, *Medieval Colonialism*, now in press.

19 Játiva Charter. Chivert Charter. Roca Traver, "Vida mudéjar," doc. 3 (Feb. 26, 1267).

20 Arch. Crown, Peter III, Reg. Canc. 46, fol. 100v (Aug. 12, 1283); published in Fernández y González, *Mudejares de Castilla*, appendix, doc. 52; Janer, *Moriscos de España*, doc. 26; *Colección de documentos inéditos*, VI, 196.

21 Játiva Charter: "et quod omnes sarraceni gubernentur per alcadi [*sic*] et adenantatos vestros."

faqīh was the central figure, followed closely by the *qā'id* (*alcaydus*); both recur three times and in that order, once as associated "with their successors." In this case the *faqīh* seems to be the *qāḍī* as against the military-aristocratic person of the *alcaydus*, who in turn retained his own eminence owing to the obligations of defensive war. In any case the Chivert *faqīh* was not the *amīn*, a functionary treated separately later in the surrender document.[22] At Uxó and at Alfandech the Moors could name their own "*qāḍī* and *amīn*," expressed by the charters in that order. García y García, historian of the Uxó Valley, concluded that in the thirteenth century the *qāḍī* ruled there, the *amīn* holding a subordinate position; only in the fourteenth century did a reversal occur, the *amīn* taking power and the *qāḍī* disappearing from the administrative scene.[23] No clue as to the Eslida Valley's political life emerges from its first charter, which spoke confusingly of the several "alcadi" of castles under its jurisdiction and also of a judge "alcadus." The second charter distinguished two offices, "your *alcaydus* and *alcaldus*." The *alcaydus* here cannot have been a Christian castellan; indeed, in the light of the subsequent phrase—"and he is to be lord of your aljama and elected at the will of your Saracens"—both *qāḍī* and *qā'id* may have combined in one person, as in the case of the *qāḍī* and *amīn* offices at Lérida.[24]

Though the *qāḍī* appeared with pride of place in surrender contracts, King James did not mention any under that technical name in his memoirs. This is understandable. In his essentially military narrative he concerned himself rather with the castle *qā'id* and the feudal lord. When he outlined surrender negotiations in its pages

[22] Chivert Charter.

[23] Alfandech Charter; Uxó Charter; García y García, *Historia de Vall de Uxó*, pp. 34, 80.

[24] Eslida Charter. The Second Eslida Charter put legal contracts "in posse vestri alcaydi et alcaldi et dominus sit de aliama vestra et eligatur ad cognicionem sarracenorum vestrorum." Between 1242 and 1276, the dates of the two charters, the status of Eslida castle underwent changes. The Templars still controlled it in 1258, though the king had claims on its revenues; in 1259 Galceran of Moncada was drawing its income to satisfy a debt, and William of Anglesola was scheduled to succeed him; both men were apparently bailiffs rather than castle custodians. In 1260 King James gave Eslida, Veo, and Ahín castles to his son James of Jérica; in the later revolt, the king placed Raymond Calvera of the royal household in charge of the castle (1277), but by 1283 James of Jérica was still lord.

he acted in summary fashion, showing little concern for interior organization; he saw himself as dealing with a community as such through its representative agents. He desired broad community support rather than the adherence of a principal administrator. This in itself may reveal something about the role of the aljama administrator; here it suffices to note that, when King James described the agent sent out by any single community, apart from military castellans or regional rulers standing just above the aljama, that agent was a *faqīh* together with a supporting companion. At the critical moment in Peñíscola's surrender the aljama delegated two men to handle transfer of the defenses, "the *faqīh* and one other." At Almenara—against the opposition of the castellan—"the *faqīh* and another Saracen who was locally very powerful" opened negotiations. Even at Játiva, the powerful *qā'id* sent as vizier the *faqīh* al-Mufawwiz.[25] Perhaps a political role for the *faqīh* at this early period is not unexpected; Ibn Khaldūn observed the scholar-intellectual's lust for political activism and wryly cautioned that, while the *faqīh* ought to concern himself with politics in theory and practice, he was unqualified to share in its authority.[26] A clue to this functionary's permanent role comes at the end of the century, however, from the aljama at the town of Borgia in Aragon proper; four offices reserved to crown appointment began with "the alfaquinate" and ended with "the alaminate."[27] Here *faqīh* seems to have been an alter-

[25] *Llibre dels feyts*, ch. 184: "l·alfaquim e i altre"; ch. 243: "del alfaquim e de i altre sarray que·y era molt poderos"; ch. 336. The Tortosa surrender of 1148 was made "cum alguaziris et alfachis et alchavis et cum alios homines [*sic*] de Tortoxa"; they were to choose their "alcaides" according to their "usaticos"; their pact of 1174 names only two men, the *ṣāḥib al-madīna* and the *qāḍī*, who were to represent the aljama in assessing tax property (Fernández y González, *Mudejares de Castilla*, appendix, docs. 5, 9). The Tudela Charter of 1115 has a bizarrely transcribed array of administrators; the pact is "cum alcudi" (*qāḍī*) and with "algalifos," "alforques," and "Alfabilis"; "et illa sennoria de illos moros [sit] in manu de Alfabili aut in manu de illo moro quem elegerit Alfabili" (*ibid.*, doc. 2). No "algalifus" appears in Valencia, and this *khalīfa* (representative or successor) may have filled any of several minor posts; see T. W. Arnold's article under that noun in *EI*[1], II, part 2, 881-885. The *faqīh* does not appear in the Uxó, Játiva, or Eslida charters explicitly, though perhaps should be understood as included under the other titles. The later Chelva Charter (1370) has "vuestros alfaquines" as muezzins "segun era acostumbrado."

[26] *Muqaddimah*, I, 459; II, 5.

[27] See n. 11 (1294): "alfaquinado," "alaminatge"; and also its document of 1399 with ruling *alfaquinus*.

nate title for *qāḍī*. Should each main *faqīh* arranging a surrender to King James therefore be understood as the *qāḍī* of his area? If so, then the king's omission of the *qāḍī* from his narrative becomes more apparent than real, and the *qāḍī* assumes a role in negotiations consonant with his preeminence on the surrender charters. The preeminence of the *qāḍī*, whether alone or in tandem with a *qā'id*, was natural enough. Even when Pope Innocent III urged the subject Muslims of Sicily—a region where the *qāḍī* had not developed such extraordinary political powers as in Spain—to remain loyal to their Christian king a few decades before, he addressed himself equally to the *qāḍī* and to the politico-military *qā'id* administering each town.[28]

Here and there a Valencian *qāḍī* emerges from anonymity, receiving a privilege or becoming involved by name in a legal settlement. In 1244 the authority signing first among nine witnesses to a regional concordat concerning water, for example, was the *qāḍī* of Gandía Ibn Ghumār (Avengomar).[29] At Valencia city Sa'd b. Yaḥyā (Çahat Aviniafia) comes into view in documents from 1258 to 1273; in the earliest he was *alcadus*, distinct from his relative the former *amīn*. King James grants "to you, *qāḍī* of the Saracens of Valencia, and yours forever that room which the former *amīn* of the Saracens, your father-in-law, held in the Moorish quarter of Valencia, which room is contiguous to your buildings."[30] This concession does not prove that the Valencia city *qāḍī* exercised administrative power; it serves only to locate him in time and to save the researcher befuddlement when the name and office are later misspelled. In subsequent business he appears as *alcaydus* of the Moorish quarter; the insouciant Christian usage is another warning that Christian scribes might designate a Muslim leader indifferently *qāḍī* and *qā'id*, and that wherever *alcaidus* materializes without a

[28] Amari, *Musulmani di Sicilia*, III, 266, and see pp. 260ff., 578.

[29] Roque Chabás, *Distribución de las aguas en 1244*, pp. 3-6, doc. of July 16, 1244. On the deceptive name Avengomar, see below, p. 411.

[30] Arch. Crown, James I, Reg. Canc. 10, fol. 83v (July 1, 1258). "Concedimus tibi Çahat Aviniafia alcadio sarracenorum Valencie et tuis imperpetuum illam cameram quam alaminus quondam sarracenorum Valencie socer tuus habebat in moraria Valencie, que camera est contigua domibus tuis. Quam cameram habeatis tu et tui francham et liberam . . . a celo in abissum ad dandum . . . alienandum. . . ."

Muslim-held castle in the background, it is safer to assume that he was an *alcadus*.

King James assigned a salary in 1267 to Sa'd (Çahat) as *qāḍī*, to be drawn from public funds, in an instrument which serves as a model for bureaucratic wordiness. "Through us and ours we give and concede to you, Sa'd b. Yaḥyā (Çahat Abinhaia), *alcaydus* of the Saracens of the city of Valencia, for your whole life a hundred Valencian solidi, to be taken and had annually from our revenues and fees of the butchery of the Saracens of Valencia, by reason of your aforesaid office of *alcaydus*." Sa'd was to enjoy this "in such wise that every year of your life from now on, while you exercise the said office and conduct yourself well and faithfully in it, you are to take and have the said hundred solidi from our revenues and fees of the butchery . . . for your work and office as is contained above." James concluded with instructions for Valencia city's bailiff to pay Sa'd the agreed sum every year. To this salary the *qāḍī* probably added a percentage of fees taken; at least that was the universal custom fifty years later.[31] Since Sa'd cannot have become castellan at the capital, and since his considerable salary would not have derived from the crown for his spiritual or judicial work, where a share of fines would easily have supported him, he was obviously acting as a community administrator just like his colleague the *qāḍī* of Játiva. Sa'd seems to have continued as *qāḍī* as late as 1273, when King James exempted from the public tax his "shop in the Moorish

[31] *Ibid.*, Reg. Canc. 15, fol. 85 (March 14, 1267). "Per nos et nostros damus et concedimus tibi Çahato Abinhaia alcaydo sarracenorum civitatis Valencie in tota vita tua centum solidos regalium habendos et percipiendos annuatim in redditibus et iuribus nostris carnicerie sarracenorum Valencie ratione predicti officii tui alcaydi. Ita quod tu singulis annis de cetero in vita tua, dum dictum officium exercebis et in ipso bene et fideliter te habebis, habeas et percipias dictos c solidos de redditibus et iuribus nostris carnicerie . . . pro labore et officio tuo ut superius continetur. Mandantes firmiter baiulo nostro Valencie . . . quod de redditibus et iuribus nostris predictis carnicerie predicte donetur et solvatur tibi ut dictum est annuatim c solidos." It would be difficult to find a better example of the bureaucrat in full flight, unable to put the king's message briefly. In Arch. Reino Val., the *Llibre negre* of the royal chancery has a document setting the salaries of Valencian Mudejar *alcadis* at "duos denarios regalium Valencie pro qualibet libra eorum pro quibus dabitur suum consilium," plus an expense account of two solidi daily every time they traveled outside their place of residence to give judgment (fol. 1 v [Jan. 13, 1329]; see also fols. 192v-194).

quarter of Valencia," which "faced the butchery of the Saracens of Valencia." The office was again *alcaydus*, but the surname was either misspelled or reveals a successor—not Aviniafia or Abinhaia but Abenache.[32] No minor figure could ambition such a post. The next administrative *qāḍī* was Muḥammad of Salā, described by King Peter elsewhere as a member of his household.[33]

It is tempting to think that the *ṣāḥib-aṣ-ṣalāt* retained political influence within the aljama, though the evidence is unclear. This "prayer leader," already encountered in his religious context, acquired political influence in caliphal Spain and a position as civil dignitary with his own advisory council. It is difficult to say what remained of the office at the regional and local level in the thirteenth century. The Chivert charter lists such a *ṣāḥib* by name as third in significance after the *faqīh* and *qā'id*, later speaking of a plurality of presumably lesser "çabacalani." The charters of Játiva, Aldea, and Alfandech give him room, though without adverting to his potential political influence.[34] The list of offices at Borgia in Aragon in 1294 gives him as one of four crown-appointed officials of the aljama along with the *faqīh* (*qāḍī*?), the *ḳātib* or secretary, and the *amīn*.[35] Very much later, after the murder of an *amīn* in the same region, the crown took care to send a copy of its instructions "al çalmedina."[36]

Town Councils; Sheiks or Notables

Though all signs point to the *qāḍī* as chief administrative officer within the aljama, this does not mean that he wielded absolute ruling power. Whenever the aljama manifests itself in action, both during and after the crusade, the modern observer finds it operating as a group. Below the rank of *qāḍī* or *qā'id*, inner power resided in the

[32] Arch. Crown, James I, Reg. Canc. 19, fol. 30v (July 8, 1273): "absolvimus tibi Çahat Abenache sarraceno alcaydo morerie Valencie et tuis imperpetuum illos duos morabatinos censuales quos annuatim nobis facere teneris pro nostro operatorio scito [*for* sito] in moreria Valencie"; "affrontat cum carniceria sarracenorum Valencie." If Abenache does represent a different man, conjectural reconstruction of the name is difficult; forms like Ibn 'Ā'ishah Ash'ab, Ḥākim, or 'Aqīl do not quite fit.

[33] See document in n. 75.

[34] Aldea, Alfandech, Chivert, and Játiva Charters.

[35] See document in n. 11.

[36] Macho Ortega, "Documentos," p. 152 (July 8, 1400).

community's council. At first glance, this seems part of a long tradition of town councils in Spain. The great Menéndez Pidal has described the town of Spanish Islam, during the interims of princely rule, as continuing like "a species of republic," governed "by the aljama or senate of notables under the presidency of the *qāḍī*"; in the postcaliphal era, consequently, each of the multiple political entities naturally functioned under "a republican municipal government."[37] This picture of republican institutions, drawn by excellent historians of Spain from Dozy to Cagigas, contradicts the classical view of towns throughout Islam as undifferentiated and noncorporative, almost apolitical, without municipal life, presided over by an absolute authority.[38] For such a traditional town even Berber assemblies and the Almohad princely council could do no more than provide variations on the universal theme. In this noncivic, functional town, the external state imposed officials, while neighborhood or factional associations merely provided informal accommodation to passing needs. Was the Spanish city therefore the unique exception, an anomaly in Islam? Did its assembly thus differ radically, perhaps incorporating those inchoate elements of autonomy that Cahen discerned in Middle Eastern cities, especially the factions, quarters, and solidarities that tended to coalesce, so that the city could affirm itself to a degree rather than sink into an amorphous, servile mass under the bureaucratic state?[39] Unfortunately for this approach, as Stern points out, such collectivities were never more than temporary and fortuitous groupings induced by passing crises, which aborted before they could assume institutional form. Berque observes that the assembly that was common in medieval North Africa made for "a sort of spontaneous democracy" at all levels but alongside officialdom; the phenomenon fell far short of political republicanism there and in Spain.[40]

37 *España del Cid*, I, 74, 435: "especie de república . . . por la Aljama o Senado de los notables, bajo la presidencia del cadí"; "un gobierno republicano municipal."

38 See, e.g., Planhol, *The World of Islam*, an "essai de géographie islamique," ch. I; Von Grunebaum, "The Structure of the Muslim Town," *Islam: Essays*, p. 142.

39 Claude Cahen, "Mouvements populaires et autonomisme urbain dans l'Asie musulmane du moyen âge," *Arabica*, v (1958), 225-250, and VI (1959) 25-56, 233-265.

40 Stern, in *Islamic City*, pp. 29n., 33-37. J. Berque, "Djamā'a," *EI*², II, 411-413.

A more common temptation sees the Spanish committees or groupings as derived from Roman-Visigothic antecedents. Following a tradition that includes authors like Mayer and Simonet, Ḥusayn Mu'nis has recently restated the theory in an influential study, tracing the aljama's council back to "the Roman system of city-provinces governed by their *curiae*." He depicts the conquering Arabs as having left the Roman civic organization intact, while paying a tribal chief or a functionary to provide military defense and external supervision. Despite its recurrent popularity, the explanation cannot stand scrutiny; scholars like Hinojosa and Sánchez-Albornoz have discredited its foundations. The last remnants of Roman curial organization in Spain died under the Visigoths; nothing remained for the Muslims to inherit.[41] While ruling out Roman or Visigothic continuity, one need not dismiss the possibility of synchronism between Islamic and Catalan-Languedocian neighbors in their orientation toward the assembly. Institutions, sprung from different cultures and serving quite different needs and principles, can derive extra support from contemporary elements common to both. The superficial similarities, whatever their interrelation, extended also to rural assemblies. Just as the "rural municipality," with its council and officials, repeated for scattered Christians of a countryside the functions served by the urban council, so Valencia's Islamic and Mudejar subvillages each enjoyed its own quasi-council.[42] A far cry from the corporation of

[41] Ḥusayn Mu'nis, "La división político-administrativa de la España musulmana," *RIEEIM*, v (1957), esp. pp. 94, 98, 100, 106-109, 116. Claudio Sánchez-Albornoz, *Ruina y extinción del municipio romano en España e instituciones que le reemplazen* (Buenos Aires, 1943), esp. pp. 99ff., 109ff. More recently José Lacarra has continued the work of his master, especially in his "Panorama de la historia urbana en la península ibérica desde el siglo v al x," *Settimane di studio del centro italiano di studi sull' alto medioevo* (Spoleto, 1959). Torres Balbás emphasizes that very few Spanish cities were new, Murcia being one of the rare non-Roman foundations ("Ciudades hispanomusulmanas de nueva fundación," *Études d'orientalisme*, II, 788-789).

[42] García, *Estado económico-social*, p. 65. Ibn 'Abdūn speaks of village heads, but in the context of a sociopolitical organization very different at the rural, estate level (*Séville musulmane*, p. 10). The conclusions of Archibald Lewis on the underlying "assembly" orientation of Catalonia's feudalized government system ca. 975-1050 may have a bearing on the interrelations or implications of osmotic influence between Christian and Islamic Spain (*The Development of Southern French and Catalan Society*, pp. 360-377). Thomas Bisson pursues this evolving and pervasive assembly mentality in his *Assemblies and Representation in Languedoc in the Thirteenth Century* (Princeton, 1964), summed briefly on pp. 291ff.

the Christians, the Moorish entities undoubtedly gathered strength during the decades of precrusade fragmentation but especially during the disoriented postcrusade period, eventually acquiring under Christian rule some institutional continuity. Supremely important in this process was the incorrigible manner in which Valencian crusaders viewed the aljama committee as corresponding to the town council of their own communes, just as they saw Ramaḍān as Lent and a *wālī* as a European king. By treating the assembly thus in practical affairs, the Christian overlords assimilated the Islamic phenomenon to their own, thrusting new roles upon it and effectively bringing it to institutionalization. By the fourteenth century it had become a neat little body of elected representatives. At Valldigna, for example, twenty-nine such worthies rotated by election every Christmas, an arrangement similar to that at Chelva.[43] No wonder a modern student of Mudejars thought the council elders of the crusade period equivalent to the Catalan *consellers*, an advisory board elected by the people.[44]

King James unwittingly promoted this transculturative phenomenon, whose ultimate effects must have been particularly traumatic for Mudejar society. James normally handled the whole aljama of a town, valley, or district as though it were a medieval commune. In precisely this sense he received the sheiks of Murcia city when they came to offer surrender; they were the city's "capitols," the technical term for councilmen of a Catalan commune or in an earlier meaning for canons of an incorporated cathedral chapter. In the same spirit James later addressed his Pego Mudejars as "the aljama and whole commune [*universitas*] of the Saracens of the valley of Pego." Here the king went beyond the Islamic use of aljama for both assembly and community, employing the universal technical terminology for a legal corporation—in the urban context, a commune. A king so sophisticated in the uses of Roman law, a protagonist of its evolution in statecraft, cannot have used the word carelessly. The Chivert charter noted that sixteen town leaders were acting "at the will of the other

[43] Fernández y González, *Mudejares de Castilla*, appendix, doc. 71 (1370): "por la señoría y por la aljama." Valldigna *carta puebla* of 1366 in Gual Camarena, "Mudéjares valencianos, aportaciones," p. 175. See also Cagigas, *Sevilla almohade*, p. 24, on its city council under the *qāḍī* al-Bajī.

[44] Roca Traver, "Vida mudéjar," p. 129.

probi homines," a designation recurring also in the Játiva charter and strongly reflecting the Christian commune. The contemporary tendency in James's realm toward organizing society around semiautonomous corporations enjoying legal privileges and immortality undoubtedly contributed to the strengthening of the Valencian system of Mudejar aljamas and helped assimilate them to the commune. Such was not the nature of the Valencian Islamic town, however, at the moment of surrender.[45]

These aljama assemblies varied greatly according to local circumstances. Valencia city was not the rural Uxó Valley nor the tight lordship of Játiva. The easier climate of a village assembly could allow, as Alcira or Murviedro could not, for a democratic gathering of all family heads. Within an assembly some families or individuals had more influence than others; King James sometimes worked through such people to sway the wider gathering. At some places important knights can be discerned as having a special role. The assembly existed in every kind of local context, from a metropolis like Alcira to a rural valley with villages like Nules; inevitably it became less differentiated, the smaller the community. Whether the council was large or small, the Christians called its members "elders." On occasion they varied this designation with some other revealing name—"the better men" (*meylors*) at Játiva and Villena, or "the good men" (*bons*) at Elche. Much earlier at Tortosa they had been "the more important" (*mayorales*); in contemporary Cordova they were "the leaders" (*primores*).[46] The Valencian crusaders also care-

[45] See the surrender documents above in Chapters VI and VIII. In *Llibre dels feyts*, ch. 417, he calls the deliberative body itself "la aljama." Though he does not use the term commune, it emerged later; Argel in Bougie surrendered to the Christians in 1510 as "el comun de la mi ciudad de Algezer" (Fernández y González, *Mudejares de Castilla*, appendix, doc. 94). See also the document of 1513 from Pego, concerning Ondara, in Roque Chabás, "Liquidación de notas," *El archivo*, VII (1893), 344: "nomine et vice totius universitatis aliame et sarracenorum dicte ville et eius singularium et quorumlibet eorum in solidum." Amari concluded that Sicily's Islamic communities under Christian rule tended to evolve into true communes (*Musulmani di Sicilia*, III, 291-292). On the urban corporate movement in James's realms (*universitates*), see J. M. Font y Rius, "Orígenes del régimen municipal de Cataluña," part 2, *AHDE*, XVII (1946), 423ff., 496-498.

[46] *Llibre dels feyts*, chs. 327, 410, 416. Tortosa Charter (1148). Jiménez de Rada, *De rebus Hispaniae*, lib. IX, c. 16. See the "proceres"—notables or community leaders —as distinguished both from aljama officials and from "vicini et habitatores" (or if those words modify "proceres," then from the mass of absent common folk)

lessly identified such men, as in the Játiva and Chivert charters, by the technical title "the respectable men" (*probi homines* and *prohoms*), baldly attaching them to the class of substantial or chief citizens from whom Christians drew their own officials and assemblies in towns of all sizes.[47] The preferred name, however, was elders (*veyls, veteres, viejos*), whether on the island of Minorca, at Valencia city, in Biar, or universally in a circular letter of 1283 to each of the kingdom's many aljamas. At Murcia city they were "elders and learned men of the town" ("veyls e savis homens de la vila"), where the term *savis* may be a mere convention, or indicate experience or wisdom, or more literally involve the erudite *faqīh* class.[48]

Some historians have incautiously accepted "elders" literally, imagining a sage council of the oldest residents, characterized by wisdom and equanimity.[49] This is oversimplified. King James and his contemporaries were merely following the Arabic, translating "sheik" as "elder." The Arabic word did not necessarily imply age, any more than it carried the romantic overtones associated with it by moderns. "The sheik Abū Aḥmad," listed in a medieval Arabic chronology as dying at Valencia city just after James's first siege of Peñíscola, need not have been powerful, tribal, or elderly.[50] Ibn al-Abbār, "a member of the body of sheiks" at Valencia city during its siege, was not then an old man.[51] Catalan had its own transliteration, *xec* or *xech*, but records of the Valencian crusade era rarely use it. Twice King

in the fifteenth-century document cited above in n. 10; Uxó had some 160 in this class present at the signing, and Eslida 30.

47 María del Carmen Carlé reviews the sparse references and theories on this nucleus of more important people, who were "not a class but a relational situation" in Christian communities by the thirteenth century, in her "*Boni homines* y hombres buenos," *Cuadernos de historia de España*, XXXIX (1964), 132-168. See, for Catalonia, Font y Rius, "Régimen municipal," pp. 327-388. Caro Baroja conjectured that such town councillors among Muslims were the tribal or family sheiks. Amari inclined to identify Sicily's *anciani* with sheiks, assimilating them also to the town notables acting in parallel as *buoni uomini* (*Musulmani di Sicilia*, III, 285-286, 292).

48 *Llibre dels feyts*, chs. 119-120, 355, 439. Peter's letter to the aljamas in 1283 is in Fernández y González, *Mudejares de Castilla*, appendix, doc. 52. A letter to the leaders and *veteres morarie* of Valencia city is in Roca Traver, "Vida mudéjar," doc. 30.

49 Roca Traver, "Vida mudéjar," p. 129.

50 *Spanisch-islamische Urkunden*, doc. 57, a Valencian date list (624, or 1226 in the Christian calendar).

51 Ibn Khaldūn, *Histoire des Berbères*, II, 348.

James applied it to the king of Majorca, rather as a component of his name: "he had the name Sheik Abū Yaḥyā" (Xech Abohehie). James was aware of the equivalence between *xec* and "elder," earlier conveying the same status by calling him "lo veyl."[52]

James could use "old" as an epithet of affection or respect, as when he addressed a knight "Ah, Don veyl!"[53] In a much broader way, the word had become a conventional title among Muslims. "Elder" attributed the best qualities Muslims looked for in old men—experience, stability, merit, position, and the like—without committing itself to any age group. An analogy can be found in the medieval Latin *senior*—either an old man or a person of authority—as well as in the use of the vaguely honorific *senyors* by which contemporary Catalan authors like Raymond Lull and Arnold of Vilanova addressed their readers. "Elders" in short was a synonym for solid citizens or respected men; prefaced to the name of such a man, it conveyed little more than polite regard. It also served to designate a supervisor over any number of enterprises—the *ra'īs* who moderated a mosque's functionaries, the numerous directors of law schools or pious Sufi establishments, the disciplinarian for a market or its subsection (not to be confused with the head of a trade grouping or with the *muḥtasib*), the spokesman for each neighborhood in a city, or even the leader of an organized gang of ruffians.[54]

The Christians observing both the Islamic society they encountered in Valencia at the moment of crusade impact, and the subsequent Mudejar community, understood the term rather in the traditional sense of Muslim urban notables. Applied to cities of the conquered

[52] *Llibre dels feyts*, chs. 67, 85; "el havia nom Xech Abohehie," confounded by the 1557 edition into the single name Retabohihe. The Majorcan king, appearing in ch. 67 merely as "lo veyl," mystified the editors of the recent Casacuberta edition, who conjecture the modern Catalan equivalent "el vell (?)"; but there is no doubt that this is the "Xech."

[53] *Ibid.*, ch. 83.

[54] Lapidus offers a broad range of examples of supervisory personnel and notables bearing the name, in his *Muslim Cities*, pp. 73, 92, 156 (head of a quarter), pp. 111-112 (head of mosque personnel), p. 96 (disciplinarians in a market section), p. 112 (supervisor of law school), and passim. See also Tyan, *Droit public musulman*, I, 84. Goitein, *Mediterranean Society*, I, xvii. Levy explains a more technical meaning the word can bear (*Social Structure of Islam*, p. 73). In late thirteenth-century Cordova, the "jeque mayor" or "anciano" paid a thousand *maravedis* for his title and heard the aljama's cases, so that he seems to have been the main *qāḍī* (Orti Belmonte, "Fuero de Córdoba: mudéjares," p. 40).

kingdom, "elders" obviously comprised a mixed bag of substantial or prestigious leaders of varied profession or position; in smaller towns and villages they might translate as important locals or merely heads of households; where tribal patterns still dominated, perhaps in some pastoral sector, these men might be chieftains. The king's memoirs leave the impression that they were numerous. At Játiva the hundred chief men of the town surrendered; at Bairén the elders of the town and villages appointed a delegation of twenty to wait on the king; at Nules the king had to prepare special presents of clothing for twenty such leaders, and at Uxó for thirty. The Chivert charter named sixteen as a partial delegation.[55]

A primary meaning of sheik nevertheless remained "an old man," and within a body of notables the elderly enjoyed special status. King James noticed that the governor of Minorca, who gathered over three hundred "of the better men" into "a more complete council" during the island's crisis, took advice as well from the oldest among the notables.[56] His contemporary Joinville admired the title sheik precisely because Muslims, "of all people, most honor old men"; and down into Morisco days, each family or line in the Granadan kingdom honored its oldest representative of direct paternal primogeniture as its sheik.[57] If old men held honored place in the Valencian council, how old was "old"? King James described two Muslim oldsters ("antichs homens") with whom he dealt at Biar as over fifty years of age. This accords with the understanding of Muslim authors generally, who applied sheik in its chronological sense to men over fifty.[58] This over-fifty category must have comprised a fairly numerous body of active older men, since a Valencian lawsuit of 1267 over ownership of two towns involved consultation with "the oldest Moors," an even older category of men seventy, eighty, and ninety.[59] From study of skulls along the eastern coast of Spain, anthropologists

[55] *Llibre dels feyts*, chs. 250, 252, 314-315, 327. Chivert Charter.

[56] *Llibre dels feyts*, chs. 120-121. The Minorca assembly may be regarded rather as the princely council expanded to its limits in an emergency, though in fact the expansion would undoubtedly have come by addition of the *probi homines* (see *Llibre dels feyts*, ch. 121).

[57] Joinville, *Histoire de St. Louis*, ch. 62. Caro Baroja, *Moriscos*, p. 103.

[58] *Llibre dels feyts*, ch. 355: "qui eren antichs homens, que cascu havia plus de l anys." A. Cour, "Shaikh," *EI*[1], IV, 275.

[59] Arch. Crown, James I, Reg. Canc. 15, fol. 82 (Feb. 27, 1267): "de lxx e de lxxx e de xc anos."

have concluded that 27 percent of the thirteenth-century population lived beyond sixty, with 22 percent filling the forty-to-sixty bracket; the over-sixty segment thus comprised a third of the adult (over twenty-one) populace.[60] Ethnic distinctions in these statistics would favor a larger percentage of oldsters among Muslims.[61]

Ibn Khaldūn, with his customary originality, explored the wider question of life-span and relative age. He thought 120 years a life-span theoretically natural to man, observed that some Muslims lived to the age of 100, and others to 50, 70, or 80, and concluded that the normal life lasted between 60 and 70 years; growth ended at 40, followed by a plateau of existence "for a while" before decline began to set in, so that three overlapping generations from grandfather through grandson could be expected to cover 100 years.[62] His Valencian contemporary Eiximenis, familiar with the region's Mudejars, observed that "the Saracens have more old men than the Christians, because they are more temperate in their diet"; where a Christian consumed quantities of meat—a trait Lull also noted in the Catalans—with sauces, bread, and wine, the Muslim contented himself with eight or ten figs, toasted bread, and some water.[63] Early in the fourteenth century, John of Montecorvino was to complain from his arduous Peking mission of being old before his time, at fifty-eight. In the light of such evidence, an "old" assemblyman in Valencia must have been over fifty and probably very much older.

Principal Assistants

If the council constituted the seat of administration in city and village, with the *qāḍī* or an equivalent *faqīh* its principal though not single representative, where did the intervening *adelantados* stand? The name is equivalent to the Arabic *muqaddam*, meaning "placed

[60] Jaime Vicens Vives, *An Economic History of Spain*, trans. F. López-Morillas (Princeton, 1969), p. 175; in Roman days here only 16 percent lived beyond sixty, 22 percent filling the forty-to-sixty bracket; taken together, these statistics demonstrate a step in the dramatic rise in life expectancy from Neolithic to medieval times.

[61] See n. 63.

[62] *Muqaddimah*, I, 343; see also pp. 278-282, 346.

[63] Eiximenis, *Terç del crestià*, in Soldevila, *Historia de España*, II, 157: "los sarrains per tal han més hòmens vells que los cristians car son pus temprats en llur menjar."

in front," much like the Roman title *praefectus*. A *muqaddam* might head a ship, troops, monastery, or police. This chameleon quality, common to most terms designating authorities in Islam, makes it difficult to define the office covered here. General histories of aljama administration for the realms of Aragon speak of the *adelantados*, or in Catalan-speaking regions the *adelantats*, as a smaller council or administrator's cabinet of executive assistants. A standard account by Giménez Soler describes them as the two lieutenants helping the *amīn* govern an aljama. Esteban Abad recently outlined the aljama government at Daroca in Aragon proper as "very simple": an *amīn* with two annually elected *adelantados* or *clavarios*. Roca Traver likened the Valencian *adelantats* to the Christian jurates, elected to cooperate with the ruling *amīn* and meeting thrice weekly. Macho Ortega makes them aides, assisted in complex *morerías* by some six elected "councillors."[64]

Adelantats were prominent in the fourteenth and later centuries of Valencian Mudejarism; Valldigna had three, while places like Carlet, Chivert, and Ribesalbes each had two.[65] The crown in 1376 addressed the Valencia city Moors as "you the aljama, *adelantats*, and elders of the Moorish quarter."[66] General interpretations about *adelantats* require cautious examination. Analogy from past and future, or from a similar region or situation, can illumine a problem; on occasion, however, it can compound the difficulties. The converging influence of Christian forms and of the more evolved Jewish and Mudejar colonial exemplars seems to have transformed both name and function of these officials; by the time they had acquired the

[64] Giménez Soler, *Corona de Aragón*, p. 293. Esteban Abad, *Ciudad y comunidad de Daroca*, p. 216. Roca Traver, "Vida mudéjar," p. 128. Macho Ortega, "Mudéjares aragoneses," pp. 158-159. *Adelantado* is a more common form than the Catalan *adelantat*, since both office and name were borrowed from Castile and Aragon proper.

[65] Gual Camarena, "Mudéjares valencianos, aportaciones," p. 177. The document of 1404 above in n. 11 lists as separate "clavarios, adelantados, jurados, alamines, e biellos."

[66] Roca Traver, "Vida mudéjar," doc. 30 (July 18, 1376): "vobis aljame, adelantatis, et veteribus morarie predicte Valencie," each position considered as a continuing "officium." A suit brought in Calatayud in 1382 by the local aljama was led by three "sarraceni aliame sarracenorum civitatis Calatayubii" together with unspecified "adelantati eiusdem aliame" (Fernández y González, *Mudejares de Castilla*, appendix, doc. 69). Charles V addressed the Moors of Valencia kingdom in 1525 as "alami, iurados et aliama" (*ibid.*, doc. 98).

designation jurates they had probably assumed that role for the Mudejar community.

Thirteenth-century Valencia affords almost no record of the office. The surrender charters, the king's memoirs, and the orders addressed to aljamas are silent. This does not prove that the *adelantat* did not exist among the other functionaries named; it does suggest that his office had not yet gained prominence, or that it lay disguised under another name, or that it had not yet fully differentiated from some more inclusive office. The one exception comes in Játiva's charter, where "you may have four Saracens as *adelantats*, whomever you want to elect from among you, who is to care for and maintain you and your property and your rights." The duties (*custodire et manutenere*), together with the range of objects covered, point to an activity wider than execution of administrative detail, as though these men were representatives of the popular interest. Later this charter plainly states that all its "Saracens are to be governed by your *qāḍī* and *adelantats*."[67]

One other area furnishes a hint concerning the thirteenth-century *adelantado* or *adelantat*—the administrative history of Jewish aljamas in the realms of Aragon. Early in the thirteenth century these communities began imitating Christian municipalities by electing a set number of communal officers—*neëmanim* or *muḳademin*—called *adelantados* or eventually on occasion "jurates." Their number varied; Calatayud in 1229 elected from its *probi homines* four *adelantados*, whereas other places deliberately multiplied them so that important families might enjoy the status that accrued from having a relative as incumbent. Their duties differed from place to place. Unusually wide powers at Calatayud allowed them to arrest and punish malefactors, even to the death penalty, and to administer communal affairs; their administrative decisions, if backed by a majority of the elders or council, became valid for the aljama. At Zaragoza in 1264 the elected four *adelantados* effectively replaced the council and elders as principal administrators; they represented the wealthy aristocrats in a tense social struggle there, though by 1280 the revised body of twenty-five *adelantados* had a broader base.

An inner council of administrative-judicial nature thus tended to assume control of Jewish aljamas during the course of the thirteenth

[67] Játiva Charter. The form used is Latin *adenantatus*.

century; but by the witness of Ben Adret, there was no uniformity as late as 1264, so that Murviedro, for example, dispensed with *adelantats*.[68] The situation continued fluid throughout the century, differing from place to place. The pace of evolution was slower and less uniform than in the Christian towns. Since Valencian Muslims came under Christian control only in the second quarter of the century, and since they formed a preponderant mass of population less easy to influence at the grass-roots level, their evolution, too, was undoubtedly slow. The date of the Játiva charter, significantly 1252, may well signal the first experiment by the crown in Valencia, with the *adelantat* inserted as part of the post-*qā'id* reform of government for that city.

In Latin documents the Jewish *adelantats* became *secretarii*. In Islamic Valencia the office of *scriptor* or secretary was something quite different, either the princely or the notarial *kātib*. Always a personage of importance at an Islamic court, the *kātib* had particularly flourished in the Almohad corpus of functionaries, outranked only by the grand vizier. A pale reflection of his glory was the more prosaic public scribe who drafted public instruments and elaborated common contracts according to a formulary. Ibn Khaldūn discourses on the nature of the princely secretary's office, its evolution and varied fortunes, and the forms it assumed under different dynasties. He recommends "that the person in charge of this office must be selected from among the upper classes and be a refined gentleman of great knowledge and with a good deal of stylistic ability." He must be familiar with "the principal branches of scholarship" insofar as they are likely to come up in the ruler's gatherings, and he must have character and "good manners."[69]

In the dying years of the Islamic kingdom of Valencia, while the crusaders were gobbling up castle after castle, the historian Ibn al-Abbār adorned the office of *kātib*. He had previously served Abū 'Abd Allāh and his son Abū Zayd; he was at the side of Abū Zayd during the Calatayud pact with King James but soon defected to Zayyān. When James set siege to Valencia city in 1238, Ibn al-Abbār led the diplomatic mission that persuaded Tunis to dispatch a naval expedition. After the fall of Valencia he held the same post at Tunis,

[68] Baer, *Jews in Christian Spain*, I, 217-226.
[69] *Muqaddimah*, II, 26-35, esp. p. 28.

rising to be premier or vizier until his fall and execution. Another princely secretary was the scholar Abu 'l-Qasīm (Abolcaçim), "the main secretary" (*escriva major*) of Játiva, who conducted that city's surrender negotiations. To secure his help in the council of the *qā'id*, King James bribed him by promising "more riches than ever you had." Obviously Abu 'l-Qasīm was no bureaucratic scribe or public notary.[70]

Lesser scribes must certainly have abounded in the Valencian kingdom, given the insatiable demand for contracts in the daily life of contemporary Spanish Muslims. Hoenerbach has studied this class and has transcribed a model of their work, the marriage contract at Murviedro drawn along classical lines sixty years after the Christian conquest.[71] It stands as the lone survivor from thirteenth-century Valencia of a genre whose exemplars must once have been common as grass. Possibly the notarial scribe is hidden from us under the more generic title of *faqīh*. The Christian municipal chancery may supply a clue to the local aljama notariate. The supervisory office of municipal secretary was a desirable plum in Christian Valencia, even for a town as inconsequential as San Mateo. Parish rectors defied royal prohibitions to exercise this rewarding craft, and by 1283 at the capital city the notaries were among the large guilds who won a share of municipal powers.[72] An analogous position of aljama secretary appears among the prime offices of Mudejar Valencia. Though it is possible to identify him with the *adelantat* or some executive adjutant along the lines of chamberlain, he almost surely fulfilled the notarial or scribal function. Ibn 'Abdūn describes this office for twelfth-century Seville as demanding some literary talent and considerable legal knowledge for the redaction of marriages and other contracts.[73]

[70] *Llibre dels feyts*, chs. 350-353: "mes que anch no·m hagues." Huici has a sketch of Ibn al-Abbār in his *Historia musulmana de Valencia*, III, 265-270.

[71] *Spanisch-islamische Urkunden*, introductory essay on *escribano* and *kātib*, pp. xxi-xxxv. On the *kātib* as adviser, secretary, and judicial collaborator of the *qāḍī*, see Tyan, *Organisation judiciaire*, pp. 255-258.

[72] Burns, *Crusader Valencia*, pp. 35, 126, 405, and index under "notaries"; in 1230 a city like Toulouse supported thirty-two such scribes. See García, *Estado económico-social*, p. 64, on the seignorial notariate in Christian Valencian settlement as a public revenue source which a lord could retain, sell, or otherwise exploit.

[73] Ibn 'Abdūn, *Séville musulmane, le traité*, pp. 27-28. See the listing of this office in 1294 as one of the four major posts of the aljama, above, n. 11.

The *amīn* Muḥammad, lifetime "scriptor" at Chelva from 1269, appears to have received a supervisory notarial post much like that in a Christian town; along with his governing powers he possessed a profitable monopoly.[74] Muḥammad of Salā ("de Sale"), scribe and later *qāḍī* of the Valencia city Moorish quarter, seems to have been in the same position.[75] Beyond these fragments, vision fails; one must either have recourse to an analogy from outside Valencia, as with the Mudejar "scrivania" at Cortes where "le scribano" operated in the mosque,[76] or else turn again to the impressive model from Murviedro and project from it the scribal profession flourishing a generation after the crusade. Carreras y Candi, in a careful study of the notariate in the realms of King James, concluded that "almost always the notaries of the Saracens were Jews"; he cited as illustration the monopoly conferred on Judah Bonsenyor in 1294 for all notarial functions of Muslims in the territory of Barcelona.[77] Valencia would seem to have constituted an exception, however, especially in the postcrusade generation, unless the generalization retains some truth for lesser subnotaries, or unless a supervisory or licensing monopoly involving tax-farmers is in question.

In the larger Moorish quarters, other petty officials must have been plentiful; but the Christian overlords showed little interest in preserving their titles or duties for posterity. Given the undifferentiated administration of the medieval aljama, where administrative, judicial, commercial, and religious powers shaded into one another, the list of administrators might be extended to include functionaries already encountered in other spheres, such as the ubiquitous *muḥtasib* and his helpers, the *ṣāḥib al-madīna*, the *ṣāḥib ash-shurṭa*, the *saio*, and tax people like the *mushrif*. The *clavarius* appears in the Chivert

[74] See doc. of Jan. 14, n. 17 above: "sis alaminus et scriptor."

[75] Arch. Crown, Peter III, Reg. Canc. 44, fol. 190 (Sept. 6, 1280), appointing "vobis Mahometo de Sale de domo nostra alcaidiam et scribaniam sarracenorum morarie Valencie"; he held the "office" under the conditions usual for "other holders." Though the name may represent Ibn Ṣāliḥ, the derivative *de* suggests a place; Salé (Salā) near Rabat, in later times home of the ex-Morisco Sallee Rovers or pirates, was an Atlantic port with regular trade to Spain in the thirteenth century. Alternatively, as-Sahla was another name for the region west of Valencia, al-Barrasīn.

[76] "Documentos para la reconquista del Ebro," 3d series, *EEMCA*, v (1952), doc. 399 (ca. 1234).

[77] Carreras y Candi, "Institució notarial en lo segle xiii," p. 765.

charter as "gatekeeper or porter." Roca Traver makes him *mushrif*, an elected tax-collector and administrator of public monies. Semantically this *claver* or *clavario* relates better to *ḥājib*, the chamberlain or keeper of entry. At the lower extreme of the bureaucratic scale, can he be simply the night watch, who went under the name gatekeeper in Islamic Spanish cities because of the many gates to quarters, each with its armed watchman and dog?[78] The Christian *merí* or *merino* assigned to every Mudejar aljama in the description of Giménez Soler does not turn up in early Valencian records, at least under that name; nor does an aristocratic protector of the people appear in the city, like the converted son of Baeza's ruler who lived in the Moorish quarter of contemporary Seville as the *Infante* or Prince Fernando Abdelmon.[79]

A ruler wields power directly, as well as presiding over its wider exercise by his corps of bureaucrats; around him like planets in a stately circle move the entrenched institutions, semiautonomous groupings, and similar informal reservoirs of power. This governmental complex, however widely considered, reveals the political power structure only imperfectly. A missing dimension leaves the mechanisms flat and unreal, a mere physiology of the body politic bereft of vivifying force. The next chapter supplies that dimension by breathing a kind of soul into the mechanisms of Islamic and Mudejar Valencia.

[78] The Spanish gatekeeper is explained in al-Maqqarī, *Mohammedan Dynasties in Spain*, I, 105. *Clavario* might also be the *saio* above on p. 237.

[79] Giménez Soler, *Corona de Aragón*, p. 293. Ballesteros, *Sevilla en el siglo xiii*, p. 101; he was the son of Ibn Muḥammad. *Merí* derives from Latin *maiorinus*. On *mushrif* see above, p. 367 and note. Macho Ortega found the later *clavario* only in major aljamas, administering a tax-collecting office ("Mudéjares aragoneses," p. 160; see also the petty staff on pp. 161-162).

CHAPTER XVII

The Islamic Establishment: Vertical Power

THE TERM establishment, though victim of journalistic abuse, best describes the coalescive bond siting a governmental authority firmly within its community. It designates the loose agglomeration of office-holders, wealthy merchants, landlords, men of religion, scholars, literary intellectuals, professionals, military figures, and the like, who represent residual power or who influence the executors of power. This alliance is strongest at its upper levels, where the principal representatives of each species meet and mingle. Present usage lays stress on privileged inner circles that wield indirect power, enveloped in a protective larger periphery of people who are either influential with such circles or support them because of their own stake in the *status quo*; the usage implies self-serving and reactionary complacency, with overtones of sinister near-conspiracy as interlocking interests manipulate the larger society.[1] The cliché parodies a reality that is operative in any community and constitutes almost the prime reality in some political societies. For the medieval Muslim world, no analysis of the visible political framework conveys an understanding of the politico-social community unless it takes into account this profoundly powerful combination. Neglect of its role in Valencian affairs has left previous explanations of Mudejar communities strangely formal and lifeless.

Such an establishment was not the only bonding factor in the Valencian social order; solidarities of various kinds cut across the diversity of subcommunities. The Malikite school of law dominated Spain, creating a unity as did no other factor or power at this time; local leaders, combining wealth, political office, and the often authoritative charism of religion, constituted an unparalleled unitive

[1] See the penetrating essay by Henry Fairlie, who is responsible for the expression's vogue, "Evolution of a Term," *New Yorker*, XLIV, no. 35 (1968), 173-206; and Fowler, *Modern English Usage* (Gowers edn.), p. 169.

force. Sects, loyalties, trade associations, and brotherhoods all contributed their measure. Their impact remained partial, however, or lacked that constant, universal, sociopolitical effectiveness achieved by the amorphous entity that somehow subsumed these inferior organizing factors.

The Coordinating Elite

Having analyzed the main administrative offices and located the centers of specifically political power, one might easily conclude that the task of reconstructing the Valencian political scene in the precrusade and Mudejar years had been completed. The illogical interpenetration of functions, their tendency to alter shape while retaining a traditional title, and the kaleidoscopic variety of ill-defined political forms flourishing like mushrooms in the dark of the Almohad collapse do conspire, of course, to leave the picture somewhat murky. If the map of political power in its main features is now reasonably clear, however, the clarity is deceptive. A society so amorphous, so passionately fragmented and removed from its rulers, could hardly have survived if held together only by the sheer will of a local usurper. Something in the picture is missing.

The Western mind tends to supply corporative groups, elected representatives, defined professions and interests—a balance of church organizations against civil, for example, and labor or school entities against both. In the final analysis, however, the Muslim aljama was not a commune, and it lacked the self-governing, relatively autonomous kinds of Western association. To describe such a town in terms of community officials consequently makes little sense. Yet what else is left to do? To detail each discernible unity such as the tribe, the rural wealthy class, the city neighborhood, the literary clique, and the prominent families does not suffice to reveal the Valencian aljama's inner reality. Lapidus has opened a way around the impasse, offering an alternative method for studying Muslim communities.[2] He finds a set of informal patterns of

[2] Ira Lapidus, *Muslim Cities*, esp. pp. 107-115 and chs. 3, 4; and his contribution to *Middle Eastern Cities*, pp. 49ff. See also the comments of Hourani and Stern in *Islamic City*, chs. 1 and 2. Cahen offers supporting elements in his "Mouvements populaires et autonomisme urbain," passim.

social activity that circle around and through a religious elite. Beyond parochial divisions and the officials relevant to a bureaucratic central government, the town with its region exhibits an inner life, a cohesion and stability springing not from institutions and formal structures but from a social configuration. While not exactly forming a government below the government, it did amount to a common social order, a normative pattern.

The erudites of Islamic religious tradition provided its nucleus. To render the reality in more exact image, they were the spirit informing the sociopolitical body, giving it dynamism and direction. Because religious law penetrated everywhere, shaping the unitary whole, the religious elite were either identified or associated with the managerial, familial, economic, professional, and propertied elite, and also had points of contact at every other level of society. Since the notables of Islam were relatively undifferentiated—a *qāḍī* might also be a merchant, or a carpenter, or a part-time teacher—this relationship comprised less a parallelism, or even a nuclear positioning of the elite in society, than an interpenetration.

This higher elite was not a class, for it cut across all social divisions, integrating them and channeling their energies. The full or part-time religious figure was present among the bureaucrats in secretarial, consultative, and administrative posts; among the wealthy as patrician jurist, merchant-teacher, learned client, and famed *qāḍī*; among the artisans as scribe, court officer, prayer leader, mosque functionary, and teacher; and even among the despised masses as popular preacher, holy man, and supporter of some *qāḍī*. Learning or piety conferred status as surely as did wealth; social mobility ensured constant immigration from all classes into the religious elite, as well as emigration by that elite into the familial and other subelites. Certain families or tribal groupings traditionally contributed members to this coordinating elite, though Islamic biographers exaggerated the duration of these families; three or four such generations were unusual.[3]

[3] Lapidus, *Muslim Cities*, p. 110; cf. the similar findings of Ibn Khaldūn as below in n. 20, with qualification by Caro Baroja. As a function of familial fluidity, coordinate leadership later passed to the wealthier Mudejars, who assumed the *faqīh* role as intellectuals and cult functionaries; this helps explain why Valencia's Moriscos, isolated by broken geography, bad communications, and lack of unified life style, still spoke with one voice on the eve of expulsion, as "la nación de los

The elite supplied focal points, around which cliques and their wider circles of more indifferent supporters drew together, representing all classes from patron to mob; this center might be anything from a pious or learned figure in a mosque to an official or a school. This inner ordering of Islamic society was mirrored in the bazaar, where a jumble of shop, mosque, school, inn, administrative office, and service amenities allowed the individual to interchange roles and easily to shift activities. Crisscrossing and overlapping, this part-time interchange with its nuclear focal points managed to achieve many ends which specialized agencies or more formal associations did in the Christian West.

Lapidus makes two important reservations. The pattern did not comprise the whole social order but only the principal coordinating and normative element; the protection, order, and economic progress that is indispensable to all the elites had to come, for example, from the superimposed state, just as the state required the cooperation of the coordinating elite for communication, legitimation, and broad support. Secondly, emphasis on this factor in Islamic society does not deny an analogous if less important pattern within the highly structured Christian communes; on the contrary, "stress on cities as process rather than cities as form" now allows the student of comparative urbanism "to transcend the dichotomies between European and Asian."[4] These insights, drawn from the Near East, can be fruitfully applied to Valencia. Differences between the two regions were pronounced. The military and state systems of Valencia were not the disembodied and alien dictatorship characteristic of the Mamluks, but instead comprised part of a native, more integrated social mechanism; its rural and chivalric orders related intimately to the civic population. Constant warfare demanded structures more

---

cristianos nuevos de moros del reino de Valencia" (Halperín Donghi, "Recouvrements: Valence," p. 163). On Islamic Valencian families, studied for themselves as above in Chapter IV rather than in the present elitist context, only fragmentary researches have been made. See the articles of Ribera Tarragó in Chapter XIII, n. 1; the political figures in Huici, *Historia musulmana de Valencia*, I, ch. 2, and passim; pertinent sections of Ibn Ḥazm in Terés, as well as the works of Lautensach, Mateu y Llopis, Sanchis Guarner, Sanchis Sivera, and especially Vernet, all as cited above in Chapter IV, n. 7.

[4] Lapidus, *Muslim Cities*, p. vii.

formal, while institutional osmosis with the past and with the enemy influenced the evolution of such structures. Valencian society nevertheless illustrates the same general pattern of a coordinating religious elite contributing form to a society divided and seemingly amorphous at any level other than the parochial.

The analogy between East and West can be seen, for example, in the facile surrender of Valencian towns by their notables. The ultimate loyalty of elite-coordinated notables in the East was not to a given regime or faction but to the stable governance of society by military power; when circumstances required, submission to a conqueror and eager cooperation with his desires recommended itself at any price, except of course that of sacrificing a properly Muslim life and good order. "Nowhere was there a hint of resistance or obstruction, or shame at the lack of it"; the notables saw surrender as "imperative because order was imperative."[5] In Valencia this psychology manifested itself by the Muslims' open, friendly switch from foe to loyal subject of the Christian king. What formerly seemed anomalous in the Valencian experience, explicable perhaps by the Spanish past, we can now recognize as emerging from the deeper social order of the Islamic town.

The assortment of religiously oriented functionaries might be reassembled here from their scattered positions in other parts of the book and made to illustrate the interpenetrating clerisy. It will be more useful instead to examine specific localities, supplementing them with illustrative individuals and families. This task involves adumbrating as well the allied elite of wealth; to a lesser extent than the religious elite, it also cut across the social lines that separated landed aristocrat, military adventurer or caste, patrician merchant, rural sheik, and independently rich jurist. Explanation of this point is doubly necessary, since the impression prevails that early Valencian Mudejars almost exclusively comprised farmers or at best small-craftsmen. The disdainful Desclot must bear some blame for the image, as do those scholars who survey several centuries of Mudejarism until the dimly documented early years assimilate to the retrograde later situation. Besides, agricultural people did predominate numerically in any urban society up to and into modern times,

[5] *Ibid.*, pp. 132-133.

even though their presence and occupation never altered the dominant fact of urban-dynamic control.[6]

Elite of Wealth; Patrician Families

The extensive wealthy class of the preconquest kingdom appears not only in general evidence of prosperity and mercantilism but explicitly in episodes like the sale of valuables during expulsion from the fallen capital. Outside the main city, so small a place as Moncada yielded to the crusaders "much rich loot, and pearls, and necklaces, and bracelets of gold and silver, and much silk cloth and many other valuables," spoils worth a hundred thousand besants.[7] Long after Játiva's surrender, its aljama, when threatened with a later expulsion, was able to offer a bribe of "100,000 besants of taxes" to cool the king's anger.[8] Mudejar ruler-aristocrats, who received sufficient attention in a previous context, were obviously not the only type of rich men.

The affluent classes were visible everywhere. Eslida Mudejars, though relatively backward and rural, owned additional properties in other parts of the kingdom; their charter of 1242 explicitly provided that "they may recover their estates [*hereditates*] wherever [these] shall be, except in Valencia and Burriana"; the latter cities by unconditional surrender had lost their countrysides, not at the owner-farmer but at the rent-collecting landlord level. The rebel leaders who had their estates seized at Uxó in 1250 amounted to a half dozen; their several farms were sizable.[9] A stray marriage contract surviving at Murviedro reveals that the widowed mother of the bride disposed of extensive properties "in Murviedro and in the surrounding countryside on both banks" of the lower Palancia, including "farms,

[6] Desclot, *Crònica*, ch. 65; Desclot's disdainful view of *sarrains paliers* as unwarlike farmers became, in the interpretation of Quadrado and modern historians, a belief that they were serfs. Gual Camarena describes the thirteenth-century Mudejars as "predominantemente agricultores y artesanos" ("Mudéjares valencianos en la época del Magnánimo," p. 469); the observation is acceptable in the framework just given.

[7] *Llibre dels feyts*, ch. 202: "molta bona roba, e perles, e sarces de coyl, e brassaderes d·aur e d·argent, e molt drap de seda e d·altres robes moltes; si qu·entre·ls sarrains e ço qu·n exi, que ben puja a c milia besans."

[8] *Ibid.*, ch. 368: "c milia besants de renda."

[9] Eslida Charter. García, *Historia de Vall de Uxó*, p. 51.

vineyards, fields, houses, clothing, furnishings, and olive groves" as well as "the whole field of white [fallow] earth."[10] Not only the mother's holdings but the size of the dowry, 300 gold pieces, shows that the family's social rank was high; rather than local farmers of means or aristocrats, they were a wealthy provincial family.

To reinforce the impression of a middling-rich class, any number of records locate or describe Mudejar properties, usually by way of locating some Christian land grant. Wealthier Mudejars built large town houses so commonly that the 1252 Játiva charter set a special house tax upon the category of residence (*staticum*) constructed by throwing three or four buildings into one. This constitution also allowed Mudejars to purchase buildings and farms without hindrance anywhere in the kingdom.[11] When the Valencian *Furs* forbade "Christian men or women slaves or Christian nurses" to the Mudejar, it is unlikely that the general law had application only to the relatively infrequent noble; it conjures up a more general class of slaveholders, from the modest household with a servant or two to the large domestic establishment of the city patrician.[12] Studying the graceful figures that people the Mudejar ceramics of Valencia—sharp-nosed warriors, serene and unveiled women—one is tempted to think that the Mudejar upper classes influenced the portraiture, though the figures were more plausibly Christian.[13]

Both the religious and the wealthy elite were represented at the surrender of Almenara, in the persons of the most important town erudite and another "very influential" Moor; the two operated initially by "private" connivance "with their friends."[14] Such "friends" represented that combination of caste and family encountered in the charters. Chapter IV has already adverted to the sparse data on Valencian kin groups, with their circles of immediate household, actively involved *consanguinei*, and "friends," together with the englobing "lineage" or tribal and subtribal houses that lent the generic family

[10] *Spanisch-islamische Urkunden*, doc. 5. See above, p. 225. See Gaudefroy-Demombynes, *Muslim Institutions*, ch. 8 on marriage and dowry. On the condition of women in Spanish Islam, see Lévi-Provençal, *España musulmana*, v, 258, 260-261; Berber influence must have elevated her status further. Mudejar women could contract or be obligated as much as men; see, e.g., the Tudela situation in Ibarra, "Cristianos y moros, documentos aragoneses y navarros," p. 81.

[11] Játiva Charter.

[12] *Furs*, lib. I, rub. VIII, c. 1, 2.

[13] See Chapter V, n. 14.

[14] *Llibre dels feyts*, ch. 243.

name. The chapters on aristocrats and patriots supplied examples at an exalted ruling level. Ibn Khaldūn provided insight into divisions among these groupings, such as old-versus-*arriviste*, native-versus-Berber, and military-versus-urban, each of them an inadequate or overlapping category. Can further examples be discovered, but from the now obscure class of urban and village notables? Can their names yield any model for reconstructing kin groups at that level?

The surrender negotiations for mighty Játiva involved especially a *faqīh* with an unnamed notable as companion. The *faqīh* was "Almofois," the most celebrated scholar at Játiva and a member of "the upper class" (*meylors homens*).[15] Here was an excellent example of the erudite who incorporated in his person the elites of religious learning, patrician family, wealth, and political power. Only one family in Spanish Islam bore the name Benimofauaz, whose syllables the vulgar pronounced as Mofois.[16] This was the Banū Mufawwaz or Mufawwiz, a Játiva branch of the great Banū Ma'āfir. Distinguished not only for learning but for holiness, the Banū Ma'āfir had a reputation in literary-scientific circles at Cordova; some were regarded as saints. At Játiva they exercised high office. During the late twelfth century the clan supplied the main *qāḍī* both at Játiva and at Alcira; indeed the last *qāḍī* of Játiva about whom details survive came from this family (d. 1194). The crusade figure may well have been Játiva's *qāḍī*, but King James was too dazzled "by your repute" to bother to record his precise office.[17] This luminary's influence, like that of his counterpart the Almenara *faqīh*, had another field of play—the city council. This fits the contemporary pattern visible at places like Seville where the *qāḍī*, a theologian-jurist from a principal local family, presided over a town council dominated by an oligarchy of patrician families like the Banū Khaldūn.[18]

[15] *Ibid.*, ch. 336. See above, p. 173n.

[16] Ribera y Tarragó, "Tribu de Maáfar: los Benimofáuaz de Játiva," pp. 236-243. See above, pp. 172-173. The name puzzled Gayangos, who suggested "the horsemen" or else a derivative of *al-makhārif*. Was the *qā'id* of Játiva in the Cid's time, "Ben Mahcor," a variant, with f, h, and hard c interchangeable (Menéndez Pidal, *España del Cid*, I, 313-314)?

[17] *Llibre dels feyts*, ch. 337.

[18] Cagigas, *Sevilla almohade*, p. 21. Ibn Khaldūn, *Muqaddimah*, Rosenthal's intro., p. xxxv.

When the Játiva council became identified with local government after the extrusion of the Banū ʿĪsā as vassal-lords under King James, the 1252 charter showed two and probably three of the Banū Maʿāfir clan in power, including the first signatory and the vizier. "Almafar" and "Abmafar" appear as variants of Maʿāfir; "Almehiz" might be al-Muʿizz, but is suspiciously close to the local variant for Mufawwiz that King James recorded as Mofois. The pact presented clearly the leading Mudejar families. Of the fourteen aljama notables named, the Banū Maʿāfir contributed three, the al-Banika (Alfanequi) family three, and eight other families one apiece. There is one Ghālib (Galip), a common name but perhaps connected with the Banū Ghālib (Avingalib), represented at the Elche surrender by Muḥammad and in Murcian affairs by Abū ʿAmrūs (Abuambre).[19] The list as caught by Catalan ears ran thus: Jahia Almehiz, Abutinum Abudarecha, Abdalla Alfanequi, Ali Alfanequi, Abuzach Alfanequi, Almafar Algaccel, Abmafar Almiquineci, Mahomat Abnecebit, Abdalla Exambra, Galip Adaroez, Iahie Abenraha, Mahomet Abbacar, Abdalla Alcaçes, and Mahomet Abdolucet.

Without extrinsic evidence it is difficult to do more than surmise the originals of these names. "Abutinum" may represent one of the Berber Spanish Banū Dhi 'n-Nūn or Dhu 'n-Nūn; "Adaroez" ʿAbd ar-Raʾīs; "Abuzach" Abū Isḥāq; and "Abbacar" Abū Bakkār. Could "Abdolucet" conceal ʿAbd al-ʿAzīz? "Algaccel" approximates *alguacil*, Romance for *al-wazīr*; if it is a name, rather than a title, al-Ghazzāl will serve. "Alcaçes" may relate to a form like al-Qazzāz rather than 'l-Casis, or -Qāsim. "Abnecebit" suggests Ibn Thābit. "Almiquineci" could connect with the Spanish Banū Miknāsa, or denote some place of origin like Mequinenza near Lérida. If "Alfanequi" is not al-Banika, it may have something in common with Romance *alfaneque*, white eagle or tent. These notables, proud in their own day, can be rescued from oblivion only by painstaking paleographical reexamination, combined with comparative etymology, some ingenuity in coping with careless scribes, and familiarity with chance fragments from other periods of Valencian history.

At Chivert the principal leaders appeared on the surrender constitution, fifteen names representing ten families. The main citizen

[19] *Llibre dels feyts*, ch. 416 (Elche). Fernández y González, *Mudejares de Castilla*, appendix, doc. 47 (1266). Vernet has ʿAmrūs become Ambros in Catalan.

was the *faqīh* 'Abd Allāh b. Yūsuf b. 'Abd al-'Alī or 'Abd al-A'lā (Abdelale); he headed the list, probably as *qāḍī.* His son 'Alī stood fifth among the fifteen. Two members of the al-Ghāzī clan were among the first to sign—Ḥakam b. Yūsuf al-Ghāzī (Facam son of Juceff Algazi) and Ḥakam b. 'Alī al-Ghāzī (Defecan son of Aliagazi). Low on the list were Muḥammad and 'Alī b. Ḥabīb (Abinfabib), while two men named Abū Bakr (Ubaquer) seem to belong together. Perhaps 'Abd Allāh b. Sharīf (? Avinxarifet) and 'Alī "Arunxaxit" were misspelled relatives. Other families contributed one man apiece; they fell upon the scribal ear as Aucat son of Bintuper, Coloymme Abdelgobar, Moferich son of Sala, Abdeluasit Avinçamege, and Çoleymen Axaquot; the charter later concerned itself with the coveted estate of Aug Almucer and his wife Eva Abintigarra, tentatively awarding it to Aug's brother or relative (*frater*) 'Alī Azmon Abdelle the Younger and to the Ḥakam b. Yūsuf seen above. Idiosyncrasies of Christian ear and pen discourage hope of exact reconstruction of these families, though a number of them find echo in Valencian topography. The Ubaquer duo recall Beniboquer near Alcira, mentioned in the crusaders' land division, as well as the Valencian rebel Bocor, and the common Abū Bakr. Towns like Salem, Benisalem, Benigalip, Benetuser, Beniayso, and the like suggest at least that these family names were not strange to the region. It is tempting to see Mufarrij b. aṣ-Ṣālaḥ in Moferich, son of Sala. Aug and Aucat resemble Wakī' and Wāqidī, rather than exotic Spanish elements such as al-Qūṭī (Gothic), Huqu (Hugo), or primitive Auca (as in Dar-ūca, Daroca). Conjecture can supply variations for the more difficult names, but it may also mislead. Topography is an inadequate guide, as Ibn Khaldūn noted, both because tribalism was weak in Spain and because notable families so commonly fell back into obscurity after three to four generations.[20]

[20] *Muqaddimah,* I, 61, 279-280, 334-335, with psychological reasons why nobility and leadership must normally run their course within four generations. Caro Baroja takes issue with Ibn Khaldūn and other Islamic sources for exaggerating both the loss of tribal spirit and the perdurance of lineage (*Moriscos,* pp. 37-53); but the point at issue is the general pattern rather than the possibly frequent exceptions. The Chivert list runs: "alfachino nomine Abdalla filio de Juceff Abdelale et de alcaido Aucat filio de Bintuper et Cabacalano nomine Coloymme Abdelgobar et Defecan filio de Aliagazi et Ali filio alfachimi Abdelale iuvene et Facam filio de

Leadership in the neighborhood of Bairén, still fairly intact in 1244, left its outline in the signatures to an irrigation dispute. To settle litigation between the Christian immigrant communities of Bairén and Benietos over water distribution, authorities appealed to past practice as attested by Mudejar notables. The first signatories were the *qāḍī* Avengamer and Gomar Avengomar. They may perhaps transliterate as Ibn 'Āmir and Ibn 'Umar. If the two were relatives, carelessly copied, they might have belonged to the Berber Banū Ghumāra or more probably to the Gomar family (Gomà, Gumà), which survived widely in eastern Spain from Visigothic Godomar antecedents. The other seven witnesses went onto the document as Muḥammad b. Ghāyyib (Gayep), Aḥmad b. Darrāj (Abendarraix), Ibrāhīm ar-Ra'uf (Arragueff), Ibrāhīm al-Makīn (Almocant), Muḥammad b. Sālim (Avencalima), Muḥammad b. Aḥwar (Ahuor), and an interpreter Yūsuf. Again multiple names represent the dominant clan, but again a spread of differing names betrays the broad base of families in a local class of notables. The concentration of influence in the Avengomar leaders recalls the nepotistic situation seen at the Valencia city Moorish quarter in 1258, where the son-in-law of its former *amīn* turned up in power as *qāḍī*.[21] With two or more notables of a family visible in a record, especially in a list of leaders, the familial structure of a given council stands out. Elsewhere it is hard to distinguish a functionary or *faqīh* from a family representative. The envoy from Játiva to King James—"Setxi, very powerful in the town and in the council of the *qā'id*"—can be inserted into Játiva's establishment with confidence if not

---

Juceff Algazi iuvene et Abdelam Avinxarif et Ali Arunxaxit et Moferich filio Çale et Ubaquer Alguarbi et Abdeluasit Avinçamege et Çoleymen Axaquot et Maffomet Abinfabib et Ali Abinfabib et Ubaquer Abdelfeure, voluntate omnium aliorum proborum hominum." Abdelale later becomes Abdelle. Others appear in the text.

[21] Chabás, *Distribución de las aguas en 1244*, pp. 3-6 (July 16—not August 4—1244): "e de sarracenos alcadi Avengamer e Gomar Avengomar e Mahomet Abengayeb, testes trugaman Juceffaucortina e el çequiero Abrahim Arragueff e Abrahim Almocant e Mahomet Abencalima e Mahomet Ahuor e Hamet Abendarraix." The interpreter's last name Aucortinna is a puzzle, but is not, e.g., al-Qarṭājannī. The Valencia city document is above in Chapter XVI, n. 30. In *Llibre dels feyts*, ch. 79, the Majorcan king exhorted his council of island notables to defend not only "nostres moylers e nostres filles" against conquest by the Christian host, but also characteristically "nostres parents"—the family clan.

with precision of placement. The same is true of Ibn Faraḥ (Abenferri), prominent at Liria, who transferred to the service of Játiva after his town surrendered. The name Setxi might be as-Sājī; more probably it relates either to the Visigothic line Sais and Saisa of this region (from Germanic Saxo), or to the place Saix or Sax between Elda and Villena (from Latin *saxum*) which gave the Valencian family name Saixó. Abenferri may be Ibn Fihr or al-Fihrī, whose ancient Arabic military family settled in Játiva, Denia, Valencia, and their environs; derivatives from the Latin *ferro* also persisted in the Valencian region, and appear today under forms like Ferrús, Ferràs, and Ferris.[22]

Ibn Khaldūn, whose family had belonged to Seville's notables, observed that when an Islamic kingdom collapsed leadership usually devolved upon "members of great and noble houses who are eligible for the positions of elders and leaders in a city." He also discoursed on the tendency toward intermarriage, which eventually unified a town at the level of notables until, like a tribe, it split again into factions during time of crisis, each group seeking dominant power by alliance with "clients, partisans, and allies." Previous pages have sufficiently adverted to the subsidiary phenomenon of partisanship at all levels in Valencia; here the clear outlines of local organization impose themselves on the observer.[23]

The existence of a class of local notables in Mudejar Valencia is evident, as is its cross-class leadership of erudites and religious figures. These people did not flee in such numbers as to strip their communities, except at the siege-points of Burriana and the capital. They survived the early rebellion, at towns as different as Uxó and Játiva; presumably many survived the later troubles. When did they disappear then, and why? This mystery belongs to the complicated

[22] *Llibre dels feyts*, chs. 318 to 327 passim and ch. 353 have both Setxi and Abenferri, though the Casacuberta edition confounds them as one man in ch. 325; "era molt poderos en la vila e era del conseyl del alcayt"; "qui era estat de Liria," where context and perhaps the grammar indicate his station. Abenferri is susceptible of reconstructions like Ibn Faraḥ, who was a poet captured at the fall of Seville in 1248, or even Ibn Faraj, common in eastern Spain at this period (Farax, Farag, Farach, Faraix) and prominent in the Valencia of the Cid (Banū al-Faraj). Until the crusade the Valencian village of Tiu had belonged to "Ali Abuferri" (*Itinerari*, p. 190).

[23] *Muqaddimah*, II, 303-305; on the merchant capitalist class see also II, 285, 343-345.

story of Valencian emigration and expulsion. Here it suffices to note that local society remained for a time intact, with the organization and influence it implied. The paradox is that a country so rent by factionalism as to fall before the crusaders, piece by piece, was by reason of that very fragmentation tough enough to survive at its lower levels.

Autumn of the Creative Class

Did intellectual and artistic life survive the crusade? Historians tend to assume that it did not. Aguilar concluded that the creative class fled, since no distinguished names appear in the postcrusade period.[24] Michavila y Vila believed that the patron groups must have abandoned the country to fanatical and Berber influences of the ignorant lower classes.[25] Arabic writers of the time convey the same impression—a wave of invaders crushed Spanish Islam, silencing its voice and plunging it into sad darkness. This view has merit but does not tell the whole story. Intellectual and creative elements continued to function in Mudejar society, doubtless at diminished levels of intensity that dimmed more and more as the decades wore on. It is probable that provincial culture especially survived. Arabic commentators exaggerated beyond measure in their descriptions of Valencia's fate, voicing with poetic force their cosmic distress; it is unwise to isolate this one note of their threnody as more than an echo of historical fact. The premises of modern historians—that there was a lack of distinguished individuals and that the upper classes had fled en masse—do not sufficiently support their conclusion. To assume a distinct class of patrons supporting a creative class, both existing in suspension above the ignorant mob, is fatal; Islamic society was at once more complex and less differentiated. The survival of local, regional, and urban religious personnel, for example, indicates some survival of learning.

The scholar *faqīh* abounded on the Mudejar scene; the *qāḍī*

[24] Aguilar y Serrat, *Noticias de Segorbe*, I, 96.

[25] Antonio Michavila y Vila, "Apuntes para el estudio de la vida social del reino de Valencia en la época de los reyes de la casa de Aragón," *III Congrés*, II, 121. Torres Fontes concluded that Murcia's Islamic cultural level had fallen drastically by the early fourteenth century, affected by wars and emigration ("Alcalde mayor," pp. 139, 142).

dominated his aljama; pilgrims embarked for overseas and returned; courts sat "as in the time of the Saracens"; and the mosque-centers preserved preaching and schooling. The commercial and propertied classes stayed on in strength. Valencia's pattern of surrender intact, and its capacity for sustained revolt, point to an integral if wounded community. Aljamas as rooted as Játiva or Alcira continued to function under their oligarchic notables; even the victim-city Valencia soon boasted a bustling Moorish quarter as focus for the huerta's Mudejars. Dominican erudites seeking converts suffered from no lack of Mudejar faculty to hire for their schools, or of educated disputants on the Muslim side.[26] One may question the quality of postcrusade literary-religious culture or plausibly posit its diminution, especially as the city populations shrank or disappeared; but it is unreasonable to assert its precipitate collapse.

A potent objection intrudes. If learning and beauty survived, as we have argued, why are no distinguished men or products in evidence? This paradox of creative classes who leave no evidence of their existence in the history of art and letters might find an aprioristic answer in the assumption that mere survival imposed a creative level lower than distinction, in a time so troubled as to drive the best men to the greener pastures of Granada or North Africa and to disorient the hapless who remained. A community suffering the rule of an infidel overlord, surrounded by emblems of his victory, with patronage reduced and intellectual life withdrawn into provincial aljamas, must have had to content itself largely with the derivative and the second-rate. Perhaps little change was visible in the first decades, masked by the confusion of reconstruction. As time passed, with the Christian presence increasing and town aljamas becoming fewer and smaller, Islamic culture would have grown correspondingly ever more crippled.

A more exact response to the problem is at hand. Valencian culture had ceased to be distinguished even before the crusade. Ribera Tarragó found that the most eminent man of letters at Játiva, al-Mufawwiz, went entirely unnoticed by Arabic authors; his name and reputation live only by courtesy of the Christian King James.[27] It

[26] See the details in my "Christian-Islamic Confrontation," including the personal experience recounted by Ibn Rashīq al-Mursī.

[27] See pp. 172-173.

is improbable that this luminary's colleagues or successors would have attracted any more attention. This region had been outstanding less for science or medicine than for poetry and history, together with some law and philosophy; but the golden age of letters had already passed. Ibn Sa'īd is considered to have written the last testament of Andalusian poetry, so far had it declined under the Almohads. The Almohad era, though not the desert some would make it, marked a decline of quality in literature, the arts, and science. Le Tourneau concludes that, especially from Las Navas in 1212, Almohad "civilization was struck by impotence and stupor, and the wonderful artistic and literary flow of the second half of the twelfth century came to an abrupt end"; at its best, that flow had been a court culture for a tiny elite and several cities, unshared by the empire at large and providing "only a veneer." García Gómez still finds much to admire in the Almohad century of Andalusia, essentially creative and liberated from the dead weight of the East; but he too admits that "at bottom, Islamic Spain was in decline" culturally.[28] In terms of architecture and inscriptions the period as a whole makes a poor showing in eastern Spain. Terrasse observes that "Almohad art [and architecture] is hardly known to us except by African monuments"; Las Navas had opened "a new epoch" both in North African and Hispano-Islamic art, marked by divergence from the East, uncreative fixity, isolated parochialism, and a defeatist psychology. Africa began two centuries of an artistic "history without grandeur."[29]

The kingdom of Valencia retains very little of Islamic build-

[28] Le Tourneau, *Almohad Movement*, pp. 100-101. Emilio García Gómez, *Poesía arábigoandaluza, breve síntesis histórica* (Madrid, 1952), pp. 82-84; *Poemas arábigoandaluces*, pp. 40-43. Reynold A. Nicholson, *A Literary History of the Arabs*, 2d edn. (Cambridge, [1929] 1962), pp. 432-434. On the limited impact of "impractical" and suspect philosophy, despite Spain's great names, see Ribera Tarragó, *Enseñanza*, pp. 49, 56; see also W. M. Watt, "Philosophy and Theology under the Almohads," *Primer congreso de estudios árabes e islámicos* (Madrid, 1964), pp. 103, 107.

[29] Henri Terrasse, *L'art hispano-mauresque des origines au xiii siècle* (Paris, 1932), pp. 377, 416, 460, 467. Lévi-Provençal, *Inscriptions arabes d'Espagne*, p. xv and ch. 13. Torres Balbás, "Játiva y los restos del palacio de Pinohermoso," esp. comments on pp. 143-144, 152, 156-157, 170. For background see his brief survey, *Artes almoravide y almohade*; with great patience, one can glean the remaining fragments of information on architectural remains from his *Ciudades hispanomusulmanas*, vol. II, passim. See also Martínez-Ferrando, *Baixa edat mitjana*, pp. 1062ff., 1092.

ing from the precrusade era. She has nothing to show for the Almohad era like Seville's Giralda; her filigree of stone and sunlight, endlessly multiplied in less substantial edifices, has long since evanesced. The city of Valencia, whatever face of glory it presented to the conquering crusaders, had suffered grievous architectural loss a century before; the vindictive heirs of the Cid, withdrawing before the Almoravid surge, had put the city to the torch, apparently selecting as targets the principal public buildings.[30] The waning creative forces in Almohad Valencia, and the dependence upon past achievements, carried over into the postcrusade architecture; Mudejar construction, frequent in Aragon proper but rare in the Catalan parts of the confederated kingdom, is fairly absent from Valencia. Thus Islamic survivals of any kind are rare—some bath ruins dating perhaps from after the crusade, fragments of a town-house room ca. 1225, and unstudied elements in castles or walls. Valencia's flourishing industrial arts[31] found no echo in this bulkier Mudejar field. By the vigil of the Christian invasion, Valencia's Islamic civilization had grown increasingly stagnant and less adventurous, retreating within its traditionalism. The dynamism of the crusading West burst over Valencia at the very period when a curious passivity was descending upon Islam. The long, withdrawing roar of the receding tide had begun before the invaders reached the shore.

Many talented men undeniably moved to greener pastures after the crusade; any number of patronal families relocated; and cultural life to that degree became poorer. Some of the talented would have drifted away in any case in such a restless, opportunistic ambience—as had al-Ḥarīrī of Alcira, who died in Seville the day it fell in 1248; or the prolific polygraph and greatest of Muslim mystics, Ibn al-'Arabī of Murcia, who died in the Near East shortly after the Christians installed themselves at Valencia city; or his fellow Murcian and philosopher-mystic Ibn Sab'īn, who seems to have committed suicide at Mecca in 1270; or the scandalous Valen-

[30] Al-Ḥimyarī reports that the Christians "burned it during the evacuation" (*Kitāb ar-rawḍ al-mi'ṭār*, p. 102). Ibn 'Idhārī says that Alfonso "set fire to the main mosque, the alcazar, and some houses" (*Al-Bayān al-mugrib*, p. 101). The *Historia Roderici* has Alfonso give orders, "totam urbem igne cremari," and describes the victor reoccupying "the blackened ruin" (part 6, ch. 76, esp. p. 581).

[31] See Chapter V, section 1.

cian Ibn Diḥya, deposed after twice serving as Denia's *qāḍī* to die abroad in 1235. The period after the catastrophe of Las Navas was bloody and disturbed, with the Christian invasion only culminating the wrack of the body social.

A number of eminent scholars demonstrably disappeared as a result of the crusade. Abu 'r-Rabī' b. Sālim, the colleague and disciple of Averroes who climaxed his literary career as *qāḍī* of Valencia city, fell fighting in the battle of Puig that sealed his city's fate. (Previously the learned *faqīh* of Játiva, Aḥmad b. Hārūn, had died fighting at Las Navas.) Ibn al-Abbār of Onda, secretary to the last three rulers of Valencia and one of the great historians of his era, betook himself to Tunis and a new career. Another distinguished historian, Ibn 'Amīra al-Qāḍī of Alcira, also fled Valencia city in 1238; he became state secretary in Morocco, *qāḍī* several times over, and eventually state secretary at Tunis. He left a rueful poem from Valencia city's last hours, commemorating his chagrin when the ruler Zayyān paid for a haircut but neglected to recompense his "verse trimmer's" efforts; "I see the one who brought a razor rewarded, but empty is the hand that brought a poem."[32] The celebrated calligraphic school at Valencia city, part of its flourishing book industry, was a casualty of the 1238 general expulsion. The year before the city fell, the calligrapher Abū Ḥāmid b. Abī Zāhir (Abuhamid Benibizaher) died, and with the exiles the style itself soon removed to Tunis, largely supplanting the native style there. A whole group of Sufi mystics belonging to the Banū Sīd-bono of Denia and Valencia removed to Granada, where they founded a popular center.[33]

If talent bled away from the region during the last years of the Almohads and especially after the Christian victory, the solidly established tradition of high learning must have persisted at centers like Alcira, Játiva, Liria, Onda, and the Valencian huerta; a number of lesser places must have proudly remembered their eminent sons. When Ibn Sa'īd compiled his autumnal anthology of Islamic Spanish poetry, *The Pennants*, in 1243 and arranged the contributions by locale, he allowed space for Alcira, Denia, Lorca, Murcia, and Va-

[32] Nykl, *Hispano-Arabic Poetry*, p. 334.

[33] Ribera Tarragó, "Escuela valenciana de calígrafos árabes," pp. 305, 308; see also Ibn Khaldūn, *Muqaddimah*, II, 352, 377. See also Chapter IX, n. 45.

lencia city; in keeping with what was said about an undifferentiated society coordinated by the erudite, he subdivided each locale under such classes or professions as civil servant, notable, and jurist.[34] That all this heritage disappeared overnight is a thesis sustainable only on the assumption of brutal conquest, rearrangement of regional and local society, and the loss of most of the landed, commercial, and jurist classes; each assumption, as relevant chapters have shown, is false. Moreover in the one area for which Valencian artistry remained vital, the industrial arts, a Mudejar creativity did emerge, growing in strength as the postrevolt decades wore on.

At another level, loss of culture and identity proved real. Muslim writers and commentators in the wider world of Islam spared little attention for a lost province like Mudejar Valencia with its pathetic productions. For Christian writers, all of Valencia's learned Muslims might as well have sat on the moon, except on those occasions when they demanded attention—when taxes were to be collected, "medical men of their law or sect" regulated,[35] or irreverence suppressed. The colonialist dominant culture, euphorically dynamic, submerged the massive Muslim majority. "They effected this in the traditional way of colonials: by creating an urban and landlord superstructure, endowing their immediate surroundings with every quality they could borrow from the homeland, and treating the native population as a lesser caste to be tolerated in ghettos apart."[36] Ibn Khaldūn, with his eye on conquered Spain in the next century, discoursed about the paralyzing effect that benevolent colonialism exerts upon its victims, so that they lose hope, lose the energy generated by hope, and lose the creative, civilizing, and commercial

[34] 'Alī b. Mūsā b. Sa'īd al-Maghrībī, *Moorish Poetry, a Translation of the Pennants: An Anthology Compiled in 1243 by the Andalusian Ibn Sa'īd*, trans. A. J. Arberry (Cambridge, 1953).

[35] Monzón parliament (Peter IV) in Fernández y González, *Mudejares de Castilla*, appendix, doc. 70 (1363): "Los iueus empero e serrahins, metges, hajen esser examinats per metges de lur ley o secto." Though a long lifetime after our period, the profession being regulated had not just sprung up. Mudejar doctors had to swear "be e lealment praticar, ans que a la pratica sien admesos." Piles Ros has a license for a fifteenth-century Mudejar physician in Valencia, Sa'd Zayd (Çaat Zeyt), *faqīh* of Onda, who "uset et puxets usar de medecina"; another appears in connection with a public inquest after the death of his patient ("Moros de realengo en Valencia," p. 237).

[36] Burns, *Crusader Valencia*, I, 303, and see the concluding chapter in general.

results of that energy; disintegration at this point "is in human nature" and inevitable for the conquered society.[37]

This son of an exiled Sevillian clan, still Spanish in his loyalties, offered further insights into the fate of places like Valencia. Just before the final crusade, Spanish Islam had achieved a height of "sedentary culture," the culmination and goal of "civilization" with roots stretching back into Visigothic society, such as "had not been reached in any other [Islamic] region except reportedly in Iraq, Syria, and Egypt," boasting "all the various kinds of crafts" refined to perfection. Ibn Khaldūn shrewdly added that the resultant "coloring remained in that civilization and did not leave it until it was totally destroyed." Before this could happen, "many people from eastern Spain who were exiled in the seventh [thirteenth] century" exported aspects of this Valencian culture.[38] By his own era, a century after the crusade, cultural life appeared dead in the captured land; "civilization there has deteriorated and the enemy has gained control over most of it, except for a few people along the coast" at Granada, "who are more concerned with making a living than with the things that come after it."[39]

Ibn Khaldūn also observed that Spanish scholarship had been declining for centuries, the Almohad era being particularly disastrous, and that Granadan jurisprudence soon became an empty shadow. He diagnosed the ills of Almohad Spain, its factionalism and "group feeling." He particularly noted that the mere removal of a capital could kill an Islamic city: a dynasty pulled together the city's elements, so that departure of its dignitaries left it a mass of uncorrelated commercial and negligible elements. As for cultural decline in relation to the thirteenth-century crusade, he stressed two factors. Spain saw its most creative children go into exile; those remaining behind soon "had no leisure to occupy themselves" with literature. Islamic social organization regressed, as did its attendant arts and letters, except at Granada. He traced the tragedy ultimately to loss of the Islamic dynasties, who by religious guidance and civil rule presided over the shaping of civilization, much as over an eduction of metaphysical "form" from passive "matter."[40]

[37] *Muqaddimah*, I, esp. ch. 2, sections 22-23, and ch. 3, section 5.

[38] *Ibid.*, II, 288, 350.

[39] *Ibid.*, II, 430.

[40] *Ibid.*, II, 299-300, 352, 427-428, 430; III, 117-118, 364-365; see also III, 104, and the definition of civilization on p. 137.

A civilization may decline and disappear, though remnants remain alive. After the thirteenth century, intercommunication among the depressed learned classes did persist. Muslim pilgrims and merchants still made their way to far corners of their world. Mudejar craftsmen exercised their high talents. An occasional prodigy flourished, like Játiva's historian, biographer, and traveler 'Abd Allāh b. Aḥmad (d. 1323) or the sage called ash-Shāṭibī, "the Játivan" (d. 1446). They were footprints of a glory now departed. There had been an epic quality to the inner disintegration of Valencia. In its early Mudejar phase, the great civilization lingered, dying. Perhaps it is fitting that the decline played itself out in silence, decently obscured from the historian's gaze behind the busy facade of the Christian colonial regime. It is important to recognize, however, that death was approaching: its stages, lengthy details, and final moment may be hidden, but not its reality. The crusaders did not kill Islamic Valencian culture, though they dealt it mortal wounds. Unwittingly, without intending final damage, they gave these wounds to a body already in its last throes from self-inflicted injuries. The accidents of military strategy allowed the vanquished society to breathe on and even to move about its business for a while, whole but doomed. A generation passed away in its twilight, warmed by its setting sun.

BIBLIOGRAPHY

My *Crusader Kingdom of Valencia* provided both direct and background bibliography for thirteenth-century Valencia, including archival and bibliographical tools. The supplementary list offered here is essentially a selection from over six hundred titles cited in the course of the present book, repeating only important elements from the previous bibliography. Besides Mudejar materials proper, it includes representative studies on collateral themes involved, such as the Holy Land colonies, Jews, Moriscos, and Mozarabs, and especially Islamic history. In a general way it excludes those aspects of Mudejar life reserved for the further volumes on society as illumined by tax records and on Christian-Islamic interrelations. While remaining a selection from works cited, therefore, with dimensions to be supplied from the previous bibliography and with a number of background titles, it does comprise an integral bibliography by itself.

The Preface has already provided bibliographical orientation in establishing the place of this book in Mudejar studies. The absence of Islamic documentation for Valencia has also been noted there, and the consequent function of the Arabic sources as contributing only background and contemporary flavor. For the elements of Arabic names—the choice of elided al-, and unbarred Abu 'l—see pp. xxvi-xxvii, and on the occasionally unaccented *mudéjares* see Chapter IV, note 1. Where a modern author commonly employs both Arabic and Western names, I have provided both, cross-referring to the Arabic form where necessary. Medieval Arabic authors appear under the element by which they are best known in current Spanish scholarship, with the full name in parentheses to facilitate further investigation. My previous bibliography has explained such problems as the eccentricities of Catalan-Castilian names and my manner of resolving them.

Primary Sources

Manuscript

The bibliography for *The Crusader Kingdom of Valencia* devoted five pages to analyzing thirty-five pertinent archival collections. Though many of these affected the structure of the present volume, I have only expressly cited the following nine collections.

Archivio Segreto Vaticano, Rome.
Archivo de la Catedral, Tortosa.

Archivo de la Catedral, Valencia.
Archivo de la Corona de Aragón, Barcelona.
Archivo General del Reino, Valencia.
Archivo Histórico Nacional, Madrid.
Archivo Municipal, Valencia.
Biblioteca, Universidad de Barcelona.
Biblioteca, Universidad de Valencia.

Since *Islam under the Crusaders* is essentially an archival study resting upon many thousands of documents examined during the past nearly twenty years, the outline of subdivisions and fonds in these collections offered in the previous bibliography has particular pertinence.

Published

'Abd al-Wāḥid ('Abd al-Wāḥid b. 'Alī, Abū Muḥammad, al-Marrākushī). *Kitāb al-mu'ŷib fī taljīṣ ajbār al-Magrib.* Translator, Ambrosio Huici Miranda. Colección de crónicas árabes de la reconquista, 4. Tetuán: Instituto General Franco de estudios e investigación hispano-árabe, 1955.

Abū Bakr aṭ-Ṭurṭūshī (Muḥammad b. al-Walīd b. Khalaf, Abū Bakr, al-Andalusī aṭ-Ṭurṭūshī). *Lámpara de los príncipes por Abubequer de Tortosa.* Translator, Maximiliano Alarcón y Santón. 2 vols. Madrid: Instituto de Don Juan, 1930-1931.

Abu 'l-Fidā' (Ismā'īl b. 'Alī, Abu 'l-Fidā', al-Malik al-Mu'ayyad). *Géographie d'Aboulféda traduite de l'arabe en français et accompagnée de notes et d'éclaircissements.* Translator, M. [J. T.] Reinaud, 2 vols. in 3. Paris: Imprimerie nationale, 1848-1883.

Al- (adaptive variants ad-, an-, ar-, ash-, at-, az-, etc.). See element following, as al-Ḥimyarī under Ḥ.

Aldea Charter. Carta puebla de Aldea, February 12, 1258. In "Colección de cartas pueblas," no. 60, *Boletín de la sociedad castellonense de cultura,* XVI (1935), 289-291.

Alfandech Charter. Carta puebla de Alfandech, April 15, 1277. See Primary Sources, Manuscript: Archivo de la Corona de Aragón [James II, Reg. Canc. 196, fol. 164].

Alfonso X the Learned (Wise), King. *Primera crónica general de España que mandó componer Alfonso el Sabio y se continuaba bajo Sancho IV en 1289.* Editor, Ramón Menéndez Pidal *et alii.* 2 vols. Madrid: Universidad de Madrid, 1955.

———. *Las siete partidas del sabio rey don Alfonso el Nono, nueuamente glosadas.* Editor, Gregorio López. 7 vols. in 3. Salamanca: Andrea de Portonariis, 1565.

'Alī Abū Bakr aṣ-Ṣanhājī al-Baidhak. "Histoire des almohades." *Documents inédits d'histoire almohade* (*q.v.*), pp. 75-246.

Arié. See Ibn 'Abd ar-Ra'ūf.

Aureum opus regalium priuilegiorum ciuitatis et regni Valentie cum historia cristianissimi regis Jacobi ipsius primi conquistatoris. Editor, Luis de Alanya. Valencia: Diego de Gumiel, 1515.

Benjamin b[en] Jonah of Tudela. *The Itinerary of Benjamin of Tudela. Critical Text, Translation, and Commentary.* Editor, Marcus Nathan Adler. London: Henry Frowde, 1907. Also in *Contemporaries of Marco Polo*, part 4. Translator, Manuel Komroff. New York: Boni Books, 1928.

Ben-Shemesh. See *Taxation*; Qudāmah; Ya'qūb.

Bibliotheca arabico-hispana escurialensis sive librorum omnium MSS. quos arabice ab auctoribus magnam partem. . . . Editor, Miguel Casiri. 2 vols. Madrid: Antonio Pérez de Soto, 1760-1770.

Bofarull y de Sartorio. See *Rentas.*

Bofarull y Mascaró. See *Repartimiento de Mallorca; Repartimiento de Valencia.*

Chelva Charter. Carta puebla de Chelva, August 17, 1370. In *Colección de documentos inéditos para la historia de España* (*q.v.*), XVIII, 69-74. Also in Fernández y González, *Mudejares de Castilla* (*q.v.*), appendix, doc. 71.

Chivert Charter. Carta puebla de Chivert, April 28, 1234. In "Colección de cartas pueblas," no. 76, *Boletín de la sociedad castellonense de cultura*, XXIV (1948), 226-230. Also in *Homenaje á Codera* (*q.v.*), pp. 28-33.

Código de las costumbres de Tortosa. Editor, Bienvenido Oliver. In his *Historia del derecho en Cataluña* (*q.v.*, secondary sources), vol. IV.

Colección de crónicas árabes de la reconquista. Translator, Ambrosio Huici Miranda. 4 vols. Tetuán: Instituto General Franco de estudios e investigación hispano-árabe, 1952-1955.

Colección de documentos inéditos del archivo general de la corona de Aragón. Editors, Próspero de Bofarull y Mascaró *et alii.* 41 vols. Barcelona: Imprenta del archivo, 1847-1910.

Colección de documentos inéditos para la historia de España. Editors, Martín Fernández Navarrete, Miguel Salvá, Pedro Sáinz de Baranda *et alii.* 112 vols. Madrid: Viuda de Calera *et alibi*, 1842-1896.

Colección de documentos para la historia de Gandía y su comarca. Editor, José Camarena Mahiques. Gandía: Casa Ferrer, 1961.

Colección de documentos para la historia del reino de Murcia. Editor, Juan Torres Fontes. 2 vols. to date. Murcia: Academia Alfonso X el Sabio, 1963ff.

Colección de fueros municipales y cartas pueblas de los reinos de Castilla, León, corona de Aragón y Navarra coordinada y anotada. Editor, Tomás Muñoz y Romero. (Vol. 1, *unicum.*) Madrid: J. M. Alonso, 1847.

Colección diplomática. Citation used only for Huici, immediately below.

Colección diplomática de Jaime I, el Conquistador. Editor, Ambrosio Huici Miranda. 3 vols. Valencia: Hijo de Francisco Vives Mora, 1916-1920; Renovación tipográfica, 1922.

Colección diplomática de los documentos a que se refiere la disertación del feudalismo particular e irredimible de los pueblos del reino de Valencia, de donde salieron expulsos los moriscos en el año 1609. Editors, Miguel Salvá and Pedro Sáinz de Baranda. In *Colección de documentos inéditos para la historia* (*q.v.*), vol. XVIII.

Collectio maxima conciliorum omnis Hispaniae et novi orbis, epistolarumque decretalium celebriorum, necnon plurium monumentorum veterum ad illam spectantium, cum notis et dissertationibus, quibus sacri canones, historia ac disciplina ecclesiastica, et chronologia, accurate illustrantur. Editors, José Sáenz de Aguirre and Giuseppe Catalani. 6 vols. Rome: A. Fulganius, 1753-1755.

Corpus iuris canonici. Editors, Emil Friedberg and E. L. Richter. 2d edn. 2 vols. Leipzig: B. Tauchnitz, 1879-1881.

Cortes de los antiguos reinos de Aragón y de Valencia y principado de Cataluña. 26 vols. in 27. Madrid: Real academia de la historia, 1896-1922.

Crónica de San Juan de la Peña. Latin text. Editor, Antonio Ubieto Arteta. Textos medievales, 4. Valencia: Gráficas Bautista, 1961.

Crònica general de Pere III el Cerimoniòs, dita comunament crònica de Sant Joan de la Penya. Old Catalan text. Editor, Amadeu J. Soberanas Lleó. Barcelona: Alpha, 1961.

Crónica latina de los reyes de Castilla. Editor, María Desemparados Cabanes Pecourt. Textos medievales, 11. Valencia: J. Nácher, 1964.

Desclot, Bernat. *Crònica.* Editor, Miguel Coll y Alentorn. 4 vols. Barcelona: Editorial Barcino, 1949-1950.

———. *Chronicle of the Reign of King Pedro III of Aragon.* Translator, F. L. Critchlow. 2 vols. Princeton: Princeton University Press, 1928-1934.

Ad-Dimashqī (Shams ad-Dīn Muḥammad b. Abī Ṭālib, ad-Dimashqī). *Manuel de la cosmographie du moyen âge.* Translator, A. F. Mehren. Copenhagen: C. A. Reitzel, 1874.

Documentos de Alfonso X el Sabio. In *Colección de documentos para . . . Murcia* (*q.v.*), vol. 1.

"Documentos para el estudio de la reconquista y repoblación del valle del Ebro." Editor, José M. Lacarra. *Estudios de edad media de la corona de Aragón*, II (1946), 469-574; III (1947-1948), 499-727; V (1952), 511-668.

"Documentos relativos a la condición social y jurídica de los mudéjares aragoneses." Editor, Francisco Macho y Ortega. *Revista de ciencias jurídicas y sociales*, V (1922), 143-160, 444-464.

Documents inédits d'histoire almohade, fragments manuscrits du "legajo" 1919 au fonds arabe de l'escurial. Editor, Évariste Lévi-Provençal. Textes arabes relatifs à l'histoire de l'occident musulman, I. Paris: Paul Geuthner, 1928.

Durán i Sanpere, A. "Un document de la morería de Valencia en l'any 1408." *Boletín de la real academia de buenas letras de Barcelona*, VIII (1916), 505-507.

Elogio del Islam español. See ash-Shaqundī.

Eslida Charter. Carta puebla de Eslida, May 29, 1242. In "Colección de cartas pueblas," no. 63, *Boletín de la sociedad castellonense de cultura*, XVIII (1943), 159-160. Also in *Colección de documentos inéditos de España* (*q.v.*), XVIII, 55-58; *Colección diplomática* (*q.v.*) doc. 241; Fernández y González, *Mudejares de Castilla* (*q.v.*), appendix, doc. 17; Janer, *Moriscos de España* (*q.v.*), appendix, doc. 15. See also Second Eslida Charter.

Fori antiqui Valentiae. Editor, Manuel Dualde Serrano. Escuela de estudios medievales, textos, 22. Valencia: Consejo superior de investigaciones científicas, 1967.

Fori regni Valentiae. Monzón: Impressi imperiali, 1548. [Cited as *Furs.*]

Fuero de Córdoba. Editor, M. A. Orti Belmonte. In Orti Belmonte, "El fuero de Córdoba" (*q.v.*, secondary sources), pp. 67-84.

Furs e ordinacions fetes per los gloriosos reys de Aragò als regnícols del regne de València. Valencia: Lambert Palmart, 1482.

Al-Garsīfī, 'Umar. See Ibn 'Abd ar-Ra'ūf.

Gayangos. See Gebir; James I, "Leyes"; secondary sources, al-Maqqarī.

Gebir, Içe de. "Suma de los principales mandamientos y devedamientos de la ley y çunna." Editor, Pascual de Gayangos. *Memorial histórico español* (*q.v.*), V, part 2.

González. See *Repartimiento de Sevilla.*

Al-Ḥimyarī (Muḥammad b. Muḥammad b. 'Abd al-Mun'im, al-Ḥimyarī). *Kitāb ar-rawḍ al-mi'ṭār.* Translator, M. P. Maestro González. Textos medievales, 10. Valencia: Gráficas Bautista, 1963.

———. *La péninsule ibérique au moyen-âge d'après le Kitāb ar-rawḍ al-mi'ṭār fī ḫabar al-akṭār d'Ibn 'Abd al-Mun'im al-Ḥimyarī. Texte arabe des notices relatives à l'Espagne, au Portugal et au sud-ouest de la France, publié avec une introduction, un répertoire analytique, une traduction annotée, un glossaire et une carte.* Editor and translator, Évariste Lévi-Provençal. Publications de la fondation de Goeje, 12. Leiden: E. J. Brill, 1938.

Historia de la corona de Aragón (la más antigüa de que se tiene noticia) conocida generalmente con el nombre de crónica de San Juan de la Peña. Editor, Tomás Ximénez de Embún. Biblioteca de escritores aragoneses, sección histórico-doctrinal, 1. Zaragoza: Diputación provincial de Zaragoza, 1876.

Historia Roderici. In R. Menéndez Pidal, *España del Cid* (*q.v.*), II, 904-970.

Hoenerbach. See Ibn al-Khaṭīb; *Spanisch-islamische Urkunden.*

Al-Ḥulal. See Ibn as-Sammāk.

Huici. See *Colección de crónicas; Colección diplomática*; Ibn Abī Zar'; Ibn 'Idhārī; Ibn as-Sammāk.

Ibarra, Eduardo. "Cristianos y moros, documentos aragoneses y navarros." *Homenaje á Codera* (*q.v.*, secondary sources), pp. 80-92.

Ibn al-Abbār (Muḥammad b. 'Abd Allāh b. Abī Bakr b. al-Abbār, al-Balansī). "Un traité inédit d'Ibn al-Abbār à tendance chiite." Translator, A. Ghedira. *Al-Andalus*, XXII (1957), 31-54.

Ibn 'Abd al-Mun'im. See al-Ḥimyarī.

Ibn 'Abd ar-Ra'ūf and 'Umar al-Garsīfī. "Traduction annotée et commentée des traités de *ḥisba* d'Ibn 'Abd al-Ra'ūf et de 'Umar al-Garsīfī." Translator, Rachel Arié. *Hespéris-Tamuda*, I (1960), 5-38, 199-214, 349-386.

Ibn 'Abdūn (Muḥammad b. Aḥmad b. 'Abdūn, at-Tujībī). *Séville musulmane au début du xiie siècle, le traité d'Ibn 'Abdūn traduite avec une introduction et des notes.* Translator, Évariste Lévi-Provençal. Paris: Editions G. P. Maisonneuve, 1947.

Ibn Abī Zar' ('Alī b. 'Abd Allāh b. Abī Zar', al-Fāsī). *Rawḍ al-qirṭās.* Translator, Ambrosio Huici Miranda. 2d edn. 2 vols. Textos medievales, 12, 18. Valencia: Editorial Anubar, 1964.

Ibn 'Askar ('Abd ar-Raḥmān b. Muḥammad b. 'Askar). See secondary sources, Vallvé Bermejo.

Ibn Baṭṭūṭa (Muḥammad b. 'Abd Allāh b. Muḥammad b. Ibrāhīm b. Baṭṭūṭa, aṭ-Ṭanjī). *Voyages d'Ibn Batoutah.* Editors and translators, C. Defrémery and B. R. Sanguinetti. 4 vols. Paris: Imprimerie nationale, 1857-1874.

———. *Travels.* Translator, H.A.R. Gibb. 3 vols. Hakluyt Society Publications, second series, 110, 117, 141. Cambridge: Cambridge University Press, 1958-1971.

Ibn Ḥazm ('Alī b. Aḥmad b. Ḥazm, al-Andalusī). *The Ring of the Dove.* Translator, E. J. Arberry. London: Luzac, 1953.

———. "Linajes árabes en al-Andalus según la 'Ŷamhara' de Ibn Ḥazm." Translator, Elías Terés. *Al-Andalus*, XXII (1957), 55-111, 337-376.

Ibn 'Idhārī (Aḥmad b. Muḥammad b. 'Idhārī, Abu 'l-'Abbās, al-Marrākushī). *Al-Bayān al-mugrib fi ijtiṣār ajbār muluk̠ al-Andalus wa al-Magrib: Los almohades.* Translator, Ambrosio Huici Miranda. In *Colección de crónicas árabes de la reconquista* (*q.v.*), 2, 3. 2 vols. Tetuán: Instituto General Franco de estudios e investigación hispano-árabe, 1953-1954.

Ibn Jubayr (Muḥammad b. Aḥmad b. Jubayr, al-Kinānī). *The Travels of Ibn Jubayr, Being the Chronicle of a Mediaeval Spanish Moor Concerning His Journey to the Egypt of Saladin, the Holy Cities of Arabia, Baghdad the City of the Caliphs, the Latin Kingdom of Jerusalem and the Norman Kingdom of Sicily.* Translator, R.J.C. Broadhurst. London: Jonathan Cape, 1952.

Ibn Khaldūn ('Abd ar-Raḥmān b. Muḥammad Walī ad-Dīn b. Khaldūn). "Histoire des Benou'l Ahmar, rois de Grenade." Translator, Maurice Gaudefroy-Demombynes. *Journal asiatique*, 9th series, XII (1898), 309-340.

———. *Histoire des Berbères et des dynasties musulmanes de l'Afrique septentrionale.* Rev. edn. Editors, Paul Casanova and Henri Pérès. Translator, William MacGuckin, baron de Slane. 4 vols. Paris: Paul Geuthner, 1925-1956.

———. *The Muqaddimah: An Introduction to History.* Translator, Franz Rosenthal. Bollingen Series, 43. 3 vols. 2d edn. Princeton: Princeton University Press, 1967.

———. *Les prolégomènes historiques d'Ibn Khaldoun.* Translator, William MacGuckin, baron de Slane. 3 vols. Paris: Académie des inscriptions et belles lettres, [1862-1868] 1934-1938.

Ibn Khaldūn, Yaḥyā. See Yaḥyā b. Muḥammad.

Ibn Khallikān (Aḥmad b. Muḥammad b. Khallikān, al-Andalusī). *Biographical Dictionary.* Translator, William MacGuckin, baron de Slane. 4 vols. Paris: Oriental Translation Fund of Great Britain and Ireland, 1843-1861.

Ibn al-Khaṭīb (Muḥammad b. 'Abd Allāh b. al-Khaṭīb, Lisān ad-Dīn). *Islamische Geschichte Spaniens, Übersetzung der A'māl al-a'lām und ergänzender Texte.* Translator, Wilhelm Hoenerbach. Zürich: Artemis Verlag, 1970.

Ibn al-Khaṭīb. See secondary sources, al-Maqqarī.

Ibn Sa'īd ('Alī b. Mūsā b. Sa'īd, al-Andalusī al-Maghrībī). *Moorish Poetry: A Translation of the Pennants, an Anthology compiled in 1243 by the Andalusian Ibn Sa'īd.* Translator, A. J. Arberry. Cambridge: Cambridge University Press, 1953.

Ibn as-Sammāk (Muḥammad b. Abu 'l-Ma'ālī b. as-Sammāk al-Malaqī, Abū 'Abd Allāh, attribution moot). *"Al-Ḥulal al-mawšiyya," crónica árabe de las dinastías almorávide, almohade, y benimerín.* Translator, Ambrosio Huici Miranda. Colección de crónicas árabes de la reconquista, I. Tetuán: Instituto General Franco de estudios e investigación hispano-árabe, 1951.

Al-Idrīsī (Muḥammad b. Muḥammad b. Idrīs, al-Idrīsī, Abū 'Abd Allāh). *Description de l'Afrique et de l'Espagne.* Editors and translators, Reinhart Dozy and M. J. de Goeje. Leiden: E. J. Brill, [1864-1866] 1968.

———. *Géographie d'Édrisi.* Translator, P. Amedée Jaubert. 2 vols. Paris: L'Imprimerie royale, 1836-1840.

Itinerari. See secondary sources, Miret y Sans.

James I, King (Spanish Jaime; Catalan Jacme or Jaume). *Crònica [Llibre dels feyts].* Editor, Josep M. de Casacuberta. Collecció popular barcino, 15, 21, 185, 186, 196, 197, 199, 200. 9 vols. in 2. Barcelona: Editorial Barcino, 1926-1962.

———. *The Chronicle of James I, King of Aragon, Surnamed the Conqueror (Written by Himself).* Translator, John Forster; introduction, notes, appendix, and glossary by Pascual de Gayangos. 2 vols. London: Chapman and Hall, 1883.

Játiva Charter. Carta puebla de Játiva, January 23, 1251 or 1252. In *Colección de documentos inéditos de España (q.v.)*, XVIII, 62. Also in *Colección diplomática (q.v.)*, doc. 412; Fernández y González, *Mudejares de Castilla (q.v.)*, appendix, doc. 24; Janer, *Moriscos de España (q.v.)*, appendix, doc. 18.

Jiménez de Rada, Rodrigo (attribution moot). *De rebus Hispaniae*, lib. IX, c. 13. In his *Opera*, editor, M. D. Cabanes Pecourt, 1 vol. to date. Textos medievales, 22. Valencia: Editorial Anubar, [1793] 1968.

Lévi-Provençal. See al-Ḥimyarī; Ibn 'Abdūn.

"Leyes de moros del siglo XIV." *Tratados de legislación musulmana.* Editor, Pascual de Gayangos. In *Memorial histórico español (q.v.)*, V, 428-448.

Libros de habices del reino de Granada. Editor, María del Carmen Villanueva Rico. 2 vols. Madrid: Instituto hispano-árabe de cultura, 1961.

Llibre dels feyts. See James I, *Crònica.*

Lull, Ramón [Ramon]. *Obres de Ramon Lull, edició original feta en vista dels millors i més antics manuscrits.* Editors, Mateo Obrador y Bennássar, Salvador Galmés *et alii.* 21 vols. to date. Palma de Mallorca. Comissió editora lulliana, for Institut d'estudis catalans, 1906ff.

Al-Malaqī. See Ibn as-Sammāk.

Al-Maqqarī. See secondary sources.

Al-Marrākushī. See 'Abd al-Wāḥid; Ibn 'Idhārī.

Martí, Ramón. See *Vocabulista.*

Mas Latrie. See *Traités.*

Memorial histórico español: colección de documentos, opúsculos y antigüedades. 48 vols. Madrid: Real academia de la historia, 1851-1918.

Muntaner, Ramón. *Crònica.* Editor, Enrique Bagué. 9 vols. in 2. Collecció popular barcino, 19, 141-148. Barcelona: Editorial Barcino, 1927-1952.

———. *The Chronicle of Muntaner Translated from the Catalan.* Translator, Lady Henrietta Margaret Goodenough. Hakluyt Society Publications, second series, 47, 50. 2 vols. London: Hakluyt Society, 1920-1921.

An-Nāṣirī. See secondary sources.

An-Nuwayrī (Aḥmad b. 'Abd al-Wahhāb, an-Nuwayrī) [En Nuguairi]. *Historia de los musulmanes de España y África.* Translator, Mariano Gaspar Remiro. 2 vols. Granada: Centro de estudios históricos de Granada y su reino, 1917-1919.

"Primera contribución conocida impuesta a los moros del reino de Valencia." Editor, Roque Chabás. *El archivo,* I (1886), 255-256.

Primera crónica. See Alfonso X.

Qudāmah b. Ja'far b. Qudāmah, al-Kātib al-Baghdādī. *Kitāb al-kharāj.* In *Taxation in Islam* (*q.v.*), II, 17-68.

Rationes decimarum Hispaniae (1279-1280). Editor, José Rius Serra. Textos y estudios de la corona de Aragón, 7, 8. Barcelona: Consejo superior de investigaciones científicas, 1946-1947.

Ar-Rāzī (Aḥmad b. Muḥammad b. Mūsā, ar-Rāzī). *La crónica denominada del moro Rasis.* Translator, Pascual de Gayangos. Memorias, 8. Madrid: Real academia de la historia, 1952.

———. "Description de l'Espagne." Translator, Évariste Lévi-Provençal. *Al-Andalus,* XVIII (1953), 50-108.

Rentas de la antigua corona de Aragón. Editor, Manuel de Bofarull y de Sartorio. *Colección de documentos inéditos del archivo general de la corona de Aragón* (*q.v.*), vol. XXXIX.

El "Repartiment" de Burriana y Villarreal. Editor, Ramón de María. Valencia: J. Nácher, 1935.

Repartiment de Valencia. Facsimile edition. Editor, Julián Ribera y Tarragó. Valencia: Centro de cultura valenciana, 1939.

Repartimiento de Mallorca. Editor, Próspero de Bofarull y Mascaró. In *Colección de documentos inéditos del archivo general de la corona de Aragón* (*q.v.*), XIII, 1-141.

Repartimiento de Murcia. Editor, Juan Torres Fontes. Escuela de estudios medievales, textos, 31. Madrid: Consejo superior de investigaciones científicas, 1960.

Repartimiento de Sevilla. Editor, Julio González. Escuela de estudios medievales, textos, 15, 16. 2 vols. Madrid: Consejo superior de investigaciones científicas, 1951.

Repartimiento de Valencia. Editor, Próspero de Bofarull y Mascaró. In *Colección de documentos inéditos del archivo general de la corona de Aragón* (*q.v.*), XI, 143-656.

"Repàs d'un manual notarial del temps del rey en Jaume I." Editor, Joan Segura, *Congrés I* (*q.v.*, secondary sources), pp. 300-326.

Schiaparelli. See *Vocabulista.*

"Sección de documentos." Editor, Roque Chabás. Series irregularly published in *El archivo.*

Second Eslida Charter. Carta puebla de Eslida, June 27, 1276. See Primary Sources, Manuscript: Archivo de la Corona de Aragón [James I, Reg. Canc. 83, fol. 3v].

Shams ad-Dīn. See ad-Dimashqī.

Ash-Shaqundī (Ismā'īl b. Muḥammad, ash-Shaqundī). *Elogio del Islam español* (*Risāla fī faḍl al-Andalus*). Translator, Emilio García Gómez. Escuelas de estudios árabes de Madrid y Granada, B series, 2. Madrid: E. Maestre, 1934.

Slane, William MacGuckin, baron de. See Ibn Khaldūn; Ibn Khallikān.

Spanisch-islamische Urkunden aus der Zeit der Naṣriden und Moriscos. Editor, Wilhelm Hoenerbach. University of California Publications, Near Eastern Studies, 3 [Bonner orientalistische Studien, neue serie, bd. 15; Orientalischen seminars der Universität Bonn]. Berkeley: University of California Press, 1965.

Tales Charter. Carta puebla de Tales, May 27, 1260. In "Colección de cartas pueblas," no. 84, *Boletín de la sociedad castellonense de cultura,* XXVIII (1952), 437-438.

Taxation in Islam. Editor and translator, Aharon Ben-Shemesh. 2d edn. rev. 3 vols. to date. Leiden: E. J. Brill, 1965-1969.

Torres Fontes. See *Repartimiento de Sevilla.*

Tortosa Charter. Carta puebla de Tortosa, December 1148. In *Colección de documentos inéditos de la corona de Aragón* (*q.v.*), IV, 130-134.

Also in Fernández y González, *Mudejares de Castilla* (*q.v.*), appendix, doc. 5 (misdated).

Traités de paix et de commerce et documents divers concernant les relations des chrétiens avec les arabes de l'Afrique septentrionale au moyen âge recueillis par ordre de l'empereur et publiés avec une introduction historique. Editor, Louis (comte de) Mas Latrie. 2 vols. Research and Source Works, 63. New York: Burt Franklin, [1866] 1963.

Tudela Charter. Carta puebla de Tudela, March 1115. In *Colección de fueros municipales y cartas pueblas* (*q.v.*), p. 415. Also in Fernández y González, *Mudejares de Castilla* (*q.v.*), appendix, doc. 2.

Usāmah b. Murshīd b. Munqidh, al-Kinānī ash-Shayzārī. *An Arab-Syrian Gentleman and Warrior in the Period of the Crusades: Memoirs of Usāmah ibn-Munqidh* (*Kitāb al-I'tibār*). Translator, Philip K. Hitti. Records of Civilization, Sources and Studies. New York: Columbia University Press, 1929.

Usatges de Barcelona i commemoracions de Pere Albert. Editor, Josep Rovira i Ermengol. Barcelona: Editorial Barcino, 1933.

Uxó Charter. Carta puebla de Uxó, August 1250. In *Colección de documentos inéditos de España* (*q.v.*), XVIII, 42-50. Also in *Colección diplomática* (*q.v.*), doc. 383; Fernández y González, *Mudejares de Castilla* (*q.v.*), appendix, doc. 23.

Valencia Capitulation. Surrender treaty for Valencia city, September 28, 1238. In *Colección de documentos inéditos de España* (*q.v.*), XVIII, 84-86. Also in Fernández y González, *Mudejares de Castilla* (*q.v.*), appendix, doc. 15; Tourtoulon, *Don Jaime I el Conquistador* (*q.v.*), I, appendix, doc. 15.

Villanueva Rico. See *Libros de habices.*

Vocabulista in arabico, pubblicato per la prima volta sopra un codice della biblioteca riccardiana di Firenze. Dubious attribution to Ramón Martí. Editor, Celestino Schiaparelli. Florence: Successori Le Monnier, 1871.

Al-Wansharīshī. See secondary sources, Idris.

Al-Waṭwāṭ (Muḥammad b. Ibrāhīm b. Yaḥyā, al-Kutubī al-Waṭwāṭ). *Extraits inédits relatifs au Maghreb* (*géographie et histoire*). Translator, Edmond Fagnan. Algiers: Bastide-Jourdan, 1924.

Ximenez. See Jiménez.

Yaḥyā b. Muḥammad b. Khaldūn, Abū Zakarīyā'. *Histoire des Benī 'Abd-el-Wâd, rois de Tlemcen, jusqu'au règne d'Abou H'ammou Moûsa II.* Translator, Alfred Bel. 3 vols. Algiers: Pierre Fontana, 1903-1913.

Ya'qūb b. Ibrāhīm, Abū Yūsuf al-Anṣārī. *Kitāb al-kharāj.* Abridged in *Taxation in Islam* (*q.v.*), II, 69-78.

Yāqūt b. 'Abd Allāh al-Ḥamawī ar-Rūmī. *The Introductory Chapters of Yāqūt's Mu'jam al-Buldān.* Translator, Wadie Jwaideh. Leiden: E. J. Brill, 1959.

Az-Zarkashī (Muḥammad b. Ibrāhīm az-Zarkashī). *Chronique des almohades et des hafçides.* Translator, Edmond Fagnan. Constantine: Société archéologique du département, 1895.

Secondary Sources

Aḥmad b. Naṣr ad-Dāwūdī al-Mālikī. *Kitāb fīhi al-amwāl.* Editor and translator, H. H. Abdul Wahab and F. Dachroaui. In "Le régime foncier en Sicile au moyen âge (ixe et x siècles)." *Études d'orientalisme* (*q.v.*), II, 401-444.

Albertini, Eugène. *Les divisions administratives de l'Espagne romaine.* Paris: E. de Boccard, 1923.

Alemany, José. "Milicias cristianas al servicio de los sultanes musulmanes de Almagreb." *Homenaje á Codera* (*q.v.*), pp. 133-169.

Almagro Basch, Martín *et alii. Historia de Albarracín y su sierra.* 4 vols. to date. Teruel: Instituto de estudios turolenses, 1959ff.

Aluch, Abdelkrim. "Organización administrativa de las ciudades en el Islam español." *Miscelánea de estudios árabes y hebraicos,* X (1961), 37-68.

Amari, Michele. *Storia dei musulmani di Sicilia.* 2d edn. 3 vols. Catania, Sicily: R. Prampolini, 1933-1939.

Aragó Cabañas, Antonio M. "La institución 'baiulus regis' en Cataluña en la época de Alfonso el Casto." *Congrés VII* (*q.v.*), III, 139-142.

Ardit Lucas, Manuel, "El asalto a la morería de Valencia en el año 1455." *Ligarzas* (Valencia), II (1970), 127-138.

Arié, Rachel. "Quelques remarques sur le costume des musulmans d'Espagne au temps des naṣrides." *Arabica,* XII (1965), 244-261.

Arranz Velarde, F. *La España musulmana* (*la historia y la tradición*). Madrid: Talleres gráficos Marsiega, 1941.

Arribas Palau, Mariano. *Musulmanes de Valencia apresados cerca de Ibiza en 1413.* Tetuán: Centro de estudios marroquíes, 1955.

Asín Palacios, Miguel. *Contribución a la toponimia árabe de España.* 2d edn. Madrid: Consejo superior de investigaciones científicas, 1944.

Badía Margarit, Antonio M. "'Alcalde,' difusión de un arabismo en catalán." *Homenaje a Millás-Vallicrosa* (*q.v.*), I, 67-82.

Baer, Yitzhak [Fritz]. *A History of the Jews in Christian Spain.* Translator, Louis Schoffman. 2 vols. Philadelphia: Jewish Publication Society of America, 1966.

Ballesteros y Beretta, Antonio. *Alfonso X el Sabio.* Barcelona: Salvat Editores, 1963.

———. *Sevilla en el siglo xiii.* Madrid: Juan Pérez Torres, 1913.

Bayerri y Bertoméu, Enrique. *Historia de Tortosa y su comarca.* 8 vols. to date. Tortosa: Algueró y Baiges, 1933ff.

Bel, Alfred. *La religion musulmane en Berbérie, esquisse d'histoire et de sociologie religieuses.* 2 vols. Paris: Paul Geuthner, 1938.

Ben-Ami, Aharon. *Social Change in a Hostile Environment: The Crusaders' Kingdom of Jerusalem.* Princeton: Princeton University Press, 1969.

Bencheneb. See Ibn Shanab.

Beuter, Pedro Antonio. *La coronica general de toda España y especialmente del reyno de Valencia.* 2 vols. Valencia: Pedro Patricio Mey, [1538-1551] 1604.

Boix y Ricarte, Vicente. *Historia de la ciudad y reino de Valencia.* 3 vols. Valencia: Benito Monfort, 1845-1847.

Boronat y Barrachina, Pascual. *Los moriscos españoles y su expulsión, estudio histórico-crítico.* 2 vols. Valencia: Francisco Vives Mora, 1901.

Bosch Vilá, Jacinto. *Albarracín musulmán.* In Almagro, *Historia de Albarracín* (*q.v.*), vol. II.

———. "Algunas consideraciones sobre 'al-Ṯaġr en al-Andalus' y la división político-administrativa de la España musulmana." *Études d'orientalisme* (*q.v.*), I, 23-33.

———. "Establecimiento de grupos humanos norteafricanos en la península ibérica, a raíz de la invasión musulmana." *Atti del I congresso internazionale di studi nord-africani*, pp. 147-161. Cagliari: Università di Cagliari, 1965.

Bousquet, Georges Henri. *Le droit musulman.* Paris: Armand Colin, 1963.

———. *L'Islam maghrébin: Introduction à l'étude générale de l'Islâm.* 4th edn. rev. Algiers: Maison des livres, 1954.

Branchát, Vicente. *Tratado de los derechos y regalías que corresponden al real patrimonio en el reyno de Valencia y de la jurisdicción del intendente como subrogado en lugar del antiguo bayle general.* 3 vols. Valencia: José y Tomás de Orga, 1784-1786.

Brockelmann, Carl. *Geschichte der arabischen Literatur.* 5 vols. (including supplements). Leiden: E. J. Brill, 1898-1942. Vols. I and II rev., 1943-1949.

Brockelmann, Carl. *History of the Islamic Peoples.* Translators, Joel Carmichael and Moshe Perlmann. 2d edn. rev. in trans. New York: G. P. Putnam's Sons, 1947.

Brunschvig, Robert. *La Berbérie orientale sous les ḥafṣides.* Publications de l'Institut d'études orientales d'Alger, 8, 11. 2 vols. Paris: Adrien-Maisonneuve, 1940-1947.

Burns, Robert Ignatius. "Baths and Caravanserais in Crusader Valencia." *Speculum,* XLVI (1971), 443-458.

———. "Christian-Islamic Confrontation in the West: The Thirteenth-Century Dream of Conversion." *American Historical Review,* LXXVI (1971), 1386-1434.

———. *The Crusader Kingdom of Valencia: Reconstruction on a Thirteenth-Century Frontier.* 2 vols. Cambridge, Mass.: Harvard University Press, 1967.

———. "How to End a Crusade: Techniques for Making Peace in the Thirteenth-Century Kingdom of Valencia." *Military Affairs,* XXXV (1971), 142-148.

———. "Irrigation Taxes in Early Mudejar Valencia: The Problem of the *Alfarda.*" *Speculum,* XLIV (1969), 560-567.

———. "Journey from Islam: Incipient Cultural Transition in the Conquered Kingdom of Valencia (1240-1280)." *Speculum,* XXXV (1960), 337-356.

———. "A Mediaeval Income Tax: The Tithe in the Thirteenth-Century Kingdom of Valencia." *Speculum,* XLI (1966), 438-451.

———. "The Muslim in the Christian Feudal Order (the Kingdom of Valencia, 1240-1280)." *Studies in Medieval Culture,* V, in press.

———. "The Parish as a Frontier Institution in Thirteenth-Century Valencia." *Speculum,* XXXVII (1962), 244-251.

———. "Renegades, Adventurers, and Sharp Businessmen: The Thirteenth-Century Spaniard in the Cause of Islam." *Catholic Historical Review,* LVII (1972), 341-366.

———. "Le royaume chrétien de Valence et ses vassaux musulmans (1240-1280)." *Annales, économies, sociétés, civilisations,* XXVIII (1973), 199-225.

———. "Social Riots on the Christian-Moslem Frontier: Thirteenth-Century Valencia." *American Historical Review,* LXVI (1961), 378-400.

———. *Medieval Colonialism: Postcrusade Exploitation of Islamic Valencia.* Princeton: Princeton University Press, in press.

Busquets Mulet, Jaime. "El códice latinoarábigo del repartimiento de Mallorca." *Homenaje a Millás-Vallicrosa* (*q.v.*), I, 243-300.

Cabanes Pecourt, María Desamparados de. "Aportación al estudio de la situación social de los mudéjares valencianos." *Congresso luso-espanhol de estudos medievais.* Oporto: Câmara municipal, in press.

Cagigas, Isidro de las. *Andalucía musulmana: Aportaciones a la delimitación de la frontera del Andalus.* (*Ensayo de etnografía andaluza medieval.*) Madrid: Consejo superior de investigaciones científicas, 1950.

———. *Los mozárabes.* Minorías étnico-religiosas de la edad media española, 1, 2. 2 vols. Madrid: Consejo superior de investigaciones científicas, 1947-1948.

———. *Los mudejares.* Minorías étnico-religiosas de la edad media española, 3, 4. 2 vols. Madrid: Consejo superior de investigaciones científicas, 1948-1949.

———. *Sevilla almohade y últimos años de su vida musulmana.* Madrid: Consejo superior de investigaciones científicas, 1951.

Cahen, Claude. "La féodalité et les institutions politiques de l'orient latin." *Atti del convegno di scienze morali, storiche, e filologiche, 27 Maggio-1 Giugno 1956, tema: oriente ed occidente nel medio evo,* pp. 167-197. Rome: Accademia nazionale dei Lincei, 1957.

———. "Mouvements populaires et autonomisme urbain dans l'Asie musulman du moyen âge." *Arabica,* v (1958), 225-250, vi (1959), 25-56, 233-265.

———. "Notes sur l'histoire des croisades et de l'orient latin: le régime rural syrien au temps de la domination franque." *Bulletin de la faculté des lettres de Strasbourg,* xxix (1951), 286-310.

———. *La Syrie du nord a l'époque des croisades et la principauté franque d'Antioche.* Institut français de Damas, Bibliotheque orientale, 1. Paris: Paul Geuthner, 1940.

Caro Baroja, Julio C. *Los moriscos del reino de Granada, ensayo de historia social.* Madrid: Instituto de estudios políticos, 1957.

———. *Los pueblos de España, ensayo de etnología.* Colección histórica Laye, 5. Barcelona: Editorial Barna, 1946.

Casas Torres, José Manuel. *La vivienda y los núcleos de población rurales de la huerta de Valencia.* Madrid: Consejo superior de investigaciones científicas, 1944.

Casey, James. "Moriscos and the Depopulation of Valencia." *Past and Present,* L (1971), 19-40.

Castejón Calderón, Rafael. *Los juristas hispano-musulmanes* (*desde la conquista, hasta la caída del califato de Córdoba—años 711 a 1031 de C.*). Madrid: Consejo superior de investigaciones científicas, 1948.

Castro, Américo. *España en su historia: cristianos, moros y judíos.* Buenos Aires: Editorial Losada, ct. 1948. Rev. in trans. as *The Structure of Spanish History.* Translator, E. L. King. Princeton: Princeton University Press, 1954.

——. *The Spaniards: An Introduction to their History.* Translators, W. F. King and S. Margaretten. Berkeley: University of California Press, 1971.

Cavanilles, Antonio J. *Observaciones sobre la historia natural, geografía, agricultura, población y frutos del reyno de Valencia.* 2 vols. Madrid: Imprenta Real, 1795-1797. (Second printing, much reduced in size and maps, 2 vols. Zaragoza: Consejo superior de investigaciones científicas, 1958.)

Chabás y Lloréns, Roque. "La capitulación de Valencia." *El archivo,* IV (1890), 221-223.

——. "Çeid Abu Çeid." *El archivo,* IV (1890), 215-221, V (1891), 143-166, 288-304, 362-376.

——. *Distribución de las aguas en 1244 y donaciones del termino de Gandía por D. Jaime I.* Valencia: Francisco Vives Mora, 1898.

——. "Don Jaime el Conquistador y Alazrach." *El archivo,* IV (1890), 280-282.

——. "Glosario de algunas voces oscuras usadas en el derecho foral valenciano." *Anales del centro de cultura valenciana,* XII (1944), 3-27, 76-79, 128-150. Repaged offprint, Valencia: Imprenta Diana, 1946.

——. *Historia de la ciudad de Denia.* Editor, F. Figueras Pacheco. Instituto de estudios alicantinos, 3, 4. 2 vols. 2d edn. Alicante: Diputación provincial, 1958-1960.

——. "El libro del repartimiento de la ciudad y reino de Valencia." *El archivo,* III (1888-1889), 73-98; VI (1892), 240-250; VII (1893), 365-372.

——. "Los mozárabes valencianos." *El archivo,* V (1891), 6-28.

——. "Zahen y los moros de Uxó y Eslida." *El archivo,* I (1886), 262-263.

Circourt, A. [Anne M.J.A.], comte de. *Histoire des mores, mudejares et des morisques ou des arabes d'Espagne sous la domination des chrétiens.* 3 vols. Paris: G. A. Dentu, 1845-1848.

Codera y Zaidín, Francisco. "Apodos ó sobrenombres de moros españoles." *Mélanges Hartwig Derenbourg, recueil de travaux d'érudition dédiés a la mémoire d'Hartwig Derenbourg par ses amis et ses élèves,* pp. 323-334. Paris: Ernest Leroux, 1909.

Conde, José Antonio. *Historia de la dominación de los árabes en España, sacada de varios manuscritos y memorias arábigas.* Madrid: Marín y Compañía, 1874.

Congrés [*I*] *d'història de la corona d'Aragó, dedicat al rey en Jaume I y a la seua época.* 2 vols. paginated as one. Barcelona: Ayuntamiento de Barcelona, 1909-1913.

III Congrés d'història de la corona d'Aragó, dedicat al període compres entre la mort de Jaume I i la proclamació del rey Don Ferrán d'Antequera. 2 vols. Valencia: Diputación provincial, 1923.

IV Congrés d'història de la corona d'Aragó. 2 vols. Palma de Mallorca: Diputación provincial, 1959-1970.

VII Congrés d'història de la corona d'Aragó. 3 vols. Barcelona: Ayuntamiento de Barcelona, 1963-1964.

Congreso [*primer*] *de estudios árabes e islámicos, Actas* [1962]. Madrid: Comité permanente del congreso, 1964.

Cortabarría Beitia, A. "L'état actuel des études arabes en Espagne." *Mélanges de l'institut dominicain d'études orientales du Caire,* VIII (1964-1966), 75-129.

Coulson, N. J. *A History of Islamic Law.* Islamic Surveys, 2. Edinburgh: University of Edinburgh Press, 1964.

Danvila y Collado, Manuel. *Estudio acerca del poder civil de los árabes de España durante el período de su dominación.* Madrid: Jaime Ratés, 1906.

———. "Saco de la morería de Valencia en 1455." *El archivo,* III (1889), 124-129.

Ad-Dāwūdī. See Aḥmad.

Dermenghem, Émile. *Le culte des saints dans l'Islam maghrébin.* 6th edn. Paris: Gallimard, 1954.

Dozy, Reinhart P. A. *Histoire des musulmans d'Espagne jusqu'à la conquête de l'Andalousie par les Almoravides* (*711-1110*). Editor, Évariste Lévi-Provençal. 3 vols. Rev. edn. Leiden: E. J. Brill, 1932.

———. *Supplément aux dictionnaires arabes.* 2 vols. 3d edn. Leiden: E. J. Brill, 1967.

——— and Willem H. Engelmann. *Glossaire des mots espagnols et portugais dérivés de l'arabe.* 2d edn. rev. Leiden: E. J. Brill, [1869] 1965.

Dualde Serrano, Manuel. "Misión moralizadora del lugarteniente general Juan de Lanuza en el reino de Valencia." *Estudios de edad media de la corona de Aragón,* V (1952), 474-498.

Dubler, César E. *Über das Wirtschaftsleben auf der iberischen Halbinsel vom xi zum xiii Jahrhundert, Beitrag zu den islamisch-christlichen Beziehungen.* Romanica helvetica, series linguistica, 22. Erlenbach-Zurich: Eugen Rentsch Verlag, 1943.

Dufourcq, Charles Emmanuel. *L'Espagne catalane et le Maghrib aux xiiie et xive siècles, de la bataille de Las Navas de Tolosa (1212) à l'avène-*

ment du sultan mérinide Abou-l-Hasan (1313). Bibliothèque de l'école des hautes études hispaniques, Université de Bordeaux, 37. Paris: Presses universitaires de France, 1966.

———. "Les relations du Maroc et de la Castille pendant la première moitié du xiiie siècle." *Revue d'histoire et de civilisation du Maghreb*, v (1968), 37-62.

Enan, Mohamed Abdulla. See 'Inān.

Enciclopedia lingüistica hispánica. Editors, M. Alvar, A. Badía *et alii*. 2 vols. plus supplement. Madrid: Consejo superior de investigaciones científicas, 1960-1962.

Encyclopaedia of Islam. A Dictionary of the Geography, Ethnography, and Biography of the Muhammadan Peoples. Editors, M. T. Houtsma *et alii*. 4 vols. and supplement. Leiden: E. J. Brill, 1913-1936. 2d edn. rev. [*EI*²]. Editors, H.A.R. Gibb, J. H. Kramers, E. Lévi-Provençal *et alii*. 4 vols. to date. Leiden: E. J. Brill, 1960ff.

Epstein, Isidore. *The "Responsa" of Rabbi Solomon Ben Adreth of Barcelona (1235-1310) as a Source of the History of Spain. Studies in the Communal Life of the Jews in Spain as Reflected in the "Responsa." And the Responsa of Rabbi Simon B. Ẓemaḥ Duran as a Source of the History of the Jews in North Africa*. 2 vols. in one. New York: KTAV Publishing House, [1925-1930] 1968.

Escolano, Gaspar. *Décadas de la historia de la insigne y coronada ciudad y reino de Valencia*. Editor, Juan B. Perales. 3 vols. Valencia: Terraza, Aliena y Compañía, [1610-1611] 1878-1880.

Estenaga Echevarría, Narciso. "Condición social de los mudéjares en Toledo durante la edad media." *Real academia de bellas artes y ciencias históricas de Toledo*, vi (1924), 5-27.

Études d'orientalisme dediées a la mémoire de Lévi-Provençal. 2 vols. Paris: G. P. Maisonneuve et Larose, 1962.

Fernández y González, Francisco. *Estado social y político de los mudejares de Castilla, considerados en sí mismos y respecto de la civilización española*. Madrid: Real academia de la historia, 1866.

Ferrandis e Irles, Manuel. "Rendición del castillo de Chivert á los templarios." *Homenaje á Codera (q.v.)*, pp. 23-33.

Fischer, August. "Zur Syntax der muslimischen Bekenntnisformel." *Islamica* (Leiden), iv (1931), 512-521.

Fischer, Christian Augustus. *A Picture of Valencia, Taken on the Spot; Comprehending a Description of that Province, Its Inhabitants, Manners and Customs, Productions, Commerce, Manufactures, etc., with an Appendix, Containing a Geographical and Statistical Survey of*

Valencia and of the Balearic and Pithyusian Islands; Together with Remarks on the Moors in Spain. 2d edn. London: Henry Colburn, 1811.

Fonseca, Damián. *Relación de la expulsión de los moriscos del reino de Valencia.* Valencia: La sociedad valenciana de bibliófilos, [1512] 1878.

Font y Rius, José M. "La comarca de Tortosa a raíz de la reconquista cristiana (1148), notes sobre su fisionomía político-social." *Cuadernos de historia de España,* XIX (1953), 104-128.

———. *Instituciones medievales españolas: La organización política, económica y social de los reinos cristianos de la reconquista.* Madrid: Consejo superior de investigaciones científicas, 1949.

———. "La reconquista y repoblación de Levante y Murcia." In J. M. Font y Rius *et alii, La reconquista española y la repoblación del país,* Escuela de estudios medievales, 15, pp. 85-126. Zaragoza: Consejo superior de investigaciones científicas, 1951.

Fontavella González, Vicente. *La huerta de Gandía.* Zaragoza: Consejo superior de investigaciones científicas, 1950.

Fórneas, José María. "Sobre los Banū Ḥawṭ Allāh (-Ḥawṭella) y algunos fenómenos fonéticos del árabe levantino." *Al-Andalus,* XXXII (1967), 445-457.

Fuster, Juan. *Poetes, moriscos, y capellans.* Valencia: L'Estel, 1962.

Galmés de Fuentes, Álvaro. "El mozárabe levantino en los 'Libros de los repartimientos de Mallorca y Valencia.'" *Nueva revista de filología hispánica,* IV (1950), 313-346.

G[arcía] de Valdeavellano y Arcimís, Luis. *Curso de historia de las instituciones españolas de los orígenes al final de la edad media.* Madrid: Revista de occidente, 1968.

———. "Las instituciones feudales en España." Appended to F. L. Ganshof, *El feudalismo,* translator F. Formosa, pp. 229-305. Barcelona: Ariel, 1963.

———. "Les liens de vassalité et les immunités en Espagne." In *Les liens de vassalité et les immunités* as *Recueils de la société Jean Bodin pour l'histoire comparative des institutions,* I (1958), 222-255. 2d edn. rev.

García y García, Honorio. "Los elementos germánico y musulmán en los 'Furs' (estudios de derecho foral valenciano)." *Boletín de la sociedad castellonense de cultura,* XXXI (1955), 80-85.

———. *Estado económico-social de los vasallos en la gobernación foral de Castellón.* Vich: Imprenta Ausetana, 1943.

———. "El 'Libre del repartiment' y la práctica notarial de su tiempo." *Boletín de la sociedad castellonense de cultura,* XXV (1949), 493-499.

García y García, Honorio. *Notas para la historia de Vall de Uxó*. Vall de Uxó: Ayuntamiento de Uxó, 1962.

García Gómez, Emilio. *Poemas arábigoandaluces*. Colección austral, 162. 4th edn. Madrid: Espasa-Calpe, 1959.

———. *Poesía arábigoandaluza, breve síntesis histórica*. Madrid: Instituto Faruk 1° de estudios islámicos [Editorial Maestre], 1952.

———. See also Lévi-Provençal, *España musulmana*; and primary sources, ash-Shaqundī.

García Sanz, Arcadio. "Mudéjares y moriscos en Castellón." *Boletín de la sociedad castellonense de cultura*, XXVIII (1952), 94-114.

———. "Tales y sus cartas pueblas." *Boletín de la sociedad castellonense de cultura*, XXVIII (1952), 439-442.

Gardet, Louis. *La cité musulmane, vie sociale et politique*. Études musulmanes, 1. Paris: J. Vrin, 1954.

Gaspar Remiro, Mariano. *Historia de la Murcia musulmana*. Zaragoza: Andrés Uriarte, 1905.

Gaudefroy-Demombynes, Maurice. *Muslim Institutions*. Translator, J. P. MacGregor. 2d edn. rev. New York: George Allen Unwin, 1961.

Gautier-Dalché, J. "Des mudejars aux morisques [en Valence]: deux articles, deux méthodes." *Hespéris*, XLV (1958), 271-289.

Gazulla, Faustino D. *Jaime I de Aragón y los estados musulmanes*. Barcelona: Real academia de buenas letras, 1919.

———. "Las compañías de zenetes en el reino de Aragón (1284-1291)." *Boletín de la real academia de la historia*, XC (1927), 174-196.

Geografía general del reino de Valencia. Editor, F. Carreras y Candi. 5 vols. Barcelona: Alberto Martín, 1920-1927.

Gibb, Hamilton A. R. *Arabic Literature: An Introduction*. 2d edn. rev. Oxford: The Clarendon Press, 1963.

———. See primary sources, Ibn Baṭṭūṭa.

——— and Harold Bowen. *Islamic Society and the West*. London: Oxford University Press, 1957.

Gibert y Sánchez de la Vega, Rafael. "Los contratos agrarios en el derecho medieval." *Boletín de la universidad de Granada*, XXII (1950), 305-330.

Giménez Soler, Andrés. "Caballeros españoles en África y africanos en España." *Revue hispanique*, XII (1905), 299-372.

———. *La corona de Aragón y Granada, historia de las relaciones entre ambos reinos*. Barcelona: Casa provincial de caridad, 1908.

———. *La edad media en la corona de Aragón*. 2d edn. rev. Colección labor, ciencias históricas, 223, 224. Barcelona: Editorial Labor, 1944.

Giner Bolufer, Carmelo. "Topografía histórica de los valles de Pego." *Anales del centro de cultura valenciana*, XV (1947), 46-74.

Glick, Thomas F. *Irrigation and Society in Medieval Valencia.* Cambridge: Harvard University Press, 1969.

———. "*Muḥtasib* and *Mustasaf*: A Case Study of Institutional Diffusion." *Viator*, II (1971), 59-81.

——— and Oriol Pi Sunyer. "Acculturation as an Explanatory Concept in Spanish History." *Comparative Studies in Society and History*, XI (1969), 136-154.

Glossarium mediae latinitatis Cataloniae, voces latinas y romances documentadas en fuentes catalanas del año 800 al 1100. Editors, Mariano Bassols de Climent *et alii*. One vol. to date. Barcelona: Universidad de Barcelona, 1960.

Goitein, Solomon D. *A Mediterranean Society: The Jewish Communities of the Arab World as Portrayed in the Documents of the Cairo Geniza.* 2 vols. to date. Berkeley: University of California Press, 1967ff.

———. *Studies in Islamic History and Institutions.* Leiden: E. J. Brill, 1966.

Goldziher, Ignácz. "Los árabes españoles y el Islam" [1876]. *Congreso de estudios árabes (q.v.)*, pp. 3-77.

González, Julio. *Alfonso IX.* 2 vols. Madrid: Consejo superior de investigaciones científicas, 1944.

———. *El reino de Castilla en la época de Alfonso VIII.* Escuela de estudios medievales, textos, 25. 3 vols. Madrid: Consejo superior de investigaciones científicas, 1960.

González Martí, Manuel. *Cerámica del levante español, siglos medievales.* 3 vols. Madrid: Editorial Labor, 1944-1952.

González Palencia, Ángel. "La España musulmana." In Luis Pericot García *et alii, Historia de España, gran historia general de los pueblos hispanos*, II, 157-332. 5 vols. Barcelona: Instituto Gallach, 1936-1943.

———. *Historia de la España musulmana.* 4th edn. rev. Colección labor, ciencias históricas, 69. Barcelona: Editorial Labor, 1945.

———. *Historia de la literatura arábigo-española.* Barcelona: Editorial Labor, [1928] 1945.

———. *Los mozárabes de Toledo en los siglos xii y xiii.* 4 vols. Madrid: Instituto de Valencia de Don Juan, 1926-1930.

Grau Monserrat, Manuel. "Mudéjares castellonenses." *Boletín de la real academia de buenas letras de Barcelona*, XXIX (1961-1962), 251-273.

Grunebaum. See Von Grunebaum.

Gual Camarena, Miguel. "Una cofradía de negros libertos en el siglo XV." *Estudios de edad media de la corona de Aragón*, V (1952), 457-463.

Gual Camarena, Miguel. "Contribución al estudio de la territorialidad de los fueros de Valencia." *Estudios de edad media de la corona de Aragón*, III (1947-1948), 262-289.

———. "La corona de Aragón en la repoblación murciana." *Congrés VII* (*q.v.*), II, 303-310.

———. "Mudéjares valencianos, aportaciones para su estudio." *Saitabi*, VII (1949), 165-199.

———. "Los mudéjares valencianos en la época del Magnánimo." *Congrés IV* (*q.v.*), I, 467-494.

———. "Precedentes de la reconquista valenciana." *Estudios medievales* [Valencia], I (1952), 167-246. Repaged offprint. Valencia: Consejo superior de investigaciones científicas, 1953.

———. "Reconquista de la zona castellonense." *Boletín de la sociedad castellonense de cultura*, XXV (1949), 417-441.

Guichard, Pierre. "Le peuplement de la région de Valence aux deux premiers siècles de la domination musulmane." *Mélanges de la casa de Velázquez*, V (1969), 103-158.

Guillén Robles, F. *Málaga musulmana. Sucesos, antigüedades, ciencias y letras malagueñas durante la edad media*. Málaga: Ayuntamiento de Málaga, [1880] 1957.

Halperín Donghi, Tulio. "Un conflicto nacional: moriscos y cristianos viejos en Valencia." *Cuadernos de historia de España*, XXIV-XXV (1955), 5-115; XXV-XXVI (1957), 82-250.

———. "Recouvrements de civilisation: les morisques du royaume de Valence au XVIe siècle." *Annales, économies, sociétés, civilisations*, XI (1956), 154-182.

Hinojosa, Eduardo de. "Mezquinos y exáricos, datos para la historia de la servidumbre en Navarra y Aragón." *Homenaje á Codera* (*q.v.*), pp. 523-531.

Hitti, Philip K. *History of the Arabs, from the Earliest Times to the Present*. 10th edn. London: Macmillan, 1970.

———. *Islam and the West: An Historical Cultural Survey*. Princeton: D. Van Nostrand, 1962.

———. *Arab-Syrian Gentleman*. See primary sources, Usāmah.

Hoenerbach. See primary sources, *Spanisch-islamische*; Ibn al-Khaṭīb.

Homenaje á D[on] Francisco Codera en su jubilación del profesorado. Estudios de erudición oriental. Editors, Eduardo Saavedra *et alii*. Zaragoza: Mariano Escar, 1904.

Homenaje a Jaime Vicens Vives. Editor, J. Maluquer de Motes. 2 vols. Barcelona: Universidad de Barcelona, 1965.

Homenaje a Millás-Vallicrosa. 2 vols. Barcelona: Consejo superior de investigaciones científicas, 1954-1956.

Hommage à Georges Marçais. In *Mélanges d'histoire* (*q.v.*), vol. II.

Hopkins, J.F.P. *Medieval Muslim Government in Barbary until the Sixth Century of the Hijra*. London: Luzac and Co. Ltd., 1958.

Hourani. See *Islamic City*.

Houston, J. M. "Land Use and Society in the Plain of Valencia." In *Geographical Essays in Memory of Alan G. Ogilvie*, editors R. Miller and J. W. Watson, pp. 166-194. London: Thomas Nelson and Sons Ltd., 1959.

Huici Miranda, Ambrosio. *Las grandas batallas de la reconquista durante las invasiones africanas* (*almoravides, almohades, y benimerines*). Madrid: Consejo superior de investigaciones científicas, 1956.

———. *Historia musulmana de Valencia y su región, novedades y rectificaciones*. 3 vols. Valencia: Ayuntamiento de Valencia, 1969-1970.

———. *Historia política del imperio almohade*. Tetuán: Instituto General Franco de estudios e investigación hispano-árabe, 1956-1957.

———. See primary sources, Huici.

Ibn Shanab (Bencheneb). "Notes chronologiques principalement sur la conquête de l'Espagne par les chrétiens." *Mélanges René Basset, études nord-africaines et orientales*, I, 69-77. 2 vols. Paris: Ernest Leroux, 1923-1925.

Idris, Hady Roger. *Berbérie orientale sous les zīrīdes, xe-xiie siècles*. 2 vols. Publications de l'institut d'études orientales (d'Alger), 22. Paris: Adrien-Maisonneuve, 1962.

———. "Le mariage en occident musulman d'après un choix de Fatwās médiévales extraites du Mi'yār d'al-Wanšarīšī." *Studia islamica*, XXXII (1970), 157-167.

Imām ad-Dīn (Imamuddin), S. M. *A Political History of Muslim Spain*. Dacca: Najmah and Sons, 1961.

———. *Some Aspects of the Socio-Economic and Cultural History of Muslim Spain, 711-1492 A.D.* Medieval Iberian Peninsula Texts and Studies, 2. Leiden: E. J. Brill, 1965.

'Inān [Enan] (Muḥammad 'Abd Allāh 'Inān). *The Age of the Almoravides and Almohads in Maghreb and Moslem Spain*. English title, Arabic text. 2 vols. Cairo: Lajnat at-ta'līf Press, 1964-1965.

———. *The End of the Moorish Empire in Spain and the History of the Moriscos*. English introduction, Arabic text. 2d edn. rev. Cairo: Miṣr Press, 1958.

The Islamic City: A Colloquium. Editors, A. H. Hourani and S. M. Stern. Near Eastern History Group of Oxford University and Near Eastern Center of the University of Pennsylvania, Papers on Islamic History, 1. Philadelphia: University of Pennsylvania, 1969.

Itinerari. See Miret y Sans.

Janer, Florencio. *Condición social de los moriscos de España, causas de su expulsión y consecuencias que este produjo en el orden económico y político.* Madrid: Real academia de la historia, 1857.

Julien, Charles André. *Histoire de l'Afrique du nord. Tunisie-Algérie-Maroc, de la conquête arabe à 1830.* Editor, Roger Le Tourneau. 2 vols. 2d edn. rev. Paris: Payot, 1951-1952. Vol. II translated as *History of North Africa: Tunisia, Algeria, Morocco, from the Arab Conquest to 1830.* Editors, Roger Le Tourneau and C. C. Stewart; translator, John Petrie. New York: Praeger, 1970.

Klüpfel, Ludwig. *Die äussere Politik Alfonsos III von Aragonien (1285-1291).* Abhandlungen zur mittleren und neueren Geschichte, 35. Berlin: W. Rothschild, 1911-1912.

Lacarra, José M. *La reconquista española.* See Font y Rius.

———. "La repoblación de Zaragoza por Alfonso el Batallador." *Estudios de historia social de España,* I (1949), 205-223.

———. See primary sources, "Documentos . . . del Ebro."

Ladero Quesada, M. A. *Granada, historia de un país islámico (1232-1571).* Biblioteca universitaria Gredos, 2. Madrid: Editorial Gredos, 1969.

———. *Los mudéjares de Castilla en tiempo de Isabel I.* Valladolid: Instituto Isabel la Católica de historia eclesiástica, 1969.

Lapeyre, Henri. *Géographie de l'Espagne morisque.* École pratique des hautes études, Démographie et sociétés, 2. Paris: S.E.V.P.E.N., 1959.

Lapidus, Ira Marvin. *Muslim Cities in the Later Middle Ages.* Harvard Middle Eastern Studies, 11. Cambridge, Mass.: Harvard University Press, 1967.

———, editor. See *Middle Eastern Cities.*

Lautensach, Hermann. *Maurische Züge im geographischen Bild der iberischen Halbinsel.* Bonner geographische Abhandlungen, geographischen Institut der Universität Bonn, 28. Bonn: Ferd. Dünmlers Verlag, 1960.

Le Tourneau, Roger. *The Almohad Movement in North Africa in the Twelfth and Thirteenth Centuries.* Princeton: Princeton University Press, 1969.

———. "L'occident musulman du milieu du viie siècle à la fin du xve siècle." *Annales de l'institut d'études orientales* (d'Alger), II (1936), 147-176.

Lenguaje técnico. See Rodón Binué.

León Tello, Pilar. "Carta de población a los moros de Urzante." *Congreso de estudios árabes (q.v.),* pp. 329-343.

Lévi-Provençal, Évariste. *Las ciudades y las instituciones urbanas del occidente musulmán en la edad media.* Instituto General Franco de estudios e investigación hispano-árabe, publicaciones fuera de serie. Tetuán: Editora marroquí, 1950. Also in French, *Conférences* (*q.v.*), pp. 75-119.

———. *La civilisation arabe en Espagne, vue générale.* Islam d'hier et d'aujourd'hui, 1. 3d edn. Paris: Maisonneuve-Larose, 1961.

———. *Conférences sur l'Espagne musulmane, prononcées à la faculté des lettres en 1947 y 1948.* Cairo: Imprimerie nationale, 1951.

———. *Histoire de l'Espagne musulmane.* 3 vols. 2d edn. rev. Paris: G. P. Maisonneuve, [1950-1953] 1967. Revised in translation by Emilio García Gómez, *España musulmana hasta la caída del califato de Córdoba (711-1031 de J.C.).* 2 vols. In Ramón Menéndez Pidal *et alii, Historia de España* (*q.v.*), vols. IV, V.

———. *Inscriptions arabes d'Espagne.* Leiden: E. J. Brill, 1931.

———. *Islam d'occident, études d'histoire médiévale.* Islam d'hier et d'aujourd'hui, 7. Paris: G. P. Maisonneuve, 1948.

———. "Notes de toponomastique hispano-maǵribine: les noms des portes, le *bāb aš-šarīʿa* et la *šarīʿa* dans les villes d'occident musulman au moyen-âge." *Annales de l'institut d'études orientales* (d'Alger), II (1936), 210-234.

———. *Péninsule ibérique.* See primary sources, al-Ḥimyarī.

———. *Séville musulmane.* See primary sources, Ibn ʿAbdūn.

———. See also *Études d'orientalisme*; and primary sources, *Documents inédits*, ar-Rāzī.

Levy, Reuben. *The Social Structure of Islam.* [2d edn. of *The Sociology of Islam*]. Cambridge: Cambridge University Press, 1957.

Lewis, Bernard. "Raza y color en el Islam." *Al-Andalus*, XXXIII (1968), 1-51.

Liauzu, Jean-Guy. "Un aspect de la reconquête de la vallée de l'Ebre aux xie et xiie siècles, l'agriculture irriguée et l'héritage de l'Islam." *Hespéris-Tamuda*, V (1964), 5-13.

———. "La condition des musulmans dans l'Aragon chrétien aux xie et xiie siècles." *Hespéris-Tamuda*, IX (1968), 185-200.

Lloréns y Raga, P. L. "Los sarracenos de la Sierra de Eslida y Vall d'Uxó a fines del siglo xv." *Boletín de la sociedad castellonense de cultura*, XLIII (1967), 53-67.

López Martínez, Celestino. *Mudéjares y moriscos sevillanos: Páginas históricas.* Seville: Tipografía Rodríguez, Giménez y compañía, 1935.

López Ortiz, José. *Derecho musulmán*. Colección labor, ciencias jurídicas, 322. Barcelona: Editorial Labor, 1932.

———. "Formularios notariales de la España musulmana." *La ciudad de Dios*, CXLV (1926), 260-272.

———. "La jurisprudencia y el estilo de los tribunales musulmanes de España." *Anuario de historia del derecho español*, IX (1932), 213-248.

Lourie, Elena. "Free Moslems in the Balearics under Christian Rule in the Thirteenth Century." *Speculum*, XLV (1970), 624-649.

———. "A Society Organized for War: Medieval Spain." *Past and Present*, XXXV (1966), 54-76.

Macdonald, Duncan B. *Development of Muslim Theology, Jurisprudence and Constitutional Theory*. Oriental Reprints, II. Beirut: Khayats, [1903] 1966.

Macho y Ortega, Francisco. "Condición social de los mudéjares aragoneses (siglo XV)." *Memorias de la facultad de filosofía y letras de la universidad de Zaragoza*, I (1922-1923), 137-319.

———. See primary sources, "Documentos . . . de los mudéjares."

Al-Maqqarī (Aḥmad b. Muḥammad, at-Tilimsānī al-Maqqarī). *The History of the Mohammedan Dynasties in Spain: Extracted from the Nafhu-t-tíb min ghosni-l-Andalusi-r-rattíb wa táríkh Lisánu-d-dín Ibni-l-khattíb*. Translator and abridger, Pascual de Gayangos. Oriental Translation Fund, 53. 2 vols. London: W. H. Allen and Company, [1840-1843] 1964.

Maravall Casesnoves, José M. *El concepto de España en la edad media*. Madrid: Instituto de estudios políticos, 1954.

Marçais, George. *L'architecture musulmane d'occident. Tunisie, Algérie, Maroc, Espagne et Sicile*. Paris: Arts et métiers graphiques, 1954.

Marçais, William [Guillaume]. "L'Islamisme et la vie urbaine." In his *Articles et Conférences*, pp. 59-67. Publications de l'institut d'études orientales (d'Alger), 21. Paris: Adrien-Maisonneuve, 1961.

Martínez-Ferrando, J. E. *Baixa edat mitjana (segles xii, xiii, xiv i xv)*. In Ferran Soldevila, *Història dels catalans* (*q.v.*), vol. II.

———. *Catálogo de los documentos del antiguo reino de Valencia*. 2 vols. Madrid: Cuerpo facultativo de archiveros, bibliotecarios, y arqueólogos, 1934.

———. *La València de Jaume II, breu aplec de notícies*. Colecció l'espiga, 49. Valencia: Editorial Torre, 1963.

Martínez Ortiz, José with Jaime De Scals Aracil. *Colección cerámica del museo histórico municipal de Valencia, ciclo Paterna-Manises. Catálogo-inventario con un estudio preliminar*. Archivo municipal de Valencia, 1st series, 1. Valencia: Ayuntamiento de Valencia, 1962.

Masiá de Ros, Ángeles. *La corona de Aragón y los estados del norte de África, política de Jaime II y Alfonso IV en Egipto, Ifriquía y Tremecén.* Barcelona: Instituto español de estudios mediterraneos, 1951.

Massignon, L. "Ibn Sab'īn, et la 'conspiration ḥallāgienne' en Andalousie, et en orient au xiiie siècle." *Études d'orientalisme* (*q.v.*), II, 661-681.

Mateu Ibars, Josefina. *Los virreyes de Valencia: Fuentes para su estudio.* Archivo municipal de Valencia, 3d series, 2. Valencia: Ayuntamiento de Valencia, 1963.

Mateu y Llopis, Felipe. *Alpuente, reino musulman.* Valencia: Editorial F. Domenech, 1944.

———. "Hallazgos cerámicos en Valencia." *Al-Andalus*, XVI (1951), 165-167.

———. "Nómina de los musulmanes de las montañas de Coll de Rates del reino de Valencia en 1409." *Al-Andalus*, VI (1942), 299-335.

———. "La repoblación musulmana del reino de Valencia en el siglo xiii y las monedas de tipo almohade." *Boletín de la sociedad castellonense de cultura*, XXVIII (1952), 29-43.

Mat[t]heu y Sanz, Lorenzo. *Tractatus de regimine urbis et regni Valentiae sive selectarum interpretationum ad principaliores foros eiusdem.* Valencia: Bernardo Nogués, 1654.

Mélanges d'histoire et d'archéologie de l'occident musulman. 2 vols. Algiers: Gouvernement générale de l'Algérie, 1957.

Menéndez Pidal, Ramón. *La España del Cid.* 4th edn. rev. Obras completas, 6, 7. 2 vols. Madrid: Espasa-Calpe, 1947.

———. *España y su historia.* 2 vols. Madrid: Ediciones minotauro, 1957.

——— *et alii. Historia de España.* 12 vols. to date. Madrid: Espasa-Calpe, 1957ff.

Mez, Adam. *Renaissance of Islam.* Translators, S. Khuda Bukhsh and D. S. Margoliouth. London: Luzac and Co., 1937.

Middle Eastern Cities: A Symposium on Ancient, Islamic, and Contemporary Middle Eastern Urbanism. Editor, Ira Lapidus. Berkeley: University of California Press, 1969.

Millet, René. *Les almohades, histoire d'une dynastie berbère.* Paris: Société d'éditions géographiques, maritimes et coloniales, 1923.

Miret y Sans, Joaquín. "La esclavitud en Cataluña en los ultimos tiempos de la edad media." *Revue hispanique*, XLI (1917), 1-109.

———. *Itinerari de Jaume I "el Conqueridor."* Barcelona: Institut d'estudis catalans, 1918.

Mitjavila, Josep Albert. *Mossarabs, mudèixars, moriscos.* Valencia: Centro de cultura valenciana, 1963.

Mobarec Asfura, Norma. "Condición jurídica de los moros en la alta edad media española." *Revista chilena de historia del derecho,* II (1961), 36-52.

Momblanch y Gonzálbez, Francisco de P. "El rey D. Jaime y las guerras de Alazrach." *VII Asamblea de cronistas de Valencia* [1968]. Repaged offprint. Valencia: Marí Montañana, 1970.

Monés. See Mu'nis.

Monroe, James T. *Islam and the Arabs in Spanish Scholarship (Sixteenth Century to the Present).* Medieval Iberian Texts and Studies, 3. Leiden: E. J. Brill, 1970.

Monzó Nogués, Andrés. *La vall d'Alcalá y sus egregias figuras Ahmet ben Almançor, Çaida, y Çoraida.* Carlet, Valencia: Centro de cultura valenciana, 1954.

Mu'nis, Ḥusayn. "La división político-administrativa de la España musulmana." *Revista del instituto egipcio de estudios islámicos en Madrid,* V (1957), 79-135.

Nakosteen, Mehdi Khan. *History of Islamic Origins of Western Education A.D. 800-1350, with an Introduction to Medieval Muslim Education.* Boulder: University of Colorado Press, 1964.

An-Nāṣirī (Aḥmad b. Khālid an-Nāṣirī). *Kitāb el-istiqça li-akhbar doual el-Maghrib el-aqça* [part 3], *Les almohades.* Translator, Ismāʿīl Ḥāmid. As *Archives marocaines,* vol. XXII (1927).

Neuman, Abraham A. *The Jews in Spain: Their Social, Political and Cultural Life During the Middle Ages.* 2 vols. Philadelphia: Jewish Publication Society of America, 1942.

Nicholson, Reynold A. *A Literary History of the Arabs.* 2d edn. rev. Cambridge: Cambridge University Press, 1962.

Noth, Albrecht. *Heiliger Krieg und heiliger Kampf in Islam und Christentum.* Bonner historische Forschungen, 28. Bonn: Ludwig Röhrscheid, 1966.

Nykl, A. R. *Hispano-Arabic Poetry and Its Relations with the Old Provençal Troubadours.* Baltimore: J. H. Furst, 1946.

Oliver, Bienvenido. *Historia del derecho en Cataluña, Mallorca y Valencia. Código de las costumbres de Tortosa.* 4 vols. Madrid: Miguel Ginesta, 1876-1881.

Orellana, Marcos Antonio de. *Valencia antigua y moderna.* 3 vols. Valencia: Acción bibliográfica valenciana, 1923-1924.

Oriola-Cortada, E. Antonio de. "La couronne d'Aragon et les hafsides au xiiie siècle (1229-1301)." *Analecta sacra tarraconensia,* XXV (1952), 51-115.

Orti Belmonte, Miguel Ángel. "El fuero de Córdoba y las clases sociales en la ciudad: mudéjares y judíos en la edad media." *Boletín de la real academia de Córdoba*, xxv (1954), 5-94.

P., J.M.E. de la. "Sello de Ceyt Abuzeyt rey moro de Valencia." *Revista de archivos, bibliotecas, y museos*, v (1875), 20, 31, 93-96, 277-281, 389-393.

Pascual y Beltrán, Ventura. "La conquista de Játiva por Jaime I no pudo ser en 1249." *Anales del centro de cultura valenciana*, xvii (1949), 41-50.

———. "Recuerdos de un insigne mozárabe valenciano [San Pedro Pascual], su estatua, su casa, sus libros." *Anales del centro de cultura valenciana*, xii (1944), 82-97.

Pastor de Togneri, Reyna, and Marta Bonaudo. "Problèmes d'assimilation d'une minorité: les mozarabes de Tolède (de 1085 à la fin du xiiie siècle)." *Annales, économies, sociétés, civilisations*, xxv (1970), 351-390.

Pauty, Edmond. "Villes spontanées et villes créees en Islam." *Annales de l'institut d'études orientales*, ix (1951), 52-75.

Pedregal y Fantini, José. *Estado social y cultural de los mozárabes y mudéjares españoles*. Seville: Revista de tribunales, 1898.

Pérès, Henri. "Les éléments ethniques de l'Espagne musulmane et de la langue arabe au ve-xie siècle." *Études d'orientalisme* (*q.v.*), ii, 717-733.

———. *L'Espagne vue par les voyageurs musulmans de 1610 à 1930*. Publications de l'institut d'études orientales (d'Alger), 6. Paris: Adrien-Maisonneuve, 1937.

———. "La langue arabe et les habitants de l'Andalousie au moyen âge." *Revue de l'académie arabe*, xix (1944), 393-408.

Piles Ibars, Andrés. *Valencia árabe*. Vol. i (*unicum*). Valencia: Manuel Alafre, 1901.

Piles Ros, Leopoldo. "La situación social de los moros de realengo en la Valencia del siglo xv." *Estudios de historia social de España*, i (1949), 225-274.

Planhol, Xavier de. *Le monde islamique: essai de géographie religieuse*. Paris: Presses universitaires de France, 1957. Translated as *The World of Islam*. Ithaca, N.Y.: Cornell University Press, 1959.

Poliak, A. N. "Classification of Lands in the Islamic Law and its Technical Terms." *American Journal of Semitic Languages and Literatures*, lvii (1940), 50-62.

———. "La féodalité islamique." *Revue des études islamiques*, x (1936), 248-265.

Pons Boïgues, Francisco. *Ensayo bio-bibliográfico sobre los historiadores y geógrafos arábigo-españoles.* Madrid: Establecimiento tipográfico de San Francisco de Sales, 1898.

Prawer, Joshua. *The Crusaders' Kingdom: European Colonialism in the Middle Ages.* New York: Praeger Publishers, 1972.

———. *Histoire du royaume latin de Jérusalem.* Translator, G. Nahon. Rev. in trans. 2 vols. Paris: Centre national de la recherche scientifique, 1969-1970.

Prieto y Vives, Antonio. *Formación del reino de Granada.* Discurso de recepción. Madrid: Real academia de la historia, 1929.

Reglá Campistrol, Juan. *Estudios sobre los moriscos.* Valencia: Universidad de Valencia, 1964.

Ribera y Tarragó, Julián. *Disertaciones y opúsculos.* 2 vols. Madrid: Estanislao Maestre, 1928.

———. *La enseñanza entre los musulmanes españoles.* 3d edn. Córdoba: Real academia de ciencias, bellas letras, y nobles artes de Córdoba, 1925. Reprinted in *Disertaciones* (*q.v.*), I, 229-359.

———. *Opúsculos dispersos.* Tetuán: Instituto General Franco de estudios e investigación hispano-árabe, 1952.

Richard, Jean. *Le royaume latin de Jérusalem.* Paris: Presses universitaires de France, 1953.

Riquer, Martín de, and Antonio Comas. *Història de la literatura catalana.* 4 vols. to date. Barcelona: Edicions Ariel, 1964.

Roca Traver, Francisco A. "La gobernación foral del reino de Valencia: una cuestión de competencia." *Estudios de edad media de la corona de Aragón,* IV (1951), 177-214.

———. "Un siglo de vida mudéjar en la Valencia medieval (1238-1338)." *Estudios de edad media de la corona de Aragón,* V (1952), 115-208.

Roda Soriano, Salvador. "El camino de dolor del estilo mudéjar en el reino de Valencia." *Anales del centro de cultura valenciana,* XVIII (1957), 2-24.

Rodón Binué, Eulalia. *El lenguaje técnico del feudalismo en el siglo xi en Cataluña (contribución al estudio del latín medieval).* Filología clásica, 16. Barcelona: Consejo superior de investigaciones científicas, 1957.

Rodrigo y Pertegás, José. "La morería de Valencia, ensayo de descripción topográficohistórica de la misma." *Boletín de la real academia de la historia,* LXXXVI (1925), 229-251.

———. "La urbe valenciana en el siglo xiv." *Congrés III* (*q.v.*), II, 279-374. Repaged offprint, Valencia: Hijo de F. Vives Mora, 1924.

Romano Ventura, David. "Los funcionarios judíos de Pedro el Grande de Aragón." *Boletín de la real academia de buenas letras de Barcelona,* XXVIII (1969-1970), 5-41.

———. "Los hermanos Abenmenassé al servicio de Pedro el Grande de Aragón." *Homenaje a Millás-Vallicrosa* (*q.v.*), II, 243-292.

Rosenthal, Erwin I. J. *Political Thought in Medieval Islam: An Introductory Outline.* Cambridge: Cambridge University Press, 1958.

Rosselló Bordoy, Guillem. *L'Islam a les illes balears.* Palma de Mallorca: Editorial Daedalus, 1968.

Rull Villar, Baltasar. "La rebelión de los moriscos en la Sierra de Espadán y sus castillos." *Anales del centro de cultura valenciana,* XXI (1960), 54-71.

Sánchez-Albornoz y Menduiña, Claudio. *La España musulmana según los autores islamitas y cristianos medievales.* 2 vols. 2d edn. rev. Barcelona: El Ateneo, 1960.

———. *Ruina y extinción del municipio romano en España e instituciones que le reemplazan.* Buenos Aires: Instituto de la cultura española, medioeval y moderna, 1943.

Sanchis Guarner, Manuel. "Dictados tópicos de la comarca de Denia, Pego y La Marina." *Revista valenciana de filología,* V (1955-1958), 7-62.

———. "Època musulmana." See Tarradell *et alii, Història del país valencià.*

———. *Els parlers romànics de València i Mallorca anteriors a la reconquista.* 2d edn. rev. Biblioteca de filología, instituto de literatura y estudios filológicos, 6. Valencia: Diputación provincial, 1961.

———. "De toponímia aràbigo-valentina." *Revista valenciana de filología,* I (1951), 259-271.

Sanchis y Sivera, José. *Nomenclátor geográfico-eclesiástico de los pueblos de la diócesis de Valencia con los nombres antiguos y modernos de los que existen o han existido, notas históricas y estadísticas. . . .* Valencia: Casa de beneficencia, 1922.

Sá Vall. See Vall.

Sayous, A. *Le commerce des europeens à Tunis depuis le xiie siècle jusqu'à la fin du xvie. Exposé et documents.* Paris: Société d'éditions géographiques, maritimes et coloniales, 1929.

Schack, Adolfo Federico von. *Poesía y arte de los árabes en España y Sicilia.* Translator, Juan Valera. 3 vols. 2d edn. Madrid: M. Rivadeneyra, 1872.

Schact, Joseph. "Droit byzantin et droit musulman." *Atti del convegno di scienze morali, storiche e filologiche, 27 Maggio-1 Giugno 1956:*

Oriente ed occidente nel medio evo, pp. 197-218. Rome: Accademia nazionale dei Lincei, 1957.

———. *An Introduction to Islamic Law*. Oxford: The Clarendon Press, 1964.

Schiaparelli. See primary sources, *Vocabulista*.

Schramm, Percy Ernst. "Der König von Aragon, seine Stellung im Staatsrecht (1276-1410)." *Historisches Jahrbuch*, LXXIV (1955), 99-123.

Shneidman, J. Lee. *The Rise of the Aragonese-Catalan Empire, 1200-1350*. 2 vols. New York: New York University Press, 1970.

Simonet, Francisco J. *Historia de los mozárabes de España deducida de los mejores y más auténticos testimonios de los escritores cristianos y árabes*. Memorias, 13. Madrid: Real academia de la historia, 1897-1903.

———. *Glosario de voces ibéricas y latinas usadas entre los mozárabes precedido de un estudio sobre el dialecto hispano-mozárabe*. Amsterdam: Oriental Press, [1888] 1967.

Sivan, Emmanuel. *L'Islam et la croisade; idéologie et propagande dans les réactions musulmanes aux croisades*. Paris: Librairie d'Amérique et d'Orient, 1968.

Smail, R. C. *Crusading Warfare (1097-1193)*. Cambridge: Cambridge University Press, 1956.

Smith, Robert S. "Fourteenth-Century Population Records of Catalonia." *Speculum*, XIX (1944), 494-501.

Sobrequés Vidal, Santiago. "Patriciado urbano." In Jaime Vicens Vives *et alii, Historia social y económica de España y América*, II, part 1. Barcelona: Teide, 1957.

Soldevila, Ferran. *Història de Catalunya*. 3 vols. 2d edn. rev. Barcelona: Alpha, 1962.

———. *Pere el Gran*. Memòries de la secció històrico-arqueològica, 11, 13, 16, 22. 2 parts in 4 vols. Barcelona: Institut d'estudis catalans, 1950-1962.

———. *Els primers temps de Jaume I*. Memòries de la secció històrico-arqueològica, 27. Barcelona: Institut d'estudis catalans, 1968.

———. *Vida de Jaume I el Conqueridor*. Biblioteca biográfica catalana, 14. Barcelona: Aedos, 1958.

——— *et alii*. *Història dels catalans*. 3 vols. to date. Barcelona: Edicions Ariel, 1961.

Sordo, Enrique. *Moorish Spain. Cordoba, Seville, Granada*. New York: Crown Publishers, 1963.

Sourdel, D. "'Wazīr' et 'Ḥāǧib' en occident." *Études d'orientalisme* (*q.v.*), II, 749-755.

Spuler, Bertold, *et alii. The Muslim World: A Historical Survey.* Translator, F.R.C. Bagley. Rev. in trans. 3 vols. to date. Leiden: E. J. Brill, 1960ff.

Steiger, Arnald. *Contribución a la fonética del hispano-árabe y de los arabismos en el ibero-románico y el siciliano.* Madrid: Revista de filología española (supplement, 17), 1932.

Stern. See *Islamic City.*

Tarradell Mateu, Miguel. "Una hipótesis que se desvanece: el papel de África en las raíces de los pueblos hispánicos." *Homenaje a Jaime Vicens Vives (q.v.)*, I, 173-181.

———, Manuel Sanchis i Guarner, *et alii. Història del país valencià.* Estudis e documents, 5. 1 vol. of 4 to date. Barcelona: Edicions 62, 1965.

Teixidor, Josef. *Antigüedades de Valencia: observaciones críticas donde con instrumentos auténticos se destruye lo fabuloso dejando en su debida estabilidad lo bien fundado* [*1767*]. Editor, Roque Chabás y Lloréns. Monumentos históricos de Valencia y su reino, 1. 2 vols. Valencia: Sociedad el archivo valentino, 1895.

Terés Sádaba, Elías. "Textos poéticos árabes sobre Valencia." *Al-Andalus*, xxx (1965), 291-307.

———. See primary sources, Ibn Ḥazm.

Terrasse, Henri. *L'art hispano-mauresque des origines au xiii siècle.* Publications de l'institut des hautes études marocaines, 25. Paris: Editions G. van Oest, 1932.

———. *Histoire du Maroc des origines à l'établissement du protectorat français.* 2 vols. Casablanca: Éditions Atlantides, 1950.

———. *Islam d'Espagne: une rencontre de l'orient et de l'occident.* Civilisations d'hier et d'aujourd'hui. Paris: Plon, 1958.

———. See Torres Balbás, *Ciudades.*

Toledo Girau, José. *El castell i la vall d'Alfandech de Marinyèn des de sa reconquesta per Jaume I, fins la fundació del monestir de Valldigna per Jaume II.* Obras de investigación histórica, 11. Castellón de la Plana: Sociedad castellonense de cultura, 1936.

———. *El monasterio de Valldigna, contribución al estudio de su historia durante el gobierno de sus abades perpetuos.* Valencia: Hijo de F. Vives Mora, 1944.

Torres Balbás, Leopoldo. *Algunos aspectos del mudejarismo urbano medieval.* Madrid: Academia de la historia, 1954.

———. *Artes almoravide y almohade.* Madrid: Consejo superior de investigaciones científicas, 1955.

Torres Balbás, Leopoldo. *Ciudades hispanomusulmanas*. Editor, Henri Terrasse. 2 vols. Madrid: Instituto hispano-árabe de cultura, 1971.

———. L. Cervera, F. Chueca, P. Bidagor. *Resumen histórico del urbanismo en España*. Madrid: Instituto de estudios de administración local, 1954.

Torres Fontes, Juan. "Jaime I y Alfonso X, dos criterios de repoblación." *Congrés VII* (*q.v.*), III, 329-340.

———. "Los mudéjares murcianos en el siglo xiii." *Murgetana*, XVII (1961), 57-90.

———. *La reconquista de Murcia en 1266 por Jaime I de Aragón*. Murcia: Diputación de Murcia, 1967.

———. "El reino musulmán de Murcia en el siglo xiii." *Anales de la universidad de Murcia*, x (1952), 259-274.

———. *La repoblación murciana en el siglo xiii*. Murcia: Academia Alfonso X el Sabio, 1963.

———. See primary sources, *Colección, Documentos,* and *Repartimiento.*

Torres Morera, Juan R. *Repoblación del reino de Valencia después de la expulsión de los moriscos*. Valencia: Ayuntamiento de Valencia, 1969.

Tourtoulon, Charles (baron de). *Don Jaime I el Conquistador, rey de Aragón, conde de Barcelona, señor de Montpeller, según las crónicas y documentos inéditos*. Rev. in trans. Translator, Teodoro Llorente y Olivares. 2 vols. Valencia: José Doménech, 1874.

Tritton, Arthur Stanley. *Materials on Muslim Education in the Middle Ages*. London: Luzac and Co., 1957.

Tyan, Émile. *Institutions du droit public musulman*. 2 vols. Paris: Recueil Sirey, 1954-1956.

———. *Histoire de l'organisation judiciaire en pays d'Islam*. 2d edn. rev. Leiden: E. J. Brill, 1960.

Ubieto Arteta, Antonio. "La conquista de Valencia en la mente de Jaime I." *Saitabi*, XII (1962), 117-139.

Valdeavellano. See G[arcía] de Valdeavellano.

Vall, Guillem de Sá. "Rendición del castillo de Xivert." *Boletín de la sociedad castellonense de cultura*, XXIV (1948), 231-233.

Valls-Taberner, Ferran. *Obras selectas*. Editors, Ramón d'Abadal and J. E. Martínez-Ferrando. 3 vols. Barcelona: Consejo superior de investigaciones científicas, 1952-1957.

Vallvé Bermejo, Joaquín. "Una fuente importante de la historia de al-Andalus, la 'Historia' de Ibn 'Askar." *Al-Andalus*, XXXI (1966), 237-265.

Verlinden, Charles. "La condition des populations rurales dans l'Espagne médiévale." In *Le servage*, pp. 172-196. Brussels: Société Jean Bodin, 1937.

———. *L'esclavage dans l'Europe médiévale*. Rijksuniversiteit te Gent, faculteit van de letteren, 119. One vol. to date, *Péninsule ibérique, France*. Bruges: Universiteit te Gent [Ghent], 1955ff.

Vernet, Ginés, Juan. "Antropónimos de etimología árabe en el levante español: ensayo metodológico." *Revista del instituto egipcio de estudios islámicos en Madrid*, XI-XII (1963-1964), 141-147.

———. "Antropónimos musulmanes en los actuales partidos judiciales de Falset y Gandesa." *Homenaje a Jaime Vicens Vives* (*q.v.*), I, 123-127.

———. *Los musulmanes españoles*. Barcelona: Sayma ediciones, 1962.

———. "Toponimia arábiga." *Enciclopedia lingüistica hispánica* (*q.v.*), I, 561-579.

———. "El valle del Ebro como nexo entre oriente y occidente." *Boletín de la real academia de buenas letras de Barcelona*, XXIII (1950), 249-286.

Véronne, Chantal de la. "Recherches sur le chiffre de la population musulmane de Valence en 1238 d'après le 'Repartimiento.' " *Bulletin hispanique*, LI (1949), 423-426.

Viciana, [Rafael] Martín de. *Crónica de Valencia* [*Segunda parte; Tercera parte*]. 2 vols. Valencia: Sociedad valenciana de bibliófilos, [1564] 1881-1882.

Von Grunebaum, G. E. *Classical Islam: A History, 600-1258*. Translator, Katherine Watson. London: George Allen and Unwin, 1970.

———. *Islam. Essays in the Nature and Growth of a Cultural Tradition*. Comparative Studies of Cultures and Civilizations, 5. New York: Barnes and Noble, 1961.

———. *Medieval Islam: A Study in Cultural Orientation*. Oriental Institute Essay. Chicago: University of Chicago Press, 1947.

Watt, William Montgomery. *Islamic Political Thought: The Basic Concepts*. Islamic Surveys, 6. Edinburgh: University of Edinburgh Press, 1968.

——— and Pierre Cachia. *A History of Islamic Spain*. Islamic Surveys, 4. Edinburgh: University of Edinburgh Press, 1965.

Wieruszowski, Helene. "Peter der Grosse von Katalonien-Aragon und die Juden, eine Politik des gerechten Ausgleichs." *Homenatge a Antoni Rubió i Lluch, miscellània d'estudis literaris històrics i lingüistics*, pp. 239-262. 3 vols. Barcelona: Institut d'estudis catalans, 1936.

The World of Islam. Studies in Honor of Philip K. Hitti. Editors, James Kritzeck and R. Bayly Winder. London: Macmillan, 1960.

Zurita y Castro, Jerónimo de. *Anales de la corona de Aragón*. 7 vols. Zaragoza: Colegio de S. Vicente Ferrer (vol. VII: Universidad de Zaragoza), 1610-1621.

——. *Indices rerum ab Aragoniae regibus gestarum ab initiis regni ad annum mcdx*. Zaragoza: Dominicus a Portonariis de Ursinis, 1578.

INDEX

Alconstantini, Bahye (Bahiel), 253, 254n
Alconstantini, Moses, son of Bahye, xxviii, 47
Alconstantini, Solomon, son of Bahye, 253, 254n
alcopzi (mosque properties), 199n, 212-13
Alcora, 93
Alcoy, 23, 25, 43, 57, 59, 153n, 325, 331, 360; cemetery, 210; festival of al-Azraq, 332; mosque, 203-204
Alcoy massif, 15, 325, 337
Alcudia de Veo, 378, 380
Aldaya, 242
Aldea (Tortosa), 123, 227, 246, 267, 379, 386; cemetery, 210; Islamic worship, 191, 192, 205
aldea (*ḍay'a*, farm-hamlet), 60
Alenz, 316
Alexander III, Pope, 97n
Alexander IV, Pope, 287
Alfandech, 43, 59, 93, 127-28, 145, 259; government, 382; charter and treaty, 190-91, 226, 291, 379, 386; Islamic worship, 190-92, 194, 205; siege, 336; surrender, 131, 133, 137, 166
alfaquí, Muslim jurist, see *faqīh*
alfaquín (incorrectly *alfaquí*), Jewish erudite, 222, 253-54n
Alfarp, 205
Alfonso I (the Battler), King of Aragon, 156, 217n, 228
Alfonso III, King of Aragon, 247, 292n, 316
Alfonso IV, King of Aragon, 269
Alfonso IV, King of León, 312n
Alfonso VI, King of Castile, 162, 186
Alfonso VIII, King of Castile, 358
Alfonso X, King of Castile, xv, 20, 22, 39, 129, 133, 144, 146, 176n, 264n, 356; al-Azraq meets, 304, 305; death, 45; education patronized by, 201; laws, Castilian code, 215; in Muslim revolt, 40, 42, 44, 45; Muslims in armies of, 288, 294
Alfonso XI, King of Castile, 298n
Alfonso, Prince (son of James I), 46; al-Azraq's homage to, 283, 325, 326, 367
Algar, 132, 316
'Alī (diplomat), 170
'Alī (spy), 295
'Alī al-Baqā', 306
'Alī al-Gadaslī, 206
'Alī al-Khaṭṭāb, 61
Alicante (city), 18, 20, 21, 25, 36, 39, 40, 44
Alicante (modern province), 15
aljamas (communities), 62, 70, 71, 72n, 99, 130-31, 156, 185; elite in, 402-403; in feudal system, 284-85; government, 374-86; surrender charters, 107, 123, 130-31, 138
Almácera, 181
Almazora, 57; surrender parley, 166, 168
Almenara, 52, 54, 59, 107, 302, 383, 407, 408; migrants from, 83, 86; *qā'id*, 369; siege, 160-61; surrender parleys, 166-69, 171; surrender terms, 127, 133; treaty ceremony, 180
Almizra, 59; treaty, 20, 319, 325, 342
almogàvers (irregular troops), 95, 294, 296n
Almohads, 26-32, 34, 51, 68, 94, 221, 229, 297, 355, 359, 365, 366, 379, 387, 397, 402, 419; caliphs, 26, 28; harem, 215-16; judicial system, 231, 235; literature and arts, 415-17; rebellions against, 30-31; Spanish Muslim attitude toward, 28
Almonacid, 264
Almoravids, 68, 94, 197, 375; names derived from, 307n
Alpuente, 50, 51, 53-55, 300, 302, 361
alquerias (farm-hamlets), 55, 58, 60-62
Altea, 23, 59, 132, 325, 327-29, 332
Altura, 130
Amari, Michele, 391n
amīn (local administrator), 233-36, 238, 240-41, 244, 246, 262, 264, 353, 386, 395; functions, 376-81
'Āmir b. Idrīs, 38
Andalusia, 415; conquest, 29; Islamic rule, 26, 30; population, 79
Andarella, 210
Andilla, 302
Andrew of Odena, 261

20; conquests by, 20; farming, 104; feudal system, 278, 287; French alliance with, 45; laws, 215, 224; legal system, 264-65n; in Muslim revolts, 38-39, 42, 44, 45; population, 79, 80n; treaties with, 14, 15, 20, 32, 193
castles, 308, 313-22; conquered, 117-18; as fortresses, 164-65; towns and, 55-59
Castro, 107, 127, 180, 369; surrender parleys, 166, 169
Catalan Grand Company, 296-97
Catalans, 11, 388; in Castile, 20; as lawyers, 178; as merchants, 97; in Valencia, 20, 22, 311; in Valencia (city), 84, 86
Catalonia, 11; farming, 104; feudal system, 274-75, 282, 283; population, 74-75, 79, 80
Cazola, treaty, 339n
Celtiberians, 66
cemeteries, Islamic, 203-205, 207-10
ceramics, 93, 407
Cervera, 54, 57, 166; surrender terms, 127
Cerveri Ça Nera, 98
Ceuta, 222
Chábas y Lloréns, Roque, xxi, 86, 142-43, 144, 151, 363
charters, settlement (*cartas pueblas*), 177-78; *see also* surrender terms; names of cities
Chella, 152
Chelva, 23, 44, 54, 230, 302, 380, 389, 399; surrender, 133-34, 180n
Chelva River, 134
Chíu, 58
Chiva, 145, 211
chivalry, 311-12
Chivert, 142, 151, 166, 167, 182; cemeteries, 210; charter and surrender terms, 61, 99, 112, 118-19, 126-28, 131, 175, 188, 190-91, 193-97, 203, 205, 211, 215, 218, 290, 371, 386, 389-91, 399-400, 409-10; families, names, 409-10; feudal system in charter, 281, 285; government, 379-82, 389-90, 395; Islamic worship, 188, 190-91, 193-95, 197; law in charter, 224, 226, 227, 229, 230, 234, 237, 244, 251, 259, 264, 265; legal system, seignorial, 267, 268; mosques, 203, 205, 211; Muslims as Christian allies, 290
Christians: legal authority in Muslim courts, 234, 236, 249-52, 264-70; legal rights, 163; in Islamic cities, quarters, 128, 144, 152, 163; relations with Muslims, *see* Muslims
Chronicles of St. Denis, 160
Chulilla, 130, 302
church and state, Christian, 185
church bells, Muslims' hatred of, 187
Cid, the, 14, 54, 55, 125, 289, 376; judicial authority, 249-50; Valencia principality, 156, 186
Cirat, 302
Circourt, Anne M.J.A., comte de, xviii
circumcision, 214
cities, 81-88; as administrative units, 49-55; expulsion of Muslims from, 142-47, 153-54, 158; in feudal system, 278; medina (central area), 143, 144; Islamic, character of, 81-82, 87-88, 143-45; Mudejar quarters in, 143-52, 206; names of districts, 86-87; population, 74-75
city-states: councils, 386-94, 408-409; in feudal system, 277, 311; government officials, 374-400
classes, social, 89-113; artisans, 90-96; farmers, 99-108; merchants, 96-99; military aristocracy, 300-22; Muslims' view of, 89-90; slaves, *see* slaves
clavarius, meaning of office, 399-400
Cocentaina, 57, 59, 61, 66, 133, 144, 295, 331; legal system, 230, 236, 243, 245, 246, 250, 260-61, 263
Colin, Georges, xxvii
communes, 284-85, 390n
Conde, José Antonio, 341n
Confrides, 133, 230, 245
Contestanes, 51, 66
contracts, 224-26; *see also* marriage, contracts
Corbera, 55, 59

Cordova (city), 20, 29, 38, 69, 139, 390, 408; divisions, 86; fall of, 356; mosques, 202; Muslim books from, 193
Cordova (province), 51
Cordova caliphate, 51, 375, 379
Cornel, Peter, 161
Cortes, near Tudela, 399
Corts family, 330
council: in Jewish communities, 396-97; of Muslim ruler, 359-60; town or city, 386-94, 408-409
crafts (craftsmen), 90-96
Crevillente, 295, 365
Crónica de San Juan de la Peña, 331, 344n
crowds, estimates of size, 76-77
Cuart, 131, 192, 199, 226, 380; legal dispute, 268
çucac (street), 86
Cuenca, 291
Cuevas de Vinromá, 56, 126, 127
Culla, 55, 56, 127
Cullera, 5, 7, 24, 36, 54, 55, 59, 62, 75, 108, 128, 131, 140, 158, 361; siege, 160, 179; trade, 98
customs, collection, 78

Damascus, 67, 69; mosque, 200
Daniel, Norman, xviin, 192
Dante Alighieri, 313n
Danvila y Collado, Manuel, xxi, 150n
Daroca, 82, 85, 86, 156, 264, 395
Deçpont, Raymond, bishop of Valencia, 205
Denia, 18, 23, 25, 32-36, 50, 53-55, 58, 59, 128, 133, 143, 165, 227, 246, 361, 417; Islamic worship, 191-92, 197; shipyards, 93, 94n; trade, 98
Denia (province), 51, 52
Desclot, Bernat, 5-6n, 39, 129-30n, 132, 320-21, 327, 332, 337, 350, 351, 405
dhimmī (protected nonbeliever), 157
ad-Dimashqī, 52, 53
Diocletian, Emperor, 51
Dodge, Bayard, 198n
Domeño, 302
Dominic of Puigvert, 330
Dominicans, 44-45, 414
Dos Aguas, 218
Dozy, Reinhart P. A., 236-37, 305, 387
Dubler, César E., 90n
Dufourcq, Charles Emmanuel, xxii, 74-75, 81, 97-98
Du Guesclin, Bertrand, 297

Ebo, 326; Valley, 330
Ebro Valley, 67, 103, 156
Edetanes, 66
education, Islamic, 198-201
Egypt, Muslims from, 68
Eiximenis, Francesc, 87, 394
Elche, 69, 129, 188, 380, 390, 409; Muslim law, 229; surrender parleys, 166-69, 170; treaty, 173-74, 176, 179, 181
elders in councils, 390-94
Eleazar b. Joel Halevi, rabbi, 297
elections, 380
Elías de Tejada, Francisco, 278n
elite, 402-13; disappearance of, 412-13; families in, 403-12; intellectual and creative life, 413-20; religious, 403, 405, 407; Valencian notables, 404-405; of wealth, 406-13
Enguera, 51, 57, 166, 167
Ennueyo, 73
Epstein, Isidore, 215n
Escrivá, Arnold, bailiff, 346-47
Escrivá family, 330
Eslida, 43, 44, 73, 120, 348, 370; aljama, 374; cemeteries, 210; charters and surrender terms, 99, 119-21, 132, 170, 180n, 188, 192, 195, 199, 212, 215, 243, 371, 374, 382, 406; feudalism in charter, 280; government, 378, 382; irrigation system dispute, 242, 255-57, 357; Islamic education, 198, 199; Islamic worship, 186, 191, 192, 205; law in charter, 221, 224-26, 233, 244; *see also* Sierra de Eslida
Espioca, 210
Estenaga Echevarría, Narciso, xix
exarici (share-farmers), 102-104
exortins (bodyguards), 305

Fairlie, Henry, 401n
families: in elite, 403-12; kinship groups, 70-72, 407-408; names, 409-12

influence on, 223-24; Jews and, 228, 230-31n; king as supreme authority, 249; Romanized code, 14, 21, 251; Valencian *Furs*, 90n, 97, 104-105, 109-10, 214, 217, 231, 277, 407
law, Islamic, 214, 220-48; appointments and appeals, 243-48; capital crimes, 250-52, 262-63, 270; Christians in legal system, 234, 236, 249-52, 264-70; criminal jurisdiction, 259-63; Jews in legal system, 234, 247n, 249n, 259n, 260, 264, 265; jurisdictions and personnel, 231-43; king as supreme authority, 249-51; Malikite school, 221, 224, 226, 375, 401; oaths, 179, 216-18; public and private, 228; punishments, 250-52, 258n; in surrender terms, 120, 121, 123-24, 126, 128, 132-33; *see also* Hadith; Sunna
law, Roman, 356
lawyers (advocates), 222
Ledesma Rubio, M. L., xix
Lérida, 20, 46, 382; Jews, 83n, 228; judicial system, 238; migrants from, 82, 83, 86
Le Tourneau, Roger, 415
Lévi-Provençal, Évariste, 49, 191, 200, 215, 221, 236, 239n, 248, 367n
Lewis, Archibald, 388n
Liauzu, Jean-Guy, xix, 103
Liria, 23, 24, 43, 54, 55, 59, 66, 67, 70, 75, 302, 361, 379, 417; mosque, 204
literature, Islamic, 414-18
livestock, 107-108
Lloréns y Raga, Peregrín, 126
Lobo (Lūb), King of Valencia, 33, 360
Lombar, 202
López, Peter, of Pomar, 338
López Martínez, Celestino, xix
Lorca, 39, 69, 129, 417
lords, *see* feudal lords
Louis IX, King of France, 176n
Lourie, Elena, xix
Luchente, 23, 59; battle of, 43, 296
Lull, Raymond, 13, 189-90, 196, 198-99, 250, 268, 310, 392, 394
Lyons, ecumenical council, 349
Ma'āfir, Banū, 67, 70, 172, 408-409
Macho y Ortega, Francisco, xix, 178n, 247, 376-77n, 377, 379, 395
Maghrib, 42, 68; as West, 237, 366, 379, 405
Majorca, 20, 69, 86, 135, 158, 190, 310, 320, 355, 357, 359, 367; conquest, 5, 16, 159, 161-62, 166, 167, 304-305; government, 361, 392; legal system, 265; military aristocrats, 307; population, 79; surrender parleys, 168
Makhzūm, Banū, 70
al-Makhzūmī, 364n
Málaga, 41, 365
malik (king), 26n, 356; assumed title, 337
Malikite school (law), 221, 224, 226, 375, 401
Mamluks, 404
al-Ma'mūn, caliph, 29-30
Manresa, 94
manuscripts, *see* books
al-Maqqarī, 124, 222, 248, 339n
Mardanīsh, Banū, 33, 306, 338, 365
Margarida, 327
Marinids, 29, 345; in rebellions, 38, 41, 45
Marrakesh, 26, 29, 32, 38, 69, 345, 355
marriage: in charters, 215, 224-25; contracts, 219, 224-26, 398, 399, 406-407; dowry, 223, 226; polygamy, 214-16
Marseilles, 22
Martí, Raymond, 64, 367
Martínez-Ferrando, J. E., 335
Masalavas, 70
Mateu y Llopis, Felipe, xxi
Mayer, Ernesto, 353n, 388
Mazahéri, Aly Akbar, 198n
maẓālim (courts), 232-33, 237
Mecca, pilgrimage to, 194-96
medina (central area of city), 143, 144
Menéndez Pidal, Ramón, xiiin, 125, 142, 387
merchants, 96-99
merí (*merino*), 400
merum et mixtum dominion, 268-70
Michavila y Vila, Antonio, 413
Mijares River, 23, 44, 62, 66, 79

Library of Congress Cataloging in Publication Data

Burns, Robert Ignatius.
Islam under the crusaders.

Bibliography: p.
1. Valencia—History. 2. Mudéjares.
3. Jaime I, King of Aragon, 1208-1276.
4. Pedro III, el Grand, King of Aragon, 1239-1285.
5. Crusades.
I. Title.
DP302.V205B83 946'.76 72-4039
ISBN 0-691-05207-7